Handbook of
Parent Training

Handbook of Parent Training

Parents as Co-Therapists for Children's Behavior Problems

Second Edition

Edited by
James M. Briesmeister
Charles E. Schaefer

John Wiley & Sons, Inc.

New York • Chichester • Weinheim • Brisbane • Singapore • Toronto

Library of Congress Cataloging-in-Publication Data:

Handbook of parent training : parents as co-therapists for children's
    behavior problems / edited by James M. Briesmeister, Charles E.
    Schaefer. — 2nd ed.
        p.   cm.
    Includes bibliographical references and indexes.
    ISBN 0-471-16343-0 (cloth : alk. paper)
    1. Behavior disorders in children—Study and teaching. 2. Child
psychotherapy—Study and teaching.   3. Child psychotherapy—Parent
participation.   I. Briesmeister, James M.   II. Schaefer, Charles E.
RJ506.B44H26   1998
618.92'8914—dc21   97-20446

Printed in the United States of America.

10 9 8 7 6 5 4 3 2 1

Contributors

Arthur D. Anastopoulos, Ph.D.
Associate Professor
Director, AD/HD Specialty Clinic
The University of North Carolina
Greensboro, North Carolina

Sharon L. Berry, Ph.D.
Children's Memorial Hospital
Chicago, Illinois

Elaine A. Blechman, Ph.D.
Professor, Psychology Department
University of Colorado
Boulder, Colorado

Stephen R. Boggs, Ph.D.
Associate Professor of Clinical and Health Psychology
University of Florida
Department of Clinical and Health Psychology
Gainesville, Florida

Phyllis Booth, M.A.
Director of Training
The Theraplay Institute
Chicago, Illinois

Sue Bratton, Ph.D.
Director, Child and Family Resource Clinic
University of North Texas
Denton, Texas

James M. Briesmeister, Ph.D.
Private Practice
Shelby Township, Michigan

Karen S. Budd, Ph.D.
DePaul University
Department of Psychology
Chicago, Illinois

Cary S. Chugh
DePaul University
Chicago, Illinois

Andrew Eisen, Ph.D.
Assistant Professor
Fairleigh Dickinson University
Teaneck, New Jersey

Linda Engler, Ph.D.
Staff Psychologist
Hackensack University Medical Center
Hackensack, New Jersey

Sheila Eyberg, Ph.D.
Professor of Clinical and Health Psychology
University of Florida
Department of Clinical and Health Psychology
Gainesville, Florida

Wendy S. Freeman, M.A.
Doctoral Fellow
Department of Psychology
The University of British Columbia
Vancouver, Canada

Beata Geyer
Doctoral Fellow
Fairleigh Dickinson University
Teaneck, New Jersey

Lois Hancock, M.S.
Therapist
University of Washington
Parenting Clinic
Seattle, Washington

Arthur C. Houts, Ph.D.
Professor and Director of Clinical Training
The University of Memphis
Memphis, Tennessee

Charlotte Johnston, Ph.D.
Associate Professor
Department of Psychology
The University of British Columbia
Vancouver, Canada

Christopher Kearney, Ph.D.
Associate Professor
Psychology Department
University of Nevada Las Vegas
Las Vegas, Nevada

Terrence Koller, Ph.D.
Private Practice
Evanston, Illinois

Juliana R. Lachenmeyer, Ph.D.
Professor
Psychology Department
Fairleigh Dickinson University
Director, Anxiety Treatment Program
North Shore University Hospital
Teaneck, New Jersey

John R. Lutzker, Ph.D.
University of Judaism
Los Angeles, California

Sean C. McDevitt, Ph.D.
Scottsdale, Arizona

Michael W. Mellon, Ph.D.
University of Arkansas for Medical Sciences
Arkansas Children's Hospital
Section for Behavioral Pediatrics
Little Rock, Arkansas

Laurie S. Miller, Ph.D.
Assistant Professor of Clinical Psychology in Psychiatry
College of Physicians and Surgeons of Columbia University
New York, New York

Tami Roblek
Graduate Student
Clinical Psychology
University of Nevada
Las Vegas, Nevada

Charles E. Schaefer, Ph.D.
Professor of Psychology
Fairleigh Dickinson University
Teaneck, New Jersey

Lisa Sheeber, Ph.D.
Research Scientist
Oregon Research Institute
Eugene, Oregon

Stephanie E. Steed, M.A.
Behavior Change Associates
Anaheim, California

Carolyn Webster-Stratton, Ph.D.
Director, Parenting Clinic
University of Washington
Seattle, Washington

Lillie Weiss, Ph.D.
Private Practice
Center for Psychotherapy and Dream Analysis
Phoenix, Arizona

Sharlene Wolchik, Ph.D.
Professor
Psychology Department
Arizona State University
Tempe, Arizona

Amy R. Wolfson, Ph.D.
Assistant Professor of Psychology
College of the Holy Cross
Worcester, Massachusetts

Preface

The Handbook of Parent Training, first published in 1989, was impressive as a compilation and review of some of the most relevant research, theories, and clinical applications of behavioral parenting available at that time. The book described the theoretical constructs, empirical studies, and clinically tested parent training formats of pioneers and innovators in the field. Since its inception, parent training has fostered a burgeoning body of empirical and clinical literature and has gained wide acceptance as a method of choice for resolving and modifying childhood disorders and adjustment conflicts. Considerable progress has occurred in the field of parent training since the first volume was written. Most notably, parent training has been applied to a wider and more divergent array of childhood and adolescent clinical disorders. This edition provides a comprehensive review and update of some of the most recent innovations in the field of parent training. Some of the authors in this revised edition of the *Handbook* will be familiar to those acquainted with the original text. All of the contributors are specialists in the field of behavioral child research and therapy who have continuously strengthened, evaluated, and refined their unique parent intervention strategies. The approaches submitted by these influential authors offer even more expansive and sophisticated procedural formats and implementations. The parent instructional tactics have become increasingly diverse while remaining practical and applicable.

Parent training is an intervention format grounded in behavioral modification constructs and the principles of learning theory. The clinician instructs and coaches the parents in new parenting and child management skills. The parents learn new and effective ways of relating, communicating, and responding to their youngsters. Parent training is a collaborative endeavor in which the parents are trained to become agents of therapeutic change; they are given the tools necessary to become effective cotherapists. Although the various intervention techniques are multimodal, multifaceted, and individualized to address the needs of a particular child with a specific problem, all parent training approaches share the common goal of systematically training parents in the most appropriate and effective behavioral modification methods. The instructional formats are intended to impart information and skills that better equip parents to identify, assess, remedy, and resolve the child's maladaptive and disordered behaviors and interactional patterns. The therapist instructs, guides, and supervises parents as they acquire greater mastery and competency in the understanding, development, and implementation of parenting skills. Parents learn how to effect constructive changes in the child and enhance relationships within the family. Effective parent training not only benefits the child, but by its very structure elicits positive changes within the context of the parent-child constellation and the family.

Parents are in a unique position to know their youngsters. In a very real sense, they are specialists when it comes to their own children. In a similar manner, mental health professionals know the complexities and nuances of behavioral analysis; they are specialists in the application of behavioral principles. Parent training is a reciprocal relationship, in which the participants share their respective expertise to the advantage of the child and family. The approach is not only child-focused, it is also problem-focused. It is prescriptive in that the intervention strategies are designed to ameliorate specific childhood problems.

This book is intended to serve as a practical and comprehensive guide for practitioners in a number of areas of child care, including the fields of psychology, psychiatry, social work, nursing, pediatrics, education, and related areas. Every chapter offers scientifically based research grounded in the principles of behavioral and developmental psychology. However, the authors do not describe their respective intervention approaches in an empirical vacuum. Each approach has been clinically tested, critically evaluated, and reevaluated through follow-up studies. The authors are also mental health consultants and practitioners. They illustrate the appropriate procedures and application of their intervention formats through extensive case material. The reader is privy to the combined and integrated techniques and sequential steps employed in each treatment session to remediate and modify the problems of troubled children and the frustrations experienced by their families.

While emphasizing the prescriptive approach, the authors also recognize that any given problem-focused intervention tactic may not necessarily be appropriate or effective with every child who manifests that problem. This text is certainly not in-tended to be a standardized, one-size-fits-all panacea. Even the best and most valid time-tested procedures cannot be applied to every problem situation. Our aim is to share professional knowledge and expertise. In implementing these skills, however, therapists must be creative and resourceful in adopting and adapting these procedures to the specific needs and expectations of the parents and children with whom they work. No definitive formula, no fail-safe gimmick, no "cookbook recipe" can guarantee the parents' and/or child's active and collaborative participation and efficacious treatment outcomes. The authors in this book articulate groundbreaking intervention strategies that are theoretically and empirically sound and clinically tested. In their thought-provoking presentations, the authors deliver appealing and impressive suggestions and directives as they uncover fertile ground for further re-search and the implementation of the divergent approaches enumerated in this book. The readers are invited to adopt these perspectives and strategies to their own intervention scenarios. When appropriate, these programs can be combined and integrated with other treatment alternatives. Within these pages, the authors offer programs that can improve parent-child relationships, enhance communication and listening skills, and modify the child's disruptive behaviors. They also offer the readers appealing challenges and directives for further professional creativity, involvement, and collaboration.

JAMES M. BRIESMEISTER
CHARLES E. SCHAEFER

Shelby Township, Michigan
Teaneck, New Jersey
November 1997

Contents

Introduction

THE NATURE OF PARENT TRAINING

THE ADVENT of behavioral parent training can be traced to the 1960s (Hawkins, Peterson, Schweid, & Bijou, 1966; Wahler, Winkel, Peterson, & Morrison, 1965). Even before it was well established, parent training was perceived as an innovative approach that sparked curiosity, enthusiasm, and optimism as a viable form of intervention for childhood problems. From its introduction, parent training was hailed as an ingenious and multifaceted format that not only modified negative behaviors of children but also strengthened the family unit and offered parents new resources for enhancing their skills and efficacy in the demanding task of parenting. Training parents to become effective cotherapists steadily evolved into a systematic and empirically grounded approach that typically relied on stylized interventions designed to instruct parents in practical and clinically tested techniques for modifying the disruptive, maladaptive, and undesirable behaviors of their children. The pioneering formats for parent training characteristically taught parents how to change their children's behaviors through behavioral engineering; the application of social-learning principles; and newly acquired parental monitoring, intervention, and relational competencies and abilities. Mental health professionals guide the parents in the accurate identification of childhood problems, implement assessment measures that help define the problem and its intensity, and educate parents in the treatment plans that would be best suited for the specific childhood conflicts they confront in their individual family situations. In essence, the parent training approach utilizes parents as the primary agents of change for their children. It is, after all, the parents who construct and manage the child's environment. One of the most crucial tasks of parenting is the formation of an environment

1

in which children can learn to recognize, appreciate, and develop appropriate social behaviors and skills.

Few would argue that the word *parenting* may be used interchangeably with the term *socialization.* Parents set the standards, roles, expectations, and demands for their children. Parents have the primary responsibility for molding their young wards into responsible, productive, and caring members of society—assets to the human community. It follows, then, that the parenting role is essential to the overall welfare of the family, community, and society as a whole. Parent training is, in essence, a form of behavioral family intervention. As such, the approach may be described as a therapeutic process in which the parents serve as cotherapists. The process is directed at effecting changes and remediations in a child's behavior and adjustment by altering aspects of the family environment that affect the problematic behavior of the youngster (Sanders & Dadds, 1993). Therefore, it is a logical, practical, and expedient format for instructing and influencing positive changes within the child, the family, and the community at large.

Any discussion about parent training must take into account the target child's age and developmental level or stage. For any intervention strategy to be effective, it must be appropriate and in accord with the child's level of personal, cognitive, emotional, social, and psychological growth. Parent training is child-focused. If an intervention technique is age- or stage-inappropriate, it will not only prove ineffectual, it may also confuse and anger the youngster, thereby aggravating and compounding an already stressful situation. Intervention ploys that are too young and simplistic will bore the child. Those that are too challenging or demanding will frustrate the child. In either case, the child is lost. In a discussion of childhood depression and psychological disorders, Bemporad (1978) asserts that any consideration of therapeutic intervention with young children must assess, evaluate, and treat the symptoms within the context and framework of the developmental process. The parent training approach acknowledges, respects, and works within the parameters of the child's developmental process.

THE CONTENT AND STRUCTURE OF PARENT TRAINING FORMATS

Parent training is grounded in the empirical and applied concepts of behaviorism as well as the principles of social learning theory. These notions are communicated to the parents in several ways. Although the instructional process, as well as the research and clinical application, is systematic, parent training is not a unidimensional approach. It involves complex, multimodal, and multifaceted intervention strategies that are determined by the needs of the target child, the unique parent-child relationship, the idiosyncratic needs inherent in the family structure, and the nature of the problem. All interventions share in the common goal of teaching parents how to modify and remedy destructive and dysfunctional patterns of family interaction in order to produce lasting and constructive changes (Patterson, 1969). Parent training particularly seeks to modify the reciprocal patterns of antecedents and consequences of problematic child behavior as well as faulty styles of child management. The parents are in a position to determine and control the child's rewards and punishments. The behavioral parent training format may also employ didactic measures and verbal instructions that teach parents the ways of communicating or interacting with their children which are most likely to result in a positive relationship and desirable behaviors for all involved. In addition, they may be trained to use behavioral management and contingency schedules that help parents determine the most effective forms of differential reinforcements and the most successful reinforcement regime. Instructional manuals, problem-focused check-lists, and shaping may also be warranted and in accord with the specific needs of the family and target child's issues. Parents may be trained, in the effective use of time-out, which, essentially, means removing children from provocative or destructive environmental stimuli by having them go to another room or sit in a chair for a designated period. The use of contingency schedules may involve training the parents to ascertain whether it would prove more effective and long-lasting to reward the child should every time a desirable behavior occurs (continuous reinforcement) or to reward the child only occasionally (intermittent reinforcement)? The behavioral parent training procedure is determined by specific problems and needs. Different schedules of reinforcement, stimulus control techniques, and extinction may be prescribed for different children and distinct problematic situations.

Along with the most effective application of contingency schedules and contingency management, parent training formats may also emphasize *active* training methods, such as modeling, rehearsal, feedback, and structured homework assignments. Mental health professionals may offer guided practice in modeling. Therapists might use videotapes, case presentations and examples, group procedures, and the like to demonstrate the appropriate techniques necessary to achieve improved parent-child communications, relations, or the resolution of specific problems. The theoretical foundation of social learning theory, and in particular the research findings of Bandura (1977), are invaluable in understanding the impact of modeling as an instructional format and a technique for changing a child's disruptive behavior. The clinician is able to offer feedback regarding the parents' performance. In fact, through the aid of videotapes, the parents themselves may be able to view their own modeling techniques and interactions with the child. As such, the parents are able to offer their own feedback and critique their own performance. They can identify their potential strengths and weaknesses and correct any existing shortcomings.

One of the many beneficial side effects of modeling involves the parents' enhanced sense of empathy with their child and the child's difficulties. For example, parents could be taught to model management skills, frustration tolerance, and impulse control for their child. The goal is to move toward the eventual internalization of self-management and self-monitoring in the child. Consequently, the positive impact of the parent training procedures should continue even in the parents' absence. The approach strives for generalizability as well as self-management. Through modeling, parents can also learn how to improve their communication skills. Parents as well as children can learn to communicate, listen, and respond more effectively. When parents model appropriate behaviors and responses for their children and, perhaps, children model their interpretation of the parents' statements, behaviors, or expectations, it can be quite an awakening for both parties. Modeling, then, can be utilized to improve mutual understanding, reciprocity, and empathy within the family structure.

Parent training has made significant progress over the past years. The instructional procedures have included and exceeded many of the more traditional formats. Current strategies involve a combination of behavioral and social learning gamets with exciting, prolific, and promising results. The formats include such factors as innovative assessments, early intervention programs, training procedures, and follow-up studies. Many of the current advances in parent training address the need for early clinical intervention suggested by empirical research in child behavior and development. For example, research on conduct disorder and antisocial behavior has consistently emphasized the need for the early identification of risk factors as well as early intervention (Offord & Bennett, 1994; Pakiz, Reinherz, & Giaconia, 1997; Reid, 1993). A number of the authors in this book (see Chapters 2, 3, 5, and 16) focus on early interventions that employ the parent training format to reduce risks for antisocial behavior using the parent training format. Recent developments in parent training have centered on an ecobehavioral approach (see Chapter 9) that involves identifying and assessing the families' social ecology (Lutzker & Campbell, 1994) and examining possible influences—constructive and destructive—that may impact the family unit.

A review of the progress and advances in parent training discloses that the intervention procedures extend beyond seeking to resolve children's clinical disorders and behavioral problems. Contingency schedules, child management techniques, and social learning principles combine with a host of concepts, theories, and tactics. New advances integrate the behavioral and social learning principles with attribution theory (see Chapter 6), the theoretical structure and content of play therapy (see Chapter 10), and home-based treatment (see Chapter 12). Research in child development and family relations emphasize the correlation between healthy sibling relationships and mental health and adjustment (Stocker, 1994; Volling, Youngblade, & Belsky, 1997). Consistent with empirical data, new and creative parent instructional formats have been designed to improve sibling relationships (see Chapter 4). Parent training has become increasingly more sophisticated, ingenious, penetrating, and prescriptive. Some parent training formats now focus on the impact of differential child temperament styles (see Chapter 15). The approach is structured to meet the temperament styles of the target child and also to address the problems that may surface if the child's temperament style is not a good fit with the parents' styles and behaviors. Furthermore, since therapy occurs within the context of the family, culture, and historical time, it is affected by the moral standards of the family and the society at large (see Chapter 16) as well as by modern technology and contemporary theories. Therefore, it is not surprising that videotape-based parent training programs have become more prevalent (see Chapters 3 and 5).

Because parent training formats are multimodal and multifaceted, the content of the programs can be individually formulated, structured, and designed to meet specific needs of the child, family, and parent-child unit. Furthermore, the myriad modalities allow for generalizability; the newly acquired skills can be applied variously and in divergent situations. The theoretically grounded concepts of systematic behavioral analysis and the principles of social-cognitive learning are generic and applicable to a wide range of problematic circumstances. Parent training procedures tend to be problem-focused. In fact, an essential research priority of the parent training format is to determine which type of training technique is best suited for different parents, children, and problems (Blechman, 1981). However, even though the behavioral and social learning precepts used to improve parenting abilities and child management may be prescribed for a particular problem, the behavioral instructional techniques are generalizable. They can be effectively applied to a multitude of problematic situations.

HISTORICAL ANTECEDENTS OF PARENT TRAINING

Since its inception, parent training has had a profound impact on the field of developmental psychology and child therapy; it has become a prominent intervention strategy in the treatment of numerous childhood disorders. In one of the earliest recorded cases of therapeutic intervention involving a child, Freud (1909/1955) presented the analysis of Little Hans, a youngster approaching 5 years of age. In this classic case study, Freud did not treat Little Hans directly. Instead, he instructed the boy's father in viable strategies for resolving Hans's underlying phobic impulses and symptoms. However, considerable time elapsed before the occurrence of similar recorded instances in which parent training played a significant role in therapy with children.

Many researchers have investigated and compared the effectiveness of differential parent training programs in reducing childhood conflicts (e.g., Blechman, 1985; Flanagan, Adams, & Forehand, 1979, Forehand & McMahon, 1981; O'Dell, Flynn, & Benlolo, 1979). Nay (1975) conducted one of the earliest systematic comparisons of differential instructional techniques. An in-depth comparison was made among five different methods of instructing mothers of young children in time-out procedures: written, lecture, and videotape presentations; videotape modeling coupled with role playing; and a no-treatment condition. The parents benefited from all the training techniques; the results did not show any statistically significant differences among the various instructional procedures. Parent training as an effective method of intervention fared very well in these early reviews, comparisons, and critiques. It has evolved as a viable empirically supported and clinically tested approach for working with a wide range of childhood problems and dysfunctions. Two decades ago, Graziano (1977) argued convincingly that the parent training approach has revolutionized clinical interventions and services for children, adding that it may be one of the most significant achievements in the field of child therapy. Today, that statement remains as valid an assessment of the status of parent training as it was then. Given the abundance of research and successful clinical applications, the revolution appears to be continuing at an impressive pace.

In the relevant research and literature of the 1980s, there is evidence of a growing interest in, and confirmation of, the value and impact of training parents as cotherapists. Wells and Forehand (1981), for example propose that the approach has benefits for such problems as childhood antisocial behaviors and conduct disorders. Extensive descriptions and reviews of the efficacy and applicability of behavioral parent training procedures are presented in Dangel and Polster (1984), Kendall and Braswell (1985), Milne (1986), and in the original edition of Schaefer and Briesmeister (1989). Each of the various intervention techniques offered in these reviews aims to equip parents with the most essential, efficient, and effective behavioral management tactics and social learning skills. The reviews recount detailed descriptions of crucial theoretically grounded and empirically tested intervention approaches. The researchers whose studies are described in these reviews employ numerous case studies to illustrate the relevancy, applicability, impact, efficacy, and generalizability of the divergent strategies as they are applied to childhood problems and dysfunctions.

ADVANCES IN PARENT TRAINING AND ITS APPLICATION

The growing success of the parent training approach has spawned numerous empirical studies and has prompted a broader application of the methods and principles of training parents as cotherapists. Researchers and clinicians continue to discover the advantages of the parent training format. Zacker (1978) points out that parents quickly master and apply the principles of social-cognitive learning and behavioral modification. Because behavior therapy is based on natural and observable phenomena, it is readily accepted by parents without great resistance or hesitation. It also affords the parents a sense of efficacy, esteem, and competence in the parenting role. Some researchers have noted that family dysfunction is at core a generic risk factor for an array of childhood disorders and adjustment maladies (e.g., Dadds, 1987; Rutter, 1985). At the same time, one of the major criticisms of empirical research is that it is difficult to translate into an applicable treatment strategy. Research that centers on clinical practice has been criticized for focusing on a standardized, one-size-fits-all solution or format (Persons, 1991). Given that dysfunctional behavior is at the root of family conflicts, treatment interventions must address the idiosyncratic manner in which the particular dysfunction is manifested. Parent training offers a prescriptive approach. The principles involved in the training process are suitable for the remediation and modification of situation-specific, child-specific, and family-specific problems all of which involve some dysfunctional factors.

A brief and admittedly condensed review of the history of research and clinical application of these intervention principles and procedures confirms that parent training has been applied to the modification of myriad problematic situations. Parent training has been used in the remediation and resolution of oppositional and conduct-disordered youngsters (Forehand & Long, 1988; Serketich & Dumas, 1996; Webster-Stratton & Hammond, 1990; Webster-Stratton, Kolpacoff, & Hollinsworth, 1988; Wells & Egan, 1988). The parent instructional approach has also been used to address and remedy attention-deficit/hyperactivity disorder (Abikoff & Hechtman, 1996; Anastopoulos & Barkley 1990; Anastopoulos, Shelton, DuPaul, & Guevremont, 1993; Pisterman, Firestone, McGrath, & Goodman, 1992). In addition, attempts have also been made to train parents in the reduction of childhood fears, anxieties, and obsessive-compulsive symptoms (Kearney & Silverman, 1995; Knox, Albano, & Barlow, 1996). The parent training intervention approach has also been applied to abused and neglected children (Lutzker, 1992; Wolfe, Edwards, Manion, & Koverola, 1988) as well as youngsters with developmental disabilities (Baker, Smithen, & Kashimal, 1991; Harrold, Lutzker, Campbell, & Touchette, 1992; Huynen, Lutzker, Bigelow, Touchette, & Campbell, 1996). This selected and abridged review of parent training formats is but a small representation of the heuristic value, fertile and prolific clinical application, and growing acceptance of parent training.

PARENTS AS AGENTS OF THERAPEUTIC CHANGE

Traditionally, mental health professionals who work with children have sought to effect change directly with their young patients. Within the parent training process, however, the therapist educates the parents in the proper application of those procedures that elicit socially desirable changes in behavior and reduce or eliminate socially undesirable actions. Braswell (1991) proposes that the notion of the patient-client relationship as a collaborative effort is a tenet of the behavioral and cognitive-behavioral modalities. Parent training has its origins within the applied behavioral analysis traditions. One of the key premises of applied behavioral analysis is that a child's behavior, whether adaptive or maladaptive, desirable or undesirable, is a product of the youngster's history and present interactions with people and circumstances that impact on the child. Consequently, the training approach views the parents as the primary caregivers and managers of the child's environment. Parents become the primary mediators to bring about long-term therapeutic change in the children (Patterson, 1969). Any effective intervention strategy must assess and modify those aspects of the child's social environment that contribute to, maintain, and exacerbate problems. Parents are trained in viable and clinically tested techniques that have been proven to ameliorate childhood conflicts. To accomplish this complex and challenging goal, parents must be instructed in the systematic application of the most effective principles of behavioral management and social learning theory. Training parents in the appropriate use of differential social contingencies for the reduction of specific conflicts affords them a bevy of viable intervention formats.

Family therapy approaches and multisystemic intervention models (e.g., Haley, 1976; Minuchin, 1974) propose that behavioral problems of the child are best understood within the context of the family as an interrelated system. This empirically grounded stance insists that parents are intimately enmeshed in the child's life, adaptive styles, and maladaptive actions. Changes in the parenting strategies directly affect the child in obvious as well as subtle ways. Furthermore, this influence and impact on the child remains long after the termination of formal therapy with a mental health professional. The parents' impact on the child is unquestionably long-lasting and far-reaching. Parental influence and impact, like the parent-child relationship, extends over the entire lifespan. Although the intensity of the impact may differ at various developmental levels, it is, nonetheless, very real. A review of the extensive and growing body of literature on parent training makes it clear that the behavioral training approach does not merely serve as an adjunct to child therapy. In fact, it is an intervention maneuver that is at the very core of the treatment process. In this approach parents and the family environment no longer serve as a backdrop for therapy. Similarly, although they acknowledge and utilize the professionals' expertise and experience, parents are the cotherapists, the agents of change. In this manner, the parent-child relationship is the most essential and integral variable within the therapeutic endeavor. Consequently, the parents' role involvement in therapy is not one of passive observation in which parents sit on the sidelines and wait for the mental health professional to "cure" their child's disorder or dysfunction. Instead, the parents are an essential variable in the therapeutic paradigm. Their role is that of an active therapeutic agent of change. This approach recognizes and enhances the efficacy, competency, and skills of the parents.

ADVANTAGES OF THE
PARENT TRAINING FORMAT

One of the many benefits and advantages of the behavioral parent training approach is that it allows parents to develop a well-established and, at times, hard-earned, sense of mastery and confidence in their parenting skills (Donofrio, 1976). It also reaffirms the primary importance of the parent-child unit. In a number of instances, the parents learn to communicate and interrelate constructively with their child for the first time. What once may have been a situation that was out of control now appears positive, rewarding, and filled with promise for the parents as well as the child. In this approach, the parents do not place the child in therapy with the expectation that the expert will "fix" the problem. Instead, the perception and expectation is that the clinician will show the parents how they can remedy their child's problem. The therapist reinforces the parents' competencies and abilities to cope with their child and resolve the youngster's current and future conflicts.

Another major advantage of the active parental involvement, which is at the core of behavioral parent training is the realization that parents are more likely to maintain their children in therapy if, in fact, the parents are an integral and essential part of that treatment orientation. In contrast, many traditional therapeutic formats occasionally invite the parents to participate in the child-clinician's therapeutic relationship. Parents are allowed to join in select treatment sessions, receive didactic information about the therapeutic process or goals, ask questions, and are given updates on the child's therapeutic status and future prognosis. This approach may instill in the parents the perception that they are unable to mange their child's problems; they must rely on an outside agent, a mental health professional, to enable them to cope with their child's maladies. In the parent training format, the parents are the cotherapists. With this integral involvement, in which the parents are at the core of the therapeutic process, parents are more likely to continue with the training and keep their child in treatment. They are also more likely to comply with follow-up studies.

As mentioned in discussing the content and structure of parent training, the multicomponent intervention strategies can be applied in different situations. The ability to generalize clinical treatment effects is certainly one criterion of the effectiveness, success, and value of any intervention process. Parents and children need to generalize the newly acquired management skills beyond the boundaries of the training sessions. Parents typically master behavioral management skills that increase the child's ability to adapt and cope as well as enhance parenting abilities and confidence. At some point, therefore, the parents as well as the youngster are likely to apply the bounty of new knowledge to future problems and situations. Parents may generalize the skills across time, children, circumstances, conflicts, and settings. If new challenges and difficulties surface, they can implement their training experiences. In some instances, parents will make the generalizations automatically and in an appropriate and correct manner. On the other hand, some parents may require further training and interventions to implement effective generalizations (Sanders & Glynn, 1981).

The child will also generalize learned skills such as self-monitoring, self-management, impulse control, attentional enhancements, and improved communications and interactional styles. In fact, generalization is more likely to ensure when parents treat their own children at home, because behaviors are being modified and formed in the same environment in which they have occurred and will continue to occur (Donofrio, 1976). The child, like the parents, may generalize without any prompting or may require some instructions in the appropriate application of the positive skills to different situations. If a child participated in a home-based intervention, the skills and gains will transfer to school. Conversely, if the treatment program was school-based, therapeutic gains should transfer to the home environment. The impact of the intervention and remediation can be extensive and broad. The social and communication skills that a child acquires in a parent training strategy aimed at improving sibling relationships can generalize to relationships with parents, grandparents, teachers, classmates, and peers. Skills that help the child reduce school phobia and anxiety can also decrease the youngster's resistance to unfamiliar environments and situations. By learning impulse control techniques in parent training sessions, the child is better able to reduce acting-out behaviors in school, at play, and while shopping with the parents.

Today, stepfamilies, restructured second and third families, and amalgamated families, in general, are more common than ever (Baa, Sweet, & Martin, 1990). The conflicts associated with single-parenting, custodial disputes, joint custody, and nontraditional family configurations are increasingly taking center stage. Parent training intervention is well suited to the needs of families in transition because it is multimodal, integrates divergent concepts and tactics, utilizes parents as primary agents of therapeutic change and incorporates the target child and parents in a collaborative effort within any family context. Not all therapeutic formats adequately address the unique and complicated needs of restructured families. Lawton and Sanders (1994) propose that even some traditional forms of parent training have been inadequate when confronting the conflicts inherent in restructured families; these formats need to be modified and reformulated in light of the delicate and, at times, undefined role of parents within stepfamilies. To meet this need, Lawton and Sanders have developed a behavioral stepfamily intervention program which includes techniques to enhance partner support and highlights the value of shared family activities to reduce the child's oppositional and conflictual behavior.

Any discussion of the advantages and benefits of parent training would be incomplete without considering a very practical issue, cost. In this era of managed care and ongoing cuts in mental health programs, the burden of cost often falls on the family. Quite often, the families who need mental health services for their children are not in a position to afford the costs. Due to its very nature and structure, parent training tends to be a cost-effective form of treatment. Typically, the intervention is home-based and short-term. Despite the variations within a behavioral family training approach, the therapeutic contract and format that the clinician establishes with the parents is clearly delineated and designed to accomplish two tasks: first, to teach parents positive and effective techniques for child management; second, to decrease problematic behaviors within the family (Crane, 1995). These goals and the overall education of adults can also be accomplished within a group setting. A number of parent training approaches extend beyond the home-based implementation.

Many programs are specifically designed for a school setting, classroom, play setting, child treatment facility, clinic, hospital, and various child-care agencies.

Research evaluating and comparing the treatment outcomes of group training approaches across age and problem situations has yielded interesting results. Ruma, Burke, and Thompson (1996) used hierarchical regression analysis to test the effects of a number of variables, including site of training, age of the youngsters, and the severity of the presenting problems. In terms of clinical significance, when comparing the effects of age, adolescents had the lowest rate of recovery. However, when a logistic regression analysis was completed, age was not a significant predictor of treatment success and recovery. The best predictor was the severity of the target child's problems. Group approaches tend to be less effective for children with the most severe problems. With the possible exception of extreme clinical disorders, the judicial use of group parent training is a viable approach. In fact, less professional time and expense is needed to instruct parents than to treat the child in a mental health setting. Furthermore, therapists typically need time to develop a therapeutic alliance and trust with the child. The child's trust of the parents has already been established, thereby saving time and the expense of therapy sessions. Group parent training results in significant savings of time, energy, and costs. Furthermore, when parent-child units are placed in behavioral training groups with other parents and children who share similar (or related) problems, all participants learn from each other. A form of peer instruction, modeling and coaching takes place. This further reduces time and costs and faciliates the therapeutic process.

FUTURE DIRECTIONS

Although parent training intervention approaches have been effective with many families, there is still room for improvement and the need for ongoing progress and refinement. As successful as any intervention tactic may be, it cannot afford to rest on its laurels; ongoing transformation and evolution are essential. Theories, concepts, and clinical implementations must be continuously redefined, reevaluated, and reapplied in increasingly more sophisticated ways. Attempts to update the parent training content, structure, format, and process must be consistent with current empirically based and clinically tested constructs in child and adolescent development, family therapy, child treatment strategies, and related intervention methods. Researchers and mental health practitioners who work with children and their families must strive for more systematic and heuristic research and theory development as well as pragmatic and cost-effective clinical applications. Professionals in the field of parent training are certainly on the right course when they highlight the importance of follow-up studies to measure the strengths and deficits of treatment outcome, the long-term maintenance and impact of treatment, the generalizability of the newly acquired skills and techniques, and the overall and long-term impact of the intervention ploy on the child and parents.

Similarly, research and follow-up studies must continue to focus on the development of assessment strategies and measures to predict, control, and prevent relapse once the intervention program has been completed. Further research needs to focus on the efficacy of intervention programs that are structured to include occasional "retraining" and "refresher" sessions. In a very real sense, the therapeutic process may be "interminable." Parents need the reassurance that if the dysfunctional behaviors resurface or, for whatever reason, maintenance and generalizability do not persist, they can return to the mental health specialist for a reinstatement of the parent training procedures.

Increasing attention must be concentrated on the bidirectional nature and impact of the parent-child relationship. Not only does the parents' behavior affect the child; the childs' behavior, actions, and temperament also reciprocally affect the parents' responses to the child. Mental health researchers and professionals need to foster studies akin to Sheeber and McDevitt's temperament-focused parent training (Chapter 15). The success of future parent training formats may be contingent on a continued awareness and investigation of the subtle but powerful influence of personality and temperament variables, adjustment patterns, and coping styles of the parents and children.

Admittedly, traditional parent training intervention formats have concentrated on the identification, assessment, resolution, and remediation of children's problems within the context of the family structure. It is equally as important to prevent or avert problems and maladaptive actions and reactions well before their inception or at least before the disruptive influence spreads throughout the family and overwhelms its members. Empirical research must focus on the importance of preventive tactics and measures. We must continue to develop and test effective assessments and evaluative instruments that identify variables in the behavioral patterns of children and parents placing them at risk for future catastrophe. Every attempt must be made to identify these risk factors and intervene as early as possible. This early identification and intervention process is, in essence, preventive. Just as the prescriptive approach is structured and designed to meet the needs of particular problems and maladjustment issues, so too, differential prevention and identification maneuvers must address specific problems, the needs of the individual child, and the idiosyncratic parent-child interactive pattern. Since the early development of parent training formats, the generic theories of behavioral analysis and the general principles of social-cognitive learning have been molded and tempered to fit the individual child, parent-child constellation, and family, not vice versa. Furthermore, this individualized sculpting process must occur early and it must include preventive as well as remedial aspects.

THE APPROACH OF THIS BOOK

This book is intended to serve as a practical and comprehensive handbook of theoretically sound and empirically tested approaches to training parents as cotherapists. This book is a revised update of an earlier version (1989). Parent training remains primarily behavioral in focus and grounded in learning theory and the principles of conditioning and behavior modification. However, provocative, inventive, and prolific insights and conceptualizations have occurred since the original publication of *The Handbook of Parent Training*. The growing body of research in this field is heuristic and fertile and offers thought-provoking directions for future studies and implementation. The clinical application has become increasingly more ingenious and diverse. The parent training approach can also be used in conjunction with a wide range of intervention theories and formats. The authors represented in this book come from divergent theoretical backgrounds and orientations. They are particularly knowledgeable in theoretical constructs regarding child and adolescent development and growth. Many of these authors are pioneers in the field of parent training and family therapy. In addition, they are skilled researchers and clinicians. Their clinical expertise is based on an integration of empirical knowledge, clinical experience, and professional creativity and farsightedness.

This text reflects a prescriptive approach to therapy. The authors present specific childhood disorders, problems, and difficulties in coping and adjusting. They then describe parent training modalities for each conflictual situation. Any consideration of childhood disorders must be understood against the backdrop of the developmental process as well as the individual child's level or stage of development. Any and all expectations regarding the child's physical, cognitive, emotional, social-interpersonal actions and behaviors must also be made within the framework of the developmental process and within the context of the family unit. Knowing this, the authors who have contributed to this handbook have an expertise in family and group intervention procedures as well as child development and child psychology. They are also specialists in behavioral theory and social-cognitive learning principles. The range of childhood disorders is vast, complex, and overwhelming. Therefore, therapeutic attempts at resolution must address and integrate numerous variables, constructs, and treatment approaches. The contributors to this book present descriptions and case material that demonstrate their approaches to diagnosing, assessing, evaluating, and resolving childhood disorders and adjustment problems.

The ability to individualize treatment and to prescribe remedies or modification techniques that meet the needs of each child requires a bewildering amount of technical knowledge. Despite our dedication and involvement as professionals in the field of child, family, and adolescent care, we are understandably limited in our knowledge, time, energy, and resources. In today's quick-paced and busy world, it is difficult to keep abreast of the ever growing and expansive changes in the field of mental health. This book attempts to fill those technical gaps. The authors in this book have assembled and reviewed a vast array of empirical and technical research and treatment strategies. Furthermore, they have evaluated, modified, and refined their respective parent training approaches. These efforts afford readers an opportunity to increase their own fund of knowledge and repertoire of therapeutic skills and aptitudes and, perhaps, to narrow the expanse of their own technical gaps.

The prescriptive approach used throughout this book is also an applied approach. The authors have implemented and tested their particular parent training formats. They can offer guidelines, precautionary suggestions, indications and contraindications, and invaluable recommendations for each intervention program. Some of the intervention strategies are directive and delineate straightforward child management maneuvers, whereas others are less structured and become defined as the instructional program progresses. All the training programs, however, involve active participation on the part of parents and the child. Parental input is essential at all stages of the treatment process: diagnosis, assessment, intervention proper, evaluation, and follow-up studies regarding treatment outcome. Similarly, all the procedures in this book are family-, child-, and problem-focused. They address a unique family constellation, an individual child, and a particular problematic issue.

THE FORMAT OF THIS BOOK

Many books that focus on therapy with children begin with a broad theoretical orientation and then attempt to relate the theory to specific maladaptive and dysfunctional behaviors. In contrast, our approach identifies some prevalent and specific childhood behavioral problems. We then describe multimodal parent training approaches to identify, assess, and modify these specific behavior disorders. Each contributor to this

Handbook offers unique multifaceted therapeutic techniques that integrate theory, research, and implementation strategies. Many of the authors are recognized pioneers and specialists in the field of parent training and child therapy. All of them are well versed and experienced researchers and clinicians who have developed, tested, and refined practical treatment strategies and have made significant contributions to the growing body of parent training literature. The book has five parts, which center on major and specific disorder categories and topics.

The authors in Part One of the book concentrate on intervention strategies that ameliorate and remedy externalizing disorders. These are behaviors that characteristically turn against others in their environment. It can include such disorders as antisocial behaviors, attention-deficit/hyperactivity disorders, maladaptive relationships with others, and, in general, acting-out.

In Chapter 1, Anastopoulos offers a rationale for applying parent training to the treatment of attention-deficit/hyperactivity disorder. The author expounds on the direct and more subtle impact that this disorder may have on other externalizing behaviors and symptoms and presents a step-by-step intervention format.

In Chapter 2, Eyberg and Boggs elaborate on a psychosocial intervention treatment program for preschool youngsters with conduct disorder. They emphasize techniques that develop, maintain, and enhance positive parent-child relationships and reduce the risk factors for continued problems.

In Chapter 3, Webster-Stratton and Hancock introduce the reader to a videotape-based parent training program for the management of oppositional and conduct-disordered children. A multitude of tested and proven child management maneuvers are illustrated in this videotaped modeling and instructional tactic.

In Chapter 4, Johnston and Freeman tackle the all-too-prevalent problem of sibling conflict and rivalry. Their creative training approach gives parents effective problem-solving skills as well as ways in which they can foster positive antecedent conditions within the family, thereby improving the well-being of all its members.

In Chapter 5, Miller points out that early conduct problems may be precursors of antisocial behaviors. The author then enumerates on the Enhanced Parent Training Program, which is designed to reduce and alter destructive risk factors.

The authors in Part Two of the Handbook direct attention to internalizing disorders. They apply treatment strategies aimed at reducing the negative impact and problems associated with separation anxiety and school refusal.

In Chapter 6, Eisen, Engler, and Geyer discuss a multifaceted intervention program that uses cognitive-behavioral procedures to modify and reduce a child's separation anxiety. The authors also present timely strategies for assessing and evaluating the intensity of childhood anxiety disorders.

Kearney and Roblek, in Chapter 7, review an extensive spectrum of school refusal problems and the impact of school refusal on the youngster, parents, and family, in general. The authors offer a muticomponent assessment process and intervention approach that identifies a number of key variables which may associated with school refusal. Each approach seeks to address and resolve the key factors.

Part Three of the book focuses on conflicts related to developmental lags and deficits. The authors in this section identify and address problems that may interfere with the natural process of physical, cognitive, emotional, social, and psychological growth and development.

In Chapter 8, Lachenmeyer discusses and describes the difficulties associated with a failure to thrive syndrome. The author examines parent training intervention formats that can be adapted to a wide spectrum of situations in which poor nutritional intake is negatively affecting a child's growth and causing conflicts for all the members of the family.

In Chapter 9, Lutzker and Steed review and evaluate an impressive number of historic parent training approaches. They outline the steady progression and evolution of parent training modalities particularly as they apply to the modification of problems related to developmental disabilities. The authors describe and illustrate an ecobehavioral model of parent training intervention.

Booth and Koller submit a discussion of Theraplay in Chapter 10. Theraplay is an inventive short-term, goal-oriented intervention modeled on the reciprocity that is inherent in the relationship between parent and child. This approach is best suited to the treatment of underlying relationship problems, such as training parents of failure-to-attach children.

In Part Four of the text, the authors concentrate on some representative problems common to children. Faulty sleep patterns, enuresis, and food refusal are typical examples of conflictual situations that can be a source of immense stress within the family. The chapters in this section of the book offer detailed, step-by-step programs that seek to reduce some of the more prominant and disturbing features of these maladaptive childhood conflicts.

In Chapter 11, Wolfson discusses the wide range of normal sleep patterns and cycles seen in infants. The author then cites mechanisms for distinguishing normal from disturbed infant sleep patterns. Wolfson emphasizes the prevention as well as the remediation of faulty sleep patterns and the influence that parents have on the infant's sleep/wake habits.

Mellon and Houts offer a home-based treatment for primary enuresis. In Chapter 12, they present some traditional approaches that have been instrumental in the treatment of this childhood disorder. The crux of the chapter, however, describes the Full Spectrum Home Training, which incorporates research-based and time-tested strategies for controlling and reducing enuresis.

In Chapter 13, Budd, Chugh, and Berry articulate the scope of children's food refusal problems. Following a clarification and distinction of the characteristics of chronic food refusal from a failure to thrive syndrome, the authors elucidate on the impact of the parents' behaviors on the child's feeding or eating dysfunctions. They offer clinical cases that demonstrate the effectiveness of specific parent training procedures in reducing and modifying children's food refusal problems.

Part Five addresses some of the unique problems that might be experienced by special needs parents and children. The chapters in this section focus on restructured and transitional families. The authors also discuss the impact of child temperament and the fit or misfit of the parent-child temperament interaction. Groundbreaking strategies designed to instill moral and prosocial behaviors within the family context are also illustrated.

In Chapter 14, Weiss and Wolchik present an empirically based intervention program geared toward training mothers to help their children adjust to the traumatic impact of divorce. The "New Beginnings" program emphasizes skill acquisition as well as the effective reduction of stressors associated with divorce.

In Chapter 15, Sheeber and McDevitt offer an intervention program based on an understanding of children's temperament to modify and enhance parent-child relations. The authors demonstrate a temperament-focused approach that illustrates how different childhood temperamental styles affect the parents as well as parental responses and parenting techniques.

Blechman, in Chapter 16, points out some of the major deficits in coping patterns of high-risk adolescents. The author discloses an ingenious intervention program. Prosocial Family Therapy, which takes place within a moral context and is constructed to help parents of antisocial youth promote prosocial coping behaviors.

In Chapter 17, Bratton presents an original parent training intervention strategy that seeks to improve the quality of the parent-child relationship following a divorce. Parents are trained to become agents of therapeutic change through the structured Filial/Family Play Therapy methodological approach. The approach discussed in Chapter 17 facilitates the child's adjustment to the divorce process and instills in the parents a sense of mastery and competency in essential parenting skills.

REFERENCES

Abikoff, H. B., & Hechtman, L. (1996). Multimodal therapy and stimulants in the treatment of children with attention-deficit hyperactivity disorder. In E. D. Hibbs & P. S. Jensen (Eds.), *Psychosocial treatments for child and adolescent disorders: Empirically based strategies for clinical practice* (pp. 341–369). Washington, DC: American Psychological Association.

Anastopoulos, A. D., & Barkley, R. A. (1990). Counseling and training parents. In R. A. Barkley (Ed.), *Attention deficit hyperactivity disorder: A handbook for diagnosis and treatment* (pp. 397–431). New York: Guilford Press.

Anastopoulos, A. D., Shelton, T., DuPaul, G. J., & Guevremont, D. C. (1993). Parent training for attention deficit hyperactivity disorder: Its impact on parent functioning. *Journal of Abnormal Child Psychology, 21,* 581–596.

Baa, I., Sweet, J., & Martin, T. C. (1990). Changing patterns of remarriage. *Journal of Marriage and the Family, 52,* 747–756.

Baker, B. L., Smithen, S. J., & Kashimal, K. J. (1991). Effects of parent training on families of children with mental retardation: Increased burden or generalized benefit? *American Journal on Mental Retardation, 96,* 127–136.

Bandura, A. (1977). *Social learning theory.* Englewood Cliffs, NJ: Prentice-Hall.

Bemporad, J. (1978). Psychotherapy of depression in children and adolescents. In S. Arieti & J. Bemporad (Eds.), *Severe and mild depression* (pp. 344–357). New York: Basic Books.

Blechman, E. A. (1981). Toward comprehensive behavioral family intervention: An algorithm for matching families and interventions. *Behavior Modifications, 5,* 221–236.

Blechman, E. A. (1985). *Solving child behavior problems: At home and at school.* Champaign, IL: Research Press.

Braswell, L. (1991). Involving parents in cognitive-behavioral therapy with children and adolescents. In P. C. Kendall (Ed.), *Child and adolescent therapy.* New York: Guilford Press.

Crane, D. R. (1995). Introduction to behavioral family therapy for families with young children. *Journal of Family Therapy, 17,* 229–242.

Dadds, M. R. (1987). Families and the origins of child behavior problems. *Family Process, 26,* 341–357.

Dangel, R. F., & Polster, R. A. (Eds.). (1984). *Parent training: Foundations of research and practice.* New York: Guilford Press.

Donofrio, A. F. (1976). Parent education vs. child psychotherapy. *Psychology in the Schools, 13*(2), 176–184.

Flanagan, S., Adams, H. E., & Forehand, R. (1979). A comparison of four instructional techniques for teaching parents how to use time-out. *Behavior Therapy, 10,* 94–102.

Forehand, R. L., & Long, N. (1988). Outpatient treatment of the acting out child: Procedures, long term follow-up data, and clinical problems. *Advances in Behavior Research and Therapy, 10,* 129–177.

Forehand, R. L., & McMahon, R. (1981). *Helping the noncompliant child.* New York: Guilford Press.

Freud, S. (1955). The analysis of a phobia in a 5-year-old boy. In J. Stachey (Ed. & Trans.), *The standard edition of the complete psychological works of Sigmund Freud* (Vol. 10, pp. 149–289). London: Hogarth Press. (Original work published 1909)

Graziano, A. M. (1977). Parents as behavior therapists. *Progress in Behavior Modification, 4,* 251–298.

Haley, J. (1976). *Problem solving therapy.* San Francisco: Jossey-Bass.

Harrold, M., Lutzker, J. R., Campbell, R. V., & Touchette, P. E. (1992). Improving parent-child interactions for families with developmental disabilities. *Journal of Behavior Therapy and Experimental Psychiatry, 23,* 89–100.

Hawkins, R. P., Peterson, R. F., Schweid, E., & Bijou, S. W. (1966). Behavior therapy in the home: Amelioration of problem parent-child relations with the parent in a therapeutic role. *Journal of Experimental Child Psychology, 4,* 99–107.

Huynen, K. B., Lutzker, J. R., Bigelow, K. M., Touchette, P. E., & Campbell, R. V. (1996). Planned activities training for mothers of children with developmental disabilities: Community generalization and follow-up. *Behavior Modification, 20,* 406–427.

Kearney, C. A., & Silverman, W. K. (1995). Family environment of youngsters with school refusal behavior: A synopsis with implications for assessment and treatment. *American Journal of Family Therapy, 23,* 59–72.

Kendall, P. C., & Braswell, L. (1985). *Cognitive-behavior therapy for impulsive children.* New York: Guilford Press.

Knox, L. S., Albano, A. M., & Barlow, D. H. (1996). Parental involvement in the treatment of childhood obsessive-compulsive disorder: A multiple baseline examination incorporating parents. *Behavior Therapy, 27,* 93–115.

Lawton, J. M., & Sanders, M. R. (1994). Designing effective behavioral family interventions for stepfamilies. *Clinical Psychology Review, 14,* 463–496,

Lutzker, J. R. (1992). Developmental disabilities and child abuse and neglect: The ecobehavioral imperative. *Behavior Change, 9,* 149–156.

Lutzker, J. R., & Campbell, R. V. (1994). *Ecobehavioral family interventions in developmental disabilities.* Pacific Grove, CA: Brooks/Cole.

Milne, D. (1986). *Training behavior therapists: Methods, evaluation and implementation with parents, nurses and teachers.* Cambridge, MA: Brookline Books.

Minuchin, S. (1974). *Families and family therapy.* Cambridge, MA: Harvard University Press.

Nay, W. R. (1975). A systematic comparison of instructional techniques for parents. *Behavior Therapy, 6,* 14–21.

O'Dell, S. L., Flynn, J. M., & Benlolo, L. A. (1979). A comparison of parent training techniques in child behavior modification. *Journal of Behavior Therapy and Experimental Psychiatry, 8,* 261–268.

Offord, D., & Bennett, K. J. (1994). Conduct disorder: Long-term outcomes and intervention effectiveness. *Journal of the American Academy of Child and Adolescent Psychiatry, 8,* 1069–1078.

Pakiz, B., Reinherz, H. Z., & Giaconia, R. M. (1997). Early risk factors for serious anti-social behavior at age 21: A longitudinal community study. *American Journal of Orthopsychiatry, 67*(1), 92–101.

Patterson, G. R. (1969). Behavioral techniques based on social learning: An additional base for developing behavior modification technologies. In C. M. Franks (Ed.), *Behavior therapy: Appraisal and status* (pp. 341–374). New York: McGraw-Hill.

Persons, J. B. (1991). Psychotherapy outcomes studies do not accurately represent current models of psychotherapy. *American Psychologist, 46,* 99–106.

Pisterman, S., Firestone, P., McGrath, P., & Goodman, J. T. (1992). The role of parent training in treatment of preschoolers with ADHD. *American Journal of Orthopsychiatry, 62,* 397–408.

Reid, J. B. (1993). Prevention of conduct disorder before and after school entry: Relating interventions to developmental findings. *Development and Psychopathology, 5,* 243–262.

Ruma, P. R., Burke, R. V., & Thompson, R. W. (1996). Group parent training: Is it effective for children of all ages? *Behavior Therapy, 27,* 159–169.

Rutter, M. (1985). Family and school influences on behavioral development. *Journal of Child Psychology and Psychiatry, 26,* 349–368.

Sanders, M. E., & Dadds, M. R. (1993). *Behavioral family intervention.* Needham Heights, MA: Allyn & Bacon.

Sanders, M. R., & Glynn, T. (1981). Training parents in behavioral self-management: An analysis of generalization and maintenance. *Journal of Applied Behavior Analysis, 14,* 223–237.

Schaefer, C. E., & Briesmeister, J. M. (1989). *Handbook of parent training: Parents as co-therapists for children's behavior problems.* New York: Wiley.

Serketich, W. J., & Dumas, J. E. (1996). The effectiveness of behavioral parent training to modify antisocial behavior in children: A meta-analysis. *Behavior Therapy, 27,* 171–186.

Stocker, C. (1994). Children's perceptions of relationships with siblings, friends, and mothers: Compensatory processes and links with adjustment. *Journal of Child Psychology and Psychiatry, 35,* 1447–1459.

Volling, B. L., Youngblade, L. M., & Belsky, J. (1997). Young children's social relationships with siblings and friends. *American Journal of Orthopsychiatry, 67*(1), 102–111.

Wahler, R. C., Winkel, G. H., Peterson, R. F., & Morrison, D. C. (1965). Mothers as behavior therapists for their own children. *Behaviour Research and Therapy, 3,* 113–134.

Webster-Stratton, C., & Hammond, M. (1990). Predictors of treatment outcome in parent training for families with conduct problem children. *Behavior Therapy, 21,* 319–337.

Webster-Stratton, C., Kolpacoff, M., & Hollinsworth, T. (1988). Self-administered videotape therapy for families with conduct-problem children: Comparison with two cost effective treatments and a control group. *Journal of Consulting and Clinical Psychology, 56,* 558–566.

Wells, K. C., & Egan, J. (1988). Social learning and systems family therapy for childhood oppositional disorder: Comparative treatment outcome. *Comprehensive Psychiatry, 29,* 138–146.

Wells, K. C., & Forehand, R. (1981). Child behavior problems in the home. In S. M. Turner, K. Calhoun, & H. E. Adams (Eds.), *Handbook of clinical behavior therapy.* New York: Wiley.

Wolfe, D. A., Edwards, B., Manion, I., & Koverola, C. (1988). Early intervention for parents at risk of child abuse and neglect: A preliminary investigation. *Journal of Consulting and Clinical Psychology, 56*(1), 40–47.

Zacker, J. (1978). Parents as change agents. *American Journal of Psychotherapy, 37*(4), 572–582.

EXTERNALIZING DISORDERS

THE DIFFERENTIAL categories of "externalizing/internalizing" allow for a classification of troubled children on the basis of psychiatric symptoms manifested at the time of referral. Externalizing symptoms characteristically include such features as acting-out and antisocial behaviors. These are behaviors that typically turn against others. The chapters in Part One focus on the innovative use of parent training techniques that help parents recognize, assess, clarify, and correct maladaptive and dysfunctional externalizing disorders.

In Chapter 1, Anastopoulos addresses the persistent pattern of inattentive and/or hyperactive impulsive behaviors known as attention-deficit/hyperactivity disorder (AD/HD). Interest in this disorder has spawned a vast body of empirical research, theoretical concepts, and multifaceted therapeutic approaches. It is not surprising that parent training intervention strategies have also been applied. Indeed, Anastopoulos delineates the clinical advantages of using parents as cotherapists in AD/HD treatment programs. He also considers some of the current biological, psychological, and psychosocial conceptualizations of this diagnostic syndrome. The author postulates a strong and appealing rationale for using parent training in the clinical management of a child's AD/HD symptoms.

Anastopoulos points out that even though the features of AD/HD may differ from child to child, the core issue remains an underlying deficit in behavioral inhibition processes. This deficit can have a significant negative impact on the psychosocial functioning of the target child as well as that of the parents and siblings. Anastopoulos discloses the ways in which AD/HD features may underlie and interact with other externalizing problems, such as conduct disorders and oppositional-defiant behaviors. The author addresses the relevancy of parent training as a viable treatment system. He presents a multimethod assessment approach and a multimodal intervention format that offers a step-by-step technique aimed at informing parents about the nature and logistics of parent training. This sequential program also helps parents understand the subtle and intricate nature of parent-child conflicts. In addition, it offers parents insights on when, and under what circumstances, it is beneficial to attend to certain problems and when it might be wise to ignore them.

Eyberg and Boggs present an integrated approach to the treatment of preschool children with conduct disorders. In Chapter 2, they describe and focus on the conflicts associated with a dysfunctional relationship between parent and child. The format of Parent-Child Interaction Therapy is conducted within the context of a natural play setting. The approach incorporates both behavioral and traditional issues relevant to treatment. Eyberg and Boggs distinguish between two essential phases of treatment, each of which consists of multiple components. They offer a technique that facilitates a positive relationship between parents and their children. The authors prescribe a psychosocial intervention treatment program that focuses on defined pretreatment, midtreatment, and posttreatment assessments. They also devote considerable attention to establishing constructive child- and parent-directed interactions as well as crucial follow-up evaluations. Eyberg and Boggs's approach employs viable techniques for establishing a positive parent-child relationship. It also instructs parents and children how to identify and acquire prosocial behaviors.

In Chapter 3, the reader is introduced to a groundbreaking videotape-based parenting program for the management of oppositional and conduct-disordered children. The program by Webster-Stratton and Hancock is also a community-based prevention approach for families at risk for abuse and child conduct problems. The authors conducted a 15-year research study to develop and evaluate videotape modeling group discussion parent training formats. They describe their original 12-week parent program BASIC, which encompasses 10 videotapes with over 250 vignettes. This program employs parental participation, open discussions and modeling in teaching parents interactive play and reinforcement skills. In conjunction with BASIC the authors also incorporate a more recently developed supplemental program: ADVANCE. The supplemental program addresses related family risks, such as depression, marital stress, or poor coping skills.

Webster-Stratton and Hancock point out that the videotape modeling parent training program is active and collaborative. While acknowledging the expertise of professionals, the program fosters a reciprocal relationship based on the skills, knowledge, and strengths of the parents as well as the clinician. This collaborative approach strengthens the parents' competencies and "efficacy expectations." The parents become empowered rather than dependent on the therapist. Still further, this empirically based and theoretically sound integrated approach achieves its goals. The BASIC program has proven effective in improving parental attitudes and parent-child interactions. It also trains the parents in the use of non-physical and nonabusive alternatives to violent forms of child discipline. Similarly, the ADVANCE program promotes the parents' use of effective problem-solving and communication skills.

The authors promulgate a practical and time-tested nonviolent modalities of discipline and parent training. They describe and evaluate the judicious use of praise, ignoring skills, time-out, and related limit-setting techniques. They highlight the importance of teaching parents and children problem-solving skills. Their approach helps the parents to generate plausible solutions with their youngster and instruct the child in the appropriate ways of implementing these solutions. In this manner, for instance, the child can learn constructive alternatives to crying, hitting, or running to the parents when problems surface. Therefore, the child learns how to manage problems and also develops a sense of mastery and "self-efficacy."

Following a description of normative sibling relationships and the ways in which parenting behaviors impact on sibling interactions, Johnston and Freeman define and assess some of the typical conflicts that may occur in the sibling relationship. In Chapter 4, they hone in on a systematic review of parent intervention ploys that are age-appropriate and focus on specific problems, solutions, and populations. They present studies and descriptions that provide informative data and techniques for reducing sibling conflict. Strategies from operant conditioning, social skills training, and child management have been investigated, evaluated, and utilized.

Johnston and Freeman offer parents directives in effective problem solving as well as ways in which they can foster antecedent conditions within the family that promote positive interactions between children. They propose tactics that, in essence, involve environmental engineering. They discuss the rules and standards necessary to alter antecedent conditions in a desirable direction. Johnston and Freeman's presentation offers procedures for educating parents in operant techniques that can reduce conflicts by presenting negative consequences or can reinforce appropriate sibling interactions with positive consequences. The authors also emphasize the importance and impact of training children to become effective conflict managers. These skills can generalize to problem solving and management in many situations.

In Chapter 5, Miller presents empirical and clinical evidence of significant developmental findings that suggest early conduct problems may be precursors of antisocial behaviors. She also cites data suggesting that parenting practices are strong predictors of childhood conduct problems. As such, improving parenting practices may reduce child behavior problems. Miller bases the Enhanced Parent Training on the Videotape Modeling Programs developed by Webster-Stratton and discussed in Chapter 3. Miller's adaptation involves two major features: the BASIC Parent Training Videotape Modeling Program and The Family Training Videotape Modeling Program. Miller's implementation of these two programs includes parenting skills training, children's playgroups, positive parent-child interaction training, and home visits designed to facilitate the generalization of newly acquired skills.

The author also investigates issues regarding the relevance and clinical application of the proposed parent training program including a section on therapist training and the applicability of the preventive approach. The results of pilot tests also illustrate the program's acceptability with inner-city families who may be at high risk for antisocial behavior. Enhanced Parent Training is a preventive approach that assists parents in positively altering the deviant and destructive course of at-risk children.

CHAPTER 1

A Training Program for Parents of Children with Attention-Deficit/Hyperactivity Disorder

ARTHUR D. ANASTOPOULOS

ATTENTION-DEFICIT/HYPERACTIVITY DISORDER (AD/HD; American Psychiatric Association, 1994) is a childhood condition for which clinicians and researchers have frequently employed parent training (PT) interventions. As is the case for other childhood disorders, part of the rationale for utilizing PT in the treatment of AD/HD stems from a consideration of the many clinical advantages inherent in the use of parents as cotherapists. Along with these generic arguments, however, there are many other reasons specific to AD/HD that provide further justification for its use with this population. A major objective of this chapter therefore, is to bring much of this rationale to light.

Some understanding of AD/HD as a disorder is first necessary. This chapter therefore begins with an overview of AD/HD, emphasizing matters that have direct bearing on the rationale for using PT as well as highlighting many of the important clinical issues that often arise in the context of counseling parents about this disorder. Against this background, the theoretical and clinical arguments for using PT with AD/HD populations will be presented. This will be followed by a review of the limited research that has examined the clinical efficacy of this form of treatment. This chapter will then provide a detailed description of one of the most widely used PT programs for AD/HD, accompanied by a PT case presentation, illustrating not only therapeutic benefits but also some of the common obstacles that arise in clinical application.

OVERVIEW OF AD/HD

Primary Symptoms

Clinical descriptions of children with AD/HD frequently include complaints of "not listening to instructions," "not finishing assigned work," "daydreaming," "becoming bored easily," and so forth. Common to all of these referral concerns is a diminished capacity for vigilance; that is, difficulties sustaining attention to task (Douglas, 1983). Such problems can occur in free play settings (Routh & Schroeder, 1976), but most often surface in situations demanding sustained attention to dull, boring, repetitive tasks (Milich, Loney, & Landau, 1982). Clinic-referred children with AD/HD may exhibit impulsivity as well. For example, they may interrupt others who might be busy, or display tremendous difficulty waiting for their turn in game situations. They may also begin tasks before directions are completed, take unnecessary risks, talk out of turn, or make indiscreet remarks without regard for social consequences. When hyperactivity is present, this may be displayed not only motorically but verbally. Descriptions of physical restlessness might include statements such as "always on the go," "unable to sit still," and so forth. As for the verbal component, descriptions often center around the child's "talking excessively" or being a "chatterbox or motor mouth." Whether mild or severe, what makes all of these behaviors manifestations of hyperactivity is their *excessive, task-irrelevant,* and *developmentally inappropriate* nature.

Although these symptoms traditionally have been viewed as distinct and separate components of the disorder, the validity of this assumption has recently been questioned. At a theoretical level, Barkley (1997) has proposed that all three primary symptoms, as well as many associated features, may stem from an underlying deficit in behavioral inhibition processes. From a strictly empirical point of view, recently reported factor analytic results have further suggested that while inattention symptoms do indeed tend to cluster apart from symptoms of impulsivity and hyperactivity, these latter two symptoms nonetheless routinely cluster together (DuPaul et al., in press).

Diagnostic Criteria

Within North America today, the currently accepted criteria for making an AD/HD diagnosis appear in the fourth edition of the *Diagnostic and Statistical Manual of Mental Disorders* (*DSM-IV;* American Psychiatric Association, 1994). At the heart of this decision-making process are two 9-item symptom listings—one pertaining to inattention symptoms, the other to hyperactivity-impulsivity concerns. Parents and/or teachers must report the presence of at least 6 of 9 problem behaviors from either list to warrant consideration of an AD/HD diagnosis. Such behaviors must have an onset prior to 7 years of age, a duration of at least 6 months, and a frequency above and beyond that expected of children of the same mental age. Furthermore, they must be evident in two or more settings, have a clear impact on psychosocial functioning, and not be due to other types of mental health or learning disorders that might better explain their presence.

As is evident from these criteria, the manner in which AD/HD presents itself clinically can vary from child to child. For some children with AD/HD, symptoms of inattention may be of relatively greater concern than impulsivity or hyperactivity problems. For others, impulsivity and hyperactivity difficulties may be more prominent. Reflecting these possible differences in clinical presentation, the new *DSM-IV* criteria not only allow for, but require, AD/HD subtyping. For example, when more than 6 symptoms are present from both lists and all other criteria are met, a diagnosis of AD/HD, Combined Type is in order. If 6 or more inattention symptoms are present, but less than 6 hyperactive-impulsive symptoms are evident, and all other criteria are met, the proper diagnosis would be AD/HD, Predominantly Inattentive Type. Those familiar with prior diagnostic classification schemes will quickly recognize these *DSM-IV* categories as similar, but not exact, counterparts to what previously was known as Attention-Deficit Hyperactivity Disorder and Undifferentiated Attention Deficit Disorder in *DSM-III-R* (American Psychiatric Association, 1987) and Attention Deficit Disorder with or without Hyperactivity in *DSM-III* (American Psychiatric Association, 1980). Appearing for the first time in *DSM-IV*, however, is the subtyping condition known as AD/HD, Predominantly Hyperactive-Impulsive Type, which is the appropriate diagnosis to make whenever 6 or more hyperactive-impulsive symptoms arise, less than 6 inattention concerns are evident, and all other criteria are met. Along with these major subtyping categories, *DSM-IV* also makes available two additional classifications that have primary bearing on adolescents and adults. For example, a diagnosis of AD/HD, In Partial Remission, may be given to individuals who have clinical problems resulting from AD/HD symptoms that currently do not meet criteria for any of the above subtypes, but nonetheless were part of a previously documented AD/HD diagnosis. In similar cases, where an earlier history of AD/HD can not be established with any degree of certainty, a diagnosis of AD/HD, Not Otherwise Specified, would instead be made.

ASSOCIATED FEATURES

In addition to their primary symptoms, children with AD/HD frequently display secondary or comorbid difficulties that can adversely affect school performance, family relations, peer relations, and many other areas of psychosocial functioning (Barkley, 1990). For example, noncompliance, argumentativeness, temper outbursts, lying, stealing, and other manifestations of Oppositional-Defiant Disorder and Conduct Disorder may occur in up to 65% of the clinic-referred AD/HD population (Loney & Milich, 1982). Virtually all children with AD/HD experience some type of school difficulty. An especially common problem is that their levels of academic productivity and achievement are significantly lower than their estimated potential (Barkley, 1990). As many as 20% to 30% may also exhibit dyslexia or other types of specific learning disabilities (Barkley, DuPaul, & McMurray, 1990). As a result of such complications, a relatively high percentage typically receives some form of special education assistance (Barkley, 1990). Significant peer socialization problems may occur as well (Pelham & Bender, 1982). At times, such difficulties involve deficiencies in establishing friendships (Grenell, Glass, & Katz, 1987). More often than not, however, maintaining satisfactory peer relations is of even greater clinical concern. Due to their inability to control their behavior in social situations, children with AD/HD frequently alienate their peers, who in turn respond with social rejection or avoidance (Cunningham & Siegel, 1987). Possibly as a result of such behavioral, academic, and/or social problems, children with AD/HD very often exhibit low self-esteem, low frustration tolerance, symptoms of depression and anxiety, and other emotional complications (Margalit & Arieli, 1984).

IMPACT ON FAMILY FUNCTIONING

Whether alone or in combination with various comorbid conditions, AD/HD can have a significant impact on the psychosocial functioning of parents and siblings. Research has shown, for example, that parents of children with AD/HD very often become overly directive and negative in their parenting style (Cunningham & Barkley, 1979). In addition to viewing themselves as less skilled and less knowledgeable in their parenting roles (Mash & Johnston, 1990), they may also experience considerable stress in their parenting roles, especially when comorbid oppositional-defiant features are present (Anastopoulos, Guevremont, Shelton, & DuPaul, 1992). Depression and marital discord may arise as well (Lahey et al., 1988). Whether these parent and family complications result directly from the child's AD/HD is not entirely clear at present. Clinical experience would suggest that they probably do, at least in part, given the increased caretaking demands that children with AD/HD impose on their parents. These include more frequent displays of noncompliance related to the child's difficulties in following through on parental instructions (Cunningham & Barkley, 1979). In addition, parents of these children often find themselves involved in resolving various school, peer, and sibling difficulties, which occur throughout childhood (Barkley, 1990) and into adolescence as well (Barkley, Anastopoulos, Guevremont, & Fletcher, 1991).

EPIDEMIOLOGY

Prevalence

Depending on the criteria employed, estimates of the incidence of AD/HD may vary a great deal, ranging from as low as 2% up to as much as 25% to 30%. Using the diagnostic criteria put forth by *DSM-IV,* approximately 3% to 5% of the general child population will meet criteria for some type of AD/HD diagnosis (American Psychiatric Association, 1994). Although its actual incidence may fluctuate somewhat within the general population, AD/HD is by no means specific to any particular subgroup. For example, it may be found among the rich and the poor, as well as among those with either very little or very high levels of education. It also cuts fairly evenly across diverse ethnic, racial, and religious lines. As is the case for other externalizing problems, however, AD/HD does occur much more often in boys than in girls. The ratio within clinic samples, for example, has been reported to be as high as 6:1, whereas in community samples it occurs on the order of 3:1 (Barkley, 1990).

Developmental Course and Outcome

Some children show evidence of AD/HD in early infancy (Hartsough & Lambert, 1985). Most, however, first display clear signs of developmentally deviant behavior between 3 and 4 years of age (Ross & Ross, 1982). For a smaller number of children, AD/HD symptoms may not surface until 5 or 6 years of age, coinciding with school entrance. During middle childhood, AD/HD symptoms often become more chronic and pervasive, even though they may appear somewhat improved at times. It is during this same period that secondary complications, such as academic underachievement or oppositional- defiant behavior, frequently arise. Contrary to popular opinion, most children do not outgrow their AD/HD problems upon reaching adolescence. As many as 70% will continue to exhibit developmentally inappropriate levels of inattention and, to a lesser extent, symptoms of hyperactivity-impulsivity during their teen years (Weiss & Hechtman, 1986). Although the pattern of secondary complications accompanying AD/HD in adolescence is highly similar to that found in younger AD/HD populations (Barkley et al., 1991), certain differences do exist. Upon reaching adolescence, for example, additional problems may arise in pursuit of meeting occupational responsibilities. Moreover, teens with AD/HD are at increased risk for becoming involved in automobile accidents and traffic violations (Barkley, Guevremont, Anastopoulos, Du-Paul, & Shelton, 1993). Although adolescent and adult outcome data are scant, what research is available suggests that, while many children with AD/HD continue to display these symptoms well into adolescence and adulthood, the vast majority will learn to compensate for these problems, and therefore make a satisfactory adult adjustment (Weiss & Hechtman, 1986; Wender, 1995). For those who do not, comorbid problems, such as depression or alcoholism (Farrington, Loeber, & van Kammen, 1987), are often of relatively greater clinical concern than their AD/HD symptoms.

Theoretical Models

Biological Conceptualizations

Within the field today, there is a consensus that neurochemical imbalances play a central role in the etiology of AD/HD. There may be abnormalities in one or more of the monoaminergic systems, involving either dopamine or norepinephrine mechanisms (Zametkin & Rapoport, 1986). The locus of this dysfunction purportedly lies within the prefrontal-limbic areas of the brain (Lou, Henriksen, Bruhn, Borner, & Nielsen, 1989). For a majority of children with AD/HD, such neurological circumstances presumably arise from inborn biologic factors, including genetic transmission and pregnancy and birth complications (Biederman et al., 1987; Deutsch, 1987; Edelbrock, 1995; Streissguth et al., 1984). For relatively smaller numbers of children carrying this diagnosis, it can be acquired after birth, via head injury, neurological illness, elevated lead levels, and other biological complications (Ross & Ross, 1982). Despite their widespread public appeal, there is relatively little support for the assertions of Feingold (1975) and others that the ingestion of sugar or other food substances directly causes AD/HD (Wolraich et al., 1994).

Psychological Conceptualizations

Over the years, numerous psychological theories have been put forth to explain the manner in which AD/HD affects psychosocial functioning. Many of the early accounts, which did not have the benefit of the above-noted etiological findings, focused almost exclusively on psychological processes that were believed to be at the core of AD/HD difficulties. Among these were theories implicating core deficiencies in the regulation of behavior in response to situational demands (Routh, 1978), in self-directed instruction (Kendall & Braswell, 1985), in the self-regulation of arousal to environmental demands (Douglas, 1983), and in rule-governed behavior (Barkley, 1981). Although differing somewhat in their theoretical emphasis, each of these views shared the belief that poor executive functioning was a central problem.

Building on what is now known about the biology of AD/HD, more recent theories have taken on a very distinctive neuropsychological flavor. Quay (1989), for example, has proposed that AD/HD stems from an impairment in a neurologically-based behavioral inhibition system. In an extensive elaboration of this same theme, Barkley (1997) has also contended that a deficit in behavioral inhibition is central to understanding the cognitive, behavioral, and social deficits observed within AD/HD populations. Although less comprehensive in their scope, the theoretical views of many other investigators in the field are consistent with the notion that deficits in behavioral inhibition are at the core of many AD/HD problems (Schachar, Tannock, & Logan, 1993; Sergeant, 1995).

Psychosocial Conceptualizations

Although a few environmental theories have been proposed to explain AD/HD (Block, 1977; Willis & Lovaas, 1977), these have not received much support in the research literature. Thus, there would seem to be little justification for claiming that poor parenting or chaotic home environments are in any way causally related to AD/HD. When AD/HD is found among children who come from such family circumstances, one might reasonably speculate that the parents of such children may themselves be individuals with childhood and adult histories of AD/HD. If so, this would help to explain why their homes might be so chaotic and, at the same time, provide support for a genetic explanation for the child's AD/HD condition. Under this same scenario, the resulting chaos in the home might then be viewed as a factor exacerbating, rather than causing, the child's preexisting, inborn AD/HD condition.

ASSESSMENT

Despite the existence of relatively clear diagnostic guidelines, establishing an AD/HD diagnosis remains a difficult matter. One factor contributing to this situation is the situational variability of AD/HD symptoms. Contrary to the belief of many, AD/HD is not an all-or-none phenomenon, either always present or never. Instead, it is a condition whose primary symptoms show significant fluctuations in response to different situational demands (Zentall, 1985). AD/HD symptoms, for example, are much more likely to occur in situations that are unstructured, low in feedback, or boring (Barkley, 1977; Douglas, 1983; Luk, 1985). Presumably due to increased demands for behavioral self-regulation, group settings are also more problematic for children with AD/HD than one-to-one situations. Because being aware of the situational variability of AD/HD symptoms is central to understanding the frequently irregular clinical presentation of this disorder, it is imperative for clinicians to obtain information from individuals who observe identified children across different settings. At the very least, this should include input from parents and teachers. When appropriate, other significant caretakers, such as day-care providers and babysitters, should provide input from observation.

Another critical factor affecting the evaluation process is the increased likelihood that children and adolescents with AD/HD will display comorbid conditions. Thus, it is critical for clinicians to incorporate assessment methods that address not only primary AD/HD symptoms, but also other aspects of the identified child's or adolescent's psychosocial functioning. Of additional importance is the need for gathering assessment data pertaining to parental, marital, and family functioning. Although gathering this type of parental and family information may not shed much light on whether or not AD/HD is present, it nevertheless provides a context for understanding how problem behaviors may be maintained. Moreover, such information often serves as a basis for determining how likely it is that parents and other caretakers will implement recommended PT and other treatment strategies on behalf of their child or adolescent.

Implicit in the preceding discussion is that clinical evaluations of AD/HD must be comprehensive and multidimensional, so as to capture its situational variability, its comorbid features, and its impact on home, school, and social functioning (Barkley, 1990). This multimethod assessment approach may include, for example, not only the traditional methods of parent and child interviews, but also standardized child behavior rating scales, parent self-report measures, direct behavioral observations of AD/HD symptoms in natural or analogue settings, and clinic-based psychological tests.

TREATMENT APPROACHES

Many of the same factors that complicate the assessment process can affect treatment outcome as well. Foremost among these are the cross-situational pervasiveness of primary AD/HD symptoms and the relatively high incidence of co-occurring or comorbid conditions. Such circumstances make it highly unlikely that any singular treatment approach can satisfactorily meet all of the clinical management needs of children and adolescents with AD/HD. For this reason, clinicians must often employ multiple treatment strategies in combination, each of which addresses a different aspect of the child's or adolescent's psychosocial difficulties.

Among those treatments that have received adequate, or at the very least preliminary, empirical support are pharmacotherapy, parent training in contingency management methods, parent counseling, classroom applications of contingency management techniques, and cognitive-behavioral training. These interventions should not be viewed as *curative* of AD/HD; instead, their value lies in their temporary reduction of

AD/HD symptom levels and in their reduction of related behavioral or emotional difficulties. When these treatments are removed, AD/HD symptoms very often return to pretreatment levels. Thus, their effectiveness in improving prognosis presumably rests on their being maintained over long periods of time.

RATIONALE

In light of the preceding treatment discussion, an important question arises: On what basis is there justification for using PT in the clinical management of children with AD/HD? Although by no means comprehensive, part of the answer to this question stems from a consideration of the following clinical, theoretical, and empirical points.

CLINICAL CONSIDERATIONS

Although stimulant medication therapy is by far the most commonly used treatment in the clinical management of children with AD/HD (Barkley, 1990), 10% to 20% of those who take such medication do not show clinically significant improvements in their primary AD/HD symptomatology (Taylor, 1986). Even when a favorable response is obtained, some children experience side effects that are of sufficient frequency and severity to preclude continued use of stimulant medication. Independent of these issues, many parents prefer not to use any form of medication in treating their child. To the extent that there are children with AD/HD for whom stimulant medication therapy, as well as other medications, are not a viable treatment option, alternative treatments must be used. Among these, PT is certainly worthy of further consideration.

PT can also be helpful to children with AD/HD who are stimulant medication responders. For example, in an effort to reduce the risks for insomnia and various other side effects, most physicians limit their stimulant prescriptions to two or three doses per day. For similar reasons, some physicians further limit the child's medication regimen to school days only. What this means from a practical standpoint is that there are substantial portions of any given day, usually in the late afternoons and early evening, when children are not deriving any therapeutic benefits from stimulant medication. For parents and other caretakers, this necessitates finding other means for handling their child's behavioral difficulties in the home. Here again, PT can play a useful role.

Additional justification for utilizing PT stems from a consideration of the potential for comorbidity. As was noted earlier, children with AD/HD often display oppositional-defiant behavior, aggression, conduct difficulties, and other externalizing problems. Because such secondary features can not be fully addressed through the use of medication, alternative treatment approaches need to be considered. In view of its highly success-ful track record with noncompliant (Forehand & McMahon, 1981) and conduct disordered (Patterson, 1982) populations, PT is well suited to this purpose.

Of additional clinical importance is that raising a child with AD/HD can place enormous strains on family functioning. In particular, levels of parenting stress parental guilt can be quite high, along with a diminished sense of parenting competence. Such circumstances are not usually due to faulty parenting. On the contrary, many parents of children with AD/HD use parenting strategies that work fine for normal siblings in the family. Alerting parents to this reality begins the process of alleviating their distress. Teaching them more effective ways of dealing with their child with AD/HD, through the use of PT, can also go a long way toward facilitating their own personal adjustment.

As is evident from the preceding discussion, there are many commonly encountered clinical situations that provide a basis for using PT in the overall management of children with AD/HD. Additional justification for implementing this form of treatment comes from a consideration of a number of theoretical matters.

THEORETICAL CONSIDERATIONS

Noted earlier in this chapter is the recent shift in the way that AD/HD is conceptualized as a disorder. Many experts in the field today have begun to view AD/HD as a condition characterized by neurologically-based deficits in behavioral inhibition (Barkley, 1997; Quay, 1989; Schachar et al., 1993). To the extent that deficits in behavioral inhibition are central to understanding this disorder, it suggests that children with AD/HD will not be very adept at thinking through the consequences of their ac-tions. Working from this assumption, it would then seem reasonable to consider increasing the child's awareness of the connection between their behavior and its consequences. More so than many other forms of treat-ment, PT lends itself especially well to meeting this therapeutic objective.

Further theoretical justification stems from a consideration of the appar-ent relationship that exists among AD/HD, Oppositional-Defiant Disorder (ODD), and Conduct Disorder (CD). Recent findings from the field of de-velopmental psychopathology have implicated the possibility of a develop-mental pathway, leading from AD/HD to these comorbid conditions (Loeber, Keenan, Lahey, Green, & Thomas, 1993). If having AD/HD greatly increases the risk for developing ODD or CD at a later point in time, then it would seem to be of utmost clinical importance to begin treatment as soon as possible to reduce this risk among children not yet affected by these co-morbid conditions. Although research of this sort has yet to be conducted, the fact that PT has worked so well with noncompliant (Forehand & McMahon, 1981) and conduct disordered (Patterson, 1982) populations provides a basis for considering its use in such a preventive role.

EMPIRICAL FINDINGS

Despite the plethora of research on PT in behavior modification (Dangel & Polster, 1984), very few studies have examined the efficacy of this approach with children specifically identified as having AD/HD. What few studies exist can be interpreted with cautious optimism as supporting the use of PT with such children (Anastopoulos, Shelton, DuPaul, & Guevremont, 1993; Erhardt & Baker, 1990; Pisterman, Firestone, McGrath, & Goodman, 1992; Pisterman, McGrath, Firestone, & Goodman, 1989). Most of these interventions utilized weekly therapy sessions in either group or individual formats that were short-term in nature, spanning 6 to 12 weeks. Most of these programs served to train parents in the use of specialized contingency management techniques, such as positive reinforcement, response cost, and/or time out strategies. Some, however, combined contingency management training with didactic counseling, aimed at increasing parental knowledge and understanding of AD/HD (Anastopoulos et al., 1993; Pisterman et al., 1992). In addition to producing changes in child behavior, PT interventions have also led to improvements in various aspects of parental and family functioning, including decreased parenting stress and increased parenting self-esteem (Anastopoulos et al., 1993; Erhardt & Baker, 1990; Pisterman et al., 1989).

Information about the efficacy of PT also comes from studies in which this form of treatment was combined with other interventions, such as pharmacotherapy (Abikoff & Hechtman, 1996; Pollard, Ward, & Barkley, 1983) and self-control therapy (Horn, Ialongo, Pascoe, & Greenberg, 1991; Ialongo, Horn, Pascoe, & Greenberg, 1993). In contrast to what is found when used alone, many of these multimodal intervention studies, especially those involving medication, have noted that PT contributes very little to outcome, above and beyond that accounted for by the other treatment. Because so few of these studies have been conducted to date, it would seem premature to discount the potential therapeutic benefits of PT in a multimodal intervention package. Fortunately, further clarification of this matter is forthcoming (Richters et al., 1995).

THE PARENT TRAINING PROGRAM

Although there are many ways to conduct PT programs for children with AD/HD (Newby, Fischer, & Roman, 1991), little is known about their relative efficacy. Thus, it would not be unreasonable to present any one of them to illustrate how PT is applied in clinical practice. For the purposes of this chapter, however, the one that will be presented is the one that was originally developed by Barkley (1987) and later modified by his colleagues at the University of Massachusetts Medical Center (Anastopoulos & Barkley, 1990).

Therapist Qualifications

At face value, delivering PT to parents of children with AD/HD might seem to be a relatively easy task. If all that is done is didactic in nature, that is, simply presenting the program to an attentive and cooperative parent, then it can be. More often than not, however, this is not the case. Thus, its delivery typically requires the skills of a qualified therapist.

One's professional degree is perhaps the least important of these qualifications. What is of utmost relevance, however, is the depth of the therapist's understanding of AD/HD, as well as his or her familiarity with and expertise in using behavior management strategies. Having these skills is especially critical to the success of the program because a one-size-fits-all approach just doesn't work. Finding ways to tailor PT to fit the needs of individual parents requires a great deal of flexibility and creativity, and these attributes typically come from extensive experience and in-depth knowledge.

Although not necessary for many purely behavioral PT applications, possessing cognitive therapy and family therapy skills can also play an important role in delivering this form of treatment. Such skills can be used to overcome parental difficulties in utilizing recommended PT strategies. Related to the use of these skills, it is also highly desirable for therapists to be well-versed in adult and child psychopathology.

Client Characteristics

One of the most frequently misunderstood aspects of PT is that it is not appropriate for all children who receive an AD/HD diagnosis. Generally speaking, it is intended for parents of children with AD/HD between 4 and 12 years of age. Of even greater clinical importance is that there needs to be some indication that the child's AD/HD is directly causing home management difficulties. This need not be limited to hard-to-manage child behavior. It may also encompass elevated levels of parenting stress and other types of family disruption that would benefit from PT intervention.

A parent's capacity for undergoing PT also needs to be taken into account. Parents who are troubled by significant levels of psychological distress or marital discord may not be good candidates for this form of treatment. Depending on the situation, some parents may need to defer starting PT until such clinical matters are resolved. Others may find it more appropriate to address such problems at the same time that they are participating in PT.

SPECIFIC TRAINING STEPS

Although the PT program typically can be completed in 8 to 12 sessions, it does not confine clinicians to a specific number of treatment sessions that must be followed inflexibly. Instead, it allows them to guide parents through treatment in a step-by-step fashion, taking as many sessions as is necessary to bring about desired therapeutic change. There are 10 steps that make up the intervention program (Table 1.1). Readers interested in learning more about this program are encouraged to see Barkley (1987), in conjunction with Anastopoulos and Barkley (1990).

Table 1.1
Summary of Training Program for Parents of Children with
Attention-Deficit/Hyperactivity Disorder

Session	Therapeutic Content
1	Overview of Attention-Deficit/Hyperactivity Disorder.
2	Discussion of four-factor model of parent-child conflict; review of behavior management principles and request-noncompliance cycle.
3	Using positive attending and ignoring skills during special play time.
4	Using positive attending and ignoring skills to promote appropriate independent play and compliance with simple requests; issuing commands more effectively.
5	Setting up a reward-oriented home token or point system.
6	Using response cost for minor noncompliance and rule violations.
7	Using time out from reinforcement for more serious rule violations.
8	Handling child behavior problems in public.
9	Handling future problems; fading out home program; discussion of school system's role; review of commonly used classroom interventions; (e.g., daily report card systems); termination and disposition issues.
10	Booster session to review progress and troubleshoot as needed.

Step 1: Program Orientation and Overview of AD/HD

The objectives of the first step are (a) to acquaint parents with the mechanics of participating in the treatment program, (b) to begin increasing their knowledge of AD/HD, (c) to set appropriate expectations for therapeutic change, and (d) to begin addressing any faulty perceptions that they may have about themselves or about their children.

The session typically starts with parents' providing a brief update of their status since the completion of the diagnostic evaluation. If necessary, additional assessments are done to evaluate the emergence of any new child behavior problems and to provide a more accurate baseline against which future therapeutic changes may be gauged. Having completed the updating process, the rationale, purpose, and content of the training program are discussed. Also covered at this time are the boundaries of confidentiality and relevant billing matters.

Following this program orientation, an overview of AD/HD, similar to that covered earlier in this chapter, is presented. This includes a review of its history, its numerous label changes, its core symptoms, its currently accepted diagnostic criteria, and its prevalence rates. Also covered are many of the commonly encountered associated features of AD/HD, including oppositional defiant behavior, aggressiveness, academic underachievement, social skills deficits, and emotional immaturity. This is generally followed by a discussion of what is known about the immediate and extended families of children with AD/HD. Up-to-date information about the developmental course of this disorder is presented as well. Attention is then directed to etiological concerns. In the context of this discussion, emphasis is placed on the view that, for most children, AD/HD is a biologically-based inborn temperamental style that predisposes them to be inattentive, impulsive, and physically restless. Special efforts are also made to clarify the confusion surrounding the situational variability of this disorder's primary symptoms. Against this background, the importance of using a multimethod assessment approach is discussed. In the ensuing treatment discussion, emphasis is placed on the need for taking a multimodal intervention approach.

Presentation of this information should be as brief as possible, allowing parents to focus more attentively upon the main points. It is also helpful for clinicians to limit their references to summary statistics and percentages obtained from the AD/HD population as a whole. As so many parents have so frankly stated, they are not interested in facts and figures that have little to do with their child. The more that the presentation relates to the parents' particular child, the more likely it is that they will grasp the clinical and theoretical points that need to be made. Another precaution for clinicians to bear in mind as they describe the general AD/HD population is that some parents will incorrectly infer that their child is doomed to a life filled with comorbidity, failure, and misery. For this reason, clinicians must be sure to clarify that: (a) what applies to the AD/HD population as a whole does not necessarily apply to any one individual, and that; (b) outcome is determined by a large number and variety of factors, of which AD/HD is just one influence, albeit an important one.

Although it is certainly possible to conduct this first session in a lecture format, most clinicians would agree that its therapeutic impact is much greater when parents have an opportunity to ask questions, to voice their emotional reactions to what they just heard, and to discuss expectations for the program. Should parents feel overwhelmed by the sheer volume of new AD/HD information, they are reminded that processing such information will occur gradually over time. Should they wish to facilitate their acquisition of such knowledge, they are also alerted to the availability of pertinent texts and encouraged to review videotaped presentations on the topic. As for their emotional reactions, to the extent that parental feelings of shock, guilt, sadness, or anger arise, therapeutic attention must then be directed to addressing such negative emotions. For this purpose, cognitive restructuring and other cognitive therapy techniques are especially helpful. Similar therapeutic efforts can be utilized to address unrealistic parental expectations for treatment outcome—unrealistic in the sense that changes in child behavior are expected to occur in a rapid, continuous fashion. As an alternative to this viewpoint, clinicians might instead suggest that therapeutic change will occur in a gradual and variable manner. Moreover, they must remind parents that what they learn needs to become part of their everyday parenting style, not just what they do during the treatment program. To the extent that parents can continue to use these skills after the program ends, their chances for bringing about improvements in their child's behavior increase dramatically.

Step 2: Understanding Parent-Child Relations

The purpose of this step is two-fold: to present parents with a four-factor model for understanding parent-child conflict and to increase parental knowledge of behavior management principles as they apply to children with AD/HD.

After reviewing carryover concerns from the previous session, clinicians provide parents with a conceptual framework for understanding deviant parent-child interactions and their therapeutic management. Initially, the theoretical views of Bell (Bell & Harper, 1977) and Patterson (1982) are introduced in general terms. In this context, parents are alerted to four major factors which, in various combinations, can contribute to the emergence and/or maintenance of children's behavioral difficulties.

The first of these involves the child's characteristics. Prominent among these is the youngster's inborn temperamental style, which encompasses general activity level, attention span, emotionality, sociability, responsiveness to stimulation, and habit regularity. Along with the child's characteristics, a like number and variety of parent characteristics are cited as circumstances that can place children at risk for conflict with their parents. Additional attention is directed to the goodness of fit between various child and parent characteristics. Stresses impinging upon the family are recognized as well. In particular, parents are taught several ways in which family stress can contribute to the emergence and/or maintenance of behavioral difficulties by altering parental perceptions of the child, by altering the child's emotional well-being directly, and/or by preoccupying parents to the point that they become highly variable and inconsistent in their disciplinary approach. The way that parents respond to child behavior is also discussed. In particular, attention is directed to explaining how certain parenting styles (e.g., excessive or harsh criticism, inconsistency), while not the cause of AD/HD, nevertheless can complicate the management of this disorder and its associated features. Against this background, attention is called to the fact that the model predicts that altering any of the four factors should lead to reductions in parent-child conflict. By noting that parenting style is by far the one most amenable to change, clinicians are thus able to provide parents with a clear rationale for conducting the remainder of the program.

At this point in the session, clinicians provide parents with an overview of general behavior management principles as a way of preparing them for later coverage of specific behavioral techniques. This overview may be introduced with a discussion of how antecedent events, as well as consequences, can be altered to modify children's behavior. Included as part of this discussion are different types of positive reinforcement, ignoring, and punishment strategies; the need for using such consequences in combination; and the advantages of dispensing them in a specific, immediate, and consistent fashion. In this portion of the session, special attention is also directed to the role played by negative reinforcement. In particular, parents are first taught that children often misbehave or exhibit noncompliance either to gain positive consequences or to avoid unpleasant or boring situations. An especially useful way to illustrate this latter situation is to describe the request-noncompliance cycle—that is, the cycle of multiple parental requests, following multiple instances of child noncompliance, that generally leads to escalating emotions and coercive interactions, not to mention an increased likelihood of further noncompliance from the child. Throughout this entire discussion, parents are reminded that the behavior management needs of children with AD/HD can be somewhat different from those of other children at times. For example, because children with AD/HD become bored rather easily and quickly, parents must be sure to use consequences that are particularly salient and meaningful, and to change such consequences periodically to keep them interesting and motivating.

Although no formal between-session assignment is given, parents are encouraged to begin observing their own parenting efforts in the context of the above discussed behavior management principles.

Step 3: Increasing Positive Attending Skills during Special Time

The main objective of this step is to begin teaching parents positive attending and ignoring skills in the context of special time. This step begins with a clarification of any carryover concerns and a review of how the informal between-session assignment went. Next, the importance of attending positively to individuals of any age is discussed. Because children with AD/HD frequently engage in behaviors that can be rather aversive at times, many parents prefer not to interact with them. When parent-child interactions do occur, parents often assume that negative child behavior will arise and therefore adopt a parenting style that is overly directive, corrective, coercive, or unpleasant. This in turn contributes to children becoming even less willing to behave in a compliant manner.

For these reasons, the "special time" assignment is presented. Unlike other types of special time, which simply involve setting aside time with the child, special time in this program requires that parents must remain as nondirective and as noncorrective as possible. Doing so allows them to see their child's behavior in a different light, allowing them the opportunity to "catch 'em being good." This leads to opportunities to attend positively to the child, which in turn helps to rebuild positive parent-child relations.

This is accomplished in the following manner. Parents first set aside a daily time period, usually 15 to 20 minutes on average, for interacting with their child. Ideally this should be scheduled in the absence of major time pressures or other types of interference. During special time, the child is allowed to decide what to do, within broad limits, of course. Parents must refrain from asking too many questions and avoid the temptation to suggest alternative play or interaction approaches. While continuing to observe their child in this manner, they must try to narrate the ongoing play activities in positive terms, while ignoring any mildly inappropriate behavior that may arise.

Those who have tried special time are well aware of how difficult it is to do. This difficulty, along with various other complications (e.g., busy daily schedules), are called to the attention of parents for the purpose of setting realistic expectations for its implementation. To be sure that parents get sufficient practice, they are encouraged to catch their children being good, not just during special time, but throughout the day as well. Such spontaneous opportunities can be used for increasing the amount of positive attention that children receive.

To assist parents in their efforts to practice these techniques between sessions, they are given a written handout summarizing the procedure. Should any unforeseen problems arise in their efforts to practice, they are encouraged to telephone for assistance.

Step 4: Extending Positive Attention to Other Situations; Giving Commands More Effectively

This step attempts to extend positive attending skills to two additional situations: (a) when children are displaying appropriate behavior that allows parents to engage in activities uninterrupted, and (b) when children comply with parental requests. Also covered in this step are instructions for issuing commands more effectively.

First, parental efforts to carry out the between-session assignment are discussed. As needed, clinicians give suggestions for improving implementation of special time and/or spontaneous positive attending. Parent and child emotional reactions are processed as well.

Once it is clear that parents have become sufficiently adept at using positive attending strategies, it becomes possible to expand these skills to other situations. Many children, especially those with AD/HD who have difficulty waiting for things, become disruptive when parents are engaged in home activities, such as talking on the telephone, preparing dinner, or visiting with company. After calling attention to the fact that parents generally do not hesitate to interrupt an ongoing activity to address disruptions, the following questions are posed: Should parents stop what they are doing to attend positively to children when they are engaged in independent play that is not disruptive? Most parents do not think so, citing the "let sleeping dogs lie" philosophy as their rationale. This assumption is first examined from a cognitive therapy perspective—specifically, in terms of the fact that it is an example of jumping to conclusions (in this case, a negative future outcome). Parents are then asked how certain they are that dispensing positive attention in this manner will be disruptive. Most often they state that they are pretty sure, but not 100%. While acknowledging that parents might in fact be correct in their prediction, clinicians also point out that they may not be. Until their "sleeping dogs" philosophy is put to empirical test against an alternative hypothesis, neither can be confirmed or disconfirmed. Additional justification for putting these competing assumptions to test may be inferred from what was learned earlier in the review of general behavior management principles. More specifically, parents are reminded that when any behavior—in this case, appropriate independent play—is ignored, this decreases its probability of occurring. This in turn increases the likelihood that various disruptive behaviors will develop inadvertently. If attended to positively, however, such independent play is much more likely to reappear in the future. Recognizing that initial parental attempts to reinforce appropriate independent play may at first be disruptive, parents are reminded that children eventually become accustomed to this change in parental response. This then leads to gradual improvements in their tendency to behave appropriately while their parents are busy.

Positive attending skills may also be applied to parental command situations. Although most parents have little trouble pointing out the various ways in which children with AD/HD do not comply with their requests, it is much harder for them to identify request situations that elicit compliance. Some even get to the point of believing that their child "does nothing that I ask him (or her) to do." While it is certainly true that children with AD/HD are frequently noncompliant, it is equally important for parents to recognize an unintentional tendency on their part to ignore instances of compliance when they occur. In cognitive therapy terms, parents are selectively attending to the negative aspects of their child's responses to their requests. In behavior therapy terms, they are discouraging compliance through their ignoring, and encouraging noncompliance through their attention to it. Against this background, clinicians point out the importance of paying positive attention to children whenever they are compliant. In addition, parents are advised to set the stage for practicing their use of such positive attending skills, by having them issue brief sequences of simple household commands that have a high probability of eliciting compliance from their child. Over time this should lead to a gradual increase in the child's overall compliance with parental requests, including those of relatively low probability.

The final topic for this step is the manner in which commands are given. Verbal and nonverbal parameters of how parents communicate commands to children are examined. This includes coverage of the following recommendations:

- That parents only issue commands they intend to follow through on;
- That commands take the form of direct statements rather than questions;
- That commands be relatively simple;
- That they be issued in the absence of outside distractions, and only when direct eye contact is being made with the child, so as to increase the likelihood of the child's attending to such instructions; and

- That commands be repeated back to the parents, so as to give them an opportunity to clarify any misunderstanding before the child responds.

Like all other steps in this training program, this session ends with a specific request for parents to practice these techniques prior to the next session. To assist them in doing so, they receive written reminder handouts summarizing all that was covered in this session. Parents are also reminded to continue practicing special time and spontaneous positive attending. In anticipation of the next step, clinicians furthermore ask parents to begin developing lists of requests and privileges that will be used in the home-based token system.

Step 5: Establishing a Home Poker Chip/Point System

Setting up a reward-oriented home token system is the major focus of this step. Such a system serves to provide children with AD/HD the external motivation they need to complete parent-requested activities that may be of little intrinsic interest and/or a trigger for their defiance. Another reason for using such a system is because positive attending and ignoring strategies are often insufficient for managing children with AD/HD, who generally require more concrete and meaningful rewards.

Following review and refinement of the therapeutic skills taught in steps 3 and 4, clinicians embark on a somewhat philosophical, yet practical, discussion of what are children's rights and what are their privileges. Such a discussion often serves to alert parents to how they have inadvertently been treating many of their child's privileges as if they were rights. This in turn makes it easier to set up the home-based poker chip or point system described next.

First, parents are asked to generate two lists: one list of daily, weekly, and long-range privileges that are likely to be interesting and motivating to the child; the other list pertaining to regular chores and/or household rules that parents would like done better. Such target behaviors should include not only instances of noncompliance and defiance, but also those situations where a child doesn't follow through because of loss of interest, distractions, and other AD/HD problems. Later at home, parents may wish to incorporate input from the child as to any other items that should be included in these lists.

Point values are then assigned to each list. For children 9 years old and under, plastic poker chips are used as tokens. Earned poker chips are collected and stored in a home "bank" that a child has set aside specifically for that purpose. For 9- to 11-year-old children, points are used in place of chips and are monitored in a checkbook register or some other type of notebook of interest to a youngster. Generally speaking, children can earn predetermined numbers of poker chips or points for complying with initial parent requests and for completing assigned tasks, which previously may have been left incomplete due to lack of interest or motivation in doing them. In addition, parents can dispense bonus chips or points for especially well-done chores or independent displays of appropriate behavior. At no time, however, should chips or points be taken away for noncompliance in this phase of the training program. Instead, encountered noncompliance should be handled in the same way that parents have dealt with such situations previously.

Parental motivation, which may have been quite high up until now, may begin to waver for several reasons. Some parents may once again tell us, "I've done something like this before and it doesn't work." As described earlier, cognitive therapy strategies may be used to correct this type of faulty thinking, which has the potential to interfere with parental efforts to institute a home token system. Another potentially self-defeating assumption that parents may express is "I don't think my child will go along with this." When this is stated, it becomes necessary to discuss the issue of who is in charge—parent or child? In the context of such a discussion, parental control is framed as a constructive responsibility, one that children may not like or appreciate immediately, but nevertheless one that is ultimately in their best interests. When they look at it in this light, most parents are at the very least willing to give the home token system a try.

Having made sure that parents fully understand the working mechanics of this token system, clinicians provide them with a detailed handout summarizing this phase of the program. This serves as a useful reminder of what to do as they practice this technique at home prior to the next session. They are also reminded to continue practicing all other facets of the program and to call immediately for consultation, should problems arise.

Step 6: Adding Response Cost to the Program

The primary goal of this step is to refine the home token system, including the addition of response cost strategies for minor misbehavior. It begins with a careful review of parental efforts to implement the home token system. Because problems inevitably arise, most of this session is set aside for clarifying confusion where needed and for making suggestions for increasing the effectiveness of this system.

Following this discussion, the response cost technique is introduced, which represents the first time in the treatment program that a penalty or punishment approach has been considered for use. More specifically, parents are instructed to begin deducting poker chips or points for noncompliance with one or two particularly troublesome requests on the list. Similar penalties may be used for one or two "don't behaviors"—that is, don't hit, don't talk back, and so on—that may be added to the program. At this stage, not only does the child with AD/HD fail to earn chips or points that would have resulted from compliance; previously earned chips or points are now also removed from the bank for displays of non-compliance. The number of chips or points lost is equal to the number of chips or points that would have been gained, had compliance occurred. For many children with AD/HD, who over the past week may have learned how to expend minimal effort to get the privileges that they desire, adding a response cost component to their token system often increases their overall level of compliance with parental requests, because they now have the additional incentive of trying not to lose what they have already earned. Clinicians also routinely caution parents to avoid getting into punishment spirals, whereby so many chips are taken away that a debt is incurred. As a rule, parents should not employ response cost more than twice in a row for the same noncompliant behavior. If needed, backup penalties, such as time out, can be employed instead. Furthermore, parents need to take steps to ensure that a child's token reserves do not approach a zero balance, which might diminish his or her interest in the program. If the balance gets low, parents must dispense bonus tokens for any display or appropriate child behavior, whether or not it happens to be on the list.

Unlike the other steps of the program, this step does not include a handout for parents to take home for review. With the exception of the addition of response cost, their assignment for the week is essentially the same—to continue using the home-based poker chip or point system. Should problems arise, parents are to call for assistance prior to the next session.

Step 7: Using Time-Out from Reinforcement

The focus of this step is to introduce the use of time-out strategies for dealing with more serious forms of noncompliance and/or rule violations.

After reviewing the home token system and making whatever adjustments are deemed necessary, clinicians begin discussing "time-out from reinforcement," or simply time-out. Although most types of noncompliance will continue to be handled via response cost, parents are encouraged to identify one or two especially resistant or serious types of noncompliance or rule violations (e.g., hitting a sibling) that may become the targets of time-out. Once these are identified, attention is then focused on teaching the mechanics of implementing the time-out procedure. Like the token system, time-out is a rather difficult technique to employ. Its use must be explained very carefully before asking parents to practice it at home.

Critical to the success of this technique is that three conditions must be met prior to releasing the youngster from time-out. First, the child must serve a minimum amount of time, generally equal in minutes to the number of years in his or her age. Once this condition is met, parents may approach the time-out area only when the child has been quiet for a brief period of time. This avoids the problem of inadvertently dispensing parental attention for inappropriate behavior. Next, and perhaps most importantly, parents must reissue the request or command that initially led the youngster to be placed into time-out. In cases where the child does not comply with the reissued directive, the entire three-step time-out cycle is repeated as many times as is necessary, until compliance is achieved. Thus, under no circumstances does the child avoid doing what was asked. Once compliance is achieved, parents thank the child in a neutral manner for doing what was asked, but no tokens are dispensed. A few moments later, however, parents should look for an opportunity to reinforce the child with poker chips or points, thereby balancing out their use of punishment.

In addition to covering these facets of time-out, clinicians routinely address other aspects of this procedure, including how to select a location for serving time-out and what to do if the child defiantly leaves the time out area. In regards to this latter point, various back-up penalty strategies may be employed, such as response cost, privilege removal, grounding, and/or physical restraint.

More so than any of the other procedures in this program, time out is a strategy that usually has been tried previously in one form or another. Thus, many parents have firm beliefs about its potential for success, or lack thereof. Such biases need to be addressed via cognitive restructuring techniques. Failure to do so runs the risk that parents will not be properly motivated to incorporate this treatment strategy in the manner in which it was intended. This in turn may increase parental frustration and diminish any further interest in participation in the program.

Parents leave with a written handout on time-out and are reminded to call for assistance as needed prior to the next session.

Step 8: Managing Behavior in Public Places

The major objective of this step is to begin expanding use of the entire home-based program to settings outside the home. Initially, parental efforts to incorporate time-out strategies are reviewed and refined as needed. All other facets of the program are reviewed and refined as well. If the home-based program is judged to be running relatively smoothly, attention is directed to a discussion of settings outside the home in which problem behaviors arise. Among the many settings that are often identified by parents as problematic are grocery stores, department stores, malls, movie theaters, restaurants, churches, and synagogues. Disciplinary strategies previously employed in such settings are reviewed and analyzed in terms of their overall ineffectiveness.

Against this background, the importance of anticipating such problems in public is discussed. In particular, parents are advised to have a plan of action before entering a predictably problematic public situation. This may be accomplished as follows. First, parents must review their expectations for his or her behavior in this setting. Next, they must establish some incentive for compliance with these rules. Finally, they must specify what types of punishment will be applied, should noncompliance with these rules ensue. Of equal importance to the success of this plan is to have the child state his or her understanding of these rules and consequences prior to entering the public situation. This allows parents an opportunity to clarify any misunderstanding on the part of the child that may result from confusion or from inattentiveness.

Generally speaking, modified versions of the strategies used successfully within the home are incorporated into this plan. These may include, for example, dispensing poker chips for ongoing compliance with parental requests such as "stay close, don't touch, don't beg," or removal of poker chips for noncompliance with these same requests. Modified versions of time-out may also be employed by parents, using quiet, out-of-the-way public areas for this purpose.

In contrast with their eagerness to try out various home management techniques, many parents are much less enthusiastic about experimenting with these techniques in public places. The perceived threat of public embarrassment is often cited. After all, "what will people think?" The mind-reading aspects of this particular situation are highlighted as the basis for their jumping to such a conclusion. Alternative viewpoints of what people might think, and the relative importance of what others think when it pertains to their child's welfare, are discussed. Addressing parental perceptions of this situation in this manner generally makes it possible to reduce their uneasiness and to increase their motivation for trying such a new and challenging approach.

Parents are asked to practice these procedures on at least two separate occasions prior to the next session. To facilitate these efforts, a written handout on the topic is distributed.

Step 9: School Management Issues and Preparing for Termination

This step serves many purposes: to increase parental knowledge of relevant school issues; to discuss how to handle future problems that might arise, and; to begin preparing for termination, including instructions on how to fade out the home-based program.

In addition to reviewing and fine-tuning parental efforts to deal with problem behavior in public places, clinicians also review and refine all other aspects of the training program. Parental feedback about the training program may be elicited as this time as well. Such comments often serve as a backdrop against which handling of future behavior problems may be discussed.

Parents also discuss what they believe might be problematic for them in the future and how they might handle such problematic situations. Attention is then directed to the various ways in which many parents slip away from adherence to this program. While some degree of slippage or departure from the protocol is acceptable, and in fact encouraged, too much may lead to increased behavioral difficulties. For this reason, parents are informed how to run a check on themselves to ascertain where fine-tuning of their specialized child management skills is required. A written handout summarizing this self-check system is distributed at this time.

Another important feature of this session is to discuss the child's current school status, including what modifications, if any, are being employed to deal with his or her AD/HD. This is followed by a description of the legal rights of children with AD/HD within the school system. In the context of this discussion, emphasis is placed on the child being in the least restrictive educational environment. How and when to consider special education accommodations is covered as well. Independent of placement issues, parents receive numerous suggestions for modifying their child's classroom environment to accommodate their AD/HD. Particular attention is directed to the mechanics of setting up a daily report card system. In this system teachers monitor specific classroom behaviors (e.g., finishes assigned tasks) by providing ratings on an index card, which is sent home on a daily basis. These teacher ratings are then converted into either token gains or losses, proportional to the quality of behavior and performance displayed by the child that day. One major advantage to using home-based consequences in this system is that they are consistently more meaningful and effective than stickers, extra recess, or other types of consequences typically available in school. Another significant advantage is that it imposes very little burden on classroom teachers, who must also direct their time and energy to meeting the needs of other students in the class. Of more general importance is that the daily report card system incorporates many of the behavior management principles specific to children with AD/HD. For example, implicit in its use is an attempt to provide extremely specific, immediate, and frequent feedback, all of which should serve to facilitate classroom performance.

Although much of what is discussed with parents might suggest an insensitivity to the needs of the teacher or the other students in the class, nothing could be further from the truth. On the contrary, parents are made aware of the various budgetary constraints, personnel limitations, and so forth that might make it most difficult to implement all of what they might like for their child. In light of this possibility, they are strongly encouraged to work with school personnel in as collaborative and cooperative a manner as possible.

The final portion of this session is used to address termination and/or disposition issues. In addition to agreeing upon an appropriate booster session date, efforts are made to determine whether any other types of clinical services are needed. This might include, for example, the need for adding a medication component or for scheduling school consultation visits to address classroom management concerns directly with school personnel.

Step 10: Booster Session

Although any length of time may be deemed acceptable, it is customary to meet with parents for a booster session approximately 1 month after conducting step 9. One objective of this session is to readminister pertinent child behavior and parent self-report rating scales and questionnaires, which serve as indices of any posttreatment changes that may have occurred. Further review and refinement of previously learned intervention strategies is conducted as well. Also established at this time is a mutually agreed-upon final clinical disposition. If desired, this may include scheduling of additional booster sessions.

CASE MATERIAL

The following case was referred to the AD/HD Clinic, a subspecialty child unit in the Department of Psychiatry at the University of Massachusetts Medical Center.

REASON FOR REFERRAL

Nathan is an 8-year-old boy who was initially referred to the AD/HD Clinic for an evaluation of longstanding home and school difficulties. Of particular concern to his parents and third-grade teacher at the time of his referral were his problems finishing assigned tasks, his frequent interruptions of others, and his constant fidgeting.

BACKGROUND INFORMATION

Nathan's mother's pregnancy, delivery, and neonatal course were unremarkable. His infant health and temperament were well within normal limits. According to his parents, he reached all of his major developmental milestones at age-appropriate times. Throughout his lifetime, Nathan had maintained excellent physical health.

The middle of three children, Nathan and his siblings live with their biological parents in a middle-class suburban home. Nathan maintained fairly typical relations with his siblings, neither of whom posed any major medical, learning, behavioral, or emotional problems. Both of Nathan's parents were in good health. Neither had a history of significant childhood or adult problems. Nathan's father was college educated and working full time as an engineer. His mother had two years of college training but had not worked outside of the home for several years. Nathan's parents had been married for 15 years, during which time there had been some strains in their relationship, but not to the point of separations or marital counseling. No major lifestyle changes or psychosocial stressors had occurred within 12 months of Nathan's diagnostic evaluation.

Nathan attended nursery school for two years prior to entering kindergarten. From kindergarten to his current enrollment in third grade he had been enrolled in the same public school setting. Throughout his schooling Nathan's teachers had described him as "bright, but lazy, more interested in playing, and not working up to his ability." Of particular concern was that his academic productivity and achievement in almost all subject areas were well below grade level in quality. Moreover, Nathan's classmates were beginning to shy away from him, as they did not appreciate his intrusiveness or his tendency to get into trouble with the teacher.

DIAGNOSTIC FORMULATION AND TREATMENT RECOMMENDATIONS

Input about Nathan and his family was obtained via multimethod assessment. The results of this evaluation confirmed that he did indeed meet *DSM-IV* criteria for a diagnosis of AD/HD, Combined Type, which was moderate in overall severity and manifested across both the home and school settings. No other *DSM-IV* diagnostic concerns emerged with respect to other areas of Nathan's learning, behavioral, emotional, or psychiatric functioning. In the absence of such findings, Nathan's AD/HD was viewed to be a major factor contributing to his diminished academic productivity and achievement, his emerging peer relationship problems in school, his misbehavior at home, and his parents' extremely high levels of parenting stress.

To address Nathan's AD/HD both at home and at school, several intervention strategies were recommended for incorporation into his overall treatment plan. This included: PT; parent and teacher education about AD/HD as a disorder; numerous curriculum, teaching style, and classroom environment modifications; school-based social skills training, and; pharmacotherapy, using Ritalin or some other form of stimulant medication therapy.

Based on stories that they had read in their local newspaper, Nathan's parents were not at all interested in considering stimulant medication therapy as a treatment option for him. Given that they had "tried everything and nothing works," they were also not especially eager to begin the PT program. Likewise, they expressed a great deal of pessimism about the prospects of enlisting the support and cooperation of Nathan's third-grade teacher, given that all other teachers up to that point had not been very responsive to meeting his individual classroom needs.

As for their assessment of the efficacy of PT, it was first necessary to point out that what they had tried previously were traditional parenting techniques, which work well for normal children but not so for children with AD/HD. What they needed to be using were specialized parenting techniques, to meet Nathan's special behavioral needs. Several examples of how the recommended PT strategies were very different from what they had tried before were presented, as were research findings pertinent to the efficacy of this form of treatment. Such information served to increase their willingness to participate in this program. Similar cognitive restructuring strategies were employed to address the fortune-telling nature of their negative expectation that they would not be able to enlist the cooperation of Nathan's teacher. As for their concerns about medication, it was agreed that their preference not to medicate would be honored. At the same time, however, they were encouraged to take on an empirical approach to this matter. More specifically, they were advised to implement the recommended home and school-based psychosocial treatments. After a period of 4 to 6 months, they and Nathan's teacher would need to evaluate his response to these treatments. If his level of improvement was less than satisfactory at that time, they would need to reconsider the merits of a stimulant medication trial. In the meantime, they agreed to begin receiving counseling about the advantages and disadvantages of using stimulant medication, so as to acquire an understanding of this form of treatment that was more accurate and comprehensive than that available from the popular media.

COURSE OF TREATMENT

The above treatment plan was implemented over a period of several months. At various points during their participation in PT, Nathan's parents occasionally slipped into unrealistic, negative thinking patterns that interfered with their willingness to try out new parenting strategies. For example, the recommended home poker chip system initially reminded them of something that they had previously tried unsuccessfully, and therefore they were disinclined to consider its use. Once again, it was necessary to point out how what was being recommended was different from what they had done before. With clinician encouragement, this information made it easier for them to test the hypothesis that these new parenting strategies might work better.

Although the poker chip system worked well for several weeks, Nathan began to display some resistance and deterioration in his behavior. This led both parents to the faulty conclusion that they were right, the program did not work. It was pointed out that this was not an unusual occurrence for children with AD/HD, given that they are prone to become bored easily. They were encouraged to make minor modifications in his poker chip system, so as to increase its novelty, salience, and meaningfulness to Nathan. It was hypothesized that if they did, he very likely would regain interest in the program. When put to test, this prediction was supported.

In the midst of this PT program, a school meeting was conducted, involving Nathan's teacher, principal, and parents. The purpose of this meeting was to educate school personnel about AD/HD in general, to alert them as to how it affected Nathan, and to emphasize the need for collaborative team work between school personnel and his parents. Contrary to their expectations, Nathan's parents were pleasantly surprised to discover that his teacher and principal were highly receptive to this suggestion and that they would begin immediately incorporating modifications to meet his AD/HD needs in the classroom and in other areas of the school where behavior problems might arise (e.g., recess).

After several months, it was clear that these home and school-based interventions had brought about many improvements in Nathan's psychosocial functioning. Of additional importance is that Nathan's parents reported feeling less stress and guilt in their roles as parents. Moreover, both parents indicated that they had learned to view and accept Nathan's AD/HD in a different light. This in turn reduced some of the marital disagreements and conflict that they had been having over parenting issues. Amidst such gains, however, there was still room for improvement, particularly in terms of Nathan's home and school behavior. This, coupled with the fact that they had acquired a better understanding of the potential benefits and side effects of stimulant medication therapy, set the stage for Nathan's parents to request that he undergo a double-blind, placebo-controlled stimulant trial to determine if this form of treatment might bring about further normalization of his behavior. It did. Thereafter, Nathan was placed on a longer term trial of medication, in combination with the other treatments already in place.

CONCLUSION

What should be readily apparent from the preceding discussion is that PT would seem to have a place in the overall clinical management of children with AD/HD. One of the major advantages to using PT is that it can be used to target not only the child's primary AD/HD symptomatology, but also many of their comorbid features, including oppositional-defiant behavior and conduct problems. Moreover, because PT interventions often utilize parents as cotherapists, many parents themselves derive indirect therapeutic benefits from their involvement in treatment. Although it remains to be seen what the long-term impact of PT interventions might be, preliminary evidence would seem to suggest that treatment-induced improvements in psychosocial functioning can be maintained in the absence of ongoing therapist contact, at least in the short run.

As was noted earlier, much of the research to date has focused on the clinical efficacy of PT interventions when used alone. One benefit of pursuing this type of research is that it has allowed for a better understanding of the unique impact that this form of treatment can have on outcome within an AD/HD population. Examining PT by itself has also provided important insight into its therapeutic limitations, including the fact that not everyone benefits from PT. Of additional concern is that in multimodal interventions, PT thus far has not added a great deal to treatment outcome, above and beyond that accounted for by other treatments, such as medication. Although some individuals might view such limitations as contraindications for using PT, one could also view them as an impetus for conducting further research. For example, such information could be used to guide research that addresses: (a) With which treatments might PT be combined to maximize therapeutic outcome? and, (b) For which children and their families is the combination of PT with other treatments a viable intervention approach?

REFERENCES

Abikoff, H. B., & Hechtman, L. (1996). Multimodal therapy and stimulants in the treatment of children with attention-deficit hyperactivity disorder. In E. D. Hibbs & P. S. Jensen (Eds.), *Psychosocial treatments for child and adolescent disorders: Empirically based strategies for clinical practice* (pp. 341–369). Washington, DC: American Psychological Association.

American Psychiatric Association. (1980). *Diagnostic and statistical manual of mental disorders* (3rd ed.). Washington, DC: Author.

American Psychiatric Association. (1987). *Diagnostic and statistical manual of mental disorders* (3rd ed. Rev.). Washington, DC: Author.

American Psychiatric Association. (1994). *Diagnostic and statistical manual of mental disorders* (4th ed.). Washington, DC: Author.

Anastopoulos, A. D., & Barkley, R. A. (1990). Counseling and training parents. In R. A. Barkley (Ed.), *Attention deficit hyperactivity disorder: A handbook for diagnosis and treatment.* New York: Guilford Press.

Anastopoulos, A. D., Guevremont, D. C., Shelton, T. L., & DuPaul, G. J. (1992). Parenting stress among families of children with attention deficit hyperactivity disorder. *Journal of Abnormal Child Psychology, 20,* 503–520.

Anastopoulos, A. D., Shelton, T., DuPaul, G. J., & Guevremont, D. C. (1993). Parent training for attention deficit hyperactivity disorder: Its impact on parent functioning. *Journal of Abnormal Child Psychology, 21,* 581–596.

Barkley, R. A. (1977). A review of stimulant drug research with hyperactive children. *Journal of Child Psychology and Psychiatry, 18,* 137–165.

Barkley, R. A. (1981). *Hyperactive children: A handbook for diagnosis and treatment.* New York: Guilford Press.

Barkley, R. A. (1987). *Defiant children: A clinician's manual for parent training.* New York: Guilford Press.

Barkley, R. A. (1990). *Attention deficit hyperactivity disorder: A handbook for diagnosis and treatment.* New York: Guilford Press.

Barkley, R. A. (1997). Behavioral inhibition, sustained attention, and executive functions: Constructing a unifying theory of ADHD. *Psychological Bulletin, 121,* 65–94.

Barkley, R. A., Anastopoulos, A. D., Guevremont, D. C., & Fletcher, K. E. (1991). Adolescents with AD/HD: Patterns of behavioral adjustment, academic functioning, and treatment utilization. *Journal of the American Academy of Child and Adolescent Psychiatry, 30,* 752–761.

Barkley, R. A., Anastopoulos, A. D., Guevremont, D. C., & Fletcher, K. E. (1992). Adolescents with attention deficit hyperactivity disorder: Mother-adolescent interactions, family beliefs and conflicts, and maternal psychopathology. *Journal of Abnormal Child Psychology, 20,* 263–288.

Barkley, R. A., DuPaul, G. J., & McMurray, M. (1990). A comprehensive evaluation of attention deficit disorder with and without hyperactivity defined by research criteria. *Journal of Consulting and Clinical Psychology, 58,* 775–789.

Barkley, R. A., Guevremont, D. C., Anastopoulos, A. D., DuPaul, G. J., & Shelton, T. L. (1993). Driving-related risks and outcomes of attention deficit hyperactivity disorder in adolescents and young adults: A 3- to 5-year follow-up survey. *Pediatrics, 92,* 212–218.

Barkley, R. A., Guevremont, D. C., Anastopoulos, A. D., & Fletcher, K. F. (1992). A comparison of three family therapy programs for treating family conflicts in adolescents with ADHD. *Journal of Consulting and Clinical Psychology, 60,* 450–462.

Bell, R. Q., & Harper, L. (1977). *Child effects on adults.* New York: Wiley.

Biederman, J., Munir, K., Knee, D., Armentano, M., Autor, S., Waternaux, C., & Tsuang, M. (1987). High rate of affective disorders in probands with attention deficit disorders and in their relatives: A controlled family study. *American Journal of Psychiatry, 144,* 330–333.

Block, G. H. (1977). Hyperactivity: A cultural perspective. *Journal of Learning Disabilities, 110,* 236–240.

Cunningham, C. E., & Barkley, R. A. (1979). The interactions of hyperactive and normal children with their mothers during free play and structured task. *Child Development, 50,* 217–224.

Cunningham, C. E., & Siegel, L. S. (1987). Peer interactions of normal and attention-deficit disordered boys during free-play, cooperative task, and simulated classroom situations. *Journal of Abnormal Child Psychology, 15,* 247–268.

Dangel, R. F., & Polster, R. A. (Eds.). (1984). *Parent training: Foundations of research and practice.* New York: Guilford Press.

Deutsch, K. (1987). *Genetic factors in attention deficit disorders.* Paper presented at the symposium on Disorders of Brain, Development, and Cognition, Boston, MA.

Douglas, V. I. (1983). Attention and cognitive problems. In M. Rutter (Ed.), *Developmental neuropsychiatry.* New York: Guilford Press.

DuPaul, G. J., Power, T. J., Anastopoulos, A. D., Reid, R., McGoey, K. E., & Ikeda, M. J. (in press). Teacher ratings of attention-deficit/hyperactivity disorder symptoms: Factor structure and normative data. *Psychological Assessment.*

Edelbrock, C. E. (1995). A twin study of competence and problem behaviors of childhood and early adolescence. *Journal of Child Psychology and Psychiatry, 36,* 775–785.

Erhardt, D., & Baker, B. L. (1990). The effects of behavioral parent training on families with young hyperactive children. *Journal of Behavior Therapy and Experimental Psychiatry, 21,* 121–132.

Farrington, D. P., Loeber, R., & van Kammen, W. B. (1987). *Long-term criminal outcomes of hyperactivity-impulsivity, attention deficit and conduct problems in childhood.* Paper presented at the meeting of the Society for Life History Research, St. Louis, MO.

Feingold, B. (1975). *Why your child is hyperactive.* New York: Random House.

Forehand, R., & McMahon, R. (1981). *Helping the noncompliant child: A clinician's guide to parent training.* New York: Guilford Press.

Grenell, M. M., Glass, C. R., & Katz, K. S. (1987). Hyperactive children and peer interaction: Knowledge and performance of social skills. *Journal of Abnormal Child Psychology,* 1–13.

Hartsough, C. S., & Lambert, N. M. (1985). Medical factors in hyperactive and normal children: Prenatal, developmental, and health history findings. *American Journal of Orthopsychiatry, 55,* 190–201.

Horn, W. F., Ialongo, N., Pascoe, J. M., & Greenberg, G. (1991). Additive effects of psychostimulants, parent training, and self-control therapy with ADHD children. *Journal of the American Academy of Child and Adolescent Psychiatry, 30,* 233–240.

Ialongo, N. S., Horn, W. F., Pascoe, J. M., & Greenberg, G. (1993). The effects of multimodal intervention with attention-deficit hyperactivity disorder children: A 9 month follow-up. *Journal of the American Academy of Child and Adolescent Psychiatry, 32,* 182–189.

Kendall, P. C., & Braswell, L. (1985). *Cognitive-behavioral therapy for impulsive children.* New York: Guilford Press.

Lahey, B. B., Piacentini, J., McBurnett, K., Stone, P., Hatdagen, S., & Hynd, G. (1988). Psychopathology in the parents of children with conduct disorder and hyperactivity. *Journal of American Academy of Child & Adolescent Psychiatry, 27,* 163–170.

Levin, P. M. (1938). Restlessness in children. *Archives of Neurology and Psychiatry, 39,* 764–770.

Loeber, R., Keenan, K., Lahey, B. B., Green, S. M., & Thomas, C. (1993). Evidence for developmentally based diagnoses of oppositional defiant disorder and conduct disorder. *Journal of Abnormal Child Psychology, 21,* 377–410.

Loney, J., & Milich, R. (1982). Hyperactivity, inattention, and aggression in clinical practice. In D. Routh & M. Wolraich (Eds.), *Advances in developmental and behavioral pediatrics* (Vol. 3, pp. 113–147). Greenwich, CT: JAI Press.

Lou, H. C., Henriksen, L., Bruhn, P., Borner, H., & Nielsen, J. B. (1989). Striatal dysfunction in attention deficit and hyperkinetic disorder. *Archives of Neurology, 46,* 48–52.

Luk, S. (1985). Direct observations studies of hyperactive behaviors. *Journal of the American Academy of Child Psychiatry, 24,* 338–344.

Margalit, M., & Arieli, N. (1984). Emotional and behavioral aspects of hyperactivity. *Journal of Learning Disabilities, 17,* 374–376.

Mash, E. J., & Johnston, C. (1990). Determinants of parenting stress: Illustrations from families of hyperactive children and families of physically abused children. *Journal of Clinical Child Psychology, 19,* 313–328.

Milich, R., Loney, J., & Landau, S. (1982). The independent dimensions of hyperactivity and aggression: A validation with playroom observation data. *Journal of Abnormal Psychology, 91,* 183–198.

Newby, R. F., Fischer, M., & Roman, M. A. (1991). Parent training for families of children with ADHD. *School Psychology Review, 20,* 252–265.

Patterson, G. R. (1982). *Coercive family process.* Eugene, OR: Castalia Press.

Pelham, W. E., & Bender, M. E. (1982). Peer relationships in hyperactive children: Description and treatment. In K. D. Gadow & I. Bialer (Eds.), *Advances in learning and behavioral disabilities* (Vol. 1, pp. 365–436). Greenwich, CT: JAI Press.

Pisterman, S., Firestone, P., McGrath, P., & Goodman, J. T. (1992). The role of parent training in treatment of preschoolers with ADHD. *American Journal of Orthopsychiatry, 62,* 397–408.

Pisterman, S., McGrath, P., Firestone, P., & Goodman, J. T. (1989). Outcome of parent-mediated treatment of preschoolers with attention deficit disorder with hyperactivity. *Journal of Consulting and Clinical Psychology, 57,* 636–643.

Pollard, S., Ward, E. M., & Barkley, R. A. (1983). The effects of parent training and Ritalin on the parent-child interactions of hyperactive boys. *Child and Family Therapy, 5,* 51–69.

Quay, H. C. (1989). The behavioral reward and inhibition systems in childhood behavior disorder. In L. M. Bloomingdale (Ed.), *Attention deficit disorder: III. New research in treatment, psychopharmacology, and attention* (pp. 176–186). New York: Pergamon Press.

Richters, J. E., Arnold, L. E., Jensen, P. S., Abikoff, H., Conners, C. K., Greenhill, L. L., Hechtman, L., Hinshaw, S. P., Pelham, W. E., & Swanson, J. M. (1995). NIMH collaborative multisite multimodal treatment study of children with ADHD: I. Background and rationale. *Journal of the American Academy of Child and Adolescent Psychiatry, 34,* 987–1000.

Ross, D. M., & Ross, S. A. (1982). *Hyperactivity: Current issues, research, and theory* (2nd ed.). New York: Wiley.

Routh, D. K. (1978). Hyperactivity. In P. Magrab (Ed.), *Psychological management of pediatric problems* (pp. 3–48). Baltimore: University Park Press.

Routh, D. K., & Schroeder, C. S. (1976). Standardized playroom measures as indices of hyperactivity. *Journal of Abnormal Child Psychology, 4,* 199–207.

Schachar, R. J., Tannock, R., & Logan, G. (1993). Inhibitory control, impulsiveness, and attention deficit hyperactivity disorder. *Clinical Psychology Review, 13*, 721–739.

Sergeant, J. A. (1995). Hyperkinetic disorder revisited. In J. A. Sergeant (Ed.), *Eunethydis: European approaches to hyperkinetic disorder* (pp. 7–17). Amsterdam, The Netherlands: Author.

Streissguth, A. P., Martin, D. C., Barr, H. M., Sandman, B. M., Kirchner, G. L., & Darby, B. L. (1984). Intrauterine alcohol and nicotine exposure: Attention and reaction time in 4-year-old children. *Developmental Psychology, 20*, 533–541.

Taylor, E. (1986). *The overactive child.* Philadelphia: Lippincott.

Weiss, G., & Hechtman, L. (1986). *Hyperactive children grown up.* New York: Guilford Press.

Wender, P. H. (1995). *Attention-deficit hyperactivity disorder in adults.* New York: Oxford Press.

Willis, T. J., & Lovaas, I. (1977). A behavioral approach to treating hyperactive children: The parent's role. In J. B. Millichap (Ed.), *Learning disabilities and related disorders* (pp. 119–140). Chicago: Yearbook Medical.

Wolraich, M. L., Lindgren, S. D., Stumbo, P. J., Stegink, L. D., Appelbaum, M. I., & Kiritsy, M. C. (1994). Effects of diets high in sucrose or aspartame on the behavior and cognitive performance of children. *New England Journal of Medicine, 330*, 301–307.

Zametkin, A. J., & Rapoport, J. L. (1986). The pathophysiology of attention deficit disorder with hyperactivity: A review. In B. Lahey & A. Kazdin (Eds.), *Advances in clinical child psychology* (Vol. 9, pp. 177–216). New York: Plenum Press.

Zentall, S. S. (1985). A context for hyperactivity. In K. D. Gadow & I. Bialer (Eds.), *Advances in learning and behavioral disabilities* (Vol. 4, pp. 273–343). Greenwich, CT: JAI Press.

CHAPTER 2

Parent-Child Interaction Therapy: A Psychosocial Intervention for the Treatment of Young Conduct-Disordered Children

SHEILA M. EYBERG and STEPHEN R. BOGGS

THIS CHAPTER describes Parent-Child Interaction Therapy (PCIT) and its application to the treatment of preschool children with conduct problems. Although we focus in this chapter on children with severe and persistent conduct problems, PCIT is used clinically with parents and children whose dysfunctional relationships may reflect multiple individual or social problems of one or both members of the dyad such as temperament or personality disorders, medical or neurological impairments, traumatic stress or adjustment disorders, cognitive deficits or poverty. Indeed, significant conduct problems in young children are rarely present in isolation.

Children with conduct problem behavior constitute the majority of children referred to mental health clinics (Offord, Boyle, & Racine, 1991; Schuhman, Durning, Eyberg, & Boggs, 1996). Conduct problems in young children show considerable stability during childhood (Campbell & Ewing, 1990) and epidemiological research suggests that these early behaviors may be a common pathway for a wide range of psychological disorders in adolescence and adulthood (Fischer, Rolf, Hasazi, & Cummings, 1984; Lerner, Inui, Trupin, & Douglas, 1985) including delinquency and criminal behavior. Therefore, early and effective treatment for these young children has important implications for the child and his or her family and for society as well.

As noted by Schaeffer and Briesmeister (1989), parent training with these youngsters has historically taken one of two primary approaches to treatment: the relationship enhancement approach as exemplified by Guerney (1964); and the behavioral approach as exemplified by Patterson (1974, 1982) and Wahler (1965). The approach described here, Parent-Child Interaction Therapy, is an integrated approach to the treatment of preschool children with conduct problems that incorporates both behavioral and traditional concerns (Eyberg, 1988). Consistent with the behavioral approach, Parent-Child Interaction Therapy assumes that conduct problem behavior is established or maintained by the child's interaction with the parent. Even when the child's problem behaviors originate from biological characteristics such as difficult temperament or the neurological deficits suspected in hyperactive, developmentally delayed, or autistic children, many of the conduct problems are intensified by the parent-child interactional patterns. For example, the hyperactive child is often thought to be neurologically different from the normally active child, but Barkley (1990) has demonstrated that altering parent response to child behavior during instruction-giving sequences can significantly impact the degree of overactivity, impulsivity, and inattention observed in these children.

Consistent with traditional play therapy approaches to child treatment, PCIT recognizes that creating or strengthening a trusting, close bond between parent(s) and child will influence the child's behavior positively (McNeil, Hembree-Kigin, & Eyberg, 1996). Changing parent-child relationships in this way encourages generalized behavior change by establishing a pervasive, mutually rewarding context for all family interactions. For example, a child with a history of frequent, high-quality, positive interactions with a parent will respond more rapidly to the parent's requests and direction than a child who is accustomed to only negative feedback. The changes in family relationship patterns contribute positively to maintenance of change in child behavior as well.

Parent-Child Interaction Therapy is conducted within the context of natural play situations between parent and child. This play setting is important because play is a primary medium through which young children learn new skills and work through developmental problems (Russ, 1993). In addition, a play setting provides abundant opportunities for parents to practice the techniques of communication and authority necessary to establish a positive influence on their children.

Parent-Child Interaction Therapy consists of two phases of treatment labeled Child-Directed Interaction (CDI) and Parent-Directed Interaction (PDI). Each phase consists of multiple components designed to impact both the parent's and the child's behavior.

The CDI focuses on changing the quality of the parent-child relationship. Parents are taught nondirective interaction skills to provide a safe and therapeutic context that allows the child to experiment with change. Interpersonal factors such as parental warmth, attention, and praise serve as nontangible incentives that assist the child toward developing internal attributions of self-control (Robinson, 1985). Differential reinforcement of child behavior through praise directed toward the child's appropriate play and consistent ignoring of any undesirable activity provides a positive form of behavior management throughout this phase.

In PDI, methods of incorporating clearly communicated and age-appropriate instructions to the child are taught. Using techniques based directly on operant principles of behavior change, parents are taught to provide consistent positive and negative consequences following the child's obedience and disobedience. In addition, the therapist assists the parent to learn ways of understanding how a child's behavior is shaped and maintained by the child's social environment and how methods of behavior change learned throughout PCIT can be applied to new problems as they arise. These functional problem-solving skills serve to increase the generalization of clinic-based parent training efforts (Boggs, Stokes, & Danforth, 1986).

The specific goals of PCIT are to teach parents to build a positive relationship with their child, to teach their child desirable prosocial behaviors, and to decrease their child's inappropriate behaviors. The treatment model provides a detailed structure within which parents and children learn a global set of positive interaction skills that can be readily applied to their own unique problems.

THE TREATMENT PROGRAM

THE PRETREATMENT ASSESSMENT

Parent-Child Interaction Therapy depends on assessment information to delineate the problems to be addressed, guide the course of treatment, and evaluate outcome. At the initial, pretreatment assessment, we ask parents to complete a *DSM-IV* Rating Scale that serves as a broad screening for Oppositional Defiant Disorder, Attention Deficit Hyperactivity Disorder, Conduct Disorder, Generalized Anxiety Disorder, and Major Depressive Disorder. Any area(s) of concern is followed up with a *DSM-IV* Structured Interview, addressing the severity and pervasiveness of the symptoms for diagnostic purposes. This general screening is followed by a clinical interview with the parents that covers the child's developmental, medical and social history and includes a behavioral analysis of the child's presenting problems, and a detailed history of the parents' discipline strategies that encompasses precise descriptions of how they are used, their frequency and perceived effectiveness, and the parents' beliefs and attitudes about their use. Parents are also asked about common discipline methods (e.g., spanking, rewards) if they have not mentioned them.

A play interview with a child (Boggs & Eyberg, 1990) is included to assess the child's responsiveness to social reinforcement and to adults other than the child's parents. A brief cognitive screening of the child with the Peabody Picture Vocabulary Test—Revised (Dunn & Dunn, 1981) is conducted to determine the child's receptive language skills. Parent rating scales including the Eyberg Child Behavior Inventory (Eyberg, 1992, in press-a), the Parenting Stress Index (Abidin, 1995), and the Parental Locus of Control—Short Form (Rayfield, Eyberg, Boggs, & Roberts, 1995) are administered to assess the child's behavior problems and important aspects of parent functioning. The Sutter-Eyberg Student Behavior Inventory (Eyberg, 1992, in press-b) is administered to the child's teacher to assess problematic behaviors in school situations. Finally, direct observations of the interactions between each parent and the child are recorded using the Dyadic Parent-Child Interaction Coding System II (DPICS-II; Eyberg, Bessmer, Newcomb, Edwards, & Robinson, 1994) to assess the quality of the parent-child interaction in three, five-minute standardized situations that vary in the degree to which parental control is required. The DPICS-II Clinic Version, a quick (and easy) paper-and-pencil method of assessing basic parenting skills and child compliance and disruptive behavior, is used so that we can give parents immediate feedback about the kinds of skills we will emphasize in PCIT.

STRUCTURE OF THE TREATMENT SESSIONS

PCIT contains two distinct phases of therapy, labeled Child-Directed Interaction and Parent-Directed Interaction. Each phase is first presented in one didactic session in which the specific techniques and their rationales are explained and modeled for the parents and role-played with them. Handouts summarizing the basic techniques are given to the parents for their review. In subsequent sessions, following brief reviews of weekly home progress, each parent practices the interaction in a play situation with the child in the playroom while the spouse and therapist observe the interaction through a one-way mirror. (If one-way mirrors are not available, the therapist, and often the spouse, may observe from within the playroom.) The therapist first codes the relevant interaction (CDI or PDI) for five minutes and then uses those data to determine the primary area to emphasize in coaching the parent. In our clinic, the parent wears an ear device through which the therapist coaches the parent.

Coaching consists of frequent, brief statements giving parents immediate feedback on their demonstrated skills (e.g., "Good labeled praise," "Nice imitating her play"), their manner (e.g., "Perfect timing," "Sounds very genuine"), or their effect (e.g., "He likes your touch," "Your soft voice calmed him down") and at times providing gentle corrections ("Oops, a little leading") or suggestions ("How about a hug with that praise?"). At the end of each session, the therapist reviews with each parent a summary data sheet showing the number of times they used each skill during the five-minute coded interaction from the current and each previous session. By jointly examining their progress, parents are able to select their own goal for the week in terms of the skill(s) they will work hardest to master.

CHILD-DIRECTED INTERACTION

A primary goal of the CDI is to create or strengthen a strong, positive parent-child relationship, in which negative attitudes of resistance or frustration are lessened to allow effective behavior change. The CDI incorporates the techniques of differential social attention and client-centered play therapy with the parent in the role of therapist. The basic rule for the parents' play is to follow the child's lead. In order to follow, parents are taught specifically how to avoid leading behaviors, such as commands and questions. When children are given the lead, oppositional behaviors rarely occur, leaving the parent free to attend to the child's appropriate talk and play. Parents are also taught very specifically how to attend by describing and imitating the child's play, answering the child's questions, reflecting the child's statements, and praising the child. If undesirable behaviors occur, parents are taught to avoid criticizing the child by ignoring the behavior when possible. If potentially harmful behaviors occur, parents are told to discontinue the CDI. The rationale for each of these techniques that is emphasized is individually tailored to the families' unique problems and abilities. The techniques are presented to the parents in the form of the "rules of CDI," which are summarized on a handout (Table 2.1) given to the parents at the end of the didactic session. This handout includes the rationale as well as specific examples of each technique to aid parents during early home practice sessions.

During treatment sessions, parents are guided and coached in the use of the CDI skills with their child until data from the five-minute coded interaction at the beginning of the session show that the parents have met the minimal criteria for mastery: (a) 10 behavioral descriptions; (b) 10 reflective statements (if the child is verbal); (c) 15 praises (at least 8 of them labeled); and (d) no more than 3 total across questions, commands, and criticisms. Additionally, parents must ignore every occurrence

Table 2.1
Parent-Child Interaction Therapy—Child-Directed Interaction

Rule	Reason	Examples
1. *Describe* your child's appropriate behavior	Allows child to lead Shows child that you are interested Teaches concepts Models speech Holds child's attention Organizes child's thoughts about play	You have a red block. You're making a tower. You drew a smiling face. You're putting on two more pieces.
2. *Describe* objects and events involved in the game	Lets child lead Shows child that you are involved in the game Teaches concepts Models speech Organizes child's thoughts about play	That sign says "Go Slow." I'm driving the red car. Ernie and Bert are playing near the farm. The train track curves around the mountain.
3. *Imitate* appropriate play	Lets child lead Approves child's choice of play Shows child that you are involved Teaches child how to play with others (e.g., basis of taking turns) Tends to increase child's imitation of what you do	Child: I'm putting baby to bed. Parent: I'll put sister to bed, too. Child: I'm making a sun in the sky. Parent: I'm going to put a sun in my picture, too.
4. *Reflect* appropriate talk	Doesn't control the conversation Shows the child that you are really listening Demonstrates acceptance and understanding of child Improves child's speech Increases verbal communication	Child: I made a star. Parent: Yes, you made a star. Child: The camel got bumps on top. Parent: It has two humps on its back. Child: I like to play with this castle. Parent: This is a fun castle to play with.
5. *Praise* appropriate behavior	Causes the behavior to increase Lets the child know what you like Increases child's self-esteem	That's terrific counting! I like the way you're playing so quietly. You have wonderful ideas for this picture.

Table 2.1 *(Continued)*

Rule	Reason	Examples
	Adds to warmth of the relationship	I'm proud of you for being polite.
	Makes *both* parent and child feel good!	You did a nice job on that building.
6. *Ignore* negative behavior (unless it is dangerous or destructive) a. don't look at the child, smile, frown, etc. b. be silent c. ignore every time d. expect behavior to increase at first	Helps the child to notice the difference between your responses to good and bad behavior Although behavior may increase at first, *consistent* ignoring decreases many behaviors	Child: (sasses parent and picks up toy) Parent: (ignores sass; praises picking up) Child: (hits parent.) Parent: (GAME STOPS. This can't be ignored.)
7. *Don't* give commands	Doesn't allow child to lead Can cause unpleasantness Child obedience will be taught later	*Indirect Commands:* Will you hand me that paper? Could you tell me the alphabet? *Direct Commands:* Give me the red box. Please tie your shoe. Come here.
8. *Don't* ask questions	Leads the conversation instead of following Many questions are commands and require an answer May seem like you aren't listening or disagree with child	It's big, isn't it? That's a blue one, right? What color is this? Are you having fun? You want to play with the wastebasket? Will you help me?
9. *Don't criticize*	Doesn't work to decrease bad behaviors Often increases the criticized behavior May lower the child's self-esteem Creates an unpleasant interaction	You're being naughty. I don't like it when you talk back. Don't scribble on your paper. No, honey, that's not right. That design is ugly.

of nonharmful inappropriate behavior (e.g., whining, yelling, sassing). Once the parents have reached these criteria, the second phase of PCIT—the Parent-Directed Interaction—is added. Because the CDI skills continue to be important, however, the therapist continues to code five minutes of CDI at the beginning of each therapy session. If a parent has fallen below the criterion on any of the skills, CDI is coached briefly before the PDI interaction is begun. The five-minute CDI home play sessions also continue.

Parent-Directed Interaction

The primary goals of the PDI are to increase low-rate prosocial behaviors and to decrease inappropriate behaviors that are too harmful to be ignored, are controlled by reinforcers other than parental attention, or do not extinguish easily. The PDI incorporates several techniques based on social learning theory including differential attention, social reinforcement, punishment, skills training, and strategies for enhancing generalization and maintenance following treatment, such as problem-solving skill training.

In PDI, the parents continue to give positive attention to appropriate behavior and to ignore inappropriate behavior. But, instead of just responding to behavior initiated by the child, the parent leads the activity by giving verbal directions to the child and by applying specific consequences for compliance and noncompliance. The PDI provides the parents with a consistent procedure for obtaining compliance in a way that is fair to the child because the child clearly understands what is expected and knows exactly what will happen if he or she obeys or disobeys.

In PDI, parents are first taught to use clear, direct commands when it is important that the child obey, such as "Please sit down while you draw," or "Put the blocks away gently this time." Rules for effective commands are described and explained to parents and are summarized on a handout (Table 2.2) that the parents can take with them.

Parents are next taught precise steps to follow once they have given their child a command. Specifically, they are taught to ignore inappropriate behavior and to attend only to whether the child obeys or disobeys. If the child obeys, parents are instructed to give a labeled praise and return to CDI techniques before they issue another command. If the child disobeys, parents are instructed to initiate the timeout procedure. Parents are taught never to ignore noncompliance. Noncompliance is reinforced by more than parental attention: Getting out of doing what they don't want to do is often highly reinforcing to a child.

The time-out procedure in Figure 2.1 provides parents with a standard, concrete, easily-administered set of steps, consisting of three levels: warning, chair, and back up. The child has a choice at each point in the

Table 2.2
PDI: Rules for Effective Commands

1. *Commands should be direct rather than indirect.* Direct commands should leave no question in the child's mind that he/she is being told to do something. Indirect commands give the child an illusion of choice. They are often expressed in question form.

   Examples: Please hand me the block. (Direct Command)
   instead of
   Will you please hand me the block? (Indirect Command)

   Put the train in the box. (Direct Command)
   instead of
   Let's put the train in the box. (Indirect Command)

2. *Commands should be positively stated.* Tell the child what "to do" rather than what *"not to do."* Avoid "Don't" commands.

   Examples: Come sit beside me. (Positively stated)
   instead of
   Don't run around the room!

   Please put your hands in your pocket. (Positively stated)
   instead of
   Stop touching that crystal.

3. *Commands should be given one at a time.*

   Examples: Please put your shoes in the closet. (Simple)
   instead of
   Please put your shoes in the closet, take a bath, and brush your teeth.

   Please put your dirty clothes in the basket. (Simple)
   instead of
   Clean your room. (This command is very general and contains many hidden commands)

4. *Commands should not be vague.* Be sure to tell the child specifically what to do.

   Examples: Get down off the chair. (Specific)
   instead of
   Be careful.

   Talk in a quiet voice. (Specific)
   instead of
   Behave!

5. *Commands should be simple.* The child should understand your command and be able to do what you tell him/her to do.

   Examples: Put the blue Lego in the box.
   instead of
   Please change the location of the azure plastic construction block from the floor to its container.

   Draw a square.
   instead of
   Draw a hexagon.

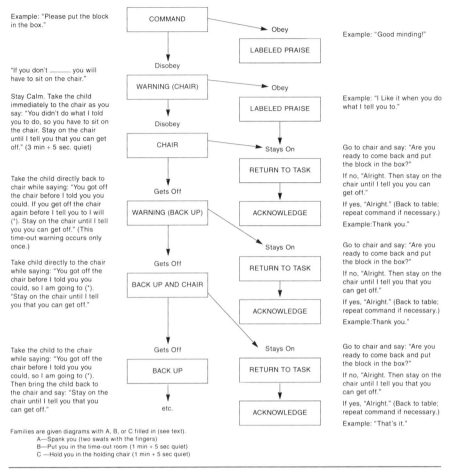

Example: "Please put the block in the box."

COMMAND

Obey

Example: "Good minding!"

LABELED PRAISE

Disobey

"If you don't _____ you will have to sit on the chair."

WARNING (CHAIR)

Obey

Example: "I Like it when you do what I tell you to."

Stay Calm. Take the child immediately to the chair as you say: "You didn't do what I told you to do, so you have to sit on the chair. Stay on the chair until I tell you that you can get off." (3 min + 5 sec. quiet)

LABELED PRAISE

Disobey

CHAIR

Stays On

Go to chair and say: "Are you ready to come back and put the block in the box?"

RETURN TO TASK

If no, "Alright. Then stay on the chair until I tell you you can get off."

Gets Off

Take the child directly back to chair while saying: "You got off the chair before I told you you could. If you get off the chair again before I tell you to I will (*). Stay on the chair until I tell you you can get off." (This time-out warning occurs only once.)

WARNING (BACK UP)

ACKNOWLEDGE

If yes, "Alright." (Back to table; repeat command if necessary.)

Example:Thank you."

Stays On

Go to chair and say: "Are you ready to come back and put the block in the box?"

Gets Off

Take child directly to the chair while saying: "You got off the chair before I told you you could, so I am going to (*). "Stay on the chair until I tell you that you can get off."

RETURN TO TASK

If no, "Alright. Then stay on the chair until I tell you that you can get off."

BACK UP AND CHAIR

ACKNOWLEDGE

If yes, "Alright." (Back to table; repeat command if necessary.)

Example:Thank you."

Gets Off

Stays On

Go to chair and say: "Are you ready to come back and put the block in the box?"

Take the child to the chair while saying: "You got off the chair before I told you you could, so I am going to (*). Then bring the child back to the chair and say: "Stay on the chair until I tell you that you can get off."

BACK UP

RETURN TO TASK

If no, "Alright. Then stay on the chair until I tell you that you can get off."

etc.

ACKNOWLEDGE

If yes, "Alright." (Back to table; repeat command if necessary.)

Example: "That's it."

Families are given diagrams with A, B, or C filled in (see text).
    A—Spank you (two swats with the fingers)
    B—Put you in the time-out room (1 min + 5 sec quiet)
    C —Hold you in the holding chair (1 min + 5 sec quiet)

Figure 2.1   Time-Out Diagram.

sequence to end the procedure, by complying with the command. The procedure does not stop until the child obeys the original command.

The Warning

The warning is given after the child's first failure to obey. The warning is the statement: "If you don't [original command], then you will have to sit on the chair." If the child obeys the warning, the parent gives the child a labeled praise and the play continues.

The Chair

If the child does not obey the warning, the parent takes the child calmly but immediately to the time-out chair, while saying, "You didn't do what I told you to do, so you have to sit on the chair." This statement reminds the child of the reason for the punishment and reiterates the connection between noncompliance and its consequence. As soon as the child is on the chair, the parent says, "Stay on the chair until I tell you that you can get off." This statement is very different from a statement such as "Stay here until you're ready to behave." It is important that the parent maintain control of the time spent on the chair. If a child can get off the chair whenever he or she wants to, the chair is much less effective as a punishment (Bean & Roberts, 1981).

After the child is on the chair, the parent is told to ignore all behaviors of the child on the chair. The child is required to sit on the chair for three minutes, plus five seconds of quiet at the end. The five seconds of quiet are required so that the child will not think that some misbehavior performed just before the time limit expired was a successful tactic that might work again to get off the chair. As soon as the time period is complete, the parent is instructed to walk over to the child and ask, "Are you ready to come back and [original command]?" If the child's response is judged to be "no," the parent is instructed to say, "All right, then stay on the chair until I tell you that you can get off." In this case, the parent then immediately leaves the area of the chair and begins the three-minute time period again. If the parent judges that the child's response to the question indicates "yes," the parent says, "All right," walks the child back to the task and, if necessary, may repeat the command. A child rarely refuses to obey at this point, but if the child did not obey, the parent would say again, "You didn't do what I told you to do, so you have to sit on the chair," and follow through as before.

When the child does obey the command after having been on the chair, the parent acknowledges the child's compliance by saying, for example, "thank you." The parent does not give extensive praise for the behavior at this point because the child did not comply until after he or she was punished. Instead, the parent immediately gives the child another similar but very simple command. The child is likely to obey this command, and it is at this point that the parent gives the child highly enthusiastic labeled praise for minding. In this way, children begin to differentiate between the responses that follow obeying immediately, and the responses that follow obeying after having to be punished first.

Time-out on the chair is the only punishment the child is given for noncompliance, and it is quickly established as the only punishment the parent uses. Because the time out on the chair has limited effectiveness with conduct-disordered children if they can get off whenever they choose to, however, a back-up punishment is necessary for these children, to teach them to stay on the chair.

The Back-Up Procedures

Historically and to the present, psychologists have engaged in controversy about the appropriateness and the relative efficacy of the time-out chair back-up procedures that have been used in the treatment of young, conduct-disordered children (Larzelere, 1993; McNeil, Clemens-Mowrer, Gurwitch, & Funderburk, 1994). The procedures used in PCIT (spank, room, or hold) have received empirical support for their effectiveness (Bean & Roberts, 1981; McNeil et al., 1994; Roberts & Powers, 1990). The therapist determines the most appropriate back-up for an individual family based on a review of information from the assessment interview and any additional information that may be relevant (e.g., parent beliefs and attitudes, abuse history, physical limitations, foster status, therapist attitudes). We do not advise describing the alternatives to parents.

As shown in Figure 2.1, the first time the child gets off the time-out chair without permission, the parent places the child back on the chair while giving a back-up warning: "You got off the chair before I told you that you could. If you get off the chair again, I will (describe consequence)." The back-up warning is given only once. For some children this warning is sufficient because they believe that the parent will follow through. Some children, however, must test this new rule.

Throughout PDI training, we emphasize to the parents that the child is not to receive the back-up consequence for any behavior except getting off the chair. Because of the consistency of the back-up following getting off the chair, the child learns very quickly not to get off. The average number of backups during treatment is four, including both clinic and home counts. The result is that the chair becomes a highly effective punishment, and parents have no need thereafter to use the back-up as a disciplinary measure.

The Spank. To use the spank as a back-up consequence, the parent sits on the chair and places the child squarely across his or her lap, facing down, gives the child two swats with the fingers of one hand, usually to the child's bare bottom, and then returns the child to the chair. Then the parent says calmly, "Stay on the chair until I tell you that you can get off." The parent makes no other statements after this one, but leaves the area immediately and begins the three-minute timing again.

The Room. To use the room as a back-up consequence, the parent firmly, but gently, leads the child to the time-out room. After placing the child in the room and closing the door, the parent begins timing the one-minute duration of this back-up punishment. In addition to the one-minute, a five-second period of quiet is required before the door is opened. When the door is opened, the child is returned to the chair and told, "Stay on the chair until I tell you that you can get off." The three-minute duration of the chair time-out then begins again.

The Hold. The hold requires the use of a second, usually smaller, "holding chair" placed in close proximity to the child's usual time-out chair. The parent leads the child to the holding chair, places the child in the chair, and holds the child by sitting or kneeling behind the child's chair and holding the child's (crossed) wrists securely. After the child has been held for one minute plus five seconds of quiet, the parent returns the child to the time-out chair. The parent says, "Stay on the chair until I tell you that you can get off," and the three-minute timing begins again.

COURSE OF PDI SESSIONS

After the PDI skills have been presented in the didactic session, the parents are instructed to memorize the procedure from the diagram hand-out, but not to practice it with the child until the next therapy session. Parents are coached through their first use of the procedure with their child in the clinic. The therapist coaches the parent at first to give commands that are likely to be obeyed, in order to maximize the possibility that the child will first experience the positive consequences of compliance. Following this, parents are coached in the use of commands that may elicit noncompliance, in order to maximize the probability that the parent will be able to conduct the procedure correctly the first time, and will have emotional support from the therapist if they find the procedure difficult.

In coaching subsequent PDI sessions in the clinic, the therapist must keep in mind the child's unique problems. If a treatment goal includes increasing a certain behavior, the therapist coaches the parent to give commands for that behavior periodically. For example, to increase social skills, the parent might say, "I gave you the piece you asked for, so say, 'thank you'," and then praise the child's obedience ("I'm proud of you for saying thank you when someone shares with you."). If a treatment goal is to teach a new skill, the therapist coaches the parent to break down the skill into simpler component skills that the child has already mastered, and then build up to mastery of the new skill through practice and labeled praise. If a treatment goal is to decrease a particular behavior, the parent is coached to issue commands for incompatible behaviors that can replace the problem behavior. The incompatible behavior can be increased with carefully planned labeled praise. To decrease yelling, for example, an appropriate command might be, "Please use your indoor voice" followed by labeled praises for quiet talking as well as obeying: "Thank you for minding. I like to listen to you when you use your indoor voice."

INCORPORATING STRATEGIES TO ENHANCE GENERALIZATION AND MAINTENANCE

Throughout the PDI phase of treatment, the therapist guides the parent in applying the principles and procedures of both CDI and PDI to the child's behavior at home and in other settings. Several strategies to enhance generalization and maintenance are introduced. Initially parents are instructed simply to practice the PDI skills in brief daily practice situations that could be play sessions or "work situations," such as picking up the toys after the CDI play session. Homework assignments proceed gradually to use of the PDI steps whenever parents need to direct their child's behavior at home, and in public. Parents are taught modifications of basic PCIT procedures for specific situations and learn to assume increasing responsibility for applying the principles creatively to new situations.

A useful strategy in generalization training is teaching parents to use *house rules* (see Table 2.3). In contrast to the "running commands" used in the standard PDI, house rules are "standing commands" or commands that are always in force. They are particularly useful for eliminating aggressive and destructive behaviors that cannot be prevented easily with running commands for incompatible behaviors. They are also useful in helping children stop habitual behaviors that are emitted impulsively, such as sassing.

Parents are taught to use house rules after they have mastered the PDI skills. In order to implement a house rule, parents are instructed to choose a neutral time to speak to the child: a time distant from the occurrence of misbehavior. A parent describes the problem to the child, points out that it has been difficult for the child to remember instructions about the problem in the past, and explains that a new rule will be started in the home that will help the child to remember. Parents then explain to the child that any time the behavior occurs in the future, the child will be sent to the time-out chair immediately. When the house rule is disobeyed subsequent to this discussion, the parent labels the rule violation and sends the child to the chair as in the standard PDI procedure ("You hit your sister, so you have to sit on the chair."), but does not give the warning statement before the time-out and does not ask the "Are you ready . . . " question when time-out is completed.

The therapists teach parents to use the house rules strategy by explaining the rationale and procedure and by providing individualized examples of the types of behaviors most applicable to their family. The importance of using house rules only for specific behaviors that can be easily defined for the child is stressed (vague house rules, such as "Don't be bad," are as confusing for a child as vague commands, such as "Be good") and the parents are instructed to initiate only one house rule at a time. Parents are asked to keep a record of each house rule and the daily frequency of rule violations so that the effectiveness of the technique can be evaluated during the therapy session. Because most

Table 2.3
House Rules Handout

House rules are used for behaviors that:

1. Persist despite praising incompatible (opposite) behaviors.
2. Occur unpredictably and before a command can be given.
3. Cannot be ignored due to potential harm.

Before you begin the house rules procedure:

1. Select the misbehavior to be stopped.
   (strangling the cat)
2. If possible, choose a word for the misbehavior that your child understands.
   ("hurting" the cat)
3. If not possible, teach your child a word for it before proceeding.
   (label the behavior for 3–4 days when it occurs; "That's hurting")
4. Explain the new house rule to the child at a neutral time.
   ("You've been nice to the cat this morning and I like that. But sometimes you forget. I am starting a house rule to help you remember. It goes like this: Any time you hurt the cat, you'll have to go to the chair. But if you remember to play gently with the cat, like this morning, you won't have to go to the chair.")

Using the house rule:

1. Do not use a warning if the child breaks a house rule. If the misbehavior occurs, take your child immediately to the chair for 3 minutes plus 5 seconds of quiet.
2. Take your child to the chair every time the misbehavior occurs.
3. On the way to the chair, say nothing except the brief statement of why ("You hurt the cat . . .") and what happens (". . . so you have to go to the chair").
4. When you leave the chair, say, "Stay here until I tell you you can get off."
5. If your child gets off the chair, use the same back-up that you use in PDI.
6. After your child has been on the chair for 3 minutes plus 5 seconds of quiet, say "You can get off the chair now." Do not mention the misbehavior at this time.
7. Praise an incompatible (opposite) behavior as soon as possible. ("I'm glad you're playing gently with the cat.")

To begin another house rule:

You may begin a new house rule after your child has learned to obey the previous one. Your child should have no more than two "active" house rules at a time. Once your child has learned to obey a house rule, it is no longer "active" but it is still a house rule. If your child breaks an earlier house rule, you will take him to the chair for the misbehavior.

house rules are effective quickly, the appropriateness of this strategy for a particular problem can usually be determined at the next clinic session.

Other modifications to the basic procedures have been developed with (or by) parents to deal with noncompliance and misbehavior in grocery stores, in church, when visiting, when traveling, and less common trouble spots. The variations are based on the principles and skills that the parents and child have already mastered, and they are therefore easy to implement. For many families the generalization across settings seems to occur naturally. Still, we think it important for maintenance to teach a problem-solving strategy throughout treatment.

Problem-solving skills training teaches parents to apply the principles learned throughout therapy to problems other than those explicitly observed during the clinic sessions. The therapist does not provide a series of interventions to match each new behavior problem presented by the family. Instead, the therapist guides the parents to functionally analyze new problems and plan their own interventions. To do this, the therapist prompts the parents to describe specifically the child's behavior and its possible controlling conditions, to decide which of the techniques they have learned may be used to alter these conditions, and to develop a concrete plan for implementing and evaluating their plan. The general algorithm (Boggs et al., 1986) used by the therapist for this purpose is shown in Table 2.4.

Teaching the parent to use functional problem solving is most often accomplished during regular discussions of the week's progress and problems. The therapist at first uses many prompts and suggestions to establish the parents' use of the problem-solving model and then gradually fades this verbal guidance as parents begin to use the model naturally to analyze how best to respond to their child's behavior. A handout containing the algorithm shown in Table 2.4 is sometimes used in the session to illustrate the model more tangibly; parents may be asked to write their responses to the problem-solving prompts. For any plan initiated in the therapy session, the therapist adds an additional column to the homework record sheet so that the parents can track its success. At subsequent sessions, the plan can be discussed and modified if needed, and the parents can be reinforced for their independent child management skills.

When the therapists determine that termination criteria have been reached and the parents agree that their goals for treatment have been met, a posttreatment assessment is scheduled. This assessment closely parallels the pretreatment assessment. A parent interview is conducted involving a review of the presenting problems and the changes that have occurred. Coded behavioral observations and parent and teacher rating scales are re-administered. In addition to these measures that were used

Table 2.4
Problem-Solving Skills Training Guide

General Information
1. Describe the general situation: _____

2. Describe the child's behavior that currently occurs in the situation: _____

_____

    When? _____

    Where? _____

    How often? _____

3. What are the current consequences for this behavior? _____

4. Should the behavior increase or decrease? _____

If Behavior Should Increase:
1. Does the child ever perform this behavior? _____

    If not, are you sure the child can perform this behavior? _____

    If not sure, how will you teach the child the behavior? _____

2. What possible consequences might strengthen the desired behavior? _____

_____

3. How will you arrange for these consequences to occur? _____

    Plan of Action:
    When will the consequences be provided? _____

    Where? _____

    Who will provide them? _____

    How often? _____

    How will you know when you are successful? _____

If Behavior Should Decrease:
1. What desired behavior could occur instead of the problem behavior? _____

_____

2. What positive consequences could follow the desired behavior? _____

3. What consequences could follow the problem behavior? _____

4. How will you arrange for these consequences to occur? _____

    Plan of Action:
    When will the consequences be provided? _____

    Where? _____

    Who will provide them? _____

    How often? _____

    How will you know you are successful? _____

at pretreatment, the parents complete the Therapy Attitude Inventory (Eyberg, 1993) to provide a measure of consumer satisfaction.

FOLLOW-UP AND BOOSTER SESSION

Four months after the family completes treatment, a follow-up assessment and booster session is scheduled. The purpose of this session is to assess whether the family has maintained treatment gains and to provide a brief, posttreatment intervention to assist the family if indicated.

These sessions are divided into two one-hour segments. During the first hour, the therapist interviews the parents about the child's progress and about any new problems encountered in the past four months. Then the parents each complete an ECBI and participate in DPICS-II observations. A break is then taken by the family while the therapist uses the information collected during the first hour to assess what to address in the booster session during the next hour.

If the parents have reported few or no concerns about their child's behavior and the ECBI and DPICS-II data suggest good maintenance of appropriate child behavior and parenting skills, the second hour is spent in a brief review of CDI and PDI skills followed by discussion of any "active" house rules. Parents are encouraged to anticipate challenging future situations and to problem-solve ways to prevent or deal with difficult behavior should it occur. At the end of the second hour, the family is congratulated on their progress and encouraged to contact the therapist should they have any questions in the future.

If information collected during the first hour suggests that any problem is recurring or that the parents' interaction skills have fallen below mastery criteria, most of the booster-session hour involves discussion and coaching of specific skills. Parents are first shown their DPICS-II results and their performance is compared to their final therapy session to focus their attention on the skills they have "down pat" and the skills they want to improve. All the skills or rules for CDI and PDI are reviewed, and then each parent is coached in play situations with the child with coaching emphasis on the identified skills to improve. After coaching, the therapist guides the parents to problem-solve ways that the specific skills could be used to deal with reported child behavior problems. A "behavior prescription" is written that lists recommendations for skill practice at home, house rules, or public behavior rules. We encourage parents to post the behavior prescription on their refrigerator at home to remind them to implement the plans made at their booster session. At the end of the session, we congratulate the family on the positive aspects of their progress and encourage them to contact us if they have any difficulty with implementing their new plans.

RESEARCH ON PARENT-CHILD
INTERACTION THERAPY

PCIT outcome research has demonstrated statistically and clinically significant improvements in child conduct problem behavior (Eisenstadt, Eyberg, McNeil, Newcomb, & Funderburk, 1993; Eyberg & Robinson, 1982; Zangwill, 1984). Studies have documented significant change in parents' interactional style, as evidenced by increases in the proportion of praise and decreases in the proportion of criticism in their speech during play sessions with their child (Eyberg, Boggs, & Algina, 1995). These changes are reflected in significant improvements in child compliance and disruptive behaviors which have been shown to generalize to the home (Boggs, 1990), to the school (McNeil, Eyberg, Eisenstadt, Newcomb, & Funderburk, 1991), and to untreated siblings (Brestan, Eyberg, Boggs, & Algina, 1997). Newcomb (1995) demonstrated maintenance of treatment gains at one-year follow-up for both children and parents, although by two years following treatment approximately half of the treated children again met diagnostic criteria for a disruptive behavior diagnosis, which suggested the need for regular "checkups" (Kazdin, 1995) and the booster sessions we have incorporated into the treatment program.

CASE ILLUSTRATION

The following case illustration presents a hypothetical case that demonstrates typical events families bring to treatment as well as the session-by-session procedures that define PCIT. A more extensive treatment manual is available for clinicians (Hembree-Kigin & McNeil, 1995). We emphasize that although PCIT is typically a brief treatment, it is not time-limited and may be significantly longer with individual families that evidence greater parent psychopathology or family adversity.

BACKGROUND INFORMATION

Nathan C. is a five-year-old boy who was referred by his pediatrician for treatment of his oppositional and aggressive behaviors at home and school. He lives with his parents, Mr. and Mrs. C., and his three-year-old brother Timothy. Mr. C. is a thirty-year-old junior associate in a local law firm and Mrs. C. is a twenty-seven-year-old nurse at a health center. Nathan is currently in kindergarten in a private school where his brother Timothy attends nursery school.

During the intake evaluation, Nathan was described as a healthy, active child, although he was described as having had a difficult temperament "from day one." His oppositional behaviors were apparent as early as two years of age, although Mrs. C. attributed this behavior to the birth of Timothy and said she had expected that he would grow out of it. Mr. C. had felt that his wife was too lenient during that time and it was then that marital conflict centering around child discipline began to develop.

School problems began to emerge three months prior to our evaluation when Nathan entered kindergarten. Nathan was reported to be aggressive on the playground and disruptive in class. For example, the teacher reported to the parents that Nathan had difficulty staying seated in the circle during story time, often poking at the other children, and when reprimanded would have temper tantrums which included loud sassing, throwing and jumping on toys, and tearing pages out of books. The teacher had told the parents that if his behavior did not improve he would need to be removed from that school.

Nathan's behavior was becoming similarly out of control at home. Mrs. C. was clearly distressed in describing Nathan's noncompliance and the lack of support she felt from his father. Mr. C. admitted that he was home very little when the children were awake due to his job responsibilities, but stated somewhat angrily that Nathan "almost never" disobeyed him. He did complain of Nathan's taunting and fighting with Timothy on the weekends, and expressed anger that Mrs. C. would allow Nathan to argue and talk back to her incessantly. Both parents expressed concern about Nathan's denial of his actions when confronted.

When Mr. and Mrs. C. were asked about their typical methods of disciplining Nathan, Mr. C. stated that he has found that stern words and an occasional swat were sufficient. Mrs. C. described her most typical method of discipline as explaining to Nathan what he did wrong. She also reported threatening to take away toys if Nathan doesn't obey, but acknowledged that she rarely actually takes away toys because Nathan will apologize before that is necessary. She reported that she spanks on occasion, as a last resort.

PRETREATMENT ASSESSMENT RESULTS

Nathan was generally cooperative during administration of the PPVT-R. Results from this measure indicated that Nathan's receptive language skills were in the high average range. During a play interview Nathan was cheerful and easily engaged in play. During a game of tic-tac-toe, he responded gleefully to praise, but was reluctant to respond to suggestions from the interviewer regarding turn-taking. Initial DPICS-II observations indicated that Mr. C. was very verbal and directive in all three situations. In the CDI, he tended to lead the play using a high rate of indirect commands and questions. He used few behavioral descriptions or reflections and no praise. His feedback to Nathan consisted primarily of acknowledgments and "corrective" critical statements. His PDI and Clean Up interactions were similar to CDI except that most of his commands were direct. Over all three situations, Nathan was compliant to 34% of first commands, but Mr. C. tended to repeat disobeyed commands more loudly until they were obeyed. Nathan whined at a high rate in all three situations, but showed no other deviant behaviors.

In contrast, Mrs. C. tended to speak to Nathan at a much lower frequency than average in all situations. In CDI, she followed Nathan's play well, giving no commands and playing along with him using the same toys. Her few verbalizations were primarily information descriptions and questions. Her PDI was similar to the CDI situation. Although instructed to lead the play, she continued to follow Nathan's lead. Nathan obeyed only 20% of his mother's commands in this situation and exhibited no deviant behaviors. In Clean-Up, Mrs. C. attempted to cajole Nathan into putting the toys away by trying to make it into a game. When that was unsuccessful, she began putting the toys away herself, pleading with Nathan to put one block in a box. Nathan did not want to stop playing and yelled at her to stop putting toys away, working himself into a tantrum in which he threw himself on the floor kicking, screaming, and crying. As soon as Mrs. C. had finished putting the toys away, she picked Nathan up and held and rocked him.

On the ECBI, both parent's scores were in the problem range (intensity scores >132; problem scores >15), and behavioral ratings by Nathan's kindergarten teacher on the SESBI were within the conduct problem range as well. The teacher's scores on the SESBI yielded an intensity score of 154 and a problem score of 16.

On the Parenting Stress Index, Mrs. C. obtained a Total Stress Score at the 90th percentile, indicating significant stress in the parent-child system. Significant scores in the Child Domain indicated that she viewed Nathan as highly demanding and that she may have been overly committed to being a model parent. It also appeared that she did not view Nathan as a source of positive reinforcement and may in fact have felt rejected by Nathan. Significant scores in the Parent Domain suggested that she experienced her parenting role as restricting her freedom and may have felt frustrated in her attempts to maintain her own identity. Her responses suggested a limited range of child management skills. Also, she expressed feeling a lack of emotional and active support by Mr. C. in the area of child management. Mr. C.'s scores on the PSI were in rather sharp contrast to Mrs. C.'s. His Total Stress Score was at the 75th percentile, suggesting that he did not view his interactions with Nathan as greatly upsetting. Mr. C.'s Child Domain and Parent Domain Scores were not clinically significant, although an elevation on one subscale of the Child Domain indicated that he viewed his relationship with Nathan as not particularly rewarding.

Mr. and Mrs. C.'s PLOC-SF results suggested that both parents believed that external factors aside from their own parenting skills and abilities accounted for Nathan's behavior. Mrs. C's score on the PLOC-SF was 84, slightly more than one standard deviation above the mean of similar mothers referred for parent management training. Mr. C.'s score on this measure was 70, at the mean of fathers referred for help with their children's behavior problems. Clearly, both parents felt that they had little personal control over Nathan's behavior.

CHILD-DIRECTED INTERACTION

Both parents arrived promptly for the initial CDI didactic session. The parents appeared to learn the rules of the CDI quickly as demonstrated by their performance during the role-plays. Mrs. C. quickly assumed a natural, relaxed interaction style, but Mr. C. appeared somewhat uncomfortable, frequently breaking the role and joking. At the end of this first session, he raised a number of concerns about the necessity of "play" and specifically questioned whether Nathan should be praised for behavior that children should be expected to do. We acknowledged that is not an uncommon concern at this early point in treatment but that in our experience these relationship building skills provide an important foundation upon which to build effective discipline strategies. Mrs. C., who had been very enthusiastic about CDI, began to tear during her husband's comments. Noticing her reaction, Mr. C. told her that he would give treatment a try.

At the next meeting, Nathan came bounding in ahead of his parents, asking when they would get to play. While Nathan played with the toys available in the room, we spoke briefly with the parents about the first week of home practice. Mr. C. had not brought in his homework record sheet, explaining that he had to work late almost every evening. He reported attempting to engage Nathan in play on one occasion on Saturday morning but that he could not get Nathan's attention away from the cartoons. Mrs. C.'s homework sheet indicated that she had practiced every day. She stated that she enjoyed the play sessions but expressed some concern that she had allowed the play to extend past the suggested five-minute limit. Nathan volunteered that he liked this new game and wanted it to be a long time. We explained that five minutes was recommended because it is long enough to have positive effects and that we did not want the time involved to feel burdensome for her, but that if she and Nathan both enjoyed extending the time occasionally it was fine.

We began the first interaction with Mr. C. and Nathan. In the first five minutes, when we simply observed and coded, Mr. C. appeared uncomfortable and spoke much less frequently than he had during the baseline interaction. He did appear to be trying to follow the rules. He attended closely to Nathan's play with the Legos, nonverbally placing pieces in front of Nathan and pointing to suggest where they might go. He was successful at avoiding giving verbal directions or critical statements although he showed some displeasure facially when Nathan whined or ignored his pointing. His few descriptive statements were somewhat stilted and frequently their intonation turned them into questions. No praise or reflection was yet evident in this situation.

In coaching Mr. C. for this first session, we focused on praising him extensively for his close attending to Nathan's play. Our first goal for Mr. C. was to increase his verbalizations. We praised every descriptive statement but also praised him for "ignoring" when Nathan's behavior displeased him. We pointed out opportunities for behavioral descriptions of appropriate play behavior by making occasional short descriptions, and he was responsive in repeating these phrases. As Mr. C. began to increase his independent use of descriptions, Nathan began to talk more frequently, laughed, and moved closer to his father. We noted these changes aloud to the father. Behind the mirror, Mrs. C. initially made negative comments about her husband's performance. Rather than responding to these comments, we limited our responses to descriptions of Nathan's behavior.

Midway through the session, we asked Mr. and Mrs. C. to trade places. During her first five minutes of uncoached interaction, we observed a high rate of descriptive statements. It is typical for parents who have just watched coaching to demonstrate vicarious benefit. She also attempted several reflective statements but, like her husband, the intonation turned most of these phrases into questions (e.g., "That's a steeple?"). She also gave Nathan many unlabeled praises and two labeled praises during these five minutes. In coaching the mother, we praised each of her descriptive and reflective statements while ignoring all questions during this first coaching session.

In discussing the progress of the first session with the parents, we first commented to them about how well the session had gone, noting that Nathan seemed to enjoy their play and pointing out how much less whining had occurred in this session. We acknowledged to Mr. C. how hard it is not to lead a child's task when it is so clear to an adult how the child could improve it. We also noted that it is more difficult to be the first parent observed during the first session. We asked for his thoughts about his interaction with Nathan. He said he was frustrated by the constraints but was surprised at some of Nathan's creative ideas in construction. We then asked Mr. C. how he might be able to arrange his work schedule to fit in practice at home. He appeared hesitant to commit himself but thought it might be easier to play with Nathan in the morning before work. Turning to Mrs. C., we first told her how remarkable it was for a parent to use so many praises in the first session. We also praised her attempts to reflect Nathan's speech, noting how hard it is to avoid questioning intonations. To assist Mrs. C. to "hear" her own questions in order to "catch them," we modeled two short verbal interactions. In the first, one of us made 10 descriptive statements and the other made reflective questions after each statement. In the second, one of us made the same 10 descriptive statements and the other reflected each as a statement. She immediately noticed the differences and we role-played this with her briefly. We encouraged her to practice "catching" her questions and switching them to statements during her CDI practice sessions at home.

When the Cs arrived at the next session, we observed that Mrs. C. appeared warmer while speaking to her husband, and she told us that Nathan had been talking all week about putting together a Lego space shuttle set with his father. Mr. C. had practiced four days, and Mrs. C. had once again practiced daily. Mr. C. reported that it was easier to get Nathan involved in play than he had anticipated. Mrs. C. reported that she had worked on reflections but was still finding it hard to avoid turning them into questions. She also mentioned that Nathan seemed less whiny during the week.

Mrs. C. was observed first this week with Nathan, and her data showed that 10 of her 35 descriptive statements were behavioral descriptions, all of her 5 praises were labeled, and she made 15 reflective statements with only 4 reflective questions. We commented to Mr. C. behind the mirror that "this is a hard act to follow," and were pleased that he responded by saying he was impressed with her skill rather than making a defensive response. During coaching with Mrs. C., we praised every reflection and labeled praise, noting that both skills increased steadily. She caught most of her questions without prompting and changed them to reflections.

Mr. C.'s precoaching data showed a still low rate of reflection and praise with several questions and indirect commands ("you want to . . . ") but he made 40 descriptive statements. Before coaching, we commented positively on his high rate of descriptions. Although his verbal and non-verbal directive play had decreased substantially, the indirect commands suggested to us that it was still difficult for Mr. C. to follow Nathan's play. Coaching focused on imitation and reflection. We praised "following rather than leading" each time these behaviors occurred. When he had not made a directive comment or gesture for five minutes, we gave him feedback on this, pointing out Nathan's age-appropriate talk and obvious delight in the play.

During the discussion at the end of the session, Mrs. C. expressed her concern that Timothy had been interrupting her play sessions with Nathan and stated that she was feeling guilty leaving him out of the play. She asked if the play session could include both boys. We explained that Nathan's special "alone time" with her is important but questioned whether it would be possible to give special time alone to Timothy, too. She agreed that would be a good solution but that she still did not know how she would keep either boy from interrupting the other. We encouraged the couple to discuss possible solutions to the problem. After discussion, they decided to practice simultaneously in the mornings with each boy and then switch.

At the third coaching session, Mr. and Mrs. C. reported that the morning play periods had worked out well. In fact, Mr. C. had practiced every day for the first time. The increased practice was reflected in the parents' precoaching data which indicated continued improvement on all CDI skills. We observed that Mr. C. consistently followed Nathan's play without attempting to direct it, and that his interactions with Nathan appeared more relaxed and natural. We also noted that Nathan did not whine throughout the session.

In contrast to recent weeks, Mr. and Mrs. C. arrived at the fourth coaching session obviously angry with each other and with Nathan. They related that two nights previously Nathan had cut some pages out of several law books. When Mr. C. discovered Nathan with his books, he had apparently lost control of his temper, had yelled at Mrs. C. for not keeping Nathan out of his study, and had spanked Nathan with his belt. Mrs. C. had reacted with equal anger, defending Nathan by asserting that Nathan did not understand the value of books, declaring that it was not her responsibility any more than her husband's to keep Nathan out of the study and that punishing Nathan so severely was not appropriate. Mr. C. sat in angry silence while Mrs. C. reported to us that her husband had not practiced CDI since the incident and that he had stated that he did not feel that treatment was working. At this point, we reflected how discouraged they both must have felt by that incident after having worked so hard with Nathan and having seen so few changes yet. We explained that Nathan had been misbehaving for a long time and that we knew he still presented many problems, some of which would require the disciplining techniques that would be the focus of the second phase of treatment. We pointed out that both of them were getting very close to the criteria for moving to the second phase. Mrs. C. appealed to her husband to give it a chance. Mr. C. said it would take some time for him to think about it. We then suggested that we go ahead with Mrs. C.'s coaching.

We coded Mrs. C. and then began coaching. Behind the mirror we pointed out aloud positive attributes we observed about Nathan such as his creativity in play. After coaching Mrs. C. for 10 minutes, we asked Mr. C. if he would be willing to give it a try. He somewhat reluctantly agreed, and during the initial five-minute interaction, we observed that although he was talking very little to Nathan, the relative rate of questions was nevertheless decreased. During coaching, we praised Mr. C.'s skills with the goal of again increasing his talk. During this coaching, Mr. C. gradually became more involved in Nathan's play.

After coaching, we emphasized that even after such a difficult week we were encouraged to see that both of them had demonstrated high levels of progress. Interestingly, Mr. C. then told us that Nathan had actually been better behaved that week except for the one major problem. Mrs. C. also noted that Nathan's teacher had sent home a positive progress report. The session ended with Mr. C. agreeing to continue for now.

At the fifth coaching session, Mr. and Mrs. C. told us that they had a long talk after the last session and had decided that they did not want to let Nathan's behavior cause their personal relationship to suffer again. They had committed themselves to finishing treatment as a team and wanted us to know that. Both parents had practiced regularly and had in fact twice coached each other while playing with Nathan.

It was Mr. C.'s week to begin the interaction with Nathan first. During the initial coding period, he reached the CDI criteria, and we informed him of his accomplishment. Mrs. C. expressed some nervousness about her forthcoming performance but said she was determined to reach criteria, too. She in fact significantly exceeded the CDI criteria during that session. We congratulated both parents on their success. At that time, we gave the parents the midtreatment ECBI and SESBI for completion during the week. We scheduled the PDI didactic session for the following week.

MIDTREATMENT ASSESSMENT

Mr. and Mrs. C. returned the completed ECBIs and a SESBI prior to the PDI didactic session. Mr. C. obtained an Intensity Score of 124 and a Problem Score of 12, while Mrs. C. obtained an Intensity Score of 129 and a Problem Score of 16. Clearly, both parents had perceived some improvement since the beginning of treatment, but still reported significant behavior problems. The SESBI Intensity Score had changed very little since the teacher's first assessment of Nathan's school behavior, decreasing from 170 to 162. However, the teacher did note a fewer number of problems at midtreatment (Problem Score = 15).

PARENT-DIRECTED INTERACTION

Mr. and Mrs. C. came in alone for the PDI teaching session. Both parents learned the PDI procedures easily as judged by their role-play. Mr. C. was quite enthusiastic about the time-out procedure and stated that he thought this sort of structure was exactly what Nathan needed. Mrs. C. agreed that a consistent approach to discipline was needed, but she was worried that Nathan might get upset and questioned if this could possibly harm him psychologically. She also stated that she was concerned that Nathan might not love them as much if they use the procedures. Both parents were glad that they would not be practicing PDI during the next week.

Mr. and Mrs. C. were asked to continue practicing CDI and to memorize the PDI handout shown in Figure 2.1, but not to use PDI at home until we had practiced it together in the clinic first. We suggested that they handle discipline at home during the next week as they normally would.

At the first PDI coaching session, both parents stated that they had reviewed the PDI handout and felt that they knew the procedure. Mrs. C. appeared anxious, so we suggested that Mr. C. be coached first. We then turned to Nathan and explained the plan to him in simple words, watching for his attention:

> You and your mom and dad are coming here so we can help you all to get along better. Now, along with your special play time, we have a new game. This game is to help you learn to do what your parents ask. In this new game, your mom or dad will tell you some things to do. It is very important that you do what they tell you. That will make the game fun. But if you don't do what they ask, they have to put you on the time-out chair (pointing). After you sit on the chair and are quiet, they will give you another chance to do what they ask. If you have to sit on the chair, it's very important that you don't get off the chair before they tell you. If you get off the chair before they tell you, they have to spank you. So it's important not to get off the chair. But if you do what they ask, you will have fun playing with them. What do you think about this game?

Nathan listened to the explanation quietly and intensely, but when asked about his opinion he simply shrugged.

We then left Mr. C. and Nathan in the playroom, telling Mr. C. to start playing CDI as they had in the past. From the observation room, we first coached CDI for a few minutes until both appeared relaxed and engaged. We then prompted Mr. C. to explain to Nathan that they would be switching now to the new rules where Nathan would follow his father's instructions. Nathan pouted when his father said this, but we coached Mr. C. to ignore the pout.

We had Mr. C. start with very simple commands that Nathan was likely to obey. In the CDI warm-up, Nathan had chosen to play with the farmhouse and animals. We provided Mr. C. with the first command: "Tell him to put the cow in the barn." Nathan obeyed and Mr. C. started to give another command. We interrupted and reminded him to give a labeled praise for obedience and then switch back to CDI. We praised Mr. C. for success in obtaining compliance to his first command. After about 20 seconds, we instructed Mr. C. to give another simple command. He gave an appropriate simple command, Nathan again complied, and Mr. C. remembered to praise. After brief CDI, Mr. C. gave a third command that required Nathan to change activities ("Bring the coloring book over here"). Nathan whined that he was not finished building his fence. Mr. C. issued the warning in a harsh voice without needing a prompt and successfully ignored the whine. Nathan obeyed, but Mr. C. forgot to praise, and when prompted his praise sounded artificial. We instructed him to switch back to CDI for a moment. We commented to Mr. C. about how well he did at ignoring the whine. We then said that Nathan seemed to make him a little angry and we suggested that he continue CDI for a while. When he appeared more relaxed, we commented on the effectiveness of his timely warning, suggesting that he try it the next time with a soft, matter-of-fact voice, to see if that would work as well.

This provides an example of how PDI typically starts. In this case, Nathan never did disobey his father's warnings in the first session, and Mr. C. continued giving appropriate commands and improving in remembering to praise compliance. His praises became increasingly genuine-sounding like his praise in CDI had been.

After 20 minutes of coaching Mr. C., we switched to Mrs. C. She had remained tense and we let her practice CDI with Nathan for 10 minutes with the farm animals until she appeared relaxed. When she explained to Nathan, "Now we are going to switch to my rules," Nathan yelled, "No, I don't want to." Mrs. C. paled and looked toward the mirror with an expression of panic. We praised her for ignoring and encouraged her to relax ("Nice ignoring Nathan's yell; everything is okay; just relax silently for a minute . . . "). When she nodded that she was ready, we prompted her to say, "Put the cow in the barn." Nathan responded, "You do it." We immediately prompted through the earpiece, "Tell him, 'If you don't put the cow in the barn, you will have to sit on the chair.'" She repeated the statement exactly, but Nathan again refused. Mrs. C. repeated the next statement appropriately and took Nathan to the chair. He screamed on the chair, and Mrs. C. barely returned to the table before Nathan got off the chair. Even though we were confident that she had learned the sequence, we continued to direct every step. After the spank warning step, Nathan again got off the chair and we coached Mrs. C. through the spank. Nathan sat screaming and crying on the chair and Mrs. C. sat holding back tears at the table. We reflected her feelings, encouraged her to breathe deeply, reinforced her perfect performance, and reminded her how important it was for Nathan to learn to obey. We pointed out that Nathan was staying on the chair this time, a sign that he was beginning to learn.

After two minutes of tantruming on the chair, Nathan got off and ran toward Mrs. C., saying, "Hug me, mommy!" However, Mrs. C. had been forewarned and was able to take him back and complete the spank procedure correctly. She again had tears but turned her head away from Nathan so that he could not see her emotion. Throughout this time, we continued praising and supporting Mrs. C. through the earpiece.

Nathan stayed on the chair this time but cried for five minutes. As soon as he was quiet for five seconds, Mrs. C. asked him if he was ready to put the cow in the barn. Nathan nodded yes, returned to the table, and complied. We then coached Mrs. C. with the acknowledgment and a second command, "Thank you. Please put the horse in the barn," which Nathan also obeyed. Mrs. C. praised Nathan effusively and gave him a hug. We then had Mrs. C. switch back to CDI and had her continue this for five minutes. During this time, Nathan returned to cheerful and energetic play, giving us the opportunity to point out to Mrs. C. that Nathan was enjoying playing with her and that Nathan's relationship with her did not show any negative effect as a result of prior discipline. She expressed tentative agreement and appeared pleased. When we all joined her in the playroom, Mr. C. complimented his wife genuinely and they hugged each other.

We discussed the session in some detail, letting the parents know that although the PDI procedure is stressful the first time, they handled everything extremely well and that Nathan had already begun to respond. Both of them felt that they were ready to practice the PDI in 5-minute daily sessions. We suggested that they practice it right after CDI practice when they are both at home so that they could support each other and that they call us if they had any problems or questions.

At the second PDI coaching session, Mr. and Mrs. C. both reported practicing CDI and PDI every day. Mr. C. stated that he had to follow through with the entire sequence at home and had spanked Nathan once. He estimated needing to give warnings after about "one-tenth" of his commands. Mrs. C. estimated needing to use the chair warning for about 80% of her commands. Her records indicated that Nathan had gone to the chair from one to four times the first three days but that he had stayed on the chair, and that he had responded to all warnings after that.

During coaching with each parent, both Mr. and Mrs. C. demonstrated excellent skills. All of their commands were direct, and they spontaneously praised almost every compliance without prompting. At one point, Mr. C. began to issue commands rapidly without interspersing descriptions or reflections between the command-obey-praise sequences, but with a brief reminder, he slowed down this pace. Nathan remained cheerful throughout most of the session, whining his discontent after warnings, but requiring warnings to only 20% of commands, and never disobeying a warning.

Both parents felt ready to use PDI for "real" commands rather than just in play sessions and we shared with them our confidence that they were ready. We praised Nathan for how well he was learning to obey, and explained that now his parents would be expecting him to obey all the time.

The third PDI coaching session began with both parents expressing delight in how well Nathan had done at home during the previous week. He had never had to go to the chair and both parents estimated that they had needed to use warnings after fewer than half of their commands. They informed us that they had decided to try PDI with Timothy, too, and that he had been sent to the time-out chair twice but had never attempted to get off without permission. They thought Timothy had likely learned about the time-out procedure from observations of Nathan.

They also reported that Nathan had not had a tantrum all week although he still seemed whiny, especially with Timothy, and was still aggressive with his brother. We decided that because the parents had mastered the PDI techniques and were implementing them so effectively, it was an appropriate time to teach them the house rules strategy. Because "whining" is not well defined in many families, we asked them if Nathan knew what whining meant. They were uncertain and had difficulty defining it themselves, although they felt they both clearly recognized a whine when they heard it. We suggested that, in order to teach Nathan what a whine is, they label it, and its opposite, for Nathan during the next week. They were to say matter-of-factly, "That's a whine" when they noticed whining, and to ignore subsequent talk until it was in his "normal voice," which they chose to label and praise as his "big boy voice." We added to their record sheet a column to tally each whine episode that occurred. We told them that if Nathan's whining did not decrease over the course of the week, we would be ready to implement a house rule.

CDI coding showed, as usual, they were maintaining their skills. PDI was coded for the first time. Both parents did a nice job of giving clear, direct commands and interspersing CDI skills. They remembered to praise compliance every time and Nathan required only one warning by each parent. During the brief feedback discussion at the end of the session, the parents informed us that the school open house was coming up during the next week and that they were anxious to hear how Nathan had been doing since he had been getting lots of "happy faces" sent home in the past two weeks.

In the initial coding and coaching of the fourth PDI session, Nathan was 100% compliant with both parents in session. The parents proudly reported that the school visit had gone quite well and that the teacher had described Nathan as "like a different child" at school. She had reported that he seemed calmer in class and stayed in the circle now during group activities, although he still annoyed other children during recess.

The parents' data on whining showed it occurred about five to ten times per day. Mr. and Mrs. C. said they had been diligent about labeling it. We explained the technique of house rules and its application to whining, and asked the parents to continue to record the occurrence of whining each day.

At the fifth PDI session, coaching was brief because the parents demonstrated excellent CDI and PDI skills and home practice. Once during the PDI interaction with his mother, Nathan whined and Mrs. C. demonstrated her use of the house rule, sending Nathan to the time-out chair. He remained quietly on the chair for three minutes and then he and Mrs. C. resumed their play. In reviewing the home data on whining, Mr. and Mrs. C. reported that the rule had been effective. Nathan's whining had decreased rapidly to only once in the last two days. We encouraged them to continue this house rule whenever a whine recurred.

Mr. and Mrs. C. reported that they were still very concerned about the fighting between Nathan and Timothy and wondered if this could be handled using a house rule. We used this opportunity to utilize the problem-solving technique explicitly. In describing the problem, the parents said that fights happened almost every night, most often late in the evening when the boys played together in the TV room. Mrs. C.'s typical method of dealing with the fighting had been to separate the boys and try to determine who had started it. Mr. and Mrs. C. recognized that trying to find out who had started a fight seemed to increase the time and stress associated with dealing with it. We asked them to think about all the techniques they had learned and how they might be applied to this problem. They first discussed how they might apply a house rule for both boys, realizing that this would reduce the attention the boys received for fighting as well as reducing their own stress. They were concerned about whether it would be fair to punish both boys, but in talking it through, concluded that "it takes two to fight." They discussed how they could include in their talk to the boys about the new house rule some ways to avoid fighting when the other boy starts it. They also discussed how to implement the plan and decided that Mrs. C. would take Timothy to one chair and Mr. C. would take Nathan to another. After supporting this initial plan, we asked them to think of any principles from their CDI training that might further enhance their success. Mrs. C. suggested that they could praise the boys for playing cooperatively, and we asked if that would be easy to remember. Mr. C. offered to put a reminder chart up on the wall that the parents could check off each time they remembered to praise cooperative play. At the end of this session, we added another column to their data sheets to record the occurrence of fights.

At the sixth PDI session, data from coding again demonstrated excellence in the parents' skills and in Nathan's behavior in both CDI and PDI. Although the parents continued formal 5-minute CDI and PDI practice sessions at home each day, they told us they were actually using a combination of CDI and PDI during all of their interactions with the boys. They reported that Nathan had not whined during the week but that the boys were still fighting quite a bit, even though they had consistently used the house rule procedure and had praised cooperative play many times. According to their records, there were two fights the first night they implemented the house rule and four other fights throughout the week. We indicated that we thought their techniques were sound and probably just needed more time. They told us that they had instituted a house rule on their own to deal with Timothy's jumping on their water bed, and anticipated that he would stop that misbehavior rapidly.

Mr. and Mrs. C. reported that other than fighting, Nathan no longer seemed to be presenting any important problems at home. We asked about Nathan's lying and they reported that they had not noticed that problem for quite some time. We wondered aloud if it seemed that we were getting close to therapy termination. Mr. and Mrs. C. mentioned that they had talked about that, too, and felt they could probably handle things on their own except for the fighting. We suggested they continue using the fighting house rule for two weeks and that if the fighting had substantially decreased by then, we would have the next session be a wrap-up session and final assessment. We gave them the SESBI to have Nathan's teacher fill out and bring with them.

The parents came to the last session excited to report that only two fights had occurred during the past two weeks. They commented that they knew the boys would always fight some, but they felt that it was now manageable. We congratulated them on their excellent progress, and conducted posttreatment assessment.

POSTTREATMENT ASSESSMENT

In the post DPICS-II observations, Mr. and Mrs. C. looked almost identical in their interactions with Nathan. All three situations were notable for high rates of positive verbal and nonverbal interaction. Nathan exhibited no deviant behaviors in any situation. In CDI both parents were successful in letting Nathan lead the play and joined in his activity enthusiastically. Nathan eagerly led the play, laughing frequently. In PDI and Clean Up, Nathan was 90% compliant to first commands with Mrs. C. and obeyed the two warnings given. Nathan was 100% compliant with his father. Both parents were at criterion skill levels in all interactions.

On the ECBI, both parents' scores were in the normal range. Mrs. C. obtained a Problem Score of 4 and an Intensity Score of 93. Mr. C. also obtained a Problem Score of 4 and an Intensity Score of 105. Additionally, Mrs. C.'s completion of the Parenting Stress Index was within the normal range on all scales. Her score on the Relationship with Spouse Scale confirmed our clinical impression that the initial marital disharmony had been primarily related to child management issues that were now resolved. Mr. C.'s PSI scores were even lower than at pretreatment, and the Child Domain subscale relating to his view of Nathan as reinforcing was much improved. The PLOC-SF results for both Mr. and Mrs. C. demonstrated that they now attributed to themselves the ability to teach new behaviors and to change problematic ones. On the TAI, both parents rated all items at the most positive level, expressing their high degree of satisfaction with the results of therapy. Nathan's teacher also rated Nathan's behavior in the normal range on the SESBI with a problem score of 6 and an intensity score of 86.

After giving feedback to the family on the very positive results of their posttreatment assessment, we conducted the "TV show." We all viewed edited segments of the DPICS-II observation from before and after therapy. Mr. and Mrs. C. expressed surprise at Nathan's, and their own, pretreatment behavior. Nathan hid his head in his mother's lap during a part of the pretreatment Clean Up segment. After watching the posttreatment segments, Nathan told us he was "bigger" now. The parents commented on how much warmer and interactive their relationship with Nathan was now. We gave Nathan a blue ribbon to show what a big boy he is.

Four-Month Follow-Up and Booster Session

At the four-month follow-up session, Mr. and Mrs. C. reported that they had continued to practice CDI regularly and found it one of the most pleasurable parts of their day. They reported that sibling fighting remained infrequent and that they had continued to use house rules for both whining and fighting when they did occur. They reported having instituted one new house rule for taking food out of the refrigerator and had successfully resolved that problem. In general they reported feeling very confident in their parenting skills and described Nathan as "having turned into quite a little gentleman." Nathan's follow-up ECBIs were both within the normal range, and DPICS-II observations showed good maintenance of parenting skills across the CDI, PDI, and Clean Up situations.

Because there was no need for further coaching of PCIT skills during the second hour, the specific rules for CDI and PDI were only briefly reviewed. We spent some time talking to the parents about any problems they might anticipate with Nathan's behavior in the future. They were somewhat concerned that Nathan's school behavior might deteriorate when he began first grade next year. We asked the parents to generate ideas about what they might do to help Nathan's teacher get a good start with him. They decided that their best option was to meet his new teacher before school started, explain the behavior management program they had been implementing, and suggest ways that she might handle Nathan's misbehavior should it occur. They also decided it was important to let the teacher know that Nathan was highly responsive to praise and to attention for good behavior. Finally, we encouraged Mr. and Mrs. C. to contact us any time they wished to discuss Nathan's adjustment and ended the follow-up session by congratulating the parents for having made so much progress with Nathan.

SUMMARY AND CONCLUSION

This chapter has presented the conceptual foundation, empirical validation, and step-by-step procedures used in PCIT for the treatment of preschool-age youngsters with conduct problems and their families. In illustrating this approach to parent training, we highlighted the importance of integrating behavioral and traditional therapeutic techniques and dealing with family issues within the structure of the dyadic treatment model. The importance of the continuous link between assessment and treatment to establish therapy goals, guide the course of treatment, and evaluate the outcome was emphasized.

Studies to date have demonstrated a successful outcome of PCIT with families in which a child presents with disruptive behavior. Changes in child behavior have been shown by observational and rating scales data in multiple settings. Clinically significant reductions in frequency and number of conduct problems have shown generalization to the child's classroom, and long-term maintenance of changes in the parent-child interaction and in the child's school behaviors have been demonstrated following this brief therapy.

The interactional approaches to parent training, with its emphasis on improving communication and relationship skills within families, shows promise for interventions with a wide variety of child and family dysfunctions. The principles and procedures that produce behavior change

in the oppositional child and family are the same as those that would reduce distress in many family situations. Empirical validation of PCIT
within such diverse contexts will be an important next step.

REFERENCES

Abidin, R. R. (1995). *Parenting stress index—Manual* (3rd ed.). Odessa, FL: Psychological Assessment Resources.

American Psychiatric Association. (1994). *Diagnostic and statistical manual of mental disorders* (4th ed.). Washington, DC: Author.

Barkley, R. A. (1990). *Attention deficit hyperactivity disorder: A handbook for diagnosis and treatment.* New York: Guilford Press.

Bean, A. W., & Roberts, M. W. (1981). The effect of time out release contingencies
on changes in child noncompliance. *Journal of Abnormal Child Psychology, 9,*
95–105.

Boggs, S. R. (1990, August). *Generalization of treatment to the home setting: Direct observation analysis.* Paper presented at the annual meeting of the American Psychological Association, Boston.

Boggs, S. R., & Eyberg, S. M. (1990). Interviewing techniques and establishing
rapport. In A. LaGreca (Ed.), *Childhood assessment: Through the eyes of a child.*
Newton, MA: Allyn & Bacon.

Boggs, S. R., Stokes, T. F., & Danforth, J. (1986, August). *Functional problem-solving
skills: Increasing the generality of parent training.* Paper presented at the annual
meeting of the American Psychological Association, Washington, DC.

Breston, E., Eyberg, S. M., Boggs, S., & Algina, J. (1997). Parent-child interaction
therapy: Parent perceptions of untreated siblings. *Child and Family Behavior
Therapy, 19,* 13–28.

Campbell, S. B., & Ewing, L. J. (1990). Follow-up of hard-to-manage preschoolers:
Adjustment at age 9 and predictors of continuing symptoms. *Journal of Child
Psychology and Psychiatry, 31,* 871–889.

Dunn, L. M., & Dunn, L. M. (1981). *Peabody picture vocabulary test-Revised: Manual.* Circle Pines, MN: American Guidance Service.

Eisenstadt, T. H., Eyberg, S. M., McNeil, C. B., Newcomb, K., & Funderburk, B.
(1993). Parent-child interaction therapy with behavior problem children: Relative effectiveness of two stages and overall treatment outcome. *Journal of
Clinical Child Psychology, 22,* 42–51.

Eyberg, S. M. (1988). Parent-child interaction therapy: Integration of traditional
and behavioral concerns. *Child and Family Behavior Therapy, 10,* 33–46.

Eyberg, S. M. (1992). Parent and teacher behavior inventories for the assessment
of conduct problem behaviors in children. In L. VandeCreek, S. Knapp, &
T. L. Jackson (Eds.), *Innovations in clinical practice: A source book* (Vol. 11). Sarasota, FL: Professional Resource Press.

Eyberg, S. M. (1993). Consumer satisfaction measures for assessing parent training programs. In L. VandeCreek, S. Knapp, & T. L. Jackson (Eds.), *Innovations
in clinical practice: A source book* (Vol. 12). Sarasota, FL: Professional Resource
Press.

Eyberg, S. M. (in press-a). *Eyberg child behavior inventory: Professional manual.* Odessa, FL: Psychological Assessment Resources.

Eyberg, S. M. (in press-b). *Sutter-Eyberg student behavior inventory: Professional manual.* Odessa, FL: Psychological Assessment Resources.

Eyberg, S. M., Bessmer, J., Newcomb, K., Edwards, D., & Robinson, E. (1994). *Manual for the dyadic parent-child interaction coding system-II* (Social and Behavioral Sciences Documents, Ms. No. 2897). (Available from Select Press, P. O. Box 9838, San Rafael, CA 94912)

Eyberg, S. M., Boggs, S. R., & Algina, J. (1995). Parent-child interaction therapy: A psychosocial model for the treatment of young children with conduct problem behavior and their families. *Psychopharmacology Bulletin, 31,* 83–92.

Eyberg, S. M., Edwards, D., Boggs, S., & Foote, R. (in press). Maintaining the treatment effects of parent training: The role of "booster sessions" and other maintenance strategies. *Clinical Psychology: Science and Practice.*

Eyberg, S. M., & Robinson, E. A. (1982). Parent-child interaction training: Effects on family functioning. *Journal of Clinical Child Psychology, 11,* 123–129.

Fischer, M., Rolf, J. E., Hasazi, J. E., & Cummings, L. (1984). Follow-up of a preschool epidemiological sample: Cross-age continuities and predictions of later adjustment with internalizing and externalizing dimensions of behavior. *Child Development, 55,* 137–150.

Guerney, B. G., Jr. (1964). Filial therapy: Description and rationale. *Journal of Consulting and Clinical Psychology, 28,* 303–310.

Hanf, C. (1969). *A two stage program for modifying maternal controlling during mother-child (M-C) interaction.* Paper presented at the meeting of the Western Psychological Association, Vancouver, BC.

Hembree-Kigin, T., & McNeil, C. (1995). *Parent-child interaction therapy.* New York: Plenum Press.

Kazdin, A. E. (1995). Scope of child and adolescent psychotherapy research: Limited sampling of dysfunctions, treatments, and client characteristics. *Journal of Child Clinical Psychology, 24,* 125–140.

Larzelere, R. E. (1993). Empirically justified uses of spanking: Toward a discriminating view of corporal punishment. *Journal of Psychology and Theology, 21,* 142–147.

Lerner, J. A., Inui, T. S., Trupin, E. W., & Douglas, E. (1985). Preschool behavior can predict future psychiatric disorders. *Journal of the American Academy of Child Psychiatry, 24,* 42–48.

McNeil, C. B., Clemens-Mowrer, L., Gurwitch, R. G., & Funderburk, B. (1994). Assessment of a new procedure for timeout escape in preschoolers: Authors' response to Lutzker's rejoinder. *Child and Family Behavior Therapy, 16,* 51–56.

McNeil, C. B., Eyberg, S. M., Eisenstadt, T. H., Newcomb, K., & Funderburk, B. W. (1991). Parent-child interaction therapy with behavior problem children: Generalization of treatment effects to the school setting. *Journal of Clinical Child Psychology, 20,* 140–151.

McNeil, C. B., Hembree-Kigin, T., & Eyberg, S. M. (1996). *Short-term play therapy for disruptive children.* King of Prussia, AL: Center for Applied Psychology.

Newcomb, K. (1995). *The long term effectiveness of parent-child interaction therapy with behavior problem children and their families: A two-year follow-up.* Unpublished doctoral dissertation, University of Florida, Gainesville.

Offord, D. R., Boyle, M. C., & Racine, Y. A. (1991). The epidemiology of antisocial behavior in childhood and adolescence. In D. J. Pepler & K. H. Rubin (Eds.), *The development and treatment of childhood aggression* (pp. 31–54). Hillsdale, NJ: Erlbaum.

Patterson, G. R. (1974). Interventions for boys with conduct problems: Multiple settings, treatments, and criteria. *Journal of Consulting and Clinical Psychology, 42,* 471–481.

Patterson, G. R. (1982). *Coercive family process.* Eugene, OR: Castalia Press.

Rayfield, A., Eyberg, S. M., Boggs, S., & Roberts, M. (1995, November). *Development and validation of the parenting locus of control-short form.* Paper presented at the annual meeting of the AABT Preconference on Social Learning and the Family, Washington, DC.

Roberts, M. W., & Powers, S. W. (1990). Adjusting chair timeout enforcement procedures for oppositional children. *Behavior Therapy, 21,* 257–271.

Robinson, E. A. (1985). Coercion theory revisited: Toward a new theoretical perspective on the etiology of conduct disorders. *Clinical Psychology Review, 5,* 597–625.

Russ, S. (1993). *Affect and creativity: The role of affect and play in the creative process.* Hillsdale, NJ: Erlbaum.

Schaeffer, C. E., & Briesmeister, J. M. (Eds.). (1989). *Handbook of parent training: Parents as co-therapists for children's behavior problems.* New York: Wiley.

Schuhmann, E., Durning, P., Eyberg, S. M., & Boggs, S. (1996). Screening for conduct problem behavior in pediatric settings using the Eyberg Child Behavior Inventory. *Ambulatory Child Health, 2,* 35–41.

Wahler, R. (1965). Mothers as behavior therapists for their own children. *Behavior Research and Therapy, 3,* 113–124.

Zangwill, W. M. (1984). An evaluation of a parent training program. *Child and Family Behavior Therapy, 5,* 1–16.

CHAPTER 3

Training for Parents of Young Children with Conduct Problems: Content, Methods, and Therapeutic Processes

CAROLYN WEBSTER-STRATTON and LOIS HANCOCK

THIS CHAPTER describes a comprehensive videotape-based parenting program that has been proven effective both in clinical treatment programs for young children referred for conduct problems and in community programs for families at increased risk for abuse and child conduct problems because of the risk factors associated with poverty (Webster-Stratton, 1994, 1995, in press-a; Webster-Stratton, Hollinsworth, & Kolpacoff, 1989). The program was designed with the broad goals of (a) strengthening parenting competence, especially the use of nonviolent discipline approaches; (b) increasing positive family support networks and school involvement; (c) promoting child social competence; and (d) decreasing child conduct problems.

The program targets parents of young children ages 3 to 8 years. There are several reasons for targeting this age range. First, epidemiological studies have indicated that conduct problems among preschool children are more common than was once thought (Landy & Peters, 1991). In one of the first studies to examine the prevalence of behavior problems in

This research was supported by the NIH National Center for Nursing Research Grant No. 5 R01 NR01075–12 and Research Scientist Development Award MH00988–05 from NIMH.

young children, Richman and Graham (1975) found that 15% of 3- to 4-year-olds had mild behavior problems and 7% had moderate to severe behavior problems. Similarly, Earls (1980) reported significant behavior problems among 24% of the preschoolers in his sample. In another study of parents of children ages 6 weeks to 5 years, the number and intensity of parental concerns peaked when children were ages 3 to 4 years; the major complaints involved difficulties with behavior management and discipline (Jenkins, 1980). Relatively high proportions of parents of 4-year-olds complain of more general problems with noncompliance, limited self-control, and poor relations with siblings and peers (Kazdin, 1985; Ogbu, 1978). Richman, Stevenson, and Graham (1982) reported that 12.9% were described by their mothers as overactive and restless, 10.7% were seen as difficult to control, and 9.2% were seen as attention seeking. A large-scale screening study of day-care attendees (ages 2–4 years) in rural Vermont (Crowther, Bond, & Rolf, 1981) found that, according to teachers, at least 20% of the children exhibited high frequencies of aggressive and disruptive behaviors, with the most severe forms observed among preschool boys.

In our own study with 500 low-income mothers of 4-year-old children from eight Head Start centers, we found that 43.6% of mothers perceived their children as being in the clinical range (above normative cutoff point) for conduct problems on the Eyberg Child Behavior Inventory (ECBI); (Robinson, Eyberg, & Ross, 1980); 25% were in the severe range (above 15 behavior problems). According to mother reports on the Child Behavior Checklist (CBCL; Achenbach & Edelbrock, 1991), 35.5% of the children were above the normal cutoff T-scores for externalizing problems (85th percentile) and 20% for internalizing problems; 15% were in the severe range for externalizing problems (i.e., a T score above 67, which reflects the 95th percentile). Moreover, independent home observations of mother-child interactions indicated that the mean base rate of total child aggressive and noncompliant behaviors during home observations was 15.2 per 30 minutes, that is, one every 2 minutes. These base rates are notably higher than previously reported epidemiological studies regarding aggression in the general population of preschoolers, suggesting that poverty places children at higher risk for early-onset conduct problems. These data are also supported by Offord, Boyle, and Szatmari (1987), who found in their epidemiological study that conduct problems among children ages 3 to 7 occurred at higher rates in low-income families on welfare than in middle- or upper-income families.

The second reason for targeting hard-to-manage young children ages 3 to 8 is that these "aggressive" children are at increased risk for rejection by their peers (Coie, 1990b) and for abuse by their parents (Reid, Taplin, & Loeber, 1981), as well as for school dropout, alcoholism, drug abuse, depression, juvenile delinquency, antisocial personality, interpersonal problems, poor physical health, marital disruption, and criminal activities later in life (Kazdin, 1985). Studies have shown high continuity between oppositional and externalizing problems in the early preschool years and conduct disorders in adolescence (Egeland, Kalkoske, Gottesman, & Erickson, 1990; Fisher, Rolf, Hasazi, & Cummings, 1984; Richman et al., 1982; Rose, Rose, & Feldman, 1989). Campbell's review (1991) of a series of longitudinal studies of hard-to-manage preschoolers reveals a surprising convergence of findings. At least 50% of preschool children with moderate to severe externalizing problems continued to show some degree of disturbance at school age, with boys doing more poorly than girls. Of those with continuing behavior problems, 67% met the diagnostic criteria for Attention Deficit/Hyperactivity Disorder (ADHD), Oppositional Defiant Disorder (OD), or Conduct Disorder (CD) by age 9. Moreover, Eyberg (1992) points out that although this percentage is high, it may be an underestimate since many of the children from the most dysfunctional families were lost to follow-up.

Developmental theorists have suggested that there may be two developmental pathways related to conduct disorders: the "early starter" versus "late starter" pathway (Kazdin, 1985; Loeber, 1990; Patterson, DeBaryshe & Ramsey, 1989). The hypothesized "early onset" pathway begins formally with the emergence of conduct problems (e.g., noncompliance, hitting, yelling at high rates) in the early preschool period, progresses to aggressive (e.g., fighting) and nonaggressive (e.g., lying and stealing) symptoms of conduct disorders in middle childhood, and then develops into the most serious symptoms by adolescence (Lahey, Loeber, Quay, Frick, & Grimm, 1992), including interpersonal violence and property crimes. In addition, there is an expansion of settings in which the problem behaviors occur, from home to day care or preschool settings, then to school settings, and finally to the broader community. For the adolescent ("late starter") onset conduct disorders, the prognosis seems more favorable than for adolescents who have a chronic history of conduct disorders stemming from their early preschool years. Adolescents who are most likely to be chronically antisocial are those who first evidenced symptoms of aggressive behavior in the preschool years (White, Moffit, Earls, & Robins, 1990). These children with early-onset conduct problems also account for a disproportionate share of delinquent acts in adolescence. Thus early-onset conduct problems are a sensitive predictor of subsequent CD, and the primary developmental pathway for serious conduct disorders in adolescence and adulthood appears to be established in the preschool period (Campbell, 1991; Campbell & Ewing, 1990; Loeber, 1991).

Based on the evidence that a significant number of children who become chronically antisocial and delinquent first exhibit aggressive symptoms during the preschool and early school years, it is surprising that there have not been more early screening and prevention/intervention studies targeted at this age group. Intervention while these children are preschoolers is particularly strategic. Intervention programs for parents of preschool and early school-age children can help these parents teach their children to behave appropriately before aggressive behaviors result in peer rejection, well-established negative reputations, and school problems (Bierman, Miller, & Stabb, 1987; Coie, 1990a, 1990b; Dodge, Coie, Pettit, & Price, 1990), not to mention academic failure. Data suggest that fewer than 10% of young children with conduct problems who need mental health services actually receive them (Hobbs, 1982).

PARENT TRAINING PROGRAM

THEORETICAL BACKGROUND

In developing this parenting program, we have been strongly influenced by the seminal theoretical work (Loeber, 1985) on conduct-disordered behaviors by G. R. Patterson (1982, 1986). His social-learning model emphasizes the importance of the family socialization processes; in his "coercion hypothesis," negative reinforcement plays an important role in developing and maintaining both the child's deviant behaviors and the parents' critical or coercive behaviors. His research demonstrates that as this coercive process continues over time, the rate and intensity of parent and child aggressive behaviors escalate. Moreover, the parents' increasingly frequent use of negative discipline provides the child the opportunity for further modeling (observational learning) of aggression (Patterson, 1982). This pioneering research indicates that harsh and inconsistent parenting skills are at least partly responsible for the development of conduct problems. Patterson's success in reducing conduct problems by training parents of preadolescents, suggested to us that working with at-risk families to train parents in supportive, noncoercive parenting skills while their children were still very young could alter the poor long-term prognosis for these children.

SUMMARY OF PARENTING PROGRAM AND RESEARCH FINDINGS

For the past 15 years, we have conducted a program of research to develop and evaluate videotape modeling for group discussion parent training programs for families of children with conduct problems (ages 3–8 years). Our original 12-week parent program, titled BASIC (10 videotapes with more than 250 vignettes) was heavily guided by the modeling literature and focused on teaching parents interactive play skills and reinforcement skills based on the early work of Hanf (1970) and Eyberg and Matarazzo

(1980), as well as a specific set of nonviolent discipline techniques including Time-Out and Ignore as described by Patterson (1982) and Forehand and McMahon (1981) logical and natural consequences, and problem-solving strategies (D'Zurilla & Goldfried, 1971; D'Zurilla & Nezu, 1982). In 1987, we developed a supplement to the program *(ADVANCE)* that addressed other family risk factors (e.g., depression, marital distress, poor coping skills, lack of support). In 1992, we revised our training videotapes to make the program more culturally sensitive, more prevention-oriented, and more usable outside the Pacific Northwest; for example, we included a higher percentage of people of color (40%). In addition, we developed a new program titled *Supporting Your Child's Education* to address the risk factors related to children's lack of academic readiness and weak home/school connections. All three programs involved videotapes and group discussion.

Researched in a series of randomized studies with over 600 children referred for conduct problems (ages 3–7 years), the BASIC program has been shown to be effective in significantly improving parental attitudes and parent-child interactions, along with significantly reducing parents' use of violent forms of discipline and reducing child conduct problems (Webster-Stratton, 1982, 1984, 1989, 1990b, 1994; Webster-Stratton et al., 1989). The ADVANCE program has been shown to be highly effective in promoting parents' use of effective problem-solving and communication skills, reducing maternal depression, and increasing children's social and problem-solving skills (Webster-Stratton, 1994). Both programs have received high consumer satisfaction and low dropout rates regardless of the family's socioeconomic status. Effects have been sustained up to 4 years' postintervention (for a complete review of the clinic-based research, see Webster-Stratton, 1996, 1997).

We also examined the effectiveness of using a shortened version of the BASIC program as a selective prevention intervention in a randomized trial with 500 Head Start families. Head Start social service staff were trained to lead the parent groups. Results indicated that mothers who attended the parenting program made significantly fewer critical remarks, made less use of physically negative discipline, and were more positive, appropriate, and consistent in their discipline style when compared with control mothers. Intervention mothers perceived their family service workers (group leaders) as more supportive than did control mothers; furthermore, teachers reported that mothers who had attended the parenting program were more involved in their children's education than control mothers. In turn, children of parents who had been trained were observed at home to exhibit significantly fewer negative behaviors, less noncompliance, more positive affect, and more prosocial behaviors than children of control parents. These data supported the hypothesis that strengthening parenting competence and increasing parental involvement in children's school-related activities in a high-risk sample of welfare mothers is a useful strategy for decreasing conduct problems (Webster-Stratton, 1995).

SPECIFIC CONTENT OF BASIC PARENTING PROGRAM

Play Skills

The training begins with a focus on play. Therapists discuss with parents the importance of play and present effective ways of playing with children. The unfortunate fact is that many parents of children with conduct problems do not want to play with their children; their interactions are simply too stressful. Typically, there is negativity on both sides: These parents feel negative toward their children out of anger and frustration concerning their children's misbehavior, and their children in turn are negative toward their parents. Therefore the first step in breaking this negative cycle of behaviors and feelings is to infuse some positive feelings into the relationship through play. For parents of highly aggressive children, playtimes can be the first pleasurable times they have had with their children in months or even years.

Regular daily parent-child playtimes help build warm relationships between family members, creating a "bank" of positive feelings and experiences that can be "drawn on" in times of conflict. This is particularly important for parents of children with conduct problems who may be feeling resentful, critical, angry, distant, or hopeless about their relationships with their children. Play with parents not only helps children feel deeply loved, thereby fostering a secure base for their ongoing emotional development, but just as importantly, promotes parents' feelings of attachment and warmth toward their children.

Teaching parents how to have good playtimes with their children not only fosters warmth in the relationship but also helps children learn some other important skills such as the vocabulary they need for communicating their thoughts and feelings. It also helps them learn the social skills of turn-taking and fosters their ability to understand the feelings and perspectives of others. Through play, parents can help their children learn to solve problems, test out ideas, and use their imaginations. Moreover, play is a time when parents can respond to their children in ways that promote children's feelings of self-worth and competence. In fact, studies have shown that children tend to be more creative, to have increased self-confidence, and to have fewer behavior problems if their parents engage in regular playtimes with their children and, when doing so, give them their supportive attention. However, many parents do not play in supportive ways; they use playtime to "teach," to correct, to instruct; or they compete with their child, criticize his or her actions, undermine, or inter-fere with their child's play. Or it may be a matter of giving only divided attention. The BASIC program focuses first on teaching parents how to engage in supportive, child-directed play.

In the first three 2-hour sessions of the BASIC program, parents view and discuss more than 50 videotaped vignettes of parents and children playing together in both appropriate and inappropriate ways. Parents are asked to play with their children at home for at least 10 minutes every day, using the skills they learned in the weekly group sessions. Thera-pists discuss the most common pitfalls that parents encounter when play-ing with their children. The following principles are stressed:

Points to Remember When Playing with Children

- Follow the child's lead.
- Pace at the child's level.
- Engage in role play and make-believe with the child.
- Praise and encourage the child's ideas and creativity.
- Use descriptive comments instead of asking questions.
- Be an attentive and appreciative audience.
- Curb the desire to give too much help; encourage the child's prob-lem solving.
- Don't expect too much—give the child time to think and explore.
- Avoid too much competition with children.
- Don't criticize.
- Reward quiet playtimes with parental attention.
- Laugh and have fun.

Praise

Parents of children with conduct problems often find it hard to praise their children. Perhaps believing that children should behave appropri-ately without adult reinforcement or that praise should be reserved for exceptionally good behavior or outstanding performance, many parents would never think of praising their children for playing quietly or for doing their chores without complaining. Although some parents believe they should not have to praise their children for everyday behaviors, many others simply do not know *how* or *when* to give praise and encour-agement. They themselves may have received little praise from their own parents when they were young; not accustomed to hearing praise, the words may seem awkward or artificial. Or perhaps they are so stressed and angry with their children for misbehaviors that they cannot see any praiseworthy behavior even when it does occur.

Consequently, our therapists teach parents to identify the behaviors they want to promote, to look for those behaviors, and to praise them. Here are the major points we emphasize:

Points to Remember about Praising Your Child

- Don't worry about spoiling children with praise.
- Catch the child when he or she is being good—don't save praise or perfect behavior.
- Make praise contingent on positive behavior.
- Praise immediately.
- Give labeled and specific praise.
- Praise with smiles, eye contact, and enthusiasm.
- Give pats, hugs, and kisses along with verbal praise.
- Praise in front of other people.
- Praise wholeheartedly, without qualifiers or sarcasm.
- Increase praise for difficult children.
- Model self-praise.

Sometimes parents will say that their child is so deviant that they can find nothing to praise. Many times, these are depressed parents who cannot see the prosocial behaviors in their child. Watching the videotapes of parent-child interactions helps such parents to identify positive behaviors that they can reinforce.

Many parents who don't praise their children don't praise themselves, either. If they listened to their internal "self-talk," they would find that they are rarely or never saying things like, "You're doing a good job of disciplining Johnny," or "You handled that conflict calmly and rationally," or "You've been very patient in this situation." Instead, they are quick to criticize themselves for every flaw or mistake. Therapists teach parents how to speak to themselves in positive statements and to create positive experiences for themselves as incentives or rewards for following through with their playtimes each week. We believe that if they can do this for themselves, they will be more likely to continue praising and playing with their children.

Incentives

For some oppositional and conduct-disordered children, parental praise is not sufficient reinforcement initially to turn around a difficult problem behavior. In these cases, incentives or tangible rewards can be used by parents to help motivate the child. Incentives or rewards include things the child particularly enjoys such as a special treat, additional privileges, a toy or a favorite activity, stickers, additional time with a parent, or having a friend overnight. Incentives can be used to encourage such positive behaviors in children as using the toilet, playing cooperatively with siblings or friends, getting dressed, getting ready for school on time, completing homework, cleaning up the playroom, and so on. When teaching parents about using incentives, our therapists stress the importance of continuing to provide social rewards as well; each type of reward serves a different purpose. Social rewards such as praise and physical affection should be used to reinforce the small efforts children make to master a new skill or behavior, whereas tangible rewards can be used to reinforce the achievement of a specific goal. Once children learn the desired behavior, tangible rewards can be phased out and the social reward of parental praise will maintain the existing behavior.

The therapists teach parents two ways of using rewards. The first is for the parent to surprise the child with a reward whenever he or she behaves in some desired way, such as sharing or sitting still in the car. This approach works if the child already exhibits the appropriate behaviors fairly regularly and the parent wants to increase the frequency with which they occur. The second approach is for the parent to *plan the reward in advance* with the child (or explain to the child in advance)—as in a contract. This program is recommended when parents want to increase an infrequent behavior. For example, a parent might set up a sticker chart for two children who fight frequently. She could start by telling both children that they will receive a sticker for every half hour that they play cooperatively. Then she could discuss with them a reward they would like to work for, such as having a friend overnight, reading an extra story at bedtime, going to the park with Dad, choosing their favorite cereal at the grocery store, going to a movie, picking something from a surprise grab bag, and so forth. It is a good idea to make the reward list fairly long and include nonmaterial as well as material rewards and inexpensive items as well as more expensive items. This list can be altered over time as children come up with new suggestions. Whereas preschool children (ages 3–4 years) may be rewarded by the sticker itself without needing a backup reinforcer, 5- to 6-year-olds should be able to trade in stickers for something each day if they like, and 7- and 8-year-olds can wait a few days before getting a reward.

We give parents the following list of principles to use when starting incentive programs:

Points to Remember about Incentive Programs

- Define the desired behavior clearly.
- Choose effective rewards (i.e., rewards that the child will find sufficiently reinforcing).

- Set consistent limits concerning which behaviors will receive rewards.
- Make the program simple and fun.
- Make the steps small.
- Monitor the charts carefully.
- Follow through with the rewards immediately.
- Avoid mixing rewards with punishment.
- Gradually replace rewards with social approval.
- Revise the program as the behaviors and rewards change.

Parents are given the home assignment of identifying one or two positive behaviors they want to increase and then setting up an incentive program with their child (charts and stickers are sent home with parents). When they return the following week, they present their plans and reward charts to the group and the therapist and other parents spend time reviewing and revising the charts and troubleshooting possible pitfalls.

It usually takes six to seven group sessions to cover the topics of play, praise, and tangible rewards. The objective of this first part of the training is to foster more positive relationships between parents and children and to help parents promote more appropriate social behaviors in their children. We often see behavior problems improve in this part of the program even though we have not discussed discipline. As we move into the next phase of the parenting program, we frequently refer to the pyramid (see Figure 3.1) to remind parents of the foundation (play and positive reinforcement) and to reiterate the importance of building this positive base as we begin to focus on strategies designed to decrease inappropriate behavior.

Limit Setting

The first aspect of discipline that we discuss is the importance of clear limit setting. However, we also remind parents that *all* children test their parents' rules and standards. Young children scream or throw temper tantrums when a toy is taken away. School-age children argue or protest when barred from something they want. This is a healthy expression of a child's need for independence and autonomy. Research shows, in fact, that normal children fail to comply with their parents' requests about one third of the time. What makes the oppositional defiant or conduct-disordered child different is that he or she is noncompliant about two thirds of the time. This means that these parents are engaged in power struggles with their child the majority of the time, making it very difficult for them to adequately socialize their child.

We teach parents that children test parents' rules not only to assert their autonomy, but also to see whether their parents are going to be

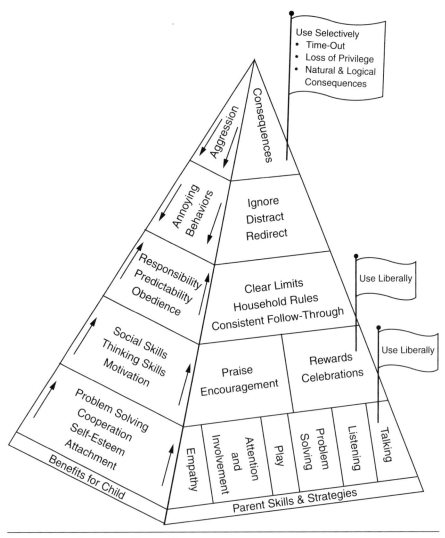

Figure 3.1 Parenting Pyramid.

consistent, for it is only by breaking a rule that children can determine whether it is actually a rule or just a one-time command. Only consistent consequences will teach a child what is expected. If parents' rules have been inconsistent in the past, or if parents have not enforced their rules or have enforced them inconsistently, then their children have learned from experience that they can get their parents to back down if they protest long enough and hard enough, and they will escalate their noncompliance accordingly.

The therapist helps prepare parents for this testing. Parents are helped to understand these are not personal attacks, but learning experiences for their children, in which their children explore the limits of their environment and learn which behaviors are appropriate or inappropriate. Our therapists explain that consistent limit setting and predictable responses from parents help give children a sense of stability and security. They reassure parents that children who feel a sense of security regarding the limits of their environment have less need to constantly test it. While stressors such as marital discord, single parenting, poverty, unemployment, depression, and lack of support may make it difficult for parents to be consistent, strengthening parents' sense of commitment to limit setting can help buffer the disruptive effects of these stressors on parenting. One of the ways the therapists elicit this commitment is to engage the parents in an exercise of listing the advantages as well as the possible barriers to limit setting. The subsequent discussion helps parents grasp the importance of consistent limit setting for their children's eventual adjustment and define the reasons for their inconsistency. We highlight the following major points:

Points to Remember about Limit Setting

- Be realistic in your expectations and use age-appropriate commands.
- Give one command at a time.
- Use commands that clearly specify the desired behavior.
- Make commands short and to the point.
- Use "do" commands and "when-then" commands.
- Make commands positive and polite.
- Give children options whenever possible.
- Give children ample opportunity to comply.
- Praise compliance or provide consequences for noncompliance.
- Give warnings and helpful reminders.
- Don't use "stop" or "don't" commands.
- Don't give unnecessary commands.
- Don't threaten children.
- Support your partner's commands.
- Strike a balance between parent and child control.

Ignoring Skills

Young children with conduct problems engage in irritating behaviors such as whining, teasing, arguing, swearing, and tantrums at rates higher than normal children. Although these inappropriate behaviors are usually not dangerous to others, they frequently lead to peer rejection and isolation, which are damaging to children's self-esteem. Yet these misbehaviors can often be eliminated through systematic ignoring.

Ignoring is one of the most difficult approaches for parents to use; many parents argue that ignoring is not discipline at all. Thus, it is particularly important for the therapist to explain the rationale for this approach. The rationale for ignoring is straightforward. Children's behavior is maintained by the attention it receives. Even negative parental attention, such as nagging, yelling, and scolding, can be rewarding to children. When misbehavior is ignored, on the other hand, children receive no payoff, so that if the ignoring is consistently maintained, children will eventually stop what they are doing. And as they receive approval, attention, and incentives for appropriate behaviors, they learn that it is more beneficial to behave appropriately than inappropriately.

The following are the key principles we emphasize:

Points to Remember about Ignoring

- Limit the number of behaviors to ignore.
- Choose specific behaviors to ignore and make sure you can ignore them.
- Be consistent.
- Physically move away from the child but stay in the room if possible.
- Avoid eye contact and discussion while ignoring.
- Return attention to the child as soon as misbehavior stops.
- Be prepared for testing.

Time-Out Skills

We teach parents to use time-out for high-intensity problems, such as fighting, hitting, and destructive behavior. The therapist explains to parents that time-out is actually an extreme form of parental ignoring in which children are removed for a brief period from all sources of positive reinforcement, especially parental attention. Not only does time-out assure that the child's misbehavior is not being reinforced by attention, but time-out models for children the parent's use of self-control and a nonviolent response to a conflict situation. Time-out gives the child (and the parents) time to cool down, get control over misbehavior, and reflect on what has happened. Because time-out forces children to reflect and calm down, they are more likely to develop appropriate guilt, and an internal sense of responsibility or conscience over time. We also help parents understand that time-out is a discipline approach that fosters a warm, respectful relationship rather than a fearful, power-based relationship (i.e., based on fear of being hit by parent); one that contributes to open communication rather than devious sneaky behavior on the part of the child who wants to avoid punishment. Here are the key principles we emphasize:

Points to Remember about Time-Out

- Monitor your own anger to avoid exploding suddenly; give warnings.
- Don't threaten time-out unless prepared to follow through.

- Carefully limit the number of behaviors for which time-out is used.
- Use time-out consistently for chosen misbehaviors.
- Be as polite and calm as possible in sending child to time-out.
- Give 5-minute time-outs, requiring that the last 2 minutes be silent.
- Ignore child while in time-out.
- Be prepared for testing.
- Use nonviolent approaches, such as loss of privileges, as backup for not going to time-out.
- Hold children responsible for messes in time-out.
- Support a partner's use of time-out.
- Don't rely exclusively on time-out—combine with other techniques, such as ignoring, logical consequences, and problem solving.
- Build up "bank account" with praise, love, and support.

Parents are often quite resistant to using time-outs, for various reasons. First, it is inconvenient: It requires advance planning in terms of the procedure and the location. Second, it can be time-consuming and may require that parents keep themselves under control for long periods. Third, it can be frustrating for parents because the child's misbehavior may get worse in time-out, since children often scream, bang on the walls, or break something. Some parents resist time-out because they don't think it produces enough remorse and pain in children, which they think are necessary for punishment to work effectively (some children even indicate they like time-out). Still other parents resist time-out because they feel it communicates rejection to the child.

Conversely, many parents prefer spanking as a discipline strategy because it is efficient and immediate, and most likely will stop the inappropriate behavior in the short-term. It can even feel good to some parents because it "evens the score." That is, parents may feel they have obtained revenge for the child's misbehavior by inflicting pain as punishment. For some parents, the use of spanking is important because it allows them to feel dominant and maintain control of the situation. However, research has shown that spanking, lecturing, criticism, and expressions of disapproval are ineffective methods of discipline and usually result in parents finding themselves spiraling into more and more uncontrolled spanking and yelling to get their children to respond. We help parents understand that in fact, nagging, criticizing, hitting, shouting, and even reasoning with children while they misbehave are forms of parental attention which actually reinforce the particular misbehavior; these approaches also result in children learning to nag, criticize, hit, shout, or argue in response to their parents. Spanking and yelling also teach children that it is all right for someone who loves you to hit or yell at you when displeased with your behavior. Moreover, the violence of spanking increases children's resistance, resentment, and anger toward the parent and erodes the parent-child relationship. Consequently, rather than the child reflecting on his or her mistake and feeling guilt and remorse for it, the child externalizes the event by directing resentment and blame toward the parent for hitting him or her.

We have found it useful to bring the issue of spanking to the foreground through a values exercise wherein we brainstorm (without judgment) the advantages and disadvantages of spanking, followed by the advantages and disadvantages of time-out. This discussion usually leads most parent groups to the insight that spanking has many advantages (to the parent) in the short-term but disadvantages in the long-term (to the child). On the other hand, time-out is inconvenient (to the parent) in the short-term but has more long-term advantages for the child's social and emotional development. Helping parents to shift their perspective from their child's present misbehavior to his or her future development is a critical step, with potential to greatly empower parents; they realize that they can make a difference for their child's future by the way they parent and socialize their children.

Natural and Logical Consequences

More so than time-out or ignoring, natural and logical consequences teach children to take responsibility for their own behavior. A natural consequence is whatever would result from a child's action or inaction in the absence of adult intervention. For example, if Ryan slept in or refused to go to the school bus, the natural consequence would be that he would have to walk to school. If Caitlin did not want to wear her coat, then she would get cold. In these examples, the children experience the direct consequences of their own decisions—they are not protected from the possibility of an undesirable outcome of their behavior by their parents' commands. However when implementing consequences, assuring the safety of the child should be of primary importance. For example, the child should not be permitted to walk to school if he is very young or the neighborhood is unsafe. A logical consequence, on the other hand, is designed by parents who hold children accountable for their behavior. A logical consequence for a youngster who broke a neighbor's window would be to do chores in order to make up the cost of the replacement. A logical consequence for stealing would be to take the object back to the store, apologize to the store owner, and do an extra chore or to lose a privilege.

Natural and logical consequences are most effective for recurring misbehaviors where parents are able to decide ahead of time how they will follow through if the misbehavior recurs. For example, the parent who says, "If you aren't dressed for school by 8:00 A.M., you will have to go in your pajamas," or "If you spend all your allowance on candy, you'll have no money for that movie you want to rent," is informing the child ahead of time what will be the consequence of continuing the behavior. In effect, the child has a choice and is responsible for the outcome. On the other hand, the parent who does not specify the consequence ahead of time is not helping the child see the connection between the behavior and the negative outcome. We emphasize the following principles concerning natural and logical consequences:

Points to Remember about Consequences

- Make consequences age-appropriate.
- Be sure you can live with the consequences you have set up.
- Give the child a choice; specify consequences ahead of time.
- Involve the child whenever possible.
- Use consequences that are short and to the point.
- Make consequences immediate.
- Make consequences safe and nonpunitive.

CONTENT OF ADVANCE PARENTING PROGRAM

A number of studies have indicated that a family's ability to benefit from parenting training is influenced by factors such as maternal and paternal depression (McMahon, Forehand, Griest, & Wells, 1981; Webster-Stratton & Hammond, 1990), marital conflict and hostility (Dadds, Schwartz, & Sanders, 1987; Webster-Stratton, 1994), isolation (Dumas & Wahler, 1983), negative life stressors (Dumas & Wahler, 1983; Webster-Stratton, 1985b), and socioeconomic status (Webster-Stratton, 1985b, 1990a; Webster-Stratton & Hammond, 1990). Other researchers examining parenting training interventions have found similar factors to be associated with treatment relapses (Dumas & Wahler, 1983; Forehand, Furey, & McMahon, 1984; Griest et al., 1982; Patterson, 1986). These findings suggest that parenting training programs need to emphasize partner involvement, parent support, problem-solving, communication, and coping skills, and depression management. Although therapy cannot alter a family's life stressors and economic situation, it can help parents and children cope more effectively in the face of stressful situations.

As a result of these research findings, we developed the ADVANCE videotape parent program, which is offered following completion of the BASIC program in an additional 8 to 10 sessions. The focus of these sessions is on parents' communication, anger management and other coping skills, and problem solving. We help parents realize that children are constantly learning from observing their parents' interactions with each other and with others in their community, including teachers and neighbors (see Figure 3.2).

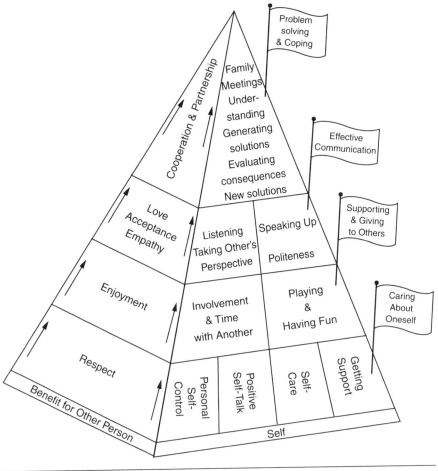

Figure 3.2   Pyramid for Building Relationships.

Communication Skills

Many parents—whether or not their children have conduct problems—find themselves in disagreement over how to discipline their child. This is to be expected, given that they have had different childhood experiences of parenting. Yet all too often, these different perspectives result in anger, even open conflict, between couples over how to raise their children. In the case of conduct problems, this parental conflict only aggravates the problem. Frequent marital conflict and negative affect can lead to ineffective parenting, which contributes to child conduct problems which, in turn, contribute to further marital distress and depression. Moreover, children become increasingly aggressive with peers when they frequently observe the negative interactions between their parents. A similar pattern can occur for single parents, the only difference being that they may be angry at an ex-partner, a teacher, another family member, or someone in their community for the lack of support and inability to understand their difficulties raising a child single-handedly. In teaching communication skills as part of our parenting program, we hope not only to enable them to resolve current problems and avert future ones, but also to model these skills for their children.

Listening. The first skill we teach is effective listening—listening without interrupting, giving advice, criticizing, or arguing. We call this "giving the other person the floor," and for humor as well as to make the point concrete, we quite literally give them a piece of floor tile. We emphasize paraphrasing, summarizing, and validating statements as part of listening skills.

Speaking Up. Among the parents who come to us for help with their children's conduct problems, we have identified a subgroup of "conflict avoiders"; because they dislike arguments, these parents store up grievances and resentments until they finally explode in anger. Teaching parents how to bring up issues as they occur involves helping them become more comfortable with conflict. This is a long-term process, but we try to develop a higher tolerance for conflict by establishing some ground rules that parents are encouraged to adopt at home as well as in the training sessions. These include:

- **Politeness.** It is amazing but true that families are much more likely to say mean or insulting things to the people they know and love than to strangers. Family members frequently interrupt each other, put one another down, and hurt each other's feelings. Put-downs evoke anger, resentment, defensiveness, and guilt or depression, and they undermine effective communication and problem solving. We teach parents that politeness is extremely important in the effective resolution of a situation regardless of how their child or partner is acting, and ask parents to make a conscious decision to be polite to each other. Just because someone else is rude and childish does not make it acceptable to behave similarly. This means parents must do a bit of editing before they speak.

- **Permission to Stop (Truce).** We teach parents to call a "stop" or "truce," and to halt all discussion when they find themselves becoming increasingly critical or angry. The therapist helps the parents decide in advance exactly how they are going to signal the need for a "stop" or "truce." They might simply say, "I need to stop talking about this right now," or "I'm getting upset. Could we talk about this later when I calm down?" (Note the use of "I" messages.) Everyone in the family needs to agree that even if only one person gives the signal, the discussion will end temporarily. The person who calls the truce is then responsible for setting another time for resuming the discussion. Cooling-off periods should be no longer than 24 hours, or the parents may avoid resolving the problem altogether.

Feeling Talk.   We also teach parents the importance of speaking up about feelings—both their own and their children's. Many parents talk to their children about ideas and facts, but rarely their feelings or their children's. Research suggests that boys are likely to be criticized for crying or being emotional. Girls are more likely to be taught that direct expression of angry feelings is unfeminine. As a result, boys learn to express angry feelings, and girls learn to express feelings of depression.

Parents need to be encouraged to model feeling talk for their sons and daughters. "I enjoyed our time together today. I feel happy," "I understand you feel angry about not going to the movie," and "I feel sad that your puppy died," are all examples of effective feeling-talk that involve "I" statements and are based in the present. We warn parents that expression of feelings does not include license to "let it all hang out" in a tirade of negative feelings. In fact, we educate them about the dangers of parental hostility and open conflict for children's social and emotional development. We teach them that if they express negative feelings or have disagreements in their marital relationship, it is important to reassure their children that they are not to blame. Moreover, we teach them the importance of children observing their parents discussing differences of opinion calmly and coming up with mutually agreed-on solutions to their problems. For if children can see their parents engaged in effective problem solving, their anxiety about conflict will be greatly alleviated, whereas if they see (or sense) marital conflict but do not see any resolution, they will remain anxious and be sensitized to future conflict.

Avoiding Mixed Messages.   We cover "mixed messages" in our parenting training because this type of communication, when habitual, can have such devastating psychological effects on children; even when it occurs only infrequently, it undermines the parent-child relationship. When one aspect of a parent's communication conveys approval while another conveys criticism, a child is confused and his or her self-esteem suffers. When a parent's words say one thing and his or her behavior another, the child does not know what to believe, what to trust, and loses confidence in his or her own perceptions.

Parents undermine themselves when they deliver mixed messages. Our therapists emphasize the importance of parents being clear and consistent, so that the content and feeling of their communication match, as should the verbal and nonverbal messages. Research indicates that when there is a discrepancy, the listener tends to weight the nonverbal or feeling messages as truer. Thus, even if the words are positive, when the affect is negative, the child or partner will hear the message as negative.

Making Requests.   Probably the most difficult communication transaction between partners, and the most common between parent and child, is that of asking someone to do something—a request or command. In relationships where an ongoing conflict exists, these can be particularly troublesome. A direct request for a specific behavior may be perceived as authoritarian and compliance might then be felt as an acceptance of the hierarchy rather than simple cooperation. People in such relationships find themselves arguing over the specific request when the real issue is the power struggle—who is in control. We teach parents about the importance of being able to make requests in a polite way and the necessity of complying with requests in any relationship; reciprocality in the relationship is emphasized as the goal as opposed to one person dominating the other.

Managing Upsetting Thoughts

All parents have their moments of anger, depression, frustration, and guilt—sometimes all at the same time—when dealing with their children's misbehaviors. Upsetting feelings are not only to be expected, but are beneficial in that they signal the need for change and provide motivation. Danger arises, however, when these feelings so overwhelm parents that they are immobilized or lose control. In our parenting training, then, our aim is to help parents learn to cope with their emotional responses to parenting in a manner that preserves their feelings of efficacy.

We ask parents to identify some of their common negative self-statements; and then we teach them to defuse these negative thoughts in the following four ways:

1. *Use Thought Interruption.* As soon as the parent is aware of having a negative thought, he or she is told to stop the thought by saying, "I am going to stop thinking about that now." Some parents wear a rubber band on their wrist and snap it every time they have a negative thought to remind them to stop it. "Stop worrying. Worrying won't help anything."

2. *Reschedule Worrying or Anger Time.* For parents who constantly revisit all the ways their children have made them angry or compulsively review a list of all their worries, we ask them to schedule "anger time" or "worry time" into the day. For example, they will allow themselves 30 minutes at 9:30 A.M. to be as angry as they want; during the rest of the day they will not allow these thoughts to interfere with their mood, work, or play. For some parents, we will suggest a "telephone time" when they can call the therapist and tell them their angry thoughts. The paradox of this approach is that when it comes time to "vent," the parent often doesn't feel as angry and finds it difficult to do.

3. *Objectify the Situation.* The third approach we teach for stopping negative self-talk is for parents to ask themselves during moments of conflict whether what they are thinking or doing is helping them reach their goal. Some researchers have called this the "turtle technique" because parents withdraw into a shell momentarily to assess their behavior. One father in a parent group gave us an example: He was trying to leave for work and his son wasn't ready to go. He put him in his bedroom and the boy started screaming. The father's anger increased until he opened the door and grabbed his son saying, "You want negative attention, you're going to get it!" Suddenly, he thought about what he was doing and realized that this was getting him nowhere. He left the room, went outside, and a few minutes later his son joined him fully dressed. The father discussed how he was able to become more objective, to stand back and assess what was happening and realize that losing control or getting revenge would only aggravate the situation.

4. *Normalize the Situation.* The fourth approach that therapists help parents learn is to objectify or normalize a situation by remembering that all relationships have conflict and all children have behavior problems. Moreover, all parents and children have feelings of guilt, depression, anger, and anxiety. The group process is very effective for helping with normalization because parents soon realize most of the parents in the group have had similar thoughts and reactions.

Once parents have learned to normalize thoughts and to stop the negative ones then they need to learn how to increase their positive thoughts, because reducing the number of negative thoughts does not automatically increase positive ones. We teach six steps to help increase positive thoughts:

1. Dispute negative self-talk; refute negative labels.
2. Substitute calming or coping thoughts for negative ones.
3. Time projection—paint a positive future.
4. Think and verbalize self-praise.
5. Use humor. Laugh.
6. Model positive, coping self-talk out loud.

Therapists help parents identify negative labels they may carry about their children's or partner's personalities (e.g., he's totally irresponsible) and to refocus rather on specific behaviors they want to encourage. Therapists can dispute negative thinking by asking the parents, "Is that always true?" or "Is that totally accurate?" or by encouraging parents to ask themselves these questions. Most likely, the behavior is only true for the moment. When parents move from the behavior to the specific behavior that is annoying them, they may be able to come up with a coping statement. Diane's dad might say to himself, "I seem to be labeling her. She's not really lazy. She's just having trouble remembering to take out the garbage. I'll talk to her about ways to remember." The therapists can help remind parents that all children throw tantrums, disobey, forget to do chores, and behave aggressively from time to time.

Negative labels go hand-in-hand with defeatism. A mother who has worked with her son but finds he continues to get poor grades may say to herself, "I'm tired of this. Why try at all? Nothing will work"; or "I can't deal with this. He's just not capable." The adoption of a defeatist attitude usually results in withdrawal from the problem, avoidance of discipline, and a simmering level of annoyance or anxiety. Eventually, parents will either explode with anger or become depressed. Moreover, saying that a child is not capable of changing has the possibility of becoming a self-fulfilling prophecy. We teach parents to think, "This is frustrating and I'm tired but I can cope," or "No one can make me give up. Things will get better. It just takes time." The important message for parents to give themselves and their children is that they can *all* cope with the situation. Even if things are bleak, parents can reflect a positive outlook for the future.

A related tendency is what we call "negative prophecy"—predicting a dismal future. Parents of conduct problem children often come to expect that because negative behaviors have occurred, they will continue and will determine future events: Five-year-old Connie has been stealing small things around the house, and her father thinks, "She will become a delinquent and drop out of school." Other examples of negative fortune-telling are, "He'll never stop," "Oh no, it's starting again. It will be just the same as last time." This kind of gloomy prophesying causes parents to feel depressed, behave passively, and withdraw from helping their children act more appropriately. Moreover, negative predictions set up a self-fulfilling prophecy. If parents are convinced that their children will never behave any better, then they probably won't.

Our therapists strive to help parents to think more positively so that they focus on coping and present children with more hopeful messages about their capabilities. One strategy is prediction—mentally traveling forward to a time when the stressful period will have ended and a positive outcome has been achieved. The mother of 6-year-old twins who fight constantly might say to herself, "It is hard to have two 6-year-olds. They bicker all the time. But in a few years they will probably get along well and be good friends." Sometimes parents say to themselves, "This isn't fair! Why do I have to have a child like this? I don't deserve this. My child deserves to be punished." They feel victimized by their children and their life circumstances, and their anger serves the purpose of justifying their revenge. They may think they are in control of the situation even though their anger is out of control. Indeed, it is hard to let go of anger, especially if parents feel they are the victim of unfair treatment. Being angry can help them feel righteous, energized, and powerful. Giving it up can be difficult because it is sometimes confused with loss of power. In such situations, we find it is useful to help parents think in terms of long-term goals rather than the short-term satisfaction of revenge. Parents are encouraged to say to themselves, "In the long term, it is better for my child to see me cope by taking charge of my anger rather than to let it control me." Another constructive self-statement would be, "The long-term cost of letting my anger explode would be far greater than the momentary satisfaction of showing my child (or partner) I won't be pushed around."

Some parents assume they know why their child or spouse behaved in a certain way. Often they attribute motives to misbehaviors and act on these beliefs as if they were true. We call this "mind-reading." These assumptions can become self-fulfilling prophecies. For example, two children are bickering in the den while their mother is trying to watch the news. She mind-reads, "They are being loud on purpose. They want to make me mad!" Or a father comes home from grocery shopping and finds his wife talking on the phone while the kids mess up the living room. He mind-reads, "Nobody cares about me. If she cared about me, she would make the kids behave properly." This kind of negative mind-reading is bound to increase resentment and anger toward his wife and children.

We help parents understand the importance of focusing on the behavior they want to change and to avoid speculating about motives. Instead of the mother thinking, "They are doing it on purpose to make me mad," she might say to herself, "I don't know what has upset them today. Perhaps I should ask them." She asks them about their problem instead of making assumptions. In the second example, the father might tell himself, "I need to talk to her about helping the kids keep the living room tidier." He avoids mind-reading and focuses on the behavior he wants to change. He has chosen to see himself as a facilitator of change rather than a victim of his family.

As parents learn to use coping, calming thoughts when confronted with a problem, we encourage them to say them out loud (see Table 3.1). While a family is seated at the dinner table, Mom might say to Dad, "Peter, I think I coped well with Alice's problem at school. I told myself not to overreact, that all children have difficulty at school from time to time. I set up an appointment with her teacher to talk about ways we can help her learn to share better. I feel good about that." Here Alice's

Table 3.1
Coping Thoughts

Upsetting Thoughts	Coping Thoughts
"My child is a monster. This is ridiculous."	"My child is testing to see if he can get his own way. My job is to stay calm and help him learn better ways to behave."
"I'm sick of being her maid. Things are going to change or else!"	"I need to talk to Bethany about her leaving her clothes around. If we discuss this calmly, we should be able to reach a good solution."
"He's just like his father. I can't handle it when he's angry."	"I can handle this. I am in control. He has just learned some powerful ways to get control. I need to develop a plan to teach him more appropriate ways to behave."
"I can't take this. Why did I have to end up with a child like her?"	"She's difficult because she's only 5 years old. She's learning and it will get easier."

Other Calming and Coping Thoughts
I don't like it when she acts like that, but I can handle that.
My job is to stay calm and help him learn better ways to ask for what he wants.
I can help her learn better ways to behave.
He is just testing the limits, I can help him with that.
This is not the end of the world. She is a bright child and I'm a caring mother. We will make it over this hump.
He really doesn't do that much any more, and has been quite good lately. This is a temporary setback.
I shouldn't blame my impatience on her. I'll talk to her about it.
I am doing the best I can to help them learn more positive behaviors.
I can develop a plan to deal with it.
I have a lot of coping techniques I can call upon.
This stress I'm feeling is exactly what the therapist said I might feel, it is a reminder to use my coping exercises.
She doesn't really understand what those swear words mean. I'm not going to let it upset me.
Don't be so hard on myself—nobody's perfect. One step at a time.
We're getting through this—each day it gets a little better.
I don't need to take care of everything right now; all I need to do is take care of today.

Examples of Self-Praise Thoughts
I have good self-control.
I like people.
I can cope.
No one can make me mad; it's up to me.
I can control my thinking and my anger.
I'm a good parent.
I try hard.

mother not only is modeling how she stopped herself from overreacting, but also is modeling self-praise.

Managing Stress through Personal Time-Out

Once parents have learned to recognize upsetting thoughts and substitute coping thoughts, we move to the topic of handling stress. The first step is becoming aware of their physiological responses to stressful events and thoughts. Many people report that in stressful situations they experience levels of physical tension, rapid heartbeat, headache, hypertension, and muscle tension that interfere with their behavior and thinking processes. One of the myths about stress is that it happens only in crises or emergencies. In fact, studies show that everyday hassles may actually produce more stress. And parenting certainly can produce a lot of stress. The daily tensions—getting everyone ready to leave for work and school, rushing around doing errands, meeting deadlines, trying to find a baby sitter, not having enough money to pay for school pictures or a birthday present—take their toll. Stress results not only from major life events like divorce or moving, but also by seemingly little things, such as children misbehaving or being ill, cereal spilled on the floor, or a pile of dirty clothes. The causes of stress are highly individual. What brings one person to the verge of "losing it" may not bother another person at all. Helping parents learn to manage their stress levels is essential to helping them learn to become skillful, consistent parents.

Modifying negative self-talk and developing a repertoire of coping thoughts help parents lower their levels of stress. We also recommend to parents that they develop the habit of taking personal "time-outs" from stress to provide an opportunity for physical, mental, and emotional relaxation and recuperation. In most sports, there is provision for time-out. These breaks give the coach and team a chance to catch their breath, regroup, and then reenter the game with renewed energy. In our daily lives, however, there are very few time-outs. Even coffee breaks are usually filled with stimulation rather than relaxation. Certainly there are very few opportunities for recuperation in the average parent's day, especially for at-home parents of young children. And yet it is the at-home parent who is particularly in need of opportunities to rest, strategize, and reenter the "game" of parenting with renewed energy.

The essence of parental time-out is for parents to *step back from the stress* of interacting with their child and refocus on what is essential. Once parents have gained perspective on the situation and calmed down their physiological reactions such as racing heart or muscle tension, they have robbed it of the power to overwhelm them. Parental time-outs may last a minute or they may last an hour—whatever is possible given the circumstances. Here are some variations on parental time-out: One to two sessions are devoted to this topic, although aspects of these themes are interwoven throughout every session:

- *Time-Out for a Breather.* This involves breathing deeply and slowly ideally in a quiet place. If possible, the parent also practices deep relaxation. Actually, the mere act of deep breathing will result in some degree of muscle relaxation.
- *Time-Out on the Go.* This technique can be used anywhere, while grocery shopping, doing the dishes, or sitting at a desk. Parents are taught to systematically tense and relax certain muscle groups and to visualize their muscles relaxing and releasing tension. For example, breathe in, tensing one arm and fist as tightly as possible. Hold for a count of four, then relax fully while breathing out. Repeat for other parts of the body.
- *Time-Out for Visualizing.* A third use of time-out is to visualize or imagine a calm scene. Parents choose their own personal visualization—a cloudless sky, an expanse of ocean, a quiet library. They can use it when they find themselves becoming tense.
- *Time-Out to Control Anger.* While some parents believe that "blowing off steam" by shouting and swearing will drain off violent energy and reduce aggression, we teach them that rather than having a cathartic or beneficial effect, outbursts of anger inflame aggression and violence. Studies have shown that couples who yell at each other do not feel less angry afterward; they feel more angry. The reason for this is that angry outbursts are self-reinforcing because they give people a false sense of power. They often feel that their anger forces others to take them seriously or results in others' compliance. Therapists help parents to look at the long-term effects of anger on themselves and on their children. When parents are taking a time-out to control anger, we ask them to practice their deep breathing and visualization exercises and focus on coping self-statements.
- *Time-Out for Self-Talk about Stress.* Parents are taught to use their self-talk as a way to manage stress, that is, to stop stressful thoughts by refuting or disputing them, or putting the stress in perspective. For example, tell yourself, "This is normal. Stress is a reasonable and normal response to what I'm dealing with today. This is the way I usually feel when I begin a time-out." Parents learn to use these feelings of tension as allies in coping with the situation. They serve as signals for parents to say to themselves, "Relax, take a slow breath. Take it easy." We teach parents to expect their stress will rise at times and to remember, the objective is not to eliminate it totally but to keep it manageable. The idea is for parents to normalize stress and recognize it as a part of family life. They are helped to think

about it as temporary rather than ongoing, to focus on what is controllable instead of what is uncontrollable, to focus on coping rather than on feelings of being overwhelmed, and to define steps they can take rather than blaming others.

- *Time-Out for Fun.* Here parents are urged to use time-out for doing something pleasurable such as reading, going for a walk, taking a bath. We focus on pleasures involving little or no expense and that are nurturing rather than destructive to one's health.

All the preceding uses of parental time-out can help parents release tension and anger, regain a calmer physiological state, and gain a greater sense of control over their own emotional state and their own behavior—thereby helping them be better parents. All might be termed "self-care."

In our experience with parent training groups, we have found the notion of parental self-care to be a foreign concept—especially with low-income families, who are typically so overwhelmed with daily tasks and depressed about their life circumstances that they feel unable to focus on self-care. As we talk with them about time-outs for personal, no-cost, or inexpensive pleasures, we meet resistance: "I can't take care of myself—I can't afford a sitter and I can't leave my children alone to take a walk," or "I can't go to a movie—I don't have a car or any money!" or "You've got to be kidding—I've got enough to do!" Our first homework assignment on this topic is, therefore, for parents to make a list of things they could do to give themselves a pleasurable break from parenting. Another homework assignment is to list typical daily stressors and come up with a positive strategy for handling the stress. Our discussion on this topic includes an exercise where parents list all possible obstacles to following through with their plan to reduce stress and think about ways to counteract some of these obstacles. As groups hear themselves talk in terms of devaluing themselves and their needs and feeling trapped, they begin to brainstorm ways they could help each other to accomplish this goal. We teach parents several ways to take personal time-out for the release of tension and anger, and the attainment of self-control.

Problem Solving

Although many people might like to think that the ideal family or couple has no conflict, we know otherwise. Conflicts and disagreements are inevitable in families and couples because of competing needs, differences in individual viewpoints, developmental pressures, and so on. What marks a resilient family or couple is not the absence of disagreements and conflict, but the ability to resolve them to everyone's satisfaction (more or less). Families and couples that can successfully negotiate their differences and can accept compromise, resolving problems collaboratively so that all the participants have and feel the resolution takes into account their position (although it may not be exactly what they want), will be better able to maintain satisfying relationships in the face of those inevitable difficult periods in their lives; families and couples who cannot do so will break apart under the strain. In the next two portions of the training program, we focus on teaching parents problem-solving skills that can help them cope with the inevitable conflicts in all relationships.

Therapists explain that problem solving is not like other types of discussion. It is neither spontaneous nor natural; it is highly structured. Problem solving involves a specific set of methods designed to enhance one's ability to think effectively about the issues and to work toward resolution of the conflict. However, being structured does not mean that it must be dull. On the contrary, many families report that the structure underlies an interesting process that brings them together by encouraging flexibility and collaboration.

Problem-solving skills incorporate the communication and cognitive skills learned in the prior sessions. It is important that these be taught first, before the problem-solving content. Anger can cause a narrowing of vision that blocks the ability to define issues and perceive options. It may also fuel the belief that other people have deliberately caused a problem and an attitude that action must be taken immediately, without time for deliberation. Depression can cause withdrawal from the process or a passive attitude toward problems. Parents must have some control over feelings of intense anger or depression before effective problem solving can begin.

We teach six steps to effective problem solving:

1. *Set Aside a Time and Place and Decide on an Agenda.* We recommend that parents not try to resolve conflicts at the time they arise. Most people are too emotionally aroused in the "heat of the battle" to go through the problem-solving process in a rational manner. Discussing a problem at a *neutral* time makes it much more likely that it will be resolved effectively. To prepare for problem solving, parents need to determine a specific time and place to have discussions. Many decide to meet at the same time each week. Often this will be at night after the children are in bed. We advise that they take the phone off the hook (or turn on the answering machine and turn down the volume), turn off the television, and eliminate as many other distractions as possible. We also tell them to set the agenda in advance, so that both people can be thinking about it, and to limit it to only one problem. We advise them to spend no more than 45 minutes on a problem. Few people can tolerate more than 45 minutes of problem solving without becoming exhausted.

2. *Describe and Define the Problem.* In describing the problem, each person needs to present his or her viewpoint, including:

   a. Situation : What is the problem?

                 : Who is involved?

                 : What aspect of it bothers you?

                 : How frequently does it happen (per day, per week)?

                 : Where and when does it happen?

                 : How does it happen? What sets it off or follows its occurrence?

                 : What happened last time?

                 : Why do you think it is happening, or what reasons do others give?

   b. Response : How do you feel when the problem is occurring?

                 : What do you do and say while it is occurring?

                 : How do you feel afterward?

                 : Why do you respond that way?

It is important that parents have a collaborative attitude and share responsibility for problem solving. Only one problem should be dealt with at a time. If one person does sidetrack in this manner, the other can say, "I think we are supposed to be discussing when you come home, not my discipline techniques." Although one parent might feel that he or she is the victim of a situation and that the other person is the cause of the problem, these feelings need to be put aside to encourage a sense of working together. Difficult as it is, each parent must listen carefully to the other person's point of view. Even if only one person in the family considers a situation to be a problem, it is critical that the family address it as a *mutual* problem that both people (or the whole family) must help resolve. This contributes to the well-being of the entire family.

After both have described the problem situation from their point of view, they should define the problem concisely. The definition should be oriented toward change desired in the future rather than focusing on the past.

3. *Outline Goals and Expectations.* Once the problem has been defined, the parents should again summarize the problem and then state the desired goal. For example, "I would like you to be home by 7:00 p.m.," or, "I would like him to be able to share better." The goal should then be assessed to be sure (a) it would resolve the problem, and (b) it is realistic (expecting a tax accountant to be home by 7:00 p.m. during tax season isn't realistic).

4. *Brainstorm Solutions.* We then teach parents to brainstorm—to generate possible solutions. Parents are encouraged to generate as

many solutions as they can conceive, without evaluating them. No further discussion of the problem should occur. The focus here is on creativity and productivity, so any judgments about the possible solutions or assessment of their merits should be avoided at this stage. We encourage parents to suggest several humorous ideas to lighten up the discussion.

5. *Make a Plan.* The fifth step in the process is to go through the list of possible solutions one at a time, eliminating any far-fetched and impossible ones and combining any that naturally go together. Then the pros and cons of each solution should be discussed in detail, keeping in mind the following:

- Is it realistic and practical?
- What are the best and worst possible outcomes?
- Are the best outcomes short- or long-term?
- How well do the best outcomes match the goal that we defined?

Then a plan of action should be formulated. This may combine several ideas from the list and should state clearly what each person will do and who will be responsible for what. The agreement should be written down and a follow-up meeting should be scheduled to review how the plan of action is working and determine any necessary revisions.

6. *Evaluation of Outcome.* At a follow-up meeting, the solutions should be evaluated by answering several questions. First, was the strategy carried out as planned? For example, if the plan was that Dad would be home by 7:00 P.M. 3 nights each week and spend Saturday mornings with the family, was this done consistently? If not, what prevented him from doing so? Second, if the plan was designed to improve a behavior, how was the behavior affected? If the goal was to have their child in bed by 9:00 by using stickers, then some record should be kept of the child's actual bedtimes. Finally, do the goals and observed outcomes match? Do the changes actually create the desired outcome? If not, then a new strategy may need to be developed.

Often when parents begin to discuss a problem with their partner or children, they find themselves arguing about who caused the problem. But arguments of this sort inevitably involve blaming and accusations; as we know, they usually escalate into bickering. They are powerful methods for undermining the problem-solving process and are sometimes even used for that purpose (though usually unconsciously). Our therapists try to impress on parents the importance of an attitude of collaboration in problem solving; that is, both parents must share responsibility for the problem. We urge upon parents the necessity of putting aside feelings of victimization or self-righteousness and substituting a commitment to problem solving. The goal is not to decide who is at fault, but to define the nature of the problem and how to solve it.

Of course, one problem-solving session is not going to resolve a problem if it is a difficult one. But even a small step in the desired direction can be a real turnaround for a couple. Our therapists reinforce this progress and urge parents to praise each other's problem-solving efforts. Such positive feedback sets the stage for future sessions. If couples and families can learn to successfully problem-solve together, they are more likely to maintain flexible, satisfying relationships over a long period of time.

This content usually takes three to four sessions to complete. Homework assignments for the first week include practicing defining problems clearly and using the listening and speaking communication skills. The following week, the parents are asked to outline goals and brainstorm possible solutions. We have parents practice these skills with a fairly easy problem first, and then gradually move to more difficult ones.

Teaching Children to Problem-Solve

When young children react to their problems by crying, hitting, or running to their parents, these responses do little to help them resolve the problem; in fact, they create new problems. But research shows that children resort to inappropriate strategies because they do not know other ways to respond. Parents can help by teaching their children problem-solving skills.

First and foremost, parents can teach these skills by modeling them. It is a rich learning experience for children to watch parents discussing problems with other adults, negotiating and resolving conflict, and evaluating the outcome of their solutions in an appropriate, nonhostile manner. Although parents may not want their children to observe all their problem-solving meetings, many daily decisions they make provide good opportunities for them to learn. For example, children learn from noticing how their parents say "no" to a friend's request. They watch with interest as Dad receives Mom's suggestion to wear something different. Is Mom sarcastic, angry, or matter-of-fact in her request? Does Dad pout, get angry, cooperate, or ask for more information? Watching parents decide which movie to see on Saturday night can teach children much about compromise and negotiation. Watching them discuss financial problems teaches children how to carry on a problem-solving discussion in the face of stress and worry.

Besides modeling problem-solving skills, parents can teach these to their children directly. But many parents confuse telling their children what to do with helping them learn to problem-solve. There are many obvious problems with this approach; parents may tell their children what to do before they have found out what the actual problem is, that is, from the child's viewpoint. Thus one of the first tasks for parents when their children are engaged in conflict is to understand the problem from their child's point of view. Parents need to learn to ask questions like, "What happened?" "What's the matter?" or "Can you tell me about it?" and to deliver them in a nonaccusatory tone so that the child will be more likely to talk openly about it. This questioning not only helps the child to clarify the problem in his or her own mind, but also ensures that the parent won't jump to the wrong conclusion about what's going on, for any solution must be relevant to the child's perception of the situation. And when children believe that their parents understand their point of view, they are more likely to be willing to deal with the problem cooperatively. Rather than being encouraged to learn *how to think*, they are told what to think and the solution is imposed on them.

We teach parents to help their children learn the following five steps to problem-solve successfully:

1. What is my problem?
2. What are some plans (brainstorm solutions)?
3. What are the consequences? What is the best plan (evaluate consequences)?
4. Am I using my plan (implementation)?
5. How did I do (evaluate the outcome and reinforce efforts)?

Throughout the process, parents can encourage children to talk aloud as they think and can praise their ideas and attempts at solutions. In this way, parents reinforce the development of a style of thinking that will help them to deal with all kinds of problems.

Our therapists begin by helping parents set up hypothetical problem situations with their children. Through the use of stories or puppets, parents can create problem scenes and ask their children to come up with as many solutions as possible. We give parents a list of possible "suppose games" they can play with their children at home for problem-solving practice. For example: Suppose a child much younger than you started hitting you. What would you do? or, Suppose a boy had been playing for a long, long time with a toy, and you wanted to play with it. What would you do?

After proposing a hypothetical problem, parents encourage their children to think about their feelings as well as those of the other person in the situation and, on that basis, to describe the problem. Parents then invite them to come up with as many solutions as they can. If children cannot think of any to begin with, parents suggest a few. The objective for parents is to make these problem-solving discussions fun by using cartoons, stories, or puppets. They might even suggest that they write a story together. Parents are cautioned to avoid criticizing or ridiculing any of their children's ideas, no matter how silly they are. Instead, they are urged to encourage creative thinking and to model creative solutions themselves.

After generating possible solutions, the next step is to help children look at what would happen if each solution were carried out. Parents help their children imagine the possible consequences. Often, children are surprised or upset when things don't go as envisioned. This reaction can partially be avoided if they stop and predict several outcomes that might result from their behavior. A child might say that tricking or hitting a friend to get a toy is a solution. The parent would then help the child to consider the possible outcomes, such as losing a friend, getting into trouble, or getting the toy. The consequences of asking the friend for the toy might include being turned down or ignored—or it might get the child the toy. After reviewing possible outcomes, parents help their children decide which one or two might be the best. For children between the ages of 3 and 8, the second step of generating possible solutions is the key skill to learn. While implementation and evaluation are more easily done by older children, youngsters first need to consider possible solutions and to understand that some solutions are better than others.

The fourth step is for parents to help children actually implement a solution (if the problem is a real-life problem). Real-life problem solving is, of course, much harder than problem solving in a hypothetical or neutral situation. In conflict situations, children may be so angry and upset that they cannot think clearly. Parents will need to be able to calm them through discussion, so they can come up with some solutions. Sometimes children may be so emotional that they need to go for a brief time-out until they cool off. Occasionally, a problem is so distressing that it is best discussed later when both parents and their children have had time to calm down and gain some perspective.

We teach parents to guide their children into thinking about what may have caused the problem in the first place and to invite them to come up with a possible solution. If parents want to help their children develop a habit of solving their own problems, they need to be encouraged to think for themselves. Parents can teach their children how to think about a problem but should not teach them what to think about it. The only time parents need to offer solutions is when their children don't have any ideas, but this should not be confused with teaching problem solving.

The opposite occurs when parents think they are helping their children learn problem solving by telling them to work it out for themselves. This presumes that their children already have good problem-solving skills; but for most young children, this approach will not work. If two children are in conflict over a toy, parental ignoring will probably result in continued arguing and the more aggressive child getting the toy. The more aggressive child will be reinforced for inappropriate behavior (because he got what he wanted) and the other is reinforced for giving in (because the fighting ceased when he backed down). The children learn from this situation, but it is not a lesson we would want them to learn.

PARENT TRAINING METHODS

Videotape Modeling

Because the extent of conduct problems has created a need for service that far exceeds available personnel and resources, we were convinced of the need to develop an intervention that would be cost-effective, widely applicable, and sustaining. Videotape modeling promised to be both effective and cost-efficient. Bandura's (1977) modeling theory of learning suggests that parents could improve their parenting skills by watching videotaped examples of parents interacting with their children in ways that promote prosocial behaviors and decreased inappropriate behaviors. Moreover, this method of training would be more accessible, especially to less verbally oriented parents, than other methods (e.g., didactic instruction, written handouts, group discussion) and could promote better generalization (and therefore long-term maintenance) by portraying many models in a wide variety of situations. Furthermore, videotape modeling has a low individual training cost when used in groups, and lends itself to mass dissemination.

Thus, we developed a program that relies heavily on videotape modeling as a therapeutic method. Therapists present 16 videotape programs composed of more than 250 brief vignettes showing parents and children of different sexes, ages, cultures, socioeconomic backgrounds, and temperamental styles. Parents are shown interacting with their children in natural situations, such as during mealtime, getting children dressed, toilet training, handling disobedience, and playing together. Scenes depict parents "doing it right" and "doing it wrong." The intent in showing negative as well as positive examples is to demystify the notion of "perfect parenting" and to illustrate how parents can learn from their mistakes. The videotapes are used as a catalyst to stimulate group discussion and problem solving, with the therapist ensuring that the discussion addresses the intended topic and is understood by the parents. As noted earlier, our research has indicated that therapist-led group discussion utilizing videotape modeling is superior to therapist-led group discussion without videotapes, as well as to videotape alone (Webster-Stratton, 1990b; Webster-Stratton et al., 1989; Webster-Stratton, Kolpacoff, & Hollinsworth, 1988). When showing a videotape vignette, the therapist pauses the tape to give parents a chance to discuss and react to what they have observed. Sometimes group members are uncertain about whether the kinds of parenting they have just observed are appropriate or not. Thus, the therapist asks open-ended questions such as, "What do you think about this parent's approach to the situation?" or "How would you feel if your child did that?" (Suggested questions and discussion topics are included in therapist manual.) If participants are unclear about specific aspects of the parent-child interaction, or if they have missed a critical feature of the vignette, the therapist rewinds the tape and has the group watch the scene again. The goal is not only to have parents grasp the intended concept, but also to have parents become actively involved in problem solving and sharing ideas about the vignette. The therapist can facilitate integration of the concepts by asking how the concepts illustrated in the vignettes apply or don't apply to parents' own situations. For example, a mother makes the following comment after watching a few of the play vignettes:

MOTHER: I don't have any toys at home. I can't afford toys like those shown on the tapes—I'm living on a welfare check.

THERAPIST: You know, even if you had the money it is not important to have fancy toys. In fact, some of the best toys for children are things like pots and pans, empty cereal boxes, dry macaroni, and string—why don't we brainstorm some ideas for inexpensive things you could use to play with your child at home?

This interaction between the therapist and mother illustrates the importance of collaborating with parents to be sure the concepts shown on the videotapes are relevant for their particular cultural and socioeconomic situation.

Therapists' Do's and Don'ts of Using Videotapes

1. Pace vignettes throughout the entire session. Avoid waiting until the last half of the program to show the majority of vignettes.
2. Allow for discussion following every vignette. If you are short of time, you may verbally highlight key points in the vignette. Do not run vignettes together without dialogue.
3. Allow for parents' first impressions (insights) to be expressed *before* you offer analysis and interpretation.
4. If parents' reactions are critical of the behavior shown in a vignette, balance their perspective by noting some positive features of the parents' behaviors. (If you allow a group to go too negative, parents may feel you could be just as critical of their mistakes.)
5. Remember to model a realistic perspective of parenting.

Role Play and Rehearsal

Role playing or rehearsal of unfamiliar or newly acquired behaviors is one of the most common components of parent training programs and has been shown to be quite effective in producing behavioral changes (Eisler, Hersen, & Agras, 1973; Twentyman & McFall, 1975). Role plays help parents anticipate situations more clearly, dramatizing possible sequences of behavior. We recommend doing three to four brief role plays during each session.

Many parents, however, feel inadequate regarding their parenting behavior, and therefore may be reluctant to undertake role playing. Besides presenting a clear rationale for conducting the role play, we have found that it is often best for the therapist to do the first role play to reduce parents' self-consciousness and anxiety. It also helps to make the role play humorous through exaggeration. For example, the therapist role-playing the parent may go out of the room and shout from a distance (e.g., kitchen) for the child (role-played by parent) to put away the toys. This usually raises chuckles of recognition, for there is no way for the parent to know whether the child is complying or not, or whether the child has even registered the command.

After the therapist has done the first role play, we then break the parent group into pairs to practice particular skills such as play, praise, time-out, or problem solving. We often find it is a good idea to first instruct parents to "do it the worst way possible," and then follow this with, "Now use as many of the positive strategies we talked about as possible." The contrast helps reduce performance anxiety over projected demands for perfection. Later on, as parents become more comfortable, they can role-play a situation in front of the whole group; for example, role playing the use of time-out with a "difficult child." In this case, one parent plays the child and another the child's parent. The rest of the group act as coaches for the "parent." It is often helpful to "freeze-frame" the role play and ask the group questions such as, "Now what should she do?" or "What is the child trying to say by behaving like that?"

Role playing can also be useful in the case of the long-winded parent who wants to describe in detail some situation at home. We can shortcut the discussion and clarify the problem by asking, "Why don't you be the child or parent and show us exactly what happens?" This allows us to role play alternative responses for the parent to try at home.

Our weekly evaluations indicate that parents find the role plays extremely useful. Usually it is the therapist who is most resistant to the idea of doing role plays, for effective role playing requires that the therapist allow him- or herself to take risks, to be playful, to be vulnerable, and to relinquish control.

WEEKLY HOME ASSIGNMENTS

As we have seen from the description of the program content, for every session there is a home assignment. Parents need to understand the purpose for the assignments. They should be presented as an integral part of the learning process:

THERAPIST: You can't learn to drive a car or play the piano without practicing, and this is also the case with the parenting skills you are learning here—the more effort you put into the assignments, the more success you will have with the program.

The assignments help transfer what is talked about in group sessions to real life at home. They also serve as a powerful stimulus for discussion at the subsequent session. Moreover, assignments convey the critical message that sitting passively in the group is not "magic moondust"; parents must collaborate with the therapist by working at home to make changes.

Parents are provided with the book, *The Incredible Years,* as part of the training materials (Webster-Stratton, 1992). Each week they are asked to read a chapter to prepare for the subsequent session. For those parents who cannot read, audiotapes of the chapter are provided. Along with the reading assignment, homework usually involves asking parents to do some observing of behavior or recording of thoughts at home and trying out a particular parenting strategy. At the start of every group session, the therapist asks parents to share their experience with the home assignment and reading for the week. This enables the therapist to see how well the parents are integrating the material into their daily lives. Parents are more likely to take the assignments seriously if they know the therapist is going to begin each session by reviewing the assignment from the previous week.

When a parent questions the usefulness or feasibility of an assignment, this should be explored immediately, in a collaborative spirit. For example, a single parent with four young children says she is unable to do 15 minutes of playtime each day with an individual child. The therapist responds:

THERAPIST: I imagine you barely have 2 minutes to yourself all day—let alone 15 minutes with an individual child. Let's talk about ways to practice the play skills with several children at the same time. Or, would it be possible to play in brief bursts of 2 or 3 minutes throughout the day? Or, are there any times when you have only one or two children at home?

If the therapist does not pursue the issue, parents may conclude that the therapist is not really committed to the assignments or does not really want to understand parents' particular circumstances. Similarly, when a parent fails to complete an assignment from the previous session, the therapist should explore the problem with questions such as, "What made it hard for you to do the assignment?" "How have you overcome this problem in the past?" "What advice would you give to someone else who has this problem?" "What can you do to make it easier for you to complete the assignment this week?" "Do you think there is another assignment that might be more useful for you?"

Therapists review assignments each week and give parents personal written feedback as well as surprise stickers, chocolate, cartoons, or cards in their folder to applaud a particular parent's achievement. Each week when the parent arrives at group, they put in their individual folder the week's assignment, check off whether or not they were able to do the assignment, and they pick up the therapists' comments on the prior week's assignment. The individual folders offer quiet group members another channel for communication with the therapist. They are also a private place for communicating questions and comments that the parent does not want to share with the entire group. The checklists encourage parents to self-monitor; we frequently find parents asking us if they can still get credit for the homework assignment if they do it the following week!

WEEKLY EVALUATIONS

Each group session is evaluated by having parents complete a brief Weekly Evaluation Form. This gives the therapists immediate feedback about how each parent is responding to the therapist's style, the group discussions, and the content presented in the session. When a parent is dissatisfied or is having trouble with a concept, the therapist may want to call that parent to resolve the issue, or if the difficulty is shared by others, bring it up in a subsequent session.

PHONE CALLS AND MAKE UP SESSIONS

Therapists "check in" with parents every couple of weeks with a telephone call, asking how things are going and whether parents are having any difficulty with the home assignments. These calls allow therapists and parents to get to know one another outside the group—particularly useful in the case of quiet or reluctant parents—and promote engagement with the program, as well as revealing how well parents are assimilating the material presented in group. We recommend an individual call to any parent who has two neutral or negative weekly evaluations in a row regarding any aspect of the program (therapist, group discussion, or content), to let the parent know the therapist is concerned about the issues raised in the evaluations and will try to meet that parent's learning needs.

When a parent misses a session, therapists call them right away to let the parent know the therapist is concerned about his or her participation and takes absences seriously. It also gives the therapist an opportunity to help the parent make up the session and do the assignment before the next session.

PARENT TRAINING PROCESS

PARENT TRAINING AS COLLABORATION

There are many competing parent intervention programs, each with different sets of assumptions about the causes of family problems, the role of the therapist, the nature of the relationship between parent and therapist, and the level of responsibility assumed by the parent and the therapist. What they have in common is that in most parent training, the model is *hierarchical:* The therapist's role is that of an expert who is responsible for uncovering and interpreting past experiences and family dynamics to the family; and the parent's role is that of a relatively passive recipient of the therapist's knowledge and advice. The child's misbehavior is evidence that the parent is unable to effectively parent, and the therapist's role is to diagnose and repair the deficit within the parent.

In contrast, our training model for working with families is active and collaborative. In a collaborative relationship, the therapist does not set him- or herself up as an expert dispensing advice to parents about how they *should* parent more effectively. With a root meaning of "to labor together," collaboration implies a reciprocal relationship based on utilizing equally the therapist's and the parents' knowledge, strengths, and perspectives. A collaborative model of parent training is nonblaming and nonhierarchical. This approach to parent training has been described in detail in a recently published book (Webster-Stratton & Herbert, 1994).

As professionals, we have considerable expertise in our fields. Does the collaborative therapist have to renounce this expertise? Not at all. Yet the collaborative training model acknowledges that expertise is not the sole property of the therapist: The parents function as experts concerning their child, their particular family, and their community, and the therapist functions as expert concerning child development, family dynamics in general, behavior management principles, and so on. The collaborative therapist labors with parents by actively soliciting their ideas and feelings, understanding their cultural context, and involving them in the therapeutic process by inviting them to share their experiences, discuss their ideas, and engage in problem solving. Collaboration implies that parents actively participate in setting goals and the intervention agenda. Collaboration also implies that parents evaluate each session, and the therapist is responsible for adapting the intervention in response to their evaluations.

Another aspect of the collaborative therapist's labor is working with parents to adapt concepts and skills to the particular circumstances of those parents and the particular temperament of their child. A parent who lives in a one-room trailer is unlikely to have an empty room for time-out and will even have difficulty finding a suitable spot to put a time-out chair. A parent living in an apartment where walls are not soundproof will be acutely sensitive to the possible reactions of neighbors when he or she tries to ignore the screaming child; with good reason, that parent may resist using the ignore technique. These parents may raise objections—possibly unrelated from the therapist's point of view—to the use of time-out or ignoring. In traditional (hierarchical) therapy, these would be seen as instances of resistance, and the therapist would labor to overcome the parents' resistance. In contrast, the collaborative therapist would operate from the assumption that the parent had legitimate grounds for resisting this aspect of the training, would attempt to understand the living situation and other circumstances of each family and involve the parents in problem solving to adapt the concepts to their particular situation. Highly active, impulsive children will not be able to sit quietly and play attentively with their parents for long periods. Such children will also have more difficulty sitting in time-out than less active children. Other children are not particularly responsive to Tangible Reward programs. Therapists need to be sensitive to these differences in child temperament so that they can begin to collaborate with parents in defining the approaches that will work for them and their child.

A noncollaborative approach is didactic and nonparticipative—the therapist lectures, the parents listen. The noncollaborative therapist presents principles and skills to parents in terms of "prescriptions" for successful ways of dealing with their children. Homework assignments are rigid, given without regard for the particular circumstances of an individual family. We reject this approach because, for one thing, it is unsuccessful: It is likely to lead to higher attrition rates and poor long-term maintenance. Furthermore, it is ethically dubious to impose goals on parents that may not be congruent with their goals, values, and lifestyles and that may not suit the temperament of their child. This is particularly important when there are cultural or class differences between the therapist and the group, where assumptions arising from the therapist's own background or training may simply not apply. The collaborative model implies that, insofar as possible, the therapist stimulates the parents to generate solutions based on their experience with their child, and based on their family's cultural, class, and individual background. When parents come up with solutions they view as appropriate, the therapist can then reinforce and expand on these ideas.

A collaborative style of leadership is demonstrated by open communication patterns within the group and the therapist's attitude of acceptance toward all families in the program. By building a relationship based not on authority but on rapport with the group, the therapist creates a climate of trust, making the group a safe place for parents to reveal their problems and to risk new approaches. The collaborative therapist is a careful listener who uses open-ended questions when exploring issues, for they are more likely to generate discussion and collaboration. He or she encourages debate and alternative viewpoints, treating all viewpoints with respect. The therapist's empathic understanding is conveyed by actively reaching out to the parents, eliciting their ideas, and attempting to understand rather than analyze.

PARENT TRAINING AS EMPOWERMENT

This partnership between parents and group therapist has the effect of giving back dignity, respect, and self-control to parents who, because of their particular situation, may be in a vulnerable time of low self-confidence and intense feelings of guilt and self-blame (Spitzer, Webster-Stratton, & Hollinsworth, 1991). It is our hypothesis that a collaborative approach is more likely to increase parents' confidence and perceived self-efficacy than all other therapeutic approaches. The essential goal of collaborative intervention is to "empower" parents so that they feel confident about their parenting skills and about their ability to respond to new situations that may arise when the therapist is not there to help them. Bandura (1977) has called this strategy strengthening the client's "efficacy expectations," that is, parents' conviction that they can successfully change their own and their child's behaviors. Bandura (1982, 1989) has suggested that self-efficacy is the mediating variable between knowledge and behavior. Therefore, parents with high "self-efficacy" will tend to persist at tasks until they succeed. The literature also indicates that people who have determined their own priorities and goals are more likely to persist in the face of difficulties and less likely to show debilitating effects of stress (e.g., Dweck, 1975; Seligman, 1975).

Moreover, this model is likely to increase parents' engagement in the intervention. Research (Backeland & Lundwall, 1975; Janis & Mann, 1977; Meichenbaum & Turk, 1987) suggests that the collaborative process has the multiple advantages of reducing attrition rates, increasing motivation and commitment, reducing resistance, increasing temporal and situational generalization, and giving parents and the therapist a joint stake in the outcome of the intervention. On the other hand, controlling or hierarchical modes of therapy, in which the therapist analyzes, interprets, and makes decisions *for* parents without incorporating their input, may result in a low level of commitment, dependency, low self-efficacy, and increased resistance (Janis & Mann, 1977; Patterson & Forgatch, 1985), as well as resentment of professionals. In fact, if parents are not given appropriate ways to participate, they may see no alternative but to drop out or resist the intervention as a means of asserting their control over the therapeutic process.

In short, the net result of collaborative parent training is to empower parents by strengthening their knowledge and skill base, their self-confidence, and their autonomy, instead of creating dependence on the therapist and inadvertently perpetuating a sense of inadequacy or helplessness. There is a further reason for this model: Since we want parents to adopt a participative, collaborative, empowering approach with their own children, it is important to use this approach with them in the parent program (i.e., to model with them the relationship style we wish them to use with their children). This form of training leads to greater internalization of learning in children (and very likely adults).

PARENT TRAINING GROUPS AS SUPPORT SYSTEMS

It is debatable whether there are clearly differentiated criteria for choosing between one-on-one intervention and group training. Our own research with clinic families has shown that group training utilizing videotape modeling is at least as therapeutically effective as one-on-one intervention and certainly more cost-effective (Webster-Stratton, 1984, 1985b). But aside from the obvious economic benefits, there is another benefit to the group format: greater parental engagement with the program, a particularly compelling benefit in the case of low-income single mothers, who have been reported by Wahler (Wahler & Afton, 1980) and others to be "insular"—socially isolated, with little support and few friendships. Insular parents frequently report feeling criticized and otherwise rejected in their relationships with relatives, professionals, case workers, spouses, and friends. Parent groups can become an empowering environment for these parents, decreasing their insularity and giving them new sources of support.

Many of the parents in our studies initially were reluctant to participate in groups, preferring the privacy of individual counseling. However, after completion of the training, 87.7% reported that group discussion was a very useful training method. After having had a successful group experience, many parents were for the first time willing to consider serving on PTA boards or participating in other school and community-related group functions.

In the parent group, parents learned how to collaborate in problem solving, how to express their appreciation for each other, and how to cheer each other's successes in tackling difficult problems. They also learned to share their feelings of guilt, anger, and depression, as well as experiences that involved mistakes on their part or misbehaviors from their children. These discussions served as a powerful source of support. Through this sharing of feelings and experiences, commonalty was discovered. Feelings of isolation decreased, and parents were empowered by the knowledge that they are not alone in their problems and that many of their problems are normal. And this sense of group support and kinship increased parents' engagement with the program. The following comments were made in one of our groups:

FATHER: You know when this program is finished, I will always think about this group in spirit.

MOTHER: This group is all sharing—it's people who aren't judging me, who are also taking risks and saying, "Have you tried this? or have you considered you might be off track?"

One of the ways we helped our groups become support systems was by assigning everyone a parent "buddy" in the second session. Buddies were asked to call each other during the week to share how the homework assignment (e.g., praising, limit setting) was going. New "buddies" were assigned every few weeks throughout the program. Parents were initially hesitant about making these calls, but as they experienced the sense of support they received from these phone conversations, they expressed a desire to continue these calls. Many fathers voiced that this was the first time they had ever talked to another father about parenting. If a parent missed a session, the buddy would call right away to tell the parent he or she was missed and to fill the person in on the week's material.

BUILDING PARENT SUPPORT OUTSIDE THE GROUP

Parents often reported conflicts with partners and grandparents over how to handle the child's problems, resulting in stressed relationships and stressed individuals. Therefore, in addition to building the support system within the parent group, the program also emphasized building support within the family and home life. The program encouraged every parent to have a spouse, partner, close friend, or family member (such as grandparent) participate in the program to provide mutual support. (Our own follow-up studies as well as others' have indicated that the greatest likelihood of relapse occurs in families in which only one person was involved in the intervention (Herbert, 1987; Webster-Stratton, 1985a). During parent groups, partners were helped to define ways they could support each other when one was feeling discouraged, tired, or unable to cope.

Frequently, the energy required to care for children, coupled with financial constraints, leaves parents feeling exhausted and too tired to make plans to spend time with each other or with adult friends, let alone interact with them. Yet time away from the child with a partner or a friend can help parents feel supported and energized. It helps them gain perspective so they are better able to cope with parenting. Wahler's (Wahler & Afton, 1980) research has indicated that single mothers who have contact with other people outside the home fare much better in their parenting than mothers without such contacts, whereas maternal insularity or social isolation results in the probability of intervention failure (Dumas & Wahler, 1983). In our group, sometimes parents seemed almost to have forgotten their identity as individuals. Thus, one of the home assignments was to do some "self-care" activity in which parents did something nice for themselves. Paradoxically, the result of spending some time away in "self-care" activities was often a feeling of support and understanding from one's partner or the other adult who made it possible.

THERAPIST STRATEGIES

THERAPIST QUALIFICATIONS

Therapists in our programs have represented several disciplines including nursing, social work, education, psychology, and psychiatry. These individuals have had master's or doctoral degrees in their professions and a strong background in child development, counseling, and clinical work with families. But we have found that therapists' effectiveness as group leaders in our program is determined not by their educational or professional background but by their degree of comfort with a collaborative process and their ability to promote intimacy and assume a friendship role with families—that is, the kind of friend who listens, asks for clarification, is reflective and nonjudgmental, tries to understand what the parent is saying through empathy, and helps problem-solve and does not command, instruct, or tell the parent how to parent. At the same time, the therapist must also be able to lead and teach—to explain behavioral principles and provide a clear rationale for them, to challenge families to see new perspectives, to elicit the strengths of the parent group, and to provide clear limit setting within the group when necessary.

Advocacy

Therapist approaches such as self-disclosure, humor, and positive reinforcement serve the overall purpose of building a supportive relationship. The therapist can also actively support parents by acting as advocates for them, particularly in situations where communication with other professionals may have become difficult. In the role of advocate, the therapist can bring relevant persons, programs, and resources to the family, or bring the family to them. For example, the therapist can arrange and attend meetings between parents and teachers so as to help the parents clarify the child's problems, agree on goals, and set up behavior management programs that are consistent from the clinic to home and to school.

It must be emphasized that the ultimate goal of this advocacy role is to strengthen the parents' ability to advocate for themselves and for their children. The danger of advocacy is that it can become a "rescue" or an "expert" role; and as a result, the parents may feel dependent or uncommitted. An example of this might be the therapist who makes recommendations to a child's teacher, without the parent being involved. Our approach to advocacy in this situation would be to say to the parent, "We want you to share with the teacher the strategies that you are trying to use at home to see whether the teachers might consider setting up a similar program at school." We accompany the parent and try to provide support. By giving parents the responsibility for their own advocacy, sharing their own solutions, and advocating *with* (rather than *for*) parents, we again emphasize the collaborative process.

Identifying Goals of Group

At the initial parent group, parents are asked to share some of their personal experiences with their children, as well as their goals for the training program. These goals for each parent are posted on the wall so that they can be referred to throughout the program. This initial discussion often produces immediate group rapport as parents realize they have similar difficulties and are working toward similar goals. Throughout the training, parents are given home assignments to write down the child behaviors they want to see increase or decrease. These targeted behaviors (e.g., go to bed at 8:00 P.M.; not interrupt when someone is on phone) become the focus of group discussion and brainstorming. Several times during the program, the therapist draws up a composite list of behaviors parents are working on so that group members can see the similarities in their issues. This promotes ongoing group cohesion, as well as attention to individual goals, thereby increasing parents' commitment to the program.

Ensuring Group Safety and Sufficient Structure

One of the most difficult aspects of the therapist's role is to prevent the group experience from becoming negative. If this should happen, dropout is a certainty. Consequently, during the first meeting, we ask group members to generate rules that would help them feel safe, comfortable, and accepted in the group. These rules are kept posted on the wall to be added to or referred to if necessary during weekly sessions. Examples include (a) only one person may talk at a time, (b) everyone's ideas are respected, (c) anyone has a right to pass, (d) no "put downs" are allowed, and (e) confidentiality within the room. After identifying the rules, we ask the group to discuss why they think these rules are important.

For groups that are very verbal and tend to get sidetracked or to digress, it is helpful at the beginning of each session to select a parent to act as a cotherapist. The job of this parent cotherapist is to be a timekeeper, to make sure all vignettes are covered, to help identify participants who are sidetracking the discussion, and to keep the group focused on the main topics for the session. Our evaluations indicate that parents become frustrated and disengaged if the discussion wanders, and they appreciate having enough structure imposed to keep the discussion moving along. By rotating the job of cotherapist, the task of monitoring the group discussion becomes everyone's responsibility; everyone is committed to the group's functioning well.

The group process can also be disrupted by a participant who challenges the therapist's knowledge or advocates inappropriate child-rearing practices. It is important that the therapist not seem critical or frustrated with this person's comments, for this is the "coercion trap" many parents have experienced in the past. Instead, the therapist looks for the relevant points in what the person has said and reinforces them for the group. By conveying acceptance and warmth, even toward a parent who is an obviously difficult group member, the therapist models acceptance and helps group members see that the goal is to understand and respect everyone.

Explanation as Persuasion

Therapeutic change depends on persuasion. This implies that parents must be given the rationale for each component of the program. It is important for the therapist to voice clear explanations based on valid information and knowledge of the developmental literature as well as hard-earned practical wisdom and experience. The treatment principles, objectives, and methods should not be shrouded in mystery. Research has indicated that parents' understanding of the social learning principles underlying the parent training program leads to enhanced generalization or maintenance of treatment effects (McMahon & Forehand, 1984).

However, it is also important that these rationales and theories be presented in such a way that the parent can see the connection with his or her stated goals. For example, when providing the rationale for child-directed play interactions, the therapist explains how this approach fosters the child's self-esteem, social competence, and eventual success in school, while at the same time decreasing his or her need to obtain control over parents by negative behaviors. In this example, supplying the rationale is important not only because parents may not immediately see the connection between playing with their children more and helping their child be less aggressive, but also because of the connection made between this new aspect of the program, and the parents' original reason for seeking help (their child's aggressiveness). If they do not understand the rationale for the play sessions, they may not be motivated to do them at home.

Reframing

Therapeutic change depends on providing explanatory "stories," alternative explanations that help parents to reshape their perceptions of and their beliefs about the nature of their problems. Reframing by the therapist or cognitive restructuring is a powerful interpretive tool for helping parents understand their experiences, thereby promoting change in their behaviors. It involves altering the parent's emotional and/or conceptual viewpoint of an experience by placing the experience in another "frame" that fits the facts of the situation well, thereby altering its meaning.

One type of reframing that we frequently use is to take a problem a parent is having with a child and reframe it in terms of child development. Reframing a difficult child's behavior in terms of a psychological or emotional drive such as testing the security of limits, or reacting to the loss of a parent, or moving toward independence, helps the parents see the behavior as appropriate or normal—in some cases even positive. Seen in this light, problematic behaviors are the expression of normal emotions and developmental stages. Viewing situations in this light, parents can see that they are participating in a process of growth for the child. This attitude enhances coping and decreases feelings of anger and helplessness. Understood in terms of children's needs to test the security of their environment or to test the love of their parents, parent-child conflicts become less overwhelming and parents are more able to remain committed to the hard work of parenting.

Generational Issues

Another strategy that increases parents' commitment, promoting empathy and bonding between parent and child, is to help the parents see the connections between their own childhood experiences and those of their child. When parents acknowledge similarities between their personality and their child's, the therapist can help parents see how these similarities may result in conflicting reactions for them as a parent, yet give the parents intuitive insight into what parenting strategies might be most useful with their child.

The therapist can also help parents see how their reactions and responses as parents are based on their own experiences as a child (either imitating or reacting to the parenting they experienced) and how these influences may create resistance to alternative parenting styles. There is therefore a place in the collaborative model for brief consideration of the child's and parents' past. These stories are often negative, filled with pain, anger, self-deprecation, bitterness, and regret. It may be necessary for the therapist to help parents "lay the ghosts" to rest before they can apply themselves wholeheartedly and with optimism to problems in the here-and-now.

Reframing the Future

Parents are often skeptical about their ability to change, especially if they see in their behavior a family pattern, for patterns often seem fixed and irreversible. Thus another function of the therapist is to counter that skepticism with positive expectations for change. For example, one parent said, "My mother beat me, now I beat my children." In response, the therapist expressed her confidence in the parent's ability to break the family cycle. Each small step toward change—even the step of coming to a parent training program in the first place—can be pointed to as evidence that the problem is *not* fixed or irreversible.

Therapists strive to convey optimism about the parents' ability to successfully carry out the strategies required to produce positive changes in the child's behaviors. According to Bandura (1989), all psychological procedures are mediated through a system of beliefs about the level of skill required to bring about an outcome and the likely end result of a course of action. Efficacy expectations are thought to be the most important component. Thus, successful treatment depends on the ability of the therapist to strengthen parents' expectations of personal efficacy ("I am able to do it").

Generalizing and Contextualizing

Generalization—the ability to apply specific skills learned in the training to one's own situation, and also the ability to extrapolate from current concerns to future parenting dilemmas—is enhanced by participation where group members are exposed to many family life situations and

approaches to solving problems. Another means of enhancing generalization is by group problem solving. The therapist compiles a list of behaviors that parents want to encourage or discourage and asks the group to
come up with as many ideas as possible for dealing with those behaviors.
Generalization is also enhanced by what we call "principles *training*"—
pointing out or having a group member state the basic principle that can
be applied across multiple situations. These principles can be listed on a
poster and brought to each session to facilitate continued applications of
the principle. Each principle could be identified by the group member's
name who first stated that principle (i.e., Jim's principle: Behaviors that
receive attention occur more often).

We also engage the families in a process we call "contextualizing"—
asking parents to identify the particular circumstances in which they
find it difficult or impossible to apply what they have been learning in
the training. Often parents will identify high stress times of the day,
such as the first 30 minutes when they get home at night from work, or
are late for an appointment, or have relatives visiting. We encourage
parents to identify these vulnerable periods and to strategically plan
ways to deal with them. When parents have been successful in maintaining control during a stressful situation, we encourage them to reflect on this and to share their strategies by asking such questions as,
"What made it possible for you to maintain control in such a stressful
situation? What were you thinking to yourself at the time? How did
you do that?" Here the therapist aims to help the parents recognize
their positive coping skills.

Preparing for Termination and Predicting Relapses

Preparing for the end of the parenting program is critical. Usually we
find parents beginning to raise the issue 4 to 6 weeks before the end of
the training, as they begin to worry about what they will do when they
are without the support of the group and the therapist. Therapists prepare parents for the inevitable relapses in their parenting skills and children's misbehavior both during the training program and after the
program has ended, brainstorming and helping parents rehearse what
they will do when there is a relapse. Parents have suggested calling another parent in the group for advice and support, contacting the group
therapist, practicing the program exercises in the workbook again beginning with praises and play periods, identifying the problem behaviors
and reviewing the techniques presented in the course for dealing with
them, arranging for some time away from the children to refuel and ener-
gize, and focusing on positive alternatives rather than becoming im-
mersed in feelings of failure or frustration. Therapists reassure parents
that mistakes and relapses are "normal" and to be expected, stressing

that the important point is to develop strategies to counteract relapses so that family life doesn't become too disrupted.

Preparing for the Long Term

We also brainstorm with parents how they can continue to feel supported after the program ends. The following are some of the ideas our groups have discussed:

How to Continue to Feel Supported as a Parent

- Continue to meet as a group to support each other once a month. Study some of the other videotape learning modules together.
- Identify two parents from the group who are willing to act as "touch points"—who will keep a set of the tapes and provide a place to meet to discuss parenting issues that arrive.
- Put notes on the refrigerator, telephone, or steering wheel to remind yourself to use specific concepts such as praising good behavior, ignoring inappropriate behavior, and so on.
- Review the notes and handouts with a partner or a friend once every 2 weeks. Reread or listen to audiotape portions of the book.
- Reward yourself once a week for working on parenting skills by going out for coffee or to a movie with a partner or a friend.
- Plan discussions of parenting issues with a partner or friend once every 2 weeks.
- Tell yourself you are doing a good job!
- Set aside some time to relax and refuel your energy on a daily basis.
- Recognize that it is okay for parents and children to make mistakes.

An ongoing theme reiterated by the therapist throughout the training program is that it is not easy to be a parent. It is a difficult challenge that very few of us are adequately prepared for. One of the most common mistakes that adults make in relating to children is to go for the short-term payoffs (e.g., give in to a child's tantrum to stop the unpleasant behavior) at the expenses of the long-term consequences (the child learns to have tantrums to get what he or she wants). We emphasize that although the parenting skills presented in this program need to be repeated *hundreds* of times and take a lot of work, the long-term benefits make it worth the effort—helping a child to become a self-confident, creative, nonviolent, and happy individual. As one of our parents so aptly put it, *"You mean there is no magic moondust?"* No, we have no magic moondust to sprinkle here; rather, our objective is to encourage parents to be patient with themselves and to be committed to their growth as parents as well as their children's growth and development.

CONCLUSIONS

This chapter has provided a description of a research-based parent training program designed to prevent and treat conduct problems in young children. Research studies have given us clear guidelines about some of the critical elements of successful parenting programs. The content of parenting programs needs to be broadly based, focusing on contextual and family interpersonal issues as well as specific parenting skills. It needs to include cognitive, affective, and behavioral components. The methods need to be performance-based, including creative use of role plays, videotape modeling, direct feedback, and home practice assignments. Another essential ingredient in successful parenting training is the elusive, difficult-to-define therapeutic mix of applied science, creativity, and caring. We believe that it is the creative art of collaboration with parents that is key to the success of parenting programs. The therapist must be extraordinarily skilled in collaborating with families in ways that promote parents' self-management, sense of competency, empowerment, and hope for themselves and their children. Additionally, by promoting collaboration not just between the therapist and parent, but also among groups of parents and with teachers and other community members, we aim to strengthen parents' awareness of the tremendous and largely untapped support that can be developed both within their families and in their communities. If we can achieve these aims, we have a structure that has a possibility of strengthening families and communities over time.

REFERENCES

Achenbach, T. M., & Edelbrock, C. S. (1991). *Manual for the child behavior checklist and revised child behavior profile.* Burlington, VT: University Associates in Psychiatry.

Backeland, F., & Lundwall, L. (1975). Dropping out of treatment: A critical review. *Psychological Bulletin, 82,* 738–783.

Bandura, A. (1977). *Social learning theory.* Englewood Cliffs, NJ: Prentice-Hall.

Bandura, A. (1982). Self-efficacy mechanisms in human agency. *American Psychologist, 84,* 191–215.

Bandura, A. (1989). Regulation of cognitive processes through perceived self-efficacy. *Developmental Psychology, 25,* 729–735.

Bierman, K. L., Miller, C. M., & Stabb, S. (1987). Improving the social behavior and peer acceptance of rejected boys: Effects of social skill training with instructions and prohibitions. *Journal of Consulting and Clinical Psychology, 55,* 194–200.

Campbell, S. B. (1991). Longitudinal studies of active and aggressive preschoolers: Individual differences in early behavior and outcome. In D. Cicchetti &

S. L. Toth (Eds.), *Rochester Symposium on Developmental Psychopathology* (pp. 57–90). Hillsdale, NJ: Erlbaum.

Campbell, S. B., & Ewing, L. J. (1990). Follow-up of hard-to-manage preschoolers: Adjustment at age 9 and predictors of continuing symptoms. *Journal of Child Psychology and Psychiatry, 31*(6), 871–889.

Coie, J. D. (1990a). Adapting intervention to the problems of aggressive and disruptive rejected children. In S. R. Asher & J. D. Coie (Eds.), *Peer rejection in childhood* (pp. 309–337). Cambridge, England: Cambridge University Press.

Coie, J. D. (1990b). Toward a theory of peer rejection. In S. R. Asher & J. D. Coie (Eds.), *Peer rejection in childhood* (pp. 365–398). Cambridge, England: Cambridge University Press.

Crowther, J. K., Bond, L. A., & Rolf, J. E. (1981). The incidence, prevalence, and severity of behavior disorders among preschool-aged children in day care. *Journal of Abnormal Child Psychology, 9,* 23–42.

Dadds, M. R., Schwartz, M. R., & Sanders, M. R. (1987). Marital discord and treatment outcome in behavioral treatment of child conduct disorders. *Journal of Consulting and Clinical Psychology, 16,* 192–203.

Dodge, K. A., Coie, J. D., Pettit, G. S., & Price, J. M. (1990). Peer status and aggression in boys' groups: Developmental and contextual analyses. *Child Development, 61*(5), 289–309.

Dumas, J. E., & Wahler, R. G. (1983). Predictors of treatment outcome in parent training: Mother insularity and socioeconomic disadvantage. *Behavioral Assessment, 5,* 301–313.

Dweck, C. S. (1975). The role of expectations and attributions in the alleviation of learned helplessness. *Journal of Personality and Social Psychology, 31,* 674–685.

D'Zurilla, T. J., & Goldfried, M. R. (1971). Problem-solving and behavior modification. *Journal of Abnormal Psychology, 78,* 107–126.

D'Zurilla, T. J., & Nezu, A. (1982). Social problem-solving in adults. In P. C. Kendall (Ed.), *Advances in cognitive behavioral research and therapy* (Vol. 1). New York: Academic Press.

Earls, F. (1980). The prevalence of behavior problems in 3-year-old children. *Archives of General Psychiatry, 37,* 1153–1159.

Egeland, B., Kalkoske, M., Gottesman, N., & Erickson, M. F. (1990). Preschool behavior problems: Stability and factors accounting for change. *Journal of Child Psychology and Psychiatry, 31,* 891–909.

Eisler, R. M., Hersen, M., & Agras, W. S. (1973). Effects of videotape and instructional feedback on nonverbal marital interactions: An analogue study. *Behavior Therapy, 4,* 510–558.

Eyberg, S. M. (1992). Assessing therapy outcome with preschool children: Progress and problems. *Journal of Clinical Child Psychology, 21*(3), 306–311.

Eyberg, S. M., & Matarazzo, R. G. (1980). Training parents as therapists: A comparison between individual parent-child interaction training and parent group didactic training. *Journal of Clinical Child Psychology, 36*(2), 492–499.

Fisher, M., Rolf, J. E., Hasazi, J. E., & Cummings, L. (1984). Follow-up of a preschool epidemiological sample: Cross-age continuities and predictions of later adjustment with internalizing and externalizing dimensions of behavior. *Child Development, 55,* 137–150.

Forehand, R. L., Furey, W. M., & McMahon, R. J. (1984). The role of maternal distress in a parent training program to modify child noncompliance. *Behavioral Psychotherapy, 12,* 93–108.

Forehand, R. L., & McMahon, R. J. (1981). *Helping the noncompliant child: A clinician's guide to parent training.* New York: Guilford Press.

Griest, D. L., Forehand, R., Rogers, T., Breiner, J., Furey, W., & Williams, C. A. (1982). Effects of parent enhancement therapy on the treatment of outcome and generalization of a parent training program. *Behaviour Research and Therapy, 20*(5), 429–436.

Hanf, C. (1970). *Shaping mothers to shape their children's behavior.* Portland: University of Oregon Medical School.

Herbert, M. (1987). *Behavioural treatment of children with problems: A practice manual.* London: Academic Press.

Hobbs, N. (1982). *The troubled and troubling child.* San Francisco: Jossey-Bass.

Janis, I. L., & Mann, L. (1977). *Decision making: A psychological analysis of conflict, choice, and commitment.* New York: Free Press.

Jenkins, S. (1980). Behavior problems in preschool children. *Journal of Child Psychology and Psychiatry, 21,* 5–18.

Kazdin, A. (1985). *Treatment of antisocial behavior in children and adolescents.* Homewood, IL: Dorsey Press.

Lahey, B. B., Loeber, R. L., Quay, H. C., Frick, P. J., & Grimm, J. (1992). Oppositional defiant and conduct disorders: Issue to be resolved for *DSM-IV. Journal of the American Academy of Child and Adolescent Psychiatry, 31*(3).

Landy, S., & Peters, R. D. (1991, February). Understanding and treating the hyper aggressive toddler. *Zero to Three,* 22–31.

Loeber, R. (1985). Patterns and development of antisocial child behavior. In G. J. Whitehurst (Ed.), *Annals of child development* (Vol. 2, pp. 77–116). New York: JAI Press.

Loeber, R. (1990). Subtypes of conduct disorder [letter]. *Journal of the American Academy of Child and Adolescent Psychiatry, 29*(5), 837–838.

Loeber, R. (1991). Antisocial behavior: More enduring than changeable? *Journal of the American Academy of Child and Adolescent Psychiatry, 30,* 393–397.

McMahon, R. J., & Forehand, R. (1984). Parent training for the noncompliant child: Treatment outcome, generalization, and adjunctive therapy procedures. In R. F. Dangel & R. A. Polster (Eds.), *Parent training: Foundations of research and practice* (pp. 298–328). New York: Guilford Press.

McMahon, R. J., Forehand, R., Griest, D. L., & Wells, K. (1981). Who drops out of treatment during parent behavioral training? *Behavioral Counseling Quarterly, 1,* 79–85.

Meichenbaum, D., & Turk, D. (1987). *Facilitating treatment adherence: A practitioner's guidebook.* New York: Plenum Press.

Offord, D. R., Boyle, M. H., & Szatmari, P. (1987). Ontario Child Health Study II: Six month prevalence of disorder and rates of service utilization. *Archives of General Psychiatry, 44,* 832–836.

Ogbu, J. (1978). *Minority education and caste: The American system in cross-cultural perspective.* New York: Academic Press.

Patterson, G. R. (1982). *Coercive family process.* Eugene, OR: Castalia Press.

Patterson, G. R. (1986). Performance models for antisocial boys. *American Psychologist, 41*(4), 432–444.

Patterson, G. R., DeBaryshe, B. D., & Ramsey, E. (1989). A developmental perspective on antisocial behavior. *American Psychologist, 44*(2), 329–335.

Patterson, G. R., & Forgatch, M. S. (1985). Therapist behavior as a determinant for client noncompliance: A paradox for the behavior modifier. *Journal of Consulting and Clinical Psychology, 53*(6), 846–851.

Reid, J., Taplin, P., & Loeber, R. (1981). A social interactional approach to the treatment of abusive families. In R. B. Stuart (Ed.), *Violent behavior: Social learning approaches to prediction management and treatment* (pp. 83–101). New York: Brunner/Mazel.

Richman, N., & Graham, P. (1975). A behavioral screening questionnaire for use with 3-year-old children: Some preliminary findings. *Journal of Child Psychology and Psychiatry, 16,* 277–287.

Richman, N., Stevenson, L., & Graham, P. J. (1982). *Pre-school to school: A behavioural study.* London: Academic Press.

Robinson, E. A., Eyberg, S. M., & Ross, A. W. (1980). The standardization of an inventory of child conduct problem behaviors. *Journal of Clinical Child Psychology, 9,* 22–28.

Rose, S. L., Rose, S. A., & Feldman, J. (1989). Stability of behavior problems in very young children. *Development and Psychopathology, 1,* 5–20.

Seligman, M. E. P. (1975). *Helplessness.* San Francisco: Freeman.

Spitzer, A., Webster-Stratton, C., & Hollinsworth, T. (1991). Coping with conduct-problem children: Parents gaining knowledge and control. *Journal of Clinical Child Psychology, 20,* 413–427.

Twentyman, C. T., & McFall, R. M. (1975). Behavioral training of social skills in shy males. *Journal of Consulting and Clinical Psychology, 43,* 384–395.

Wahler, R. G., & Afton, A. D. (1980). Attentional processes in insular and noninsular mothers. *Child Behavior Therapy, 2,* 25–41.

Webster-Stratton, C. (1982). The long term effects of a videotape modeling parent education program: Comparison of immediate and one year follow-up results. *Behavior Therapy, 13,* 702–714.

Webster-Stratton, C. (1984). Randomized trial of two parent-training programs for families with conduct-disordered children. *Journal of Consulting and Clinical Psychology, 52*(4), 666–678.

Webster-Stratton, C. (1985a). The effects of father involvement in parent training for conduct problem children. *Journal of Child Psychology and Psychiatry, 26,* 801–810.

Webster-Stratton, C. (1985b). Predictors of treatment outcome in parent training for conduct disordered children. *Behavior Therapy, 16,* 223–243.

Webster-Stratton, C. (1989). Systematic comparison of consumer satisfaction of three cost-effective parent training programs for conduct problem children. *Behavior Therapy, 20,* 103–115.

Webster-Stratton, C. (1990a). Enhancing the effectiveness of self-administered videotape parent training for families with conduct-problem children. *Journal of Abnormal Child Psychology, 18,* 479–492.

Webster-Stratton, C. (1990b). Long-term follow-up of families with young conduct problem children: From preschool to grade school. *Journal of Clinical Child Psychology, 19*(2), 144–149.

Webster-Stratton, C. (1992). *The incredible years: A trouble-shooting guide for parents of children ages 3–8 years.* Toronto, Canada: Umbrella Press.

Webster-Stratton, C. (1994). Advancing videotape parent training: A comparison study. *Journal of Consulting and Clinical Psychology, 62,* 583–593.

Webster-Stratton, C. (1995). *Preventing conduct problems in Head Start children: Preliminary short term results.* Paper presented at the meeting of the Society for Research in Child Development, Indianapolis.

Webster-Stratton, C. (1996). Videotape modeling intervention programs for families of young children with oppositional defiant disorder or conduct disorder. In P. S. Jensen & E. D. Hibbs (Eds.), *Psychosocial treatments for child and adolescent disorders: Empirically based approaches* (pp. 435–474). Washington, DC: American Psychological Association.

Webster-Stratton, C. (1997). Treating children with early-onset conduct problems: A comparison of child and parent training interventions. *Journal of Consulting and Clinical Psychology, 65,* 93–109.

Webster-Stratton, C., & Hammond, M. (1990). Predictors of treatment outcome in parent training for families with conduct problem children. *Behavior Therapy, 21,* 319–337.

Webster-Stratton, C., & Herbert, M. (1994). *Troubled families—Problem children: Working with parents: A collaborative process.* Chichester, England: Wiley.

Webster-Stratton, C., Hollinsworth, T., & Kolpacoff, M. (1989). The long-term effectiveness and clinical significance of three cost-effective training programs for families with conduct-problem children. *Journal of Consulting and Clinical Psychology, 57*(4), 550–553.

Webster-Stratton, C., Kolpacoff, M., & Hollinsworth, T. (1988). Self-administered videotape therapy for families with conduct-problem children: Comparison with two cost-effective treatments and a control group. *Journal of Consulting and Clinical Psychology, 56*(4), 558–566.

White, J., Moffit, T., Earls, F., & Robins, L. (1990). Preschool predictors of persistent conduct disorder and delinquency. *Criminology, 28,* 443–454.

CHAPTER 4

Parent Training Interventions for Sibling Conflict

CHARLOTTE JOHNSTON and WENDY FREEMAN

From the biblical story of Cain and Abel to television's depictions of Bart and Lisa Simpson, conflicts in sibling relationships have fueled numerous works of both fiction and biography, and have undoubtedly been the topic of many hours of psychotherapy. Relationships with siblings are a major aspect of most people's lives. Sibling relationships are often the only intimate, daily relationships with peers that individuals experience prior to adulthood, and bonds with siblings often last longer than any other relationship in a person's life. During childhood, sibling relationships also provide a unique training ground for the acquisition and practice of social and life skills. Given the prevalence, importance, strength, and duration of sibling relationships, one might expect them to have been the subject of great psychological scrutiny. In fact, sibling relationships have not been extensively studied. In particular, clinical psychology, perhaps because of its tendency to focus on individual differences and diagnoses, has paid little attention to problems in sibling relationships.

We express our appreciation to Georgia Tiedemann who developed a parent training program for sibling sharing and offered many insightful comments on the material of this chapter. Thanks also to members of the Parenting Lab for their comments on the chapter. This chapter was written with assistance from grants to the first author from the University of British Columbia and the British Columbia Health Research Foundation. The second author was funded by a fellowship from the National Health and Research Development Program.

This chapter begins with a brief review of the literature describing normative sibling relationships and factors that influence interactions between siblings. Following this introduction, attention switches to defining and assessing conflict in the sibling relationship. Then, the chapter focuses on descriptions of parent training interventions that have been employed to reduce sibling conflict. General characteristics of the parent training efforts are described, and the components of such interventions are outlined in detail and illustrated using case examples.

DESCRIPTION OF SIBLING RELATIONSHIPS

Historically, research on sibling interactions was focused on the influence of variables such as birth order, family size, age, and gender of the siblings, and child personalities (Furman, 1995), often producing diverse findings across studies. For example, Furman and Buhrmester (1985) found greater reported warmth, intimacy, prosocial behavior, and companionship among same-sex versus mixed-sex siblings. In contrast, Minnett, Vandell, and Santrock (1983) found more observed aggressive and dominant behavior among same- versus mixed-sex siblings. Regarding age effects, Corter, Pepler, and Abramovitch (1982) observed mixed-sex dyads and noted that older siblings were more prosocial than younger siblings and that the amount of prosocial interaction increased as the age gap between the siblings grew. In contrast, Dunn (1983) found no effects of age spacing on sibling interactions.

Individual child characteristics are also predictive of the quality of the sibling relationship. For example, Patterson (1984, 1986) has highlighted the importance of sibling relationships in families of children with aggressive behaviors. His and others' studies (e.g., Brody & Stoneman, 1987; Mash & Johnston, 1983) show that, compared with nonclinic families, the rates of sibling conflict are elevated in families of aggressive children and that siblings of aggressive children display elevated rates of deviant behavior. Patterson argues that, among these clinic-referred families, the sibling relationship serves as a training ground for deviant behavior with the siblings teaching each other a set of increasingly aversive, coercive behaviors. Dunn and Munn (1986a), studying nonclinic, preschool siblings in home interactions also found evidence of this reciprocity of sibling behavior. For example, they found significant correlations between the behaviors of the siblings (positive linked to positive and negative to negative) and that, over time, siblings were more likely to be cooperative if their siblings had been cooperative during previous interactions. An encouraging finding reported in several empirical studies is that when parents participate in parent training programs to learn how to modify a deviant child's behavior, behavioral improvements are often reported for both the target child and for the untreated siblings (e.g., Arnold, Levine, & Patterson, 1975; Eyberg & Robinson, 1982; Humphreys, Forehand, McMahon, & Roberts, 1978; Klein, Alexander, & Parsons, 1977).

Although informative, this research focusing on the configuration of the sibling dyad or on individual child characteristics has offered limited insight into the behavioral aspects of sibling relationships, how parenting behavior relates to sibling interactions, or the situational events that influence sibling behavior. From a clinical perspective, although sibling spacing and gender may have important effects on sibling conflict, such variables hold little potential in suggesting clinical interventions. However, a number of more recent studies, many of them observational in nature, have provided a glimpse into the parenting and situational stimuli related to sibling conflict. These studies inform and support strategies that can be used in the clinical context to reduce sibling conflict.

One set of variables that has received considerable research attention, with important implications for designing clinical interventions, is the role of parental presence and parental intervention in sibling conflict. Corter and colleagues have conducted both naturalistic and experimental studies of the effects of parental presence on sibling interactions (Corter, Abramovitch, & Pepler, 1983; Corter et al., 1982). The results with preschool and elementary-school ages are consistent across both correlational and experimental designs in showing that maternal presence is associated with increases in the level of conflict between siblings. However, the reason for this increased conflict in mother-present situations is less clear. Nor do many studies speak directly to the question of which parenting responses are associated with decreases in sibling conflict.

At a general level, studies have demonstrated a relationship between positive parent-child interactions and positive sibling interactions and between negative parent-child interactions and sibling conflict (Brody, Stoneman, & Burke, 1987; Dunn & Kendrick, 1982; Hetherington, 1988; Volling & Belsky, 1992). Observing mother and sibling interactions in the home, Ross, Filyer, Lollis, Perlman, and Martin (1994) found that although mothers tended to ignore sibling behaviors such as disagreeing, bossing, and verbal aggression, they were still observed to intervene in approximately 50% of sibling conflicts. When mothers did intervene, they seldom acted so as to favor one sibling over the other, and instead generally reinforced family rules and mediated equitable solutions to the conflicts. Dunn and Munn (1986b) also found that mothers intervened about half the time in preschool-age sibling disputes. Their study indicated that this maternal intervention predicted increases in both conciliation and aggression in the sibling relationship over time.

Thus, although theorists may offer clear-cut advice to parents regarding whether to intervene or to ignore sibling conflict, the empirical evidence regarding the effects of parental intervention is mixed and seldom provides a systematic consideration of which interventions are most appropriate at which child ages. Across studies with children ranging from 2 to 12 years of age, evidence can be found to indicate decreases in sibling fighting both when parents are taught to ignore the conflicts (e.g., Kelly & Main, 1979) and when parents are taught to intervene with consequences for both cooperative play and for fighting (e.g., O'Leary, O'Leary, & Becker, 1967; Olson & Roberts, 1987; Vickerman, Reed, & Roberts, 1997). Interestingly, in a small study soliciting children's opinions regarding parental interventions into sibling conflicts, Prochaska and Prochaska (1985) found that children rated rewards for cooperation, negative consequences for fighting, and distraction as equal in their impact, although all were rated as only slightly effective. Ignoring fights or imitating the fighting were parenting responses that were rated as likely to *increase* the conflict.

Another clinically relevant aspect of parental behavior that has been related to sibling relationships is the parent's differential treatment of the siblings. For example, Conger and Conger (1994) employed a cross-lagged panel design to show that differential parental hostility toward siblings predicted increases in sibling delinquency 2 years later. Other studies echo this finding of inequality in parental treatment of siblings being related to negative outcomes such as sibling conflict and child problems (e.g., Brody et al., 1987; Bryant & Crockenberg, 1980; Stocker, Dunn, & Plomin, 1989). Corter et al. (1983) found greater differences in mother's positive treatment of mixed-sex compared with same-sex siblings and suggest that this difference in maternal treatment may explain the increased antagonism often reported for mixed-sex versus same-sex sibling dyads. The Sibling Inventory of Differential Experience (Daniel & Plomin, 1985) is a parent-completed questionnaire that assesses differential parental control and affection toward siblings. Although not yet used in the clinical context, this measure may hold potential in assessing this important predictor of sibling conflict and outcome.

Finally, a scattering of studies exists looking at situational determinants of sibling conflict. Ross et al. (1994), observing sibling interactions in the home, reported that the most common source of sibling conflict was disagreement regarding rights of toy possession. Indeed, situations that involve the presentation of a limited number of highly desirable toys (Oden, Wheeler, & Herzberger, 1984; Ramsey, 1986), a reduction in the number of previously available toys (Getz & Berndt, 1982), or giving children toys as personal possessions (Tiedemann, Cross-Calvert, Johnston, Palme, & McMahon, 1987) all act to decrease sharing and increase conflict among children. The preceding studies have been conducted with preschool and early elementary-school-age children. Different situations would be expected to be problematic among older children and adolescents.

PREVALENCE AND ASSESSMENT OF SIBLING CONFLICT

From studies concerned with sibling relationships in nonclinical samples, one can ascertain that, although most sibling interactions are of a positive nature (Newman, 1994; Prochaska & Prochaska, 1985), conflict is *not* a rare event nor is it always benign. Across a range of studies, conducted both in home and laboratory settings, sibling conflicts have been observed to occur up to eight times per hour (Berndt & Bulleit, 1985; Dunn & Munn, 1986b). The results from epidemiological or survey studies confirm these observational findings. For example, Steinmetz (1978) reported that, in a sample of 57 randomly selected families with preschool to adolescent children, approximately 70% reported physical violence between siblings. Straus, Gelles, and Steinmetz (1980) found that, although most conflict among siblings is relatively mild (e.g., slapping, shoving), in a 1-year period, 42% of children were kicked, bitten, or punched by siblings, and 3% of children used a weapon in a fight with a sibling.

Despite the increasing recognition of the prevalence and potentially dangerous severity of sibling conflict, the topic remains infrequently targeted within the clinical literature. Among the many factors that stand as potential contributors to this neglect, the lack of assessment methods and classification schemes for describing sibling relationship problems are an obvious obstacle to both empirical and clinical advancements. For example, although the *DSM-IV* (American Psychiatric Association, 1994) and *ICD-10* (World Health Organization, 1992) both assign sibling relationship problems diagnostic categories, the categories are relatively vaguely defined (*ICD-10* having greater precision and empirical basis than *DSM-IV*). In addition, few psychometrically sound assessment tools exist, and the normative information on which to base classification decisions is not readily available (Carter & Volkmar, 1992; Mash & Johnston, 1996).

Much of the empirical work on sibling relationships has relied on observational methods for assessing behavior in the sibling relationship. For example, Corter et al. (1982) coded discrete child-to-sibling behaviors as being either prosocial (e.g., sharing, cooperating), antagonistic (e.g., physical aggression, object struggles), or imitative. Dunn and Munn (1986a) also observed sibling interactions in the home, and recorded a range of behaviors including affectionate touches, helping, imitation, smiling, taking objects away, restraining, and appealing to the mother. Although these observational systems and others like them have demonstrated their reliability and worth within the research context, their adaptability to the clinical context has not been investigated. One intriguing development in this area is an analogue measure created by Roberts, Arnold, and Mangum (1992). The Sibling Conflict Resolution Scale presents sibling conflict scenarios and asks children to "show me what you would do." Children's responses to the conflict situations are videotaped and coded as sophisticated verbal coping, verbal coping, neutral, verbal coercion, or motoric coercion. This measure has demonstrated good interrater reliability in coding, reasonable stability, and expected correlations with child characteristics. Although the authors caution that the measure is not yet validated as a clinical instrument, preliminary data suggests that it is sensitive to treatment changes.

Pencil-and-paper measures also have been developed to assess either children's or parents' perceptions of the sibling relationship. For example, using items based on children's reports of their relationships, Furman and Buhrmester (1985) created the Sibling Relationship Questionnaire, which taps four dimensions of sibling relationships including warmth and closeness, relative power and status, conflict, and rivalry. This measure was developed using children in Grades 5 and 6, has revealed good psychometric properties, and shows meaningful correlations with family constellation variables, such as age spacing of siblings and gender composition of sibling dyads. Normative data are not available. Graham-Bermann and Cutler (1994) have also developed a questionnaire concerning sibling relationships, The Brother-Sister Questionnaire. This measure is appropriate for adult subjects and was designed to discriminate normative from dysfunctional sibling relationships. Factor analysis of this 35-item measure revealed four factors: empathy, boundary maintenance, similarity, and coercion. The measure has good psychometric properties and reliably discriminates abusive and nonabusive sibling dyads. Again, normative data are not available.

Although several potentially promising measures exist, further developments in the assessment and classification of sibling relationships and relationship problems are sorely needed. The developmental status of siblings and age-appropriate normative information are particular areas of concern in the development of assessment and classification techniques. Advances in assessment will serve to facilitate the development and evaluation of effective treatments for this common childhood problem.

PARENT TRAINING INTERVENTIONS
FOR SIBLING CONFLICT

A small and rather eclectic literature exists describing interventions that parents have been taught with the aim of improving sibling relationships.

These interventions cover a range of child age groups, treatment formats, and treatment techniques. However, treatment outcome studies evaluating the efficacy of parenting interventions for sibling conflict using comparative treatments, no-treatment, or wait-list control group designs are rare. Also rare are systematic comparisons of the effects of interventions across gender and child age. For example, it appears reasonable that in resolving sibling conflicts, more directive parenting strategies will be needed when children are younger and have not yet acquired skills for negotiating conflict. As siblings age, more effective parenting strategies may focus less on parent-imposed solutions and more on promotion of child-generated resolutions. This proposition is reasonable, but, empirical evidence is lacking. Nevertheless, several studies and case descriptions of parenting interventions that improve sibling relationships exist and, combined with descriptions of school interventions to promote positive peer relations, provide a basic outline of effective strategies that can be incorporated into parent training to reduce sibling conflict. In describing the existing sibling interventions, we begin with a review of the range of clients, therapists, and formats that have been reported in the literature. Then, several recommended components for a parent training intervention to reduce sibling conflict are outlined.

CLIENT CHARACTERISTICS

Interventions to improve sibling relationships have been proposed for several target populations. For example, interventions have been developed for children with mental retardation (e.g., Powell, Salzberg, Rule, Levy, & Itzkowitz, 1983) and autism (e.g., Belchic & Harris, 1994; Celiberti & Harris, 1993; Strain & Danko, 1995), who do not spontaneously initiate normative levels of interaction with their brothers and sisters. The interventions applied with these populations typically focus on building positive relations among these children and siblings with normal development.

Other parenting interventions have focused specifically on the reduction of sibling conflict in either community (e.g., Leitenberg, Burchard, Burchard, Fuller, & Lysaght, 1977; Sloane, Endo, Hawkes, & Jenson, 1990) or clinic-referred families (e.g., Olson & Roberts, 1987). These interventions have been conducted with single mothers (e.g., Kelly & Main, 1979) as well as in two-parent families (e.g., Reid & Donovan, 1990). In some cases, the sibling-directed behavior of a specific child has been targeted for intervention (Allison & Allison, 1971; Houghton, 1991), and in others the interactive behavior of two or more siblings is targeted for treatment (e.g., Leitenberg et al., 1977; Olson & Roberts, 1987). Finally, interventions for sibling conflict have been proposed for children spanning several age groups ranging from preschoolers (e.g., Ramamurti & Devi, 1986) to adolescents (e.g., Houghton, 1991).

THERAPIST CHARACTERISTICS

A range of individuals have served as therapists in sibling interventions. In interventions designed to encourage the initiation of interactions between children with social skill deficits and their siblings, both therapists (e.g., Belchic & Harris, 1994) and parents who have been trained by therapists (e.g., Powell et al., 1983; Strain & Danko, 1995) have been employed to implement the treatments. Other investigations have implemented intervention strategies by both a therapist/experimenter and parent sequentially. O'Leary et al. (1967) used a trained experimenter in the first phase of treatment to implement a token reinforcement system and a time-out from reinforcement procedure. In the second phase of treatment, control over implementation of the procedures was transferred to the mother. In addition, normally-developing brothers and sisters have been trained to implement interventions to facilitate social interactions with their targeted sibling. Celiberti and Harris (1993) describe a treatment program in which a therapist taught children skills to enhance play interactions with their siblings with autism. These children were trained to elicit and praise play behaviors, and to prompt their sibling with autism when he or she was unresponsive to the child's initiation efforts.

Looking at interventions to reduce sibling conflict, there are reports in the literature of therapists and parents implementing the treatment program (e.g., Leitenberg et al., 1977; Olson & Roberts, 1987), reports of parents implementing the intervention after being trained by a therapist (e.g., Houghton, 1991), and reports of parents implementing the intervention after reading self-instructional booklets (e.g., Sloane et al., 1990).

PARENT TRAINING FORMAT

Several formats have been reported for training parents to manage sibling relations. Some papers report training only mothers to manage sibling interactions (e.g., Tiedemann & Johnston, 1992), whereas others describe interventions involving the entire family (e.g., Kelly & Main, 1979; Reid & Donovan, 1990). Studies of interventions targeting sibling relationships have also had families meeting individually with a therapist (e.g., Houghton, 1991) or in group formats with several families together meeting with a therapist (e.g., Tiedemann & Johnston, 1992). One study that compared an individually-administered and group-administered parent training program to promote sharing between young siblings found that the two treatment formats did not differ on most outcome measures (e.g., parent reports of child behavior), although only the individual format produced a significant improvement in observed sibling behavior (Tiedemann & Johnston, 1992). Training parents to manage sibling relationships has also occurred in both the clinic setting (e.g., Olson & Roberts, 1987; Tiedemann & Johnston, 1992) and in family's homes (e.g., Leitenberg et al., 1977). Finally, parents have been successfully trained using booklets rather than direct therapist contact (Sloane et al., 1990).

COMPONENTS OF PARENT TRAINING INTERVENTIONS FOR SIBLING CONFLICT

GENERAL INFORMATION

Because parents may lack accurate or adequate knowledge, an early component in a program of parent training for sibling conflict might involve imparting basic information to parents regarding child behavior or sibling relationships. John McDermott (1980), in his book titled *Raising Cain (and Abel Too)*, outlines many myths concerning sibling relationships that parents may believe (e.g., everyone else's children get along well, siblings will be reasonable with each other if parents spend enough time reasoning with the children). Thus, early in treatment the therapist is wise to examine parents' assumptions about siblings and sibling relationships and to work to dispel any inappropriate or erroneous beliefs. The provision of normative developmental information about sibling relationships and conflict may help parents to gain realistic expectations with regard to their children's interactions with one another and how these interactions may change over time. Following this principle, in a parent training program to promote sharing between young siblings, Tiedemann and Johnston (1992) devoted the first treatment session to providing information about the development of sharing and sibling relationships, and to assisting mothers in establishing age-appropriate expectations for sibling sharing.

A mother who presented at our clinic with serious concerns regarding the lack of sharing between her two young children, provides an illustration of the importance of providing developmental information to parents. In particular, the mother described her 18-month-old son as very selfish. When asked to operationalize this description, she reported that, over the past couple of months, he had begun to frequently declare his ownership of toys and household possessions, and seemed unable to understand that his older sister also wanted to play with the toys. She said that her son's favorite expression was "mine!" The therapist began by providing developmental information to the mother regarding egocentrism and the development of autonomy and identity during toddlerhood. This information, suggesting that many of the child's behaviors were developmentally appropriate and reflected his stage of development, rather than disposition, relieved the mother's anxiety and allowed her to develop more appropriate expectations for relations between her children.

Values, Goals, and Rules

Another early component in parent training might involve collaborative work between the parents and therapist to clarify the parents' values and goals regarding sibling conflict and sibling relationships. Once these are clarified, the therapist and parents can move to develop "house rules" and parenting guidelines for managing sibling conflict that are congruent with those parental goals and values. Providing information about parenting approaches that promote healthy child development and prosocial child behaviors (e.g., warm and responsive care, emphasis on positive behaviors and proactive techniques, firm and consistent discipline) can assist parents in formulating their own approaches to parenting and in setting boundaries around the parenting strategies they will employ in responding to sibling conflict.

Consideration of the family's ethnic background as well as the match between the values of this background and the assumptions underlying particular intervention strategies is also essential (Short & Johnston, 1994). Many of the assumptions of North American-developed, behavioral parenting programs (e.g., a focus on the nuclear family), may be incongruous with the values of various ethnocultural groups (e.g., a focus on extended families).

Because favoritism and inequality in parental treatment of siblings have been related to sibling conflict, interventions should encourage parents to develop equitable (not necessarily identical) ways of treating siblings and to avoid comparing siblings in areas such as appearance, achievement, or ability (Leung & Robson, 1991). One example of the importance of helping parents develop fairness in their allocation of time and attention between siblings is presented by Kelly and Main (1979). This case study describes a single mother who reported intense conflict between her 5- and 8-year-old sons. Included in the 10-session intervention was the initiation of "special time" between the mother and each child. After experimenting with various time arrangements, the mother established 30 minutes of one-to-one time with each of her children on alternating evenings just before bedtime. This, in combination with other strategies, resulted in significant improvement in the children's interactions. Also, a parent training program developed by Cunningham (1990) devotes one session to discussing strategies for parents to use in attending simultaneously to two siblings and in balancing this attention.

In working with two-parent families or blended families, coparenting issues may also need to be addressed in early sessions of parent training. Parental disagreement with regard to resolving sibling disputes can lead children to reject parental authority in conflict resolution (Reid & Donovan, 1990). Empirical studies routinely find an association between coparenting disagreement and child behavior problems (e.g., Dadds & Powell, 1991; Johnston & Behrenz, 1993; Jouriles et al., 1991). Furthermore, the exhibition of interparent conflict may provide a model of sibling antagonism for children (Emery, 1982). Reid and Donovan (1990) describe a family intervention in which initial treatment sessions are spent developing a working alliance between the mother and father and assisting them in negotiating mutually agreed-on parenting rules. In this program, once the parents can present with a united front, the parents and children are seen together, and the therapist guides the family in problem-solving tasks surrounding sibling conflict.

Reid and Donovan provide a case example of this program's use with a couple complaining of frequent physical fighting among their three sons, aged 17, 15, and 13 years. Intervention for this family comprised 20 sessions, the first 10 of which involved only the parents and focused on their disagreement over discipline. In a not uncommon presentation, the wife considered her spouse too strict, and the husband considered his wife too lenient in dealing with the sons. The therapist guided the couple in problem solving, and new rules were developed for both parents to follow in disciplining the children (e.g., no physical punishment, reflect before assigning consequences for misbehavior, follow through with consequences). The remaining 10 sessions involved both the children and parents and during these sessions, specific rules were generated for the boys to follow in sibling interactions (e.g., "back off" when provoked rather than attack).

Antecedents

Another important component of treatment is training parents to recognize and foster antecedent conditions that promote positive interactions between their children, and to reduce exposure to situations that promote sibling conflict. These strategies can be thought of as environmental engineering; rearranging or avoiding environmental situations that often lead to sibling conflict and setting up situations conducive to positive sibling relationships. For example, upon the birth of a new sibling, authors have stressed the importance of making existing children feel that they are an essential part of the family, encouraging older siblings to be active participants in the care of the new sibling, and praising older siblings for their assistance (e.g., Leung & Robson, 1991). In a study by Ramamurti and Devi (1986) involving 60 families with children aged between 0 and 4 years of age, mothers were instructed in ways to involve the older sibling in the day-to-day care and handling of the younger child. Families were interviewed and observed before this intervention and 2 months following treatment, and a significant reduction in sibling rivalry (i.e., older children's overt expressions of jealousy, hostility, and intolerance toward their younger siblings) was found.

Regarding more proximal antecedents to cooperative versus conflictual sibling interactions, research examining the effects of particular toys on children's interactions has consistently found that the toys most likely to be used cooperatively by young children include blocks, small toy cars and trucks, dolls and dollhouse equipment, housekeeping and kitchen toys, large toys or structures such as seesaws and climbing apparatuses, and wagons (e.g., Quilitich & Risley, 1973; Stoneman, Cantrell, & Hoover-Dempsey, 1983). On the other hand, the toys least likely to be shared and most likely to be fought over tend to be fine-motor construction materials such as Tinkertoys, beads, puzzles, and arts and crafts supplies (e.g., Hendrickson, Strain, Tremblay, & Shores, 1982). Ramsey (1986) suggests that objects which function as props in fantasy play (e.g., dolls, dishes) or which can be easily used by more than one child (e.g., wagon, climbing apparatus) are especially conducive to sharing between children, whereas objects which must be accumulated to be used (e.g., craft materials, Tinkertoys) are not easily shared and incite conflict.

Sloane (1988) lists several situations that commonly lead to conflict between siblings: competition for toys, television, telephone, and who goes first; and disagreements about things such as who owns what toy, whose turn it is to do the dishes, and who gets to choose the television program. Sloane goes on to describe antecedent strategies for preventing conflict in these common situations. Parents can be trained to use record keeping (e.g., posting a list in the kitchen with the date and name of the person who last took out the garbage, keeping a list to indicate whose turn it is to choose what to watch on television), labeling children's personal possessions if they are not joint possessions and are frequently fought over, and timing (e.g., limiting each child's telephone or computer time to 20 minutes, posting the rule, and putting a timer by the phone or computer). Reid and Donovan (1990), in their intervention with the family of three adolescent sons, also explored the typical precipitants to the children's conflict (e.g., name-calling and taking each other's belongings without asking) and assisted the family in problem solving to rearrange these conflict-inducing situations.

A clinical case example of the importance of situational antecedents is provided by a mother who reported extreme levels of fighting between her two preschool children. The mother described what she referred to as "the arsenic hour," indicating that the sibling fighting was worst during the hour before dinner when she was preparing the evening meal. At the encouragement of the therapist, the mother also identified situations where her children were most likely to be cooperative and to get along well. She reported that the children frequently interacted well and had fun while watching their favorite television show which played after dinner. With the help of a VCR (videocasette recorder), the mother was able to institute a change in routine that involved taping the show and playing it during the arsenic hour the next day. This simple change in antecedent conditions was reported to have an immediate effect in reducing sibling conflicts during the hour before dinner.

TEACHING CHILDREN SKILLS

In a study of normal sibling interactions, Howe and associates (1996) found that the extent to which mothers socialize their children in the expression of emotions was related to the children's ability to offer positive caretaking for younger siblings. Other research has also found that children with more advanced social cognitive skills, such as perspective taking and social sensitivity, have more positive sibling relationships (Light, 1979; Stewart & Marvin, 1984). Given these findings, teaching parents to educate their children in social skills that will enhance sibling relationships appears to be a reasonable and important component of parent training for sibling conflict.

Tiedemann and Johnston (1992) evaluated a five-session parent training program designed to promote sharing between young siblings. The program was adapted from therapist-implemented sharing interventions developed by Barton and Ascione (1979) and Bryant and Budd (1984). Parents were trained to provide children with specific instruction and practice in the component skills of sharing, to give detailed rationales and instructions regarding sharing, and to give feedback about inappropriate sharing-related behavior. The specific sharing skills that parents taught children began with "inviting" and "requesting" followed by "granting requests" and "accepting invitations." Then, parents were trained to instruct children in different ways to share and play together once an invitation or request had been accepted. Parents were also trained to teach their children the skills of "appropriate refusals" and "handling refusals." The final component of the program had parents teach strategies for handling anger and developing constructive alternatives for disputes. Tiedemann and Johnston implemented this program in both group and individual parent training formats, and found that both formats had positive effects on mother reports of sharing behavior compared with a waitlist control group. Treatment effects were generally maintained over a 6-week follow-up period.

In addition to being taught to employ prosocial behaviors in sibling interactions, research suggests that children can also be taught adaptive ways to resolve conflicts. Gentry and Benenson (1993) described an elementary-school-based peer mediation program in which children were trained to be peer conflict managers. The school intervention was implemented in three phases. First, teachers attended a 2-hour presentation describing a school-based conflict management program and were asked to add conflict-awareness exercises into their classroom curriculum for a 1-month period. Next, children in Grades 4 to 6, who were nominated by peers and teachers to be conflict managers, participated in 6 hours of training in communication and conflict resolution skills. Following training, the student conflict managers mediated the conflicts of their peers during recess periods.

Interestingly, such peer mediation programs appear not only to decrease conflicts among peers in the school setting (e.g., Johnson, Johnson, & Dudley, 1992), but also to improve children's behavior in the home setting. Gentry and Benenson (1993) found that parents of children trained to be conflict managers in a school program reported fewer conflicts between their children and siblings in the home following the intervention. Parents also reported that they had to intervene in sibling conflicts less frequently and that the conflict manager child's ability to talk productively with siblings during conflictual interactions improved. Thus, peer conflict management skills taught in school-based programs appear to have application to sibling conflicts in the home. As Tiedemann and Johnston (1992) evaluated the efficacy of a parent-led adaptation of a therapist-implemented sharing intervention, further research should be conducted to examine the efficacy of training parents to teach their children conflict mediation skills.

OPERANT TECHNIQUES

In addition to considering rules and values, altering antecedent conditions, and teaching children social skills, parents should be trained to provide reinforcement for appropriate sibling interactions and negative consequences for sibling conflict. Several such operant techniques have been found effective in the management of sibling conflict and are routinely taught, practiced, and monitored in parent training.

Starting with the reinforcement of appropriate sibling interactions, Leitenberg and colleagues (1977) examined the efficacy of two positive reinforcement techniques, omission training and the reinforcement of an appropriate alternate behavior. These techniques were tested in a sample of six families with two or three children between the ages of 2 and 10 who responded to a newspaper advertisement announcing the study.

These authors found that both reinforcement techniques were effective in reducing the frequency of sibling conflict to approximately 50% of the baseline level. Omission training consisted of reinforcing siblings for not engaging in conflict during a specified time period. During a designated hour in the early evening, siblings were each rewarded with praise and a penny for each 1-minute interval during which no conflict occurred. If conflict occurred, the parent was instructed to withhold the reward and to ignore the children's behavior. The reinforcement of alternate behavior procedure consisted of providing praise and pennies following the first occurrence of appropriate interaction in each 1-minute interval. Again, parents were instructed not to intervene in sibling conflict during the implementation of this procedure. Both of these procedures reduced sibling conflict to a similar extent, and although both procedures also lead to an increase in appropriate interaction between siblings, the increase in appropriate interaction was significantly greater when the reinforcement of appropriate interaction procedure was used.

Houghton (1991) described procedures for reinforcing appropriate sibling behavior in a 14-year-old adolescent male who was physically aggressive with his three younger siblings. The adolescent's mother reported that after school her son would routinely push and direct other physically aggressive behaviors toward his 7-, 10-, and 12-year-old siblings. The mother indicated that she and her husband had tried, unsuccessfully, to alter this behavior using strategies such as parent-child discussions, reprimands, and stopping pocket money. During treatment, a reward program was implemented in which, between 4 P.M. and 5 P.M. each day, the adolescent could earn one star for every 5 minutes of continual prosocial behavior directed toward his siblings. Prosocial behaviors included listening to the youngest sibling read and helping with homework. During the 1-hour period, a maximum of 12 stars could be earned. An agreement was made between the adolescent and his mother that, if he earned a specified number of stars during the week, he could play hockey on Saturday afternoon. Once this program had been successfully implemented, a written contract was negotiated by the child and mother outlining bonus rewards for stars earned in surplus of the number required to play hockey. Observations of aggressive behaviors showed a decline from baseline during the time the star program was in effect, and a further decline in aggressive behaviors when the contract was added to the star program.

Even when a parent reinforces appropriate sibling interactions, sibling conflicts inevitably occur. Therefore, parenting strategies for responding to conflict are essential. Some conflicts between siblings can be reduced by the parent withdrawing contingent attention. As argued by Levi, Buskila, and Gerzi (1977) and others, some of children's conflicts occur in an effort to gain parental attention. Parent intervention in such conflicts, in turn, reinforces the children for fighting and arguing. Levi and colleagues report a study in which six families with children ages 5 to 14 were instructed to not intervene in the children's conflicts and to explain to their children that they would no longer intervene, not out of lack of interest, but because the children were old enough to handle their own problems. Compared with baseline frequencies, all six families reported a reduction in the number of sibling conflicts immediately following the intervention and 8 months later. Such interventions would not be appropriate in families of younger children who have not yet developed sufficient social skills to resolve conflicts on their own.

For other conflicts, where the behavior is not maintained by parental attention, negative consequences are needed. For example, Olson and Roberts (1987) compared the effects of social skills training and time-out in families with siblings between the ages of 2 and 10. These researchers found that time-out was more effective than social skills training in reducing the frequency of aggressive sibling interactions. In the time-out intervention, children viewed four video clips depicting conflictual interactions between two children. In each video clip, an adult actor consequated the aggression by having each child serve a time-out in a chair facing a wall. After viewing each video clip, children were asked by the experimenter/therapist, "What caused the problem?" "What happened after they got into the fight?" "Why shouldn't we hit people?" "What will happen if you forget at home and hit someone?" Children and their siblings then observed their mother role-play with dolls the time-out procedure that would be used at home. Following the role play, mothers asked their children, "Why did the dolls have to go to time-out?" "Why is fighting wrong?" "What will happen if they fight again?" Mothers were then instructed to consequate all aggression between siblings in the home with time-out and to ask each child the same three questions following any time-outs. The mean frequency of sibling aggression was decreased from 10 incidents daily during an 8-day baseline period, to 3, 2, and 1 incident daily during three subsequent 8-day periods following the implementation of the intervention.

Other support for time-out as a consequence for sibling conflict comes from O'Leary et al. (1967), who reported that the combination of time-out following conflict and reinforcement following cooperative play reduced aggressive interactions between two brothers ages 6 and 3. The boys' mother reported that her 6-year-old son fought with his younger brother whenever the two children were unsupervised and that the two children would yell at and hurt one another when they played alone in the basement of their family home. Following a period during which baseline levels of conflict were recorded, a first phase of intervention was implemented in which the experimenter rewarded the children for exhibiting cooperative behavior (e.g., saying please and thank you, asking for a toy appropriately) with M&M candies and praise. At first, the experimenter rewarded every instance of cooperative behavior during a designated hour of the day with a reinforcer. On the 3rd and 4th day of the intervention, the children were rewarded for every second or fourth cooperative behavior, and on the 5th day, a token reinforcement system was introduced. The brothers were told that in addition to earning candies for cooperative behavior, they would also earn checks on a chalkboard and lose checks for deviant behavior. The chalkboard was divided in half to separately track checks for each child. Check marks could be traded for reinforcers such as candies and small toys. The number of checks required to "buy" a reinforcer was gradually increased, and on the 12th day of the token system, the use of M&Ms was discontinued and only check marks (and the backup reinforcers) were awarded for cooperative sibling behavior. The amount of cooperative play between the brothers increased to a rate of 85% of the time from a baseline level of 46%.

When the M&Ms were first discontinued, the children reacted with oppositional behavior. However, the experimenter and the mother ignored this behavior and it gradually extinguished. The token system procedure was then discontinued, and the rate of cooperative behavior decreased to a level similar to the first baseline (50%). Next, the mother reinstated the token system, and added a time-out procedure contingent on sibling conflict defined as kicking, hitting, pushing, name-calling, and throwing objects at one another. The time-out procedure consisted of placing the child who exhibited any of the preceding behaviors in the bathroom for at least 5 minutes, during 3 of which the child had to remain quiet before going back to play. Also, approximately 1 week after the reinstatement of the token system, the mother increased the number of checks needed to buy a reward. During this second phase of treatment, the rate of cooperative behavior between the two brothers rose to 90%.

Allison and Allison (1971) also found that time-out following sibling conflict was effective in reducing aggressive behavior directed by a 26-month-old girl toward her 11-month-old brother. Time-out in this case consisted of sending the girl to her room for 5 minutes following the exhibition of hitting, biting, kicking, shoving, or taking a toy away from her brother. The parents already used time-out as a consequence for other child misbehaviors, but previously responded to sibling conflict with verbal reprimands or mild physical punishment. Prior to and throughout the implementation of time-out for sibling conflict, the parents reinforced cooperative play with attention and approval. During a baseline period, the girl directed, on average, 5.7 aggressive behaviors toward her brother per 30-minute observation period. When time-out was implemented, the frequency dropped to a near zero rate (an average of .3 aggressive behaviors per observation period). When the time-out procedure was withdrawn, the rate of aggressive behavior increased to 1.5, and upon reinstatement of time-out, the rate dropped again to an average of .4 aggressive behaviors per observation period.

MAINTENANCE

Although conflict in sibling relationships is common and may be enduring, interventions are typically short-lived, ranging from a single consultation with a therapist to 10 or 12 sessions. Therefore, plans for the maintenance of treatment gains are important. Planning for treatment generalization may be particularly important in helping parents anticipate the problems that may arise as sibling pairs age. A final session (or sessions) in a parent training program should be dedicated to helping parents problem-solve issues that may arise in the future. If possible, periodic booster sessions may be provided by the therapist to monitor progress and review the general principles and techniques discussed in the treatment program. Alternately, families should be taught to self-monitor sibling conflict and to periodically reassess the extent to which they may have lapsed in their use of the strategies they learned to implement in the parent training sessions. In the case study by Kelly and Main (1979), described earlier, the final sessions of the intervention focused on the establishment of a weekly family council meeting. The weekly meeting gave the children an active role in family plans and decisions, and was intended to facilitate family unity and cooperation. Such weekly family meetings may also provide a useful forum for reviewing family rules, developing new rules for new situations, and renegotiating ongoing contracts or reward systems.

CONCLUSION

Studies and descriptions gathered from the literature offer useful information that can be used in assisting parents in reducing sibling conflict. The best developed and validated techniques are those arising from the operant tradition, including the use of time-out following sibling conflict and the reinforcement of alternate, prosocial interaction. In addition, strategies arising for the social skills training literature have also shown promise. Using parents as therapists, children have been successfully trained in positive interaction skills such as inviting, granting requests, and handling refusals. Finally, other techniques ranging from having parents alter common situational antecedents to sibling conflict, providing developmental and normative information about sibling relationships, to strengthening interparent agreement on approaches to managing sibling conflict appear as reasonable and useful components of interventions provided to parents. Combined with clinical skill in tailoring interventions to the needs of individual families, this collection of parenting strategies provides a solid beginning point for therapists in assisting families in managing sibling conflict.

Although a small literature has developed to produce the results described here, much further work is needed. Because there is a growing demand for accountability in the mental health services, studies demonstrating the efficacy and effectiveness of sibling conflict interventions are desperately needed. Many of the intervention components reviewed in this chapter have not been rigorously evaluated using controlled outcome studies. Research is needed to evaluate not only entire programs, but also the components within these programs. In addition to the groundwork necessary to validate these techniques, research must also focus on matching interventions and client characteristics. For example, there has been a glaring lack of systematic consideration of child age in the development and evaluation of interventions. Although an educated assumption is that parent-controlled operant strategies are more appropriate with younger children and collaborative problem-solving strategies with older children or adolescents, this assumption remains untested. In addition to sibling age, other variables such as family characteristics (e.g., ethnicity, one- vs. two-parent) and type of sibling problem (e.g., physical aggression, jealousy) may need to be considered in selecting an optimal treatment package. Finally, the long-term effects of parent training for sibling conflict must be assessed.

The seriousness and the prevalence of sibling conflict, in combination with the promise of empirical treatment literature, suggest that greater attention to the development of sibling interventions is warranted. We end this chapter with a call to clinical researchers to develop, describe, evaluate, and share strategies used in working with parents seeking assistance in reducing negative sibling interactions and promoting adaptive sibling relations.

REFERENCES

Allison, T. S., & Allison, S. L. (1971). Time-out from reinforcement: Effect on sibling aggression. *Psychological Record, 21,* 81–86.

American Psychiatric Association. (1994). *Diagnostic and statistical manual of mental disorders* (4th ed.). Washington, DC: Author.

Arnold, J. E., Levine, A. G., & Patterson, G. R. (1975). Changes in sibling behavior following family intervention. *Journal of Consulting and Clinical Psychology, 43,* 683–688.

Barton, E. J., & Ascione, F. R. (1979). Sharing in preschool children: Facilitation, stimulus generalization, response generalization, and maintenance. *Journal of Applied Behavior Analysis, 12,* 417–430.

Belchic, J. K., & Harris, S. L. (1994). The use of multiple peer exemplars to enhance the generalization of play skills to the siblings of children with autism. *Child and Family Behavior Therapy, 16,* 1–25.

Berndt, T. J., & Bulleit, T. N. (1985). Effects of sibling relationships on preschoolers' behavior at home and at school. *Developmental Psychology, 21,* 761–767.

Brody, G. H., & Stoneman, Z. (1987). Sibling conflict: Contributions of the siblings themselves, the parent-sibling relationship, and the broader family system. *Journal of Children in Contemporary Society, 19,* 39–53.

Brody, G. H., Stoneman, Z., & Burke, M. (1987). Child temperaments, maternal differential behavior, and sibling relationships. *Developmental Psychology, 23,* 354–362.

Bryant, B. K., & Crockenberg, S. B. (1980). Correlates and dimensions of prosocial behavior: A study of female siblings with their mothers. *Child Development, 51,* 529–544.

Bryant, L. E., & Budd, K. S. (1984). Teaching behaviorally handicapped preschool children to share. *Journal of Applied Behavior Analysis, 17,* 45–56.

Carter, A. S., & Volkmar, F. R. (1992). Sibling rivalry: Diagnostic category or focus of treatment? In B. B. Lahey & A. E. Kazdin (Eds.), *Advances in clinical child psychology* (Vol. 14, pp. 289–295). New York: Plenum Press.

Celiberti, D. A., & Harris, S. L. (1993). Behavioral intervention for siblings of children with autism: A focus on skills to enhance play. *Behavior Therapy, 24,* 573–599.

Conger, K., & Conger, R. D. (1994). Differential parenting and change in sibling differences in delinquency. *Journal of Family Psychology, 8,* 287–302.

Corter, C., Abramovitch, R., & Pepler, D. J. (1983). The role of the mother in sibling interaction. *Child Development, 54,* 1599–1605.

Corter, C., Pepler, D., & Abramovitch, R. (1982). The effects of situation and sibling status on sibling interaction. *Canadian Journal of Behavioural Sciences, 14,* 380–392.

Cunningham, C. E. (1990). A family systems approach to parent training. In R. A. Barkley (Ed.), *Attention deficit hyperactivity disorder* (pp. 432–461). New York: Guilford Press.

Dadds, M. R., & Powell, M. B. (1991). The relationship of interparental conflict and global marital adjustment to aggression, anxiety, and immaturity in aggressive and nonclinic children. *Journal of Abnormal Child Psychology, 19,* 533–567.

Daniel, D., & Plomin, R. (1985). Differential experiences of siblings in the same family. *Developmental Psychology, 21,* 747–760.

Dunn, J. (1983). Sibling relationships in early childhood. *Child Development, 54,* 787–811.

Dunn, J., & Kendrick, C. (1982). *Siblings: Love, envy and understanding.* Cambridge, MA: Harvard University Press.

Dunn, J., & Munn, P. (1986a). Siblings and the development of prosocial behaviour. *International Journal of Behavioural Development, 9,* 265–284.

Dunn, J., & Munn, P. (1986b). Sibling quarrels and maternal intervention: Individual differences in understanding and aggression. *Journal of Child Psychology and Psychiatry, 27,* 583–595.

Emery, R. E. (1982). Interparental conflict and the children of discord and divorce. *Psychological Bulletin, 92,* 310–330.

Eyberg, S. M., & Robinson, E. A. (1982). Parent-child interaction training: Effects on family functioning. *Journal of Clinical Child Psychology, 11,* 130–137.

Furman, W. (1995). Parenting siblings. In M. H. Bornstein (Ed.), *Handbook of parenting: Vol. 1. Children and parenting* (pp. 143–162). Mahwah, NJ: Erlbaum.

Furman, W., & Buhrmester, D. (1985). Children's perceptions of the qualities of sibling relationships. *Child Development, 56,* 448–461.

Gentry, D. B., & Benenson, W. A. (1993). School-to-home transfer of conflict management skills among school-age children. *Families in Society, 74,* 67–73.

Getz, S. K., & Berndt, E. (1982). A test of a method for quantifying amount, complexity, and arrangement of play resources in the preschool classroom. *Journal of Applied Developmental Psychology, 3,* 295–305.

Graham-Bermann, S. A., & Cutler, S. E. (1994). The Brother-Sister Questionnaire: Psychometric assessment and discrimination of well-functioning from dysfunctional relationships. *Journal of Family Psychology, 8,* 224–238.

Hendrickson, J. M., Strain, P. S., Tremblay, A., & Shores, R. F. (1982). Relationship between toy and material use and the occurrence of social interactive behaviors by normally developing preschool children. *Psychology in the Schools, 18,* 500–504.

Hetherington, E. M. (1988). Parents, children, and siblings six years after divorce. In R. A. Hinde & J. Stevenson-Hinde (Eds.), *Relationships within families: Mutual influences* (pp. 311–331). New York: Oxford University Press.

Houghton, S. (1991). Working with parents: A case study utilizing a triadic model approach. *Maladjustment and Therapeutic Education: The Journal of the Association of Workers for Maladjusted Children, 9,* 59–65.

Howe, N. (1996, January). Siblings and emotional development. *Center for Research in Human Development Newsletter,* 1–2.

Humphreys, L., Forehand, R., McMahon, R., & Roberts, M. (1978). Parent behavioral training to modify child noncompliance: Effects on untreated siblings. *Journal of Behavioral Therapy and Experimental Psychiatry, 9,* 235–238.

Johnson, D. W., Johnson, R. T., & Dudley, B. (1992). Effects of peer mediation training on elementary school students. *Mediation Quarterly, 10,* 89–99.

Johnston, C., & Behrenz, K. (1993). Childrearing discussions in families of non-problem children and ADHD children with higher and lower levels of aggressive-defiant behaviour. *Canadian Journal of School Psychology, 9,* 53–65.

Jouriles, E. N., Murphy, C. M., Farris, A. M., Smith, D. A., Richters, J. E., & Walters, E. (1991). Marital adjustment, parental disagreements about childrearing, and boys' behavior: Increasing the specificity of marital assessment. *Child Development, 62,* 1424–1433.

Kelly, F. D., & Main, F. O. (1979). Sibling conflict in a single-parent family: An empirical case study. *American Journal of Family Therapy, 7,* 39–47.

Klein, N. C., Alexander, J. F., & Parsons, B. V. (1977). Impact of family systems intervention on recidivism and sibling delinquency: A model of primary prevention and program evaluation. *Journal of Consulting and Clinical Psychology, 45,* 469–474.

Leitenberg, H., Burchard, J. D., Burchard, S. N., Fuller, E. J., & Lysaght, T. V. (1977). Using positive reinforcement to suppress behavior: Some experimental comparisons with sibling conflict. *Behavior Therapy, 8,* 168–182.

Leung, A. K. D., & Robson, W. L. M. (1991). Sibling rivalry. *Clinical Pediatrics, 30,* 314–317.

Levi, A. M., Buskila, M., & Gerzi, S. (1977). Benign neglect: Reducing fights among siblings. *Journal of Individual Psychology, 33,* 240–245.

Light, P. (1979). *The development of social sensitivity.* Cambridge, England: Cambridge University Press.

Mash, E. J., & Johnston, C. (1983). Sibling interactions of hyperactive and normal children and their relationship to reports of maternal stress and self-esteem. *Journal of Clinical Child Psychology, 12,* 91–99.

Mash, E. J., & Johnston, C. (1996). Family relational problems: Their place in the study of psychopathology. *Journal of Emotional and Behavioral Disorders, 4,* 240–254.

McDermott, J. F. (1980). *Raising Cain (and Abel too): The parents' book of sibling rivalry.* New York: Wyden Books.

Minnett, A. M., Vandell, D. L., & Santrock, J. W. (1983). The effects of sibling status on sibling interaction: Influence of birth order, age spacing, sex of child, and sex of sibling. *Child Development, 54,* 1064–1073.

Newman, J. (1994). Conflict and friendship in sibling relationships: A review. *Child Study Journal, 24,* 119–152.

Oden, S., Wheeler, V. A., & Herzberger, S. D. (1984). Children's conversations within a conflict of interest situation. In H. E. Syphen & J. L. Applegate (Eds.), *Communication by children and adults: Social cognitive and strategic processes* (pp. 129–151). Beverly Hills, CA: Sage.

O'Leary, K. D., O'Leary, S., & Becker, W. C. (1967). Modification of a deviant sibling interaction pattern in the home. *Behavior Research and Therapy, 5,* 113–120.

Olson, R. L., & Roberts, M. W. (1987). Alternative treatments for sibling aggression. *Behavior Therapy, 18,* 243–250.

Patterson, G. R. (1984). Siblings: Fellow travelers in coercive family processes. In R. J. Blanchard & D. C. Blanchard (Eds.), *Advances in the study of aggression* (Vol. 1, pp. 173–215). New York: Academic Press.

Patterson, G. R. (1986). The contribution of siblings to training for fighting: A microsocial analysis. In D. Olweus, J. Block, & M. Radke-Yarrow (Eds.), *Development of antisocial and prosocial behavior* (pp. 235–261). New York: Academic Press.

Powell, T. H., Salzberg, C. L., Rule, S., Levy, S., & Itzkowitz, J. S. (1983). Teaching mentally retarded children to play with their siblings using parents as trainers. *Education and Treatment of Children, 6,* 343–362.

Prochaska, J. M., & Prochaska, J. O. (1985). Children's views of the causes and "cures" of sibling rivalry. *Child Welfare, 63,* 427–433.

Quilitich, H. R., & Risley, T. R. (1973). The effects of play materials on social play. *Journal of Applied Behavior Analysis, 6,* 573–578.

Ramamurti, P. V., & Devi, P. R. (1986). Sibling rivalry in children and the effect of training the mother in handling sibling rivalry. *Indian Journal of Clinical Psychology, 13,* 15–20.

Ramsey, P. G. (1986). Possession disputes in preschool classrooms. *Child Study Journal, 16,* 173–181.

Reid, W. J., & Donovan, T. (1990). Treating sibling violence. *Family Therapy, 17,* 49–59.

Roberts, M. W., Arnold, S. B., & Mangum, P. F. (1992). The sibling conflict resolution scale. *The Behaviour Therapist, 15,* 254–255.

Ross, H. S., Filyer, R. E., Lollis, S. P., Perlman, M., & Martin, J. L. (1994). Administering justice in the family. *Journal of Family Psychology, 8,* 254–273.

Short, K. H., & Johnston, C. (1994). Ethnocultural parent education in Canada: Current status and directions. *Canadian Journal of Community Mental Health, 13,* 43–54.

Sloane, H. N. (1988). *The good kid book: How to solve the 16 most common behavior problems.* Champaign, IL: Research Press.

Sloane, H. N., Endo, G. T., Hawkes, T. W., & Jenson, W. R. (1990). Decreasing children's fighting through self-instructional parent training materials. *School Psychology International, 11,* 17–29.

Steinmetz, S. K. (1978). Sibling violence. In J. M. Eckelaar & S. N. Katz (Eds.), *Family violence: An international and interdisciplinary study* (pp. 144–177). Toronto, Canada: Butterworths.

Stewart, R., & Marvin, R. S. (1984). Sibling relations: The role of conceptual perspective-taking in the ontogeny of sibling caregiving. *Child Development, 55,* 1322–1332.

Stocker, C., Dunn, J., & Plomin, R. (1989). Sibling relationships: Links with child temperament, maternal behavior, and family structure. *Child Development, 60,* 715–727.

Stoneman, Z., Cantrell, M. L., & Hoover-Dempsey, K. (1983). The association between play materials and social behavior in a mainstreamed preschool: A naturalistic investigation. *Journal of Applied Developmental Psychology, 4,* 163–174.

Strain, P. S., & Danko, C. D. (1995). Caregivers' encouragement of positive interaction between preschoolers with autism and their siblings. *Journal of Emotional and Behavioral Disorders, 3,* 2–12.

Straus, M. A., Gelles, R. J., & Steinmetz, S. (1980). *Behind closed doors: Violence in the American family.* Garden City, NY: Anchor Press/Doubleday.

Tiedemann, G. L., Cross-Calvert, S., Johnston, C., Palme, T., & McMahon, R. (1987, June). *Sharing between preschool-aged children: Mothers' reports of teaching strategies and situational variability.* Paper presented at the meeting of the Canadian Psychological Association, Vancouver, BC.

Tiedemann, G. L., & Johnston, C. (1992). Evaluation of a parent training program to promote sharing between young siblings. *Behavior Therapy, 23,* 299–318.

Vickerman, R. C., Reed, M. D., & Roberts, M. W. (1997). Maternal intervention in sub-clinical sibling coercion. *Journal of Applied Developmental Psychology, 18,* 23–35.

Volling, B. L., & Belsky, J. (1992). The contribution of mother-child and father-child relationships to the quality of sibling interaction: A longitudinal study. *Child Development, 63,* 1209–1222.

World Health Organization. (1992). *International statistical classification of diseases and related health problems* (ICD-10, tenth revision). Geneva, Switzerland: Author.

CHAPTER 5

Preventive Intervention for Families of Preschoolers at Risk for Conduct Disorders

LAURIE MILLER

CONDUCT DISORDER is a mental health problem with significant individual, interpersonal, and societal costs. The resistance of established conduct disorders to treatments of all kinds is now well documented. It is also well known that children who develop severe conduct problems early in life are at great risk for a continuing pattern of antisocial behavior, and for impairment in other important functional domains. Despite widespread recognition of the need for effective interventions, there are few empirically-tested interventions designed specifically to *prevent* conduct disorders in young high-risk children. Unless effective *preventions* are developed, antisocial behavior among youth will continue to cost society more economically and emotionally than any other mental health problem.

This chapter describes a preventive intervention program and its application to preschoolers at high risk for developing conduct disorders. This approach toward the prevention of conduct problems is based on developmental findings regarding *risk factors* for antisocial behavior, and on the identification of potentially *effective interventions* from therapeutic investigations.

DEVELOPMENTAL FINDINGS: EARLY CONDUCT PROBLEMS AS PRECURSORS OF CONDUCT DISORDERS AND ANTISOCIAL BEHAVIOR

The evolution of conduct disorders and antisocial behavior is the most extensively studied developmental psychopathology. Similarly, the roots of adult antisocial behavior have been well investigated. The presence of childhood conduct problems emerges clearly and consistently as the most robust predictor of later antisocial behavior. There is strong empirical support for the notion that, in a substantial subgroup, antisocial behavior is stable from early childhood to adulthood (Caspi, Elder, & Bem, 1987; Huesmann & Eron, 1989; Loeber, 1982; Olweus, 1979; Robins, 1978; West & Farrington, 1977) and that these behaviors become increasingly intractable over time (Loeber, 1991). Many children who exhibit conduct problems early in life, in the form of noncompliance, and oppositional and aggressive behavior, proceed to display symptoms of conduct disorder and escalate to more serious antisocial behavior (Hinshaw, Lahey, & Hart, 1993; Loeber, 1988). In fact, the primary developmental pathway for serious conduct disorders in adolescence and adulthood appears to be established during the preschool period. Hinshaw et al. (1993) describe a prototypic early onset:

> The preschooler who throws temper tantrums and stubbornly refuses to follow adult instructions becomes the child who also initiates fights with other children and lies to the teacher. Later, the same youth begins to vandalize the school, torture animals, break into homes, steal costly items, and abuse alcohol. As a young adult, he or she forces sex on acquaintances, writes bad checks, and has a chaotic employment and marital history. This individual may also be prone to abuse partners and children. (p. 36)

As parents, such individuals perpetuate the cycle of violence across generations (Huesmann, Eron, Lefkowitz, & Walder, 1984). This persistence of conduct problems over time would not be as alarming if effective, well-established means existed for cutting short the developmental progression. The resistance of established conduct disorders to treatments of all kinds is now well documented, as reviewed by Dodge (1993), Dumas (1989), Kazdin (1987, 1993), Miller (1994a, 1994b), Offord and Bennett (1994), and Webster-Stratton (1991).

THE ROLE OF PARENTING PRACTICES IN THE DEVELOPMENT OF CONDUCT PROBLEMS

A substantial set of research findings indicates that parenting practices represent a potentially modifiable, powerful early predictor of childhood conduct problems. Studies of children with conduct disorders have found that their families are characterized by deviant parenting practices (e.g., unclear rules and commands, reinforcement of negative child behavior) (Loeber & Dishion, 1983; McCord, 1979; Patterson & Stouthamer-Loeber, 1984), limited support for social competence (Patterson, Reid, & Dishion, 1992; Wasserman, Miller, Pinner, & Jaramillo, 1996), poor supervision (Farrington, 1983; Patterson et al., 1992), physical punishment (Andrew, 1981; Eron, Huesmann, & Zelli, 1991), and parental modeling of antisocial behavior (West & Farrington, 1973). Although a host of variables have been related to conduct problems (e.g., social and economic disadvantage [West, 1982], parental psychopathology and criminality [Rutter & Giller, 1983]), these factors have been demonstrated to be mediated, at least in part, by parenting practices (Patterson et al., 1992).

Patterson's observational studies (Patterson, 1982) of the exchanges between children with conduct problems and their parents have shown that coercive parent-child interactions are particularly important in promoting children's conduct problems. When children direct deviant behaviors toward parents, these behaviors are often unintentionally reinforced, thereby increasing the likelihood that they will persist.

Complementing Patterson's model, investigators (e.g., Cicchetti & Richters, 1993; Conduct Problems Prevention Research Group, 1992; Moffit, 1993) have proposed transactional models for early onset conduct problems and their developmental progression. These models suggest that the combination of a vulnerable and difficult child (e.g., unpredictable, irritable, unresponsive) with an adverse family context (e.g., deviant parenting practices) initiates risk for a persistent pattern of antisocial behavior. The challenge of coping with a difficult child elicits a series of failed parent-child interactions. These transactional models posit that skillful parents can overcome or correct early child difficulties, but that negative family environments are likely to maintain and worsen the child's behavior problems. Without appropriate, consistent parenting for children at risk, early behavior problems are thought to escalate into more severe conduct problems, and age-appropriate social competencies fail to emerge. Over time, antisocial personalities emerge along with deficits in interpersonal relations and overall functioning. Accumulating negative consequences of children's antisocial behavior and limited social competence reduce potential for change (Vitaro, Gagnon, & Tremblay, 1990).

ALTERING CHILD CONDUCT DISORDERS WITH PARENT TRAINING

Because parenting practices are sturdy predictors of childhood conduct problems, the question arises as to whether conduct problems are reduced by improving parental behavior. Hundreds of studies have demonstrated that parent training programs can be used to improve parenting practices and reduce child behavior problems (Forehand & McMahon, 1981; McMahon & Forehand, 1984; Patterson, Cobb, & Ray, 1973; Patterson, Reid, Jones, & Conger, 1975; Spitzer, Webster-Stratton, & Hollinsworth, 1991; Webster-Stratton, 1981, 1984; Webster-Stratton & Hammond, 1997). Changes in parenting practices have been linked to changes in child conduct problems in nonclinical groups with specific behavior problems (e.g., Forgatch & Toobert, 1979), young children referred for high rates of oppositional and defiant behavior (e.g., Barkley, 1987; Eyberg & Boggs, 1989), pre-adolescent children referred for severe antisocial behavior (e.g., Patterson, 1979), adolescents at risk for delinquency and substance abuse (e.g., Dishion, Patterson, & Kavanaugh, 1992), and seriously delinquent youth (e.g., Chamberlain, 1990; Chamberlain & Reid, 1991).

There are, however, a number of important limitations of the parent training approach for reducing conduct problems in youth with *established* patterns of antisocial behavior. First, as reviewed by Reid (1992), the impact of parent training on child conduct problems has been demonstrated to be less effective with older children. Second, only a few controlled studies have examined the impact of parent training on child conduct problems in school. Two studies of the Forehand and McMahon program did not find improvement in school functioning (Breiner & Forehand, 1981), and Webster-Stratton (1982) found significant improvement in teacher reports immediately posttreatment, but not one year later. The inability of parent training alone to affect children's school behavior is a significant limitation, because school represents a major functional domain. Finally, long-term benefits of parent training programs for children with serious, stable behavior problems have not been demonstrated (Dodge, 1993; Kazdin, 1987, 1993).

EARLY INTERVENTION

There has been increasing effort toward intervening with children earlier in development. These efforts include treatment for young, clinically-referred children (e.g., Eyberg & Boggs, 1989; Webster-Stratton & Hammond, 1997; Webster-Stratton, Kolpacoff, & Hollinsworth, 1989); school-based secondary prevention programs for elementary schoolchildren identified as highly aggressive (e.g., Conduct Problems Prevention Research Group, 1992; Guerra, Tolan, Huesmann, VanAcker, & Eron, 1992; Tremblay et al., 1992), community-based interventions for school-aged children with behavior problems (Cunningham, Bremner, & Boyle, 1995) and universal school-based prevention programs (e.g., Kellam & Rebok, 1992). However, despite growing recognition of the importance of the first 5 years of life in the development of conduct problems, little work has focused on this early developmental period (Landy & Peters, 1992).

Hundreds of early intervention programs exist, but few are designed with specified social competence goals (Zigler & Freedman, 1987), and none has been designed specifically for preventing conduct problems in high-risk children. Four early intervention programs have been shown to have unanticipated positive outcomes in terms of antisocial behavior (Berrueta-Clement, Schweinhart, Barnett, Epstein, & Weikart, 1987; Johnson & Walker, 1987; Lally, Mangione, & Honig, 1988; Seitz, Rosenbaum, & Apfel, 1985), suggesting the utility of this approach. Two reviews of early intervention studies argue that a family-based approach toward early intervention is a promising strategy for the prevention of antisocial behavior and delinquency (Yoshikawa, 1994; Zigler, Taussig, & Black, 1992).

In summary, a relationship between parenting practices and child conduct problems has been established with findings from both longitudinal and treatment studies. Parenting practices have been demonstrated to be modifiable through parent training, and the most promising treatments include parent training. Although antisocial behavior has been reduced by family-based treatments, it continues in a relatively high proportion of cases. It appears that most treatments for antisocial behavior begin too late. Providing family-based intervention early on, prior to the stabilization of conduct disorders and development of secondary impairing conditions (e.g., peer rejection), may enhance the likelihood of altering the poor prognosis for high-risk children.

THE PREVENTIVE INTERVENTION PROGRAM

THEORETICAL APPROACH

In 1992, Rachel Klein and I set out to develop and test an intervention program for young children at high risk for antisocial behavior. We were interested in working with preschoolers since the preschool period has been shown to be the starting point for conduct problems for many high-risk children. We also wanted to evaluate the prevention program with children who did not yet have established conduct problems. Therefore, unlike other prevention studies, we did not use current behavior problems or level of aggression of the child as a way to select children. Instead, we included children who lived in the inner city and had a sibling with a documented history of antisocial behavior. Both inner-city residence and having a sibling with antisocial behavior have been shown to be risk factors for conduct disorders and antisocial behavior (Garbarino, Kostelny, & Dubrow, 1992; Jones, Offord, & Abrams, 1980; Patterson, 1984; Rowe & Herstand, 1986; Rowe, Rodgers, & Meseck-Bushey, 1992; Tolan & Henry, 1994; Twito & Stewart, 1982; Walter et al., 1995).

The program described in this chapter was designed for preschoolers and their families. The initial evaluation of the program was done with inner-city siblings of antisocial youth. The preventive intervention program could, however, be applied, with minor adjustments, to preschoolers from different risk levels (e.g., children of antisocial parents, inner-city children attending head start programs).

The goal of the intervention program is to instill optimal parenting practices to prevent the development of conduct disorders and enhance children's social competence. Our hypothesis is that if the program is successful in promoting long-term changes in the families of high-risk children, the transition into school will be facilitated and future problems will be avoided.

The therapeutic approach taken in the intervention program is generally cognitive behavioral and is modeled after the collaborative approach described by Webster-Stratton and Herbert (1994). Clinicians work with parents by actively soliciting their ideas and feelings, understanding their cultural context, and involving them in the process of sharing their experiences, discussing and debating ideas, and problem solving. The clinician's role is to understand the parents' perspectives, to clarify issues, to summarize important ideas and themes raised by parents, to teach and interpret in a way that is culturally sensitive, and to suggest alternative approaches and solutions to problems when needed. Because parents are given responsibility for developing solutions, with assistance from the clinicians, it is hypothesized that parents will enhance their sense of confidence about parenting and changing their children's behavior. Research suggests that such an approach reduces attrition rates, increases motivation and commitment, reduces resistance, and enhances generalization of changes over time and across settings.

PROGRAM COMPONENTS

The program tested in the pilot study had two phases: a 9-month intensive phase and a 3-month maintenance phase. The intensive phase of the intervention program includes four basic components: (a) clinic-based parenting skills training, (b) clinic-based children's play group, (c) clinic-based parent-child interaction training, and (d) home visits. During the intensive phase, parents and children attend 2-hour group sessions at the clinic twice a week and receive home visits twice a month. During the maintenance phase, families are visited twice a month in their homes. All components of the intervention are described in an intervention manual. A brief description of the components of the intervention program follows:

Parenting Skills Training

The strategies used in the parent training program are based on well-established intervention programs. It utilizes a videotape modeling series by Webster-Stratton (1987), designed for children ages 3 to 8. Webster-Stratton's program includes aspects of the widely used programs developed by Forehand and McMahon (1981) and Patterson (1982). This program has been tested extensively with referred children, ages 3 to 8 years (Webster-Stratton, 1981, 1984; Webster-Stratton & Hammond, 1997; Webster-Stratton, Kolpacoff, & Hollinsworth, 1988).

Our parenting training component includes two of Webster-Stratton's videotape programs: The BASIC 4-program Parent and Children Series and the Advanced 3-program Parent and Children Series. In the first program, parents learn to play with their children in a nondirective way and to identify and reward children's prosocial behaviors through praise and attention. Parents are taught to give effective commands and to implement time-out and ignoring procedures for noncompliance, oppositionality, and aggression. Parents also learn to use logical and natural consequences for negative behavior. In addition to learning specific strategies, parents also learn about normal variations in children's development, emotional reactions, and temperaments. The Advanced program focuses on family factors that are known to disrupt parenting practices, such as parental depressive symptoms, lack of social support, and other environmental stressors. The program teaches parents to problem solve and also helps parents teach problem-solving strategies to their children.

The group leaders show a series of videotaped interactions to the group of parents and then lead a discussion of the relevant interactions. The videotapes show parents of differing ages, cultures, and socioeconomic backgrounds, so that parents will perceive at least some of the models as similar to themselves. Such perceptions facilitate parents' view of the material as relevant. The videotapes show parent models doing some things correctly, but also making mistakes (e.g., inadvertently reinforcing negative child behavior with attention). The approach is different from other parenting programs in that the model is one of coping and interactive learning, instead of relying on the therapist to analyze the problem and recommend a solution. Parents are encouraged to watch the videos and discuss how the parent in the video might have handled the interaction differently or more effectively. This approach helps to boost parents' confidence in their own ideas and promotes their ability to analyze a variety of situations and select alternative approaches. The videotapes demonstrate behavioral principles and serve as stimuli for focused discussions, role plays, problem solving, and sharing of ideas and reactions. The group leader supports and empowers parents by teaching, leading, reframing, predicting, and role playing within a collaborative context (Webster-Stratton & Herbert, 1993).

By taking a collaborative approach to working with parents, the program is sensitive to individual cultural differences and personal values. Furthermore, the program is tailored to each family's individual needs and goals, as well as to each child's strengths and weaknesses. By providing the intervention in a group format, the program is not only more cost-effective, but it also addresses an important risk factor for conduct problems—lack of social support. The parent groups provide a parent support group that also becomes a model of parent informal support networks. Additionally, the videotaped format is ideal for parents whose literacy education level or general intellectual level is below average. Group discussions also focus on helping parents to identify inexpensive or free resources in their own communities for their children and themselves.

In our pilot study, we delivered the parent training program over a 9-month period, with sessions twice a week. We delivered the program over a relatively long period of time because of the multiple stressors that inner-city families experience. There are many factors that influence parenting practices that need to be addressed throughout the program. A portion of the parenting group session is used to review and discuss current family issues and events that are likely common to group members (e.g., older sibling returning from a juvenile facility).

Children's Playgroup

The children's playgroup was included in the program for several reasons. First, on a practical level, preschoolers are likely to be home with their parents. We did not want to add an additional obstacle to attending the program or further increase family stress by requiring parents to find child care during the group sessions. Many of the parents have neither the financial resources nor the informal support networks to provide such care. The children's group provides a controlled setting for children to play with same-age peers while their parents attend the parenting group. We use this opportunity to observe the children, identify their strengths and weaknesses, and develop techniques or strategies that seem effective with each child. This information is conveyed to parents to help them improve their interactions with their children. Furthermore, parents observe their own children during the playgroup, through a one-way mirror, and discuss with the clinicians their observations and ideas. The children's playgroup also demonstrates to parents the importance of helping their children to form positive peer relationships, and models effective ways for helping children to problem solve.

Children's playgroups are scheduled at the same time as the parent groups. Playgroup activities include: peer play, small group activities, reading, clean-up, and snack time. Observations made by intervenors during the playgroup are conveyed to parents to help them use positive parenting techniques in everyday interactions with their children. To ensure consistency, the intervenors work with the children using the same strategies that the parents are taught in the parenting group. Rules are clearly stated, praise and attention are provided for positive behavior, and time-out procedures are used for oppositional, aggressive, and noncompliant behavior. Parents observe these behaviors directly and discuss their observations of children's strengths and weaknesses, their child's response to specific behavioral strategies employed by group leaders, and their reactions or difficulties with any of the observed procedures.

Parent-Child Interaction Training

After the parent training group and children's playgroup, parents join their children for a semistructured activity (e.g., arts and crafts, reading). Under supervision and guidance from the parent and child group leaders, parents develop and practice various skills, such as giving a timeout, playing, and reinforcing positive behavior. Also, attention is paid to children's developmental skills and developmentally appropriate activities that the parents can try out at home. Additionally, parent-child interaction training includes a component that encourages parents to read to their children and to foster social competence through everyday interactions. We set up a lending library from which children select one book a week to take home. Parents are encouraged to read every day to their children. The goal is to promote positive parent-child interactions through reading, to increase the child's school readiness skills, and to expose parents to the use of a library to promote their use of libraries and other community resources.

Home Visits

This component serves many purposes. First, many inner-city families live in poor housing conditions, in small, crowded, and often unsafe buildings and neighborhoods. Home visits allow the clinicians to observe the family and neighborhood context, and to help parents generate solutions to problems that are relevant to their own circumstances. For example, it is often necessary to observe the home to help parents identify a reasonable place for a time-out chair. Furthermore, the home visits allow the clinicians to observe and work with other family members or caretakers who are hesitant to join or cannot attend the parenting groups. Importantly, the home visits are designed to facilitate generalization of parenting practices to the home environment. Other family members are encouraged to participate in the program either through home visits or by attending the parenting groups.

Home visits are provided twice a month and continue for 3 months after completion of the parenting group. The maintenance visits are designed to further enhance generalization of skills. Whereas all other components of the program are provided in group settings, this aspect is designed to address the family's individual needs. Although home visits occur only biweekly, it is important to note that the home environment is viewed as the primary setting for change. All aspects of the program aim to change parent and child behavior in the home. It is expected that, if behavioral changes occur in the home, they are likely to facilitate children's entrance into school, and generalize to peer interactions and classroom behavior.

The Parent Training Groups

The topics covered in 60 Parent Training group sessions are as follows:

Part A: Months 1–6

Session 1	Introduction to the Program
Session 2	Introduction to Children's Playgroup
Sessions 3–6	Play: How to Play
Sessions 7–10	Play: Helping Children Learn
Session 11	Review
Sessions 12–15	Praise and Rewards: Effective Praising
Sessions 16–19	Praise and Rewards: Tangible
Session 20	Review
Sessions 21–23	Effective Limit Setting: How to Set Limits
Sessions 24–26	Effective Limit Setting: Helping Children Accept Limits
Sessions 27–29	Effective Limit Setting: Dealing with Noncompliance
Session 30	Review
Sessions 31–33	Handling Misbehavior: Avoiding and Ignoring
Sessions 34–36	Handling Misbehavior: Time-Out
Sessions 37–39	Handling Misbehavior: Preventive Approaches
Session 40	Review

Part B: Months 7–9

Sessions 41–43	Communicating Effectively with Adults and Children: Active Listening
Sessions 44–46	Communicating Effectively with Adults and Children: Communicating Positively

Sessions 47–49	Communicating Effectively with Adults and Children: Giving and Support
Session 50	Review
Sessions 51–54	Problem Solving for Parents
Sessions 55–58	Problem Solving with Children
Session 59	Review
Session 60	Graduation

The format for each Parent Skills Training Group session is as follows:

Minutes	*Content*
0–30	Review of Significant Events since Last Session
31–45	Review of Implementation of New Skills at Home
46–85	Videotapes and Discussion (Webster-Stratton, 1982, 1992)
86–90	Suggestions for At-Home Activities (Review)
91–115	Parent-Child Activity
116–120	Clean-Up/Lending Library Book Selection

The following sections provide a more detailed description of each of the activities that take place during the parenting groups.

Review of Significant Events

The first 30 minutes of each session are spent reviewing significant events that may have occurred since the last group. The group leader asks if anyone has anything important going on at home to share with the group. First, each parent has the opportunity to indicate whether he or she has something specific to discuss and to briefly describe the issue. Examples include an older child coming home from a juvenile facility, a spouse losing a job, family members in town, a change in family living situation, escalation in alcohol or drug use by family member, target child broke a leg, family member diagnosed with physical illness, and anniversary of family member's death. After being made aware of all the topics that need to be discussed, the group leader allots time for each person to discuss their events. If more than 30 minutes are required, additional time is allocated and less time is spent on new material.

The goal is for parents to share important events in their lives with the group, to receive support from group members and to gain assistance with solving problems. The group leader helps parents to see how these events might influence their parenting and helps parents formulate positive ways of dealing with stressful events. Because many issues that are brought up during this time period cannot be dealt with in detail, the group leader tries to promote optimism about solving problems and conveys to the parent that these issues can be dealt with further in home visits, individual sessions, or telephone calls (as needed). On rare occasions, an event is so significant (e.g., a mother shares with the group that she has been diagnosed with a life-threatening illness), that the entire session is reserved for addressing the issue.

Review of Implementation of New Skills at Home

During the next 15 minutes, the group leader starts with an overview of the topics covered at the last session, reminding parents of the specific activities that were suggested for trying at home. The group leader might say: "Last time we discussed the importance of play for children's development. We discussed types of play that you could engage in with your child and when you could manage to fit play time into your schedule. I hope that you were able to try to play with your child since last session. Why don't you tell the group how that went?"

Parents are strongly encouraged to implement new techniques at home. The group leader asks parents to share their experiences, both positive and negative, in trying new strategies at home. Parents are reinforced by the group leader for attempting to implement new techniques, and the group leader helps the parents problem solve when they were unsuccessful. Other group members are encouraged to help trouble shoot by using their own experiences. The group leaders then summarize the experience of each parent and integrate this material into the discussion. When appropriate, the group leader asks how other family events discussed at the beginning of the session might influence parent-child interactions at home.

Videotapes and Discussion

This component lasts 40 minutes and is completely detailed in the *Parent and Child Series* manuals (Webster-Stratton, 1987). The Webster-Stratton manuals provide a description of the videotaped scenes and dialogue of the vignettes as well as discussion questions. The videotaped vignettes show parents and children interacting in many different situations. The segments show parents "doing it right" and "doing it wrong," illustrating positive as well as negative examples of parenting. The videotapes are used to stimulate group discussion and problem solving. Parents are actively involved in problem solving and share ideas with the group about their observations and experiences.

The presentation of new materials should flow naturally from the review of significant events and the discussion of the past week's at-home activities. Discussion, role play, and rehearsal focus on what went on at home and parent-child activities and strategies planned for the following week.

Summary of New Material and Suggestions for Home Activities

The group leader asks parents to summarize the new material and makes suggestions to parents about what they can do at home to promote children's development and to enhance the parent-child relationship. Activities to be tried at home that were brought up during the videotapes and discussion are summarized. The group leader predicts possible difficulties in trying some of the activities and helps parents problem solve in advance. The suggested activities are reviewed during the "Review of Implementation of New Skills at Home" section at the next parenting group meeting.

Parent-Child Activity

At each session, the children join their parents for the last 30 minutes of the group to participate in an activity. The primary goal of this component is to give parents an arena for practicing the new strategies and skills with their children under the supervision and guidance of the child and parent group leaders. A second goal is to expose parents to inexpensive activities they can do at home with all their children. During this segment, the group leader prepares the parents for the activity by telling them what materials are necessary for the activity, how they can carry out the activity or different versions of it at home, and how they can encourage their children's social skill development (e.g., listening, sharing).

The children then join the parents and the children's playgroup leader explains briefly to the parents and children what the activity will be. During the activity, the child and parent group leaders observe parent-child interactions, model appropriate behaviors for children and parents, and offer guidance to parents as needed. The parents are in charge of this activity and group leaders serve as observers and coaches.

Parent and child group leaders direct parents to focus on relevant child behaviors, verbalizations, and feelings. At first the parents may rely heavily on the group leaders for direction, but gradually they come to feel comfortable interacting with their children within the context of the group. If the parent initially has a difficult time playing with the child, the parent takes a more passive observer role while the group leader models play interaction skills for the parent. With each session, the leader encourages the parent to become more involved in the parent-child activities.

Three minutes prior to the end of the parent-child activity, the children's group leader announces that it is 3 minutes until clean-up. As in the children's group, this gives the children and parents time to finish their activity and prepare for its ending. Children are expected to clean-up under their parent's guidance. This component allows parents to try giving specific commands to their children and to try newly learned strategies (e.g., time-out) under the group leaders' supervision.

Lending Library

The purpose of the lending library is to promote parent-child interactions at home and reading readiness in the children. After the day's activities are complete, the children's playgroup leader brings in the books available from the library (in a basket or wagon). The children choose a book to take home to read with their parents. They sign out the book and are asked to return it at the next group and trade it for a new one. Over time, parents often come to recognize their children's interest in reading and view reading together as a positive, rewarding experience. Parents are encouraged to visit community libraries and bookstores to develop and enhance their children's reading-related experiences.

THERAPIST TRAINING

Therapists must be well trained in behavior management and cognitive behavioral strategies for working with adults and children. They must be well versed in normal child development, child behavior problems, and parent-child and family interactions. In addition to being knowledgeable and experienced in the content of the program, clinicians must be comfortable working within the collaborative framework. The success of the program depends, to a great extent, on the clinician's ability to work collaboratively with parents.

Training in the preventive intervention involves reading the intervention manuals, taking a 30-hour course, and participating in ongoing weekly supervision. The course is divided into four parts:

1. Training in parent-child relationships and the application of cognitive-behavioral strategies to improve parenting;
2. Training in peer interactions and the application of cognitive-behavioral strategies to improve children's social competence;
3. Training in developing a collaborative therapeutic relationship;
4. Training in special issues associated with the targeted study population and on the use of community resources.

The first section of the course presents information on the use of parenting techniques, such as playing with children in a nonintrusive way, identifying and rewarding children's prosocial behaviors through praise and attention, giving effective commands, and using time-out procedures for noncompliance, or oppositional and aggressive behavior. This section of the course is based primarily on the videotape program by Webster-

Stratton (1987), which includes videotapes of modeled parenting skills and other family issues, such as anger management, coping with depression, marital communication skills, and problem-solving strategies. This videotaped material not only serves as the basis for training the intervenors in specific behavioral strategies, but is also the primary didactic material used in the parent training groups. The staff become familiar with the training materials and therapeutic strategies by observing the taped material and participating in discussion, problem-solving exercises, and role-playing.

The second component presents information on peer relations and the social skills necessary for the development of socially competent behavior. This section is based primarily on McGinnis and Goldstein's skill-streaming book, *Skillstreaming in Early Childhood: Teaching Prosocial Skills to the Preschool and Kindergarten Child.* Videotapes of the children's playgroups from the pilot study are used as training material to demonstrate specific social skills and the intervention strategies used by the group leaders to promote the children's social skills.

The third component of the course teaches intervenors to develop a collaborative relationship with the parents. Intervenors read Webster-Stratton and Herbert's book *Troubled Families—Problem Children: Working with Parents: A Collaborative Process.* The goal of this component of training is to teach the clinicians to empower parents and to teach parents to cope more effectively with their children and other family members. The collaborative model in this intervention approach involves six roles for the intervenor (described in detail in Webster-Stratton & Herbert, 1994): (a) building a supportive relationship, (b) empowering parents, (c) teaching parents, (d) interpreting, (e) leading and challenging, and (f) predicting future problems.

The fourth and final component of training addresses issues such as making referrals for services, reporting child maltreatment, dealing with the delinquent sibling's return to the family home, spousal violence, and substance use. Therapists read vignettes of family situations to practice the application of principles targeted. Furthermore, clinicians become familiar with community resources, such as free community activities for children, libraries with special reading hours for children, and free city swimming lessons, and develop strategies for helping families to access them. After the initial training, therapists attend a 2-hour group supervision meeting once a week.

PRELIMINARY PILOT STUDY FINDINGS

We conducted a randomized controlled pilot study with 30 families to test the program's feasibility and acceptability. In general, attendance in the pilot study was very good. The average attendance across three groups was 70%. Parents in the intervention program completed a *Consumer Satisfaction Questionnaire* (Webster-Stratton, 1989). Satisfaction with the program was very high. All parents (100%) indicated that the material covered in the program was "very" to "extremely" useful and "easy" to implement. All (100%) endorsed that they would recommend the program to a friend. In addition, a number of parents who have completed the intervention program have provided us with unsolicited feedback on their child's progress.

One grandmother wrote us a letter and sent a copy of her child's positive kindergarten report card. She wrote (sic):

> I am writing this letter to tell you how well [child's name] is doing in school, and the credit goes to [the program] for giving him the head start, that head start really touches all the areas that is making him do very well in school. I really appreciate you giving me the privilege in letting [child's name] attend the program. The program really help the kids and I wish the other parent could take more time and get involve and see how good the program is. My sincere thanks goes to the entire staff.

Based on the high program attendance and high satisfaction, we believe we have been successful in designing an intervention program that is acceptable and helpful to inner-city families of high-risk children.

We compared parents in the program to parents in the control group on parenting practices observed during parent-child play interactions. Observations were made of parents and children playing for 15 minutes at prior to and immediately after the preventive intervention. Raters were unaware of the groups to which the parents and children were assigned. As hypothesized, parents who participated in the intervention were more responsive, attentive and affectionate toward their children, compared with controls.

We next examined children's behavior in a social situation with peers. Children were observed for 45 minutes in a peer group setting prior to and immediately after the intervention. These observations were made blind to group status. As hypothesized, compared to controls, children who participated in the program had substantially higher ratings on the social competence scale.

Finally, we asked parents to rate child behavior before the intervention, immediately after the program, and 6 months later. Parents of children who participated in the program reported that their children had fewer behavior problems than controls, post-intervention and at the 6-month follow-up. Thus, gains that were apparent at the end of the program were maintained 6 months later.

These results are promising and suggest that group differences between families in the intervention program and controls are apparent at the end of the prevention program, and are maintained over time. We have recently begun a federally-funded randomized clinical trial of the preventive intervention. The subjects are 100 inner-city preschoolers who have older siblings with court documented histories of delinquent behavior. If we replicate the findings from the pilot study, that is, if treated children show fewer conduct problems over time compared with controls, we will conclude that our program is successful in positively altering the developmental course of children at high-risk for developing antisocial behavior. If the program is shown to truly prevent the development of conduct problems in children at greatest risk, the policy implications would be enormous.

CASE EXAMPLE

The following is a case description of a child who participated in the pilot study. Thomas C. is an African American boy who was 5 years old when he started the preventive intervention program. When his family came to the program, Thomas lived with his 38-year-old mother, his 36-year-old father, and his half-brother and half-sister, ages 17 and 15, respectively. Mrs. C. was attending college and Mr. C. was on physical disability leave from his job as a construction worker. When Thomas entered the program, he had been attending a preschool for children with speech delays. Thomas was identified for the study through his older brother, Jerome, who was convicted for second-degree robbery. Mr. C. has bipolar disorder and alcohol abuse disorder, although he was not in treatment at the time the family entered the program. Both Thomas' brother and sister have a history of conduct disorder. Mrs. C.'s mother and sister have positive histories for depressive disorders.

At the initial intake interview, Mrs. C. expressed concern about Thomas' aggressivity with other children. During the period of evaluation, he was kicked out of preschool due to his aggressive behavior. Mrs. C. reported that Thomas would bite himself when he was angry or frustrated. Once he took a light bulb out of the socket and intentionally burned himself. He was often physically and verbally aggressive toward his mother. According to his mother, Thomas would not comply with limits set by his teacher or herself.

During the first evaluation session, Thomas spotted a dart board across the room and inquired "Whose dart board is this?" The evaluator responded, "It is for children to play with when they come to this room." "What do they do with it?" Thomas inquired. The evaluator answered, "They throw these special balls at it that stick to it." "Not me, I break it," Thomas yelled as he proceeded to break the board in half. Mrs. C. observed from the side of the room and responded, "Oh Thomas, that's not very nice."

During another evaluation session, Thomas indicated to his mother that he wanted to hold her hand. At first he reached over and held her hand gently. He then started to squeeze her hand, harder and harder, digging his nails into her skin. His mother said softly, "That hurts." Thomas continued to squeeze saying, "I want to hurt you." His mother continued to plead with him to stop, "But that hurts . . . it's not nice." Finally, when he drew blood, she pulled her hand away.

During another evaluation session, Thomas dumped all the toys in the room on the floor. His mother said, "You know you are going to have to clean all those up later." Thomas replied, "F___ you. I hate you. You're not my mother." His mother did not respond. Thomas laughed and continued to scream obscenities. Then he ran into the closet, repeatedly opening the door and screaming at her to "shut up." Mrs. C. still did not respond and then started to cry. Thomas finally came out of the closet, ran up to her and said, "Why don't you say something?"

These vignettes illustrate the typical coercive interactions that occurred between Mrs. C. and Thomas. Mrs. C. was unable to set limits with Thomas or provide consequences for his misbehavior. When she gave a command, she often used a tone of voice that did not convey seriousness. She revealed to the evaluator that she felt "completely helpless" with regard to changing her son's behavior. She reported that she feared she was "doomed to repeat the same mistakes with Thomas" that she had made with her older children. Mrs. C. provided some praise for Thomas's positive behavior, although it usually was nonspecific praise such as "you're a good boy, I love you." Mrs. C. reported that her husband was not supportive of her as a mother and often undermined her authority with Thomas. Months later she revealed that her husband had been hitting her and verbally berating her in front of the children.

In the initial session of the children's groups, Thomas displayed high levels of aggressive behavior. He was destructive with toys and kicked the therapists and other children. He had a very difficult time sharing with other children and was often noncompliant.

Through her participation in the parenting group, Mrs. C. learned to provide specific praise for Thomas's positive behavior and to spend time in free play activities with him. Importantly, she learned to give specific commands and follow up with consequences for noncompliance and misbehavior. Other group members supported her need to establish rules in the house and to "stand firm" when Thomas broke rules.

Mrs. C. was able to try out these new skills during the parent-child interaction training component. During this time, the therapists and other parents encouraged her to follow through with consequences. The first time that Thomas broke a rule, the therapist pointed this out and stated that Thomas would need to go to the time-out chair. The first few times, the therapist modeled how to give a time-out. Soon, Mrs. C. gave Thomas a time-out on her own with the therapists and other parents observing and encouraging her along the way. Within a few weeks, she started using the time-out technique at home. During home visits, the therapist observed her carrying out the procedure, giving guidance and praise to Mrs. C. Mr. C. was engaged in the therapeutic process during the home visits, and eventually took part, albeit somewhat sporadically, in the parent training groups. Home visits focused on helping Mr. and Mrs. C. work together to provide a unified approach to parenting.

Toward the end of the intervention, Mrs. C. reported decreased marital discord and increased joint problem solving and communication around parenting issues. Mr. C. eventually sought out treatment for his bipolar disorder and alcohol abuse. Mrs. C. graduated from college and obtained a job. Thomas's brother returned home and entered a city-run college preparatory program, and his sister started psychotherapy.

In response to the question, "What concerns you about your child?" Mrs. C. initially responded, "He doesn't get enough interaction with kids his age. Kids won't play with him. I'm concerned that he'll follow in his older brother's footsteps." At the completion of the program, Mrs. C. wrote, "I'm pretty content right now . . . " He plays well with others and by himself. He's a nice kid. A joy."

Even Thomas's perception of his own behavior changed. When the therapist mistakenly called Mr. C. "Thomas Sr.," Thomas corrected her by insisting, "Don't call him Thomas Sr., call him Big Thomas." The clinician queried, "If he's Big Thomas, then who are you?" Thomas smiled and replied, "I used to be wild Thomas, but now I'm calm Thomas."

CONCLUSION

This chapter presented the rationale for and a description of a preventive intervention program for young children at high risk for developing behavior problems. The program expands on a manualized treatment program (Webster-Stratton, 1981, 1984) that has been shown in numerous studies to be effective with young children who have behavior problems. In addition to parent training groups, our program includes a children's playgroup, parent-child interaction training, and home visits. We have pilot tested the program with inner-city preschoolers at high-risk for developing conduct disorders. We have demonstrated the program's acceptability with inner-city families who have children at familial risk for antisocial behavior. Preliminary findings from the pilot investigation suggest that the program may be effective in positively altering the developmental course of at-risk children. A randomized clinical trial with 100 families and a longer follow-up period is currently in progress. If the trial results in significantly more behavior problems at home and at school in the control group compared with the treatment group, we will conclude that our program is effective in preventing behavior problems in urban preschoolers at familial risk for antisocial behavior. Follow-up into adolescence would be necessary to conclude that the program prevents the development of antisocial and delinquent behavior. Given the poor showing of treatments for children who have already developed stable patterns of antisocial behavior, we hope that this program will provide an acceptable and successful approach to *preventing* the onset of behavior problems. The public health implications of such a successful intervention would be tremendous.

REFERENCES

Andrew, J. M. (1981). Delinquency: Correlating variables. *Journal of Clinical Child Psychology, 10,* 136–140.

Barkley, R. A. (1987). *Defiant children: A clinician's manual for parent training.* New York: Guilford Press.

Berrueta-Clement, J. R., Schweinhart, L. J., Barnett, W. S., Epstein, A. S., & Weikart, D. P. (1987). The effects of early educational intervention on crime and delinquency in adolescence and early childhood. In J. D. Burchard & S. N. Burchard (Eds.), *Primary prevention of psychopathology: Vol. 10. Prevention of delinquent behavior* (pp. 220–240). Newbury Park, CA: Sage.

Bierman, K. L., Miller, C. M., & Stabb, S. (1987). Improving the social behavior and peer acceptance of rejected boys: Effects of social skill training with instructions and prohibitions. *Journal of Consulting and Clinical Psychology,55,* 194–200.

Breiner, J. L., & Forehand, R. (1981). An assessment of the effects of parent training on clinic-referred children's school behavior. *Behavioral Assessment, 3,* 31–42.

Camp, B. W., & Bash, M. A. S. (1985). *Think aloud: Increasing social and cognitive skills—A problem solving program for children.* Champagne, IL: Research Press.

Caspi, A., Elder, G. H., & Bem, D. J. (1987). Moving against the world: Life-course patterns of explosive children. *Developmental Psychology, 23,* 308–313.

Chamberlain, P. (1990). Comparative evaluation of specialized foster care for seriously delinquent youths: A first step. *Community Alternatives: International Journal of Family Care, 2,* 21–36.

Chamberlain, P., & Reid, J. B. (1991). Using a specialized foster care community treatment model for children and adolescents leaving the state mental hospital. *Journal of Community Psychology, 19,* 267–276.

Cicchetti, D., & Richters, J. E. (1993). Developmental considerations in the investigation of conduct disorder. *Development and Psychopathology, 5,* 331–344.

Conduct Problems Prevention Research Group. (1992). A developmental and clinical model for the prevention of conduct disorder: The FAST track program. *Development and Psychopathology, 4*(4), 509–527.

Cunningham, C. E., Bremner, R., & Boyle, M. (1995). Large group community-based parenting programs for families of preschoolers at risk for disruptive behavior disorders: Utilization, cost effectiveness, and outcome. *Journal of Child Psychology and Psychiatry, 36,* 1141–1159.

Dishion, T. J., Patterson, G. R., & Kavanaugh, K. A. (1992). An experimental test of the coercion model: Linking theory, measurement, and intervention. In J. McCord & R. E. Tremblay (Eds.), *Preventing antisocial behavior: Intervention from birth through adolescence* (pp. 253–282). New York: Guilford Press.

Dodge, K. A. (1993). The future of research on the treatment of conduct disorder. *Development and Psychopathology, 5,* 311–319.

Dumas, J. E. (1989). Treating antisocial behavior in children: Child and family approaches. *Clinical Psychology Review, 42,* 435–442.

Eron, L. D., Huesmann, L. R., & Zelli, A. (1991). The role of parental variables in the learning of aggression. In D. J. Pepler & K. H. Rubin (Eds.), *The development and treatment of childhood aggression* (pp. 169–188). Hillsdale, NJ: Erlbaum.

Eyberg, S. M., & Boggs, S. R. (1989). Parent training for oppositional-defiant preschoolers. In C. E. Schaefer & J. M. Briesmeister (Eds.), *Handbook of parent training: Parents as cotherapists for children's behavior problems* (pp. 105–132). New York: Wiley.

Farrington, D. P. (1983). Offending from 10 to 25 years of age. In K. T. Van Dusen & S. A. Mednick (Eds.), *Prospective studies of crime and delinquency* (pp. 17–37). Boston: Kluwer-Nijhoff.

Forehand, R. L., & McMahon, R. J. (1981). *Helping the noncompliant child: A clinician's guide to parent training.* New York: Guilford Press.

Forgatch, M. S., & Toobert, D. T. (1979). A cost-effective parent training program for use with normal preschool children. *Journal of Pediatric Psychiatry, 4,* 129–145.

Garbarino, J., Kostelny, K., & Dubrow, N. (1992). *Children in dangerous environments: Coping with the consequences of community violence.* San Francisco: Jossey-Bass.

Gresham, F. M., & Nagle, R. J. (1980). Social skills training with children: Responsiveness to modeling and coaching as a function of peer orientation. *Journal of Consulting and Clinical Psychology, 48,* 718–729.

Guerra, N., Tolan, P., Huesmann, L. R., VanAcker, R., & Eron, L. (1992). *Metropolitan area child study.* Washington, DC: NIMH Workshop for Perspective Grant Applicants.

Henggeler, S. W. (1994). *Treatment manual for family preservation using multisystemic therapy.* Columbia, SC: South Carolina Health and Human Services Commission.

Henggeler, S. W., Melton, G. B., & Smith, L. A. (1992). Family preservation using multisystemic therapy: An effective alternative to incarcerating serious juvenile offenders. *Journal of Consulting and Clinical Psychology, 60,* 953–961.

Hinshaw, S. P., Lahey, B. B., & Hart, E. L. (1993). Issues and taxonomy and comorbidity in the development of conduct disorder. *Development and Psychopathology, 5,* 31–49.

Huesmann, L. R., & Eron, L. D. (1989). Individual differences in the trait of aggression. *European Journal of Personality, 3,* 95–106.

Huesmann, L. R., Eron, L. D., Lefkowitz, M. M., & Walder, L. O. (1984). The stability of aggression over time and generations. *Developmental Psychology, 20,* 1120–1134.

Johnson, D. L., & Walker, T. (1987). Primary prevention of behavior problems in Mexican-American children. *American Journal of Community Psychology, 15,* 375–385.

Jones, M. B., Offord, D. R., & Abrams, N. (1980). Brothers, sisters and antisocial behavior. *British Journal of Psychiatry, 136,* 139–145.

Kazdin, A. E. (1987). Treatment of antisocial behavior in children: Current status and future directions. *Psychological Bulletin, 102,* 187–203.

Kazdin, A. E. (1993). Treatment of conduct disorder: Progress and directions in psychotherapy research. *Development and Psychopathology, 5,* 277–310.

Kazdin, A. E., Esveldt-Dawson, K., French, N. H., & Unis, A. S. (1987). Problem-solving skills training and relationship therapy in the treatment of antisocial child behavior. *Journal of Consulting and Clinical Psychology, 55,* 76–85.

Kazdin, A. E., Siegel, T. C., & Bass, D. (1992). Cognitive problem-solving skills training and parent management training in the treatment of antisocial behavior in children. *Journal of Consulting and Clinical Psychology, 60,* 733–747.

Kellam, S. G., & Rebok, G. W. (1992). Building developmental and etiological theory through epidemiologically based preventive intervention trials. In J. McCord & R. E. Tremblay (Eds.), *Preventing antisocial behavior* (pp. 162–195). New York: Guilford Press.

Kendall, P. C., & Braswell, L. (1985). *Cognitive-behavioral therapy for impulsive children.* New York: Guilford Press.

Ladd, G. W., & Asher, S. R. (1985). Social skills training and children's peer relations: Current issues in research and practice. In L. L'Abate & M. Milan (Eds.), *Handbook of social skills training* (pp. 219–244). New York: Wiley.

Lally, J., Mangione, P., & Honig, A. (1988). The Syracuse University family development project: Long-range impact of an early intervention with low income children and their families. In D. R. Powell (Ed.), *Parent education as an early childhood intervention: Emerging directions in theory, research and practice* (pp. 79–104). Norwood, NJ: ABLEX.

Landy, S., & Peters, R. D. (1992). Toward an understanding of a developmental paradigm for aggressive conduct problems during the preschool years. In R. D. Peters, R. J. McMahon, & V. L. Quinsey (Eds.), *Aggression and violence throughout the life span* (pp. 1–30). Newbury Park, CA: Sage.

Lochman, J. E., Burch, P. R., Curry, J. F., & Lampron, L. B. (1984). Treatment and generalization effects of cognitive-behavioral and goal-setting interventions with aggressive boys. *Journal of Consulting and Clinical Psychology, 52,* 915–916.

Loeber, R. (1982). The stability of antisocial and delinquent child behavior: A review. *Child Development, 53,* 1431–1446.

Loeber, R. (1988). The natural histories of juvenile conduct problems, substance use and delinquency: Evidence for developmental progressions. In B. B. Lahey & A. E. Kazdin (Eds.), *Advances in clinical child psychology* (Vol. 11, pp. 73–124). New York: Plenum Press.

Loeber, R. (1991). Questions and advances in the study of developmental pathways. In D. Cicchetti & S. Toth (Eds.), *Rochester Symposium on Developmental Psychopathology: III* (pp. 97–115). Rochester, NY: Rochester University Press.

Loeber, R., & Dishion, T. J. (1983). Early predictors of male adolescent delinquency: A review. *Psychological Bulletin, 94,* 68–99.

McCord, J. (1979). Some child-rearing antecedents of criminal behavior in adult men. *Journal of Personality and Social Psychology, 8,* 1477–1486.

McGinnis, E., & Goldstein, A. (1990). *Skill streaming in early childhood: Teaching prosocial skills to the preschool and kindergarten child.* New York: Research Press.

McMahon, R. J., & Forehand, R. (1984). Parent training for the noncompliant child: Treatment outcome, generalization, and adjunctive therapy procedures. In R. F. Dangel & P. A. Polster (Eds.), *Parent training: Foundations of research and practice* (pp. 298–328). New York: Guilford Press.

Miller, L. S. (1994a). Preventive interventions for conduct disorders: A review. Disruptive disorders [Special issue]. *Child and Adolescent Psychiatric Clinics of North America, 3*(2), 405–420.

Miller, L. S. (1994b). Primary prevention of conduct disorder. *Psychiatric Quarterly, 65*(4), 273–285.

Moffit, T. E. (1993). Adolescence-limited and life-course-persistent antisocial behavior: A developmental taxonomy. *Psychological Review, 100*(4), 674–701.

Offord, D. R., & Bennett, K. J. (1994). Conduct disorder: Long-term outcomes and intervention effectiveness. *Journal of the American Academy of Child and Adolescent Psychiatry, 33*(8), 1069–1078.

Olweus, D. (1979). Stability of aggressive reaction patterns in males: A review. *Psychological Bulletin, 86,* 852–875.

Patterson, G. R. (1979). A performance theory of coercive family interaction. In R. B. Cairns (Ed.), *Analysis of social interactions: Methods, issues, and illustrations* (pp. 119–162). Hillsdale, NJ: Erlbaum.

Patterson, G. R. (1982). *A social learning approach: Vol. 3. Coercive family process.* Eugene, OR: Castalia Press.

Patterson, G. R. (1984). Siblings: Fellow travelers in coercive family processes. In R. J. Blanchard & D. C. Blanchard (Eds.), *Advances in the study of aggression* (Vol. 1, pp. 173–215). Orlando, FL: Academic Press.

Patterson, G. R., Chamberlain, P., & Reid, J. B. (1982). A comparative evaluation of parent training procedures. *Behavior Therapy, 13,* 638–650.

Patterson, G. R., Cobb, J. A., & Ray, R. S. (1973). A social engineering technology for retraining the families of aggressive boys. In H. E. Adams & I. P. Unikel (Eds.), *Issues and trends in behavior therapy* (pp. 139–210). Springfield, IL: Thomas.

Patterson, G. R., Reid, J. B., & Dishion, T. J. (1992). *A social interactional approach: Vol. 4. Antisocial boys.* Eugene, OR: Castalia Press.

Patterson, G. R., Reid, J. B., Jones, R. R., & Conger, R. W. (1975). *A social learning approach to family intervention* (Vol. 1). Eugene, OR: Castalia Press.

Patterson, G. R., & Stouthamer-Loeber, M. (1984). The correlation of family management practices and delinquency. *Child Development, 55,* 1299–1307.

Reid, J. B. (1992). Prevention of conduct disorder before and after school entry: Relating interventions to developmental findings. *Development and Psychopathology, 5,* 243–262.

Robins, L. N. (1978). Sturdy childhood predictors of adult antisocial behavior: Replications from longitudinal studies. *Psychological Medicine, 8*(4), 611–622.

Rowe, D. C., & Herstand, S. E. (1986). Familial influences on television viewing and aggression: A sibling study. *Aggressive Behavior, 12*(2), 111–120.

Rowe, D. C., Rodgers, J. L., & Meseck-Bushey, S. (1992). Sibling delinquency and the family environment: Shared and unshared influences. *Child Development, 63*(1), 59–67.

Rutter, M., & Giller, H. (1983). *Juvenile delinquency: Trends and perspectives.* Middlesex, England: Penguin Books.

Seitz, V., Rosenbaum, L. K., & Apfel, N. H. (1985). Effects of family support intervention: A ten-year follow-up. *Child Development, 56,* 376–391.

Spitzer, A., Webster-Stratton, C., & Hollinsworth, T. (1991). Coping with conduct-problem children: Parents gaining knowledge and control. *Journal of Clinical Child Psychology, 20,* 413–427.

Spivak, G., & Shure, M. B. (1974). *Social adjustment of young children: A cognitive approach to solving real-life problems.* San Francisco: Jossey-Bass.

Tolan, P. H., & Henry, D. (1994, October). *Patterns of psychopathology among urban poor children: The role of aggression.* Symposium presented at the 41st annual meeting of the American Academy of Child and Adolescent Psychiatry, New York.

Tremblay, R. E., Vitaro, F., Bertrand, L., LeBlanc, M., Beachesne, H., Boileau, H., & David, L. (1992). Parent and child training to prevent early onset of delinquency: The Montreal Longitudinal-Experimental Study. In J. McCord & R. E. Tremblay (Eds.), *Preventing antisocial behavior: Interventions from birth to adolescence* (pp. 117–138). New York: Guilford Press.

Twito, T. J., & Stewart, M. A. (1982). A half-sibling study of aggressive conduct disorder: Prevalence of disorders in parents, brothers and sisters. *Neuropsychobiology, 8*(3), 144–150.

Vitaro, F., Gagnon, C., & Tremblay, R. E. (1990). Predicting stable peer rejection from kindergarten to grade one. *Journal of Clinical Child Psychology, 19,* 257–264.

Walter, H. J., Vaughan, R. D., Armstrong, B., Krakoff, R. Y., Maldonado, L. M., Tiezzi, L., & McCarthy, J. F. (1995). Sexual, assaultive, and suicidal behaviors among urban minority Junior High School students. *Journal of the American Academy of Child and Adolescent Psychiatry, 34,* 73–80.

Wasserman, G. W., Miller, L. S., Pinner, E. & Jaramillo, B. (1996). Parenting predictors of early conduct problems in urban, high-risk boys. *Journal of the American Academy of Child and Adolescent Psychiatry, 35*(9), 1227–1236.

Webster-Stratton, C. (1981). Videotape modeling: A method of parent education. *Journal of Clinical Child Psychology, 10,* 93–98.

Webster-Stratton, C. (1982). The long-term effect of a videotape modeling parent education program: Comparison of immediate and one year follow-up results. *Behavior Therapy, 13,* 702–714.

Webster-Stratton, C. (1984). A randomized trial of two parent training programs for families with conduct disordered children. *Journal of Consulting and Clinical Psychology, 52,* 666–678.

Webster-Stratton, C. (1987). *Parents and children: A 10 program videotape parent training series with manuals.* Eugene, OR: Castalia Press.

Webster-Stratton, C. (1989). Systematic comparison of consumer satisfaction of three cost-effective parent training programs for conduct problem children. *Behavior Therapy, 20,* 103–115.

Webster-Stratton, C. (1991). Annotation: Strategies for helping families with conduct disordered children. *Journal of Child Psychology and Psychiatry, 32*(7), 1047–1062.

Webster-Stratton, C., & Hammond, M. (1997). Treating children with early-onset conduct problems: A comparison of child and parent interventions. *Journal of Consulting and Clinical Psychology, 65*(1), 93–109.

Webster-Stratton, C., & Herbert, M. (1993). What really happens in parent training? *Behavior Modification, 17,* 407–456.

Webster-Stratton, C., & Herbert, M. (1994). *Troubled families–Problem children.* New York: Wiley.

Webster-Stratton, C., Kolpacoff, M., & Hollinsworth, T. (1988). Self-administered videotape therapy for families with conduct disordered children: Comparisons to two other treatments and a control group. *Journal of Consulting and Clinical Psychology, 57,* 550–553.

Webster-Stratton, C., Kolpacoff, M., & Hollinsworth, T. (1989). The long-term effectiveness and clinical significance of three cost-effective training programs for families with conduct-problem children. *Journal of Consulting and Clinical Psychology, 5,* 550–553.

Wells, K. C., & Egan, J. (1988). Social learning and systems family therapy for childhood oppositional disorder: Comparative treatment outcome. *Comprehensive Psychiatry, 29,* 138–146.

West, D. J. (1982). *Delinquency: Its roots, careers, and prospects.* Cambridge, MA: Harvard University Press.

West, D. J., & Farrington, D. P. (1973). *Who becomes delinquent?* New York: Crane, Russak.

West, D. J., & Farrington, D. P. (1977). *The delinquent way of life.* London: Heinemann.

Yoshikawa, H. (1994). Prevention as cumulative protection: Effects of early family support and education on chronic delinquency and its risks. *Psychological Bulletin, 115*(1), 28–54.

Zigler, E., & Freedman, J. (1987). Evaluating family support programs. In S. L. Kagan, D. R. Powell, B. Weissbourd, & E. Zigler (Eds.), *America's family support programs: Perspectives and prospects* (pp. 352–364). New Haven, CT: Yale University Press.

Zigler, E., Taussig, C., & Black, K. (1992). Early childhood intervention: A promising preventive for juvenile delinquency. *Annuals of Psychology, 47,* 997–1006.

INTERNALIZING DISORDERS

THE CHAPTERS in Part Two focus on internalizing disorders. These typically involve symptoms such as anxiety, excessive inhibition, and depression. In Chapter 6, Eisen, Engler, and Geyer submit a parent training program that seeks to control and ameliorate the distressing symptoms of separation anxiety disorder (SAD). The authors elucidate the pertinent roles that the developmental level and cognitive processes play in understanding and determining an anxious child's functioning. They discuss, and caution the reader against the myriad subtle ways in which parents may inadvertently maintain and exacerbate childhood anxiety features. The parents need to be made aware of the impact and consequences of such behaviors as overprotection, excessive reassurance, and inappropriate and dysfunctional parent-child interactions.

Eisen, Engler, and Geyer describe the components of a parent training program designed to address separation anxiety disorder symptoms in young children. Their approach relies heavily on cognitive-behavioral procedures to educate parents in the appropriate and most effective responses to the child's separation anxiety. They outline performance-based procedures as well as cognitive interventions that have been used successfully to reduce internalizing disorders. The authors underline the importance of identifying and assessing the anxious child's coping resources, targeting the child's negative self-talk, assisting the child in formulating positive attributions, and instructing parents in parent training/contingency management and shaping procedures.

In the second half of the chapter, Eisen, Engler, and Geyer offer a case study of a 9-year-old boy who is experiencing a significant separation anxiety disorder. The case material illustrates invaluable techniques for assessing the nature and intensity of the youngster's anxiety disorder. The authors identify prescriptive treatment strategies that were applied to this case; for example self-monitoring forms for both the parents and the child. They then share the precise maneuvers applied in each session and present the rationale for incorporating separate training sessions with the parents and the child, as well as collateral training sessions for the parent-child configuration. A discussion of the essential characteristics and qualifications of therapists who engage in effective parent training has also been included.

In Chapter 7, Kearney and Roblek recount an extensive spectrum of school refusal problems ranging from those children who never attend school to those who attend intermittently to those who attend school but exhibit disruptive and interfering behaviors. The treatment of school refusal problems is grounded in certain essential conceptions. First, treatment modalities must address and include all types of children who refuse school. Second, there may be vastly divergent reasons for school refusal. Each youngster has a specific, unique, and subjective reason for refusing school. Finally, each child's reasons for refusing school determine the nature and format of the parent training intervention technique. Through the implementation of case studies, the authors demonstrate a functional treatment model that includes assessments and a prescriptive approach to the problem. The approach is geared to each child's particular reasons for refusing school. Children may refuse school to avoid anxiety-provoking and stressful situations, to escape aversive social or evaluative situations, to get attention from significant others, to pursue positive tangible reinforcement outside of school, or to achieve a combination of these goals.

To ensure that the parent training modality recognizes and addresses the specific needs of individual children with school refusal problems, Kearney and Roblek's multicomponent assessment process and intervention approach identifies fundamental core variables. These variables are empirically based and clinically pertinent in each instance of school refusal. They encompass a large and complex array of interrelated factors: the individual child's reasons for school refusal, parent variables (e.g., parenting styles, expectations, possible marital conflict), the specific nature of the parent training, and the primary elements of treatment such as the components of contingency contracting (e.g., establishing times and places for negotiation and communication, defining the specific problem, designing a written contract, and implementing the contract effectively). The authors also encourage therapists to form a working alliance with school officials, and they consider the impact of involving parents in the treatment process.

CHAPTER 6

Parent Training for Separation Anxiety Disorder

ANDREW R. EISEN, LINDA B. ENGLER, and BEATA GEYER

SEPARATION ANXIETY disorder (SAD) is the only anxiety disorder category in *DSM-IV* (American Psychiatric Association, 1994) that is specifically based on child-oriented criteria. Social phobia and generalized anxiety disorder include features of *DSM-III-R* (American Psychiatric Association, 1987) avoidant and overanxious disorders, respectively. However, these disorders no longer exist as separate diagnostic categories. The remaining *DSM-IV* anxiety disorders that children and adolescents experience (e.g., panic disorder, obsessive-compulsive disorder) are completely based on adult criteria.

For the most part, the current version of SAD has changed only marginally from that of *DSM-III-R*. The defining feature of SAD continues to be unrealistic and excessive anxiety concerning separation (APA, 1994). Since it is not uncommon for young children (2 to 3 years of age) to experience separation anxiety (Rutter, 1981), the degree of impairment must (a) exceed that expected given the child's developmental level and (b) cause significant interference in social and academic functioning (APA, 1994). A notable difference between *DSM-III-R* and its successor is the duration of disturbance requirement. The current diagnostic system necessitates a continuous disturbance of 4 weeks (as opposed to 2 weeks), which increases the likelihood that an SAD diagnosis is clinically significant.

Prevalence estimates for SAD have been slightly higher in children (3%–5%; Anderson, Williams, McGee, & Silva, 1987; Bird et al., 1988) as compared with their adolescent counterparts (.01%–2.4%; Bowen, Offord,

& Boyle, 1990; McGee, Feehan, Williams, & Anderson, 1992). SAD appears to be slightly more common in females and is frequently comorbid with overanxious disorder (Last, Hersen, Kazdin, Finkelstein, & Strauss, 1987). In addition, depression and somatic complaints frequently co-occur with SAD (Last, 1991).

TREATMENT RESEARCH

Currently, there exists a paucity of empirical studies investigating cognitive-behavioral interventions for SAD. Thus far, treatment research has been limited to case reports (e.g., Thyer & Sowers-Hoag, 1988) that have offered evidence for the effectiveness of cognitive-behavioral procedures. However, these case reports have been plagued by methodological difficulties (see Ollendick, Hagopian, & Huntzinger, 1991).

A number of investigations have also examined the utility of antidepressant medications for SAD. In a series of studies, Gittelman-Klein and Klein (1971, 1973) offered convincing evidence for the therapeutic effectiveness of imipramine (IMI) in treating symptoms of SAD. In their work, IMI was administered to 45 children with school refusal behavior for 6 weeks. The majority of the children received a SAD diagnosis but school refusal behavior was the central presenting complaint. In addition, IMI treatment was combined with behaviorally oriented therapy. The results revealed improvements on child, parent, and clinician ratings regarding somatic complaints and separation anxiety. The most notable finding, however, was IMI's superior return rate to school compared with a placebo control (81% vs. 47%).

In more recent studies, however, IMI demonstrated only marginal effectiveness compared with placebo controls (Klein, Koplewicz, & Kanner, 1992). This has been true for other pharmacological agents (clomipramine, alprazolam) as well (Berney et al., 1981; Bernstein, Garfinkel, & Borchardt, 1990). Furthermore, most studies have been hampered by methodological constraints (e.g., small sample sizes, diagnostic heterogeneity) that limit the generalizability of the findings. Overall, research has not supported the therapeutic efficacy of pharmacological agents for SAD. Carefully controlled comparative studies (cognitive-behavioral vs. medication) are greatly needed.

THEORETICAL FRAMEWORK

Kendall and colleagues (Kendall, 1985; Kendall, Howard, & Epps, 1988) have outlined a cognitive-behavioral model to explain the development and maintenance of anxious behaviors in children. The model separates cognition into four factors: structures, content, processes, and products.

Cognitive structures relate to the organization and formation of memory representations of information. A child develops a set of predicted experiences that are stored in the cognitive structures. Cognitive content is the information that the cognitive structures represent. The cognitive schema is the integration of cognitive content and structure that results in a frame of reference through which the child interprets the world. Cognitive products are the attributions that result from the combination of information with the three other cognitive factors (structures, content, and schema). As a child attempts to understand any given event, these cognitive components interact in a unique fashion. Kendall and MacDonald (1993) propose that psychopathology may be related to any of these cognitive factors and that each must be considered when planning treatment interventions.

Kendall and MacDonald (1993) make a distinction between cognitive deficiencies and cognitive distortions and their links to childhood disorders. The former entails an insufficient amount of cognitive activity (e.g., thinking, problem solving), whereas the latter involves dysfunctional thinking processes. In general, internalizing (overcontrolled) disorders are associated with cognitive distortions. These distortions relate to negative self-evaluation and a catastrophic view of the likelihood of severe negative outcomes. Meichenbaum (1986) describes three cognitive processes where distortions might occur. These include appraisal of the negative event, attribution of increased arousal, and evaluating self-competence to effectively confront the aversive event. Kendall's model suggests that for anxiety-disordered children, distortions occur at all three levels.

Although cognitive processes may play a pertinent role in determining an anxious child's functioning, the developmental level of the child serves an important function as well. This is especially true for children in the "concrete operational" stage (Piaget, 1967), where clinicians will need to focus more on concrete concepts in phrasing interview and treatment questions. A child's developmental level may also dictate the type and pace of the treatment program. Cognitive therapy may not be indicated for some youngsters, and the pace of treatment may need to progress more slowly with younger children.

RATIONALE FOR PARENT TRAINING

Parent training can be useful in working with anxious youth in general (e.g., Knox, Albano, & Barlow, 1996), and SAD in particular (Raleigh, Spasaro, & Eisen, 1995). Parents of children with SAD can fall prey to three traps that can inadvertently facilitate childhood anxiety: overprotection, excessive reassurance, and aversive parent-child interactions (Eisen & Kearney, 1995).

Parental overprotection occurs when a parent limits a child's opportunities to be exposed to anxiety-provoking stimuli. This may take the form of concealing some sources of information (e.g., television shows) or restricting activities (e.g., sports participation). In the case of SAD, a child's preoccupation with potential harm befalling a parent or themselves may fuel the caregiver's protectiveness.

In a similar vein, parents of children with SAD may find themselves frequently resorting to the use of comforting reassurance to mollify their children's fears of tragic outcomes. In doing so, the parent may limit a child's opportunities to develop independent coping skills.

Finally, because a child's separation anxiety may not generalize to every situation (e.g., remaining alone during a favorite television show), a parent may view a child's anxious behavior as manipulative. If such a scenario develops, aversive parent-child interactions (e.g., reprimands) may ensue. All three traps encourage child anxiety because the parent provides attention (positive or negative) during a child's fearful displays. Parent training can eliminate or minimize the impact of these traps by utilizing differential reinforcement, shaping, and contingency management procedures (to be discussed).

In addition to targeting traps that may exacerbate child anxiety, a parent training program for SAD should capitalize on the many roles that parents can play in their child's treatment. These roles include effective communicator, cotherapist, motivator, and educator (Eisen & Kearney, 1995).

A parent's communicative style for both verbal and nonverbal behavior can be a powerful influence in the treatment process. In the verbal realm, the frequent use of excessive reassurance and/or reprimands can actually elevate a child's anxiety. For this reason, parents should attend to their children's coping efforts and ignore signs of anxious apprehension. In the nonverbal domain, signs of parental uncertainty (e.g., facial grimaces) during a child's exposure-based homework assignments can hamper a child's success. For this reason, it is important for parents to serve as effective coping models (Kendall, 1991). This can be accomplished by having parents provide positive verbal and nonverbal feedback to their children during their coping efforts.

The likelihood of maintenance and generalization of treatment effects is enhanced when parents serve as cotherapists. The parents as cotherapist are intricately involved in their child's exposure-based homework assignments and the completion of daily diaries. The parents are largely responsible for the arrangement and implementation of exposures and, in conjunction with the therapist, can serve as a much-needed resource to remove any treatment obstacles (e.g., noncompliance). With respect to the daily diaries, the parent can assist in thought specification and recording. When working with youngsters, such assistance is invaluable.

It is not unusual for anxious youth to lack the necessary motivation to participate in a treatment program. For this reason, the parents as motivators become increasingly important. Parents can provide encouraging feedback or provide tangible rewards for compliance with treatment procedures (Silverman, 1989). A supportive family environment can help maintain a child's enthusiasm throughout the treatment process.

Finally, it is important for parents to educate their children about age-appropriate topics (e.g., relative's death, world events) and discuss their potentially negative effects. In doing so, parents can facilitate the development of problem-solving skills in their children. If a parent severely filters a child's access to unpleasant topics, anxious apprehension can result.

THE PARENT TRAINING PROGRAM

In this section, we describe the different components of a parent training program for SAD. We discuss assessment methods, therapist characteristics, and treatment procedures. Our approach combines cognitive-behavioral procedures with complementary parent training strategies.

Assessment Methods

In assessing anxious apprehension in children and adolescents, a multimethod-multisource approach using a tripartite model is recommended (e.g., cognitive, behavioral, and physiological measures; Morris & Kratochwill, 1983). To accomplish this task, diagnostic interviews, self-report measures, behavioral observations, and physiological indexes are often utilized.

The clinical interview has become one of the most prominent and widely used assessment instruments (e.g., Silverman, 1991). The Anxiety Disorders Interview Schedule for *DSM-IV* (Child and Parent versions; ADIS-C and ADIS-P; Silverman & Albano, 1995) is frequently utilized for the assessment of childhood anxiety. The section on SAD provides quantifiable data concerning anxiety symptoms, etiology, course, and a functional analysis of the disorder.

Self-report measures have also been useful in helping clinicians identify salient characteristics of childhood anxiety. Some instruments that are also useful for assessing features of separation anxiety in children include the State-Trait Anxiety Inventory for Children (STAIC; Spielberger, 1973), Fear Survey Schedule for Children-Revised (FSSC-R; Ollendick, 1983), Revised Children's Manifest Anxiety Scale (RCMAS; Reynolds & Richman, 1978), and the Child Anxiety Sensitivity Index (CASI; Silverman, Fleisig, Rabian, & Peterson, 1991). Child self-report measures are important because children possess unique information regarding their difficulties. This is especially true for internalizing disorders, which are not as easily observed as externalizing disorders.

Because there can be considerable discrepancies between parent and child reports, parent-completed measures (e.g., Child Behavior Checklist; Achenbach, 1991a) should be part of the assessment process. In addition, we recommend that parents also complete measures assessing their own levels of anxiety and depression such as the Fear Questionnaire (FQ; Marks & Mathews, 1979) and the Beck Depression Inventory (BDI; Beck, Ward, Mendelsohn, Mock, & Erbaugh, 1961). These measures are useful in assessing the impact of parental anxiety and depression on child functioning.

In the event that a child's separation anxiety is producing distress in the school environment, we recommend the administration of teacher report measures (e.g., Teacher Report Form; Achenbach, 1991b). Teacher measures are helpful to clarify the relationship between a child's academic performance and social behavior.

To avoid some of the social desirability biases inherent in diagnostic interviewing schedules and self-report measures, behavioral observations should be incorporated into the assessment process whenever feasible. Behavioral observation data can be collected in such settings as school and hospitals, and during peer interactions. If practical constraints preclude collecting data in these settings, observations during the diagnostic interview can provide clinicians with valuable information about the child's demeanor and coping skills.

Finally, psychophysiological measures can be a valuable part of a multimethod assessment. Heart rate and sweat gland activity are the most useful measures in assessing changes associated with stress and relaxation (Silverman & Kearney, 1995). In the clinic setting, however, practical constraints often preclude their use.

THERAPIST CHARACTERISTICS

Kendall (1991) highlights the versatility associated with a cognitive-behavioral theoretical orientation. For example, the cognitive-behavioral therapist needs to simultaneously fulfill the roles of consultant, diagnostician, and educator. As a consultant, the cognitive-behavioral therapist facilitates the acquisition of skills by clients and provides opportunities for enhanced coping. The role of diagnostician requires making sense of data collected from myriad sources (e.g., child, parent, teacher), developing effective treatment programs for targeted problems, and formulating *DSM-IV* diagnoses. Finally, the cognitive-behavioral therapist's role of educator should not be underestimated. Only through the dissemination of information can children and their parents begin to understand the complexities associated with SAD. Through education, a child's self-efficacy can be enhanced.

COGNITIVE-BEHAVIORAL PROCEDURES

According to Kendall (1991), cognitive-behavioral strategies use enactive performance-based procedures as well as cognitive interventions to produce changes in thinking, feeling, and behavior (p. 5). For children exhibiting internalizing disorders such as depression or separation anxiety, cognitive treatment goals include identification and modification of distorted cognitive processing. These goals can be accomplished through the teaching of new, more adaptive, cognitive strategies (Kendall & MacDonald, 1993). A cognitive coping template (Kendall, 1985) is constructed that will allow the child to cope more effectively with perceived stress.

Silverman (1989) developed the STOP acronym, which depicts a four-step self-control process toward correcting cognitive distortions related to childhood anxiety:

1. *Scared.* Recognizing that one is scared.
2. *Thoughts.* Identifying fearful thoughts.
3. *Other Thoughts.* More adaptive self-talk and other activities that foster coping.
4. *Praise.* Evaluating one's attempt at coping and applying self-rewards.

The overall goal of self-control procedures is for children to recognize signs of fearfulness and to then initiate anxiety management skills (Kendall, 1985). Once a child has mastered the anxiety management skills (STOP), a series of exposures, both in session and for homework assignments are utilized. Imaginal or in vivo exposures progress from low-fear to high-fear situations according to a hierarchy that is developed with the child and parent. In addition, children are taught to evaluate the actual data that exist, which likely disprove distorted cognitions. The goal of this aspect of treatment is for the child to evaluate him- or herself, as well as expected outcomes more realistically. Finally, modeling is used to aid the child in developing the ability to identify and challenge distorted cognitions.

The child's self-talk is an important component of this treatment approach. The child's expectations and attributions regarding individuals and the external world constitute self-talk (Kendall, 1985). Unrealistic worry about harmful outcomes involving parents or oneself tend to be the central focus for children with SAD. This chronic preoccupation of potential harm is inextricably linked with the child's reluctance to be alone. Identification of thoughts may be difficult for young children, who may not be aware of internal thoughts. However, children can be taught to identify self-talk by presenting them with cartoon figures with empty thought bubbles and asked to fill in the character's thoughts (Kendall, 1985).

In addition to targeting the child's negative self-talk, training in self-evaluation and reward is important. Because of the child's preoccupation with potential tragic outcomes to oneself and others, many children with SAD may ardently resist participation in exposure-based homework assignments. For this reason, we recommend that exposures be implemented at a gradual pace and that partial successes be emphasized. As the child with SAD experiences neutral outcomes, more realistic attributions will emerge. The use of rewards (i.e., self-praise) builds the child's confidence and self-efficacy to withstand situations eliciting greater potential fear.

Other cognitive-behavioral treatment procedures that might be used to treat SAD include relaxation training exercises and problem-solving strategies. Relaxation involves progressive relaxation of major muscle groups through tension-releasing exercises (e.g., Ollendick & Cerny, 1981). The child learns to notice muscle tension and to use that as a cue to engage in relaxation procedures. A problem-solving approach (e.g., D'Zurilla & Goldfried, 1971) involves training in problem definition, generation of alternative solutions, choice of and implementation of a chosen strategy, and evaluation of success.

PARENT TRAINING STRATEGIES

In this section, we describe parent training/contingency management procedures that can be used to treat anxious apprehension in general and SAD in particular. These include enhancing parent attention, command training, differential reinforcement, and shaping (Eisen & Kearney, 1995).

Enhancing parental attention is an essential component of a parent training program for SAD. It is not unusual for parents to exaggerate, minimize, or distort their children's difficulties. This was illustrated in our discussion of parental traps. Thus, children with SAD are receiving a great deal of attention (positive or negative) for fearful displays. The idea behind enhancing parental attention is to encourage parents to become more effective monitors of their children's behaviors. By doing so, the parent will more accurately identify a child's separation anxiety patterns that can be modified during treatment. This can be accomplished in a number of ways. A parent can maintain daily diaries listing the antecedents and consequences of a child's behavior, or the therapist can videotape parent-child interactions. The mechanism for enhanced parental monitoring is to increase the amount of time the parent observes a child.

Command training is also a useful strategy for addressing separation-related fears. Parents of children with both internalizing and externalizing disorders can deliver commands in a vague or critical manner (Barkley, 1989). Such a pattern can set the stage for parent-child power struggles that reinforce inappropriate or fearful behavior. In the case of SAD, a parental statement such as "clean your room," will often result in noncompliance on the child's part. First, the statement lacks sufficient specificity to enable the child to follow through. Second, the parent failed to take into account the amount of time the child could remain alone. Thus, the idea behind command training is to help parents deliver clear, firm commands that leave little room for misinterpretation. An example of such a command is, "Put your toys in the closet and come downstairs in five minutes."

Up to now, we have been discussing a number of ways in which parents accentuate a child's fearful displays. The idea behind differential reinforcement is to restructure this process so that parental attention becomes contingent on a child's coping efforts. This can be accomplished by having parents dispense reinforcers for a child's coping efforts and coaching them to ignore or minimize attention given for fearful displays. The therapist in conjunction with parent and child should compose a list consisting of tangible (e.g., toys, video games, favorite meals), social (e.g., parties), activity (e.g., family game, going to the zoo), and token (e.g., poker chips, gold stars to be cashed in at a later time) reinforcers (Silverman, 1989). At the outset of the program, tangibles may be necessary to motivate the child with SAD to attempt exposures. As progress becomes more apparent, it is recommended to fade tangibles and administer a greater number of social and activity reinforcers. In this way, a child's coping efforts become a source of intrinsic satisfaction.

Finally, shaping is an integral part of the parent training program. Shaping is broadly defined as rewarding successive approximations of a targeted response (e.g., Martin & Pear, 1983). This is reflected in the gradual approach to exposing the separation-anxious child to anxiety-provoking stimuli. Typical exposures simply increase the amount of time the child will remain alone. Situations could include sleeping at night, remaining in one's room, or waiting for a parent to return from an errand. In each scenario, the exposures are intensified by increasing their duration from minutes to hours. The therapist, in conjunction with the parent and child, will determine the appropriate schedule for the child. In the next section, we discuss a case example to illustrate the implementation of the parent training procedures.

CASE EXAMPLE

Description and History

Danny Kaplan presented as a bright, verbal 9-year-old boy. His engaging personality fostered a good working relationship with the therapist immediately. His most significant presenting problem was described to the therapist as intense separation anxiety, particularly on departure to school in the mornings, as well as when returning to school after having lunch at home. Danny cried when he left for school 3 to 4 mornings a week and was apprehensive of the school week ahead on Sunday nights. Many of his worries centered around attending school, where he was reported to be performing poorly, particularly in reading and English skills. This proved troubling to him, as he had a very strong desire to excel.

In addition, Danny also experienced mild social anxiety, both with the teacher, and with an older group of children who teased him. Since Danny was insecure about his own achievement, he was watchful of signs that his teacher thought poorly of him (e.g., asking the other children more questions). Rather than confronting his teacher to evaluate how realistic his concerns were, he withdrew from participating in the classroom.

The older children had found that Danny was highly sensitive to attacks on his intelligence. Therefore, they maximized the use of name-calling, which often provoked a major defensive reaction from Danny. As a result, Danny did his best to avoid these children.

In addition, Mrs. Kaplan linked Danny's separation anxiety to some recent surgeries she had undergone. She did not believe her son was confident that she would always be there for him. For this reason, many of her verbal and nonverbal communications were aimed at comforting and consoling him. Mrs. Kaplan walked Danny into his classroom on a daily basis to make his attending school as easy as possible. By doing so, Danny would not have to stand on line with the other children who teased him. On Sunday evenings, due to Danny's heightened apprehension of the week ahead, she would often spend extra time with him, cuddling and talking, trying to reassure him about the week ahead.

To complicate matters, Mrs. Kaplan also was dealing with her own symptoms of anxious apprehension. She had been diagnosed with panic disorder and was particularly fearful of many social situations (e.g., speaking publicly). Thus, she fully understood the limiting and upsetting nature of her son's symptoms. For this reason, she did not encourage Danny's confrontation of anxiety-provoking stimuli. Rather, she provided Danny with considerable attention for his crying and anxiety symptoms.

Based on the ADIS-C and ADIS-P, Danny received a principal *DSM-IV* diagnosis of SAD (moderate severity) with a comorbid social phobia (mild-moderate severity). Child self-report data (CASI, FSSC-R, RCMAS, STAIC) were consistent with diagnostic impressions. Danny scored in the clinical range on each of these measures suggesting that he was sensitive to experiencing anxiety-related symptoms.

Regarding the parent completed measures, Mrs. Kaplan reported considerable social phobic fears (FQ). Neither parent indicated depressive symptoms, and Mrs. Kaplan's CBCL score revealed some elevation on the anxiety/depression scale.

Because Danny was experiencing academic-related difficulties (poor grades), he underwent a psychoeducational evaluation (intellectual and achievement) to evaluate whether a learning disorder was present. Danny was diagnosed with a mild perceptually based learning disability. For this reason, Danny's school was informed (with parental consent) and appropriate special education services were provided.

SYNOPSIS OF THERAPY SESSIONS

After the initial evaluation, the family was invited to attend a consultation to discuss the results of the assessment and to prepare them for therapy. Child and parents were then given self-monitoring forms (Silverman, 1989) to keep track of Danny's anxiety symptoms, their accompanying situations, thoughts, and intensity. This was done to target any errors in thinking, vulnerable situations, and to begin objective monitoring of Danny's improvement.

Therapy sessions were divided into child and parent segments. Child sessions focused on the development of coping skills, role plays, and imaginal and in vivo exposures. Coping skills consisted of cognitive therapy techniques and problem-solving strategies (Kendall et al., 1992; Silverman, 1989), relaxation training and deep breathing exercises (Ollendick & Cerny, 1981). Goals of the parent sessions were to review the practical material taught to the child, to guide necessary changes in parental behavior, and to enlist the parents as much as possible as cotherapists (Eisen & Kearney, 1995; Silverman, 1989). In the following section, we outline such a program on a session-by-session basis. Unless otherwise stated, the goals of each session apply to both child and parent therapy segments.

Session 1

1. Establish rapport, review diaries.
2. Present treatment rationale.
3. Explore parental traps (parent session).
4. Construct fear/anxiety hierarchy.
5. Assign homework (HW) assignment(s).

The therapist discussed the rationale of treatment with Danny and his parents separately. First, the therapist explained how gradual exposures accompanied by the development of coping skills (cognitive therapy and relaxation training exercises) can help minimize anxiety and continued avoidance. The importance of practice and compliance with treatment was also emphasized. A preliminary hierarchy was formed, focusing around increasingly difficult separation-related situations and awkward social scenarios. Fearful situations included leaving mom by the front door at school, talking with older kids, and carpooling. The main emphasis in the parent session addressed the significance of the "reassurance trap."

Example

THERAPIST (T):   Any loving parent may inadvertantly encourage a child's anxiety by providing excessive reassurance in anxiety-provoking situations.

MOTHER (M):   How can we be expected to ignore Danny when he doesn't want to go to school?

T: You only need to develop a different focus in how to direct your love to your son. I'm sure that you would like him to learn how to cope with life's challenges. This is your chance to show him that you love him by giving him the opportunity to cope rather than to reassure him. This will encourage him to be independent in dealing with situations that have been difficult for him.

M: Of course, I want that. But what should I do when he begins crying on our way to school?

T: That's what you'll learn together, as a family. When Danny becomes better at developing coping skills, you'll be able to cue him to use these on his own, so that he can independently handle difficult situations.

The Kaplans were doing an excellent job of helping Danny monitor his anxiety. Danny appeared to be nervous every day when he went to school. They noted he had a difficult time articulating his thoughts. The therapist first assisted Danny in his half of the session, with thought specification in feared situations and possible consequences (e.g., "the kids might make me feel bad") and then explained to his parents how to offer guidance.

Sessions 2–4

1. Review diaries.
2. Finalize hierarchy.
3. Discuss cognitive therapy techniques.
4. Teach relaxation and breathing exercises.
5. Practice (model/role-play).

6. Enlist parents as cotherapists.
7. Conduct imaginal exposures.
8. Assign exposure-based HW assignments.

Danny continued to endorse negative thoughts about himself and his schoolwork. During these sessions, the STOP technique was introduced to him through therapist modeling and the use of thought bubbles. Through practice, Danny learned how to modify his cognitions from a fearful to a coping orientation.

Danny expressed great pride in himself for changing his thoughts. In addition, parental praise for school attendance and coping was emphasized. Such parental efforts helped shape Danny's approach to effortful behavior in school, as well as in practicing exposure-based HW assignments.

Treatment effects are more likely to generalize to extratherapy situations if parents are included as cotherapists. It is therefore necessary to carefully review with parents the coping skills taught to the child. In Danny's case, since he was cooperative, enthusiastic, and a quick learner, the therapist brought him into the parent session to help explain the STOP acronym.

Example

T: Danny, can you tell me what the STOP technique stands for [therapist holds up stop sign]?
D: Well, the letters of the STOP sign stand for stuff.
T: Okay, let's begin. What does the **S** stand for?
D: **S** is for scared. Scared of things like going to school, especially by myself.
T: What about the **T**?
D: **T** is for thoughts, scary thoughts, like what might happen at school, all the bad things.
T: What about the **O**?
D: **O** is for other thoughts that are, like it won't be so bad after all, and what's the worst thing that could happen to me there? I know I'll come home and that my parents won't yell or punish me if I try hard.
T: That makes sense to me. And finally, how about the **P**?
D: **P** is for proud of myself for being able to change my thoughts and being able to make myself feel better.
T: Great! It's also going to be up to you to remind your mom and dad about the STOP so they know what the letters stand for too. Can you remind them sometimes so they don't forget?
D: Sure, my memory's probably better than theirs.

Danny was administered relaxation and deep breathing training via protocol (Ollendick & Cerny, 1981), and then given a tape of the relaxation dialogue. Danny was instructed to practice the relaxation exercises at least once a day at home (15–30 minutes). The exercises were intended to "slow him down" when he became overwhelmed by anxiety-provoking situations.

Problem-solving strategies were implemented to teach Danny concrete solutions to his anxiety problems (e.g., approaching children to play a game rather than being overly defensive). Exercises specific to Danny's anxiety were formulated. It was helpful to involve his parents in his homework assignments. By doing so, they enhanced their son's ability to successfully address subsequent anxiety-provoking situations. During these sessions, the therapist conducted imaginal exposures (in session) and in vivo exposures (out of session) utilizing cognitive-behavioral strategies.

Sessions 5–6

1. Review diaries.
2. Address parental concerns.
3. Introduce contingency management system.
4. Continue to conduct imaginal and in vivo exposures.

Danny continued to experience separation anxiety despite following through with several classroom exposures. Since his mother was unsuccessful in her attempts to refocus him, she reluctantly resorted to the reassurance trap. For this reason, a contingency management program was implemented. The therapist in conjunction with Danny and his parents devised a reward list consisting of tangible, activity, social, and token reinforcers. One example included going out to dinner with his parents if Danny could enter the school building unattended for two days. The expectations for the child should be clearly defined so that there is no question of whether or not the task was successfully completed. Rewards and demands should be spelled out in a contract that all parties agree on.

Example

M: Won't Danny begin to think he should do exposures just to get things?
T: At first, it may appear that way. However, once he has achieved success experiences, his coping efforts will become more intrinsically reinforcing.
M: What if he almost made it? Should he still get the reward?
T: It is tempting to reward him even if he's partially successful. However, by setting limits with Danny, you will minimize his reassurance seeking and/or manipulative behavior. Certainly, you should provide him with praise for his coping efforts. Ultimately, your attention in the

form of verbal praise will replace other sources of reward. Remember, the idea behind the program is to expose Danny to anxiety-provoking situations at his own pace. This approach enhances his chances for success and reward.

Danny's confidence improved following the achievement of several rewards. The hierarchy was made more flexible to incorporate his own ideas about appropriate exposures and rewards. Therapist guidance ensured that his goals were realistic.

Sessions 7–9

1. Review diaries.
2. Discuss relapse prevention.
3. Address protection trap (parent session).
4. Conduct imaginal and in vivo exposures as deemed appropriate.

After a period of progress, it is not uncommon for anxious youth to backslide. A family's reaction to a lapse is crucial. For example, such an episode can result in a catastrophic reaction (e.g., everything is blown!) or it can be reframed as a learning experience that can further enhance the child's skills (Eisen & Kearney, 1995; Kendall et al., 1992). The therapist should create an expectation that the goal of the treatment program is to control rather than cure anxiety. In addition, lapses should be attributed to lessened coping efforts rather than as signs of incompetence (Kendall, 1991).

Example

M: Danny did poorly on his test. He cried for a whole hour. I'm so upset! He was doing so well and now I feel like we're back at square one.

T: Everyone has good and bad days. Danny has learned a great deal. His efforts are certainly not wasted. It's just that he found this test a little overwhelming. What can you do to help him cope better?

M: I guess by minimizing attention for his crying, not yelling, not reassuring too much. I can try to let him cope and cue him if necessary.

T: That's right. Also, it's important to focus on his efforts rather than his performance. Let him know that as long as he makes an honest effort you will be proud of him.

At this point in the treatment program, Danny's confidence was continuing to improve. He was excited about attempting more challenging exposures. Although Danny's mother was pleased with her son's progress, she reported ambivalent feelings about Danny's heightened independence. As a result, she became reluctant to expose him to situations that she perceived as dangerous, largely due to her own anxiety in these situations. For this reason, the therapist discussed the protection trap.

Example

M: I want him to go on the trip without me, but the city is a dangerous place. Maybe I should just have him stay home.

T: What message would you be giving him?

M: That I'm overprotecting him and don't trust him.

T: How could he benefit from the trip?

M: He could learn about the cultural center there, and he could be even more confident that he overcame his fear there. I know it's all in my head but I would just feel better if he stayed home.

T: It's important to be realistic about the dangers and the safety of the trip. Would the school plan such a trip if it were not safe? How are they making it safe?

M: Teachers and helpers are going, and they'll have ID on each child. It probably is safe.

T: It's perfectly natural to be concerned. But if you refuse to expose Danny to anxiety-provoking situations because of your own fears, you may limit his opportunities to develop coping skills.

M: I have to admit, I'm not sure if I like him being *that* independent.

T: What would it mean to you if he was successful?

M: I guess that he can potentially handle anxiety-provoking situations even better than I can. Maybe he won't need me anymore.

T: Your relationship may well change. He may no longer seek continual reassurance. But at the same time, he will likely appreciate the increased freedom you provide him. I wouldn't be surprised if your relationship changes for the better.

M: I know, you're right. He probably will still want me around. The transition in our relationship is a little frightening for me, though.

Sessions 10–12

1. Review diaries.
2. Review relapse prevention.
3. Review treatment progress.
4. Discuss termination issues.
5. Administer posttreatment questionnaires.

Relapse prevention consisted mainly of discussing slips. Danny and his parents were given advice to minimize the impact of relapses. These recommendations consisted of conceptualizing them as normal, by not feeling discouraged, by being confident in all the progress made to date, and by simply having Danny "pick himself up" when he experienced a slip. This was particularly important in his case, as his mother often became easily discouraged herself and was likely to communicate this to her son.

Relapses can be minimized through practice and continual exposures. With the Kaplans, it was important to also discuss the possibility that they might erroneously fall back into protecting Danny from anxiety-provoking situations. Instead, they were guided to use these slips as opportunities for further learning and confidence enhancement. In addition, positive feedback for coping should continue to be maximized.

During the last several treatment sessions, Mrs. Kaplan consistently set limits with her son. In addition, both parents were effectively shaping Danny's behavior. Careful attention was devoted to his coping efforts, whereas Danny's fearful displays were largely ignored. Thus, Danny was actively coping with his anxiety on a regular basis. He was beginning to appreciate his newfound independence and was excited about the prospect of ceasing therapy. Similarly, Danny's father felt therapeutic services for his son were no longer necessary. Mrs. Kaplan on the other hand, was still concerned about the possibility of a relapse.

Example

M: I'm not sure whether Danny is ready to end therapy.
T: Why not? He's coping well with his anxiety and we have covered every item on the fear hierarchy.
M: I know . . . but what if he slips?
T: What's the worst thing that could happen?
M: We'll be back to square one. He won't be able to go to school again.
T: How likely is that?
M: I don't know . . . probably not very likely.
T: Why is that?
M: He's learned some good coping skills.
T: That's right . . . and you and your husband have restructured your family environment so that it now encourages coping rather than fear. That is not an easy thing to do. I'm very pleased with your efforts. As long as you continue this process, I'm confident that Danny will continue to improve. My guidance is no longer necessary. Remember, you and your husband were the ones who actually carried out the program. What will you do if Danny slips?
M: I'll make sure not to overreact. Everyone has good and bad days.
T: Great! I look forward to seeing you in three months to hear about Danny's progress.

At posttreatment, Danny no longer qualified for a *DSM-IV* diagnosis. In addition, he was no longer avoiding school, the other children, or the teacher. Danny scored within normal limits on the self-report measures (CASI, FSSC-R, RCMAS, and STAIC). Parent-completed measures also were within normal limits. In addition, the combination of the parent training program and academic remediation resulted in a remarkable improvement of his grades (from C work to mostly B's).

CONCLUSION

In the *DSM-IV*, SAD is the only anxiety disorder category based solely on child criteria. Yet, the empirical treatment literature is limited in scope and utility. Pharmacological investigations have demonstrated equivocal findings, and studies of psychosocial interventions are limited to descriptive case reports. The parent training program outlined in this chapter draws on treatment techniques with empirically proven effectiveness for childhood behavior disorders. Cognitive-behavioral interventions for SAD appear promising. However, systematic evaluations of parent training programs for the treatment of SAD are needed. Identification of the therapeutic ingredients responsible for behavior change is a necessary second step so that prescriptive treatment strategies can be applied to SAD. Further research is warranted to address these issues. Perhaps then, SAD will become more fully understood and increasingly treatable.

REFERENCES

Achenbach, T. M. (1991a). *Manual for the Child Behavior Checklist/4-18 and 1991 profile.* Burlington: University of Vermont Department of Psychiatry.

Achenbach, T. M. (1991b). *Manual for the teacher's report form and 1991 profile.* Burlington: University of Vermont Department of Psychiatry.

American Psychiatric Association. (1987). *Diagnostic and statistical manual of mental disorders* (3rd ed., Rev.). Washington, DC: Author.

American Psychiatric Association. (1994). *Diagnostic and statistical manual of mental disorders* (4th ed.). Washington, DC: Author.

Anderson, J. C., Williams, S., McGee, R., & Silva, P. A. (1987). DSM-III disorders in pre-adolescent children: Prevalence in a large sample from the general population. *Archives of General Psychiatry, 44,* 69–76.

Barkley, R. A. (1989). Attention-deficit hyperactivity disorder. In E. J. Mash & R. A. Barkley (Eds.), *Treatment of childhood disorders* (pp. 39–72). New York: Guilford Press.

Beck, A. T., Ward, C. H., Mendelsohn, M., Mock, J., & Erbaugh, J. (1961). An inventory for measuring depression. *Archives of General Psychiatry, 41,* 561–571.

Berney, T., Kolvin, I., Bhate, S. R., Gauside, R. F., Jeans, J., Kay, B., & Scarth, L. (1981). School phobia: A therapeutic trial with clomipramine and short-term outcome. *British Journal of Psychiatry, 138,* 110–118.

Bernstein, G. A., Garfinkel, B. D., & Borchardt, C. M. (1990). Comparative studies of pharmacotherapy school refusal. *Journal of the American Academy of Child and Adolescent Psychiatry, 29,* 773–781.

Bird, H. R., Canino, G., Rubio-Stipec, M., Gould, M. S., Ribera, J., Sessman, W., Woodbury, M., Huertas-Goldman, S., Pagan, A., Sanches-Lacay, A., & Moscoso, M. (1988). Estimate of the prevalence of childhood maladjustment in a community survey in Puerto Rico: The use of combined measures. *Archives of General Psychiatry, 45,* 1120–1126.

Bowen, R. C., Offord, D. R., & Boyle, M. H. (1990). The prevalence of overanxious disorder and separation anxiety disorder: Results from the Ontario Child Health Study. *Journal of the American Academy of Child and Adolescent Psychiatry, 29,* 753–758.

D'Zurilla, T. J., & Goldfried, M. R. (1971). Problem solving and behavior modification. *Journal of Abnormal Psychology, 78,* 107–126.

Eisen, A. R., & Kearney, C. A. (1995). *Practitioner's guide to treating fear and anxiety in children and adolescents: A cognitive-behavioral approach.* Northvale, NJ: Jason Aronson.

Gittelman-Klein, R., & Klein, D. F. (1971). Controlled imipramine treatment of school phobia. *Archives of General Psychiatry, 25,* 204–207.

Gittelman-Klein, R., & Klein, D. F. (1973). School phobia: Diagnostic considerations in the light of imipramine effects. *Journal of Nervous and Mental Disease, 156,* 199–215.

Kendall, P. C. (1985). Toward a cognitive-behavioral model of child psychopathology and a critique of related interventions. *Journal of Abnormal Child Psychology, 13,* 357–372.

Kendall, P. C. (1991). Guiding theory for therapy with children and adolescents. In P. C. Kendall (Ed.), *Child and adolescent therapy: Cognitive-behavioral procedures.* New York: Guilford Press.

Kendall, P. C., Chansky, T. E., Kane, M., Kim, R. S., Kortlander, E., Sessa, F., Rohan, K. R., & Siqueland, L. (1992). *Anxiety disorders in youth: Cognitive-behavioral interventions.* New York: Pergamon Press.

Kendall, P. C., Howard, B. L., & Epps, J. (1988). The anxious child: Cognitive-behavioral treatment strategies. *Behavior Modification, 12,* 281–310.

Kendall, P. C., & MacDonald, J. P. (1993). Cognition in the psychopathology youth and implications for treatment. In K. S. Dobson & P. C. Kendall (Eds.), *Psychopathology and cognition.* New York: Academic Press.

Klein, R., Koplewicz, H. S., & Kanner, A. (1992). Imipramine treatment of children with separation anxiety disorder. *Journal of the American Academy of Child and Adolescent Psychiatry, 31,* 21–28.

Knox, L. S., Albano, A. M., & Barlow, D. H. (1996). Parental involvement in the treatment of childhood obsessive-compulsive disorder: A multiple baseline examination incorporating parents. *Behavior Therapy, 27,* 93–115.

Last, C. G. (1991). Somatic complaints in anxiety disordered children. *Journal of Anxiety Disorders, 5,* 125–138.

Last, C. G., Hersen, M., Kazdin, A. E., Finkelstein, R., & Strauss, C. C. (1987). Comparison of *DSM-III* separation anxiety and overanxious disorders:

Demographic characteristics and patterns of comorbidity. *Journal of the American Academy of Child Psychiatry, 26,* 527–531.

Marks, I. M., & Mathews, A. M. (1979). Brief standard self-rating for phobic patients. *Behaviour Research and Therapy, 17,* 263–267.

Martin, G., & Pear, J. (1983). *Behavior modification: What it is and how to do it* (2nd ed.). New York: Pergamon Press.

McGee, R., Feehan, M., Williams, S., & Anderson, J. (1992). *DSM-III* disorders from age 11 to age 15 years. *Journal of the American Academy of Child and Adolescent Psychiatry, 31,* 50–59.

Meichenbaum, D. (1986). Cognitive behavior modification. In F. H. Kanfer & A. P. Goldstein (Eds.), *Helping people change: A textbook of methods* (3rd ed., pp. 346–380). New York: Pergamon Press.

Morris, R. J., & Kratochwill, T. R. (1983). *Treating children's fears and phobias: A behavioral approach.* New York: Pergamon Press.

Ollendick, T. H. (1983). Reliability and validity of the revised fear survey schedule for children (FSSC-R). *Behaviour Research and Therapy, 21,* 685–692.

Ollendick, T. H., & Cerny, J. A. (1981). *Clinical behavior therapy with children.* New York: Plenum Press.

Ollendick, T. H., Hagopian, L. P., & Huntzinger, R. M. (1991). Cognitive-behavior therapy with nighttime fearful children. *Journal of Behavior Therapy and Experimental Psychiatry, 22,* 113–121.

Piaget, J. (1967). *Six psychological studies.* New York: Vintage Books.

Raleigh, H., Spasaro, S. A., & Eisen, A. R. (1995). *Prescriptive cognitive therapy for separation anxiety disorder.* Paper presented at the annual meeting of the Eastern Psychological Association, Boston, MA.

Reynolds, C. R., & Richman, B. O. (1978). What I think and feel?: A revised measure of children's manifest anxiety. *Journal of Abnormal Child Psychology, 6,* 271–280.

Rutter, M. (1981). Emotional development. In M. Rutter (Ed.), *Scientific foundations of developmental psychiatry.* Baltimore: University Park Press.

Silverman, W. K. (1989). *Self-control manual for phobic children.* Unpublished treatment protocol, Florida International University, Miami.

Silverman, W. K. (1991). Diagnostic reliability of anxiety disorders in children using structured interviews. *Journal of Anxiety Disorders, 5,* 105–124.

Silverman, W. K., & Albano, A. M. (1995). *The Anxiety Disorders Interview Schedule for DSM-IV: Child and parent versions.* Albany, NY: Graywind.

Silverman, W. K., Fleisig, W., Rabian, B., & Peterson, R. A. (1991). The Child Anxiety Sensitivity Index. *Journal of Clinical Child Psychology, 20,* 162–168.

Silverman, W. K., & Kearney, C. A. (1995). Behavioral treatment of childhood anxiety. In V. B. Van Hasselt & M. Hersen (Eds.), *Handbook of behavior therapy and pharmacotherapy for children: A comparative analysis.* New York: Pergamon Press.

Spielberger, C. D. (1973). *Manual for the State-Trait Anxiety Inventory for children.* Palo Alto, CA: Consulting Psychologists Press.

Thyer, B. A., & Sowers-Hoag, K. M. (1988). Behavior therapy for separation anxiety disorder. *Behavior Modification, 12,* 205–233.

CHAPTER 7

Parent Training in the Treatment of School Refusal Behavior

CHRISTOPHER A. KEARNEY and TAMI L. ROBLEK

OF ALL THE problems that parents must deal with in their children, perhaps none is as frustrating and perplexing as school refusal behavior. We define school refusal behavior as child-motivated refusal to attend school and/or difficulty remaining in class for an entire day (Kearney & Silverman, in press). As a result, cases of school withdrawal, where a parent deliberately withholds a child from school, are excluded here (Kahn & Nursten, 1962). School refusal behavior refers to children ages 5 to 17 years who:

1. Are completely absent from school, and/or:
2. Go to school but then leave during the course of the school day, and/or:
3. Go to school only after intense behavior problems (e.g., tantrums) in the morning, and/or:
4. Go to school with such distress that it leads to pleas for future nonattendance.

School refusal behavior thus includes a spectrum of children ranging from those who never attend school to those who intermittently attend school to those who attend school but have many interfering behaviors. In some cases, these problems spontaneously remit after a short time. Such cases of "self-corrective school refusal behavior" are common and usually last less than 2 weeks. In contrast, acute school refusal behavior lasts between 2 weeks and 1 year and is marked by significant interference in the child's and family's daily life routine. Chronic school refusal behavior lasts longer than one year and is marked by greater interference. In general, the longer a child refuses to go to school, the more severe the problem and the more difficult it will be to restore full-time school attendance (Kearney, 1995).

In this chapter, we concentrate on children whose primary problem is school refusal behavior. However, parents who refer a child with multiple behavior problems often wish to address school refusal first, and so the material in this chapter may be applicable to this situation as well.

PREVALENCE AND CLINICAL PICTURE

School refusal behavior affects about 5% of school-age children, although rates of absenteeism are considerably higher in some urban areas. The problem appears to occur in males and females with equal frequency. Peak age of onset is 5 to 6 and 11 to 12 years (Smith, 1970); entry into a new grade or building (e.g., kindergarten, junior high) is a common trigger of school refusal. In general, children with school refusal behavior have average intelligence and adequate academic achievement at least up to the point of initial absenteeism (Hampe, Miller, Barrett, & Noble, 1973; Nichols & Berg, 1970). The socioeconomic status of families with a child refusing school is considerably mixed (Baker & Wills, 1978; Last & Strauss, 1990).

A hallmark of school refusal behavior is its heterogeneity; various internalizing and externalizing symptoms mark any individual case. Common internalizing symptoms include general and social anxiety, fear, depression, social withdrawal, fatigue, and somatic complaints (especially stomachaches and headaches; Last, 1991; Last & Strauss, 1990). Common externalizing symptoms include running away from home or school, verbal or physical aggression to avoid school, noncompliance, tantrums, arguing, clinging, and refusal to move (Kearney, 1995). In most cases of school refusal behavior, youngsters show a "mixed bag" of these symptoms.

In the short term, school refusal behavior has several unfortunate consequences. These consequences include social alienation, declining school performance, increased family conflict, and a general disruption of daily activities. These problems gradually worsen as school refusal continues, especially if the behavior persists over two academic years (Kearney & Tillotson, in press). Researchers have found several long-term consequences of continued school refusal behavior as well. These consequences include school dropout, occupational and marital problems, economic deprivation, anxiety and depressive disorders, and alcohol abuse and criminal behavior (Berg, 1970; Berg & Jackson, 1985; Berg, Marks, McGuire, & Lipsedge, 1974; Flakierska, Lindstrom, & Gillberg, 1988; Hibbett & Fogelman, 1990; Hibbett, Fogelman, & Manor, 1990; Robins & Ratcliffe, 1980; Tyrer & Tyrer, 1974).

CLINICAL PROCESSES REGARDING SCHOOL REFUSAL BEHAVIOR

The seriousness, prevalence, and consequences of school refusal behavior thus demand effective ways of classifying, assessing, and treating this population. Unfortunately, these clinical processes have been hampered by substantial confusion among researchers. Historically, such confusion has been the result of:

- Using various definitions of school refusal behavior.
- Overemphasizing fear-based school refusal (i.e., "school phobia").
- Failing to agree on a uniform classification system for this population.
- Developing few assessment devices that are specific to children who refuse school.
- Advocating treatment practices that work well for some but not all children with school refusal behavior (Kearney & Silverman, in press).

As a result, therapists are often forced to rely on their own, idiosyncratically designed strategy to clinically address this population.

In our clinic, we have designed a systematic approach for classifying, assessing, and treating youngsters who refuse school. Our approach is based on three key ideas. First, we adopt the inclusive definition of school refusal behavior described earlier. Therefore, we address all types of children who refuse school, not just those who are fearful of school or those who take part in other delinquent acts (i.e., so-called "truants"). Second, we emphasize the idea that youngsters refuse school for specific reasons, or functions. Instead of focusing on the myriad symptoms that children show, we focus on the limited number of reasons why children continue to miss school. Finally, we rely on a combined assessment-prescriptive treatment approach that heavily involves parents and other family members.

In this chapter, we describe in detail our functional approach to classifying, assessing, and treating youngsters who refuse school. In doing so, we focus especially on parent training and related practices that are critical to the resolution of school refusal behavior. To begin, we outline our approach with respect to classification and assessment.

A FUNCTIONAL APPROACH TO CLASSIFYING
YOUNGSTERS WITH SCHOOL REFUSAL BEHAVIOR

We believe that youngsters refuse school primarily for one or more of four reasons. First, some youngsters refuse school to avoid aspects of school that upset them. Common aspects include school buses, hallways, classroom items, teachers, schoolmates, fire alarms, cafeterias, playgrounds, gymnasia, or specific courses or assignments. In many cases, the child is unable to say exactly what upsets him or her. Often, though, these children report unpleasant physical symptoms that make school attendance difficult (Kearney & Sims, in press). We refer to this function as avoidance of stimuli that provoke negative affectivity (general fear/anxiety/depression). Children who refuse school for this reason tend to be younger and may attend school regularly but do so with great dread.

A second reason children miss school is to escape aversive social or evaluative situations. Common avoided situations include meeting new people, having conversations with friends and acquaintances, interacting with aggressive peers, taking tests, writing on the blackboard, speaking in front of others, performing athletically (e.g., in physical education class), engaging in recitals, moving from class to class, and talking to school officials (Kearney, Eisen, & Silverman, 1995). In many of these cases, youngsters are able to identify what is bothering them. Youngsters who refuse school to escape aversive social/evaluative situations tend to be older children and adolescents. Their level of absenteeism ranges considerably. These first two functional conditions refer to children who are missing school for negative reinforcement, or to get away from something unpleasant at school. During this chapter, these two conditions will sometimes be combined.

A third reason children miss school is to get attention from significant others, usually a parent. These children often scream, cry, cling, hit, refuse to move, and/or exaggerate stomachaches and headaches to miss school and stay home. Separation anxiety is sometimes associated with this functional condition as well. Typically, these children wish to stay home with their mother; in many cases, the reverse is also true. The children may also call their parents several times during the day and elicit feelings of guilt to force acquiescence to demands (e.g., bring them home from school; Kearney & Sims, in press). Youngsters who refuse school for attention tend to be younger, and may go to school intermittently following intense behavior problems in the morning.

A fourth reason children miss school is to pursue positive tangible reinforcement outside school. These youngsters often skip school because it is more fun to be out of school. Common out-of-school activities include having day parties with friends, using alcohol and other drugs, playing videogames or watching television, playing sports, riding a bicycle, sleeping, shopping, and gambling. Family conflict, poor academic performance, and delinquent acts are also common to this group (Kearney & Silverman, 1995). Youngsters who refuse school to pursue positive tangible reinforcement tend to be older children and adolescents. Their level of absenteeism ranges considerably. These last two functional conditions refer to children who are missing school for positive reinforcement, or to pursue something attractive outside school. Therapists are more apt to receive referrals for children refusing school for positive reinforcement than for negative reinforcement.

Youngsters may also refuse school for a combination of these reasons. For example, it is not unusual for children to miss school to avoid something upsetting and to pursue the many positive aspects of staying home. Conversely, youngsters may skip school for extended periods to have fun and then become nervous at the prospect of returning to school and facing new classes, teachers, and peers. Clinicians should consider all possible combinations of reasons for school refusal when assessing a particular youngster.

In general, these four functional conditions, and combinations thereof, may serve as an adequate classification system for youngsters with school refusal behavior. In this way, clinicians do not have to be overwhelmed by the substantial number of symptoms that many of these children show. The other advantage of this system is that it can be linked directly to assessment and treatment strategies. We focus next on a brief discussion of assessment.

A FUNCTIONAL APPROACH TO ASSESSING YOUNGSTERS WITH SCHOOL REFUSAL BEHAVIOR

When assessing a child of this population, we encourage therapists to focus on the key reasons for the child's school refusal. As mentioned, these reasons are (a) avoiding stimuli that provoke negative affectivity, (b) escaping aversive social/evaluative situations, (c) getting attention, and/or (d) pursuing positive tangible reinforcement outside school. To assess why a child is refusing school, therapists may rely most on child and parent reports and direct observations of behavior.

Child and Parent Reports

As part of our multicomponent assessment process, we interview the parents and child extensively about primary symptoms and reasons for school refusal behavior. In addition, we ask each party to complete respective versions of the School Refusal Assessment Scale (SRAS; Kearney

& Silverman, 1993). The SRAS is a 16-item instrument designed to measure the relative influence of the four functional conditions previously described. A therapist solicits SRAS ratings from the parents and the child and combines the ratings into a single functional profile. From this profile, he or she can make a decision about what maintains the child's school refusal behavior. Subsequently, the therapist can decide what treatment direction to take.

For example, assume that (a) a child's mean SRAS ratings for the four functional conditions are 1.25, 2.00, 4.25, and 3.00, and (b) a parent's mean SRAS ratings for those conditions are 1.75, 3.00, 4.75, and 3.00. Ratings are averaged across all parties; in this case: 1.50, 2.50, 4.50, and 3.00. The highest scoring functional condition is considered the primary reason for the child's school refusal (in this case, the third functional condition, attention). Ratings within 0.25 points of one another are considered equal. In addition, the therapist can identify other functions that play a secondary role in maintaining school refusal behavior (in this case, the fourth functional condition, positive tangible reinforcement) as well as those that play little role. We recommend that therapists confirm these ratings using direct observations of behavior.

DIRECT OBSERVATIONS OF BEHAVIOR

Therapists may directly observe certain child behaviors and parent-child interactions to better understand how and why a child is refusing school. Observations may be done formally in the child's home or school, or a therapist may wish to closely monitor behaviors and interactions in the office setting.

For children thought to be refusing school to avoid stimuli provoking negative affectivity, therapists may compare how a child attends school under normal conditions with how he or she attends school without certain aspects of school present (e.g., not having to ride the school bus). In the office setting, therapists may watch for tearful, passive, and withdrawn behavior on the part of the child and see whether and how a parent rewards such behavior.

For children thought to be refusing school to escape aversive social/evaluative situations, therapists may compare how a child attends school under normal conditions with how he or she attends school without certain requirements (e.g., no tests given, no peers present, no physical education class scheduled). In the office setting, therapists may watch for social anxiety on the part of the child when meeting new people. Parental responses to this behavior should be closely monitored as well.

For children thought to be refusing school for attention, therapists may compare how a child attends school under normal conditions with how he or she attends school with significant others (e.g., with one's mother in the classroom). In the office setting, therapists may watch for whether a child has difficulty separating from a parent (or vice versa) or throws a tantrum to avoid a one-on-one speaking session.

For children thought to be refusing school for positive tangible reinforcement, therapists may compare a child's school attendance under normal conditions with attendance when increased rewards are made available and/or increased punishments or restricted out-of-school activities are made contingent on school absence. In the office setting, therapists may watch for youngsters who argue vigorously with their parents to force them to leave or change their answers to questions. Finally, for children thought to be refusing school for a combination of reasons, therapists should look for a variety of these behaviors under different conditions.

MAKING A DECISION ABOUT TREATING YOUNGSTERS WITH SCHOOL REFUSAL BEHAVIOR

After knowing why a child is refusing school, a decision about treatment can be made. For children refusing school for negative reinforcement, we focus on relaxation training, breathing retraining, modeling, role play, cognitive therapy, and exposure. A key aspect of treatment here is to train parents to train their children to use these techniques and maintain their use over time. For children refusing school for attention, we focus on parent training in contingency management. We concentrate on restructuring parent commands, setting up fixed routines for the morning and day, and applying consistent rewards for school attendance and punishments for school refusal. For children refusing school for positive tangible reinforcement, we focus on contracting among relevant family members. Parents are especially encouraged to initiate and develop effective contracts on their own with their child. This allows parents and children to solve problems more efficiently, reduce conflict, increase tangible rewards for school attendance, and decrease rewards and social activities for school refusal. Finally, youngsters who refuse school for multiple reasons are given combined treatment.

THE PARENT TRAINING PROGRAM AND CASE MATERIAL

Parent and Family Treatment Mediators

This section outlines our parent-family training program to address youngsters with school refusal behavior. Before doing so, we caution therapists about a key error sometimes inherent in using parent training programs. This error involves the restructuring of parenting skills without regard to the broader ecological context of the family (Shirk, in press). Clinicians should be careful not to use parent training imprudently under certain conditions (e.g., low parent motivation) that make the training program ineffective.

We therefore begin this section with a brief discussion of important parent variables that often mediate the scope and pace of treatment for youngsters with school refusal behavior. These variables include parenting/family style, attitudes and expectations about treatment, psychopathology, and marital conflict and divorce. Each of these should be watched closely by therapists during treatment. These and related issues may need to be resolved before considering the treatment programs described here.

Parenting and Family Style

Parenting style is a variable that affects all child clinical cases. In general, therapists should be wary of parents who are neglectful or rejecting, overly permissive, or strictly authoritarian (Eisen & Kearney, 1995). However, some maladaptive parent and family patterns are especially pertinent to cases of school refusal behavior. In particular, therapists should be wary of parent-family dynamics that are closely associated with specific functions of school refusal behavior.

For example, enmeshed family patterns, sometimes characterized by overprotective parents, are common to children who refuse school for attention and/or have some aspect of separation anxiety. In contrast, detached parents tend to be underinvolved in their child's activities and provide little attention to their child's thoughts and needs (Foster & Robin, 1989). Such a dynamic is common in families of youngsters who refuse school for positive tangible reinforcement. Isolated parents or families are characterized by little extrafamilial contact with others. Such a dynamic is common in families of children who refuse school to escape aversive social/evaluative situations at school. Finally, conflictive parents or families are characterized by extensive hostility and poor problem-solving behavior. Family conflict is related to all functional conditions of school refusal behavior (Kearney & Silverman, 1995). Therapists should be sensitive to the presence of each of these familial patterns and adjust treatment accordingly. For example, one may need to implement communication skills training to address family conflict during treatment for school refusal behavior.

Parent Attitudes and Expectations about Treatment

Therapists will also need to be sensitive about parent attitudes and expectations for treatment. For example, it is not unusual for parents to be quite pessimistic about their child's school refusal behavior and the likelihood for change. This is especially characteristic of parents of adolescents who have missed school for a long time. In this case, we suggest that clinicians separate legitimate parent concerns (e.g., child often breaks curfew) from those that are more suspect (e.g., child is always disrespectful to others). In addition, therapists should focus first on simple behaviors (e.g., one chore) and easier treatment practices (e.g., short contract) to help parents experience successful outcomes and perhaps become more optimistic and motivated in therapy.

Parent Psychopathology

In the school refusal population, therapists should be aware that some parents will themselves suffer from mental disorders, especially those related to anxiety and depression. Youngsters who refuse school have sometimes modeled from their parents aversive physical reactions, avoidance responses, negative patterns of thinking, aggression, and even substance abuse. Therapists should be aware of these possibilities and perhaps seek to redress the parent's mental condition first or concurrently with the child's behavior.

Marital Conflict and Divorce

In this population, parents often disagree about disciplinary procedures in general and how to handle their child's absenteeism in particular. In addition, many cases of school refusal behavior, especially those involving positive reinforcement, are marked by single-parent families and complicated family situations. Therapists are encouraged to address spousal disagreements as soon as possible, ask parents to jointly commit to a treatment plan, and make adjustments for single-parent families. Therapists should remind parents that failure to consistently provide a united front to the child will undermine the treatment process and risk future relapse.

In related fashion, therapists should be aware that parents will sometimes disagree with one another and with the child about current events in the household. Therapists should assess whether this is a deliberate attempt to absolve oneself of possible blame or to fault a spouse. If so, then it may be helpful to reframe the school refusal situation as a "family" problem that will require effort from all relevant parties. Also, it may be necessary to develop special rapport with a parent who fears he or she will be "left out" of the therapy process.

THE PARENT TRAINING PROGRAM AND CASE MATERIAL

We now describe our parent-family training program to address youngsters with school refusal behavior. Several clinical researchers (e.g.,

Kazdin, 1991) have stated that parent training programs can be divided into different types. Some of the most common types include treatment where (a) the parents help their child implement the major techniques and maintain compliance to them, (b) the parents are the primary focus of treatment, with little child contact, and (c) the parents learn to better monitor their child and apply specific techniques involving different family members.

In this section, we describe the primary treatment components for children who refuse school (a) for negative reinforcement (i.e., to avoid stimuli that provoke negative affectivity and/or to escape aversive social/evaluative situations at school), (b) for attention from significant others, or (c) for the pursuit of positive tangible reinforcement outside school. Treatment for each of these types is related, respectively, to the three types of parent training programs described earlier. Following each section, a case example is provided.

PARENT-CHILD TREATMENT FOR YOUNGSTERS REFUSING SCHOOL FOR NEGATIVE REINFORCEMENT

We first describe treatment for children refusing school to avoid stimuli that provoke negative affectivity or to escape aversive social/evaluative situations. Major treatment components for this group include relaxation training, breathing retraining, modeling/role play, cognitive therapy, and exposure or reintegration into the classroom. Of these, exposure is most critical. Each component is largely child-based, but parents are asked to play a major role in training their child and maintaining treatment gains over time. In essence, the therapist gradually "transfers control" of therapy to the parents, who then help the therapist transmit treatment information to the child currently and in the future (Silverman & Kurtines, 1996).

Relaxation Training and Breathing Retraining

To control aversive physiological reactions that may keep a child out of school, we use relaxation training and breathing retraining. Relaxation training is based on a tension-release model, whereby a child is asked to tense various muscle groups, hold the tension for 5 to 10 seconds, and then flex the muscles quickly (see Ollendick & Cerny, 1981). This is done to teach the child the difference between a tense muscle and a relaxed one, help him or her identify which muscles are most tense in a stressful situation, and provide the child with a covert strategy of controlling physiologically based anxiety. In our clinic, relaxation training is conducted directly with the child and audiotaped. We then ask the child to practice independently at least twice per day and to begin using the procedures when physically anxious during the day. This procedure is most effective for children with muscle tension (e.g., in the face, shoulders), shaking or jitteriness (e.g., in hands, knees), or "butterflies" in the stomach.

Breathing retraining is also used to control negative physical symptoms, especially those related to hyperventilation and dizziness (see Eisen & Kearney, 1995). In this procedure, the child is asked to slowly and fully breathe in through the nose and exhale slowly and fully through the mouth. The therapist emphasizes the use of regular breathing in anxiety-provoking situations. For younger children, various images are encouraged as well, such as pretending that one is a hot air balloon that needs regular fueling to reach its destination. As with relaxation training, youngsters are asked to practice this procedure during the day and especially during stressful situations.

For both relaxation training and breathing retraining, we ask parents to systematically monitor and reward their child's compliance to the assigned treatment regimen. This is particularly important for younger children who may have trouble remembering what to do from the therapy session. We ask parents to check whether the child did what was asked by the therapist, correct the child as necessary, monitor progress, and verbally praise the child for completing the therapeutic homework assignments. In general, we have found a close relationship between parent involvement and encouragement, the child's use of the therapeutic procedures, and later success.

Modeling and Role Play

To build successful social skills, particularly in youngsters who refuse school to escape aversive social/evaluative situations, we use a combination of modeling and role play. This skills training is designed to build social competence in the child and allow positive feedback and social reinforcement from others. In turn, this should encourage the child to initiate more social contacts and interact effectively in aversive situations.

In modeling and role play, the therapist identifies with the child two or three social/evaluative situations at school that are most unpleasant. Common examples include having to speak in front of others or initiating and maintaining conversations. Subsequently, the therapist asks the child to model the therapist or others who manage a social situation appropriately (e.g., give a speech in front of others without fear; carry on a productive conversation). In some cases, the child's family members or parents can act as helpful models. The child is then asked to role-play the modeled situation in front of others and receive constructive feedback (Cartledge & Milburn, 1995). Most detailed feedback will come from the therapist, although family members should provide encouragement and praise for the child's effort.

After the child has successfully practiced social interactions in the therapy setting, practice can start in real-life situations. As the child does so, parents and teachers should be active monitors of the performance. This can be done covertly by asking parents or teachers to watch the child's social interactions at school, or more overtly by asking them to place the child in progressively more challenging social situations. Verbal praise and feedback from parents, teachers, the therapist, and relevant others should continue as well. As with relaxation training and breathing retraining, there is a close relationship between a supportive and motivating parent/family milieu and successful modeling and role play.

Cognitive Therapy

To reduce the level of negative thinking that often interferes with school performance and attendance, and to enhance positive ways of thinking, we use cognitive therapy. We teach parents and youngsters about cognitive distortions like overgeneralization (e.g., "Everyone will laugh at me"), personalization (e.g., "When I hear whispers in the hall, I think they are talking about me"), all-or-none thinking (e.g., "If my speech is not perfect, it will be a disaster"), and catastrophization (e.g., "I will fail the test and get kicked out of school"; see Haaga & Davison, 1986). The youngster's verbalizations in the therapy session are scrutinized for such distortions, and the parents and youngster are asked to keep written logs of distorted thoughts and verbalizations when they are made at home and school.

Cognitive therapy in this population largely involves restructuring these thoughts and verbalizations into more realistic and logical forms. Youngsters are encouraged to stop themselves in the middle of cognitive or verbal distortions, avoid extremist phrases such as "always" or "never," hypothesis-test about the realistic probabilities of something happening in their environment, and reframe harsh thoughts or statements into more positive ones. Because many adolescents have a long history of cognitive and verbal distortions, it is important to involve parents in this process. Parents can be particularly helpful in reminding youngsters about these distortions and assisting the restructuring process. Also, in some cases, parents can work on these procedures for themselves in conjunction with their youngster.

Exposure to the School Setting

Finally, to decrease behavioral avoidance of school and to help the child practice treatment techniques in a real-life setting, we use exposure to the classroom setting. Such exposure may be imaginal if the child is already attending school with great distress or in vivo if the child is missing most days of school. In either case, exposure is likely to be the most effective component of treatment for a child refusing school for negative reinforcement (Kearney & Sims, in press). Exposure is also the component most likely facilitated by the parents.

We recommend that parents encourage school attendance from their child whenever possible. This includes the morning as the child prepares for school, at the time of expected school attendance, during the morning if the child has still not gone to school, during the afternoon if a few hours of schooltime are still available, and even on weekends. Initially, such prodding may be verbal, but later may come in the form of physically assisted school attendance (see procedures for treating school refusal motivated by attention).

CASE EXAMPLE OF PARENT-CHILD TREATMENT FOR A YOUNGSTER REFUSING SCHOOL FOR NEGATIVE REINFORCEMENT

Presenting Client and Problem

Nathan was a 10-year-old male referred by his parents, Mr. and Mrs. M., and the counselor at Nathan's elementary school. During the initial telephone screening, Mrs. M. stated that Nathan had missed only four of the previous 40 days of school, but complained about school almost every day and kept asking his parents to place him in home schooling. Nathan had intermittent problems going to school in the past, but not to the extent currently shown. Mrs. M. said that Nathan was complaining about tests in class and had physical symptoms, but that he was reluctant to give more specific information. An assessment session was scheduled within the week.

During assessment, Nathan was initially hesitant about talking with the therapist, but gradually became more expressive. He stated that school was generally not a problem except for test-taking situations and having to write or speak in front of others in his class. Nathan also said these situations brought on physical symptoms of dizziness, trembling, and nausea. He indicated that he had a small group of close friends at school, but had recently become more distant from them as these problems developed. Nathan appeared to be very concerned about receiving high grades and pleasing his parents. He said he wanted to be taught by a tutor at home so that he wouldn't have to be nervous about school.

Mr. and Mrs. M. confirmed most of this report, but also said that Nathan seemed to exaggerate some of his symptoms for attention from them and his teacher. To this point, they had resisted the idea of home schooling, but felt they should speak to a therapist about it. Mr. and Mrs. M. indicated that Nathan, the oldest of three children, had always been "fussy and nervous about things" and seemed overconcerned about his schoolwork. They also stated they wished their son would be more social and enjoy school more. A telephone interview with Nathan's teacher revealed a similar pattern of overconscientiousness, anxiety, and occasional attention-seeking behavior.

Case Formulation

Based on a comprehensive assessment, the therapist determined that Nathan was largely missing school to avoid situations that caused negative physical symptoms and to escape unpleasant social/evaluative situations (e.g., tests, performing in front of others). This determination was supported by the facts that Nathan displayed fewer school refusal problems on days when no tests or performances were required and when he could spend a lot of time with his close friends. In addition, parent and child questionnaire scores and ratings on the School Refusal Assessment Scale indicated that negative reinforcement was the key function of Nathan's school refusal behavior. Attention-getting behavior was considered a moderate secondary component.

The therapist recommended that treatment be aimed to reduce Nathan's negative physical symptoms, build skills necessary to function on tests and in front of others, and encourage more social contact. As part of this therapy approach, Mr. and Mrs. M. would actively participate in all techniques, encourage their use at home and other settings, and reward Nathan's compliance with therapeutic homework assignments. In addition, Mr. and Mrs. M. were asked to take a firmer stand against Nathan's excess attention-getting behaviors. Finally, Mr. and Mrs. M. were encouraged to refrain from home schooling at least until the therapy program ran its course.

Course of Treatment

The therapist initially concentrated on helping Nathan control the negative physical symptoms he experienced at school. In particular, relaxation training and breathing retraining exercises were used to minimize muscle tension, trembling, dizziness and, to some extent, nausea. Nathan was instructed to practice these exercises at least twice per day and in school-related situations that evoked his symptoms. In addition, Nathan's parents sat in on the procedures and listened to the therapist's rationale about their use. Each parent was instructed as to how to use and practice the procedures themselves. This allowed the therapist to give them feedback on their performance and allow the parents to adequately check whether Nathan was appropriately engaging in the procedures. The therapist and parents also set up a system of rewards and punishments for

Nathan's compliance or noncompliance, respectively, to practicing relaxation and better breathing.

As Nathan was practicing these techniques at home and school, the therapist began a program of modeling and role play to enhance Nathan's performance on tests and speaking and writing in front of others. In the office setting, the therapist asked Nathan to take a sample test provided by his teacher, give a brief reading of a newspaper article in front of a small audience of strangers, and write and solve some arithmetic problems on a blackboard in front of others. Nathan's parents were part of each audience. Following each performance over the next several sessions, Nathan was given detailed feedback about areas of strength (e.g., effort, articulation) and areas that needed improvement (e.g., timing, concentration). Initially, the therapist encouraged Nathan's parents to be supportive only. Later in therapy, Mr. and Mrs. M. were asked to give direct feedback to Nathan.

Following Nathan's repeated practice of these tasks, which involved incorporating feedback from his therapist and parents, a series of real-life practices were assigned. With Nathan's foreknowledge, Nathan's teacher was asked to place him in several test-taking and performance situations at school. Nathan was also instructed to practice relaxation and breathing retraining during these school situations. In therapy sessions, Nathan discussed his performance and what areas still needed improvement. Feedback from the teacher was also obtained weekly.

In the meantime, Mr. and Mrs. M. were asked to reward Nathan for his school attendance, particularly on those days when evaluative events were scheduled for him. The therapist also worked with Mr. and Mrs. M. to increase Nathan's participation in extracurricular activities that involved a lot of social interaction and performance in front of others.

Outcome and Prognosis

In cases like this, school attendance may not be the best barometer of successful behavior change. Instead, the use of daily parent and child ratings of anxiety and avoidance may be best. In Nathan's case, remaining problems of absenteeism and avoidance of evaluative situations were quickly resolved. However, high levels of anxiety during school performance situations remained for several weeks. By the end of therapy, these levels had decreased 70% and Nathan no longer asked to be placed in home schooling. Long-term functioning was generally good, although Nathan expressed a considerable amount of anticipatory anxiety prior to the next school year. In cases like this, we recommend that parents and school officials arrange an orientation tour for the child prior to the start of school. In this way, the child can become well acquainted with the school's structure and required procedures.

PARENT TRAINING IN CONTINGENCY MANAGEMENT FOR YOUNGSTERS
REFUSING SCHOOL FOR ATTENTION

For children who refuse school for attention or who display some aspect of separation anxiety, parent training in contingency management can be quite helpful. We have found that the most successful components of contingency management for this population are (a) restructuring parent commands toward clarity and simplicity, (b) setting up fixed routines in the morning and throughout the day, (c) implementing rewards for compliance and school attendance and punishers for noncompliance and school refusal behavior, and (d) forced school attendance under certain conditions.

Restructuring Parent Commands

In many cases of school refusal behavior motivated by attention, parents get frustrated and shout vague commands to their children (e.g., "Get ready for school!"). To counter this, parents may be taught to give commands to their child in clearer, simpler, and more direct ways. To begin, we suggest that parents write out a list of commands they gave on previous mornings. Parents should be as forthright as possible and commands should be written verbatim. This process should continue throughout therapy.

Therapists may then work to restructure the commands with the parents. As suggested by Forehand and McMahon (1981), commands should be clear, concise, and understood by the child. To accomplish this, parents may first be taught to avoid certain patterns in their commands. For example, parents should avoid questionlike commands, lecturing, vagueness, criticism, interrupted commands, incomplete commands, commands with too many steps, and commands that are eventually carried out or ignored by the parent. We suggest that therapists look for patterns of errors that parents are making in their commands and give constructive feedback as necessary.

After parents are able to avoid certain negative patterns in their commands, a therapist may help them create more effective commands. For example, parents should specify exactly when a command is to be carried out (e.g., within 5 minutes). In addition, parents should say exactly what is required of the child and keep it simple. Instead of "Go to school," for example, a parent could say, "Put on your jacket now and walk to the bus stop." Also, the child should be capable of carrying out the command, nothing else (e.g., television) should compete with the command, the command should not contain an option for the child, and the command should not be too long (Kearney & Albano, in press). During therapy, parents monitor their commands on a daily basis and make changes where needed. Soliciting input from the child may also be useful in this regard.

Setting up Fixed Routines

Because children who refuse school for attention tend to show most of their behavior problems in the morning, therapists and parents should focus on setting up a fixed routine for the early day. Such a routine will mesh nicely with more straightforward parent commands and rewards and punishments to be discussed. The therapist and parents design a morning routine that will result in certain rewards or punishments if the routine is kept or not. We recommend that the child be required to rise from bed about 90 to 120 minutes prior to the start of school. Ten minutes of lead time between waking and rising may be given. Subsequent times are set for going to the bathroom and washing, dressing and making one's bed, eating breakfast, brushing teeth, making final preparations for school, going to school by oneself or with a parent, and entering the school building and classroom.

If the child is unable to attend school, then the therapist and parents set up a supervised daytime routine. This involves having the child sit in a boring place during the day (at home or work) under the supervision of a parent or other adult. The child may also be asked to complete homework or dull household chores, but no additional verbal or physical attention should be given beyond that which is absolutely necessary. The child should not receive any satisfaction or gratification for any out-of-school activities. A child who misses the entire school day is grounded at night as well. If the child missed school during most of the week, especially on Friday, then weekend grounding or other punishments are given. The essential message to be conveyed is that school attendance is mandatory and that school absence is a serious problem that parents will deal with even at night and on weekends.

Implementing Rewards and Punishments

In conjunction with parent commands and routines, rewards are established for compliance and school attendance. Likewise, punishments are established for noncompliance and school refusal behaviors. To do so, we encourage therapists to ask parents about all types of rewards and punishments they have used in the past. Each parent rates each reward and punishment for its effectiveness, practicality, and potential usefulness. Two or three rewards and punishments are chosen that greatly impact the child and that can be given by parents immediately and consistently. Because the child is refusing school for attention, it may be best to orient rewards toward events such as additional reading time with parents, staying up later, and having a family dinner honoring the child. Conversely, punishments might include verbal reprimands, ignoring and working through misbehavior, time-out, and grounding in one's bedroom. The child should know ahead of time all rules, expected appropriate behaviors, inappropriate behaviors, and rewards and punishments.

As part of contingency management, parents link rewards and punishers to compliance or noncompliance, respectively, to parent commands and the morning routine. In addition, we suggest that parents link rewards and punishments to the absence or presence, respectively, of five school refusal behaviors that are most problematic (crying, screaming, hitting, clinging, and refusal to move). Contingencies should be given immediately and perhaps later in the day. When such contingencies are given, the child should be reminded why they are given and what behaviors are appropriate and inappropriate.

As part of this process, we encourage parents to be as emotionally neutral and forthright with their child as possible. Parents should communicate in a matter-of-fact way that school attendance is expected and that the child will receive more parental attention for compliant than noncompliant behavior. We also encourage parents to work through misbehavior as much as possible. For example, parents should dress their child and bring him or her to school despite tantrums and other problems. In addition, these children often exaggerate physical complaints to avoid school. Excess complaints should be ignored by parents; we recommend that children miss school only if they have a fever over 100 degrees Fahrenheit and/or are vomiting. If necessary, therapists and parents may want to work closely with a school nurse to monitor any symptoms, exaggerated or not, that a child shows during the school day.

Forced School Attendance

In some cases where the child remains intransigent about going to school, even after the procedures just described, it may be necessary to consider forced school attendance (Kennedy, 1965). This generally involves some physical intervention in which the child is brought to school and classroom by the parents. We suggest that this procedure be done only under certain conditions: (Kearney & Albano, in press)

1. School refusal behavior is motivated only by attention.
2. Parents and school officials are willing to participate in the process.
3. Two parents or one parent and another adult can complete the process.
4. The child understands what the process will involve.
5. The child is currently missing more school days than not.
6. The child is under age 11.

Therapists are encouraged to raise this possibility with parents if desired and solicit feedback from them. In particular, therapists should assess for parental guilt, resistance from school officials, or other circumstances that may interfere with this procedure.

If these conditions are met and the child is continuing to refuse school, then forced school attendance may be used. Parents should bring the child to school with as little verbal or physical attention as possible. In some cases, it may be necessary to initially bring the child to school for part of the day (e.g., afternoon only) and then gradually increase the amount of in-school time. In other cases, it may be necessary to initially bring the child to a nonclassroom setting (e.g., library) at school prior to reintegration into the classroom.

Most of the time, children who refuse school for attention will stop misbehaving once they are brought into school. If not, a classroom-based system of rewards and punishments may need to be set up with the child's teacher. Forced school attendance should be ended if the child displays severe anxiety or if the situation becomes unbearable or overly embarrassing for the parents.

CASE EXAMPLE OF PARENT TRAINING IN CONTINGENCY MANAGEMENT FOR A YOUNGSTER REFUSING SCHOOL FOR ATTENTION

Presenting Client and Problem

Amy was an 8-year-old female referred by her mother, Mrs. L., and the principal at Amy's elementary school. During the initial telephone screening, Mrs. L. stated that Amy had missed 18 of the previous 30 days of school. On most days when Amy had attended school, a parent had accompanied her to school and spent at least part of the day in her classroom. If her parents told Amy to go to school by herself, Amy would cry, scream, cling to objects, or become "dead weight." She also complained of mild stomachaches and begged her parents to let her stay home. On most recent days, Mr. and Mrs. L. had acquiesced to these demands. However, Amy's schoolwork was suffering considerably, disruption to the family was becoming substantial, and school officials were pressuring Mr. and Mrs. L. for a solution. Therefore, a referral was made.

These problems appeared to have been triggered by three key events: (a) movement to a new classroom, (b) the recent birth of Amy's brother, and (c) business travel that required Mr. L. to be out of town extensively. With respect to the latter, Mrs. L. indicated that her husband would only be intermittently available for assessment and treatment sessions.

During assessment, Amy was reluctant to talk in general and especially one-on-one with the therapist. When eventually coaxed to do so, Amy was quiet but reported that she often cried the night before school and in the morning before getting up. She said she had stomachaches in the morning and that her parents would let her stay home as a result. When Amy was home, her mother would read to her and allow Amy to help with tasks needed to care for the new baby. Amy stated that her mother "needs my help because Daddy is always gone." Amy said that she had no problems during weekends except for Sunday night. She also reported several things that she liked about school, including recess, her teacher, and reading.

Mrs. L. gave a similar report, but added that Amy's tantrums and other misbehaviors were becoming more frequent even during the day at home. For example, Amy was starting to scream if not allowed to care for the baby in the way she wanted. Mrs. L. also admitted that she felt guilty about not spending enough time with Amy since the birth of her brother. She stated that this may have been one reason she was quicker to "give in" to Amy's demands than her husband, who was encouraging a stricter approach. However, Amy's behaviors had reached the point of intolerability. A telephone interview with Amy's teacher revealed that Amy was generally well behaved at school, although she often complained of wanting to be with her parents and demanded a lot of attention from adults at school.

Case Formulation

Based on a comprehensive assessment, the therapist determined that Amy was largely missing school to obtain attention from her parents. This determination was supported by the facts that Amy displayed few physical or other problems on the weekend, had fewer problems attending school if a parent was with her, and was composed when with her teacher for an extended period. In addition, parent and child questionnaire scores and ratings on the School Refusal Assessment Scale indicated that attention was the key function of Amy's school refusal behavior. The therapist recommended that treatment focus on increasing the strength of parent commands, setting up clear guidelines for behavior and daily routines, and establishing a consistent pattern of rewards and punishments for school attendance and absence, respectively. The therapist and parents acknowledged that much of treatment would have to be targeted toward Amy's mother. Mr. L. would attend therapy and contribute to the treatment regimen when possible.

Course of Treatment

Although treatment was largely parent-based, Amy was required to attend each therapy session and told what to expect in the coming days. Initially, Amy's parents provided a list of commands given during the past two weeks. Many of the commands concerned chores and bedtime, with few directed toward school attendance. As a result, the therapist restructured parent commands regarding household tasks and helped build new parent commands regarding Amy's school attendance. For example, a consistent parent command was "Please clean your room." Mr. and Mrs. L. were asked to restate this command and commands like it more clearly and directly. For example, one restatement of this command was: "Go into your bedroom now, pick up all the clothes from the floor, and hang them up in your closet." In addition, specific commands were built for the morning such as "Get out of bed now," "Eat your breakfast in the next ten minutes," and "Put on your jacket now and walk to the car." The therapist also addressed issues such as Mrs. L.'s guilt that interfered with the effectiveness of the commands and allowed acquiescence to Amy's demands.

The therapist then set up a routine for the morning. Amy was to be awakened at 7:00 and required to rise by 7:10. She would then be required to go to the bathroom and wash by 7:30, dress and eat breakfast by 8:00, brush her teeth and make final preparations for school by 8:15, and get in the car to go to school by 8:30. Compliance or noncompliance to this routine would result in rewards and punishments, respectively. Specific school refusal behaviors were identified as well. In this case, rewards and punishments would be applied to the presence or absence, respectively, of screaming, clinging, and refusal to move (other behaviors were added later in therapy). If Amy still refused to attend school, then her daytime routine would consist of sitting on her bed without parental attention. She would also be grounded in her room at night and mostly on the weekends but would still complete homework sent by her teacher.

Rewards and punishments were attention-based. Rewards consisted of verbal praise, more reading time with a parent, special dinners, and staying up later with the family at night. Punishments included short verbal reprimands, ignoring, and grounding for twice the amount of time spent refusing school in the morning. Rewards and punishments were given both immediately and during the evening and weekends. In addition, Mr. and Mrs. L. were asked to ignore Amy's inappropriate behaviors (e.g., exaggerated stomachaches) and "work through" misbehaviors (e.g., tantrums) to complete the morning routine. Amy was reminded that receiving rewards or punishments was solely her choice and depended on whether she went to school.

Outcome and Prognosis

During the first week of treatment, Amy's school refusal behavior increased substantially. This was not unexpected, as many children deliberately worsen their behavior to force parental acquiescence to their demands. In this case, the parents were able to hold firm, although Mr. L. was required to leave work and physically bring Amy to school on some occasions. After one week, Amy's behavior improved somewhat. Full-time school attendance was achieved after three weeks. Long-term functioning was generally good, although Amy experienced some relapses following long weekends and extended vacations.

PARENT-FAMILY THERAPY IN CONTINGENCY CONTRACTING FOR YOUNGSTERS REFUSING SCHOOL FOR POSITIVE TANGIBLE REINFORCEMENT

For children who refuse school for positive tangible reinforcement outside school, parent-family therapy in contingency contracting can be quite helpful. We have found that the key components of contingency contracting for this population are (a) setting up times and places for negotiating a solution to a problem and communicating appropriately, (b) defining a problem, (c) designing a written contract between the parents and child to resolve the problem, and (d) implementing the contract.

Setting up Times and Places for Negotiation and Communication

Initially in therapy, we recommend that parents and family members set up a time at home for regular discussions of unresolved problems. Although the formal contracting process should be almost totally done within the therapy session at the beginning of treatment, family members should talk to one another more in natural settings. These talks may first involve general issues and possible changes in the contracts. Later in treatment, these talks should center on developing contracts independent of the therapist's help. During each family discussion, parents are encouraged to let each family member voice his or her concerns and provide solutions to family problems. In addition, family members should practice the communication skills described next.

Communication skills training is often crucial for families of children who refuse school for positive tangible reinforcement outside school. This is so because these families are usually highly conflictive and do not properly communicate during many problem-solving discussions. Initially, we suggest that therapists concentrate on having parents and family members eliminate negative speech patterns. For example, parents may be asked to discourage name-calling, insults, yelling, silence, sarcasm, interruptions, and inappropriate suggestions.

Later in treatment, we focus on building more positive interactions between parents and children. We ask parents to convey messages to their child in a simple, straightforward, and positive manner (e.g., "I like it a lot when you go to school all day"). Subsequently, we ask the youngster to paraphrase or repeat what was said to confirm that the child heard the message. Any problems must be addressed at this point. All family members then participate in this process with one another. If this is successful, both in the office and at home, the therapist then models short conversations for the family. Here, the therapist has a brief conversation with one parent in front of other family members. Then, feedback is given to everyone about appropriate messages, listening, and nonverbal behaviors (e.g., eye contact). Over time, family members practice short, positive conversations at home and audiotape some of them for the therapist to analyze. By the end of therapy, parents and family members should be able to carry on more extensive, productive, and problem-solving-oriented conversations.

Defining a Problem

Before a formal contract can be written, parents and family members must work to define a specific problem. To do so, the therapist identifies an irritating but fairly minor problem that faces the family. This problem should initially have nothing to do with school refusal behavior (e.g., chore or homework not completed, bedtime missed). Each family member should agree as to the appropriateness of the problem. In general, problems that are unsolvable, long-standing, or quite complicated should be avoided.

After choosing the problem, parents and family members are asked for their definitions of the problem. In the beginning, vast differences in definitions will be the norm, and the therapist will have to forge a compromise. For example, a parent might define a problem as "He never washes the dishes when I ask him," whereas a child might define the problem as "I have to do the dishes all the time." In this case, the therapist may derive a more precise and blameless definition: "The dishes are not being washed on a regular basis." Following any problem definition, all family members state whether it is acceptable.

As therapy progresses, more complicated problems such as those related to school refusal may be defined. We suggest that school attendance/absence, curfew, completed homework, required chores, and other items that may be key to future contracts be defined as exactly as possible by everyone. Also, parents and family members should provide these definitions more independently of the therapist over time. To test their ability in this area, therapists can intermittently give parents and family members a hypothetical, vague problem to define and give constructive feedback about their performance in doing so.

Designing a Written Contract to Resolve the Problem

After a problem is defined, the child and parents separately list as many solutions as possible. About 5 to 10 solutions should be solicited from each party and ranked in order of desirability, that is, whether the solution is practical, realistic, specific, and potentially agreeable to everyone. The lists are then compared and the therapist chooses one solution that is most desirable. Parents and family members are asked whether they agree to the choice. If so, the therapist may proceed.

The next step involves setting up tangible rewards and punishments for completing or not completing the contract. Again, each party gives input and the therapist focuses on blending everyone's viewpoint. The first contract is then formally negotiated by the therapist with the parents and child separately. The first contract, which should be quite simple so that the family experiences success with the process, may read as follows for the problem defined here: "(Child) agrees to wash the dishes on Thursday and Sunday if asked. If (child) completes this chore correctly, then (child) will receive an extra half-hour with friends on Friday night and one day during the week. If (child) does not wash the dishes when asked on these days, then he/she will be grounded for a 24-hour period determined by the parents."

Therapists must close any loopholes in the contract. In this contract, for example, one should define exactly when the dishes will be washed, who will say the dishes were washed well, and when the youngster can be with his or her friends. We usually give parents more say when closing loopholes. In addition, the contract should last no longer than a few days. In this way, the therapist can address any problems as soon as possible.

Later, contracts may become more complicated and focus directly on the youngster's school refusal behavior. Again, the main goal of these contracts is to increase tangible rewards for school attendance and decrease such rewards (and/or add punishments) for school absence. A key way of doing this is to require the youngster to attend school for the privilege of doing household chores for money. If the child misses school, the chores would still be required but no compensation would be given. A sample contract (Figure 7.1) from Kearney and Albano (in press), using a format from Stuart (1971), illustrates this point:

Implementing the Contract

Once the contract has been written, parents and family members read the contract and let the therapist know whether it is acceptable. Unacceptable conditions must be renegotiated. Once the final contract is drawn, all family members sign it and post it in an open area of the house (e.g., refrigerator door). Family members should contact the therapist as soon as possible if problems arise. In addition, we recommend that therapists contact parents and children almost daily to ensure compliance.

Therapists should be forewarned that many youngsters will comply with the contracts until formal school attendance is made part of a contract. If sudden noncompliance arises for contracts involving school

Privileges	Responsibilities
General	
In exchange for decreased family conflict and a resolution to school refusal behavior, all family members agree to	try as hard as possible to maintain this contract and fully participate in therapy.
Specific	
In exchange for the privilege of being paid to complete household chores between now and the next therapy session, (child) agrees to	attend school full-time between now and the next therapy session.
Should (child) not complete this responsibility,	he (she) will be required to complete the household chores without being paid.
In exchange for the privilege of possessing a radio and television in his (her) room, (child) agrees to	rise in the morning at 7:00, dress and eat by 7:40, wash and brush teeth by 8:00, and finalize preparations for school by 8:20.
Should (child) not complete this responsibility,	he (she) will lose the radio and television and will be grounded for one day.
In exchange for compensation of five dollars, (child) agrees to	vacuum the living room and clean the bathroom between now and the next therapy session.
Should (child) not go to school, not complete this responsibility, or complete the responsibility inadequately (to be determined by parents),	he (she) will not be paid.

(Child) and his (her) parents agree to uphold the conditions of this contract and read and initial the contract each day.

Signature of (Child) and his (her) parents:

_____

_____

Date: _____

Figure 7.1 Sample Contract

attendance, parents may have to accompany the child to school and walk him or her from class to class. In this way, school attendance is assured and the child remains eligible for the tangible rewards in the contract. Punishments may still be given for excessive behaviors such as running out of the school building. This process requires a lot of effort on the part of the parents, and must be done with the cooperation of school officials. In addition, parents will have to gradually fade themselves from the school situation.

Therapists are also encouraged to have parents closely monitor their youngster's school attendance so that any absences may be known and consequated immediately. Developing relationships with teachers, principals, attendance officers, and nurses may be helpful in this regard. Finally, youngsters in this group have often fallen behind in much of their schoolwork, so future contracts should reward the youngster for completing current schoolwork and making up past work. We have found that academic competence is usually antithetical to school refusal behavior.

Case Example of Parent-Family Therapy in Contingency Contracting for a Youngster Refusing School for Positive Tangible Reinforcement

Presenting Client and Problem

Kevin was a 14-year-old male referred by his mother, Mrs. K., and the attendance officer at Kevin's high school. As a ninth-grader, Kevin had missed 26 of the last 42 days of school and was experiencing a severe decline in his grades. During the initial telephone screening, Mrs. K., a single mother of three children, indicated that Kevin had missed school intermittently in previous years. However, his entry into high school this year seemed to be difficult and his school refusal behavior was more intense than in the past. Mrs. K. also complained that Kevin had "fallen in with the wrong crowd" and was skipping school with several new friends. Because school officials were considering expulsion if a solution was not found soon, an assessment session was scheduled for that week.

The first two scheduled sessions were postponed because Kevin refused to attend. After much pleading by his mother, Kevin agreed to speak with the therapist briefly. He indicated that he needed more independence and did not see the point of attending school, which he saw as unproductive and boring. On the days that Kevin missed, he would usually go to day parties with his friends or watch television at a friend's house. He acknowledged some concern about his grades and their effect on his ability to graduate, but said he could make up the work anytime.

Kevin's mother largely confirmed this report. She added information about Kevin's father, who was living in another state, and gave the therapist recent police reports of vandalism and illicit purchases of alcohol by Kevin. She feared she was losing control of her son and that he would become a delinquent. Mrs. K. also admitted that her work responsibilities and the demands of caring for her other children left her with little time for Kevin. Discussions with Kevin's teachers revealed little additional information because of their lack of contact with him.

Case Formulation

Based on a comprehensive assessment, the therapist determined that Kevin was missing school largely for positive tangible reinforcement outside school. This determination was supported by the facts that Kevin displayed no major internalizing symptoms, no desire to be constantly near his mother, fewer problems attending school if his mother bribed him to do so, and strong motivation to be with his friends during the school day. In addition, parent and child questionnaire scores and ratings on the School Refusal Assessment Scale indicated that positive tangible reinforcement was the key function of Kevin's school refusal behavior. The therapist recommended that treatment focus on increasing appropriate rewards for Kevin's school attendance and completed homework, increasing punishments and decreasing out-of-school activities for Kevin's school absences, and giving Mrs. K. a strategy for working with her son to negotiate solutions to family problems.

Course of Treatment

Treatment in this case focused almost exclusively on Kevin and his mother, although siblings and important others were included as necessary. Initially, the therapist spent time developing a strong rapport with Kevin, who needed to be convinced that his input would be as valuable as anyone's and that the therapist would not simply be another adult telling him what to do. In doing so, the therapist explained that a contract would involve privileges and responsibilities for all parties. Kevin acknowledged the possible usefulness of the contract but stated that his conditions would have to include some free time with his friends.

The first contract involved a simple chore, reward, and punishment similar to that described earlier. Because this contract was successful and because of the imminent consequences of Kevin's school attendance record, the therapist decided to proceed quickly to a more complex contract. This contract required Kevin to (a) attend school full-time for 4 of the next 5 school days, (b) refrain from any illicit activity, and (c) obey a curfew of 11:00 P.M. In exchange, Kevin would be allowed to (a) vacuum the house on Saturday for 10 dollars, (b) be driven by his mother to a friend's house of his choice on Sunday afternoon, and (c) go out with his friends on Friday and Saturday nights. Each party accepted the conditions of the one-week contract, signed it, and agreed to discuss the contract with one another daily. The therapist also spent time discussing Kevin's relationship with his mother, the family's communication skills, and Kevin's academic work. Finally, Mrs. K. was asked to call the school daily to check Kevin's school attendance and class assignments.

In the next session, Mrs. K. reported that the contract was only partially successful. Kevin did adhere to curfew and avoided legal trouble, but missed school 4 out of 5 schooldays. Mrs. K. allowed Kevin to see his friends on Saturday night but did not allow any other social activities or payments. The next three contracts over the next 3 weeks were modified so that (a) Kevin would experience some success with school attendance and receive appropriate tangible rewards, and (b) Mrs. K. would follow through more thoroughly on all aspects of the contract, especially punishments. These three contracts were largely successful in the latter, but Kevin's school attendance did not improve.

At this point, the therapist and Mrs. K. recruited a friend of the family who was willing to accompany Kevin to school and walk him from class to class for the next two weeks. Kevin was told that, if he skipped school again, he would be escorted in this manner. After he missed two more days of school, this procedure was implemented. Kevin then received all the tangible rewards for going to school and was not punished. Kevin's school attendance was perfect for two weeks, after which the escort was gradually faded. This was done by having Kevin escorted in the morning up to lunchtime, and then monitoring his afternoon school attendance via conversations with school officials. Over two weeks, the escort was faded until Kevin showed that he could attend school on his own. In the meantime, the therapist continued to work on other areas of conflict within the family as well as Kevin's academic standing.

Outcome and Prognosis

Kevin continued to attend school on a fairly regular basis, although relapses were common. In this population, it is not unusual for teenagers to challenge their parents' resolve by occasionally skipping school. Therefore, vigilance and consistent follow-through are critical. In addition, therapists should focus on building communication skills and reducing the conflict inherent to many families of adolescents who skip school. In this case, the therapist tried to build a better partnership between Kevin and his mother that focused on taking care of the family, negotiating solutions to problems, and easing tensions. The therapist also worked to increase Mrs. K.'s social support network to reduce her parenting burden.

Prognosis for this type of case is highly dependent on the final quality of the parent-child relationship, continued use of contracts, and improvement in and maintenance of academic work.

CONCLUSION

For therapists who address youngsters with school refusal behavior and their parents, we would like to reemphasize two key points. First, we have found it critical to include parents in many aspects of assessment for youngsters with school refusal behavior. Parents remain one of the richest sources of information about a child refusing school, particularly younger children. Therefore, parental participation is crucial during screening conversations, interviews, questionnaire administration, and direct observations of behavior. We caution therapists that initial parent reports can be frantic and overstated, but this often reflects the crisislike nature of these problems. In particular, parents will sometimes emphasize overt behavior problems in their children instead of what may be more severe anxiety and depressive problems. In addition, therapists should keep in mind that discrepancies in information between parents and children are common to this population. Therefore, a comprehensive assessment of these children is recommended.

Second, we encourage clinicians to rely on the basic ideas of our functional model for treating school refusal behavior. These ideas include using the inclusive definition of school refusal behavior presented at the beginning of this chapter and examining functions more so than the forms of school refusal behavior. The major functions discussed in this chapter were (a) negative reinforcement (avoidance of stimuli that provoke negative affectivity and/or escape from aversive social/evaluative situations at school), (b) attention from significant others, and (c) pursuit of positive tangible reinforcement outside school.

Our functional model also calls for adopting a prescriptive treatment approach from these functions that involves substantial parent input and training. Such procedures involve training parents to (a) help their child implement and maintain compliance to relaxation training, breathing retraining, modeling, role play, cognitive therapy, and exposure techniques; (b) implement some major components of contingency management, including restructured parent commands, regular daytime routines, and rewards and punishments for compliance and noncompliance; and/or (c) better monitor their child's school refusal behavior and use contracts to define problems clearly, negotiate solutions without conflict, increase appropriate tangible rewards for school attendance, and restrict activities for school absence. Future work is needed to further validate these treatment approaches for this population, but preliminary work is promising (Kearney, 1992; Kearney & Silverman, 1990).

Involving parents in the treatment process for youngsters with school refusal behavior goes beyond the mere use of techniques, however. We have found it extremely important to enlist the help of both parents, even if one is separated from daily family life; provide substantial therapist support to parents who are going through this difficult time with their child; maintain almost daily contact with parents to encourage their follow-through on treatment procedures; alleviate parent guilt, conflict, psychopathology, pessimistic attitudes, and ineffective disciplinary styles that arrest treatment progress; and provide parents with a long-term strategy they can use to remedy future occurrences of school refusal behavior. Finally, we encourage therapists to prevent more serious school refusal problems by working closely with school officials to secure early referrals and urge parents to seek treatment sooner rather than later.

REFERENCES

Baker, H., & Wills, U. (1978). School phobia: Classification and treatment. *British Journal of Psychiatry, 132,* 492–499.

Berg, I. (1970). A follow-up study of school phobic adolescents admitted to an inpatient unit. *Journal of Child Psychology and Psychiatry, 11,* 37–47.

Berg, I., & Jackson, A. (1985). Teenage school refusers grow up: A follow-up study of 168 subjects, ten years on average after inpatient treatment. *British Journal of Psychiatry, 147,* 366–370.

Berg, I., Marks, I., McGuire, R., & Lipsedge, M. (1974). School phobia and agoraphobia. *Psychological Medicine, 4,* 428–434.

Cartledge, G., & Milburn, J. F. (1995). *Teaching social skills to children and youth: Innovative approaches* (3rd ed.). Boston: Allyn & Bacon.

Eisen, A. R., & Kearney, C. A. (1995). *Practitioner's guide to treating fear and anxiety in children and adolescents: A cognitive-behavioral approach.* Northvale, NJ: Jason Aronson.

Flakierska, N., Lindstrom, M., & Gillberg, C. (1988). School refusal: A 15–20-year follow-up study of 35 Swedish urban children. *British Journal of Psychiatry, 152,* 834–837.

Forehand, R., & McMahon, R. J. (1981). *Helping the noncompliant child: A clinician's guide to parent training.* New York: Guilford Press.

Foster, S. L., & Robin, A. L. (1989). Parent-adolescent conflict. In E. J. Mash & R. A. Barkley (Eds.), *Treatment of childhood disorders* (pp. 717–775). New York: Guilford Press.

Haaga, D. A., & Davison, G. C. (1986). Cognitive change methods. In F. H. Kanfer & A. P. Goldstein (Eds.), *Helping people change: A textbook of methods* (pp. 236–282). New York: Pergamon Press.

Hampe, E., Miller, L., Barrett, C., & Noble, H. (1973). Intelligence and school phobia. *Journal of School Psychology, 11*, 66–70.

Hibbett, A., & Fogelman, K. (1990). Future lives of truants: Family formation and health-related behaviour. *British Journal of Educational Psychology, 60*, 171–179.

Hibbett, A., Fogelman, K., & Manor, O. (1990). Occupational outcomes of truancy. *British Journal of Educational Psychology, 60*, 23–36.

Kahn, J. H., & Nursten, J. P. (1962). School refusal: A comprehensive view of school phobia and other failures of school attendance. *American Journal of Orthopsychiatry, 32*, 707–718.

Kazdin, A. E. (1991). Effectiveness of psychotherapy with children and adolescents. *Journal of Consulting and Clinical Psychology, 59*, 785–789.

Kearney, C. A. (1992, November). *Prescriptive treatment for school refusal behavior.* Symposium presented at the meeting of the Association for the Advancement of Behavior Therapy, Boston, MA.

Kearney, C. A. (1995). School refusal behavior. In A. R. Eisen, C. A. Kearney, & C. E. Schaefer (Eds.), *Clinical handbook of anxiety disorders in children and adolescents* (pp. 19–52). Northvale, NJ: Jason Aronson.

Kearney, C. A., & Albano, A. M. (in press). *Therapist's guide for school refusal behavior.* New York: Psychological Corporation.

Kearney, C. A., Eisen, A. R., & Silverman, W. K. (1995). The legend and myth of school phobia. *School Psychology Quarterly, 10*, 65–85.

Kearney, C. A., & Silverman, W. K. (1990). A preliminary analysis of a functional model of assessment and treatment for school refusal behavior. *Behavior Modification, 14*, 344–360.

Kearney, C. A., & Silverman, W. K. (1993). Measuring the function of school refusal behavior: The School Refusal Assessment Scale. *Journal of Clinical Child Psychology, 22*, 85–96.

Kearney, C. A., & Silverman, W. K. (1995). Family environment of youngsters with school refusal behavior: A synopsis with implications for assessment and treatment. *American Journal of Family Therapy, 23*, 59–72.

Kearney, C. A., & Silverman, W. K. (in press). The evolution and reconciliation of taxonomic strategies for school refusal behavior. *Clinical Psychology: Science and Practice.*

Kearney, C. A., & Sims, K. E. (in press). School stress and anxiety. *In Session: Psychotherapy in Practice.*

Kearney, C. A., & Tillotson, C. A. (in press). School attendance. In T. S. Watson & F. M. Gresham (Eds.), *Child behavior therapy: Ecological considerations in assessment, treatment, and evaluation.* New York: Plenum Press.

Kennedy, W. A. (1965). School phobia: Rapid treatment of 50 cases. *Journal of Abnormal Psychology, 70*, 285–289.

Last, C. G. (1991). Somatic complaints in anxiety disordered children. *Journal of Anxiety Disorders, 5*, 125–138.

Last, C. G., & Strauss, C. C. (1990). School refusal in anxiety-disordered children and adolescents. *Journal of the American Academy of Child and Adolescent Psychiatry, 29*, 31–35.

Nichols, K. A., & Berg, I. (1970). School phobia and self-evaluation. *Journal of Child Psychology and Psychiatry, 11*, 133–141.

Ollendick, T. H., & Cerny, J. A. (1981). *Clinical behavior therapy with children.* New York: Plenum Press.

Robins, L. N., & Ratcliffe, K. S. (1980). The long-term outcome of truancy. In L. Hersov & I. Berg (Eds.), *Out of school* (pp. 65–83). New York: Wiley.

Shirk, S. R. (in press). Development and the myths of child therapy. In W. K. Silverman & T. Ollendick (Eds.), *Developmental issues in the clinical treatment of children.* Needham Heights, MA: Allyn & Bacon.

Silverman, W. K., & Kurtines, W. M. (1996). *Anxiety and phobic disorders: A pragmatic approach.* New York: Plenum Press.

Smith, S. L. (1970). School refusal with anxiety: A review of sixty-three cases. *Canadian Psychiatry Association Journal, 15*, 257–264.

Stuart, R. B. (1971). Behavioral contracting within the families of delinquents. *Journal of Behavior Therapy and Experimental Psychiatry, 2*, 1–11.

Tyrer, P., & Tyrer, S. (1974). School refusal, truancy and adult neurotic illness. *Psychological Medicine, 6*, 313–332.

PART THREE

DEVELOPMENTAL DISORDERS

SOMETIMES THE attempts to achieve mastery at various levels of development become a particularly difficult struggle and challenge for a child. This struggle may be manifested as lags, delays, or deviances in the maturation of a function, such as attachment, learning, or feeding and may also occur as significant deficits in the development process in general. In Chapter 8, Lachenmeyer discusses the failure to thrive (FTT) syndrome, which describes infants and young children who show weight loss or difficulties in gaining or maintaining weight. She notes that when there is no complete medical resolution of feeding problems, psychological treatment must be employed. Since the parents are typically the primary caregivers, they are the individuals who feed the youngster and must resolve problematic issues surrounding feeding. When remediation is necessary, the parents are usually in the best position to correct feeding dysfunctions and offer efficacious treatment. In view of these factors, parent training is a viable form of treatment intervention for FTT.

Because FTT children do not form a homogeneous group, Lachenmeyer offers parent training intervention strategies that can be applied in many situations in which poor nutritional intake is negatively affecting a child's growth. The reader is offered an intriguing spectrum of cases involving feeding interventions, tube feeding, and an investigation of some of the direct and indirect medical complications associated with poor eating. The parents are also instructed in how to maintain a Daily Food Intake Diary for the child. The author presents cognitive-behavioral techniques for reducing unpleasant associations linked with food and feeding. In addition, she outlines techniques that will increase the likelihood of pleasant associations with feeding or eating. Lachenmeyer's approach also trains parents in the proper use of operant maneuvers such as time-out, extinction, and response cost and reinforcement when dealing with failure to thrive.

Lutzker and Steed review an extensive and impressive number of parent training approaches that have been empirically studied and clinically applied with developmentally disabled children since the 1960s. The authors of Chapter 9 consider the principles of operant conditioning and the role of biology in their discussion of the etiology of mental retardation. They outline the steady progression and evolution of parent training modalities, tools, and concepts, particularly as they apply to the modification of developmental disabilities. The authors point out that even though behavioral techniques have traditionally dominated the field of parent training, several more current alternative models are applicable, such as the dynamic model, family therapy, and early intervention/education approaches.

Following their review of past behavioral strategies, Lutzker and Steed focus on the ecobehavioral model, an inventive approach that combines aspects of ecological psychology and applied behavioral psychology. In this multifaceted strategy, behavioral assessments are conducted within the family's social ecology. The major components of the ecobehavioral model are based on a combination of Planned Activities Training (PAT) and errorless compliance procedures. Planned Activities Training refers to a collection of strategies that teach parents to predict, plan, and impact positively on the behavior of their children. The technique of errorless compliance learning employs a hierarchical ranking system to increase the child's probability of successful compliance with parental instructions.

The ecobehavioral approach examined in Chapter 9 offers an alternative to contingent management training. The strategies of Planned Activities Training and errorless compliance rely on the use of antecedents that set the occasion for desired behavior and may eliminate the need for contingencies. Lutzker and Steed propose a comprehensive approach to parent training with stimulus control techniques that emphasize antecedent prevention of challenging behavior. They present case studies to illuminate the proper use of Planned Activities Training and errorless compliance and demonstrate that their approach not only reduces challenging behaviors (including noncompliance) but also promotes the development of appropriate skills and facilitates generalization across settings and behaviors.

In Chapter 10, Booth and Koller offer an extensive and well-documented description of Theraplay, a short-term, goal-oriented intervention modeled on the reciprocity involved in the interaction between parents and their child. Because Theraplay focuses on the underlying parent-child relationship, it can be custom-tailored by the therapist to guide parents in handling divergent problems. The primary objectives of Theraplay center on improving relationships and enhancing attachments. Consequently, this format is well-suited to treating underlying relationship difficulties with failure-to-attach children and their parents.

Booth and Koller focus on the importance and impact of attachment. They state that attachment is a key concept by virtue of its relationship to the individual's capacity to form relationships and to develop a sense of self. Therefore, if there is a failure or inability to form attachments, early intervention is essential. Following a summation of the primary characteristics of children with attachment problems, the authors discuss some of the major factors that may place a child at risk for a failure-to-attach disorder. They concentrate on issues associated with environmental failures, the child's sensitivities or special needs, and the impact of the child's problems and temperament on the formation and maintenance of attachment. They then outline the logistics and strategies of Theraplay that can mollify attachment and relationship problems.

In their discussion of the sequential stages of the Theraplay treatment approach to parent training, Booth and Koller give an in-depth description of the Marschak Interaction Method (MIM), a structured observation designed to assess the quality and nature of parent-child relationships. They not only present the rationale for feedback but also use case material to document the importance and validity of a feedback session. As they indicate, the parent training actually begins during the feedback session. At that time, the parents view videotapes which show their interactional styles and patterns. During this session, the parents also receive clarification of their child's responses, feelings, and needs. Furthermore, in the feedback session the nature of Theraplay is explained and the objectives of treatment are established.

Theraplay is a creative intervention format grounded in the notion that the child's secure attachment and strong sense of self develop out of early playful and responsive interactions with the mother, specifically, and parents, in general. As Booth and Koller point out in Chapter 10, it is in these interactions that the child develops the earliest primary representations of self as loved, competent, and secure. The authors present a valuable intervention strategy for the failure-to-attach syndrome that strives to instill in parents a more positive and empathic view of their child.

CHAPTER 8

Parent Training for Failure to Thrive

JULIANA RASIC LACHENMEYER

THIS CHAPTER will focus on behavioral aspects of eating problems in children and the role of the caregivers in changing these behaviors. Children with eating difficulties can be divided into two categories: those whose poor eating has led to problems in the rate of growth and who are therefore at risk for problems in neurological development and failure to thrive, and those whose rate of growth is unaffected. Children whose rate of growth has been affected by their eating history present a more serious and immediate challenge than those whose eating behavior only affects family interactions. The focus in this chapter will be on children whose growth rate is affected by their poor nutritional intake. Parental interventions in the group whose growth rate is unaffected should consist of minimizing power struggles while at the same time not catering to the child's every food preference. Children who engage in nonoral or tube feeding will be discussed, and issues in weaning these children will also be addressed.

Failure to thrive (FTT) is a syndrome that describes infants and young children who show weight loss or difficulties in gaining or maintaining weight. Roberts and Maddux (1982) apply these criteria to children under the age of 4 years and those who are below the fifth percentile in weight. The young child who fails to thrive often has developmental disabilities (Gordan & Jameson, 1979; Kotelchuck, 1980). The relationship of developmental disabilities to poor nutritional intake may be any one of the following: (a) developmental disabilities may result from poor nutritional intake, (b) developmental disabilities may actually lead to eating difficulties, (c) developmental disabilities and poor growth may be the result of a third set of variables. A child's level of developmental functioning including cognitive functioning will affect the type of intervention used as well as the rate of progress attained. Child characteristics as well as parental characteristics influence parental perceptions and caregiver-child interactions, all of which affect subsequent interactions (Sameroff & Chandler, 1975). Whereas the young child with poor nutritional intake and therefore inadequate growth is at risk for developmental and other neurological disorders, the older child is at risk for medical and psychological conditions associated with poor nutrition. Therefore, ways of intervening with the older child will also be discussed. Failure to thrive can be categorized as organic or nonorganic in etiology. According to Bithoney and Rathburn (1983) organic failure to thrive (OFTT) is a growth symptom of all serious pediatric illnesses; the common factor is the medical condition of malnutrition. Nonorganic failure to thrive (NOFTT) is a failure to grow without any diagnosable organic cause. Although this may appear to be a clear distinction, in fact, it is not. Although FTT is defined by inadequate growth that is a result of poor nutritional intake, the syndrome does not describe a homogeneous group. Sometimes the cause of the poor nutritional intake is clearly medical such as reflux (Hoffman & Ross, 1995) and a medical procedure such as medication or surgery can correct the condition. At other times, although the cause may be medical, there is no clear medical solution. Most often either the cause is unclear, or whatever the initial cause, the factor maintaining the poor nutritional status is the parent-child interaction. When there is no clear medical solution to the problem, the intervention should focus on the parent-child feeding interaction and perhaps other parent-child interactions. Lachenmeyer (1995) empirically derived the following categories of FTT based on a sample of 45 children assessed and treated over several years.

1. The poor eater who may or may not have growth-related problems.
2. The child whose eating problem has a known medical etiology for which there is medical treatment.
3. The child with either a history of or current medical problems that *do not directly* explain *current* poor nutritional intake.
4. The child with neurodevelopmental problems who may have low tone, oromotor difficulties, sensitivities, or similar problems that *directly* affect nutritional intake.
5. The child with neurodevelopmental difficulties that do not in and of themselves explain the poor nutritional intake. (Neurodevelopmental difficulties are often seen as resulting from FTT. Although this may be the case, often there is a more complex, circular interaction. Gross or even subtle neurodevelopmental problems can

cause problems with feeding. Consequent growth difficulties can also cause neurodevelopmental problems.)

6. The child who has developed a conditioned dysphagia: a conditioned aversive response that leads to food avoidance, for example, a history of choking, gagging, or vomiting that may be the result of a single incident or multiple incidents, or may be associated with diseases or treatments for certain diseases such as bone marrow transplants and chemotherapy. (This kind of food aversion may occur at any time in the life of a child or even of an adult.)

7. The child who because of medical problems has a history of nonoral or tube feeding. (Under these conditions, a child may be unaware of hunger and satiety cues and additionally may not have learned to associate oral feeding with pleasure.)

8. The child whose primary caregiver is not adequately responsive to the child's nutritional needs due to his or her own pathology, to psychosocial stressors in his or her life, or to ignorance of appropriate feeding behavior.

9. The child with multiple physical or cognitive problems none of which appear to be directly related to his or her poor nutritional status.

10. The child whose poor eating is secondary to another psychiatric disorder such as depression or obsessive-compulsive disorder (Lachenmeyer, 1997).

For all the preceding conditions—if there is no known medical condition with an appropriate medical intervention—parental work focusing on eating interactions and possibly other family or social interactions is the treatment of choice (Lachenmeyer, 1987).

PARENT TRAINING

The assumption behind parent training is that the parent is best able to carry out an intervention program. Although parents may not cause the problems of children, they are instrumental in maintaining them. And because the difficulties occur in their presence, they must respond in some way and can be taught to do so more effectively (Lachenmeyer, 1994). Parents have different ways in which they can get a child to comply: through the use of contingencies, whether implicit or explicit, including rewards, and through parental authority founded on a history of implementation of contingencies and other relationship variables. Parents can also increase the rate of occurrence of a behavior or decrease it through indirect means (e.g., in a playful way that involves an indirect focus or implicit contingencies). It is especially important with FTT that a parent not blame him- or herself for the child's poor eating and that the caregiver not attribute the problem to traits in their child (e.g., stubbornness, spitefulness, manipulative or controlling personality). It is equally important not to make negative attributions about the child's intentions, for example "she is trying to get back at me." Such attributions make the parent feel ineffectual, and less able to manage the child. Only specific behaviors can be changed. Global negative attributions are likely to affect a parent's behavior toward a child: treat the child as someone who is "willful" or "won't listen" rather than someone who is not eating sufficiently. These global attributions lead to a different definition of the problem, with a subsequent strong emotional response on the part of the parent that makes effective handling of the problem unlikely. Although parents are not the cause of the problem, they are in the best position to do something about it. With FTT, it is important to give the parents an explanation for the poor nutritional intake and then to develop a treatment plan that includes parents.

To develop a treatment plan, therapists should have training in behavioral and empirical treatment; they should know how to observe behavior and to make recommendations based on data collected. Familiarity with relaxation training, desensitization, principles of weaning, and knowledge of children and child-parent interactions are necessary. Some knowledge of nutrition is helpful. And depending on the specific case, specialized knowledge of and experience in dealing with certain medical conditions and their treatment (including tube feeding) may be necessary. Although there are technical skills that can be taught to parents, compliance is often related to the therapists' clinical skills and judgment.

The therapist must set up a collaborative relationship with the parents and a warm, positive relationship with the child. The parents must perceive the therapist as an expert who is guiding them—trust and confidence are two major components of the relationship. The relationship is collaborative in that the parents possess information on which the assessment and treatment plan are based. The parents know what they have tried in the past, what has worked or not worked, and what they are willing to do or see themselves as being able to do. By the time a family with an FTT child seeks psychological treatment, a great deal of time has passed that has often been difficult for all family members. In addition, certain interaction patterns centering around feeding and parenting in general have been established. Parents are usually tired of the feeding problem, feel hopeless about it, and yet uncertain as to what to do. By this time, the feeding problem has usually affected all relationships within the family: between spouses and between parents and FTT child. Relationships between the FTT child and siblings, parents and siblings, and even members of the extended family may have been affected.

ASSESSMENT

When working with the family of a child with FTT, a collaborative working relationship must be established with the physicians involved as well as with oromotor or speech therapists and nutritionists. Assessments in each of these areas are necessary. A medical work-up should include a history of all medical illnesses past and present. The first question is to determine possible etiology, and then if there are any *existing* medical conditions that contribute directly to the poor nutritional intake. This should include evaluations of the swallow mechanisms as well as oromotor functioning. If problems are found in any of these areas, a determination has to be made as to whether they can be treated with medicine or surgery. Oromotor difficulties or sensitivities can be worked on through oromotor exercises. The age of the FTT child is a factor in determining whether oromotor training should be undertaken, and if so, what the parent's role should be and how to best achieve compliance. If there are medical or speech interventions, they should be undertaken. Following that, the eating behavior should be assessed to determine whether the interventions were partially or completely successful. If there is no appropriate medical or oromotor intervention or if there is some residual eating difficulty despite an appropriate medical intervention, then a thorough empirical assessment of the feeding behavior should be undertaken.

Collaboration with the physician involved as well as the nutritionist or other health professionals should be ongoing. While the behavioral parent training is an independent treatment, the initial program depends on input from other professionals. The presence of medical conditions, neuropsychological findings, or oromotor findings have implications for etiology. These conditions may also maintain the eating problem and thereby affect the treatment plan. In addition, findings in these areas may set some limits on the interventions themselves. Certain medical conditions may preclude giving a child high caloric foods; oromotor difficulties may eliminate certain textured foods at the beginning of treatment.

Knowledge of a child's level of cognitive or developmental functioning is necessary in order to set up and implement contingencies. Ongoing contact between the health professionals involved is also needed because the information from one discipline may be necessary for the other (e.g., a behavioral regimen must take into account nutritional information in terms of kinds of foods and calories). Also, the professionals involved should give families similar messages about all aspects of treatment.

A behavioral assessment should include a specific assessment of the eating behavior. In addition, all areas of family functioning and child functioning should be evaluated. Individual caregiver functioning should also be assessed inasmuch as it relates to the child's eating behavior. Assessment is continuous and ongoing: Each intervention is evaluated to determine what is working and what is not working.

Following the initial telephone contact and prior to the first visit, the primary caregiver should be asked to keep a daily food intake diary. This is the primary assessment tool and consists of the time of food intake, setting and amount eaten, as well as child behaviors associated with food intake and refusal and parental behaviors associated with intake and refusal. It is a good idea for the diary to be kept in a spiral notebook. This allows the therapist to write recommendations agreed on in session as well as positive comments on achievements. The written recommendations serve as reminders and the positive comments as reinforcers between sessions. The food diary defines and delineates the eating problem. It is the basis on which the specific eating interventions are made.

An observation made by the author is that often when a parent writes down the oral intake before treatment has begun, it becomes apparent that the child eats a greater variety and even a greater amount than the parent first reported. The food diary is not only a baseline against which to measure progress so that both the therapist and the caregiver can gauge where to go but it is also a reminder of how far they have come. This is valuable feedback to a parent during what often are very difficult times spent confronting a seemingly hopeless task. Families in which a child has a history of poor feeding often have many problems, some of which are directly related to the eating problem or are even a direct result of it, and some of which are unrelated. The diary serves to focus the therapist's attention on the eating and associated behaviors rather than going too far afield into areas that have little bearing on the nutritional intake. To be successful, an assessment must be thorough enough to guarantee that all factors related to eating are evaluated, and yet must be focused enough so that interventions can be planned and successfully undertaken.

Knowledge of family routines is also important and questions related to them should be asked at the first meeting. Knowing what the daily routines are provides specific information about the impact of feeding attempts, activities that the child enjoys, and parenting styles including the amount of control parents have in other parts of their child's life and how reinforcing and supportive the parents are. For example, very often when there are feeding problems, attempts are made to feed the child throughout the day. This affects all aspects of family life and family interactions.

It is important to assess the aspects of life from which the caregivers derive satisfaction, pleasure, and feelings of competence, and how much of their daily life includes these experiences. Sources of social support are also important to assess. If caregivers are generally dissatisfied with their lives, they will have difficulty following specific recommendations centered around the child's eating.

Assessment of the family should specifically include the role that each member plays in the child's eating behavior: including when the child is fed, who does the feeding, and how the feeding is done. The ways and extent to which the eating behavior affects individual family members and the family as a whole should be assessed: How does it impact the daily life of the primary person feeding? Does it limit family activities? If one is parenting a child who has difficulty eating, regardless of the etiology of the problem, the caregiver-child interactions are likely to be affected. These interactions in turn affect other family members.

The perceived etiology of the eating problem is also likely to affect the caregiver and the family as a whole. For example, a caregiver who attributes poor nutritional intake to a medical condition beyond the child's control will act differently than one who attributes the eating problem to a personality trait of the child such as stubbornness. If the problem is seen as "not in the child's control," the parent is likely to feed into the child's problem by being reluctant to set limits. If the problem is attributed to the child's personality, the caregiver is likely to be angry and to respond accordingly. Neither leads to effective handling of the problem. Usually a caregiver vacillates between the two explanations and therefore, acts inconsistently toward the child. As mentioned earlier, if caregivers blame themselves for the problem, they will feel ineffective and not have the skills and confidence to handle what under even ordinary circumstances is a difficult situation. For these reasons, the caregivers' perceptions of the cause of the problem must be addressed. Based on the assessment, the therapist should have some working hypotheses as to etiology. These should be presented to the caregivers. Discussion of the child's control over the eating should be discouraged. Instead, the message should be given that this has been and will continue to be difficult for both the parents and child.

When the current nutritional status has been assessed, a treatment plan has to be devised to increase the child's eating. Observation of the caregiver and child interactions will provide information about the extent to which and the ways in which eating behavior has affected the interaction. From these observations, and from parental report, should come a record of problematic family interactions other than those centered around eating. For example, parental perception of lack of control over a child in one area may lead to a perception of lack of control in other areas. Children who refuse food may be seen as "powerful" and "willful." This perception may allow them to control the family in other ways as well. Often when a child is difficult, parents attribute power to the child beyond the specific behavior. For example, when one listens to the parental description of a child, very often it sounds as though a parent were describing a child older than the child in question. Reminding the parent of the child's age, putting the age on the refrigerator or referring to the child as a little "tyke" are some ways of bringing this reality home to the parent.

Although extreme difficulties in one area of parenting may affect parents' perception of a child and of the parent-child interaction, parental responses to a child's eating behavior is a sample of their parenting behavior in an area of difficulty. It is important to assess caregiver strengths as well. By looking at interactions in which the parents are more effective, the therapist can help change parental perceptions of ineffectiveness and encourage them to focus on strategies that they have used effectively: They need to realize that they do, in fact, have control over the FTT child, and they can change their behavior to be more effective.

If, once treatment has been started, a caregiver reports that he or she is unable to carry out any successful oral feeding, or if later on in treatment a caregiver feels that no further progress is being made, then direct observation of the feeding behavior by the therapist may be necessary. If the child is very young, the observation may take place in the therapist's office. For a child over the age of 3, a home visit is less obtrusive and therefore preferable. Such observations provide valuable information about the child's reactions; when and how food is presented; the length of time and amount eaten before food is refused; child behaviors associated with eating and with food refusal; the caregiver behaviors associated with food intake and food refusal; and child behaviors that precede caregiver termination of feeding. These sessions allow the therapist to coach the caregiver and even to model feeding behavior. In addition, in these sessions the therapist is able to observe subtleties in the caregiver-child interaction such as a negative look or tone or even comments that may have been previously unreported but that affect the feeding interaction.

Medical, speech, swallow, and neuropsychological assessments are needed to hypothesize an etiology and to determine whether there is a medical or oromotor solution (Woods, 1995). Regardless of etiology, if no medical or oromotor treatment sufficiently increases nutritional intake, then a behavioral assessment should be undertaken. Input from the other disciplines helps to set the parameters within which a treatment plan can be developed. The behavioral assessment includes a general assessment of family and individual members' functioning and specific assessment of eating and interactions around food. The food diary and observations of caregiver-child interactions and sometimes of feeding interactions are the primary means of assessment. Assessment is continuous throughout treatment.

TREATMENT

Focus of Sessions

The first meeting is with the primary caregivers and is used to get background information on caregiver perceptions of the problem, its etiology, maintaining factors, and its impact on the family. It is advisable to have meetings at least periodically with both caregivers and to establish this pattern from the beginning. If one caregiver is less involved, knowing that he or she is expected to participate in treatment, although attendance is less frequent than that of the primary caregiver helps to foster a commitment to the treatment as well as to encourage an understanding of what is involved. In this way, the less involved caregiver can be supportive of the primary caregiver. It may be important to have some sessions exclusively with the primary caregiver so that specific suggestions and comments can be made directly about his or her interactions with the FTT child without the added complications of the interactions between the caregivers and each's reaction to the other's interaction with the FTT child.

As mentioned earlier, the child must be evaluated. Whether the child is included in later sessions depends on the age of the child: The older the child, the more he or she should be involved in setting up the treatment plan in order to secure compliance. The older child (8 years and up) should be seen alone for part of the session and the primary caregiver should also be seen alone. By dealing directly with the older child, one is best able to gauge what he or she will actually do and to ascertain what rewards he or she will respond to. It should be remembered, however, that the work is primarily done through the caregiver. The rationale for this is readily apparent if one keeps in mind that a parent is able to put the child in a situation in which behavior can be elicited and then rewarded. This is far more effective than trying to convince a child to engage in behaviors that are negative or at least not pleasurable. These behaviors may have been previously learned and are now not performed, as in a child with a history of significantly better eating; in other instances, the requisite eating behaviors were not learned, as in a child with a history of poor or nonoral feeding. Additionally, since feeding behaviors occur in front of the parent and thus evoke a response from the caregiver, it is important to teach him or her an effective response that is likely to increase the probability of the appropriate behavior recurring.

As mentioned earlier, in the initial meeting with the child, the therapist must establish a good rapport. Parenting sessions should not include a child who is old enough to understand the recommendations being made. It is preferable for the child to see contingencies as coming from the parent. Increased effectiveness in parenting should be attributed to the parent and not to the therapist. The parent should appear to be in control of the situation and to be the one making and carrying out contingencies because the child would be less likely to comply if he or she sees the parent as ineffectual and the therapist as the one setting up the rules. Additionally, the therapist should not be seen as the "bad guy." This would decrease the likelihood of the child coming to future sessions. The therapist should be seen as the "good guy" who gets the child something he or she wants, that is, rewards. Conditions other than age that determine whether the child should attend treatment sessions include the need to observe subtleties in communication that lead to better understanding of the caregiver-child interaction, the need to observe the feeding or associated behaviors, and/or the need to model feeding or social interactions.

Rewards must be appropriate to a child's level of functioning as well as his or her interests. Higher functioning children and those with greater verbal abilities may learn faster and generalize what they have learned across situations more quickly. In this author's experience, parents of children with developmental disabilities tend to attribute the reasons for noncompliance to the child's disability. The implication is that if the child only understood, he or she would comply. This leads to inconsistent parenting with the caregiver sometimes seeing the child as able "to control" him- or herself and therefore as manipulative and other times as "unable to control" him- or herself. The therapist has to help the caregiver delineate the role that the disability plays in the eating problem. The focus should be on the child's behavior and not on perception of control or lack of control. Some general interventions do not directly involve eating behavior but are important for the treatment of FTT.

As mentioned earlier, the caregiver must be given an explanation for the child's poor nutritional intake. This is empirically derived after the intake on the feeding history and onset of the eating difficulties. The etiologies discussed earlier (Lachenmeyer, 1995) would be a good place to begin. Again, it is crucial to the treatment to avoid blaming the caregivers and to strongly and actively negate any notions of blame on their part. It should be emphasized that the caregivers can have a positive impact on the child's problem. Expectations as to how long it will be before there is significant improvement should be addressed. The caregivers should be told that to be successful, they will have to undertake hard work on a daily basis. What can be expected is slow but steady progress. There may be occasional setbacks, for example, if a child becomes ill with the flu or a cold. Children with a history of poor feeding appear to almost stop eating if they experience any physical discomfort. However, since the behavior has been learned and the positive consequences experienced, the child will regain the previous level of eating more quickly.

To make some progress immediately and to build on initial successes, sessions occur twice per week with check-in phone calls at least one other time in the week. When it is not possible to meet twice per week, phone calls between sessions can take the place of actual sessions. In this way, if the caregivers have had some success, they will benefit from positive feedback. If, on the other hand, they are stuck, it is better to make changes in the plan on the phone rather than continuing in the same way until the next session.

As one might expect, attempting to feed a child who refuses significant quantities of food is very difficult on a meal-to-meal basis. It is very important that the primary caregiver have some social support and, when possible, someone with whom to share the feeding responsibilities. She or he should also be able to engage in work or social activities that are rewarding and that do not directly include the FTT child. This will make the caregiver see him- or herself differently. Someone whose whole sense of self is based on whether or how much a child eats will be unhappy and feel ineffectual, and therefore, will have a difficult time carrying out specific recommendations.

A matter-of-fact attitude toward the child will make the caregiver more effective. If the caregiver is reminded that the child's medical and nutritional needs are being met, he or she can then be calmer and thereby avoid power struggles more easily. Expressing feelings of anger and frustration to the child are not effective means of changing a child's behavior. Strong, negative emotions may cloud a caregiver's judgment as to what is working and what further changes should be made. A parent who perceives that he or she has overreacted is likely to feel ineffectual. Emotional scenes do not benefit the child. These lead to negative effect on both parts making similar future interactions aversive. These interactions are then avoided or one of the other parties escalates to end the interaction. The caregiver can discuss his or her thoughts and feelings with the therapist who should convey an attitude of support and understanding. If a caregiver feels as though he or she has no control over the child, she or he will attribute the FTT child's eating difficulties to internal attributes. Such attributions will in turn decrease the caregiver's perception of control over the child's behavior. In fact, parents usually have more control than they think or report that they do. Looking at other areas of parent-child interaction or what parents would do if they *had to* (e.g., if some action were medically necessary) makes it clear to parents that, in fact, they have more control over the child's behavior than they thought. Caregivers can increase their control through the use of age-appropriate contingencies that will be discussed in more detail later. Sometimes changes in tone and manner can accomplish the same end.

FEEDING INTERVENTIONS

Initial goals must be clearly set with a focus on medical priorities such as weight gain. Specific interventions depend on the goals set. If weight gain is the goal, the intervention will focus on high caloric intake rather than ingesting foods of different textures or greater variety or even self-feeding. If weight maintenance is the goal, again varying the types of foods or focusing on independent eating behaviors may have to be postponed. If increase in quantity or even variety of foods eaten is the goal, then an attempt should be made to introduce foods that have the highest probability of being eaten. For a child with a history of good eating, one should reintroduce foods that had been favorites in the past. Otherwise, foods of similar taste and/or texture to the ones that the child currently eats should be presented. Before focusing on the variety of food ingested, current caloric intake would have to be adequate. Once this has been established, highly pleasurable foods might follow eating a small amount of new or less pleasurable foods.

One intervention made early in treatment is to indicate to the caregiver that all discussion of feeding and feeding behavior in front of the child should cease. Extended family should be reassured that professional help has been sought and advised that discussion of this issue, especially in front of the child, is not helpful. Another early intervention is to divide the feeding during the day into frequent small meals (5 or 6) at set times and of limited duration (30–40 minutes). Limiting meals clearly differentiates eating times from times during which there is involvement in other activities so that the entire day does not appear to be one big, aversive meal. In this way parents can put aside whatever resentments or frustrations they have about the child's eating behavior and have some pleasurable times with the child. Feeding should occur in areas with limited distraction. This is quite a change for parents who are used to dancing, jumping, and engaging in whatever distraction has been seen as necessary to get the child to eat without realizing that he or she is actually eating. In addition, feeding times in which the focus is on caloric intake should be differentiated from social eating, during which a child sits with family and/or peers during their meals. The child is then allowed to play with food or just be around people cooking and/or eating without any pressure for them to eat. The FTT child should be in the kitchen when an adult is cooking. This exposes the child to much of what makes eating pleasurable: the social context as well as smells and tastes associated with cooking. To assess the problematic behavior and to monitor progress, parents should be taught how to observe and record behavior.

Basic parenting techniques are taught to the caregivers who then apply these to parenting the FTT child as well as to food-specific issues. To decrease negative behavior, parents are taught time-out, extinction, response cost and reinforcement of incompatible behaviors. The appropriate conditions for the use of these techniques and how they should be carried out is discussed with the parents. Use of rewards including how to set up a reward system is also presented in terms of general principles and then applied to the problem at hand: eating behavior. Priority is placed on rewards with negative consequences to be used later. An attempt is also made to minimize disruptive and noncompliant behavior. Rewards should be used noncontingently (e.g., a parent just feels affectionate toward his or her child) or contingently (i.e., in response to positive behavior). Timing is very important: Rewards should not follow negative behavior. Rewards include praise, affectionate touching, and other forms of social approval, food rewards (although with FTT children these are unlikely to be rewarding at the beginning of treatment), tangible rewards, privileges, and tokens for delayed rewards.

Contingent rewards should be of two types and be given at two different times: small, immediate rewards and larger, cumulative rewards based on a certain number of trials rather than a number of days or times in a row. The child should have input into what the rewards are, and the older child should have greater input into the actual contingencies. Most importantly, both immediate and long-term rewards must be achievable. With reference to nutritional intake, eating behavior should be reinforced and noneating should be ignored. This is usually the opposite of what parents have been doing. As mentioned earlier, rewards must be achievable to work. The caregiver must accept the child's current level of eating. Rewarding the level of eating occurring at the onset of treatment is the starting point. Caregivers should understand that the child should be rewarded for what she or he has eaten, not punished for what was uneaten.

The criteria for rewards can be gradually changed usually by increasing the quantity or type of food. The eating behaviors that are to be rewarded as well as the rewards used are empirically determined for each child. The eating behaviors are established based on an evaluation of the food diary and are specific. For example, a child who stores food in his or her cheeks will be rewarded for swallowing. The rewards are age-appropriate with consideration given to the child's developmental level and interests. The criteria for rewards as well as the effectiveness of the particular rewards are continuously reevaluated. Generally, a child is rewarded for eating greater amounts and different foods.

At least one reward should be achievable at each sitting with the criteria based on the child's current level of eating. For a child with a mental or chronological age of 3 years or more, daily rewards as well as rewards for several days of eating should also be available. The point at which one food can be used as a reward for other eating behavior is a clear measure of success in treating FTT children.

It is helpful for the parent to make it look as though the rewards are the therapist's idea. The child should be told to tell the therapist if his or her caregiver is inconsistent or not quick enough in giving the rewards. In this way the child feels that the therapist is getting something for him or her. Usually the caregiver will see what the therapist is doing and support him or her in this endeavor.

After some eating has been established through the use of rewards, negative contingencies may also be used, for example, time-out following disruptive behavior (Handen, Mandell, & Russo, 1986). The child who is exhibiting refusal behavior or who cannot be contained may be removed from attention and stimulation for one minute for each year of his or her age. The clock starts *after* he or she has quieted down. Feeding should not be resumed until the next designated feeding time. It is important not to let these negative behaviors escalate to become highly charged negative interactions between caregiver and child. The adult should try to remain cool and matter-of-fact so that he or she can figure out and carry out the best plan of action. Focusing on the child's defiant behavior makes a parent angry and increases the likelihood that he or she will escalate the conflict.

It is always preferable to gain some measure of success through rewards first. A child of 3 or more years may be allowed to leave the situation after a certain amount of food has been ingested. The amount should be comparable to that eaten in the recent past. Gagging behavior may be followed by a strong reprimand. Vomiting behavior should be followed by the reintroduction of the same food, and if this is not possible because of the child's strong refusal, the child can be timed-out. Again, negative contingencies should be implemented matter-of-factly with little negative affect.

Caregivers often express concern, first, about the use of rewards or as they often call them "bribes." It should be pointed out that everyone responds to rewards. As the parents know, it is important that the child eat and grow. However, a child cannot anticipate the future consequences that he or she will experience due to poor nutritional intake. Therefore, one establishes contingencies that are meaningful to the child and that will increase the rate of the desired behavior. Caregivers are also concerned about how behavior changes will be maintained and generalized once the rewards are withdrawn. Although the behavioral research literature (Forehand & Atkeson, 1977) indicates reasons for concern, studies cited usually compare behavior initially learned in tightly controlled settings to behavior when the individual is no longer in these settings.

The feeding behavior established in a hospital or therapy setting must be generalized to the home which has less structure and probably less consistent contingencies. Inpatient feeding programs need to spend time planning maintenance of gains as well as continued increases in eating behavior once the child has gone home. This involves making sure that the primary caregiver has the necessary skills to carry out a program as well as the necessary successful experience so that he or she has the confidence to follow through. Referral to a behavioral psychologist with experience in feeding and parenting must be made.

On an outpatient basis, the issues are somewhat different. From the beginning, the primary caregiver is actively involved in setting up the program. The primary caregiver carries out the program and is instrumental in evaluating and changing the program based on the results achieved. The author indicates to parents that the priority is getting the child to eat and setting up a successful program. Results are constantly monitored and changes made. The child establishes a pattern of eating that should become reinforcing in and of itself. The child also feels good about his or her accomplishments. The caregivers feel good about themselves as parents and about the child. The relationships and interactions all become more positive. This in turn changes future interactions. Changes resulting from these interventions in fact are long-lasting and go beyond the eating behavior.

ISSUES IN TUBE FEEDING

Children who are tube fed, as a group, have a history of medical and/or feeding problems that are severe enough to warrant nonoral feeding. If such feedings are to be considered for medical reasons, they should be presented both to the caregiver and to the child as a realistic possibility rather than as a threat. When possible, nonoral feeding should be used to supplement oral feeding: it should be made contingent on the amount of oral feeding; the amount of nonoral feeding should be decreased as oral intake increases. These children have been fed based on the time of day and the amount of caloric intake that is deemed necessary for their well-being rather than on reports of hunger. They also do not have the sensory experiences associated with oral intake under conditions of hunger. Children who have experienced nonoral feeding usually are unaware of feelings of hunger and satiety. Additionally, because of medical procedures and/or unsuccessful attempts to feed, food and the stimuli surrounding food (such as smell), as well as the social interactions associated with food, are not pleasurable and are often aversive. Because of the complex or severe medical problems that led to the nonoral feeding, these children usually experience more enduring eating problems. The tube feedings, in turn, affect all family activities and interactions. Attempting to wean the child from tube feeding presents a further host of difficulties. When attempts are made to introduce or reintroduce oral feedings, even the most competent caregivers have great difficulty with the child's slow progress and occasional setbacks due to routine childhood illnesses.

The priority in tube weaning is to maintain a level of caloric intake so that growth continues despite an initial decrease in nutritional intake. Children are usually tube fed either during the night through a continuous drip, during the day, or both. Continuous feed through the night has the advantage of being less obtrusive and therefore also less intrusive in the life of the family with subsequently fewer power struggles over oral or nonoral eating. The child is fed on a schedule that has nothing to do with hunger cues. Because the feedings are done all at one time, the child is unlikely to be hungry during the day when he or she should eat normally. To increase the oral intake during the day is difficult. Day tube feedings, on the other hand, more closely approximate a normal eating schedule. Since these feedings are given at different times throughout the day, the likelihood that the child will engage in some oral feeding is greater. The day tube feedings can be given immediately following oral feedings and therefore be made contingent on the amount taken in by mouth. These feedings can be decreased contingent on the amount of oral intake. The child can be made aware of this contingency and benefit from its implementation through an increase in something pleasurable such as playtime. Also, during the day there are rewards available to which the child could respond.

Due to the difficult and frustrating time that the caregivers of these children have had, the author has found that often in a moment of intense frustration parents are likely to suggest that the tube feeding be stopped immediately and completely, assuming that the child will now "have" to eat. For a child who has had a long-standing feeding problem, abrupt termination of tube feeding usually does not lead to normal eating but rather results in rapid weight loss—greater weight loss than is healthy for the child and more than the parents are willing to tolerate. Once an effective behavioral plan has been in place and the amount of oral intake has plateaued, then assuming that it is appropriate given medical considerations, caloric intake by tube should be gradually decreased. This reduction should lead to increased hunger and correspondingly increased oral intake. Generally, a reduction of 25% of total calories at a time is recommended although the specifics of the child's weight and eating pattern must be taken into account. Before this is undertaken, the oral feeding should be well enough established so that one could expect an increase in oral feeding following reduction in tube feeding.

CASE ILLUSTRATIONS

Six brief case summaries of children with FTT, each with a different etiology and each successfully treated, will be presented.

CHILD CHARACTERISTICS/PARENT CHARACTERISTICS

Anna, 14 months old, was generally a poor eater. In her brief life, she had had a history of three viral infections. Unlike most children, when Anna had stopped vomiting, she did not resume eating. Both parents were doctors in their residency training. In discussions with the parents and through home observations, several things became clear. The mother valued her own thinness very much. Possibly for this reason, she did not pick up quickly that her daughter was not eating sufficiently. Because of the mother's own issues with food and both parents' difficulty in setting limits, they did not intervene when or as firmly as they should have. Parent training was undertaken with a focus on feeding when the child resisted and getting the mother to separate her own thoughts about thinness and to focus on her daughter's health.

CONDITIONED DYSPHAGIA/OLDER CHILD

Jessie was a 14-year-old on Total Parenteral Nutrition (TPN) feeding for one year following surgery for cancer of the jaw. Following an infection from the TPN tube, there was pressure from the medical team to get her off the tube. Jessie and her parents reported that she was initially fearful that food would get stuck in the roof of her mouth. She was also afraid of vomiting. Because of her surgery, she had no sense of smell and no saliva. She had been put on a high protein formula so that she would not feel full after a tube feeding and therefore she would be more likely to eat. However, she still reported feelings of fullness. Treatment was started when Jessie was still in the hospital. Because of her age, treatment consisted of separate meetings with her and with her parents. Since she was still coming to the hospital for chemotherapy and because her associations with the hospital were negative, frequent sessions were difficult to schedule. Treatment consisted of negotiating with Jessie what she would eat at home and at school: High caloric snacks and meals were planned. The parents were instructed to be matter-of-fact with her. Tube feedings were gradually decreased allowing her more freedom in her daily activities. Treatment was successfully concluded with Jessie entirely off the tube. Treatment focused on the feeding and also addressed some broader issues related to school, family, and illness.

MEDICAL PROBLEMS INDIRECTLY ASSOCIATED WITH POOR EATING

Kelly, 2 years old, had a history of kidney problems and hypertension. Neither of these was thought to be directly related to the poor nutritional intake. Her mother was a highly anxious woman whose whole life re-volved around her daughter. Kelly had never been with a babysitter. Kelly's mother was always home with her. The physician involved was strongly suggesting the use of tube feeding as the primary form of nutri-tional intake. The plan was to decrease the tube feeding only as oral in-take increased. This plan frightened the mother. It was also not a plan that was likely to increase oral intake. Feeding took most of the day. Kelly would also store food in her mouth. During playtime, if the mother saw the squirreled food, she would become extremely upset. The most effec-tive interventions were able to be carried out when Kelly went to pre-school. Since she was out of the house part of the day, the mother did not have complete responsibility for all oral intake. The author worked with the school. Kelly had lunch with three other girls and swallowing became a game for all of them. The mother was able to gain enough control so that she would tell Kelly that they would not leave the school premises until she drank her milk, and Kelly would drink the milk. The mother was able to set and follow through on contingencies. Kelly grew sufficiently and tube feeding was avoided.

GASTROSOMY TUBE

Jonathan, 2½ years old, had been on a gastrosomy tube from birth until he was at an age where reconstructive surgery was possible. Jonathan did not report any feelings of hunger or satiety, that is, he never asked for food. Although Jonathan's mother was not an effective parent, a program of sham feeding (Dowling, 1975) that included the mother was under-taken. At times when children are usually hungry and just prior to tube feeding, food would be put into Jonathan's mouth. Since he had a hole in his esophagus, the food would come out. The rationale for this procedure was to get Jonathan to experience the pleasurable sensations associated with food going into one's mouth and down one's throat at times of hunger and to simultaneously reward him for engaging in this behavior, every time he swallowed, his mother would hit a pop-up toy. This was done three times daily for 4 weeks prior to the surgery. Realistic expecta-tions for oral intake following surgery were set. Immediately after the surgery, Jonathan started eating and normal eating followed quickly; no other intervention was necessary.

MULTIPLY-HANDICAPPED CHILD

Sarah, 5, was a child with severe cognitive impairments as well as physical conditions that had no clear organic cause (e.g., she would develop fat pockets around her ankles). Sarah's mother was the primary caregiver and was overwhelmed. Attempts were made to give Sarah's mother some time that was her own and to increase her social supports. Then, a plan was formulated for the child's educational needs. After some changes were accomplished in theses areas, the eating issues were addressed through parenting training. Expectations of the child's progress both with food and developmental issues were realistically set. The mother was referred for supportive work in a group with parents of similarly challenged children. An effort was made to improve the mother's quality of life so that she could then attend to the specific behavioral changes that were needed for her daughter to thrive. The eating was separated from the developmental issues for which long-term support was needed. With this multifaceted approach, the mother was able to benefit from the parent training and obtain sufficient change in Sarah's eating behavior.

FAILURE TO THRIVE SECONDARY TO A PSYCHIATRIC DISORDER

Cynthia, 12, was referred because she refused to eat following an episode of choking. Treatment consisted of having her eat something in session, and setting up a reward system for generalizing gains made in session to the home. Peculiarities relative to food (e.g., wiping the flour dust off a chocolate cookie), particularly slow generalization of eating behavior from the office to the home (e.g., 8 successful trials of eating a particular food in the office before engaging in the same behavior outside the office), and hoarding behavior suggested the possibility of obsessive-compulsive disorder. A thorough evaluation with OCD as an operating hypothesis was undertaken. The treatment of the eating problem was affected in that it was now viewed as part of a broader class of behaviors. The goal of increased caloric intake was still the priority, but the focus and approach were somewhat different.

CONCLUSION

Failure to thrive is defined as poor nutritional intake that affects growth. These children do not, however, form a homogeneous group. There are several possible etiologies. Hypotheses about etiology affect assessment and inform treatment. A thorough assessment of the FTT child and family is important. When there is no complete medical resolution to the feeding problem, then psychological treatment of the eating problem and related issues must be undertaken. With children, this always involves parent training, and with young children, the work is done primarily with the parents. FTT is a biobehavioral problem with a primarily behavioral or environmental intervention.

REFERENCES

Bithoney, W. B., & Rathbun, J. M. (1983). Failure to thrive. In W. B. Levine, A. C. Carey, A. Crocker, & R. J. Gross (Eds.), *Developmental behavioral pediatrics* (pp. 557–571). Philadelphia: Saunders.

Dowling, S. (1975). Seven infants with esophageal atresia: A developmental study. *Psychoanalyic Study of the Child, 27*, 215–256.

Forehand, R., & Atkeson, B. M. (1977). Generality of treatment effects with parents as therapists: A review of assessment and implementation procedures. *Behavior Therapy, 8*, 575–593.

Gordan, A. H., & Jameson, J. C. (1979). Infant-mother attachment in patients with nonorganic failure to thrive syndrome. *Journal of the American Academy of Child Psychiatry, 18*(2), 251–259.

Handen, B. L., Mandell, F., & Russo, D. C. (1986). Feeding induction in failure to thrive children. *American Journal of Disease of Children, 140*, 52–59.

Hoffman, M. A., & Ross, A. J. (1995). Surgical management of gastroesophageal reflux in children. In S. R. Rosenthal, J. J. Sheppard, & M. Lotze (Eds.), *Dysphagia and the child with developmental disabilities*. San Diego: Singular.

Kotelchuck, C. M. (1980). Nonorganic failure to thrive: The status of interactional and environmental etiologic theories. In B. Camp (Ed.), *Advances in behavioral pediatrics* (pp. 24–51). Greenwich, CT: JAI Press.

Lachenmeyer, J. R. (1987). Failure to thrive: A critical review. In B. Lahey & A. Kazdin (Eds.), *Advances in clinical child psychology* (Vol. 10, pp. 335–357). New York: Plenum Press.

Lachenmeyer, J. R. (1994). Parent training. In M. S. Gibbs, J. R. Lachenmeyer, & J. S. Sigal (Eds.), *Community mental health*. New York: Gardner Press.

Lachenmeyer, J. R. (1995). Behavioral aspects of feeding disorders. In S. R. Rosenthal, J. J. Sheppard, & M. Lotze (Eds.), *Dysphagia and the child with developmental disabilities*. San Diego: Singular.

Lachenmeyer, J. R. (1997). *Eating disorders secondary to obsessive-compulsive disorder*. Paper presented at the meeting of the American Anxiety Association, New Orleans.

Roberts, M. C., & Maddux, J. E. (1982). A psychosocial conceptualization of nonorganic failure to thrive. *Journal of Clinical Child Psychology, 11*(3), 216–223.

Sameroff, A., & Chandler, M. (1975). Reproductive risks and the continuum of caretaker casualty. In F. D. Horowitz (Ed.), *Review of childhood developmental research* (pp. 187–197). Chicago: University of Chicago Press.

Woods, E. (1995). The influence of posture and positioning on oral motor development and dysphagia. In S. S. Rosenthal, J. J. Shepherd, & M. Lotze (Eds.), *Dysphagia and the child with developmental disabilities*. San Diego: Singular.

CHAPTER 9

Parent Training for Families of Children with Developmental Disabilities

JOHN R. LUTZKER and STEPHANIE E. STEED

IN THIS chapter, parent training approaches are reviewed from a behavioral perspective with a particular emphasis on planned activities training and behavioral momentum/errorless compliance training. The theories supporting these approaches are based on basic learning theory, especially operant conditioning. Early parent training focused primarily on the simplest principles of reinforcement and to some extent punishment (time-out and spanking). Planned Activities Training (PAT) involves more of an emphasis on antecedent prevention of challenging behavior. Thus, the focus of PAT is at least loosely based on the principles of stimulus control. Which is also true of behavioral momentum/errorless compliance training.

Although these approaches rely on some of the principles of operant conditioning, they in no way discount the role of biology in the etiology of mental retardation and specific behaviors, such as self-injury or in the eating habits of individuals with Prader-Willi Syndrome. Etiology aside, there has been a plethora of demonstrations since the 1960s as to the efficacy of these learning-based approaches in the treatment of individuals with developmental disabilities and their families. Families are best served when they receive a variety of services that affect the social ecology of the entire family (Lutzker & Campbell, 1994).

Mental retardation is a complex and common disorder. While there are no exact rates of incidence, it is estimated that in the United States there are over seven million individuals with mental retardation (Batshaw, 1991). However, there has been a revolution in the understanding of mental retardation and related disorders, such as autism, and has led to the development of many commonly practiced intervention strategies (Matson & Mulick, 1986) designed to facilitate skill development and decrease challenging behavior.

Many children with mental retardation, have difficulty in acquiring basic communication and social skills as well as normal self-help and daily living skills (Singer, Irvine, & Irvin, 1989; Webster-Stratton & Herbert, 1993). These skill deficits place many of these children at risk for developing severe challenging behaviors, including aggressive and self-injurious behavior.

These difficulties often have profound effects on the family (Lubetsky, Mueller, Madden, Walker, & Len, 1995). Families of children with developmental disabilities experience significant levels of stress in coping with their children's special needs (Baker, Smithen, & Kashimal, 1991; Bromley & Blacher, 1992; Van Hasselt, Sisson, & Aachi, 1989). The stress associated with having a child with a disability increases the likelihood of family dysfunction and crisis experiences (Kysela, McDonald, Reddon, & Gobeil-Dwyer, 1988). Parent training has been a primary strategy used to reduce stress and to facilitate behavior management skills with these families.

PARENT TRAINING STRATEGIES

The majority of the parent training strategies are based on the principles of behavior modification. The field of behavior modification emerged in the late 1960s (Turnbull & Turnbull, 1991) and soon showed that individuals with developmental disabilities could be responsive to treatments based primarily on the principles of operant conditioning (Lutzker & Campbell, 1994) and contingency management procedures (Minor, Minor, & Williams, 1983). Treatment usually consisted of teaching parents to use simple procedures such as social and primary reinforcement, extinction, time-out, shaping, and overcorrection (Lutzker & Campbell, 1994).

In addition to behavior modification, the principles of applied behavior analysis and social learning theory have also been techniques applied by researchers and practitioners (Singer et al., 1989; Tymchuk, 1986). Behavior analysis developed as a systematic attempt to investigate variables that influence behavior and to demonstrate functional relationships between treatment and outcome. Thus, behavior analysis helps to understand, prevent, and remedy behavior problems, and to promote learning (Sulzer-Azaroff & Mayer, 1991).

More recently, however, the ecobehavioral approach has been used to assist parents in managing their children's challenging behavior and for increasing functional skills. This approach involves assessing a families' social ecology (Lutzker & Campbell, 1994)—examining any possible influences on the family. It utilizes multifaceted intervention strategies.

Although behavioral techniques tend to dominate the field of parent training for children with developmental disabilities, there are several other models (Tymchuk, 1986). These include the dynamic model, family therapy, and early intervention/education approaches. The dynamic model primarily focuses on the parents and their internal conflicts with the child's disability. Although intervention within this model is designed to resolve the parents feelings and attitudes, parents are not provided with assistance in obtaining the resources or information needed to raise their children. Children with disabilities often display challenging behavior and require special assistance (speech, physical, and/or occupational therapy). This method of intervention does not lend itself to teaching parents new skills or providing them with the necessary resources often needed for day-to-day living.

During family therapy, the family members meet in a group to discuss feelings with one another and learn new and effective communication strategies and interaction styles. Although teaching parents techniques to communicate more effectively is a critical factor in parenting, this approach does not teach parents how to teach their children daily living skills, toileting, self-feeding, and dressing nor how to eliminate challenging behaviors, such as tantrums, self-injurious behavior, and aggression.

Finally, early intervention/educational approaches are developed to assist families with children who have developmental delays and physical handicaps and need support from within their community. Parenting groups increase parents' knowledge about child development, provide resources, and teach parenting techniques. This approach values the need to assist parents in finding resources and teaching skills. This method of parent skill building is usually conducted in a group setting which enables parents to receive support from other parents. Parents are able to discuss problems occurring in the home and are provided with training in general parenting techniques. Although this approach appears to provide parents with support and access to resources, the training provided and skills taught do not always generalize to the home setting because of the limited emphasis on role playing, practice, and feedback on specific skills. These elements are critical when programming for generalization across settings and behaviors.

Behavioral strategies have dominated the parent training field, placing emphasis on the role of parents as teachers and mediators of behavior change. It has been suggested that this approach has helped decrease the overall need for professional involvement and has increased the control parents exhibit over their lives and those of their children (Slentz, Walker, & Bricker, 1989). By receiving training in effective child management strategies and teaching skills, parents can then prepare their children for social and educational settings in the community (Baker, 1989). Parent training helps to ensure that children will be able to continue to live in their homes in the least restrictive environments (Bromley & Blacher, 1992; Kysela, McDonald, Reddon, & Gobeil-Dwyer, 1988).

Parent training involves teaching parents to utilize several behavioral techniques, such as identifying antecedents and consequence to challenging behaviors (Dunlap, Robbins, & Darrow, 1994; Singer et al., 1989), appropriate use of prompts and reinforcement (Lowry & Whitman, 1989; Lutzker & Campbell, 1994), and the use of shaping, fading, extinction, and time-out procedures (Hudson, 1988; Roberts & Powers, 1990). In addition, these behavioral techniques have been used to address issues such as noncompliance (Baum & Forehand, 1981; Ducharme, Pontes et al., 1994; Forehand & Wierson, 1993; Van Hasselt et al., 1989), oppositional behavior (Ducharme, Lucas, & Pontes, 1994; Robbins & Dunlap, 1992; Sallis, 1983), infant stimulation (Kravetz, Katz, & Katz, 1990; Lowry & Whitman, 1989; Minor et al., 1983), skill development (Singer et al., 1989; Plienis, Robbins, & Dunlap, 1988), and communication and language delays (Carr & Durand, 1985; Feldman et al., 1986). Further, the methods used to train parents have included lectures, modeling, role-playing, and the use of video techniques (Lutzker & Campbell, 1994) occurring in clinics, individual homes, parenting groups, or a combination of services (Baker, 1989).

PARENT TRAINING, PAT, AND ERRORLESS LEARNING

The focus here will be based on the ecobehavioral model which combines aspects of ecological psychology and behavioral psychology (applied behavior analysis and therapy). Families are viewed as social ecosystems, thus multifaceted behavioral assessments are conducted in situ and across as many individuals and situations as possible within a family's social ecology. Behavioral methodology is used in the behavioral assessment, direct observation, assessment, and treatment procedures. Humanistic counseling procedures are used by staff who deliver ecobehavioral services. Further, there is active programming for generalization of treatment effects across time, settings, and behaviors of parents and their children (Lutzker, 1994; Lutzker & Campbell, 1994). Major components of the ecobehavioral model are based on Planned Activities Training (PAT) and errorless compliance procedures (Ducharme & Popynick, 1993).

PAT is designed to teach parents that engaging children in planned and structured activities helps prevent challenging behaviors. PAT consists of several components: time management, choosing activities, activity and rule explanation, incidental teaching, feedback, and reinforcement. Errorless compliance training involves teaching parents to begin with instructions for which instruction-following (compliance) is highly probable, with gradual introduction of instructions for which compliance is least probable.

Prior to the use of PAT, contingent management training (CMT) had been the primary strategy taught to parents. CMT was used with children who demonstrated deficits in instruction-following (noncompliance) (Graziano & Diament, 1992) and focused on teaching parents to use clear commands and apply consistent consequences (Lutzker, Huynen, & Bigelow, in press).

PAT is a collection of strategies that teach parents to predict, plan, and have a positive effect on their children's behaviors. CMT, on the other hand, relies on the use of consequences and focuses less on antecedents. It originated in Australia where it was used primarily with conduct disorder children without disabilities. The parents of these hard-to-manage children were taught self-management skills to decrease their children's disruptive behavior (Sanders & Dadds, 1982) while increasing the children's engagement in productive activities.

A rationale for PAT is that it is more difficult in some settings than in others for parents to apply contingencies. It is difficult to use extinction and time out while shopping in the community. Contingencies are not always useful alternatives, they may be ineffective in some settings. For example, it is not always possible to use time out while shopping or traveling in a car (Sanders & Christensen, 1985). Thus, parents need techniques that will prove useful across a variety of settings.

An alternative to CMT is the use of antecedents that set the occasion for desired behavior and may eliminate the need for strict contingencies altogether. PAT helps parents to identify "high-risk" settings and prepare the child for home and community settings by focusing on antecedent strategies.

The effects of CMT and PAT were examined with five families who had been referred for noncompliance (Sanders & Dadds, 1982). Each family was exposed to CMT and PAT, respectively. CMT consisted of contingent reinforcement, the use of clear instructions, describing calmly what the child did wrong, describing and prompting appropriate behavior, and using time-out, when needed. PAT focused on teaching the parent to plan ahead, select and arrange activities for the setting, a brief discussion of rules, and often simulated rehearsal of the desired behavior. Consequences for appropriate and disruptive behavior were also applied when needed. CMT decreased levels of challenging behavior for only one child in the training setting and was virtually ineffective for the other children. Once PAT was introduced, however, there were reductions in the challenging behavior for three of the other children. Although sequencing effects were not examined, the data suggested that PAT reduced challenging behavior in three of the five children by enhancing CMT.

PAT combined with CMT has been effective in reducing oppositional behavior, increasing positive parent behavior, and reducing the need for contingency management in families who have children without disabilities (Sanders & Christensen, 1985). Although, noncompliant or oppositional behavior is common among children without disabilities, parents of children with developmental disabilities also report similar difficulties. Therefore, Sanders and Plant (1989) explored the use of CMT and PAT with preschool children who had developmental disabilities and who displayed noncompliance when presented with nonpreferred tasks. The two procedures were compared in the training setting and in high- and low-risk situations in the home. Three of the four children in these families showed reductions in noncompliant behavior and the parents showed increases in the use of the treatment procedures across settings. This suggested that a combination of CMT and PAT was useful in children with developmental disabilities who display challenging behaviors.

Harrold, Lutzker, Campbell, and Touchette (1992) examined the effects of sequence of PAT and CMT with families of children with developmental disabilities to determine if PAT prior to CMT would produce an outcome similar to that of CMT followed by PAT. The rationale was that if PAT produced a favorable outcome, it might suggest further exploration of its use independent of CMT. Implementing PAT prior to CMT had dramatic effects on the children's as well as the parents' behavior; therefore, it was suggested that PAT might be sufficient to bring about positive changes in the behaviors of mothers and children without the need for CMT.

The effects of PAT alone with four mothers of children with developmental disabilities was examined by Huynen, Lutzker, Bigelow, Touchette, and Campbell (1996). During training, PAT was used independently of CMT to examine its impact on the mothers' and children's behavior. Not only did PAT increase the children's appropriate behavior, but generalization occurred across three settings. This suggests that PAT is an alternative technique to the traditional use of CMT for children with developmental disabilities.

Similarly, Powers, Singer, Stevens, and Sowers (1992) examined the generalization of PAT skills across home and community settings. Three families having children with developmental disabilities were assessed in their homes and in several community settings (grocery store, mall, and church). The mothers were taught PAT in their homes and were provided with written prompts to use in the generalization settings. Two of the mothers were able to generalize the use of the techniques to novel settings, while the third mother required brief in situ training in each generalization setting. This suggests that the use of PAT generalizes across settings. Training may need to be individualized to meet the learning requirements of different parents.

In general, PAT is a useful strategy in reducing challenging behaviors promoting skill development, and facilitating generalization across settings and behaviors. Errorless compliance training is another technique that has been used to eliminate challenging behaviors, specifically noncompliance. This is especially relevant because there is evidence to suggest that compliance may be what some term a "pivotal" behavior, that once eliminated may increase the opportunity for behavioral gains in other areas (Ducharme & Popynick, 1993).

Similar to PAT, errorless compliance learning focuses on the use of antecedents to eliminate challenging behaviors and build skills. Errorless learning is a stimulus fading technique which is used to teach difficult discriminations (Ducharme, 1996). It involves creating a teaching condition in which the task to be learned is very simple. Gradually, more difficult conditions are introduced until the child complies to commands with the same high rate of correct responses as to the simple commands. This approach helps to ensure that learning is accomplished with fewer errors and undesirable responses (Ducharme & Popynick, 1993).

With errorless compliance training, the teaching strategy is designed to ensure that noncompliance rarely occurs during training. It involves a direct observational assessment to evaluate the child's compliance to a variety of instructions that are ultimately ranked according to the probability of compliance. Training begins with the parental requests for which the child will most likely comply, with reinforcement being provided after each "cooperative response." Next, requests for which compliance is less likely are gradually introduced to ensure high levels of cooperation by the child. Following training, the child responds to most requests with virtually no error (Ducharme, 1996).

Errorless learning has been used to decrease challenging behavior, set the occasion to direction following and learning, and facilitate generalization in children with developmental disabilities. Ducharme et al. (1994) used errorless learning to eliminate challenging behavior associated with specific interactive and learning tasks in a child with autism. Similarly, Ducharme and Popynick (1993) increased instruction following in four children with developmental disabilities without the use of punishment. In addition, these children generalized to untrained requests and reductions in challenging behaviors.

Errorless compliance learning is a useful strategy which, similar to PAT, relies on antecedents to increase behavior, thus eliminating the need for traditional parent training strategies that often focus on consequences.

According to Ducharme (1996), other advantages include the reduction of challenging behaviors as compliance increases. Because requests that yield a low probability of compliance are introduced gradually, children tend to experience less frustration and thus demonstrate fewer episodes of challenging behavior. Parents learn to focus on desired responses and use high levels of praise which often leads to increased self-esteem in their children. Finally, using an errorless approach helps to eliminate stress in the household. Children learn to respond to a variety of requests, parents learn to acknowledge and reinforce desired behavior, and the stress associated with confrontational disciplinary strategies is virtually eliminated.

THE PARENT TRAINING PROGRAM

THERAPIST CHARACTERISTICS

Parent training in this context means that the mediator of "treatment" is the parent. The "therapist" is the individual who trains the parent. Parent trainers can be experienced therapists or graduate students. The key element in parent training is that the therapist should be able to demonstrate to a preselected criterion the skills required for PAT and errorless compliance training. The usual model for this is for the prospective trainer to first read descriptive materials and then to pass a quiz at a 90% criterion. The trainee takes versions of the quiz and reviews the material until this criterion is met.

The next step in a training process is for the experienced therapist to model the skills to the trainee. Again, a criterion is established such that the trainee must demonstrate each newly trained component five times without a model before the skills are considered mastered. Feedback is provided by the trainer on the quality of the performance. After skills are demonstrated in simulation, the trainee observes the experienced therapist in the actual training environment—the home. The new therapist is gradually "faded" into the home situation by being asked to perform increasingly more of the training protocol with the parent(s). Again, feedback is provided by the experienced therapist.

Demonstrating PAT and errorless compliance skills do not make for a completely trained therapist. Three other components of training are required: (a) teaching skill training, (b) counseling skill training, and (c) child affective skill training. A therapist may know all of the components of PAT or any other skill-based protocol; however, this does not at all mean that the therapist knows *how* to teach (McGimsey, Greene, & Lutzker, 1995), that is, systematically teaching to criterion (through quizzes, modeling, and feedback) how to use modeling, role playing, and feedback with parents.

All parent trainers should learn to be sensitive to parents' concerns. A parent who is not comfortable with a therapist will not likely follow through with training. Thus, therapists should be systematically taught simple counseling skills. This is also done with quizzes, modeling, role playing, and feedback by using a validated manual for teaching active listening and reflective commenting skills (Borck & Fawcett, 1982). Additionally, therapists are taught how to conduct a session. Specifically, they learn how to open and close a session and how to set an agenda. Further, they are taught not to conduct parent training if the parent is having a bad day and needs to be heard instead of performing (Lutzker & Campbell, 1994).

Finally, therapists are taught affective skills with children. Once again, quizzes, role playing, modeling, and feedback are used with preset performance criteria. Lutzker, Megson, Webb, and Dachman (1985) and McGimsey, Lutzker, and Greene (1994) have validated the skills adults should display when interacting with children: making clear verbal statements, congruence between verbal and physical messages, smiling pleasant face, assume equal position of height (leveling), clear firm voice, specify how to comply with instructions, interact with appropriately behaving children, ignore minor disruptive behavior, avoid scolding, allow children passive physical contact, use assertive tone for disapproval, use assertive tone for approval, initiate active physical contact, use verbal statements rather than gestures to communicate, and have disapproving facial expression when interacting with inappropriately behaving child. Teaching therapists these skills, along with counseling skills with adults, greatly increases the likelihood of successful parent training.

CLIENT CHARACTERISTICS

PAT has been used successfully with parents and children who represent a broad range of race and ethnic groups, disorders among the children, and even with parents who have limited intellectual functioning. Social validation has shown considerable satisfaction expressed by parents about PAT. In general, parents seem initially more receptive to PAT than CMT and seem to be less resistant during PAT than CMT. It is likely that this is so because PAT more resembles naturally good parenting and teaching than CMT. Parents often complain that CMT seems artificial and are reluctant to deliver such frequent praise and tangible reinforcers.

PAT can be used with children who have a variety of disorders and intellectual deficits. Even if it is unclear that a child with mental retardation understands all that is said to him or her during incidental teaching, it is clear from the developmental psychology literature that children should be exposed to as much expressive language from parents and teachers as possible (Hart & Risley, 1995). The same is so for infants.

Logistics

PAT and errorless compliance training require minimal sessions, are efficient, and meet short-term therapy standards. Although some training has been reported to have taken place in clinics or offices, the majority of training for both procedures takes place primarily in homes and community settings. While this is more cumbersome than office-based therapy, it nonetheless promotes generalization and parents report considerable satisfaction with in situ training.

Planned Activities Training

PAT takes place across five structured sessions and involves the training of all family members and other key individuals who interact with the child. During session 1, an assessment is conducted and a general overview of PAT is provided to the family. Sessions 2 through 5 focus on practicing the techniques in home and community settings.

Training sessions are designed to teach parents to learn PAT during daily activities. Initially, parents learn to use the techniques for activities which are normally nonproblematic. Once skills are mastered, more problem activities and settings are targeted. In addition to learning the techniques, parents are also taught to evaluate their own behavior as well as the behavior of their children. Training involves intensive modeling, practice of the PAT skills, and performance feedback. Parents are required to plan ahead for each activity using a PAT checklist and write out the exact wording of what they will say to their children throughout each entire activity. Feedback is provided on the script prepared by the parents and is accompanied with a role play. This helps to ensure that the parents learn the skills and use them correctly. Training sessions are conducted in the families' homes and in all settings where challenging behavior occurs.

The Assessment

The initial PAT session begins with the counselor establishing a rapport with the family and collecting as much information as possible on the challenging behaviors. During this session, the counselor provides the parents with a Problem Setting Questionnaire, completes a functional assessment of the challenging behaviors, observes the parents and child interacting during a variety of activities, and discusses the rationale for PAT.

Parents are given a Problem Setting Questionnaire to collect information about the child's behavior during specific activities or settings. The parents are provided with a home and community problem checklist and asked to indicate the difficulty of the activity or setting on a scale of 1 to 5 (1 being easy and 5 being extremely difficult). The questions may include eating breakfast, getting ready to leave, taking a nap, dealing with arriving parents, taking a bath. The Community Problem Checklist includes specific places or events that may set the occasion for challenging behaviors, such as birthday parties, weddings, grocery shopping, medical office visits, and restaurants. This questionnaire helps identify activities and events which are high-risk situations for challenging behaviors.

Next, a functional assessment is completed to determine what the challenging behaviors include, that is, the topography, duration, frequency, and intensity of the target behaviors. Parents learn to operationally define challenging behaviors such as aggression, tantrums, and self-injury. By helping the parents to operationally define the target behaviors, the family can more accurately monitor the progress of the intervention. In addition to defining the target behaviors, parents learn to identify antecedents that set the occasion for the behavior (waiting in line, taking a bath, or being prompted to leave a desired setting), the consequences for the behavior (gaining attention, escaping a demand, or being left alone), and the conditions under which the challenging behaviors are most and least likely to occur (e.g., most likely with the mother and least likely with the father, or most likely in the afternoon and least likely in the morning). Further, information is collected about medications, diet, sleep patterns, and daily schedules to further understand their possible influence on the challenging behaviors. This information helps identify and narrow the range of potential variables that may influence the challenging behavior.

After gathering the information on the challenging behaviors, the parents and the child are observed during a play activity and/or community setting to assess their interaction skills. The parents are assessed using a PAT Checklist on how they explain the activity, use incidental teaching (described below) to engage the child, ability to give clear instructions, and use of praise. A similar checklist is used for the child to assess compliance, language, attention span, and the display of challenging behaviors. The direct observations provide an actual frequency of the behavior and information about the times of day, settings, or situations in which the challenging behavior(s) occurs, and consequences that may affect the behavior(s). These observations are used as a baseline, providing the counselor with information about how the parents naturally interact with their child.

Finally, the PAT rationale is provided to parents. They are told that they will be taught how to arrange the environment so that challenging behaviors do not occur, thus minimizing a need for any negative consequences. The session ends with a brief description and explanation of the nine PAT elements: managing time, pinpointing high-risk situations, discussing rules, planning activities, incidental teaching, attending while they are busy, reinforcement, consequences, and follow-up discussion.

The PAT Elements

The first element of PAT is *time management.* This is very important for most families. If events or activities are not planned in advance, the likelihood of problems occurring is increased. Parents should be able to plan their days and know what to expect, thus being prepared (as much as possible) for daily events. Children need the same type of planning and preparation for their daily activities and must rely solely on parents for this planning and organization. Planning ahead includes creating a schedule of the daily activities, making sure that all the supplies that will be needed for each activity are available, scheduling time to discuss the activities with the child before they occur, planning time to explain the rules or what is expected of the child prior to the activity, and having an alternative plan. Thus, the outcome of planning is: if parents take the time to plan daily events, they have the potential of preventing challenging behaviors.

A second element of PAT is *pinpointing high-risk situations.* Families engage in activities and frequent settings in which their children display challenging behavior (e.g., shopping trips, traveling in the car, waiting, mealtime). If parents identify these settings and activities and plan to engage their children more, the frequency of challenging behaviors can be reduced or eliminated. For example, going to the grocery store is often a difficult task for parents, especially with children who have developmentally disabilities. Pinpointing high-risk situations involves identifying those activities and settings in which the child is most likely to display challenging behaviors. Once parents learn to identify high-risk situations, they can properly plan for the activity and reduce the likelihood or eliminate the possibility of challenging behaviors.

A third element of PAT is *discussing the rules* of the event or activity in advance. As it is important to plan each day, it is also important to explain to children what is expected of them during each activity. Parents cannot assume that children will always remember what the rules are for each activity and setting. Also, children may not know the rules or expectations. Therefore, it is important for parents to take the time before beginning an activity or leaving for an outing to explain what is going to happen, provide the child with two to three simple rules that are easy to follow, and a brief rationale for each rule. For example, when planning a trip to the grocery store a child may be told something similar to "We are going to the grocery store to buy a few items for dinner. While in the store I need you to keep your hands to yourself and stay within arm's reach of me so that nothing gets broken and you do not get lost." In addition to planning and discussing rules, it is important to explain to the child what the consequences are for breaking rules as well as for following rules. For example, the child might be told, "If you follow the rules we will have enough time to look at the magazines before we leave. If you do not follow the rules, we will not have enough time to look at magazines and will have to go directly home." Finally, it is important to ensure that the child understands the rules. This can be accomplished by having the child repeat them back or simply reviewing them an additional time. When children know what to expect and what is expected of them, there is a greater likelihood that they will engage in appropriate behavior.

Generating a list of activities is the fourth element of PAT. When parents are prepared by having several different activities planned, the likelihood of challenging behaviors occurring is decreased. When children are engaged and provided attention, they are unlikely to display disruptive behavior.

There are several ways in which to create an activity list for children. One is to observe children at times when they are engaged and take note of the activities they seem to prefer. Another method is to involve the children in creating a list of activities in which they enjoy participating. Finally, parents can create their own lists of activities by accumulating different activities or games that may be novel to the child and only offered during special times such as high-risk situations. Activities can involve things such as games, art supplies, toys, books, a portable cassette recorder, and sports equipment. Parents should have several activities selected for each situation and should alternate activities frequently to eliminate boredom. For example, when traveling in the car, activity lists can include travel games, books, hand-held video games, and a portable tape recorder. A trip to the grocery store might include providing the child with a snack while shopping (e.g., cereal), a portable tape recorder, and/or a designated job (e.g., pushing the cart or holding the list). Finally, a list for a trip to the physician's office might include books, puzzles, paper and crayons, and a travel game.

Incidental teaching is the fifth element of PAT. It is a simple procedure that can be used to prevent challenging behaviors with children, teach new skills, and encourage language development. The development of language in children is an important step in increasing communication skills. These skills provide children with appropriate alternative behaviors, thus eliminating challenging behaviors. In time, this reduces the amount of time spent attending to the child's needs and requests. In the course of a day, adults have many opportunities to use incidental teaching in naturally occurring situations, such as during mealtime, dressing, shopping, and play time. Incidental teaching helps to keep children engaged because the parents are attending to what the child is doing and showing interest in the activity.

Hart and Risley (1975) described incidental teaching as the interaction between an adult and a single child, which arises naturally in an unstructured situation such as play and is used by the adult to transmit information or give the child practice in developing a skill. During incidental teaching, the child initiates the interaction by requesting assistance from the adult. The child's request may be verbal or nonverbal and is most frequently applied to the teaching of language skills. Incidental teaching is incorporated in natural, ongoing situations to teach functional skills and promote learning as well as to keep the child engaged (Farmer-Dougan, 1994). For example, while in the grocery store, a mother might engage her child in incidental teaching to increase language development. The mother might begin by giving the child the shopping list and explaining that she needs help finding specific items. Upon finding the first item on the list, the mother actively encourages language by asking a series of specific questions such as, "Where do you suppose we will find bananas?, Do you know where bananas come from?, Do you know what color bananas are?, How many bananas do you see on this bunch? Tell me what we can make with these bananas." Thus, incidental teaching is used to increase receptive language and appropriate expressive verbalizations made by the child.

A sixth PAT element is *attending to children* while they are engaged in activities. Attention should be given while they are engaged so that they do not have the opportunity to seek attention in inappropriate or disruptive ways. Children are more likely to continue with the activity and have little need to display disruptive behaviors when they receive attention for displaying appropriate behavior. Attention can be provided naturally and with little effort during activities by simply providing the child with a pat on the back, smiling, and/or providing a few encouraging works (e.g., "I like how you are coloring quietly"). A parent also might sit down next to a child who is drawing and talk about what the child is making.

Positive reinforcement is the seventh element of PAT. Reinforcement is critical when shaping and maintaining appropriate behavior. Children need to know when they are behaving appropriately. Reinforcement most often takes the form of tangible items or events which are received for the successful completion of an activity or outing. Parents can make a list of objects, activities, places, and food the children enjoy. Children are then provided with these items during activities or outings. For instance if a child does not like bath time, a special bubble bath may be offered to create a more positive bath experience. A parent might provide reinforcement for a child for following the rules and displaying appropriate behavior in the grocery store with a visit to the pet store once they are finished shopping. Similarly, a child may be reinforced with an extra bedtime story or staying up later at night for taking a bath in a timely matter and without a tantrum. Reinforcement can be provided in a variety of forms and is used to let children know when they are performing appropriately.

Although, PAT is based primarily on antecedent techniques to help prevent challenging behavior, consequences are sometimes needed. Thus, *consequences* are the eighth element of PAT. Just as parents are taught how to use reinforcement, they are also taught to use a hierarchy of consequences. First, parents are taught to tell children ahead of time what will happen if they display disruptive or challenging behavior. For example, a child may be told, "If you tantrum in the store shopping will take longer and we will not have time to go to the pet store." Next, parents are taught to use a hierarchy of consequences beginning with the least intrusive and gradually introducing more intrusive consequences if the behavior persists. For example, while in a store a child begins to whine and pout because he is not allowed to have some candy. The parent would begin by ignoring the whining in the hope that without any attention it will end. If the whining continues, however, the parent would give a terminating instruction and redirect into a new activity, "Robert, if you continue to whine and pout we will have to leave and go home without going to the pet store. So how about helping find cereal so that we can get this shopping done?" If the whining persists and turns into a tantrum, the task is terminated and the child is redirected into a new activity or outing, "O.K. Robert, it looks like today is not a good shopping day, so let's go home and take a rest." Consequences need to be clear and fair. Parents should only use consequences with which they plan to follow-through.

Finally, the last element of PAT includes a *follow-up discussion* upon completion of the activity. Parents are taught how to talk to their children following an activity to let them know how well they followed the rules. It is important to provide children with feedback on their performance. Parents begin discussing the activity or event by telling the child what was good and in what areas they need to improve. For example, "John, you did a great job helping me find the milk and bread at the store. You were a big help. Next time, however, I need you to work on staying within arm's reach and not running ahead of me. I know you get excited, but you need to stay with me." During this time, parents review the consequences for appropriate and inappropriate behavior and follow-through with the consequences established.

Outline of Training Sessions

During the next four sessions, the parents are taught to use the nine elements previously described during several activities and settings. Each of these training sessions includes the counselor outlining the session and modeling a home and community checklist. The parents are then provided with an opportunity to practice using both checklists with the child and receive feedback on their performance. The counselor assigns a homework task for the family to complete (e.g., practicing incidental teaching during a play time or explaining rules during a shopping trip) and answers any questions they may have. The session ends with a recap of the procedures taught and a plan for the following session.

PAT is a simple procedure to teach and implement because the elements are very natural and are taught during a variety of activities and in several settings. Because the elements are so simple and occur so naturally, parents tend to generalize the procedures to new untrained activities and settings with little additional instruction (Huynen et al., 1996). Further, the skills taught to parents maintain over time. Thus, PAT is a natural strategy that is easy to teach and learn because it is based on good, simple principles and teaching practices. PAT differs from more traditional parent training techniques in that focuses primarily on the use of antecedents to prevent challenging behaviors.

CASE EXAMPLES

The Taylor family was referred because they could not take their 6-year-old son, Zack, who had a diagnosis of autism, into public places such as the grocery store or mall. During the assessment observations, the counselor accompanied Mrs. Taylor and Zack to the mall. Upon the arrival at the mall, Zack was calm and manageable. Once inside, however, he began running up to strangers and touching them inappropriately, and darted into shops and grabbed items from shelves. When he was approached by his mother and asked to leave the situation, he screamed, cried, and threw himself on the ground. The mall was likely too stimulating for Zack. Thus, in order to increase appropriate behavior in such an environment, gradual exposure would be necessary.

PAT was taught to the mother at home during play and homework time. These times were chosen because Zack rarely displayed challenging behaviors when engaged in these tasks and it provided Mrs. Taylor an opportunity to practice all of the elements of PAT with little disruption. During training, the counselor especially focused on demonstrating how to plan ahead for events, rule discussion, use of consequences, and incidental teaching. Mrs. Taylor practiced using PAT several times in the home and on short walks in the neighborhood before returning to the mall. After this training, the counselor observed Mrs. Taylor and Zack in the mall again. This time Mrs. Taylor sat with Zack and explained to him that they were going to the mall for a short time (10 minutes). She explained that while at the mall Zack would need to stay within arm's reach of her at all times or she would have to hold his hand. Mrs. Taylor went on to explain that if he followed the rule he could purchase an ice cream before leaving; however, if he could not follow the rules they would have to leave. She then had Zack repeat the rules back to her. Once they arrived at the mall, Mrs. Taylor repeated the rules and consequences to Zack and proceeded to walk to the entrance. Upon entering the mall, Zack stayed within arm's reach of his mother only straying one time, in which case he was reminded that he was too far away and needed to come back or hold his mother's hand. Zack did so well on this short outing that he was given ice cream as reinforcement as he exited the mall.

*   *   *

The Smith family was referred for assistance because their 9-year-old daughter, Jenna, was exhibiting tantrums nightly. Jenna was an only child and had a diagnosis of mild mental retardation. The functional assessment revealed that the tantrums occurred primarily in the evening while completing her homework with her father. Mrs. Smith worked evenings, thus Jenna spent most nights at home with her father. An observation of Jenna doing her homework was conducted. It was observed that Mr. Smith prompted Jenna to do her homework and then left the room to finish the dinner dishes. When he returned, he found Jenna playing on the computer. He raised his voice and redirected her back to her studies. Jenna began to cry and yell, refusing to do her work. Mr. Smith became angry and physically prompted her to the table, sat with her while she cried, and attempted to assist her with her work.

In the subsequent five weeks, PAT was completed with Mr. Smith and Jenna. Mr. Smith learned how to use the procedures when Jenna played on the computer, helped prepare dinner, and rode in the car. During the training, the counselor demonstrated how to plan ahead by preparing a nightly schedule, discussing rules, helping Jenna begin on activities, and using incidental teaching. After the training, another observation was conducted during homework. Mr. Smith sat with Jenna and discussed the rules before it was time to do her homework. He explained that he would help her get started on her homework and if she could complete it without any crying or yelling, she could play on the computer before going to bed. Following the rule discussion, Mr. Smith helped Jenna begin her homework. Once she was engaged in the task, he exited the room for a few minutes. When he returned he sat down next to her and asked her questions about the task. When she was finished she ran to the computer and played her favorite games before going to bed.

*   *   *

The Esposito family was referred for services for (the youngest of their three children) 3-year-old, Mario, who displayed tantrums throughout the morning routine. Mario had a diagnosis of moderate mental retardation and cerebral palsy. Direct observations and a functional assessment revealed that during the morning routine, Mrs. Esposito would pick Mario up without warning and physically prompt him through diaper changing, mealtime, dressing, and tooth-brushing. During this time, Mario began to wiggle, could not sit still, and started to cry and hit his mother. While conducting these activities, Mrs. Esposito spoke very little to Mario and appeared to be rushed. She explained that the morning was a very chaotic time and that is was a struggle to get all the children to school on time.

PAT was conducted with Mrs. Esposito while the other children were at school. Training began with play and nap time, two activities which were not particularly difficult for Mrs. Esposito or Mario. Although all the elements of PAT were taught, the counselor focused on planning ahead, incidental teaching, and reinforcement. A follow-up observation was conducted during the morning routine. Mrs. Esposito went into Mario's room and gently played with him prior to picking him up. As she changed his diaper she began to talk to him and tell him the plan for the day (e.g., "After we get changed we are going to have breakfast, then get you dressed, and brush your teeth"). As they moved into the kitchen she practiced incidental teaching skills by explaining what she was making for breakfast. She continued to talk to Mario throughout the entire morning routine and subsequently he had no opportunity to display a tantrum.

Errorless Compliance Training

Errorless compliance training (Ducharme & Popynick, 1993) is designed to assist parents whose children exhibited noncompliant behavior to "errorlessly" teach their children to respond to parental requests. This strategy is labeled "errorless" because it begins with requests with which the child routinely complies and gradually introduces requests with which the child regularly does not comply (Ducharme, 1996). The procedures involve an observational assessment to determine the probability of child compliance to a variety of parental requests and hierarchical categorization of the requests according to the probability of a response. Parents initially begin with requests which have been determined to produce high probabilities of compliance and gradually introduce requests that yield low levels of cooperation.

Ducharme (1996) outlines several key components to errorless compliance training: an initial assessment, observational assessment, and hierarchical categorization of requests. Prior to training, parents are provided with a questionnaire assessment to determine the level of compliance exhibited in the home to a broad range of questions. Questions are selected from a wide array of compliance situations experienced around the home and community (e.g., demand, leisure, social, hygiene).

The parents then rank the level of compliance for each request (level 1 being most compliant and level 4 being least compliant). It is important to note that skills that have not yet been learned are not included in the ranking. Ducharme (1996) describes the level of requests as the following: level 1 as those requests "almost always followed," levels 2 and 3 as requests "usually followed," and level 4 as requests "rarely followed."

An observational assessment is conducted with the family to determine if their predictions about selected requests are accurate. The trainer lists the requests in a random order on an assessment data sheet and parents collect data on the child's compliance to each request.

Following the data collection, the parents are taught how to effectively deliver requests. The rationale for this is that parents may have problems with compliance based on the delivery of the request. By changing the manner in which requests are delivered, an increase in compliance by the child is likely to occur. Ducharme (1996) describes effective request delivery as having the following components: imperative requests, single component requests, proximity and eye contact, no repetition, polite but firm tone, no prompts or discussion, time to respond, and natural presentation.

Imperative requests are defined as requests which are delivered as a harsh command form (e.g., "come for dinner, now"). Ducharme suggests that parents utilize a more "polite" friendly style (e.g., "would you please come to dinner, now?").

Single-component requests are also suggested when delivering instructions to children. Children often have difficulty processing and following multiple-component requests (e.g., "clean your room and feed the dog"). Thus, parents are taught to use simple one-component requests to help facilitate compliance.

Proximity and eye contact are also important when delivering requests. Children who are not responding to a request may simply have not heard the instruction. Parents need to be close enough to child to gain the child's attention, make eye contact, and receive an acknowledgment for the request.

Ducharme also suggests that parents avoid repeating requests. Parents should make sure that they deliver the request clearly and in close enough range that the child hears it the first time it is given. If a child can predict that the request will be repeated, there is no need for immediate compliance.

Parents should avoid lengthy discussions about requests. The request should be delivered with a simple rationale with no further discussion about the required response. Children often engage parents in a discussion of the request to avoid completing the task.

Finally, children should be provided with an adequate amount of time to respond. Too often parents want children to respond immediately and leave little time for compliance. Parents need to wait for the child to respond once the request has been made.

Following the calculation of the probability of requests, they are ordered from highest to lowest compliance probability and treatment begins. Requests are ranked on a scale of most likely to be followed (level 1 requests) to least likely to be followed (level 2 requests). Training includes modeling of the procedures, practice, and feedback on performance. Parents are also taught to reinforce appropriate responses and to give limited attention to noncompliant behavior. Finally, parents are taught to deliver reinforcement immediately following the child's compliant behavior with enthusiasm and various forms of social interactions (hugs, pats, and kisses).

The actual intervention begins with the parents delivering the requests from the level 1 category 3 times per day. Parents are taught to collect data on the requests and responses in a manner identical to the assessment phase. Level 1 requests are continued for at least one week before beginning level 2 requests. Parents should not continue with level 2 requests until the child demonstrates a steady rate of compliance with level 1 requests.

Transition sessions are conducted before beginning level 2 requests. During these sessions, parents begin with providing level 1 requests and gradually introducing level 2 requests. Once compliance is gained for level 2 requests, level 1 requests are faded. Therefore, level 2 requests are embedded within the level 1 requests to help ensure compliance. The remaining treatment phases are identical to those used in phase 1. Parents gradually fade the level 2 requests as the child begins to comply to level 3 requests. Once level 4 requests have been introduced and the child is responding appropriately, the parents can reintroduce requests from any level.

Thus, errorless compliance training teaches parents to gain compliance by setting up the environment so that the child will succeed. With this approach, there is little opportunity for the child to make errors and the momentum of the compliance to simple requests is transferred to more difficult ones. Errorless compliance training is designed to utilize antecedents to accomplish its goal.

CASE EXAMPLES

The Bowen family was referred for services because their 12-year-old son, Jimmy, displayed noncompliance and aggressive behavior. Jimmy had a diagnosis of moderate mental retardation and autisticlike features. The functional assessment determined that Jimmy displayed noncompliant behavior and aggressive behavior when instructed to complete hygiene skills (e.g., brushing his teeth, taking a shower, washing his face and hands).

The parents were trained to use errorless compliance training to increase Jimmy's completion of daily tasks. Initially, the Bowens compiled a list of activities that included all the activities which Jimmy completed in a typical day (e.g., making his bed, getting dressed, doing homework, taking a bath, putting toys away). The parents were then asked to collect data for a week on his compliance level of each request. The list was then divided into three different levels of requests: those with which he consistently complied (level 1), those with which he occasionally complied (level 2), and those to which he rarely complied (level 3). After the lists were created and rank ordered, the counselor reviewed with the Bowens how to approach Jimmy to make a request. They reviewed how to make positive statements, provide time for him to respond, how to give simple instructions, to make sure that the instruction is heard, and to provide a sign of acknowledgment. Next, the Bowens followed the errorless compliance training procedures and began with the activities with which Jimmy most consistently complied (e.g., making his bed, putting toys away, and doing homework). They used immediate praise and reinforcement in the form of playing outside later. As Jimmy demonstrated more consistent compliance to the level 1 requests, the Bowens gradually introduced the level 2 requests, one at a time. For example, they would have Jimmy complete his homework, eat dinner (level 1 requests), and then wash his face and hands (level 2 request) before being allowed to go out and play. Gradually, all of the level 2 and 3 requests were introduced into Jimmy's schedule until he was consistently following most requests made of him and demonstrating virtually no aggressive behavior.

*   *   *

The Chan family was referred for services due to their 3-year-old daughter, Katie's, refusal to eat during mealtime. A functional assessment revealed that force feeding had been used during physical therapy when she was 6-months-old. Katie had learned to associate eating solid food with an aversive situation which produced tantrums, gagging, and vomiting. During the observation sessions, Mrs. Chan was observed carrying Katie to the table and buckling her into her booster seat as she screamed, yelled, and attempted to escape. When food was placed in front of Katie, she closed her mouth and refused to eat. Her mother tried feeding her, but Katie gagged and pushed the food away. After 15 minutes, Mrs. Chan removed Katie from the table and gave her a bottle of rice and formula.

A modified version of errorless compliance learning was used with Katie. The intervention started by having Mrs. Chan make a list of activities associated with the kitchen and eating which Katie would routinely play without becoming agitated. The activities Katie's mother suggested included playing with toy dishes, pots, and pans on a table in the family room. After successfully getting Katie to play with these items in the family room, Mrs. Chan had her play with these items in the kitchen. Next, Mrs. Chan created another list of activities in which Katie would participate, yet would only present a small amount of tantrums or gagging. These activities included helping Mrs. Chan cook simple treats in the kitchen. Katie would help make the treats by pouring ingredients into bowls, stirring, and washing dishes without being required to taste or eat anything. Next, Mrs. Chan compiled a list of foods that Katie would occasionally sample or taste (pudding, frosting, yogurt, and milkshakes). Mrs. Chan began with engaging Katie in making these items and modeled how to taste and sample the treats. She then encouraged Katie to do the same as she engaged her in conversation about the food. Eventually training sessions were gradually introduced into normal meal times and Mrs. Chan began requiring Katie to sample small portions of each meal while she used incidental teaching to talk about the food and daily events. Eventually Katie was sampling more and more food, complying to eat all of her favorites. Gradually, the bottle was faded.

*   *   *

The Henderson family was referred for services because they were unable to take their 5-year-old grandson, Mark, into the community due to his disruptive behavior and inability to follow directions. Mark had a diagnosis of autism, was nonverbal, and lived with his grandparents because his parents could not manage him. During an assessment observation, Mark and his grandmother were observed while taking a walk in their neighborhood. During the walk, the grandmother held Mark's hand very tightly so he could not run into the street and into strange homes. While she was holding his hand he screamed, cried, and attempted to bite her. When she let go, he ran down the block and was unresponsive to his name being called.

PAT and a modified version of errorless compliance training were taught to the grandmother. Initially, she was taught how to structure Mark's day using PAT during routine meal and play activities which occurred inside the family home. These tasks were selected because Mark demonstrated better instruction-following when inside the home. The grandmother was taught to plan activities (a posted schedule was used), discuss rules for each activity, explain the consequences, and use reinforcement (Table 9.1).

Next, a list of places and activities outside the house was created in which Mark would sometimes respond to his name and follow directions. These activities included playing games in the backyard and on the front porch. The grandmother practiced giving Mark simple requests (e.g., hand her toys, put toys away, kick a ball) and having him walk short distances and turn his head when his name was called. Eventually, the grandmother took Mark on short walks around the block using PAT to prepare him for the walk by explaining the rules and consequences.

Finally, it was deemed that Mark was ready for the grocery store. On the first visit, his grandmother used PAT and told Mark that they would just walk into the store and then turn right around and leave. If he followed the direction, a trip to a fast food restaurant for lunch was offered as a reinforcer. As planned, the grandmother walked into the store and gave Mark the instruction that it was time to leave and they both walked out together. In follow-up visits with the family, the grandmother expressed pride in reporting that through the use of PAT and errorless compliance learning Mark was no longer a "prisoner" of his home. He was now going to places such as the mall, the park, and was even able to eat inside the fast food restaurants.

Table 9.1
Planned Activities Training Observation

Activity	Dates			
1. Prepare all supplies in advance				
2. Pin-point high risk situations				
3. Explain activity				
4. Discuss rules (2 to 3 simple rules stated positively)				
5. Describe incentives & consequences				
6. Engage child in the activity				
7. Use incidental teaching				
8. Attend to the child during activity				
9. Use social praise and reinforcement				
10. Provide feedback on performance				
11. Provide reinforcement				
12. Implement consequences (if needed)				

Comments _____

_____

_____

_____

CONCLUSION

Behavioral parent training has been an effective strategy for teaching parents to change child behavior since the 1960s. It has been effective for families with children having behavior problems, conduct disorder, and children with developmental disabilities. Early parent training strategies usually involved teaching parents to use contingency management techniques that focus primarily upon using consequences for appropriate and challenging behaviors. More recently, Planned Activities Training (PAT) and errorless learning/behavioral momentum techniques have been shown to be quite effective for parents who have children with developmental disabilities. These strategies utilize stimulus control techniques that emphasize antecedent prevention of challenging behavior. These techniques resemble natural good parenting techniques, are easy to teach, and produce good outcome along with community generalization.

A truly comprehensive approach to parent training, that is, an eco-behavioral approach, might consider additional services to families who have children with developmental disabilities. Thus, although PAT and errorless compliance trainings are effective, nonpunitive techniques, parents might also benefit from stress reduction training, other treatments for depression, and problem-solving training (Lutzker & Campbell, 1994). The techniques reviewed in this chapter offer a new generation of strategies aimed at helping families with children who have developmental disabilities.

REFERENCES

Baker, B. L. (1989). *Parent training and developmental disabilities*. Washington, DC: American Association on Mental Retardation.

Baker, B. L., Smithen, S. J., & Kashimal, K. J. (1991). Effects of parent training on families of children with mental retardation: Increased burden or generalized benefit? *American Journal on Mental Retardation, 96*, 127–136.

Batshaw, M. L. (1991). *Your child has a disability*. Toronto, Canada: Little, Brown.

Baum, C. G., & Forehand, R. (1981). Long term follow-up of parent training by use of multiple outcome measures. *Behavior Therapy, 12*, 643–652.

Borck, L. E., & Fawcett, S. B. (1982). *Learning counseling and problem-solving skills*. New York: Haworth Press.

Bromley, B. E., & Blacher, J. (1992). Parental reasons for out-of-home placement of children with severe handicaps. *Mental Retardation, 29*, 275–280.

Carr, E. G., & Durand, V. M. (1985). Reducing behavior problems through functional communication training. *Journal of Applied Behavior Analysis, 18*, 111–126.

Ducharme, J. M. (1996). Errorless compliance training: Optimizing clinical efficacy. *Behavior Modification, 20*, 259–280.

Ducharme, J. M., Lucas, H., & Pontes, E. (1994). Errorless embedding in the reduction of severe maladaptive behavior during interactive and learning tasks. *Behavior Therapy, 25*, 489–501.

Ducharme, J. M., Pontes, E., Guger, S., Crozier, K., Lucus, H., & Popynick, M. (1994). Errorless compliance to parental requests: II. Increasing clinical practically through abbreviation of treatment parameters. *Behavior Therapy, 25*, 469–487.

Ducharme, J. M., & Popynick, M. (1993). Errorless compliance to parental requests: Treatment effects and generalization. *Behavior Therapy, 24*, 209–226.

Dunlap, G., Robbins, F. R., & Darrow, M. A. (1994). Parent's reports of their children's challenging behaviors: Results of a statewide survey. *Mental Retardation, 32*, 206–212.

Farmer-Dougan, V. (1994). Increasing requests by adults with developmental disabilities using incidental teaching by peers. *Journal of Applied Behavior Analysis, 27*, 533–544.

Feldman, M. A., Towns, F., Betel, J., Case, L., Rincover, A., & Rubino, C. A. (1986). Parent Education Project: II. Increasing stimulating interactions of developmentally handicapped mothers. *Journal of Applied Behavior Analysis, 19*, 23–37.

Forehand, R., & Wierson, M. (1993). The role of developmental factors in planning behavioral interventions for children: Disruptive behavior as an example. *Behavior Therapy, 24*, 117–141.

Graziano, A. M., & Diament, D. M. (1992). Parent behavioral training an examination of the paradigm. *Behavior Modification, 16*, 4–38.

Harrold, M., Lutzker, J. R., Campbell, R. V., & Touchette, P. E. (1992). Improving parent-child interactions for families of children with developmental disabilities. *Journal of Behavior Therapy and Experimental Psychiatry, 23*, 89–100.

Hart, B., & Risley, T. (1975). Incidental teaching of language in the preschool. *Journal of Applied Behavior Analysis, 8*, 411–420.

Hart, B., & Risley, T. (1995). *Meaningful differences in the everyday experiences of young American children.* Baltimore: Brookes.

Hudson, A. (1988). Training proficiency scale-parent version. In M. Hersen & A. S. Bellack (Eds.), *Dictionary of behavioral assessment techniques* (pp. 484–485). New York: Pergamon Press.

Huynen, K. B., Lutzker, J. R., Bigelow, K. M., Touchette, P. E., & Campbell, R. V. (1996). Planned activities training for mothers of children with developmental disabilities: Community generalization and follow-up. *Behavior Modification, 20*, 406–427.

Kravetz, S., Katz, S., & Katz, S. (1990). A goal directed approach to training parents of children with a developmental disability. *British Journal of Mental Subnormality, 70*, 17–29.

Kysela, G. M., McDonald, L., Reddon, J., & Gobeil-Dwyer, F. (1988). Stress and supports to families with a handicapped child. In K. Marfo (Ed.), *Parent-child interaction and developmental disabilities: Theory, research, and intervention* (pp. 273–289). New York: Praeger.

Lowry, M. A., & Whitman, T. L. (1989). Generalization of parenting skills: An early intervention program. *Child and Family Behavior Therapy, 11*, 45–65.

Lubetsky, M. J., Mueller, L., Madden, K., Walker, R., & Len, D. (1995). Family-centered/interdisciplinary team approach to working with families of children who have mental retardation. *Mental Retardation, 33*, 251–256.

Lutzker, J. R. (1994). Practical issues in delivering broad-based ecobehavioral services to families. *Revista Mexicana de Psicologia, 11,* 87–96.

Lutzker, J. R., & Campbell, R. V. (1994). *Ecobehavioral family interventions in developmental disabilities.* Pacific Grove, CA: Brooks/Cole.

Lutzker, J. R., Huynen, K. B., & Bigelow, K. M. (in press). Parent training. In V. B. Van Hasselt & M. Hersen (Eds.), *Handbook of psychological treatment protocols for children and adolescents.* Hillsdale, NJ: Erlbaum.

Lutzker, J. R., Megson, D. A., Webb, M. E., & Dachman, R. S. (1985). Validating and training adult-child interaction skills to professionals and to parents indicated for child abuse and neglect. *Journal of Child and Adolescent Psychotherapy, 2,* 91–104.

Matson, J. L., & Mulick, J. A. (1986). *Handbook of mental retardation.* Elmsford, NY: Pergamon Press.

McGimsey, J. F., Greene, B. F., & Lutzker, J. R. (1995). Competence in aspects of behavioral treatment and consultation: Implications for service delivery and graduate training. *Journal of Applied Behavioral Analysis, 28,* 301–315.

McGimsey, J. F., Lutzker, J. R., & Greene, B. F. (1994). Validating and teaching affective adult-child interaction skills. *Behavior Modification, 18,* 198–213.

Minor, S. W., Minor, J. W., & Williams, P. P. (1983). A participant modeling procedure to train parents of developmentally disabled infants. *Journal of Psychology, 115,* 107–111.

Plienis, A. J., Robbins, F. R., & Dunlap, G. (1988). Parent adjustment and family stress as factors in behavioral parent training for young autistic children. *Journal of the Multihandicapped Person, 1,* 31–52.

Powers, L. E., Singer, G. H., Stevens, T., & Sowers, J. (1992). Behavioral parent training in home and community generalization settings. *Education and Training in Mental Retardation, 27,* 13–27.

Robbins, F. R., & Dunlap, G. (1992). Effects of task difficulty on parent teaching skills and behavior problems of young children with autism. *American Journal on Mental Retardation, 96,* 631–643.

Roberts, M. W., & Powers, S. W. (1990). Adjusting chair timeout enforcement procedures for oppositional children. *Behavior Therapy, 21,* 257–271.

Sallis, J. F. (1983). Aggressive behaviors of children: A review of behavioral intervention and future directions. *Education and Treatment of Children, 6,* 175–191.

Sanders, M. R., & Christensen, A. P. (1985). A comparison of the effects of child management and planned activities training in five parenting environments. *Journal of Abnormal Child Psychology, 13,* 101–117.

Sanders, M. R., & Dadds, M. R. (1982). The effects of planned activities and child management procedures in parent training: An analysis of setting generality. *Behavior Therapy, 13,* 452–461.

Sanders, M. R., & Plant, K. (1989). Programming for generalization to high and low risk parenting situations in families with oppositional developmentally disabled preschoolers. *Behavior Modification, 13,* 283–305.

Singer, G. S., & Irvin, L. K. (1989). *Support for caregiving families enabling positive adaptation to disability.* Baltimore: Brookes.

Singer, G. S., Irvine, A. B., & Irvin, L. K. (1989). Expanding the focus of behavioral parent training a contextual approach. In G. Singer & L. Irvin (Eds.), *Support for caregiving families enabling positive adaptation* (pp. 85–102). Baltimore: Brookes.

Slentz, K. L., Walker, B., & Bricker, D. (1989). Supporting parent involvement in early intervention: A role-taking model. In G. Singer & L. Irvin (Eds.), *Support for caregiving families enabling positive adaptation* (pp. 221–238). Baltimore: Brookes.

Sulzer-Azaroff, B. S., & Mayer, R. G. (1991). *Behavior analysis for lasting change.* Fort Worth, TX: Holt, Rinehart and Winston.

Turnbull, A. P., & Turnbull, H. R. (1991). *Families, professionals, and exceptionality: A special partnership.* Columbus, OH: Merrill.

Tymchuk, A. J. (1986). Interventions with parents of the mentally retarded. In J. Matson & J. Mulick (Eds.), *Handbook on mental retardation* (pp. 369–380). Elmsford, NY: Pergamon Press.

Van Hasselt, V. B., Sisson, L. A., & Aachi, S. R. (1989). Parent training to increase compliance in a young multihandicapped child. *Journal of Behavior Therapy and Experimental Psychiatry, 18,* 275–283.

Webster-Stratton, C., & Herbert, M. (1993). What really happens in parent training? *Behavior Modification, 17,* 407–456.

CHAPTER 10

Training Parents of Failure-to-Attach Children

PHYLLIS B. BOOTH and TERRENCE J. KOLLER

WHAT IS THERAPLAY?

THERAPLAY IS a playful, short-term treatment method modeled on the interaction between a healthy parent and child. It is an intensive, goal-oriented approach that actively involves parents in the treatment process. Parents learn what their children need, first by watching, then by doing. Theraplay goals include, but are not limited to, enhancing the self-esteem and attachment level of both the parent and the child.

Theraplay is a method of child psychotherapy developed by Ann Jernberg (1979), based on the work of Austin Des Lauriers (1962; Des Lauriers & Carlson, 1969) and Viola Brody (1978, 1993). Des Lauriers broke from the theorists of his time by focusing on the here-and-now of the therapist-patient relationship and by introducing a more active, intrusive, and physical element into the treatment process. Ann Jernberg and her colleagues (Jernberg, 1979), at the Theraplay Institute in Chicago, applied these principles to children with a broad range of disturbance.

Theraplay actively involves parents.* The goal is to empower parents to continue, on their own, the health-promoting interactions of the treatment sessions. Training parents to be therapists for their children was a natural development of the Theraplay method. It is the parent, not the

---

*Rather than use the general word caretaker to cover all possibilities, we have chosen to use the word parents to denote the range of possible relationship to the child, biological, foster, and adopted caretakers as well as the possibility of either one or two caretakers being present.

308

child's therapist, who must live with the child 24 hours a day and thus has the greatest opportunity to influence the child for good or ill.

In describing Theraplay, Jernberg (1979) writes:

> The best way to understand the principles underlying the Theraplay method is to rediscover the basics of the mother-infant relationship: What are the typical daily pleasurable interactions in the nursery? What does a normal mother do to and for her baby? How does the healthy baby respond? What characterizes the cycle they thus set in motion between them? And what are the specific effects of their reciprocal behavior on each of the partners involved? (p. 4)

THERAPLAY DIMENSIONS

The normal playful interaction of parents includes the Theraplay elements of *Structure, Challenge, Intrusion/Engagement,* and *Nurture* that are combined in a setting that is playful, physical, and fun. Depending upon the particular needs of the child, these elements are emphasized in varying degrees when training parents.

Structure

As in the actual relationship between a parent and child, the dimension of structure in Theraplay sessions is addressed through clearly stated safety rules, through activities that have a beginning, a middle, and an end, and through activities that define body boundaries. This dimension is important for children who are overactive, unfocused, overstimulated, or who have an anxious need to be in control (Koller, 1994).

Challenge

In the parent-infant relationship, there are many opportunities to challenge the child. For example, a parent might encourage the child to "walk to Daddy" or ask the child to wave "bye bye" when a friend leaves. In treatment, challenging activities are done in partnership with the parent. For example, the therapist might challenge the child to wait for the count of three to throw a ball to his or her parent. The child is encouraged to take a risk in order to gain the reward of cheers from the adult and the intrinsic reward of accomplishment. This dimension is especially useful for shy, timid, or anxious children.

Intrusion/Engagement

Some children give off a superficial message that they want to be left alone. Others have had such bad experiences relating to others that they truly do not want to be engaged. These children need to be enticed out of their withdrawal by activities aimed at engaging them in a pleasurable relationship. As when sampling a new food, these children may not know what they are missing unless the adult encourages them to try it. The therapist must find creative ways of intruding and have a number of ways of persisting with children who are particularly resistant. The intrusive activity is always one which is intrinsically pleasurable, although this may not seem so when watching the child's reaction. These activities are especially useful for withdrawn children who avoid contact with others and appear lost in their fantasy life.

Nurture

In the parent-infant relationship, nurturing activities account for a great deal of the time spent together. For the very young infant, nurturing activities provide comfort and reassurance. Some children may not have experienced the nurturing they needed because other problems required more immediate attention. This may have been true for children whose parents were ill or who themselves experienced a severe illness. In some cases, the parent's own neediness interferes with the ability to nurture the child and a competitive relationship develops. These children benefit from increased doses of nurturing activities when they are older, although almost all benefit from some nurturing during difficult periods throughout the lifespan.

Playfulness

While not necessarily a discrete dimension, playfulness is a key element in all aspects of Theraplay. It is combined with the other dimensions in an attempt to give both the parent and child a new look at the world. This is especially important for children who are seen as too serious, intense, or worried.

THEORY

Theraplay theory developed from the study of the parent-infant interaction. The theory assumes that there is a reciprocity in the interaction and that one participant's behavior influences the other (Lewis & Lee-Painter, 1974). It is not important whether the parent or the child is the first to initiate a behavior because the reciprocal behavior can change the direction and quality of the interaction at any time. This is an important assumption underlying parent-training because it takes away blame for problems and gives parents the power to change their situation. In fact, it gives either participant this power to impact the relationship. In the simplest example of a reciprocal interaction, a mother makes a funny face at her infant who smiles back and becomes more active. This encourages the mother to make more funny faces until the child is saturated, breaks eye contact, and stops responding. The mother, sensitive to the child's signal that he has had enough, stops making faces. Later she may find other ways of engaging him when she senses he is ready. Infants benefit from the many repetitions of this type of interaction because they come to view the world as a "fun, caring, and loving place" (Jernberg, 1979, p. 5). The infant's development of social skills, language, and motor control is also enhanced through such interactions. Both the infant and the parent develop self-confidence as a result of the experience. Such interactions have a powerful impact on the parent as well. The early parent-infant interaction has been viewed as so important to both parent and infant that even routine separations of healthy mothers and infants can be disruptive for the mother (Barnett, Leiderman, Grobstein, & Klaus, 1970).

This parent-child interaction does not stop at infancy. The need for interactive, pleasurable intimacy extends throughout the life span. Adult children frequently return to their parents when the need for support arises. Adults often find mates who continue the quality of the interaction they experienced as a child. Abusive parent-child relationships can translate into abusive spousal relationships. Adults who experienced pleasurable, ego-enhancing relationships find it unfamiliar and difficult to tolerate relationships that are abusive.

The Importance of Attachment

The Theraplay approach to training parents relies heavily on attachment theory. Attachment is important by virtue of its relationship to the individual's capacity to form relationships, to the development of trust and security, and to the development of a sense of self and self-esteem. Stern (1985) describes the development of the self as an interactional process between the innately social infant and its engaged, empathic mother.

Attachment behaviors, in both parent and infant, are considered to be innately determined mechanisms that promote survival (Bowlby, 1969). These mechanisms ensure that the adult caretaker remains engaged, alert, and responsive. The infant contributes to the process by engaging the adult through its cries, looks, and smiles and ultimately by clinging and following when he or she becomes mobile. The development of attachment is a continuing dynamic process and is influenced by the unique characteristics of both the infant and the parent as well as by the quality of their interactions. Condon and Sander (1974) hypothesize that infants move in rhythm to their mother's voices and that these infant movements may reward the mother and stimulate her to continue.

The mutually enjoyable, physically intimate, and empathically responsive interaction of a healthy parent with a healthy infant has been found to lead to secure attachment (Ainsworth, 1969; Bowlby, 1969). As a result of this positive experience, the child develops a cognitive model of its parents as loving, caring, dependable, and available when needed. The key issues for a child are: How acceptable am I in my parents' eyes and how consistently available are my parents? Secure attachment is essential to the development of a strong sense of self, of feelings of self-worth, of a sense of trust and security, and of the capacity to form relationships. As a result of early attuned responses of caretakers, the infant develops the capacity to empathize with others. This is seriously lacking in some children and accounts for their cruelty, their inability to take the feelings of others into account, and their apparent lack of a conscience.

The need for attachment does not end after infancy. Adolescents who are more securely attached to their parents report higher feelings of self-esteem than do poorly attached adolescents (Armsden & Greenberg, 1987). Klaus and Kennell (1976) believe that one benefits from attachment to another at any age.

Although attachment is a natural outcome of healthy parenting, there are many things that can interfere and lead to the development of attachment problems. These range from the extreme of children raised in institutions (Spitz, 1945, 1947) where there is no opportunity to form an attachment, through disrupted attachments which result from the death of a caretaker, or removal from the home and placement in foster and adoptive homes. Insecure attachment can result when caretakers are inconsistently available either because of physical or psychological problems or because the child is unresponsive due to physical, neurological, or other developmental problems. Finally, there can be an interaction between temperament (Karen, 1994) and environmental and psychological factors that accounts for attachment difficulties. These will be discussed in detail later.

Whether a child is raised by his own biological parents or in an impersonal uncaring environment, the child will develop his or her "internal working model" of the world (Bowlby, 1969). The child will eventually formulate answers to questions like:

What kind of person am I?

What kind of world do I live in?

What can I expect when I interact with someone else?

Children deprived of a secure attachment develop a view of themselves as unlovable, of the world as cold, inconsistent, and possibly even dangerous, and expect interactions to be painful or disappointing. Ann Jernberg (1989) described the child's reaction:

Failure-to-attach children behave in ways that suggest that early in their lives they almost deliberately made these resolutions:

I will never trust anyone.
I will commit myself to no one.
I will stay safe by always keeping one foot out the door.

If I feel myself getting close to somebody and begin to feel my heart melt, I will push away from them in a hurry—really fast before that feeling gets the best of me.

I will provoke others if I have to. I will do anything I have to do just so they won't be tempted to love me (and I to love them).

These strategies were adopted in the face of abuse, abandonment, and/or exploitation. (p. 400)

The working models that these children develop of the way the world can be expected to respond can sometimes be inferred from the behavior of a failure-to-attach child. For example, when a caretaker leaves the child even for a short while, the child responds as if he thinks that the caretaker will never return. Another child might hide an accidentally broken glass for fear of severe punishment. Some children steal and hoard food and then deny it when the parent discovers it in the child's room. These behaviors in the child are difficult to understand, especially when they occur in an adoptive or foster child's new home where there is plenty of food, where the parent is sensitive to the child's fear and guilt, and where the parent always comes back. When a poorly attached child is under stress, old patterns are likely to re-emerge. The child's response is a carryover from the ways he or she learned to handle distress over the years.

Why are old patterns so persistent? Why does it take so long to change them? Part of the answer is that each individual comes to behave in predictable ways, ways that elicit a response from others. Thus, expectations tend to be confirmed. Many children prove over and over that no one cares, that no one could ever accept him or her. An example that any child therapist can understand from his or her own personal experience is how provocative a physically abused child can be toward the very adults who are trying to help.

Attachment as an Essential Ingredient in Theraplay Parent Guidance

Theraplay assumes that attachment is formed within the interaction between an engaged, empathic caretaker and his or her infant. It assumes that this interaction is not only verbal but is often a series of playful interchanges that are preverbal and intense. Thus the treatment for problems in the relationship between the parent and the child must replicate an early, healthy, playful interaction. If one is to change the child's internal models, one must present him or her with an ongoing, 24-hour-a-day positive experience. This is why parent training can be so effective in helping children with these types of problems. It is also why parents need the support of therapists. We ask them to do a very difficult and stressful job, a job that must be performed in our absence most of the time. A parent who is empathic but lacks skills is just as disadvantaged as one who has skills but lacks empathy. Theraplay parent training can help parents with either problem.

THERAPLAY VERSUS OTHER MODELS OF TREATMENT

Traditional talking therapy makes a number of assumptions that might preclude parent involvement in treatment. For example, many therapies assume that the parent played a significant role in the child's problems and must be separated from the child if the child is to get better. These theories assume that the parent will only further complicate treatment if made a part of it. They stress the importance of confidentiality because there is an assumption that the child needs to talk about something that he or she does not want the parent to know. The parents are typically left in the waiting room outside the treatment process (Axline, 1969).

Some therapies are based on a trauma theory. Here the child must re-enact a trauma or work through inner conflicts. In order to do this, the therapist must serve as a transference figure for the child and the parents have no role to play in this process. While the blame for the child's problems may not be placed on the parent, the assumption is made that the parent does not have the training, skill, nor distance necessary to achieve the results necessary.

Family therapy does include the parents in the treatment process (Haley, 1976; Minuchin, 1974). However, if there is more than one child, the family treatment process is such that focusing on one child for the purposes of attachment enhancement would not be appropriate. Family therapy primarily relies on verbal communication to attain goals and is seldom set up to engage the parent and child in a playful, physical interchange.

WHO IS INVOLVED IN THERAPLAY TREATMENT?

Theraplay treatment includes a number of players: the child, the parents, and two or more therapists. One therapist works directly with the child. A second therapist, the interpreting therapist, focuses on helping the parents understand what treatment is all about and how they should interact with their child, both in the treatment setting and at home. This second therapist is the one most actively engaged in the Parent Training aspects of Theraplay treatment and his or her role will be spelled out in the final section of this chapter: Specific Strategies for Parent Training.

THERAPISTS: QUALIFICATIONS, CHARACTERISTICS, AND TRAINING

Initially, training to become a Theraplay therapist was not restricted to persons with special qualifications for working with children. In fact,

Jernberg viewed it as one of the advantages of the technique: because it is modeled on healthy parenting responses, it could be taught to nonprofessionals. The selection of those to be trained depended more on personality characteristics than on academic qualifications. In the early days of providing Theraplay to the Chicago Head Start Program, parents of Head Start children, and young people with little formal education were trained to implement it effectively.

Jernberg's Do's and Don'ts Guidelines contain a good description of the personality characteristics she was looking for. The Theraplay therapist:

- Is confident and has leadership qualities.
- Is appealing and delightful.
- Is responsive and empathic.
- Is able to keep sessions spontaneous, flexible, and full of happy surprises.
- Is able to keep the session cheerful, optimistic, positive, and health-oriented (1979, pp. 48–49).

The Theraplay therapist must be upbeat, energetic, and empathic, and thus able to be a good role model for parents.

When Theraplay became a more established treatment modality, the requirements for certification as a Theraplay therapist became more rigorous and formalized. Candidates for training are now expected to be qualified professionals in their field, that is, to have at least a master's degree in one of the helping professions, such as social work, psychology, family therapy, or counseling. The academic requirements are meant to assure that the candidate is fully grounded in child development and in the principles of working with families. Most candidates have considerable experience working with children and families before they begin their Theraplay training.

Training in the Theraplay method includes two intensive 24-hour courses plus a year-long practicum. During the first course, the history, theory, and practice of Theraplay and the use of the Marschak Interaction Method are introduced through videotapes, observed demonstration sessions, role playing, and discussion. Work with parents is demonstrated and discussed. There is a strong emphasis on developing empathy for parents' experience dealing with their difficult children. Trainees are given an opportunity to practice playful activities that meet children's needs for Structure, Challenge, Intrusion/Engagement, and Nurture (the dimensions of Theraplay, see earlier discussion). The second 24-hour course is taken only after the candidate is well launched into the practicum.

Once a candidate has become proficient as a Theraplay therapist working directly with children, he or she then goes on to receive training as interpreting therapist with parents. Candidates are expected to take the role of interpreting therapist with several families and to develop their skills in that area.

The role of interpreting therapist is exacting. The process of parent training requires all the skills needed to work with children plus the ability to empathize, support, nurture, and structure adults. Simply giving advice will not suffice. (See section on specific strategies for parent training.)

CHILDREN: ATTACHMENT AND RELATIONSHIP PROBLEMS

Since Theraplay treatment focuses on improving relationships and enhancing attachment, the question is not what kind of child, child problem, or diagnostic category is best suited to Theraplay treatment, but rather what are the underlying relationship problems that can be effectively addressed. The Theraplay technique can be custom-tailored by the therapist to guide parents in handling a wide range of difficulties they might encounter with their children.

Many of the common diagnoses that bring children into treatment, such as school problems, the disruptive behavior disorders, and the anxiety disorders, are surface manifestations of underlying relationship problems that Theraplay is well suited to address. Attachment problems are currently receiving a great deal of attention, partly because of the growing number of angry, acting out children who are turning up in the child-care system in our country and partly because of the increase in adoptions from foreign orphanages. Diagnoses such as Reactive Attachment Disorder or labels such as Unattached or Failure-to-Attach are at the extreme end of the spectrum of the problems that Theraplay addresses.

The following is a summary of the behavior problems of Unattached or Failure-to-Attach children and of the less severe attachment disorders such as Insecure Attachment:

Problems Relating to People

These are manifested either as an inability to get close to any one person or as an indiscriminate responsiveness to many people. Sharon Gary (1995) in describing unattached children says, "Parents often feel that something is missing in [their child's] ability to give and receive love or establish a meaningful relationship." Jernberg describes them as "aloof, pseudomature, and distancing" (1989, p. 400). It follows that they often have poor peer relationships and are unable to maintain long-term friendships. Being able to relate to peers requires self-confidence, experience with give and take, and the ability to empathize with others—qualities that are often beyond the reach of the attachment-disordered child.

Problems Accepting Care from Others

This is often manifested in recklessness and accident proneness. Jernberg states, "it is not unusual to find these children covered with little scratches, bumps, and bruises" (1989, p. 400). Lieberman and Pawl (1988, p. 333) explain the recklessness as the children's attempt "to manage their uncertainty about the mother's availability as a protector by taking off on their own and courting danger. . . . " An opposite manifestation of the inability to accept care from others is a "precocious competence in self-protection" in which the child engages in self-protective behaviors usually "performed by the mother and is unusually aware of the mother's wishes and needs" (p. 334).

Problems with Change and Transitions

These children's desperate need to keep things safe and predictable (and their inability to trust that anyone will do this for them) leads them to become tyrants who insist on taking charge and calling all the shots. This need to be in control produces much of the defiant, oppositional behavior that parents encounter. The immature, explosive nature of the child's anger is also related to the attachment problems. It is in the process of becoming securely attached that a child develops the capacity to modulate the more violent expressions of emotions.

Lack of Conscience

This shows up both in cruelty to animals and to people. Other behaviors related to lack of conscience include lying, stealing, and the hoarding and gorging of food. The development of a conscience requires an awareness of others and an ability to feel empathy for them. It is through the experience of a caretaker's empathic responsiveness that children are able to develop empathy for others. The hoarding and gorging of food relates to their uncertainty that their caretakers can be trusted to provide for them.

Delayed Emotional Development

Children with attachment problems are emotionally very immature. It is therefore no surprise that their response to frustration, their awareness of others, their ability to share and to take responsibility for shared work, and so on, is like that of a younger child. The development of self-control, and of the ability to handle transitions and resist temptations is delayed.

Inhibition of Exploration

While many Failure-to-Attach children are pseudo-mature and independent, some react with clingy, immature behavior. It is as if they say to themselves, "If the world is unpredictable, then I will not try to stand on my own two feet."

In summary, it is not specific diagnostic categories that Theraplay focuses on, but rather the relationship problems that underlie a variety of behavioral problems. Such problems are seen as stemming from a range of issues subsumed under attachment. Our goal is to help parents understand the issues and to improve the quality of their relationship.

As we have defined it, a relationship or attachment problem could be seen to underlie most behavior problems. Does it follow that Theraplay should be used for all children who are brought for help? Or more specifically are there any situations where Theraplay would not be appropriate?

The most clear case is that of a traumatized child. We do not recommend that the upbeat, playful Theraplay approach be used with a child who has recently suffered a trauma, whether it be the loss of a parent, a violent war experience, a kidnapping, or physical or sexual abuse. For such children, the most urgent need is to deal with their feelings about the experience either by talking about it if they can, by acting it out with toys, or by expressing it through art.

But what about the children who were traumatized at some time in the past and whose present need is to feel better about themselves or to develop a more secure relationship with their parents before they go back to address the issue of their traumatic experiences? Or the children who are so frightened and inhibited, that they are unable to make use of the invitation to express feelings through some symbolic medium? It is less clear that such children would not benefit from some of the empathic, nurturing activities that could lead them to trust a caring, protective, and empathic adult. People experienced in working with traumatized children emphasize that part of the work involves establishing a trusting relationship with them. Before they are ready to make use of the opportunity to share their innermost fears and pain with someone else, they must first experience that person as trustworthy, caring, and empathic. Thus, at times a Theraplay approach, specially modified to meet the particular child's needs, has been found to be a helpful first step, or an approach to be used in conjunction with more traditional symbolic work.

An additional point that is often raised is the question whether a child who has been physically or sexually abused should be touched or intruded on at all. It is often argued that touch has been so painful or inappropriate for them that they would only be retraumatized by having someone move in too rapidly to touch and play with them. There is a difference between insensitive intrusion and the sensitive, but self-confident way in which a Theraplay therapist approaches a child. A cautious approach might simply reinforce the child's view that he or she is fragile, that the world is unsafe and that it is not possible to have a close physical relationship with anyone. What such children need, instead, is the reassuring experience of being touched and cared for by someone who respects their feelings and needs, yet is not afraid of being close. They need to experience good touch, good nurturing play. Parents and caretakers of children who have had bad experiences especially need to learn how to do this.

PARENT CHARACTERISTICS

What kinds of parent(s) make good candidates for training in the Theraplay approach? We have found it possible to train parent(s) from a wide variety of socioeconomic and educational backgrounds. The main requisite is that they be cooperative and motivated to help their child. Even this requirement is not always necessary. While parent(s) may come reluctantly when required by courts or childcare workers to participate in treatment, they have often been won over by the upbeat, positive Theraplay approach. The experience of seeing their child as more lovable, more appealing, and more responsive, engages the parents and helps start a more positive relationship.

Because Theraplay is based on natural, healthy responses and is aimed at a very early stage in the child's emotional development, parents do not need to be highly educated nor particularly well organized to be successful. Nor do parents have to have a great deal of skill in parenting. Parents with little experience in child rearing often turn to books for advice, but the books are not custom tailored to their children. By the time some parents come for treatment, their children's behavior has gotten so out of hand that the usual mechanisms for dealing with problems do not work. Theraplay can show these parents exactly what works and what does not work when handling their children and help them develop the parenting skills that are specifically useful with their child.

While it is a great help for a parent to have been well-parented and to have considerable ego-strength and self-confidence, it is possible for parents who are emotionally immature and needy to learn to understand and respond to their children's needs. It is essential, however, that they first have their own needs met. Such parents often benefit from having a Theraplay experience of their own, either through role playing in preparation for a session with their child or through having an individual or group experience of Theraplay directed at meeting their own needs. (See later section on Theraplay for parents.)

It is important to distinguish between the parents' current ability to respond empathically to their child and their basic parenting capacity. Many parents who come for help, particularly parents of older adopted children, appear angry and rejecting, but this may not have been their way at the beginning. The child's constant resistance and rejection of their efforts to get close leave parents hurt and angry. A parent with good basic skills may have become discouraged by a particularly unresponsive or intense child.

Empathy can be developed by building up the parent's level of confidence through support and by developing the parent's existing strengths. Role playing can also be utilized to help the parent see things from the child's point of view. Parents benefit from the support given them by a therapist who has a grasp on the big picture of the relationship and who can "hold" the parent's hand until things begin to change.

Part of treatment is an ongoing evaluation of client characteristics. Thus as the work goes on, new aspects of the child's as well as the parents' problems may surface. For example, occasionally it becomes clear that the child's mischievous, acting-out behavior amuses the parents at some unconscious level. In that case, the pattern will be pointed out to them and an attempt made to understand it and to deal with its role in perpetuating the child's difficulties. If such a confrontation does not lead to a change in the parents' behavior, there is little hope for changing the child's behavior through Theraplay. In such a case, the Theraplay sessions are ended and the parents are encouraged to seek treatment for themselves in order to explore the issues that trap them in this destructive relationship with their child.

THE COURSE OF THERAPLAY TREATMENT

Assessment Procedure

The Theraplay assessment procedure includes the following elements: an intake interview; an assessment of the child's current relationship with each parent using the Marschak Interaction Method (MIM); and a feedback session in which the initial evaluation of the problem is discussed, segments of the videotaped MIM sessions are shown to illustrate particular points, and a treatment plan is proposed. The child is not present for the intake interview or the feedback session.

The Intake Interview

The intake interview covers a range of topics but focuses especially on attachment and relationship issues. We ask about the problem as each parent sees it and how they have tried to cope with it; the child's attachment history, including the parents' dreams and expectations, the prenatal and birth experience, the child's early responsiveness, as well as losses and absences; developmental milestones; school history, behavior, achievement, and so on; current family patterns and activities; the parents' own attachment history and their current relationship with their families of origin.

The importance of learning about parents' dreams and expectations for their unborn child can be seen from the following examples:*

Mary's dreams about what her baby would be like had a powerful effect on the nature of their attachment. "I always dreamed of having a baby I could hold and rock. When Jamie came to us, he was 4 years old, but I held and rocked him anyway. Everyone said I shouldn't baby him, but I think I was right. I loved it and he loved it, too. I know it made us feel closer. Even now that he is 9, I still find that when all else fails, he will respond to my holding and rocking him." This adoptive mother's expectations stood her in good stead when faced with a difficult older adopted child.

*   *   *

In contrast, the dreams of another adoptive mother led her to overlook her daughter's need for closeness and nurture. "I dreamed of having a beautiful, intelligent daughter who could discuss literature with me." When she adopted a beautiful 3-year-old girl, her dream led her to focus her efforts on helping her child grow up, rather than on being able to get past the child's pseudomature mask to understand the needy little baby underneath.

*   *   *

A third mother who had always been active—a tomboy, a fighter—confided that she had hoped she would have a little boy with whom she could play the active games she had always enjoyed. "You know," she said, "a mother-son team." When her baby turned out to be a quiet, placid little girl, she was very disappointed. "I just couldn't get close to her. I could see that she would never be the ball-playing companion of my dreams."

The Marschak Interaction Method (MIM)

After the initial interview, the Theraplay evaluation continues using the Marschak Interaction Method (MIM), a structured observation technique designed to assess the quality and nature of the relationship between a child and each of his caretakers (Marschak, 1960, 1967; Marschak & Call, 1966). The MIM allows the therapist to see what goes on between a parent and child and to see what works and what does not work in their relationship. There is a great advantage in viewing firsthand what is taking place in the relationship rather than relying solely on the parent's subjective report. Without actually watching a mother set a limit, the therapist cannot easily determine the qualitative differences in her tone when she says "no." Even the most inexperienced child therapists viewing an MIM can make discoveries that can help formulate suggestions for a parent.

Unless the child is too young, parent and child sit side-by-side at a table on which is placed a set of cards directing them to engage in eight or nine

---

*In order to preserve confidentiality, all names and cases have been disguised.

activities. With an infant, the parent and child sit on the floor supported by pillows. Any props necessary for the task are placed in labeled containers (envelopes, boxes, etc.) near the parent.

The activities that each parent-child couple are asked to do are carefully chosen to illuminate particular aspects of their relationship. Some tasks are designed to give information about how comfortable the two are with regressive, attachment-enhancing activities, for example, "Tell child about when child was a little baby," "Rub lotion on each other," or "Feed each other." When such nurturing activities are turned into teaching tasks (for example, naming the colors of the candies or teaching the child how raisins are produced), the parent loses the opportunity to get closer to his child. Observing such an interaction, we consider that the parent needs help in this area. Other tasks are designed to assess the parent's ability to structure the situation so that the child feels safe and comfortable, for example, "Build a block structure and ask child to 'Build one just like mine.'" When the child insists that he be allowed to do it his way, or calls all the shots, we know that the family needs help. Other tasks, such as "Teach child something he or she doesn't know," assess the parents' level of expectations. If the expectations are high, can they modify them when the child has difficulty? Playful tasks alternate with those that are stressful, such as "Parent leave the room for one minute." Ambitious tasks alternate with regressive ones.

At the completion of the MIM, the therapist should be able to determine:

- The quality of the interaction.
- What it would be like to live with this child or this parent 24 hours a day.
- What works in the relationship and can be encouraged.
- What doesn't work and needs to be changed.
- What the child needs from the parent.
- What the parent needs from the child.
- How strong each is and how much each can be pushed to change.

The following are two examples of what can be seen using the MIM to observe the parent-child relationship. The first child, Sam, is an 8-year-old boy who has been living with his adoptive parents for several years. When they came for help, the parents' complaints sounded like a casebook description of the difficult behaviors of the older adopted child. In order to see how receptive Sam was to his mother's efforts to nurture him and how comfortable she was with such an activity, we chose, among others, the nurturing task, "Rub lotion on each other." Both Sam and his mother appeared to welcome what was clearly a familiar activity. The lotioning went on for several minutes as his mother gave Sam a very professional hand massage. It should have been a lovely opportunity for the two to enjoy the closeness and connectedness that would foster their attachment and comfort with each other. Yet surprisingly the whole 5-minute interaction had an impersonal air about it; there was not a word, not a bit of eye contact, no playfulness. From this single observation, it was not possible to determine who had initially set the stage for such a matter-of-fact interaction. But clearly it was a way of relating that would not lead to greater comfort and attachment. Sam and his mother needed help to get past the barriers that keep them at a distance and find ways to foster a more relaxed relationship.

Or consider the following interaction between a hypersensitive 4-year-old girl and her biological mother. From the beginning of the MIM, Tracy was angry and upset. She rejected every attempt her mother made to engage her in play with the squeaky pigs ("Each take one squeaky pig and have the two pigs play together."). Tracy pouted, cried, became bossy and demanding. Finally her mother, with only slightly disguised anger, went on to the next activity. But even then Tracy continued to resist. She pointed her finger at her mother as if she were scolding a naughty child, saying, "You never do anything right." Once again we asked ourselves, how did this situation arise? How did it happen that such a little girl should be sounding like a scolding mother and how did their relationship become so fraught with anger and recriminations? Finally, what can we do to get them back on track?

The Feedback Session

In preparation for the feedback session, we carefully analyze the MIM interaction noting both the parent's handling of the activities and the child's responses.

It is with the feedback session that parent training begins. Segments of the videotaped interaction are shown to the parents to demonstrate the patterns that have been observed. This is an opportunity to point out the positive aspects of the relationship and highlight the things the parents are already doing that work well. For example, by watching herself on videotape, a mother can see how effective it was for her to touch her child and gently redirect his out-of-control behavior. Or a father might suddenly realize how very important he is to his son as he watches how warmly he is greeted and how adoringly he is looked at when he returns to the room ("Parent leaves the room for one minute").

Sometimes children respond much more positively to one aspect of their parent's behavior than to others. For example, a child who resists her mother's usual educational or intellectual approach may be much more cooperative and responsive when her mother shifts to a more nurturing style. Seeing this difference on videotape and discussing it with the therapist has a profound effect. Being able to relate the advice to something she actually did spontaneously in the interaction makes it much more likely that she will understand that advice and be able to replicate her behavior in the future.

It is also in the feedback session that we begin to help parents understand more about their child's responses, feelings, and needs. For example, we might comment that even though his mother is very gentle as she rubs him with lotion, Timmy seems uncomfortable having it on his hands. "You have so much to offer and yet Timmy is unable to accept it because of his hypersensitivity." Or we might point out evidence of a general discomfort with anything associated with baby things. One thoughtful father speculated, "I wonder whether all that turmoil that was going on when he was a baby is still there bothering him."

During the feedback session, Theraplay is described and the goals and plan for treatment are discussed. If it is clear from the observed interaction, for example, that a child needs a lot of nurturing, the therapist will explain to the parents that the emphasis will be on nurturing activities that will meet the child's need. The expected course of treatment is outlined and the possibility of resistance and how it will be handled are spelled out. The parents are asked to predict their child's response.

At the conclusion of treatment, the MIM can be repeated as a method of evaluating progress. If videotaped, both tapes can be reviewed with the parents so they too can see how they have changed and observe the impact they have had on their child.

Sample Feedback Sessions. Betty, the 9-year-old daughter of divorced parents living with her biological father and new stepmother, was brought for treatment because among many other behavior problems, she was very hostile to her stepmother. She was also described as devious, often lying for no obvious reason. She stole, used bad language, and was extremely oppositional. "She can't get along with other kids at school. She tries to win the kids over by being the class clown."

In the MIM, it was possible to see that her clowning and smart-talk occurred whenever she was anxious. For example, when left alone, Betty acted the part of a comic TV announcer apparently unconcerned about the absence of her father. But when her Dad returned, there was a sigh of relief and a winning smile of welcome that hinted at her underlying neediness. With her stepmother, she showed in a number of subtle, easily missed ways, that she is very interested in her and that she looks to her for nurture.

In the feedback, we were able to reframe her "clowning" as covering up her pain and anxiety. "Whenever she sticks her tongue out at her stepmother, it is a sign that she is feeling anxious and uncertain how to respond. When she clowns she is saying, 'I need you to reassure me'."

The feedback begins the process of teaching parents to view their child in a more empathic, understanding manner. We point the way toward new and more effective ways of relating to their difficult child. Parents should leave the feedback session with renewed optimism that they will be able to have the relationship with their child that they have longed for.

TREATMENT

Typically, two therapists are assigned to each Theraplay case. The Theraplay therapist works with the child in the playroom while the interpreting therapist works with the parents behind a one-way mirror. It is the job of the interpreting therapist to help the parents understand what is taking place in the playroom and to prepare them for their eventual participation in the sessions. The parents watch the interaction during the first four sessions. In the remaining sessions, they enter the room for the second half of each session and begin to practice what has been found to work well with their child. The goal is that parents be able to carry on at home the Theraplay approach to their child.

Theraplay sessions are designed to follow a treatment plan that is subject to change based on the child's response to each session. Therefore the activities and therapeutic focus may differ from session to session depending on the specific needs of the child and the parents. Activities are chosen based on an assessment of the child's specific needs for Structure, Challenge, Intrusion/Engagement or Nurture. (See the discussion of Theraplay dimensions.)

Setting and Materials

The setting and materials for Theraplay are very simple. An uncluttered space with an easily cleaned floor is all that is required. Large pillows add to the comfort. A one-way mirror makes parent observation easiest, but lacking that, parents can sit in the room itself to observe. Because the Theraplay activities are so engaging, their presence causes little distraction. A video camera to record sessions is helpful. The design of the playroom matches the philosophy of treatment which focuses on the interaction and engagement between child and adult, considers the adult to be the primary playroom object, believes that healthy play can be regressive, and places the adult in charge of the action.

For each session, the therapist has available only the few simple materials needed for preselected activities. By focusing attention away from playroom props, the Theraplay therapist encourages personal interaction. This is especially important for insecurely attached or unattached children who often prefer to play with a toy than with another person.

Frequency and Duration of Treatment

An initial contract with a family usually consists of from 10 to 16 Theraplay sessions following the Intake Interview and MIM evaluation and feedback. Additional sessions may be scheduled by mutual agreement between parents and therapists.

Theraplay sessions usually take place once a week unless there is urgent need for more frequency or unless special circumstances, such as summer vacations, intervene to slow them down. We have found that a concentrated series of sessions over a few days or a week can produce a great change. However, not all families are in a position to schedule such a period of intense treatment.

Theraplay sessions are one-half hour in length and are very concentrated. Each session is preplanned to utilize every minute. Because the Theraplay therapist is providing most of the structure and is conducting the session with the belief that he or she will give to, not receive from, the child, the work is very demanding.

Treatment Stages

Typically Theraplay has six stages (see Jernberg, 1979, pp. 36–42):

Introduction. The Theraplay therapist signals that Theraplay will be active and fun, that he or she will be in charge, that there will be a clear definition of therapist and child roles and that there will be a clear structure as to time and space. This introduction begins in the waiting room and carries through the first session.

Exploration. The therapist and child get to know one another. The therapist notices the child's physical characteristics: how many freckles he has, how strong she is, how soft his skin is, how many toes she has. The therapist signals to the child that she is lovable and fun to be with.

Tentative Acceptance. This is often a beguiling phase, encouraging the therapist to breathe a sigh of relief that the child is so accepting of this new relationship and new way of interacting. Involvement may seem genuine, but is often superficial with an underlying layer of apprehension. As in the "honeymoon phase" for newly adopted children, the child's goal is to keep the therapist at bay. The therapist responds by remaining engaging, appealing and fun.

Negative Reaction. The child puts up clear resistance against intimacy. This may take the form of passive, "floppy" resistance, withdrawal, verbal threats ("I'm going to shut down your business"), or physical violence. Here the child makes use of all those defensive patterns that have been seen at home and at school. Parents often express relief when their child reaches this stage, "Finally, someone else is seeing what we go through all the time." The negative phase may last one or several sessions.

When this phase is ending, the child will become "softer;" he may relax marginally; eye contact, though fleeting, may be established; laughter and delight in an activity may slip out unintended.

Growing and Trusting.   Here, ". . . the child first experiences the pleasure of interacting with another human being in a 'normal,' reciprocally satisfying way" (Jernberg, 1979, p. 39). This is the time when much therapeutic work is accomplished. Longer periods of intimacy occur between therapist and child; reciprocal play begins; eye contact improves; in short, there is a feeling of a true partnership between therapist and child. At this point, parents or other important caregivers are introduced into the sessions so that they may begin to practice their Theraplay skills.

Termination.   This phase consists of three parts: preparation, announcement, and the final session.

PREPARATION.   When the child is able to transfer positive session behaviors into nonsession settings, and when the parents show their readiness to carry on at home, it is time to consider the conclusion of treatment. Although Theraplay is short-term in nature, and therefore transference may be less intense, termination should be well planned. Since the initial treatment plan was for a limited number of sessions, in one sense termination is anticipated from the start. However, because of the many unknowns that confront any therapist treating a child, the actual date of termination is not set until it is appropriate to do so. The therapists and parents will then agree on a termination date based not only on improvement but also on potential improvement. The expectation is that the treatment will continue with the parents as therapists, after formal Theraplay sessions have ended. To monitor the process, follow-up, or check-up sessions are scheduled at monthly intervals for one year.

ANNOUNCEMENT.   Children need warning that the special relationship they have enjoyed with the therapist is about to come to an end. The announcement is made in the context of the gains the family has made. For example, "You and your Mom and Dad are having so much fun together these days that you won't be needing to see me much longer. We'll have three more sessions together. Our final session will be a farewell party." The process of directing the child's attachment away from the therapist toward his parents that began when the parents were first brought into the sessions is accelerated at this point by having them take more and more control of the activities. Emotional reactions to termination are labeled, but not explored.

FINAL SESSION.   The final session is a party, with parents and therapists joining in the fun. The child's favorite Theraplay activities are repeated, his favorite foods are there to be eaten, and some permanent reminder of their time together is given to the child by his therapist. Sometimes a T-shirt is decorated with hand prints of everyone who has been involved in the sessions and is sent home for the child to keep. Jernberg says, "The theme of the party is a future-oriented reaffirmation of the child's [and his parents'] strengths and identity" (1979, p. 42). The child is going home with parents who are trained to be his or her full-time Theraplay therapists.

SPECIFIC STRATEGIES FOR PARENT TRAINING

Training parents to become Theraplay therapists for their children is a multifaceted operation which includes (a) a sequence of steps leading to parents' competence in using the Theraplay approach; (b) giving parents a more positive, empathic view of their child; (c) teaching parents about developmental issues and behavior management; and finally (d) meeting parents' unmet needs so that these needs will not interfere with their successful implementation of what they have learned. While some of the work is done in special sessions without the child, for example, when a parent plans and role-plays a Theraplay session in preparation for taking charge, the rest of the work is spread out over all the contacts we have with parents. Examples of each step in the Theraplay process will be discussed to clarify how these aspects of parent training are addressed.

STEPS LEADING TO COMPETENCE IN THE THERAPLAY APPROACH

The goal of parent training is to help parents become more competent as parents and to strengthen their relationship with their child. In order to accomplish this goal there is a sequence of steps including preparation and practice leading to the parent's taking full responsibility for the actual give and take of the interaction with their child.

Discussion

We begin our work (as has been noted in our section on the feedback session) by talking about our view of the child and of his needs and by explaining to parents what we will be trying to accomplish. Behind the one-way mirror, parents have an opportunity to see their child interacting with the Theraplay therapist. The interpreting therapist explains what is going on and encourages parents to ask questions about what they see and to watch how the Theraplay therapist handles whatever problem behaviors the child presents.

During Sam's first Theraplay session, the interpreting therapist pointed out to his parents how much Sam seemed to enjoy his Theraplay therapist's playful, nurturing attention, but how quick he was to take advantage of any pause in the action to take charge. "In all those years when he couldn't count on anyone's being there for him, he has formed a very strong pattern. It will take a lot of experience before he can overcome his expectation that it's up to him to make things happen. And since he has such a lot of good ideas, it will be hard for you to remember how important it is that the adult stay in charge. Watch how his therapist handles it. Sometimes she ignores it, sometimes she says, 'You have great ideas. We'll do that sometime later, but right now I want to do this with you.'"

The first sessions with Tracy posed a different problem for her parents to understand. From the very beginning, she showed her typical pattern of angry resistance to any effort to engage her. Because it was so typical, her parents were not surprised that it showed up immediately, but they needed help to understand the therapist's approach which was so different from their own pattern of alternate placating and angry withdrawal. "Watch how her therapist stays with her and continues to try to engage her," the interpreting therapist said. When Tracy suddenly stopped her angry protest and asked, "What's your name?" the interpreting therapist pointed out, "She has finally become aware that her therapist is not going to leave and she wants to know more about her." And again as the pattern of Tracy's way of controlling the situation became clear, "She works so hard. She uses all her very considerable verbal skills to stay in charge. We need to find ways to relieve her of that burden."

During the early sessions, the interpreting therapist prepares parents for the inevitable negative reaction. Unlike Tracy, most children have a honeymoon phase (see Treatment Stages above) before testing the new relationship. During this phase, it is important to prepare parents for the change that is to come. They are told that the negative reaction is important because it signals their child's beginning hope and trust that an adult will be able to stay with him even when he shows his worst side. Having the therapist, and later his parents, stay with him, calmly contain his violent behavior and not retaliate and reject him is a powerful experience (which may need to be tested many times). Following such outbursts, children often relax into the therapist's (or parents') arms for comfort as if, for the first time, they feel that someone can truly share their feelings and comfort them.

Parents are told, "This is a very important part of treatment because it signals that your child is beginning to hope that an adult can respond to the anxiety he feels when someone gets really close." Such an explanation made sense to Sam's adoptive parents because they knew his history of being rejected again and again by a series of foster parents who had inadvertently confirmed his worst fears by giving him up when he became "impossible to handle."

From the start of his fourth session, Sam began an active angry resistance that lasted for 20 minutes. He tried to hit, bite, and get away. When his therapist held him firmly and calmly reassured him, "I won't let you hurt me and I won't hurt you. I know you're mad at me! I know you don't want to be held, but I'm staying with you till you feel better." When Sam found he couldn't hit or bite his therapist, he shouted angry insults, "Let me go, you b—! I'll call the DCFS worker and tell her you abused me. You can't get away with this!" But his therapist remained calm and in control. After 20 exhausting minutes, Sam relaxed, sobbing into her arms and remained there until the end of the session. Because his parents had been prepared for this eventuality, they were able to watch the scene without too much anxiety. But they sighed with relief when it was over. "He looks so young, so vulnerable, so relaxed. We never knew it would be possible to reach him like this. On the way here he said he was going to fight her! We didn't know what he meant then, but we see now. He was thinking about her and planning this all week. It must have been very important to him." The next session once again started with a "fight," which was no surprise for Sam's parents. This time he relaxed after 10 minutes, and again snuggled into his therapist's arms for comfort. His parents reported that they had handled a temper tantrum at home in the same way as his therapist handled it in session. "We couldn't believe how much it would change our relationship. He was soft and relaxed and available for hours after it was all over. He was right there with us. It feels as if we have the key to how to help him."

For Tracy's parents who had always been there, it was more difficult to understand where her angry resistance came from. The interpreting therapist explained that because of Tracy's hypersensitivity to all kinds of stimulation, it had never been easy to soothe her. No one—not her parents, not her babysitter when mother went back to work shortly after she was born—had been able to soothe and comfort her in the way she needed. So she had grown up trusting only herself. No wonder she raged when anyone tried to take over or enter her carefully controlled world. Her parents were reassured that many children like Tracy throw tantrums and must be held until they feel better. "Don't feel embarrassed by Tracy's angry outbursts. See how she is beginning to take her therapist's presence into account. Soon she will no longer need to protest and will be able to enter into the fun." And in fact, Tracy, who was seen for a series of five sessions within one week, made a remarkable turn around. By the third session, she was laughing and playing with her therapist. By the final session, she was sitting comfortably in her mother's arms, enjoying being rocked and cuddled like the small child she really was inside.

Thus, the discussions behind the one-way mirror help parents understand the child's behavior and the reasons behind the Theraplay therapist's responses to it. Such discussions appeal primarily to the parent's cognitive understanding (though it is clear from the example of Sam, that parents often put that understanding into practice at home). Throughout Theraplay treatment, the interpreting therapist will continue to discuss and interpret the child's feelings and behavior; however, we do not depend on discussion alone to effect change.

Modeling

As parents watch the Theraplay therapist with their child from behind the one-way mirror, they see new possibilities for how they might interact with their child. Watching a Theraplay therapist count the freckles, find and take care of hurts, and rub lotion on the hands and feet of her 6-year-old son, one mother said, "Oh, I can see how much he needs this. I wish I had done it a lot more. I think I'll do it tonight before he goes to bed." Another parent noting the way her depressed daughter brightened up in the presence of her lively, energetic Theraplay therapist said, "I see that she really responds when someone is more energetic. It's not my style, but I'm going to try to be more like that."

Guided Practice

After observing three or four sessions (see Stages in Treatment), the parents enter the Theraplay room and join in the fun under the guidance of the Theraplay therapist. This is a step that must be carefully prepared for. The parents must understand that their entrance into the sessions may produce resistance and regression on the part of their child. If parents are not prepared ahead of time, they may think that they have done something wrong or be reinforced in their fears that their child doesn't like them. If they know that this is a very common response, they are better able to handle it. We explain that there are at least two reasons for such a reaction. First, children find it difficult to accept any intrusion into the relationship that is developing between themselves and the Theraplay therapist. Rather than seeing it as adding more people to their safe world, they fear it will be a loss. Second, they need to go back and test their parents just as they tested their therapist to see whether the parents can be as responsive, firm, and reliable as the Theraplay therapist is proving to be.

To help the child accept their parents' entry into the sessions, the Theraplay therapist plans activities that turn it into a game. For example, the therapist and the child may hide under pillows or a blanket and call to the parents to find them. Behind the mirror, the interpreting therapist coaches the parents to talk about the wonderful boy they are hoping to find and to respond with joy when they find him. If the child is young and restless, they will be told, "Don't make it too long before you find him. He really can't wait." With this preparation, the reunion between child and parents is joyful and leads easily to the activities which follow.

Another approach is to hide something on the child. Sometimes it is food which the parents can find and feed to their child. Sometimes it is notes that tell each parent what activities to do, for example, "Play a game of Thumb Wrestling with John" or "Give Susan a butterfly kiss."

Homework

As soon as we see that the parents are comfortable with the idea, we ask them to practice at home some of the activities that have worked well in Theraplay sessions. The mother described above who at the first session spontaneously said she would try some of the nurturing activities with her son, was clearly ready. Other parents may need to wait for awhile. But all parents need to practice at some time. At the next session, we ask how the homework went. If there were problems, we help the parents modify their approach so that it will work out better next time.

When making a homework assignment, we help parents plan carefully so that the practice will go well. "When is the best time to schedule such activities? Is there a time when you could set aside 20 minutes regularly to do these things?" And we have to prepare them for the fact that children are not always as responsive to their parents at home as they have become with their Theraplay therapist. This is almost always the case with foster and adopted children, particularly when their new mother attempts to do nurturing activities. Children who have been disappointed over and over by unavailable mothers have their greatest conflicts with the new mother who is trying to nurture them. So they test her sincerity and find it hard to accept what she has to offer.

Because a child often resists the first attempts by the parent to offer regressive nurturing (i.e., having lotion rubbed on their feet or being fed from a bottle), we suggest that parents start out with playful, challenging activities before they try quieter nurturing activities. Especially in the case of older adopted children, the Theraplay therapist makes sure that the child is comfortable with being fed and rocked, before having the mother hold the child. Only after the child is comfortable with such intimacy in the session, do we suggest that a parent add these intimate nurturing activities at home.

Playing the Adult Role

In preparation for the parents' taking a more active leading role, the Theraplay therapist and the interpreting therapist meet with parents separately to plan and role play the activities that will take place during the next session. While not all parents need this step, it is a powerful tool which we often use. Toward the end of treatment, such role playing will be geared to the parents' taking full charge of the upcoming session with the child.

Role playing serves two purposes: the obvious one of preparing parents for taking charge of sessions as well as for carrying on the Theraplay approach at home; and a more subtle one of giving them insight into how the child might feel while engaged in such activities. We will address this aspect in more detail later when we talk about helping parents achieve a more empathic view of their children.

Sample Role-Playing Session.   The following is an account of a role-playing session with a single parent who was seeking to regain custody of her 3-year-old daughter. Jane had worked very hard to meet the requirements that her DCFS worker and the courts had set up to assure that she could handle the care of her child. She had attended parenting classes, found work, arranged for an apartment, and been consistently available for all supervised visits with her little girl. But the DCFS worker felt that Jane needed more help to meet her daughter's needs for nurture and empathic responsiveness. She was, therefore, referred for an MIM and a series of eight Theraplay sessions with her child. The MIM confirmed the worker's judgment. While Jane obviously cared about her daughter, her way of showing it was through teaching. Instead of using the Feeding Task ("Feed each other.") as a way of getting close, she asked Sara to name the colors of the candy pieces and to count them. When asked why teaching was so important to her, she said, "Sara needs to know a lot if she is going to be able to get along in the world. She has had to be in so many foster homes." We felt that she and Sara would benefit from the opportunity to shift the focus of their interactions. Initially, Jane was outspoken about her frustration at what seemed to her just another roadblock in the way of getting her daughter back. "I know how to take care of her. I took care of her all the time when she was a baby. I raised all my brothers and sisters. I don't need this." But as she watched the Theraplay therapist taking good care of Sara and having fun with her, she became excited. "I could do that. My mother never played with us kids like that, but I can see that Sara really likes it." Jane entered into the sessions as a willing and eager participant.

In preparation for Jane to take charge of the seventh session, we scheduled a planning and role-playing session. Jane outlined the activities she would like to lead: paper-punch, thumb wrestling, lotion hand-prints, and so on. First Jane played the role of Sara, experiencing what it would be like for Sara to participate in such activities. She was very perceptive in her comments. "That feels good. I really like it when you put the lotion on my hands. And I can't believe how interesting it is to see my own hand-prints there on the paper." She also was able to act out some of Sara's resistance and to experience how it might feel to have a calm, but firm response from an adult.

Next Jane shifted to the role of therapist with the interpreting therapist playing the role of Sara. While Jane had a clear idea of what she wanted to do, she needed help to keep her focus on her child and to move quickly enough to stay in charge. As she played out how she would check her daughter's strong muscles before having her punch the newspaper, her eyes wandered to the other side of the room. The interpreting therapist commented, "Could you look right at her when you do that? You have such lovely warm eyes, and she would feel so much better if she could see them." When she moved slowly to introduce the next activity, the interpreting therapist, playing Sara, slipped away. Jane said, "Oh, I see that I have to move faster or I'll lose her." And thus the practice session went on, smoothing out the rough edges of her approach, preparing her to be responsive and to take charge when actually faced with her little girl.

In the process, Jane developed a stronger sense of her own powers and benefited, in her role as child, from the experience of being cared for by another adult, something she had missed out on when as a child she had to grow up quickly to take care of her younger siblings.

Taking Charge

The parent takes charge of the session with a Theraplay therapist in a supporting role. Following the preparatory role-playing session, Jane was able to take full charge of the session with Sara, having the Theraplay and interpreting therapists there as a cheering section.

GIVING PARENTS A MORE POSITIVE, EMPATHIC VIEW OF THEIR CHILD

Throughout the treatment process, beginning with the feedback to the MIM, the focus is on helping parents understand and appreciate their child. This is done in a variety of ways including (a) their observation of the Theraplay therapist's positive approach to their child, (b) through explicit guided observations, (c) through interpretation of child behaviors that parents describe as having taken place at home during the week, and (d) through taking the child's part in role playing.

Observing the Theraplay Therapist with Their Child

As they watch the Theraplay therapist with their child and notice the way the child is valued and respected, parents begin to see their child as more lovable, attractive, and appealing.

One mother, as she first observed her teenage daughter in session with her Theraplay therapist, commented, "Oh, I hate how she looks. She is so dirty and messy. I think she deliberately dresses like that to annoy me." By the fourth session, the mother said thoughtfully, "What has happened? She is so beautiful. I never noticed that before."

As they watch the Theraplay session, parents have the opportunity, free of the stress and preoccupations of everyday living, to begin to put themselves in their child's shoes. Such empathic intuiting of their child's feelings is a common experience for a new mother with her healthy baby, but has often been lost by the time a family comes for help. In order to increase the parents' empathy for their child's experience and feelings, the interpreting therapist might ask, "How do you think she's feeling right now?" or, "Notice how he smiles and relaxes when his therapist does that."

Some parents recognize how much the child is enjoying an activity, but scorn it, resent it, or say that the child is just manipulating. "He'll lap it up all right. He can behave when you're paying attention to him all the time. It's when I can't be with him that he gets into trouble." Thus at first some parents see the child only as "selfish," or manipulative, as perhaps not even deserving all this special attention. "But remember," the therapist says, "does a little baby have to earn the special attention that makes him feel so good? We are trying to fill your child up with good feelings which he can hold on to when he doesn't have you right with him."

John's parents understood this after only two sessions. John, a 6-year-old adopted boy, had once again "gotten into trouble" at school. Left alone in his classroom while the teacher attended to another child, John had taken the glue bottle from his teacher's desk and rubbed it all over himself. From the teacher's point of view—shared by his parents until just two weeks before—John had done another of his inexplicable, annoying behaviors. Now his mother said, "I understood it. With the teacher out of the room, he needed something to help hold himself together. What better choice than glue! It must have reminded him of the lotion his Theraplay therapist comforts him with." The consequence of this new understanding, was that John was not "blamed" and told he was naughty. Instead, his parents were able to tell the teacher that it is very difficult for John to maintain self-control when his teacher is out of the room. Together they made a plan so that John could be given something to steady himself whenever his teacher had to leave.

Another parent confusing her own feelings with her child's says, "He hates it. He can't stand to be touched or to have lotion put on him." The interpreting therapist responds, "Yes, that is what he is saying with his words, 'That's baby stuff.' But look closely. Is he really resisting? Would he cuddle in like that if he were totally rejecting of the closeness?"

Sometimes it is possible to give parents a more empathic understanding of their child's past behavior. For example, John's parents reported that when he first came to live with them, he would often stand silently by something he wanted rather than ask for it. In an effort to help John become more grown-up, his parents had refused to respond to his helpless silence and had insisted that he use words to let them know what he wanted. As an infant, John had never experienced the empathic, attuned responsiveness that is so important early in life. No one had been around to "read his mind." What he needed most from his new adoptive parents was that they be able to intuit his needs. This was a hard lesson for his achievement-oriented parents to keep in mind. Later when John came home exhausted from a soccer game, he was unable to tell his parents that he needed to go right to bed rather than do his homework and chores. His parents, forgetting for the moment their new understanding of his needs, felt that he ought to be able to say he was tired rather than have a temper tantrum. The conversation with their interpreting therapist went like this: "Think what a toddler would be able to do. He couldn't tell you. It would be up to you to figure it out and if you weren't able to, he would have a tantrum." "But John is not a toddler, he's 6-years-old!" "Yes, but when he's exhausted, he regresses. He can't hold it together as a 6-year-old might be able to do. At those moments, he is more like a toddler. And besides this is a wonderful opportunity for you to do the kinds of empathic caretaking that will add one more brick to the structure of his new self-esteem, and his trust that you really care and will take care of him."

Playing the Child's Role

As noted earlier, some role playing is designed primarily to teach the parent to take the therapist's role, but a second and equally important reason for the role playing is that it gives the parent an opportunity to experience what it feels like to be the child. The role playing is set up so that the parent has the opportunity to act the child's role. Often the scene enacted is some difficult behavior that the parents have asked for help in handling. The parents describe how they handled it, and the Theraplay therapist first plays the scene taking the parent's role, following the parent's script. Next, the Theraplay therapist will try a Theraplay approach to the situation. The parent is thus able to experience how each approach feels. She learns what it feels like to be held when she is upset, for example, to be stopped from doing dangerous things, or to be cuddled and comforted. Such experiences lead to increased empathy for their child's feelings. For example, one parent playing the role of his hyperactive, aggressive son, sighed with relief when the Theraplay therapist held him firmly until he relaxed. "What a relief that you finally stopped me. I felt totally out of control and really afraid that you wouldn't be able to stop me before I did something dangerous. Can that be how Tim feels? Does he wish I would stop him?"

TEACHING PARENTS ABOUT DEVELOPMENTAL ISSUES AND HOW TO MANAGE BEHAVIOR PROBLEMS

This didactic aspect of our work is common to many approaches to working with parents and children but gains added significance from parents having the opportunity to interact directly with their child and to put into practice, under the guidance of the Theraplay therapists, the information which they have been given.

Teaching Appropriate Developmental Expectations

Parents of children with attachment problems need to understand that while their child may function physically and cognitively at age level or above, they are emotionally much less mature. It is their emotional immaturity and neediness that causes so many problems. Parents of older adopted children need especially to be aware of this fact.

With an older adopted child, the issue of how well both she and her parents can handle regressive, nurturing activities is extremely important. These children who have learned that the only way to count on anything is to count on yourself, often resist the regressive, nurturing activities that are so important to establishing a secure attachment between infant and parents and so crucial in the later bonding and attachment of an older child. The child's pseudo-mature and take-charge behavior often diverts parents away from offering the kind of cuddling, holding, soothing, and caretaking that such children need. Adoptive parents often are pleased by their child's mature behavior because it assures them that he or she is making progress. Thus, there are factors on both sides, the child's and the parents', which prevent a response to the child's regressive needs. But this makes it difficult to address the child's need to develop the confidence and trust in others that will allow her to give up her desperate need to maintain control. It is through the many experiences of having her needs met by an empathic, responsive caretaker that a small child learns that her parents can be trusted to keep her safe.

In order to understand how a particular family is negotiating these issues, we look, in the MIM, at activities such as "Rub lotion on each other," "Tell child about when she first came to live with you," "Comb each other's hair," and "Feed each other." Sometimes it is clear that the parents would be happy to be more nurturing while the child resists it heartily. "That's too babyish," he may say, or "I'll put it on you instead." Sometimes the parents, too, find it difficult to be nurturing with such a large child. "What if she just stays a regressed little baby? Isn't that the way she was when she came to us? Her being more independent now seems like progress." In the feedback to such parents we say, "Look at how much she resists giving in to being taken care of. We will be working to help her feel more comfortable with that. In our experience, once a child feels truly comfortable and secure, they are very ready to move ahead."

Teaching the Concept of Internal Working Models

In order to help parents understand the importance of the playful, often regressive interactions which they see the Theraplay therapist engage in with their child we introduce them to the idea that children build up inner representations of themselves, of the world, and how others will respond to them, through the many interactions they have with others. We introduce the idea that they can understand their child's difficult behavior by understanding how he is feeling about himself, about the world and about what kinds of interactions he can expect. As they watch, we ask, "How do you think it makes him feel about himself?" "We want her to feel special, and well cared for. We want him to learn that he doesn't have to be in charge in order to get his needs met. The more he believes that, the more he will be able to relax."

With the parents of a foster child who was neglected and abused, we speculated about the view of himself and of the world that he must have built up during those early years of abandonment and neglect. "He could only believe that he was unworthy and unlovable and that adults were unresponsive and neglectful. His insistence that everything be under his control, on calling all the shots, is the only logical outcome (other than despair and giving up) of such a view of himself and of the world."

Parents are introduced to the idea that it is possible to change the child's internal working models, possible to go back and recreate the conditions under which the infant in a stable, responsive family learns to feel secure, learns to trust, and develops a strong and positive self-concept. As they watch the Theraplay therapist working with their child, they see how it is possible to do this for their own child. As soon as they are ready, they are encouraged to do the same things at home.

Every opportunity that their child offers (difficult behavior, infantile behavior, angry behavior) is a special opportunity to focus on their child's regressive needs, to recreate the kinds of interactions that foster trust and a sense of the caring, soothing presence of adults. Rather than hoping that the children will be on their best behavior, as most parents do most of the time, we welcome the misbehavior that these children show as providing the crucial opportunities for working on their underlying issues.

Consulting about Behavior Problems

The advice we give to parents about how to handle their child's difficult behavior at home is based on the Theraplay principles of clear structure with the parents being in charge, consistent follow-through, and empathic understanding of the meaning of the child's difficult behavior. Many problems become much easier to handle or disappear when the child feels understood, nurtured, and valued.

Behind the one-way mirror, the interpreting therapist asks parents how things have gone during the week. Frequently a parent will describe some difficult interaction that took place at home. Children with attachment problems often have difficulty at times of transition. One mother of a "spirited," hypersensitive, adopted 6-year-old girl complained that it is always a struggle getting her daughter ready to go to school. "Judy always creates a scene. Her clothes are too tight, her socks have lumps in them, and she can't bear to wear the gym shoes she has to have today. Nothing is right and nothing I do seems to help. The only thing that ends it is when we both get angry and she goes off to school leaving both of us feeling bad." The interpreting therapist says, "Let's think about what is going on with Judy at moments like that. How do you think she was feeling about herself? How does she feel about leaving you? What do separations mean to her? Abandonment, loneliness, pain, emptiness. Her complaints keep you with her and delay the separation. And finally they create angry feelings which make it easier at the moment for her to leave you. Those angry feelings don't help in the long run though, so we need to find a way to help her get off to school without such a difficult time." And together we work out a way for Judy's mother to get her daughter dressed in a playful, nurturing way that will leave Judy feeling more secure and better able to go off to school.

MEETING PARENTS' UNMET NEEDS

Just as the Theraplay therapist makes children feel good about themselves by being appreciative and empathically responsive, so the interpreting therapist responds to the parents. Many parents find the task of being a positive, empathic parent extremely difficult because they have not been parented in a positive, empathic manner themselves. It is essential in working with such parents to meet their needs before we can ask them to attend to the needs of their children.

Parent Support

A major component of Theraplay treatment is parent support. It is this support that makes Theraplay so effective with Failure-to-Attach children who give very little back to their parents. All parents need support, understanding, and empathy for what they are facing with their difficult child. Thus the interpreting therapist is on the alert to be empathically accepting of parents' feelings and needs. While empathy and acceptance can go a long way toward relieving an overburdened parent, often they need more than that. When this is the case, the interpreting therapist will help them find supports in the community. For example, parents of a difficult child diagnosed Pervasive Developmental Disorder or Autistic may need information about respite care.

Theraplay for Parents

Sometimes parents have had so little good parenting themselves, that they find it impossible to give to their children the nurturing and positive attention which Theraplay involves. In these cases, we offer parents the opportunity to have some Theraplay sessions for themselves. While this can be done partially through the role playing described above, which is designed to help them take charge of sessions by themselves, or to help them understand how their child feels, sometimes it is important to have the sessions designed exclusively to meet the parent's needs. Such sessions are very much like the Theraplay sessions with their children. The parent is able to experience being taken care of, being nurtured, played with, and valued just as he or she has seen his or her child cared for.

Another way of meeting parents needs is through Theraplay parent groups. For example, a group of Head Start parents met weekly for eight Theraplay group sessions. They understood that they would have the Theraplay experience in the group as preparation for sessions with their children. The group's response to the sessions followed the pattern of tentative acceptance, resistance, and final relaxation and acceptance that is typical of both individual and group Theraplay work. When the eight sessions were completed, the parents brought their children for an additional eight sessions during which they spent half the session in one-on-one Theraplay activities with their child and then joined the whole group for activities which included both child and parents. This format was very successful in helping needy parents respond and give to their children.

Dealing with Parent Issues

Sometimes it is possible to respond to the parents' marital or individual issues as part of the discussion behind the one-way mirror. A pattern developed by Evangeline Munns in her work at Blue Hills in Canada provides a more extended opportunity for family work following the Theraplay session. One Theraplay therapist takes the child (or children when there are more than one) into another playroom while the interpreting therapist and a second Theraplay therapist meet with the parents. During such sessions, it is possible to help parents resolve conflicts over parenting styles and to address marital issues that interfere with the successful parenting of their children.

Refer for Individual or Marital Work

Sometimes parents' issues and conflicts are so serious that they need to be attended to separate from the Theraplay sessions. They are then referred for individual or marital work on their own. Such work may take place concurrently with the Theraplay sessions, or it can take place after Theraplay is completed.

SUMMARY

Some children have experienced problems so severe that they are inhibited from the natural process of forming a healthy relationship with another person. These Failure-to-Attach children are best treated by establishing a healthy relationship with parents, their most logical and immediate objects of attachment. The Theraplay model keeps the family together from the outset and utilizes methods that help children and parents experience the pleasure that comes from interacting with each other. During the early, more difficult process of treatment, the Theraplay therapist is available and skilled in providing parents with support and training. The therapist serves as a model-parent, thus ensuring that parents of Failure-to-Attach children know, firsthand, what it feels like to be taken care of. As the parents develop increased skill and empathy, they become more available to their children and understanding of their needs. These children develop a relationship with their parents that will sustain them throughout their lives.

REFERENCES

Ainsworth, M. (1969). Object relations, dependency and attachment: A theoretical review of the infant-mother relationship. *Child Development, 40*, 969–1025.

Armsden, G. C., & Greenberg, M. T. (1987). The inventory of parent and peer attachment: Individual differences and their relationship to psychological well being in adolescence. *Journal of Youth and Adolescence, 16*, 427–453.

Axline, V. (1969). *Play therapy.* New York: Ballantine Books.

Barnett, C. R., Leiderman, P. H., Grobstein, R., & Klaus, M. H. (1970). Neonatal separation: The maternal side of interactional deprivation. *Pediatrics, 45*, 197.

Bowlby, J. (1969). *Attachment and loss: Vol. 1. Attachment.* London: Hogarth Press.

Brody, V. (1978). Developmental play: A relationship-focused program for children. *Journal of Child Welfare, 57*(9), 591–599.

Brody, V. (1993). *The dialogue of touch: Developmental play therapy.* Treasure Island, FL: Developmental Play Training Associates.

Condon, W. S., & Sander, C. W. (1974). Neonate movement is synchronized with adult speech: Interactional participation and language acquisition. *Science, 183,* 99.

Des Lauriers, A. (1962). *The experience of reality in childhood schizophrenia.* New York: International Universities Press.

Des Lauriers, A., & Carlson, C. F. (1969). *Your child is asleep: Early infantile autism.* Homewood, IL: Dorsey Press.

Gary, S. D. (1995). *Symptoms of unattached children.* Unpublished handout, Psychological Services, Memphis, TN.

Haley, J. (1976). *Problem solving therapy.* San Francisco: Jossey-Bass.

Jernberg, A. (1979). *Theraplay: A new treatment using structured play for problem children and their families.* San Francisco: Jossey-Bass.

Jernberg, A. (1989). Training parents of failure-to-attach children. In C. E. Schaefer & J. Briesmeister (Eds.), *Handbook of parent training: Parents as co-therapists for children* (pp. 392–413). New York: Wiley.

Jernberg, A. (1993). Attachment formation. In C. E. Schaefer (Ed.), *The therapeutic powers of play* (pp. 241–265). Northvale, NJ: Jason Aronson.

Jernberg, A., Booth, P., Koller, T., & Allert, A. (1983). *Reciprocity in parent-infant relationships.* Chicago: The Theraplay Institute.

Karen, R. (1994). *Becoming attached: Unfolding the mystery of the infant-mother bond and its impact on later life.* New York: Warner Books.

Klaus, M. J., & Kennell, J. H. (1976). *Maternal-infant bonding.* St. Louis, MO: Mosby.

Koller, T. J. (1994). Adolescent theraplay. In K. J. O'Connor & C. E. Schaefer (Eds.), *Handbook of play therapy: Vol. 2. Advances and innovations* (pp. 169–172). New York: Wiley.

Lewis, M., & Lee-Painter, S. (1974). An interactional approach to the mother-infant dyad. In M. Lewis & L. A. Rosenblum (Eds.), *The effect of the infant on its caregiver* (pp. 21–48). New York: Wiley.

Lieberman, A., & Pawl, J. (1988). Clinical applications of attachment theory. In J. Belsky & T. Nezworski (Eds.), *Clinical implications of attachment* (pp. 327–351). Hillsdale, NJ: Lawrence Erlbaum.

Marschak, M. (1960). A method for evaluating child-parent interaction under controlled conditions. *Journal of Genetic Psychology, 97,* 3–22.

Marschak, M. (1967). Imitation and participation in normal and disturbed young boys in interaction with their parents. *Journal of Clinical Psychology, 23*(4), 421–427.

Marschak, M., & Call, J. (1966). Observing the disturbed child and his parents: Class demonstration of medical students. *Journal of the American Academy of Child Psychiatry, 5,* 686–692.

Minuchin, S. (1974). *Families and family therapy.* Cambridge, MA: Harvard University Press.

Spitz, R. (1945). Hospitalism: An inquiry into the genesis of psychiatric conditions in early childhood. *Psychoanalytic Study of the Child, 1,* 53–74.

Spitz, R. (1947). *Grief: A peril in infancy* [Film]. University Park, PA: Penn State Audio Visual Services.

Stern, D. (1985). *The interpersonal world of the infant: A view from psychoanalysis and developmental psychology.* New York: Basic Books.

PART FOUR

OTHER CHILDHOOD DISORDERS

In Chapter 11, Wolfson discusses developmental changes in the sleep/ wake cycle of toddlers and preschool youngsters and the ways in which parent training strategies can prevent difficulties with sleep onset and night wakings. She notes that the rules for defining adult sleep stages cannot be applied to young children because there is a wide range of normal infant and childhood sleep. Also, infant sleep is not as clearly demarcated as that of adults. Indeed, night wakings are an important aspect of infant/toddler sleep development. Researchers attempt to determine when these wakings might be considered a problem rather than a normal part of development. In time, the infant should develop an age-appropriate sleep pattern. The author points out that one of the critical tasks of the newborn infant is to organize behavior in specific states, including waking, REM (rapid eye movement), and NREM (nonrapid eye movement) states.

In discussing the efficacious development of sleep/wake habits in infants and young children, Wolfson indicates that parent-child interactions are central to the formation of early infant sleep/wake patterns. Consequently, parent training is a logical extension of this crucial and primary interactive relationship. The intervention program presented in Chapter 11 is designed for expectant and first-time parents. The focus is on prevention and early intervention. Disruptive sleep/wake habits are easier to prevent than to curb or modify once established. To help parents ward off faulty sleep cycles in their child, Wolfson outlines some of the major influences on infant/child sleep. For example, parents must attend to the child's daily schedule, such as feeding, play, and bedtime activities. The author also alerts parents to the ways in which they may directly and indirectly contribute to the development of the child's sleep/wake patterns.

Among other factors, Wolfson's approach makes the parents aware of ways to prepare the child for bedtime and sleep. Parents become cognizant of the impact of bedtime routines and rituals. In this training approach, parents are instructed in the formation of preparatory behaviors that result in good sleep habits. Parents are offered behavior-by-behavior strategies for helping infants settle and learn techniques that encourage infants to sleep through most of the night or engage in self-soothing, whereby the infants returns to sleep on their own.

Wolfson's approach offers parents an empirically based and clinically tested format for handling problematic sleep behaviors most effectively. These problems may be related to developmental factors. Due to stranger or separation anxiety, for example, the infant may experience disruptions in sleep when in the care of a new babysitter. The sleep problems may also be associated with situational problems, such as illness or traveling. The author illustrates prescriptive and penetrating interventions for these sleep disturbances, such as systematic ignoring and scheduled awakenings with systematic ignoring. Wolfson's approach describes a number of innovative techniques all of which afford parents an understanding of the child's sleep pattern. Furthermore, this intervention modality helps parents to form age-appropriate expectations regarding their child's sleep/wake habits.

In Chapter 12, Mellon and Houts offer a review of the scientific research and clinical studies that have been instrumental in the development of Full Spectrum Home Training (FSHT), a parent training program that offers effective techniques for curbing, controlling, and correcting primary enuresis in children. The authors also present case materials and include data from actual training sessions that demonstrate the appropriate and sequential application of their approach. In this home-implemented behavioral management program, there is an emphasis on the collaboration of a behavioral psychologist, a physician/pediatrician, and the parents. To increase the probability of successful treatment and ensure that essential variables have been considered, the authors insist on the inclusion of qualified and knowledgeable professionals.

The authors point out that bed-wetting in children involves a complex interaction of physiological mechanisms within the context of behavioral factors and child development. Following a discussion of the prevalence of enuresis, Mellon and Houts offer hypothesized causes for the disorder including etiologic factors such as problems with functional bladder capacity and sleep and arousal difficulties. They review commonly employed methods for treating the disorder and training the parents of enuretic children. The authors deliver descriptions, comparisons, and evaluations of medical and behavioral approaches to this childhood problem.

The crux of the chapter focuses on Full Spectrum Home Training which is formulated from earlier research and incorporates some invaluable past approaches. For example, the authors describe and include three time-tested strategies: (a) urine alarm training, (b) retention control training, and (c) dry-bed training. In addition, cleanliness training and overlearning are part of the FSHT. Overlearning significantly reduces relapses of childhood enuresis. Mellon and Houts also emphasize recent modifications to their home-bound procedures, which are based on extensive clinical experience.

Budd, Chugh, and Berry discuss the scope of children's food refusal problems. In Chapter 13, they distinguish chronic food refusal from a failure-to-thrive syndrome. They then pose their rationale for employing a parent training approach to address the problems associated with children's food refusal. They point out that the parents are the primary feeders during infancy and early childhood and serve as the main socializing agents about food and issues related to food or feeding. The authors further note that many empirical findings point to the role of maladaptive parent-child interactions in the development of some feeding problems. Applied research also demonstrates that parents are in a position to modify children's food refusal problems by altering the social contingencies involved in feeding and mealtime interactions.

Budd, Chugh, and Berry present a taxonomy of variables, ranging from biological to environmental, that contribute to food refusal. These include medical variables, such as organic or disease processes that impact on food refusal; dietary factors; social interactions, such as the disruption of the pleasure anticipated with feeding; the environmental context; and family systems variables, such as marital conflicts or illness in the family. Following the outline of this taxonomy, the authors demonstrate behavioral parent training techniques that have proven effective in the assessment and treatment of each of the major variables which contribute to children's food refusal problems.

CHAPTER 11

Working with Parents on Developing Efficacious Sleep/Wake Habits for Infants and Young Children

AMY R. WOLFSON

AT THE LOCAL Lamaze class reunion, family gathering, first day back at work, day-care interview, and so on, parents of newborns are usually asked, "Is your baby sleeping through the night?" "How much sleep did you get last night?" However, throughout pregnancy and during the early postbirth weeks and months, parenting classes and books focus on labor and delivery, breast feeding, car seat use, early developmental milestones, and appropriate, safe baby toys. Pediatricians, early childhood educators, child psychologists, and others are less likely to systematically assist parents with their infants' sleep/wake habits.

PREVALENCE OF SLEEP PROBLEMS

In striking contrast, parent surveys show that the goal of establishing early, stable sleeping patterns is often not met; over 30% of children have sleep problems in their first 3 to 4 years (Armstrong, Dadds, & Quinn,

I would like to thank Beth Petro-Roy for her assistance in interviewing parents, providing editorial comments, and gathering research materials. Moreover, I would like to thank the countless parents that I have worked with over the years for their stories, motivation, and devotion to their children's sleep hygiene.

1994; Lozoff, Wolf, & Davis, 1985). Zuckerman, Stevenson, and Bailey (1987), in a large longitudinal sample, found that 18% of 8-month-olds and 29% of 3-year-olds had a sleep problem; 5% of the mothers of the younger infants had their own sleep disrupted by their child. Pediatricians report that 26% of their practice have sleep complaints; child psychiatrists report an alarming 61% (Coates & Thoresen, 1981). The most prevalent problematic behaviors were waking up at night and complaints of difficulty going to sleep (Armstrong et al., 1994; McGarr & Hovell, 1980; Mindell & Holst, 1991; Scott & Richards, 1990). Johnson's survey (1991) of parents indicated that resistance in going to sleep and night wakings occur regularly in 20% to 30% of 1- to 2-year-olds. Sleeping difficulties are common among young children and may affect the sleep and daytime functioning of parents.

Parents are primarily concerned with obtaining practical, reliable advice when their child's sleep/wake behaviors become problematic for the whole family. This chapter will focus on parent-child interventions and preventive approaches for handling night waking and sleep-onset, the most common sleep/wake problems for infants and young children, as well as adults. The strategies presented in the chapter are primarily geared for parents of infants and toddlers. Other sleep disturbances encountered by children include nightmares, sleepwalking, night terrors, and sleep apnea.

There is a wide range of normal childhood sleep behavior. In the following section, the normative developmental changes in sleep/wake habits are reviewed. More detailed presentations of the ontogeny of infant sleep are reviewed by Anders, Sadeh, and Appareddy (1995), Sheldon, Spire, and Levy (1992), and Wolfson (1996). In fact, beginning with Kleitman (1939/1963) and others, sleep researchers have been attempting to understand the evolution and development of sleep from infancy to adulthood and to tease apart the relationship between sleeping patterns and environmental demands for over 50 years.

DEVELOPMENTAL CHANGES IN SLEEP/WAKE PATTERNS

A critical task of the newborn infant is to organize behavior into specific states—wake, NREM, and REM sleep and to organize these states into a 24-hour rhythmic pattern. Infant sleep states are not as clearly demarcated as those of adults. However, three sleep states can be identified in the term newborn: active sleep (REM), quiet sleep (NREM), and indeterminant sleep (Anders et al., 1995). Indeterminant sleep, poorly organized sleep, is defined as a state in which criteria for neither REM nor NREM can be identified. In the newborn infant, active sleep is characterized by frequent body, limb, or face movements, irregular breathing, fast movement of the eyes, sucking, and brief smiling. Quiet sleep is exemplified by closed eyes, deep, regular breathing, virtually no movement, and an occasional body "startle" (Anders et al., 1995). Until 6 months, quiet sleep (NREM) cannot be subdivided into four EEG stages. Indeterminate sleep (or transitional sleep) diminishes over the course of the first year.

Research on the maturation of sleep/wake patterns (Anders, Keener, & Kraemer, 1985; Coons & Guilleminault, 1982) demonstrates that infants begin to differentiate day and night within 2 months; newborns sleep randomly for a total of 16 to 20 hours each day, whereas 2-month-olds spend more of their sleeping hours during the night, and their longest sleeping period generally doubles to about 8 hours between birth and 4 months.

Between 2 and 3 months of age, infants diurnal sleep/wake rhythm has not developed enough for the infant's sleep to be consolidated into a single period at night. An infant typically awakens after sleep cycles of 60 to 80 minutes. Generally, at this age, parents need to respond to such night wakings as the infant is too young to have learned to self-initiate sleep. A diurnal circadian rhythm is not well established until 3 or 4 months of age (Ferber, 1985; Parmelee, Weiner, & Schulz, 1984; Richman, 1986).

Infants do not actually remain asleep for an entire 13 to 16 hours (Anders & Keener, 1985). Night wakings are normal and even adults wake between sleep cycles. Generally, when an infant or young child falls asleep, he or she descends into Stage 4, non-REM sleep. This is a deep sleep from which the child is difficult to wake. There are usually two consecutive cycles of deep sleep with a partial waking in between. After this deep sleep, a cycle of light non-REM and REM sleep begins, usually between 12:00 A.M. and 5:00 A.M. This period corresponds to the time when night waking most frequently occurs. As infants mature, they become increasingly more able to return to sleep without signaling and without being fully conscious of having been awake. At about 1 to 2 years, developmental changes include the beginning of bedtime routines (e.g., bedtime story, song, taking a comfort object to bed), and the lengthening of time taken to fall asleep in the evening (Richman, 1986).

FACTORS THAT INFLUENCE CHILDREN'S SLEEP/WAKE PATTERNS

Sleep quality and sleep quantity varies a lot from child to child throughout development. As described earlier, night wakings are "normal"—both children and adults wake between sleep cycles. Researchers and parents, themselves, have observed that the following variables affect children's sleeping patterns (i.e., settling behaviors, night waking, sleep initiation): (a) temperament (Keener, Zeanah, & Anders, 1988; Weiss-bluth, 1981); (b) events of pregnancy and birth (e.g., low birth weight, anoxia, problematic deliveries (Anders et al., 1985; Coren & Searleman, 1985); (c) medical and developmental issues such as colic, teething (Ferber, 1985; Schmitt, 1981); and (d) environmental factors and learned associations (e.g., parenting practices, sleeping arrangements, methods of soothing, use of attachment objects, parental stress, and birth of sibling; Adair, Bauchner, Philipp, Levenson, & Zuckerman 1991; Anders et al., 1985; Medansky & Edelbrock, 1990; Paret, 1983; Van Tassel, 1985; Wolf & Lozoff, 1989; Wolfson, Lacks, & Futterman, 1992). Table 11.1 summarizes the factors that influence children's sleep from infancy through the toddler years.

Parent-child interactions are central to early infant sleep/wake behaviors. Adair et al. (1991), Ferber (1985), and France, Henderson, and Hudson (1996), and others have described the inadvertent behavior chains and behavior traps that may develop when infants and young children establish a learned association between parental presence and falling asleep. As a result, when the infant awakens, he or she desires the same circumstance (parental presence) to fall back to sleep. In fact, Adair et al. (1991) found that infants (9-month-olds) whose parents were present when they fell asleep at bedtime (40%) were significantly more likely to wake at night than infants whose parents were not present (22%). France et al. (1996) explained that repeated associations between signaling, parental attention, and resumption of sleep create a *behavior trap*. For example, if parents stop responding to the signaling, their baby will initially continue to cry. Crying is disturbing to the parents and, consequently, they, the sleepy, frustrated parents, tend to impulsively attend to their son or daughter. As a result, they inadvertently reinforce their

Table 11.1
Developmental and Environmental Factors That Affect Infant
and Young Children's Sleep/Wake Patterns

0–5 Months	5–12 Months	1–3 Years
Birth events, colic	Physical development	Separation anxiety and other fears
Nursing/weaning	Stranger/separation anxiety	Independence/dependence behaviors
Sleeping arrangements	Feeding changes such as weaning from bottle/breast	Cognitive, social, emotional development
Attachment objects, soothing techniques	Changes in sleep arrangements	Birth of sibling and other family changes

baby's awakening and crying behaviors, and reinforce the baby's need for their presence for sleep onset.

By the same token, young children's sleep/wake habits may be associated with the use of attachment objects (Wolf & Lozoff, 1989). Infants and toddlers form a learned association between objects (e.g., blanket, stuffed animal, thumb) and falling asleep at bedtime and in the middle of the night. Crowell, Keener, Ginsburg, and Anders (1987) found that the use of a comforter or attachment object is associated with fewer sleep difficulties at bed and throughout the night.

Sleeping arrangements are another way in which parents and infants/ young children interact around sleep/wake schedules. As emphasized, the manner in which a youngster falls asleep, where he or she sleeps, and the reinforced parent-child interactions that occur at bedtime and during the night are crucial aspects of sleep/wake development. Early on, differences in environmental stimuli and caregiving practices may affect the sleep/wake patterns of the newborn. In one study, rooming-in infants (e.g., slept in mother's room at night) had more contact with their caregiver than nursery infants, and rooming-in infants had significantly more quiet sleep, less indeterminate sleep, and fewer crying states than the infants who remained in the nursery at night (Keefe, 1987).

The relationship between cosleeping and other sleeping arrangements (e.g., sleeping alone, sharing bedroom with sibling, etc.) and sleep disruptions is poorly understood. Until recently, nearly all studies of infant sleep organization and development have been conducted on infants sleeping alone (McKenna et al., 1993). Likewise, over the years pediatric and psychology professionals in the United States have recommended that children sleep alone. Despite this historical advice, some degree of cosleeping has been reported in about half of the families with young children in the United States (Lozoff, 1995). The definition of cosleeping and when families choose cosleeping differs between families and across cultural groups. Some families begin cosleeping with their newborn, whereas others choose cosleeping in response to night waking or other sleep disruptions.

It is valuable to describe McKenna and colleagues' research (1993) on the impact of cosleeping on night waking, arousals, and other so-called sleep disruptions (Lozoff, 1995; McKenna et al., 1993). McKenna et al. found that cosleeping mothers and infants experience more arousals than they do when sleeping alone; exhibit overlapping arousals; spend more time in the same sleep/wake stage while in the same bed; and cosleeping mothers used pats, single touches, and so on during their infants' arousals. Additional research is needed to assess cosleeping effects.

Furthermore, children's daily schedules (e.g., feeding, play activities, bedtime routines) also contribute to the development of sleep/wake patterns. Young children's night wakings may be reinforced by extended parent-child interactions such as playing, watching television, or feeding. As a result, nighttime sleep is not consolidated; it becomes a series of naps, and the child does not develop a normal diurnal sleep pattern. In addition, some studies have found that children breast-fed through age 2 years continue to sleep in short periods with frequent night wakings (Carey, 1974; Elias, Nicolson, Bora, & Johnson, 1986). However, Adair et al. (1991) did not find a link between breast-feeding and night wakings unless the feeding is given right before bedtime or upon wakings.

Because of these influences on children's sleep, child and infant sleep patterns are quite variable. Many factors, such as maturation and medical problems, are not amenable to control. Parenting practices regarding child sleep, however, may lend themselves to alterations that facilitate healthier sleep/wake patterns in infants and children. Both child and parent influence and shape each other's responses. Optimal timing and style of response will vary from family to family, but there may be styles of parenting that are more efficacious than others with regard to sleeping patterns. Child sleep disturbance can be traced to parental anxiety, inconsistent handling, and overresponsiveness to child night waking (Coates & Thoresen, 1981; Crowell et al., 1987). Undoubtedly, treatments such as picking the child up, rocking the toddler to sleep, feeding in the middle of the night, seem to increase the prevalence of night wakings and inability to self-initiate sleep. However, studies strongly indicate that parents can increase their knowledge about infant sleep and learn to more readily respond to their child in a way that will promote good, healthy sleep patterns early on (Adair, Zuckerman, Bauchner, Philipp, & Levenson, 1992; Wolfson et al., 1992) as well as mitigate their child's existing sleep difficulties (France & Hudson, 1990; Rickert & Johnson, 1988).

DEFINITIONS: NIGHT WAKING, SETTLING, AND SLEEP INITIATION DIFFICULTIES

Young children's problematic sleep/wake behaviors are defined differently by parents, clinicians, and researchers. The situation is complex because many sleep behaviors change with age. In addition, there are numerous possible responses to the behaviors and a wide range of interpretations of the behaviors. One parent may not be bothered by having his toddler up late at night if he works during the day; in contrast, another parent might be exhausted herself and, therefore, be frustrated whenever her 1-year-old wakes up in the middle of the night.

Night wakings are an important aspect of infant/toddler sleep development. Brief awakenings from sleep are more frequent during the first 2 to 3 months than at older ages. Polysomnographic and time-lapse video studies of infants have definitely shown that infants do not sleep continuously through the night (Anders & Keener, 1985). Infants tend to awaken for momentary periods and return to sleep without parents' knowledge. Infants who put themselves back to sleep without disturbing their parents have been referred to as self-soothers, and infants who cry and awaken their parents have been called signalers (Paret, 1983).

Settling is defined as sleeping through most of the night, or in other words, as self-soothing and returning to sleep on one's own (Anders, Halpern, & Hua, 1992; Wolfson, 1996). During the first month, nearly 95% of infants wake more than once per night and signal for a parental response before returning to sleep. Laboratory studies have observed that 44% of 2-month-olds, 78% of 9-month-olds, and 60%–70% of 1-year-olds have developed the ability to settle (Anders & Keener, 1985). However, development is only one of the factors that affects night waking or not settling. Clinical studies have demonstrated that parenting practices, feeding styles, and soothing styles also influence settling behaviors and quality and quantity of night wakings (Sadeh, 1994; Wolfson et al., 1992). For the most part, as infants mature, they become increasingly more able to return to sleep without signaling and without being fully conscious of having been awake.

Child sleep researchers and clinicians have attempted to define when night waking would be considered a problem. Johnson (1991) classified infants in their study as night wakers if they woke almost twice per night, 6 nights per week, for more than 12 consecutive months. Toddlers were defined as night wakers if they woke 5.6 nights per week an average of 1 to 2 times per night for more than 18 months. France and Hudson (1990) defined night waking as "any noise from the child, sustained for more than 1 minute, heard between the time of sleep onset and an agreed upon waking time." This definition does not discriminate between sleep and a quiet awake state, yet researchers and clinicians maintain that wakefulness is not a problem unless it disrupts the child's or his/her family's life (Trilling, 1989).

STRATEGIES FOR DEVELOPING HEALTHY SLEEP/WAKE HABITS IN INFANTS AND YOUNG CHILDREN

As stated, many factors contribute to infants' developing sleep/wake behaviors. Furthermore, although most infants eventually develop a healthy, diurnal sleep/wake schedule, parents can assist their young child in forming early, nonproblematic sleep patterns. They can influence their infants by utilizing approaches that take into account their infant's schedule, habits, learned associations, and nutritional and emotional needs. From an educational and behavioral viewpoint, during their child's early development parents can (a) learn to observe behavioral differences between sleep stages; (b) become aware of the developmental changes in total sleep time from infancy to preschool age; (c) know the behavioral cues that determine whether the infant is falling asleep or alert and interacting; (d) learn to feed the infant during an awake state as opposed to a drowsy one; and (e) understand that the infant's alert states are most conducive to learning (Erikson, 1976; Wolfson, 1988).

Over the past decade, pediatricians, psychologists, journalists, and parents have written guidebooks and designed parenting programs that cover methods parents can follow to develop healthy sleep hygiene in their child (Cuthbertson & Schevill, 1985; Eberlein, 1996; Ferber, 1985; Mindell, 1997; Schaefer & DiGeronimo, 1992; Weissbluth, 1987). It is compelling to inform parents about sleep pattern development and to explain how to promote good sleep habits early on. Although intervention procedures are available and effective in treating sleep disturbances in young children, it is critical to utilize strategies that may prevent such problems in the first place.

BENEFITS OF PREVENTIVE
APPROACHES TO PARENTS

Parents who have clear expectations about parenthood feel more competent and less stressed about how to respond to their child's sleeping behaviors (Durand & Mindell, 1990; Wolfson et al., 1992). The birth of a child and the outset of parenthood, especially for first-time parents, is a stressful time. Although birth is usually viewed as a positive experience, many of the associated life changes are frequently perceived as negative or stressful (e.g., less time for self and spouse, change in sleep patterns). In families where the infant is not sleeping through the night and is developing sleep/wake disturbances, parents are often sleep deprived, less alert during the day, and therefore, highly hassled and stressed (Cuthbertson & Schevill, 1985; Durand & Mindell, 1990; Van Tassel, 1985; Wolfson et al., 1992). Furthermore, infant and toddler night wakings and other sleep disturbances may be associated with increased family arguments regarding the best solution (Durand & Mindell, 1990; Van Tassel, 1985), decreased family satisfaction (Scott & Richards, 1990; Zuckerman et al., 1987), and decreased parental competence (Wolfson et al., 1992).

Intervention during the transition to parenthood may prevent the stressful effects that parents, particularly first-timers, often experience (Markman & Kadushin, 1987; Waldron & Routh, 1981). Prevention, early intervention, or primary care programs are important in that they inform parents about associations between their behaviors and their children's behaviors so that they can avoid inadvertently strengthening problematic sleep/wake patterns. If parents help their infants develop adaptive sleep/wake habits when they are as young as 6 to 8 weeks old, they may prevent future sleep problems (Cuthbertson & Schevill, 1985; Ferber, 1985; Wolfson et al., 1992). Childhood is filled with new situations (e.g., birth of sibling) that often bring about nights of disturbed sleep. Children who sleep through the night at an early age may adapt more easily to both developmental sleep disruptions (e.g., separation anxiety) and/or situational changes (e.g., move to new home) that frequently occur in any child's life. Parents who are knowledgeable about young children's sleep hygiene, sensitive to child-parent interactions, and prepared to respond effectively will be more prepared to handle future problematic sleep behaviors.

PREVENTION AND EARLY INTERVENTION PROGRAMS

Wolfson, Lacks, and Futterman (1992), and others (Adair et al., 1992; Pinilla & Birch, 1993) demonstrated that prenatal and postbirth parent training is effective in helping infants establish early, stable sleeping patterns (e.g., sleep through the night, fewer night wakings, self-soothe to fall asleep). In Wolfson et al's. (1992) clinical study, training group parents were taught behavioral strategies to promote healthy self-sufficient sleep patterns in their infants, whereas control group parents received the same amount of personal contact without behavioral training. The preventive program was also beneficial to the parents in that the training group parents reported greater parental competence and the control group parents, by contrast, indicated increased daily hassles.

Similar findings were reported by Seymour, Brock, During, and Poole (1989) in an early intervention study with older infants and young toddlers. Seymour et al. (1989) compared a standardized group program for parents (i.e., behavior management) with a written information only group and a waiting list control group. The children in both the standardized program group and the written information only group demonstrated decreased awake time per night, whereas the waiting list control group children experienced increased awake time per night.

In the rest of this chapter, I describe our (Wolfson et al., 1992) early intervention program for teaching parents to assist their infants in developing adaptive sleep/wake habits. Before describing the nuts and bolts of the program, it is important to review the state of the field regarding assessment of infant and young children's sleep/wake behaviors.

ASSESSMENT AND MONITORING
OF SLEEP/WAKE PATTERNS

The definition of night waking or sleep initiation difficulties in very young children is controversial and variable. Studies demonstrate the need for more standardized and comprehensive assessment techniques. At this point, it is recommended that clinicians, researchers, and parents utilize a combination of measures. For example, an initial assessment of a child's sleep/wake behaviors should include (a) assessment of the presenting sleep complaint and a detailed sleep history, including at least 1 week of sleep/wake diaries; (b) general medical, psychosocial, and developmental history; and (c) physical exam. In this section, parent report measures and actigraphic monitoring are described.

Parental report is by far the most common form of assessment (Crowell et al., 1987; Ferber, 1985; Medansky & Edelbrock, 1990; Wolfson et al., 1992). Parent report provides an important perspective because of parents' initial, crucial role in the development of children's sleep/wake patterns. Parent questionnaires or interviews can identify whether the sleep problem is primary (e.g., infant never slept through the night) or secondary (infant had a clearly defined period of sleeping through the night); discover precipitating events that led up to the parents' concern about their infant's sleep; and obtain information regarding the young child's sleep environment. However, sleep charts, parent questionnaires, and interviews have obvious limitations because parents' perceived assessment of their infant/toddler's sleep behavior may be biased by variables unrelated to a child's possible sleep difficulties. Parent observation of sleep behavior is not always possible, parents rarely agree on a definition of a sleeping difficulty (i.e., getting child to go to bed vs. problem in falling asleep), and they are not able to systematically decipher sleep and awake states. Previously, researchers and some child sleep clinicians relied on time-lapse video (Anders & Keener, 1985) to more accurately assess children's sleeping patterns. In general, videotaping is reliable; however, it is intrusive and impractical.

Current technological advances have resulted in the development of the actigraph, a small solid-state computerized movement detector (Sadeh, Lavie, Scher, Tirosh, & Epstein, 1991; Webster, Kripke, Messin, Mullaney, & Wyborney, 1982). The actigraph is a wrist- or ankle-band device that monitors body movements for at least a week. In deep sleep, body movements are limited and the actigraph picks up few, if any movements. Lighter sleep and REM sleep allow for more body movements and limited wrist/ankle activity is monitored. The lighter and more restless the child's sleep becomes, the more wrist/ankle activity is picked up and the closer that child is to waking. Sadeh et al. (1991) demonstrated that actigraph measurements could discriminate between sleep-disturbed and control children (e.g., increased night wakings, lower percentages of sleep, greater sleep/wake transitions, shorter period of continuous, consolidated sleep). Actigraphs in combination with sleep/wake diaries appear to provide researchers and clinicians a reliable estimate of the amount and times of sleep and wake stages an infant or child goes through during a 24-hour period (Sadeh et al., 1991; Sadeh, Sharkey, & Carskadon, 1994). Reviews by Thoman and Acebo (1995) and Ferber (1995) provide more detailed information on monitoring sleep/wake patterns and assessing sleep problems in infants and young children.

EARLY INTERVENTION PROTOCOL: ENCOURAGING INFANTS AND YOUNG CHILDREN TO SLEEP THROUGH THE NIGHT AND ESTABLISH SLEEP HYGIENE EARLY ON

In Wolfson et al. (1992), parents were taught to gradually shape their infant's sleep to nighttime hours, to establish a nighttime focal or late night feeding, to learn to discriminate infant wakefulness, and to aid their baby to differentiate between night and day. When infants were settling ready (defined as a healthy infant of at least 6–8 weeks who is gaining weight continuously and weighs at least 9–10 lb) parents were encouraged to gradually move the focal feeding to a later time, to lengthen the time before removing a fussing baby from the crib, to stretch the time between later night feedings, and to get the baby to settle until early morning without another feeding. The early intervention program designed by Wolfson (1988, 1992) and adapted from Cuthbertson and Schevill (1985) and Ferber (1985) is described in the following section.

PROGRAM LOGISTICS

Participants and Procedures

This program is designed for expectant parents. It is particularly helpful for first-time parents. The program has the following three phases:

Phase 1. Two sessions held during the last trimester of pregnancy (session length: 60–90 min).

Phase 2. Two postbirth booster sessions (60 min) scheduled when the infant is settling ready (approximately 6–9 weeks of age).

Phase 3. Two follow-up sessions when the infants are approximately 4–6 months old.

During the sessions, parents are provided with didactic information on infant sleep and specific strategies to assist their infants in establishing early adaptive sleep habits.

Assessment

In this program, it is recommended that infants' sleep/wake patterns be assessed with a 24-hour sleep diary (Ferber, 1985; Wolfson et al., 1992; see Figure 11.1). The diary consists of a chart of 15-minute blocks of time; the parent/caretaker shades in the blocks when the baby was sleeping, leaves blank waking times, and uses designated symbols to indicate feeding the infant and other relevant activities. Diaries should be completed by one designated parent from each family for approximately 2 to 3 weeks during the postbirth sessions and for at least 2 weeks during the follow-up period. It is helpful for parents and program group leaders to calculate the following summary scores: (a) mean total sleep, weekdays, weekends; (b) mean number of sleep episodes and wake episodes; (c) number of nights infant slept continuously for more than 300 minutes; (d) bedtimes

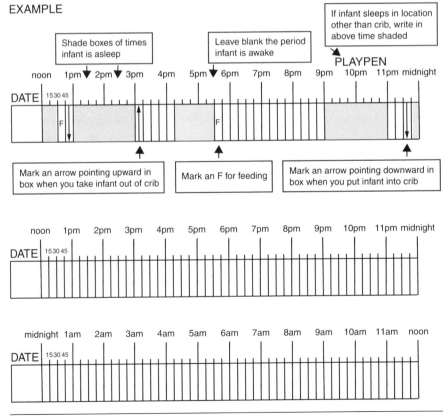

Figure 11.1 Sample Sleep Diary.

and risetimes; (e) nap times; (f) mean number of feedings; and other relevant information. In addition, it is recommended that parents complete weekly practice records (see Figure 11.2), and assess their own comprehension and satisfaction with the program, sense of self-confidence, and daily stress levels (see Wolfson et al., 1992).

EARLY INTERVENTION PROTOCOL

This section illustrates the 6-session protocol. *He* and *she* will be used alternately throughout this section when describing infants' sleep habits.

Session 1: Prenatal Introduction to Infant Sleep/Wake Patterns

I. *Introduction and Welcome*

First, the leader should introduce himself or herself and say a few words about personal background or experiences in the area of parent training, sleep, and other related subjects. Next, the leader will have the group members introduce themselves and *briefly* describe their own background, concerns, and expectations about becoming parents. This breaks the ice and makes parents feel more comfortable with the leader and each other.

II. *General Information on Infant Sleep*

A. Infant Sleep Needs

During this part of the first session, discuss how the first 4 months of life is not a period of major physical milestones, but of laying neurological groundwork and forming an environmental context for future achievements. Emphasize that during these early months newborns needs are simple, yet seem demanding; often parents are exhausted during these early weeks. Present information on the development of infant sleep/wake patterns (see earlier section on developmental changes in sleep/wake patterns).

B. Feeding and Sleeping

Discuss how newborns' sleeping patterns center around the stomach; babies are likely to wake up hungry and fall asleep after eating. Gradually this pattern changes—newborns who want to eat 10 times a day may be satisfied with only 4 larger feedings when they reach about 3 months.

C. Sleep Architecture

Following the discussion about nursing and sleep, review basic information on REM and NREM sleep (see earlier section).

D. Sleeping through the Night

It is important that parents understand that this refers *not* to having infants sleep for an uninterrupted 8 to 12 hours. Rather,

1. Briefly list your activities in getting your baby ready to go to sleep.
2. What time did you give your baby his/her focal feeding?
3. When your baby awakened at night, how quickly did you or your spouse get up to attend to the baby?
4. List the things that you did when your baby awakened in the middle of the night.
5. Did you experience any difficulties in getting your baby to settle?
6. How confident are you that your baby will sleep through the night tomorrow?

Monday _____

_____

_____

Tuesday _____

_____

_____

Wednesday _____

_____

_____

Thursday _____

_____

_____

Friday _____

_____

_____

Saturday _____

_____

_____

Sunday _____

_____

_____

Figure 11.2 Practice Record.

sleeping through the night or settling occurs when infants self-soothe and fall back to sleep on their own when they wake up.

E. Discuss myths and facts about young children's sleep/wake habits and related behaviors (see Table 11.2).

III. *Introduction to General Principles of Parent Education Program*

A. Two Principles

Present the following two principles to the parents: (1) Parents are in control of their infants' sleep and feeding, and not vice versa; and (2) Parents need to foster independence in their infant and competence in themselves.

B. Confident Parenting

Emphasize the importance and value of confident parenting. The parents' confidence in their role is a very important part of establishing good sleeping habits for their baby.

C. Importance of Routines

Infants, like their parents, benefit from a regular schedule. A routine provides an infant with security against changes in her life. Variations in individual sleep needs are large, but everyone is better off having about the same amount of sleep, at about the same time each day. The more regular and predictable routine a young child has, the more flexible parents can be, without negative effects, when exceptions arise.

IV. *Getting an Efficacious Start*

A. Statements for Discussion:

1. Parents are usually exhausted in the early weeks.

2. What can you do as parents to prevent personal and family fatigue and to guide your baby in developing good sleep habits early on?

B. Preparatory Behaviors for Good Sleeping Habits from Day 1

1. Parents should try not to hold, rock, or nurse their baby until she is asleep. They do not want to teach the baby to rely on them to fall asleep. Since building a close relationship is important in those early weeks, they should hold the baby during her wakeful times instead of sleepy times. At sleep times, they wrap the baby snugly in her blanket after feeding and changing; then they put the baby in the crib and leave the room; they can admire the baby from the doorway, but should not pick her up, which would interfere with her falling asleep on her own.

2. Babies can be taught to differentiate night from day; parents need to concentrate their baby's waking times in the daytime

Table 11.2

Myths and Facts about Infant and Young Children's Sleep/Wake Habits

Myths	Facts
Most babies wake at night.	Brief awakenings are frequent during first 2–3 months and night wakings are more of a problem when infants have trouble getting back to sleep on their own.
Bottle-fed infants are more likely to sleep throughout the night than breast-fed.	There is little association between feeding style and sleeping through the night; however, the way in which infants fall asleep is associated with how they fall back to sleep when they wake up at night.
Cosleeping is a way to cope with infant sleep disturbances.	Cultural differences in sleep/wake practices exist early on; however, cosleeping is not a solution to infant sleep disturbances for all families.
Infants share a need to wake and feed during the night with other mammals.	Middle-of-the-night feedings (e.g., 12:00 A.M. to 5:00/6:00 A.M.) of healthy infants is no longer a physical need for most babies when they are over 2 months, weigh over 10 lb, and are continuously gaining weight.
Sleep-onset difficulties and night wakings are often highly amenable to behavioral techniques.	Parents can learn strategies and ways of responding to their infants and young children that promote self-soothing at bedtime and in the middle of the night.
Systematic ignoring of a baby during the night may be harmful.	Building a close relationship with a baby is crucial. Parents can hold, rock, soothe, and snuggle with their baby during wakeful times. Systematic ignoring and related strategies are helpful for decreasing disruptive night waking.
Once a good sleeper, always a good sleeper.	Children's sleep is affected by developmental changes, transitions, and situational factors; however, children who learn to self-soothe at an early age, and whose parents are knowledgeable about children's sleep hygiene will be more prepared to handle future sleep disturbances.

Note. Adapted from France et al. (1996); Mindell et al. (1994); and Wolfson (1996).

hours, otherwise the baby will be livelier at night if he slept all day. Give the parents these helpful hints:

a. Wake your baby every few hours during the day for feedings; play with him before and after the feedings; If a visitor comes to meet the baby, do not hesitate to wake him; Mention that this may seem counterintuitive, but that this keeps the baby up at day and therefore more ready to sleep at night.

b. Do not entertain your baby at night; when you go into the baby's room, do not turn on the light (a hall light or nightlight should be sufficient); after you have fed him, try to get him back to sleep quickly.

3. Starting as early as Day 3 or 4, parents should define one *focal feeding time*; it should be in the late evening (between 10:00 P.M. and 12:00 A.M.); at this time, every evening, parents give the baby a complete feeding even if the baby doesn't wake on her own; the parents need to try not to let her fall asleep while feeding. This can be difficult.

4. Tell the parents to wait to pick up their infant until she is really complaining (not just a nondistressful whimper or a little fidgeting); If they adopt the routine of waking and feeding their baby at 10:00 to 11:00 P.M., she will most likely fall into a pattern of waking around 1:00 or 2:00 A.M., and then at around 4:00 or 5:00 A.M.; continue these demand feedings and do not be surprised if there are schedule variations.

5. Mention that they may have heard that a bottle-fed baby sleeps through the night sooner than a breast-fed baby; This is not true.

6. Parents should not wake their baby for any nightime feeding after the focal feeding time; a nursing mother whose breasts are uncomfortably full should express the milk and freeze it.

7. Point out that if they are lucky to have their baby waking only once between 11:00 P.M. and 7:00 A.M. before he is 5 or 6 weeks old, they are ahead; give themselves a gift for encouragement.

V. *Brief Review of the Program and Assignments*

Session 2: How to Help Your Infant Develop Good Sleeping Habits, or the Dress Rehearsal

I. *Review* Settling-Ready *Criteria*

At this point in the program, carefully present and discuss the four settling-ready criteria (Cuthbertson & Schevil 1985): (1) Weighs a minimum of 9 to 10 lb; (2) Age is at least 6–8 weeks; (3) Steadily gaining weight; (4) No major health problems. Emphasize that attempting to settle the baby earlier may be less successful for the baby and frustrating for parents if it does not work.

II. *Behavioral Strategies for Helping Infants Settle*
    (adapted from Cuthbertson & Schevill, 1985; Wolfson, 1988)

    A. Preparation

    1. By now, parents should be confident with the focal feeding; as parents, they are in charge. Some babies will settle or sleep through the night by 6 to 8 weeks without using any stretching approaches (to be described).

    2. It is helpful for both parents to participate at this time; have the couples discuss which parent will be in charge (who will do tasks, such as keeping the sleep diary, and/or giving the focal feeding), if they are not already doing so.

    3. Plan on devoting 3 to 5 nights to the method. Suggest to the parents that they choose Thursday, Friday, Saturday, and Sunday or Friday, Saturday, Sunday, and Monday; Weaning the baby from nighttime feedings over a weekend or other nonwork days allows the parents to regain lost sleep during the day.

    B. The Routine
       This part of the session focuses on introducing a series of steps that the parents can follow to help their baby sleep through the night.

    1. Explain to parents what to do on *Night 1:*

       Behavior 1. Have on hand a baby bottle of water.

       Behavior 2. Between 10:00 P.M. and midnight, wake baby for focal feeding; get baby back to sleep as quickly as possible.

       Behavior 3. When baby wakes at about 1:00 to 3:00 A.M., parent who did not give the focal feeding gets up. First, change baby; wrap her up and try to settle baby back to bed. Do not pick her up at this time.

       Behavior 4. Explain the following two possible directions to the parents:

       a. *If your baby falls back to sleep*—Go back to bed; when your baby does wake up, try stretching time; change him again; wrap the baby and go for a walk in the house; just do not go back into the bedroom where your spouse is sleeping.

b. *If your baby does not fall back to sleep* (after 20 min)—pick her up, comfort her, and take a walk with your baby; You might sit in a chair and watch TV (hold your baby close, but don't put her in the feeding position); At this time, hopefully you (the parent) have succeeded in stalling your baby up to an hour with what we will call stretching. (Emphasize to the new parents that they are not being harsh by not letting the baby fall asleep in their arms or by not feeding her right away.) Emphasize the importance of the stretching to the parents in both situations.

Behavior 5. Explain that at this point the parent has stretched her baby usually anywhere from 20–40 minutes. It is now time for the water prepared at the beginning of the night. Remind them that water is not formula or breast milk and a baby will give up on nighttime wakings if water, attention, and love are the only responses.

Behavior 6. Parent now changes the baby's diaper if necessary, and tries to settle her down. (Tell parents: Some of you will succeed, and some will not, as in Behavior 4.) In any event, when the baby signals you again (father/mother), go ahead and feed him. Recommend that the parents congratulate themselves on successful stretching on the first night, even if it was only until 3:00 A.M.; Remind the parents that they have started to not reinforce night-waking with food, and are, therefore, extinguishing the stimulus-response pattern of *wake up: expect to eat.*

2. Explain what to do for *Nights 2 and 3:*
   Emphasize that babies do vary in the time that it will take them to sleep through the night. Also, impress on the parents that they should review what happened the night before with each other to prepare for the next night. Remind them that they may get discouraged. Tell parents to use the following pattern:

   Behavior 1. As on the first night, prepare a bottle of water before going to bed.

   Behavior 2. Pick your baby up for her focal feeding, but make it a little later than the night before. You will be feeding her closer to midnight than 11:00 P.M.

   Behaviors 3–6. Repeat Behaviors 3 to 6 as in Night 1 (and again Night 2, etc.). By the third night, your baby may awaken at 3:30 A.M. or he may sleep until 5:30 A.M. Tell the parents that hopefully, they'll see progress, but if not, emphasize that they should not get discouraged.

3. Explain *Night 4:*
   If the baby has now already slept through until 5:00 or 6:00 A.M. (which some do by Night 3 and many more by Night 4 or 5), recommend that the parents try staying in bed, allowing the baby to fuss for about 10 to 20 minutes during this early morning hour. After all, some babies will soothe themselves back to sleep. By Night 4, many babies will go back to sleep without any intervention. However, if the baby is still waking at 3:00 to 3:30 A.M., parents continue stretching process on Night 4 (or a few more nights, if needed). Note that if baby is sick, parents should try the method again in a few weeks.

4. Explain finishing touches:
   Continue focal feeding (10:00 P.M. to midnight) until baby is 3 to 6 months old.

III. *Discussion and Role-Play Vignettes*

IV. *Hand out diaries and practice filling them out.*

Session 3: Booster Session 1, Postbirth

I. *Review Behavior-by-Behavior Method*
   Have parents discuss their own plans.

II. *Problem Solving for Parents*
   Encourage the parents to share their experiences. For example, discuss problems, either in carrying out the procedures or in the environment that make it difficult for them to follow the guidelines. Remind the parents that they are learning something new, and that these behaviors must be practiced consistently to work and to become routine. Also, remind parents of the rationale behind getting their infant to sleep through the night, and emphasize the importance of routines.

III. *Homework: Practice Records and Infant Sleep Diaries*
   Illustrate that an important part of building good, healthy sleep habits for your infant is close monitoring of sleep-related behaviors. First, go over the practice records (Figure 11.2). Recommend that the parents complete the records and bring them to the next session for discussion. Then, review the instructions for the daily infant sleep diaries (Figure 11.1).

Session 4: Booster Session 2

  I. *Review*

As in the Booster Session 1, work with the parents on problem solving and respond to their questions about infant sleep/wake patterns and settling. Congratulate those couples whose babies are sleeping through the night, and provide praise, encouragement, and support to all the parents.

 II. *Practice Records, Diaries, and Questions*

During this phase, go over in detail the data and observations that the parents recorded on the practice records and diaries in detail. Discuss problems and/or successes in carrying out any part of the behavior-by-behavior strategies, and other aspects of infant sleep hygiene.

III. *Review and Sleep Diary Completion*

Repeat the importance of trying behavior-by-behavior method if infant is not sleeping through the night, of keeping a sleep routine in their children's lives, and of completing the daily sleep diaries. Also, remind the group that there will be two follow-up sessions when their babies are approximately 4 to 6 months old.

Sessions 5 and 6: Follow-Up

  I. *Introduction to Follow-Up*

These two follow-up sessions provide information for the parents of 4- to 9-month-olds. Emphasize to the parents that this is a fun time as at this age infants become increasingly more sociable. Daytime naps and nighttime sleep are becoming more regular. Although there is considerable variation, at this age most infants sleep 13 to 15 hours in a 24-hour period. By 5 months, sleep is mainly at night with approximately two (1- to 2-hour) naps. Many infants sleep from 7:30 P.M. to 6:30 A.M., with daytime naps at 9:00 A.M. to 10:30 A.M. and 1:30 to 3:00 P.M. These two sessions focus on how to handle some of the habits and developmental and situational factors that may disrupt sleep during this developmental stage.

 II. *Sleep-Disturbing Habits*

Discuss with the parents how by 5 to 9 months of age some of the common problems are the following: unable to fall asleep on one's own; sleeping in parents' bed when this is not the parents' desire; wanting to nurse in the middle of the night and/or wanting attention and playtime during the night. These follow-up sessions will focus on helping infants with sleep onset or learning to fall asleep on their own, and with weaning infants from middle-of-the-night feedings.

A. Sleep Onset: Helping Infants Fall Asleep Alone

Discuss the following steps and guidelines for encouraging self-soothing and sleep onset for infants. These guidelines are also useful for parents of older infants and toddlers.

1. Parents should encourage the infant to become attached to a security object before trying to teach her to fall asleep alone.

2. Parents introduce a soothing, fun bedtime routine that lasts 5 to 15 minutes (e.g., parent holds baby in lap with security or attachment object while reading a book or singing), then, tells child it is bedtime and puts him in his crib with security/attachment object.

3. Parent says good night and leaves room. If child cries, say something reassuring and try to leave quickly. Try not to take her out of the crib.

4. Explain to the parents that their baby will probably complain for 3 to 5 nights, but it will end if they are consistent; remind them that crying is okay.

5. Finally, remind the parents that if they feed their baby before putting him to bed, try not to let him fall asleep. In other words, it is important to put him to bed awake.

B. Review of Strategies for Weaning Infants from Nighttime Feedings

This presentation and discussion will be largely review for parents who have participated in the entire program (e.g., prenatal, postbirth booster, and follow-up meetings). However, some parents may need a review because they are facing new difficulties or this material may be presented to parents who did not participate in the earlier sessions. The behavioral strategies are briefly reviewed. Remind the parents that it would be helpful to move the baby to his or her own room at this point, if they have not already done so. However, some parents may prefer a family bed and, as a result, some of the recommendations may be less helpful to them.

1. *Night 1:*

Behavior 1. Early evening, feed your baby his evening meal (solids, bottle, nursing), and prepare a bottle of water.

Behavior 2. Put baby to bed awake after your bedtime routine.

Behavior 3. If you are not already doing so, begin a late night or *focal feeding time* (see earlier in chapter for description). At this age, when your infant has been sleeping from the focal feeding time until early morning for about 4 weeks, you can gradually eliminate this late night feeding.

Behavior 4. When the baby wakes up in the middle of the night, it is important for the parent who did not give the earlier feeding to respond because most babies associate seeing that parent with nursing. Respond to the signaling infant only after she is really complaining. Pick her up with her security object and comfort her. If necessary, offer her a bottle of water.

Behavior 5. When your baby has settled down, put him back in his crib with his security object. Be reassuring and leave the room. Try not to linger.

Behavior 6. At this point, infants will either self-soothe, fall back to sleep, or start crying again. Explain to parents that if their baby falls back to sleep without any further assistance that this is a good indication that she will easily wean off her nighttime feedings. However, if their baby does not fall back to sleep and is crying, refer the parents back to the steps covered in the Booster Sessions materials.

2. *Nights 2–4:*

   Remind parents to discuss what happened on the previous night before proceeding with the second night, etc. Follow the strategies from the first night, but wake the baby for his/her focal feeding about 45 minutes to 1 hour later on each consecutive night. By night 4 or 5, most of the parents and infants will have achieved at least a 5–6 hour nursing-free nighttime stretch. Some families may need a few more nights of this consistent, new routine.

3. Explain finishing touches and Behavior Checklist:

   a. Continue focal feeding for 2 to 4 more weeks.

   b. Discuss with the parents how to handle early morning awakenings. For example, if their infant is waking at 5:00 A.M., they can use the same strategies for nighttime weaning to stretch her until 6:00, 6:30, or 7:00 A.M. The clinician may mention that is does not matter if she is actually sleeping after 5:00 A.M., but it is helpful for babies to feel comfortable entertaining themselves.

   c. Remind parents to put their baby down awake at both naptime and bedtime so that he continues to fall asleep on his own.

          d. If the baby struggles with night wakings again, parents should comfort her briefly, but should not return to feeding/nursing her in the middle of the night.

III. Developmental Factors That Can Disrupt Sleep

   A. Strategies for Minimizing Sleep Disruptions Related to Stranger and Separation Anxiety

      1. One common cause of sleep disruption for a baby during these months is waking up to find an unfamiliar sitter. Therefore, recommend to the parents that when they have a new or unfamiliar sitter, they should arrange for her/him and the baby to have time together when parents are around either during an afternoon or before leaving for the evening out.

      2. Vacations can also be more difficult when infants are struggling with stranger and separation anxieties. During this period, if parents are planning a trip or vacation, it might be wise to try to take the baby along. Sudden or prolonged separation from the parents may be hard on her sleep/wake patterns.

      3. During this stage, it is particularly important to make bedtime pleasant and routine. If the baby starts to cry after being put in the crib, the parent should go to him and reassure him, but try not to take him out of his crib. Mention to the parents that they might help him get comfortable again, but leave relatively quickly. This step may have to be repeated until he feels reassured enough to fall asleep. If the infant is in greater distress, some parents might try pulling up a chair and talking/singing to him as he falls asleep.

      4. Recommend that parents handle middle-of-the-night awakenings in a similar manner.

   B. Handling Gross Motor Development and Sleep/Wake Behaviors (e.g., standing in crib)

Learning to pull to a standing position and other motor developments may disrupt sleep for infants in the second 6 months of life. It frequently happens at night, either when the baby is trying to fall asleep or in the middle of the night. When an infant is going through this exciting, yet trying phase, parents can try playing more standing/sitting games during the daytime hours. During the night, if she signals and is stuck in a standing position, parents can gently sit and, then, lie her back down. Parents may have to repeat this a few times before the baby falls back to sleep. Reassure the parents that each night will be easier as she learns to get up and down on her own and to fall back to sleep.

C. Guidelines for Overcoming Occasional Sleep Disruption Due to Teething

Discuss with the parents what to do if their infant wakes up because he is teething. The first recommendation is physical comfort and reassurance. If this does not work and the parents are convinced that he is uncomfortable, they may want to ask the pediatrician about medication. Tell the parents to keep in mind, however, that teething will continue for months and medication is often only a temporary solution. Therefore, it is important to try to adhere to the earlier recommendations regarding middle-of-the-night wakings.

IV. Situations That Can Disrupt Sleep

A. Illness

Give parents these instructions: Wait until your infant's cold, ear infection, upset stomach, or other ailment has passed before you make a consistent effort to change any problematic sleep/wake habits. Then, when your baby is better, on the first 1 or 2 nights, go to her when she cries, comfort her, but try not to take her out of her crib once you have tucked her in for the night. If she does not respond to this approach after a few nights, she may have become accustomed to the nighttime attention that she received when she was sick. In this situation, return to the techniques that you used to wean her off nighttime wakings.

B. Travel

The following guidelines will help minimize sleep disruption when traveling:

1. Bring your baby's security object(s) and other familiar toys with you.

2. Without being too rigid, try to keep your baby as close to his normal naptime and bedtime schedule as possible.

3. Try to arrange his sleeping environment so that it is similar to his room and crib/bed at home. If he sleeps in his own room and you do not have an extra room for your baby to sleep in, try putting him in the corner of your vacation room, or possibly in an alcove or hallway.

On your first night home, it is helpful to go to your baby immediately to reassure her, but on subsequent nights give her a few minutes to try and settle herself. When you do go to her room, give lots of verbal reassurance and reorient her to her security object; leave her room quickly.

You may need to repeat this process several times, but try not to take her out of her crib. Over a number of nights, if she still has not returned to sleeping through the night, gradually reduce your interaction with her by calling to her from your room; your voice may be all that she needs to fall back to sleep.

WHEN PROBLEMS ARISE: HANDLING PROBLEMATIC SLEEP/WAKE BEHAVIORS DURING TODDLER AND PRESCHOOL YEARS

Behavioral methods are very well established for helping adults who experience sleep-onset and wake-after-sleep-onset insomnia. There is increasingly more information on behavioral methods for treating similar sleep difficulties in children. The techniques are straightforward, understandable to parents, increase parents' feelings of competence, and diminish their stress levels.

There are five assumptions about a child's sleep initiation and/or maintenance difficulties (Wolfson & Ricci, 1993):

1. Night wakings are part of the normal process of sleep cycling and even though the ability to maintain sleep may stabilize after early infancy, such brief wakings exist.
2. Association of falling asleep or back to sleep with such aids as rocking, nursing (for infants), security objects, a certain number of pillows, hall light, or television (for older children and adults) are a part of the sleep transition process throughout life.
3. Associations that are problematic for children are those that are not under the child's control (e.g., unable to fall asleep by him- or herself, must be rocked, fed, taken for car ride).
4. Because night wakings are a normal part of the sleep cycle, children need to learn sleep initiation at bedtime and in the middle of the night.
5. Parents' responses to wakeful behavior may reinforce or maintain the behavior; if parents change their responses, night waking will diminish over time and the child will learn to self-soothe and return to sleep on his own (Ferber, 1985; Richman, 1986).

An increasing number of studies have documented that parents can help to reverse maladaptive sleep habits in their infants and young children (see earlier reviews of treatments for children's sleep problems by Douglas, 1989; Edwards & Christophersen, 1994; France et al., 1996; Mindell, 1996; Wolfson & Ricci, 1993). Recommended treatments for ages 6 months to 2 or 3 years of age include fading (Douglas & Richman, 1982;

Ferber, 1985; Piazza & Fisher, 1991); systematic ignoring and graduated systematic ignoring (France & Hudson, 1990; Lawton, France, & Blampied, 1991; Pritchard & Appelton, 1988); systematic ignoring with parental presence (Sadeh, 1994); and scheduled awakening with systematic ignoring (Johnson & Lerner, 1985; Rickert & Johnson, 1988).

FADING

Piazza and Fisher (1991) recommended a faded bedtime approach with a response cost protocol for treatment of young children with multiple sleep problems (e.g., delayed sleep onset, night wakings, early wakings). Fading consists of putting a child to bed at the time when there is a high probability for rapid sleep onset. The bedtime is gradually made earlier on succeeding nights. The response cost component consists of removing the child from bed and keeping him or her awake for 1 hour if he/she did not fall asleep within the first 15 minutes of bedtime. Using these techniques, children showed increased sleep duration, fewer night wakings, and increased regularity of sleep (Piazza & Fisher, 1991).

SYSTEMATIC IGNORING

This behavioral technique assumes that parents play a role in children's sleeping difficulties as they reinforce the child's nonsleep behaviors by responding, giving attention, and serving as a necessary condition for sleep onset (Ferber, 1985; France & Hudson, 1990). This strategy recommends that the parent(s) use a short bedtime routine, put the infant/toddler down at a regularly scheduled time, say good night, and leave the room. Parents are told not to respond to the infant during the night (i.e., not until a scheduled rise time), unless the baby becomes sick or is in danger. France et al. (1996) describes this approach as rapid, with the worst crying and fussing over within 3 days. However, pure systematic ignoring is difficult for many parents and, therefore, noncompliance during the initial nights can increase sleep problems for some families (France et al., 1996). Other researchers and clinicians recommend graduated systematic ignoring, which many parents prefer because it is not abrupt. This involves having a parent enter the child's room for a brief period when the child awakens, verbally reassuring the child, then leaving. The parent then waits for increasingly longer periods of time before reentering the child's room (i.e., increments of 5 minutes). Several studies have demonstrated that this procedure significantly reduces night waking and bedtime disturbances in infants and toddlers, age 8 to 20 months (Durand & Mindell, 1990; France & Hudson, 1990; Lawton et al., 1991). It is noteworthy that parents reported greater marital satisfaction, decreased depressed mood, and improved family life when their child's sleep improved. Although many studies have confirmed the effectiveness of an extinction approach, there are drawbacks. One of the limitations is parents' obvious inability to consistently comply with the requirements of extinction. Implementing such a program is also difficult because children are often not receptive to less of a parent's attention, and long crying bouts and tantrums may occur at the introduction of an extinction procedure.

SYSTEMATIC IGNORING WITH PARENTAL PRESENCE

Sadeh (1994) designed an approach where the parent sleeps in the same room as the infant, but in a separate bed. Again, the infant is placed into bed and told good night. If the infant or child cries when he or she is put down for sleep, the parent lies in the other bed as if he or she were sleeping. It is recommended that the parent remain in bed until the child falls asleep, and the parent should sleep in the room with the child for about 1 week. If the child wakes up during the night, either before the parent's bedtime and/or after the parent has gone to bed for the night, it is important for the parent to ignore the cries and pretend to sleep. This approach tends to minimize infant crying and parental anxiety. Additionally, it may be helpful for parents who would like to continue to have their infant sleep in the parents' room.

SCHEDULED AWAKENINGS WITH SYSTEMATIC IGNORING

Rickert and Johnson (1988) compared a scheduled awakening technique with systematic ignoring to reduce night wakings in infants and toddlers. Scheduled awakenings consisted of a parent awakening, then feeding or consoling the child 15 to 30 minutes before usual spontaneous awakenings. Scheduled awakenings were discontinued, once spontaneous awakenings were precluded. Results revealed significant decreases in the frequency of night wakings in both the scheduled awakening group and the systematic ignoring group compared with the control group.

Although research on management of night waking and sleep initiation difficulties is in about a toddler stage, it appears that parents can be taught to alter their responses to their child's behaviors to develop an improved sleeping pattern. Taken together, a meaningful behavioral treatment for decreasing night wakings or teaching sleep initiation is to gradually help a young child learn to fall asleep by him- or herself. A child learns a new set of associations for falling asleep that no longer requires direct parental participation throughout the night. Below are general recommendations that parents can follow for improving their young child's sleep hygiene (Wolfson & Ricci, 1993).

1. Understand your child's sleep patterns and have age-appropriate expectations;
2. Use bedtime rituals that involve a soothing activity such as song, story; placing your child in crib or bed and encouraging him or her to cuddle with a transitional object (diaper, stuffed animal, blanket); and saying good night and leaving the room while your child is still awake;
3. When your child calls, return for brief reassurance and leave again; gradually lengthening time before responding to your fussing child until he or she falls asleep by him or herself;
4. When your child wakes during the night, you should respond in a similar manner as at bedtime, waiting increasingly longer between visits until your child soothes him or herself back to sleep;
5. On subsequent nights, it is helpful for you to stretch the time before responding to teach your child to self-soothe and go back to sleep without parental assistance;
6. You may find it helpful to reward your child (e.g., older toddlers and preschoolers) in the morning for falling back to sleep on their own (e.g., stickers);
7. Try sleep/wake diaries to record your child's progress and to help the family adhere to the new routine.

DISCUSSION VIGNETTES

VIGNETTE 1

Michael and Sharon are pregnant with their first child. Sharon is well into the third trimester, and she and Michael are beginning to discuss the changes the baby will bring to their lives. One of their biggest concerns is sleep, the baby's and their own. They are interested in whether or not they should wake their infant when he is sleeping to feed him on a preset schedule or just to let him sleep. They have heard that the quickest way to get a baby to sleep through the night is to allow him to cry himself to sleep; however, they are wondering at what age they should begin.

Recommendations

1. Establish a focal feeding early on.
2. Establish self-soothing early on.
3. Learn about the behavioral method for weaning infants from middle-of-the-night feedings and night wakings.

Outcome

After much deliberation, Michael and Sharon decided to participate in a program for expectant parents. The program focused on infant sleeping patterns. They learned about starting a focal feeding in the first few weeks. When their son was born, they started the focal feeding when he was 1 week old. Initially, Sharon nursed Ben between 10:00 and 12:00 A.M. and later when they introduced bottle-feeding, Mike gave the focal feeding. By 6 or 7 weeks, he was sleeping from 12:00 to 5:00 A.M., and they never used the steps for weaning infants from middle-of-the-night feedings.

VIGNETTE 2

Julie is 3 months old and waking 3 to 4 times a night. Her father feels this is perfectly normal and is quick to respond when his daughter cries. Her mother, on the other hand, feels that she should be sleeping around 8 hours a night at this point. Julie is a happy baby during the day but her mother is feeling worn out. Julie's parents have had several arguments about how to handle their daughter's sleep/wake habits and they are just not sure who is correct or what they should do.

Recommendations

1. Establish whether the baby meets the settling-ready criteria.
2. Review sleep hygiene practices.
3. Teach Julie and her parents how to gradually wean her from night wakings via the behavior-by-behavior method.

Outcome

Julie's parents talked with their pediatrician about her sleep habits and their struggles. The pediatrician referred the parents to a consulting psychologist for advice. Initially, her father was reluctant to let Julie cry at all. However, after he understood that how infants fall asleep at bedtime is associated with how they *need* to return to sleep in the middle of the night, he decided to try to wait longer before responding to Julie's cries. Her father had noticed that Julie loved to carry one of his old T-shirts around the house; he handed Julie the T-shirt at bedtime to fall asleep. After a few days, she started to fall asleep with the T-shirt. Simultaneously, Julie's parents developed a plan to gradually wean her from her night wakings. The combination of the weaning process and having the T-shirt to return to sleep decreased her night wakings to less than 1 per week.

VIGNETTE 3

Ellie, a 14-month-old, is an only child. She is being raised by her mother, a single parent. Ellie's mother is very protective of her daughter and cannot stand to hear her cry. She responds to her child very quickly during the daytime when she cries and usually remedies the situation with a bottle of juice or a treat. Mother and daughter have a very busy schedule. For example, Ellie spends the day at a sitter's or at her aunt's home while her mother works, and they do not return home until 6 or 7 P.M. She naps at least 2 hours during the day. Ellie is still waking 2 or 3 times during the night, and each time her mother responds immediately with a bottle. Ellie's mother is frustrated; she cannot stand to hear her daughter cry, but she needs her own sleep.

Recommendations

1. Establish a nap-time and nighttime sleep/wake schedule for Ellie and her mother.
2. Teach Ellie to fall asleep without feeding and establish a bedtime routine.
3. Wean Ellie from her bottle at night.

Outcome

After about 2 weeks, Ellie's mother and the two sitters were putting Ellie down for naps at about the same time each day (about 11:30 A.M.). At bedtime, she was still falling asleep before even finishing her bottle. However, her mother was determined to change Ellie's bedtime routine and end this feeding pattern. She and Ellie established a bedtime routine: (1) cuddle together in the living room, read 2 to 3 books, have juice and snack; (2) get into pajamas, wash up; and (3) place Ellie in her crib, sing two favorite songs, say good night, and leave her room. Initially, Ellie's mother continued to give her a scheduled bottle at midnight (e.g., similar to a focal feeding). After about a week, she discontinued the midnight bottle and Ellie slept through the night until early morning at 5 or 6 A.M. On a few nights, Ellie had one brief waking; however, she now returned to sleep without a feeding.

Vignette 4

Nine-month-old Cory had been sleeping through the night for about 3 or 4 months. Recently, however, he has started to cry every time his father, the primary caretaker, puts him in his crib and leaves the room. His father responds quickly to this behavior by picking Cory up each time he fusses and cries. Cory is also exhibiting similar behaviors during the daytime. At night, Cory will eventually fall asleep, but then wakes up one or two times each night. Lately, it has taken his parents over an hour to get him back to sleep. His father is very aggravated with Cory's behavior, but feels guilty if he lets him cry for more than 5 minutes.

Recommendations

1. Explain separation anxiety to Cory's parents.
2. Get Cory's father to stop picking him up immediately.
3. Wean Cory from *needing* his father to fall back to sleep during the night. Encourage Cory to use an attachment object to soothe himself back to sleep.

Outcome

Cory's parents felt much better after they understood that some children have new difficulties with night wakings when they are negotiating separation anxiety. As a result, they stopped picking him up immediately. Instead, when he started to cry, they went to him and reassured him, but did not take him out of his crib. They helped him get comfortable again, but left his room relatively quickly. During the first few days, Cory seemed particularly distressed. Therefore, his father tried pulling up a chair and singing to him as he fell back to sleep. After a few nights of this strategy, they returned to leaving the room after he was comfortable again. After about 10 days, Cory was sleeping through the night again.

VIGNETTE 5

Debra and Jon have two children. When their oldest was 4 and their youngest was a couple months old they moved to a new house. Four-year-old Anna, who had always slept through the night, started to wake up several times each night. She would wake up and come into her parents' bed. Initially, her parents decided to take turns sleeping in Anna's bed until she fell back to sleep. After 6 weeks, however, they were concerned about how to wean her from this new habit.

Recommendations

1. Review sleep hygiene for preschoolers with Anna's parents.
2. Wean Anna from needing one of her parents to fall asleep and teach her to self-soothe for falling back to sleep on her own.

Outcome

Debra and Jon had read a lot about infant and child sleep/wake habits and had taken a class before their oldest child was born. They thought that they were prepared to handle developmental disruptions. However, the move had been more stressful than they had anticipated. They went back over their parent training class notes and started to gradually wean Anna from her "new" night wakings. Simultaneously, they encouraged her to fall asleep with her favorite stuffed animal. First, they sat on the side of her bed until she fell asleep. Second, they sat on her bed until she was almost asleep. Third, they sat in a chair next to the bed. After about a week, Anna was able to fall back to sleep with her mother or father looking in from the doorway. During the following week, her parents stood in the doorway, said goodnight and returned to their own room. Throughout this process, Anna was rewarded with stickers the following morning to reinforce her falling back to sleep on her own. After about 3 weeks, Anna was no longer calling out to them in the middle of the night, and she was successfully soothing herself back to sleep.

VIGNETTE 6

Carin and Jeff have two very good 3- and 5-year-old sleepers. They have had very few problems with their boys' sleep/wake habits. Although they did not attend a class before their first son was born, they read a lot about the development of sleep/wake patterns in children. As a couple, they highly recommend establishing healthy sleep hygiene in the early weeks. In an interview, Carin explained that the following sleep hygiene practices were most helpful:

1. When the boys were only a few months old, she would put them down for the night and tell them that she would come back and look in on them in 5 minutes. This provided security and reassurance.
2. They established a structured bedtime ritual early on and stuck to it ever since the early months.
3. They encouraged both boys to use an attachment object to fall asleep. Although there have been minor disruptions (e.g., house construction, birth of the second child, allergies, etc.), Carin and Jeff felt prepared because they knew about infant/child sleep and had established healthy sleep habits early on.

CONCLUSION

This chapter discussed developmental changes in sleep/wake patterns and presented preventive strategies that parents can utilize to establish healthy sleep/wake habits for their infants and young children. Furthermore, several behavioral techniques for handling sleep onset and night waking difficulties in the toddler and preschool years are illustrated. It is recommended that parents plan and decide on the type of strategy that suits their needs, and their own child's developmental stage. Although families may make use of the recommended approaches at different stages, there are definite steps that parents can take to prevent and to treat young children's sleep difficulties. The program presented here and the majority of programs recommend: establishing a bedtime routine early on; preemptively awakening young infants for a focal feeding prior to the parents' retiring; teaching parents that healthy infants no longer physiologically need feeding in the middle of the night beginning at 2 to 5 months; giving infants an opportunity to fall asleep on their own; and gradually weaning children from night wakings by decreasing parental attention to crying and fussing.

Children are adaptable and cope with widely varying customs regarding bedtime and sleeping patterns. However, quantity and quality of sleep are an important part of every child's development, and parents who are not sleep deprived interact more effectively with their child. Preventive and early intervention programs have the potential to reduce the frequency of sleep difficulties in early childhood and to diminish stress in the family. Expanded research is needed to further assess the long-term benefits of such innovative programs.

REFERENCES

Adair, R., Bauchner, H., Philipp, B., Levenson, S., & Zuckerman, B. (1991). Night waking during infancy: Role of parental presence at bedtime. *Pediatrics, 87,* 500–504.

Adair, R., Zuckerman, B., Bauchner, H., Philipp, B., & Levenson, S. (1992). Reducing night waking in infancy: A primary care intervention. *Pediatrics, 89,* 585–588.

Anders, T., Halpern, L., & Hua, J. (1992). Sleeping through the night: Origins in early infancy. *Pediatrics, 90,* 554–560.

Anders, T., & Keener, M. (1985). Developmental course of nighttime sleep-wake patterns in full-term and premature infants during the first year of life. *Sleep, 8*(3), 173–192.

Anders, T., Keener, M., & Kraemer, H. (1985). Sleep-wake state organization, neonatal assessment and development in premature infants during the first year of life. *Sleep, 8,* 193–206.

Anders, T., Sadeh, A., & Appareddy, V. (1995). Normal sleep in neonates and children. In R. Ferber & M. Kryger (Eds.), *Principles and practice of sleep medicine in the child* (pp. 7–18). Philadelphia: Saunders.

Armstrong, K., Dadds, M., & Quinn, R. (1994). The sleep patterns of normal children. *Medical Journal of Australia, 161,* 202–206.

Carey, W. B. (1974). Night waking and temperament in infancy. *Journal of Pediatrics, 84,* 756–758.

Coates, T. J., & Thoresen, C. E. (1981). Sleep disturbance in children and adolescents. In E. G. Mash & L. G. Terdal (Eds.), *Behavioral assessment of childhood disorders* (pp. 639–678). New York: Guilford Press.

Coons, S., & Guilleminault, C. (1982). Development of sleep-wake patterns and non-rapid eye movement sleep stages during the first 6 months of life in normal infants. *Pediatrics, 69,* 793–798.

Coren, S., & Searleman, A. (1985). Birth stress and self-reported sleep difficulty. *Sleep, 8,* 222–226.

Crowell, J., Keener, M., Ginsburg, N., & Anders, T. (1987). Sleep habits in toddlers 18 to 36 months old. *Journal of the American Academy of Child and Adolescent Psychiatry, 26,* 510–519.

Cuthbertson, J., & Schevill, S. (1985). *Helping your child sleep through the night.* New York: Doubleday.

Douglas, J. (1989). Training parents to manage their child's sleep problem. In C. E. Schaefer & J. M. Briesmeister (Eds.), *Handbook of parent training: Parents as co-therapists for children's behavior problems* (pp. 13–37). New York: Wiley.

Douglas, J., & Richman, N. (1982). *Sleep management manual.* London: Hospital for Sick Children, Department of Psychological Medicine.

Durand, V. M., & Mindell, J. A. (1990). Behavioral treatment of multiple childhood sleep disorders. *Behavior Modification, 14,* 37–49.

Eberlein, T. (1996). *Sleep: How to teach your child to sleep like a baby.* New York: Pocket Books.

Edwards, K., & Christophersen, E. (1994). Treating common sleep problems of young children. *Developmental and Behavioral Pediatrics, 15,* 207–213.

Elias, M. F., Nicolson, N. A., Bora, C., & Johnson, J. (1986). Sleep/wake patterns of breast-fed infants in the first 2 years of life. *Pediatrics, 77,* 322–329.

Erikson, M. L. (1976). *Assessment and management of developmental changes in children.* St. Louis, MO: Mosby.

Ferber, R. (1985). *Solve your child's sleep problems.* New York: Simon & Schuster.

Ferber, R. (1995). Assessment of sleep disorders in the child. In R. Ferber & M. Kryger (Eds.), *Principles and practice of sleep medicine in the child* (pp. 45–53). Philadelphia: Saunders.

France, K. G., Henderson, J. M. T., & Hudson, S. M. (1996). Fact, act, and tact: A three-stage approach to treating the sleep problems of infants and young children. In R. Dahl (Ed.), *Child and Adolescent Psychiatric Clinics of North America: Sleep Disorders, 5*(3), 581–599.

France, K. G., & Hudson, S. M. (1990). Behavior management of infant sleep disturbance. *Journal of Applied Behavior Analysis, 23,* 91–98.

Johnson, C. M. (1991). Infant and toddler sleep: Telephone survey of parents in one community. *Developmental and Behavioral Pediatrics, 12,* 108–114.

Johnson, C. M., & Lerner, M. (1985). Amelioration of infant sleep disturbances: Effects of scheduled awakenings by compliant parents. *Infant Mental Health Journal, 6,* 21–30.

Keefe, M. (1987). Comparison of neonatal nighttime sleep-wake patterns in nursery versus rooming-in environments. *Nursing Research, 36,* 140–144.

Keener, M. A., Zeanah, C. H., & Anders, T. (1988). Infant temperament, sleep organization and nighttime parental interventions. *Pediatrics, 81,* 762–771.

Kleitman, N. (1963). *Sleep and wakefulness.* Chicago: University of Chicago Press. (Original work published 1939)

Lawton, C., France, K. G., & Blampied, N. M. (1991). Treatment of infant sleep disturbance by graduated extinction. *Child and Family Behavior Therapy, 13,* 39–56.

Lozoff, B. (1995). Culture and family: Influences on childhood sleep practices and problems. In R. Ferber & M. Kryger (Eds.), *Principles and practice of sleep medicine in the child* (pp. 69–73). Philadelphia: Saunders.

Lozoff, B., Wolf, A., & Davis, N. (1985). Sleep problems seen in pediatric practice. *Pediatrics, 75,* 477–483.

Markman, H. J., & Kadushin, F. S. (1987). Preventive effects of Lamaze training for first-time parents: A short-term longitudinal study. *Journal of Consulting and Clinical Psychology, 54,* 872–874.

McGarr, R. J., & Hovell, M. F. (1980). In search of the sandman: Shaping an infant to sleep. *Education and Treatment of Children, 3,* 173–182.

McKenna, J., Thoman, E., Anders, T., Sadeh, A., Schechtman, V., & Glotzbach, S. (1993). Infant-parent co-sleeping in an evolutionary perspective: Implications for understanding infant sleep development and the sudden death syndrome. *Sleep, 16,* 263–282.

Medansky, D., & Edelbrock, C. (1990). Cosleeping in a community sample of 2- and 3-year-old children. *Pediatrics, 86,* 197–203.

Mindell, J. A. (1996). Treatment of child and adolescent sleep disorder. In R. Dahl (Ed.), *Child and Adolescent Psychiatric Clinics of North America: Sleep Disorders,* 5(3), 741–751.

Mindell, J. A. (1997). *Sleeping through the night.* New York: Harper Perennial/HarperCollins.

Mindell, J. A., & Holst, S. K. (1991). Pediatricians and sleep problems in young children: Views and treatment recommendations. *Sleep Research, 20,* 105.

Mindell, J. A., Molline, M. L., Zendell, S. M., Brown, L. W., & Fry, J. M. (1994). Pediatricians and sleep disorders: Training and practice. *Pediatrics, 94*(2), 194–200.

Paret, I. (1983). Night waking and its relation to mother-infant interaction in 9-month-old infants. In J. Call, E. Galenson, & R. L. Tyson (Eds.), *Frontiers of infant psychiatry* (pp. 171–177). New York: Basic Books.

Parmelee, A. H., Weiner, N. H., & Schulz, H. R. (1984). Infant sleep patterns from birth to 16 weeks of age. *Journal of Pediatrics, 65,* 576–582.

Piazza, C. C., & Fisher, W. (1991). A faded bedtime with response cost protocol for treatment of multiple sleep problems in children. *Journal of Applied Behavior Analysis, 24,* 129–140.

Pinilla, T., & Birch, L. (1993). Help me make it through the night: Behavioral entrainment of breast-fed infants' sleep patterns. *Pediatrics, 91,* 436–444.

Pritchard, A., & Appelton, P. (1988). Management of sleep problems in preschool children. *Early Child Development and Care, 34,* 227–240.

Richman, N. (1986). Recent progress in understanding and treating sleep disorders. *Advances in Developmental and Behavioral Pediatrics, 7,* 45–63.

Rickert, V. I., & Johnson, C. M. (1988). Reducing nocturnal awakenings and crying episodes in infants and young children: A comparison between scheduled awakenings and systematic ignoring. *Pediatrics, 81,* 203–212.

Sadeh, A. (1994). Assessment of intervention for infant night waking: Parental reports and activity-based home monitoring. *Journal of Consulting and Clinical Psychology, 62,* 63–68.

Sadeh, A., Lavie, P., Scher, A., Tirosh, E., & Epstein, R. (1991). Actigraphic home-monitoring sleep-disturbed and control infants and young children: A new method for pediatric assessment of sleep-wake patterns. *Pediatrics, 87,* 494–499.

Sadeh, A., Sharkey, K., & Carskadon, M. A. (1994). Activity-based sleep-wake identification: An empirical test of methodological issues. *Sleep, 17*(3), 201–207.

Schaefer, C. E., & DiGeronimo, T. F. (1992). *Winning bedtime battles.* New York: Citadel Press.

Schmitt, B. D. (1981). Infants who do not sleep through the night. *Developmental and Behavioral Pediatrics, 2,* 20–23.

Scott, G., & Richards, M. P. M. (1990). Nightwaking in 1-year-old children in England. *Child: Care, Health, and Development, 16,* 283–302.

Seymour, F. W., Brock, P., During, M., & Poole, G. (1989). Reducing sleep disruptions in young children: Evaluation of therapist-guided and written information approaches: A brief report. *Journal of Child Psychology and Psychiatry, 30,* 913–918.

Sheldon, S., Spire, J., & Levy, H. (1992). *Pediatric sleep medicine.* Philadelphia: Saunders.

Thoman, E., & Acebo, C. (1995). Monitoring of sleep in neonates and young children. In R. Ferber & M. Kryger (Eds.), *Principles and practice of sleep medicine in the child* (pp. 55–68). Philadelphia: Saunders.

Trilling, J. S. (1989). Nighttime waking in children: A disease of civilization. *Family Systems Medicine, 7,* 17–29.

Van Tassel, E. B. (1985). The relative influence of child and environmental characteristics on sleep disturbances in the first and second years of life. *Developmental and Behavioral Pediatrics, 6,* 81–86.

Waldron, H., & Routh, D. (1981). The effect of the first child on the marital relationship. *Journal of Marriage and the Family, 43,* 785–788.

Webster, J. B., Kripke, D. F., Messin, S., Mullaney, D. J., & Wyborney, G. (1982). An activity-based sleep monitor system for ambulatory use. *Sleep, 5,* 389–399.

Weissbluth, M. (1981). Sleep duration and infant temperament. *Journal of Pediatrics, 99,* 817–819.

Weissbluth, M. (1987). *Healthy sleep habits, happy child.* New York: Fawcett Columbine.

Wolf, A. W., & Lozoff, B. (1989). Object attachment, thumbsucking, and the passage to sleep. *Journal of American Academy of Child and Adolescent Psychiatry, 28,* 287–292.

Wolfson, A. (1988). The effects of parent training on the development of infant sleeping patterns (Doctoral dissertation, Washington University, 1987). *American Doctoral Dissertations,* ADD88-12774.

Wolfson, A. (1996). Sleeping patterns of children and adolescents: Developmental trends, disruptions, and adaptations. In R. Dahl (Ed.), *Child and Adolescent Psychiatric Clinics of North America: Sleep Disorders, 5*(3), 549–668.

Wolfson, A., Lacks, P., & Futterman, A. (1992). Effects of parent training on infant sleeping patterns, parents' stress, and perceived parental competence. *Journal of Consulting and Clinical Psychology, 60,* 41–48.

Wolfson, A., & Ricci, C. (1993). Programas de intervencion y preventivos para los problemas del sueno en la primera infancia. *Focus on Psychiatry, 1*(2), 34–43.

Zuckerman, B., Stevenson, J., & Bailey, V. (1987). Sleep problems in early childhood: Continuities, predictive factors, and behavioral correlates. *Pediatrics, 80,* 664–671.

CHAPTER 12

Home-Based Treatment for Primary Enuresis

MICHAEL W. MELLON and ARTHUR C. HOUTS

THE PROBLEM OF BED-WETTING

CONSISTENT WITH the theme of this volume, we present an approach for childhood bed-wetting that requires close collaboration between behavioral psychologists, pediatricians, and parent(s) for the optimal treatment of this relatively common, yet troublesome disorder. We also emphasize a biobehavioral perspective of childhood bed-wetting. Although traditionally conceptualized as a medical or psychiatric disorder, recent advances in assessment and treatment highlight the importance of understanding childhood enuresis as an interaction of physiological mechanisms within the context of behaviorism and child development (for a more detailed discussion of this conceptualization of enuresis as a childhood elimination disorder, see Mellon & Houts, 1995). As such, childhood enuresis may represent a prototypical example of how the collaboration between pediatric psychologists, medical professionals, and parents leads to the most effective treatment.

Enuresis generally refers to accidental wetting after the age of 5 years, that occurs with a frequency of twice a week for at least 3 consecutive months or that produces considerable distress and impairment in the child's psychosocial and/or academic functioning (American Psychiatric Association, 1994). *Diurnal Enuresis* refers to daytime wetting and is distinguished from nocturnal enuresis, which applies to children who only wet the bed. This distinction is relevant because of a significantly higher incidence of medical problems such as urinary tract infection and abnormal urodynamics in diurnal enuresis (Arnold & Ginsberg, 1973; Jarvelin, Huttunen, Seppanen, Seppanen, & Moilanen, 1990). Children with daytime wetting often require further medical evaluation and treatment. However, the focus of this chapter is nocturnal enuresis without daytime wetting.

Bed-wetting has been associated with problems of emotional and social adjustment among enuretic children, though the nature of this association remains unclear. The association appears to be greatest in girls, in diurnal enuretics, and in secondary or onset enuresis, but it is important to emphasize that psychiatric disturbance is present in only a minority of enuretic children (Essen & Peckham, 1976; Kaffman & Elizur, 1977; Rutter, Yule, & Graham, 1973; Stromgren & Thomsen, 1990). Experimental studies have demonstrated that enuretic children treated for bed-wetting improve more than untreated controls on measures of self-concept and peer relations (Baker, 1969; Lovibond, 1964; Moffatt, Kato, & Pless, 1987). Continued recommendations to parents by health professionals to wait for their child to "outgrow" the disorder may now be considered inappropriate due to the potential psychosocial consequences of continued bed-wetting and the availability of effective treatment options.

Although the reported prevalence of enuresis varies (De Jonge, 1973), it is conservatively estimated that about 10% of school-age children (i.e., 5–16 years) wet their beds, with most of them doing so every night of the week (Essen & Peckham, 1976; Fergusson, Horwood, & Shannon, 1986; Jarvelin, Vikevainen-Tervonen, Moilanen, & Huttunen, 1988; Verhulst et al., 1985). Thus, an average size school of 1,000 students would be estimated to have 100 children who wet the bed each night of the week. Figure 12.1 shows the prevalance of enuresis up to age 16 based on several large-scale epidemiology studies from the United States, western Europe, Australia, and Israel.

Epidemiological studies indicate the prevalence of enuresis declines with age, and this has contributed to the belief among professionals and parents that children will outgrow the problem (Haque et al., 1981; Shelov et al., 1981). Although the spontaneous remission rate is estimated to be 16% per year, cessation of bed-wetting without treatment can take several years (Forsythe & Redmond, 1974). Moreover, as many as 3% of all enuretic children may continue with enuresis into adulthood (Forsythe & Redmond, 1974; Levine, 1943; Thorne, 1944). Less than 10% of these children have some sort of physical abnormality of the urinary tract (American Academy of Pediatrics Committee on Radiology, 1980; Jarvelin et al., 1990; Kass, 1991; Redman & Seibert, 1979; Rushton, 1989; Stansfeld, 1973) that would lead to the symptoms of day and/or night wetting. Bed-wetting appears to have a strong genetic component, and enuretic children may show signs of delayed maturation of the nervous system

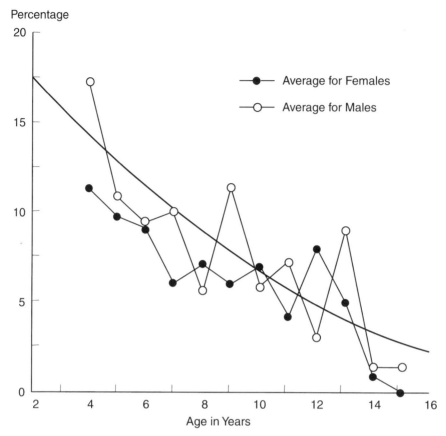

Percentage

The percentage of females and males in the general population who wet the bed from ages 4 to 15 years old (based on data collected in the United States, western Europe, Australia, and Israel).

Figure 12.1   Percentage of Children Wetting at Least Once per Week.

(Jarvelin, 1989; Jarvelin et al., 1991). Up to age 11 years, more than twice as many males as females suffer from enuresis.

WHAT CAUSES BED-WETTING?

The specific causes of nocturnal enuresis after ruling out an organic etiology are still largely unknown, and several hypotheses have been proposed to explain the problem. Current investigators recognize considerable heterogeneity among enuretic children (Geffken, Johnson, & Walker, 1986; Whelan & Houts, 1990) and do not assume that these children makeup a homogeneous group who should be treated in the same manner. Several hypothesized causes may combine to explain the problem for a particular child, whereas some hypothesized causes may in reality be only correlates of the problem. Nevertheless, factors that are significant correlates of enuresis may aid clinicians in identifying specific treatment components that may be warranted for some children depending on the presence or absence of these factors for a given child.

Enuresis is most likely the result of complex interactions between genetically transmitted physiological factors and exposure to different environments during growth and development. The major etiological hypotheses that support such a conclusion include family history, delays in physical development, and ineffective learning history. In general, there is a strong trend for enuresis to run in families. In one of the most recent studies that considered family history, Fergusson et al. (1986) found that the strongest predictor of the age of attaining nocturnal bladder control was the number of first-order relatives having a known history of enuresis. In cases where both parents have a history of bed-wetting, 77% of children are enuretic, as opposed to 44% when one parent has a positive history, and 15% if neither parent does (Bakwin, 1973). Recent basic genetic research has begun to uncover the specific markers for enuresis, but the practical application of this knowledge is as yet unknown (Eiberg, Berendt, & Mohr, 1995). What exactly is transmitted genetically is not clear, although family history findings point to delays in physical development as playing a causal role in continued bed-wetting (Jarvelin, 1989).

The leading etiological hypotheses regarding delays in physical development are those focused on deficiencies in nocturnal antidiuretic hormone (ADH) secretion and on deficiencies in muscular responses needed to inhibit urination. The first of these is often referred to as the nocturnal polyuria hypothesis and was revived by Klauber (1989) by reasoning backward from favorable outcomes of enuretic children who were treated with the synthetic ADH, desmopressin (brand name DDAVP). According to this hypothesis, enuretic children continue bed-wetting because their kidneys do not adequately concentrate urine (i.e., a mechanism of action of ADH) at night, which leads to excess nighttime urine production that exceeds ordinary bladder capacity. This failure of the kidneys to concentrate urine is believed to be caused by a lack of normal cyclic increase in ADH during sleep (George et al., 1975). This hypothesis has been supported by research conducted by Norgaard and his Danish colleagues (Norgaard, Pedersen, & Djurhuus, 1985; Norgaard, Rittig, & Djurhuus, 1989). However, studies with larger samples of enuretics suggest that the nocturnal deficiency of ADH hypothesis accounts for only about 20% of all bed-wetters (Watanabe & Kawauchi, 1994; Watanabe, Kawauchi, Kitamori, & Azuma, 1994).

The Danish research group has also reported evidence that is important for the second physiological hypothesis regarding deficiencies in muscular responses needed to inhibit urination. Norgaard (1989) observed that, during artificial filling of the bladder while enuretic children were asleep, episodes of arousal to bladder filling were preceded by increased pelvic floor activity (i.e., a "Kegel" contraction). In contrast, bed-wetting without waking was preceded by relaxation of the pelvic floor. In other words, when nighttime wetting was avoided, children appeared to be inhibiting bladder contractions by spontaneously contracting the muscles of the pelvic floor. When nighttime wetting occurred, no such inhibitory responses were observed. Instead, the relatively relaxed pelvic floor was similar to that observed in normal daytime voiding.

Not inconsistent with these hypotheses about delays in physical development, learning theorists have hypothesized that inadequate experience of certain conditions is what causes children to continue bed-wetting. By reasoning backward from the success of conditioning treatments, behavioral psychologists have speculated that simple bed-wetting is caused by children's failure to learn to attend and respond to the need to urinate while asleep (see review by Scott, Barclay, & Houts, 1990). If for any number of reasons (e.g., sleeping for long periods of time, becoming used to the discomfort of a wet bed) a child repeatedly fails to respond to the natural conditions of a wet bed, the child will fail to learn the responses necessary to avoid wetting the bed. Continued bed-wetting, then, is viewed as a failure to learn how to be dry from the naturally occurring conditions of development.

In this regard, the etiological hypothesis of ineffective learning history is complemented by hypotheses about delays in physical development. One investigation suggested that the delay in development may be at the level of the brain stem where signals from the bladder fail to be adequately processed during sleep (Ornitz, Hanna, & de Traversay, 1992). This "brain-bladder" connection is further exemplified in a study by Kawauchi, Watanabe, Kitamori, Imada, and Ohne (1993). They demonstrated that artificially filling the bladders of normal adult volunteers elicited greater plasma ADH levels than before filling, suggesting that stimulation of the bladder produces vasopressin secretion.

In another study in which infants' wetting patterns were observed during sleep, wetting episodes were preceded by arousal and, then, falling back to sleep (Duche, 1973). Duche speculated that enuresis may develop as a result of the child being unable to utilize the discriminative cues that precede micturition because neuromuscular maturation has not yet allowed the child to perform the necessary pelvic floor contraction to prevent wetting. From a biobehavioral perspective, monosymptomatic nocturnal enuresis may be viewed as caused by an interaction between delays in neurological development that are most likely genetically transmitted and behavioral experiences that can either facilitate or further delay responses needed to stop bed-wetting (Houts, 1991). In other words, the enuretic child may pass through a critical period related to gaining nighttime continence and will have been the passive victim of numerous trials of learning to not make the appropriate response (i.e., pelvic floor contraction) due to these delays.

Other hypothesized causes of enuresis that in reality may only be correlates include psychological problems; functional bladder capacity; and sleep and arousal difficulties. The hypothesis that bed-wetting is caused by emotional problems or psychic trauma was first proposed by Freud (1959), and is still commonly believed by parents and many health care professionals (Haque et al., 1981). Nevertheless, when compared with their nonenuretic peers, enuretic children do not exhibit more emotional problems. In the case of children who have stopped bed-wetting for a period of 6 months or more and then resumed bed-wetting (secondary enuretics) the onset of bed-wetting may be precipitated by a traumatic event or other significant distress. In these instances, resolving the distress may be a priority. Otherwise, any emotional difficulties experienced by children with enuresis are most likely a result and not a cause of bed-wetting (see review by Scott et al., 1990). Thus, treating the enuresis may alleviate problems such as social anxiety and low self-appraisal (Moffatt, 1989). At most, the child with emotional problems may only need extra support and encouragement during treatment.

Another hypothesized cause of enuresis is low functional bladder capacity (FBC). FBC is the volume of urine voided when a child has voluntarily postponed micturition for as long as possible after first experiencing the urge to urinate. FBC should not be confused with actual physical bladder capacity, which is a measure of bladder capacity derived from artificial filling of the bladder during catheterization. Although some investigators have reported that samples of enuretics have smaller FBCs than samples of nonenuretic controls (Esperanca & Gerrard, 1969; Starfield, 1967; Starfield & Mellits, 1968; Zaleski, Gerrard, & Shokeir, 1973), there are inconsistencies and problems with this hypothesis. Rutter (1973) found considerable overlap in the FBCs of enuretics and nonenuretics of the same age, and Starfield's (1967) research suggests that bladder capacity may be a function of the child's voiding habits rather than the determinant of those habits. Further, hypotheses that have been offered to explain low FBCs have been highly speculative (Esperanca & Gerrard, 1969), and treatment outcome research targeting methods of increasing FBC has produced inconsistent results (Geffken et al., 1986; Starfield & Mellits, 1968). Most likely, a low FBC is a correlate rather than a cause of bed-wetting, and if present for a given child, may indicate the need to add a treatment component directed toward increasing FBC.

Finally, parents and professionals have declared "deep sleep" as an important precipitating factor in enuresis, although research has never confidently confirmed this relationship (Friman, 1986). Parents of enuretic children often report that their child is difficult to wake, cannot be awakened at night, or is a "deep sleeper." Several researchers in the past have referred to enuresis as an arousal disorder (Finley, 1971; Perlmutter, 1976; Ritvo et al., 1969). Part of the problem has been due to confusion about the differentiation between depth of sleep and arousability. Depth of sleep has been operationalized in terms of sleep stages recorded on an electroencephalogram (EEG), whereas arousability refers to a behavioral measure of how easily a child can be awakened. These two measures of sleep are not, however, necessarily related (Graham, 1973).

Although some of the first studies of sleep recordings in enuretic patients suggested that enuretic events occurred in deep sleep (Pierce, Whitman, Mass, & Gay, 1961), research has since shown that enuretic episodes may occur equally in any sleep stage once the relative proportion of time spent in various sleep stages is taken into account (Mikkelsen et al., 1980; Norgaard, Hansen, Neilson, Rittig, & Djurhuns, 1989). Thus, at least as measured by EEG, depth of sleep is not a reliable correlate of wetting episodes in enuretic children. Depth of sleep is therefore unlikely to be a major cause of bed-wetting; however, arousability, or more specifically, ease of awakening may have implications for treatments like the urine alarm that require the child to be awakened.

With regard to the data on arousability, most research has compared enuretics with nonenuretic controls, and the results of these comparisons have been contradictory (Doleys, Schwartz, & Ciminero, 1981; Graham, 1973). Some studies have either reported trends suggesting enuretic versus nonenuretic differences (Bollard & Nettelbeck, 1988; Bostock, 1958; Boyd, 1960) or that children's arousability from sleep varied greatly (Barclay, 1990). In general, these studies are not inconsistent with a hypothesis that arousal may be an issue in the treatment for a subgroup of enuretic children.

Finally, a study using overnight simultaneous monitoring of EEG and cystometry obtained results that led the researchers to propose a classification system of enuresis in which two of the proposed three types are thought to be due to a disturbance in awakening (Watanabe & Azuma, 1989). The classification types Watanabe and Azuma proposed are based on the following findings from a sample of over 200 enuretic children:

1. *Type I* (61% of cases). The first bladder contraction was noticed on cystometrogram during Stage IV sleep when the bladder was full. Evidence of arousal in EEG appeared and EEG changed to a Stage I or II sleep pattern; enuresis occurred without waking.
2. *Type IIa* (11% of cases). The first bladder contraction was again noticed in Stage IV sleep, but no EEG response was observed, and enuresis occurred.

3. *Type IIb* (28% of cases). Cystometry showed uninhibited contraction of the bladder only during sleep (not on awakening). There was no change in either first bladder contraction or EEG, but enuresis occurred.

The authors consider Type I to represent a mild disturbance in awakening, whereas Type IIa is a more serious grade of awakening problem. Type IIb is thought to be due to abnormal bladder function. The authors suggested that their Type I enuresis may correspond to the "arousal" enuretic events described by Ritvo et al. (1969).

In their review of sleep research, Djurhuus, Norgaard, and Rittig (1992) speculated that the work of Watanabe and Azuma may point to some dysfunction in the pathway leading from the pontine micturition center to the cortex. This hypothesis is based on the fact that previous studies of nighttime voiding suggest that enuretic episodes reflect normal bladder function, and therefore are not the result of dysfunction between the bladder and spinal cord. This hypothesis is supported by the aforementioned findings of abnormal neurophysiological findings in the area of the brain stem near the pontine micturition center (Ornitz et al., 1992) and may soon account for the Kawauchi et al. (1993) finding of how centripetal stimulation of the bladder elicits ADH secretion in normal adults.

TREATMENTS FOR BED-WETTING

MEDICATION APPROACHES

Medication therapy for *nocturnal enuresis* began in the early 1960s when imipramine (brand name Tofranil) was found to reduce urinary incontinence in adult psychiatric patients treated for depression (MacLean, 1960). The 1970s saw the introduction of a bladder antispasmodic medication known as oxybutynin chloride (brand name Ditropan). This drug has been shown to reduce spasms of the bladder and to increase bladder capacity, in addition to being a treatment for bed-wetting (Buttarazzi, 1977; Thompson & Lauvetz, 1976). Finally, a synthetic version of the naturally occurring hormone known as vasopressin was introduced to the United States from Europe in the late 1980s. Desmopressin, or DDAVP, is currently taken intranasally to treat excessive urine production by stimulating the kidney to concentrate urine so the bladder capacity during sleep is not exceeded. A quantitative review by Houts, Berman, and Abramson (1994) reported that although pharmacological treatments produce a better outcome than no treatment, these gains are nearly lost at follow-up, and barely exceed the spontaneous remission rate.

Because of the numerous and potentially dangerous side effects of imipramine (see Werry, Dowrick, Lampen, & Vamos, 1975), and indications that oxybutynin chloride may not be more efficacious than the spontaneous cure rate of 16%, we believe desmopressin (DDAVP) is the most viable of the current pharmacological treatments for nocturnal enuresis. Imipramine, which has a slightly lower efficacy than DDAVP, might be worth considering in cases resistant to all other treatments, or in children with the added diagnosis of depression. The toxicity of the drug in overdose must be emphasized to the family.

A recent review of all controlled trials of DDAVP indicated that only 24.5% of patients achieve short-term dry ss and only 5.7% remained dry after stopping treatment (Moffatt, Harlos, Kirshen, & Burd, 1993). Houts et al. (1994) reported a more promising figure of 21% remaining dry by follow-up. However, these figures are far less impressive than the 45% lasting cure for behavioral treatments using the urine alarm alone. Therefore, the use of DDAVP for anything more than the management of bed-wetting until the child spontaneously remits is not supported by current scientific knowledge.

BEHAVIORAL APPROACHES

Behavioral treatments try to eliminate bed-wetting by directly training the child to control bladder functions during the night. Such training is usually carried out at home by parents and children. Preparing and motivating a family to carry out training procedures is a major component of these approaches. The effectiveness of these approaches depends on the willingness and ability of parents and children to correctly follow the procedures through to a conclusion.

Prior to the development of our treatment known as Full Spectrum Home Training (FSHT), three types of behavior therapy were used to treat bed-wetting: (a) urine alarm training, (b) retention control training, and (c) dry-bed training. All three have received rather extensive evaluation, and it is possible to draw conclusions about their overall effectiveness as well as their practical feasibility. Our Full Spectrum Home Training program was developed from research that evaluated these three approaches, and we incorporated into the FSHT approach those features of previous methods that seemed both useful and practical.

Urine Alarm Training, sometimes called bell-and-pad training, is the oldest form of behavior therapy. This approach was developed by Mowrer and Mowrer (1938) over 50 years ago, and subsequent research has shown this type of training to be an essential ingredient in other effective behavior therapy treatment packages . The treatment relies on a urine alarm device that consists of an absorbent pad and a battery-operated alarm.

Such devices are commercially available from Sears Roebuck and Company as a catalog-ordered item. This type of alarm uses a bed pad to detect wetting and is the one most often described in self-help books (Azrin & Besalel, 1979; Houts, Liebert, & Padawer, 1983). A newer type of device, the Wet-Stop alarm (available from Palco Labs, 8030 Soquel Avenue, Santa Cruz, CA 95062; 800-346-4488), replaces the bed pad with a small absorbent strip that is placed inside the child's underwear. This alarm is very reliable and can be used with training programs that incorporate use of a urine alarm. Similar body-worn alarm devices are also available in most drugstores but we are unfamiliar with their performance.

The basic idea of urine alarm training is to wake the child as soon as possible after wetting starts. When the child wets the bed, the alarm sounds, and the child must be awakened. Urine alarm training has been extensively used, and numerous controlled scientific investigations have demonstrated that it is very effective. About 75% of children treated with this method for an 8- to 14-week period achieve an initial arrest of bed-wetting, and by one year follow-up approximately 41% experience a relapse (Doleys, 1977). The most common cause of failure to achieve an initial arrest with this treatment is not following the procedures completely and correctly. The procedures are demanding on the family, and single parents who have problems of their own as well as couples with marital problems have been less successful than families without such problems (Dische, Yule, Corbett, & Hand, 1983).

The most common specific cause of failure is that parents do not wake the child every time the alarm sounds (Lovibond, 1964). If the child is permitted to sleep through the alarm as many children are able to do, then the child never develops the sensitivity to wake up to the alarm. A second common cause of failure is that parents permit the child to get up, turn off the alarm, and return to bed without becoming fully awake and going to the bathroom. A third cause of failure is not continuing long enough. About 12 weeks is typically required, and for children who wet more than once a night as many as 16 weeks may be needed. Families may abandon the training prematurely. Several studies show that parents who are intolerant of a child's bed-wetting and find it difficult to carry out detailed instructions tend to drop out of this training before its beneficial effects can be realized (James & Foreman, 1973; Morgan & Young, 1975).

If children become dry as a result of urine alarm training and then experience a relapse, they usually do so within the first six months after the training is completed. Evidence suggests that some children who relapse after this training can be successfully retrained with a 2- to 4-week reapplication of the urine alarm regimen (Doleys, 1977), but such retraining is not always successful. The latter problem has led some investigators to emphasize relapse prevention over relapse remediation (Houts, Peterson,

& Whelan, 1986). Also, it is still unclear why some children relapse and others remain dry. Family problems have been associated with relapse (Dische et al., 1983), and in our own research we have found that children who were previously treated with Tofranil had a stronger tendency to relapse than children who had not previously received that drug therapy (Houts, Peterson, & Liebert, 1984).

Researchers have devised a powerful method for preventing relapse from the outset. *Overlearning,* as the method is called, requires the child to drink a large quantity of fluid during the hour before bedtime. Overlearning is usually started after the child has been dry for two consecutive weeks. It is continued with the urine alarm in place until the child is dry for another two consecutive weeks. The overlearning procedure has been shown to cut the chance of relapse in half (Young & Morgan, 1972). With the addition of overlearning, the lasting cure rate of urine alarm training for simple bed-wetting is more than 60%.

Studies show that bed-wetting children have smaller bladder capacities than non-bed-wetting children (Starfield, 1967; Zaleski et al., 1973). The goal of *Retention Control Training* is to increase the child's bladder capacity, defined as how much urine the child produces after holding for as long as possible (Kimmel & Kimmel, 1970). The training itself is rather simple to do. Once a day, the parent and child do the exercises for a 2- to 3-hour period. The child drinks 8 to 16 ounces of fluid and then practices holding for as long as possible after first feeling the need to urinate. The child is given rewards for holding for longer and longer periods of time, up to 45 minutes. Retention control training produces a lasting cure in less than 30% of children with simple bed-wetting (Houts & Liebert, 1984). As a single treatment for bed-wetting, this approach is not as effective as urine alarm training, though there is some evidence to suggest that it may be a useful adjunct to standard urine alarm training either by reducing the chance of a relapse or by speeding the child's initial arrest rate (Fielding, 1980; Houts et al.,1986).

Dry-Bed Training is a behavior therapy program developed by Dr. Nathan Azrin and his colleagues (Azrin, Sneed, & Foxx, 1974). The program has been described in detail in a self-help book (Azrin & Besalel, 1979). Dry-bed training consists of four procedures. The nightly waking schedule, started by a professional who spends the night in the child's home, requires that the child be awakened every hour during the first night of training. At each waking, the child is taken to the bathroom and asked to urinate, given fluids to drink, and then encouraged to withhold urinating for the next hour. On the second night the child is awakened by the parents three hours after going to bed. If the child is dry, then the next night, the parents wake the child 2½ hours after bedtime. The waking time is moved ahead by half an hour each night following a dry bed and is stopped when the child is scheduled to be awakened one hour after going to bed. If the child wets twice in one week, the cycle of the nightly waking schedule starts over.

The second procedure, called positive practice, requires the child to lie down in the bed, count to 50, and then get up and go to the bathroom and try to urinate. The process is repeated 20 times. Twenty trials of positive practice are done in the middle of the night immediately after a wet bed and also before bedtime the next night. The third procedure of dry-bed training is the urine alarm, used as described earlier. The alarm is introduced after the first night of waking the child every hour. If the alarm signals that the child has wet, the child is awakened and reprimanded for wetting the bed. Then the fourth procedure, called cleanliness training, is done. This is done immediately after wetting the bed and requires the child to change wet clothes and bed linens. The child places all wet linens in the laundry and remakes the bed with clean sheets. After completing 20 trials of positive practice, the alarm is reactivated and the child goes back to sleep.

In keeping with the general trend to make treatments more cost effective, later research on dry-bed training sought to eliminate the alarm (Azrin & Thienes, 1978) and the use of a professional in the home (Azrin, Thienes-Hontos, & Besalel-Azrin, 1979). Two important conclusions can be drawn from research on dry-bed training. First, the inclusion of a urine alarm in this treatment package should not be considered optional, because the overall effectiveness of dry-bed training is reduced substantially if an alarm is not used. Second, there does not appear to be any appreciable gain in treatment effectiveness when a professional trainer conducts the first night of treatment than when parents do it by themselves (Houts & Liebert, 1984). Relapse after dry-bed training (39%) is virtually identical to that following simple urine alarm training (41%) (Bollard, 1982). In addition, dry-bed training is more difficult to carry out than simple urine alarm training. The requirements of the nightly waking schedule and the demands of positive practice are rather severe.

For simple, uncomplicated nocturnal enuresis, we prefer multicomponent treatments that have been demonstrated to impact the problems of speed of treatment response and relapse in urine alarm therapy by adding other behavioral procedures to the basic urine alarm treatment. Our research group has developed and modified one such multicomponent treatment called *Full Spectrum Home Treatment (FSHT)*. This approach was designed to provide parent(s) and children with an inexpensive, easy-to-use, and effective treatment for uncomplicated nocturnal enuresis. Families are provided with a detailed manual complete with support materials. Treatment has been demonstrated to be most effective if delivered by a trained professional (Houts, Whelan, & Peterson, 1987). The treatment components are (a) basic urine alarm treatment, (b) cleanliness training, (c) retention control training, and (d) overlearning. For basic urine alarm treatment, we prefer the newer urine alarm devices that are worn on the body and have been found to be more reliable than the older devices that required use of a bed pad and freestanding alarm box. Most of these newer alarm devices are turned off by removing the urine-sensitive probe from the child's underwear and drying it off.

Of the several systematic reviews of the enuresis treatment outcome literature that have been conducted over the past 30 years, only one has employed the relatively new empirical method known as meta-analysis (Houts et al., 1994). This review included the common medication approaches (i.e., imipramine, oxybutynin hydrochloride, desmopressin), verbal psychotherapies, the urine alarm alone or combined with other behavior therapies (e.g., dry-bed training, cleanliness training) in addition to assessing for moderators of treatment effectiveness such as investigator allegiance.

As previously mentioned, medication approaches when evaluated at follow-up perform disappointingly and lead to complete remission of wetting in about 17% of children. Again, this is approximately the same as the spontaneous cure rate of 16% (Forsythe & Redmond, 1974). Psychological treatments that include the urine alarm were reported to lead to a wetting cessation rate of 60% by the end of treatment with 44% remaining dry at follow-up. Houts et al. (1994) confidently concluded that behavioral treatments that include the use of the urine alarm alone or in combination with other treatment components are the treatments of choice.

We have systematically investigated Full Spectrum Home Training at the University of Memphis since the early 1980s. Figure 12.2 summarizes 1-year follow-up results from six observations of Full Spectrum Home Training, four of which are from published studies (Houts et al., 1983, 1986, 1987; Whelan & Houts, 1990). The 48 cases labeled 1988 were accumulated in a private enuresis clinic over a period of 2 years and are not from a randomized study. The 1991 sample shows outcomes from our randomized trial that compared FSHT with imipramine and oxybutynin. About 3 out of every 4 children treated with this approach can be expected to stop bed-wetting at the end of the average of 12 weeks needed to complete the treatment.

At the 1-year follow-up, 6 out of every 10 children are permanently dry. The lower relapse rates observed in the 1988 and 1991 samples were from children who did our modified overlearning where they gradually increased nighttime drinking in 2-ounce increments adjusted for their age. In the other samples, overlearning was done in the original fashion of having children consume 16 ounces of water regardless of age. We now consistently find that only about 10% of children relapse. This may be compared with 40% without overlearning and 20% with the original type of overlearning. We have not completely solved the problem of relapse,

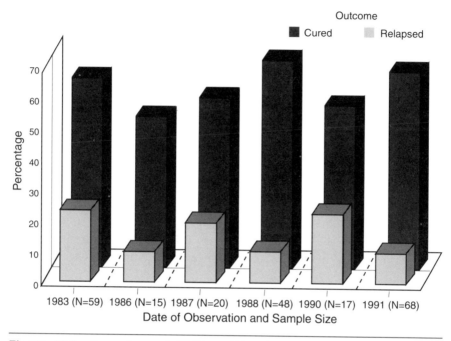

Figure 12.2 Percentage of Children Who Ceased Bed-Wetting at 1-Year Follow-Up with Full Spectrum Home Training for Six Samples.

but we have come some distance in preventing relapse after successful treatment with the urine alarm.

THE PARENT TRAINING PROGRAM— FULL SPECTRUM HOME TRAINING (FSHT)

WHAT ARE NECESSARY QUALIFICATIONS OF THE THERAPIST(S) IN FSHT?

Because enuresis has been lucidly conceptualized as a "biobehavioral" problem (Houts, 1991; Mellon & Houts, 1995) involving both environmental and physiological etiologies, its ideal management requires the collaboration of behaviorally trained psychologists and physicians. Each of these health care providers offers a unique expertise in the diagnosis and treatment of this multifaceted, yet common childhood problem.

As was previously explained, interventions based on learning processes lead to the best long-term outcomes for bed-wetting. Psychologists or other mental health providers who have been trained in the clinical application of learning principles are well suited to implement FSHT. Ideally, a pediatric psychologist who has had direct training experience with the urine alarm approach and a sensitivity to the medical aspects of the disorder could optimally manage the treatment through collaboration with a physician as needed.

Since a small percentage of nocturnal enuretics suffer from organic pathologies that can promote or prolong the problem, all children presenting with bed-wetting need to have a basic physical exam that includes a urinalysis and culture, and ideally, an ultrasound of the kidneys and bladder. In approximately 3% to 5% of children, diseases such as nephritis or diabetes will be the cause of their presenting symptoms of day- and nighttime urinary incontinence. Further, as many as 5% of boys and 10% of girls who wet the bed have urinary tract infections (Stansfeld, 1973). These medical problems and their differential diagnosis from simple bed-wetting require the services of a physician. Examination of the urine, reliable cultures, and careful questioning about medical histories and current symptoms can be performed quickly and inexpensively in an outpatient setting by a general pediatrician or family physician. Additional collaboration with a physician would also be necessary if medication treatments are to be combined with the urine alarm and other behavioral approaches.

WHAT MUST BE KNOWN ABOUT THE PATIENT IN FSHT?

Barring medical problems as a cause of bed-wetting, the treatment of choice for nocturnal enuresis includes some version of urine alarm therapy. This treatment, however, requires a large investment of time and effort not only from the child, but also the parent(s). An in-depth clinical interview of the parents and child will determine whether they are able to implement a demanding treatment, and also will help identify any associated psychopathology. Factors that have been associated with bedwetters who will successfully complete treatment and maintain those gains include information about history of enuresis, prior treatments, parental attitudes and beliefs, family and home environment, behavioral problems, and the child's current wetting pattern. The presence of relevant psychiatric symptoms or significant psychosocial stressors in the family may make a stronger argument for considering the use of medication treatment to manage the bed-wetting. Until psychosocial stressors can be reduced to subclinical levels or eliminated, behavioral treatment is unlikely to be effectively implemented.

A thorough history of a child's wetting pattern will reveal whether wetting occurred after a period of nighttime continence (6 months to a year), which is referred to as *secondary enuresis*. Medical or emotional factors may have been involved. If the onset of bed-wetting has coincided with stressful events or the presence of psychiatric symptoms, it may be useful to focus initially on minimizing current stressful events or treating psychiatric problems prior to implementing urine alarm treatment.

Carefully reviewing prior behavioral and medication interventions will often identify the reasons those treatments failed and how problems in treatment might be resolved in the future. Often, previous failure with the urine alarm is due to inadequate parental instruction and preparation. We have found that parents were not properly instructed to awaken the child, and they did not realize the treatment can require 16 weeks of effort to be successful. Frequent and careful monitoring by an experienced behavioral psychologist during treatment can prevent repeating a disappointing experience. Previous drug treatment failures are the norm rather than the exception, and parents can be reassured that the continued bed-wetting is not due to inadequate parenting.

Because some research has suggested that extremely noncompliant children are more likely to experience relapse following successful treatment (Dische et al., 1983; Sacks & DeLeon, 1973), a screening questionnaire such as the Child Behavior Checklist (CBCL) (Achenbach & Edelbrock, 1983) can identify children who need additional attention. Children with externalizing behavioral problems (Externalizing *T* score of greater than 70) are likely to be noncompliant with any parental requests, let alone the significant demands of waking to the urine alarm in the middle of the night. Likewise, internalizing behavior problems such as significant levels of anxiety and depression may interfere with the enuretic child's capacity to handle the rigors of urine alarm treatment. A clinical decision has to be made whether to train parents in contingency management prior to beginning behavioral treatment for enuresis. Failure to identify child noncompliance and internalizing problems prior to urine alarm treatment can lead to a poor outcome. Such a poor outcome will only further contribute to a child's already lowered sense of confidence and self-esteem that is typically associated with bed-wetting.

Parental attitudes and beliefs have implications for those families that enter treatment. A large survey of parents of bed-wetters (Haque et al., 1981) indicated that as many as 35% dealt with the enuresis by punishing the child when bed-wetting occurred. Butler, Brewin, and Forsythe (1986) found that the mother perceiving a greater burden for herself and attributing the cause of bed-wetting to the child were associated with greater parental intolerance as assessed by Morgan and Young's (1975) Tolerance for Enuresis Scale. This has been predictive of treatment dropout. Informing parents that bed-wetting is a deficit in physical learning rather than a willful act can lead to the family support necessary before behavioral treatment is implemented.

Because of the genetic contribution to enuresis, the problem of bed-wetting may be a common experience within the family. Young and Morgan (1973) reported a relationship between treatment dropout and positive family history of enuresis, and Fielding and Doleys (1989) have suggested that these findings may be indicative of complacency or poor motivation in these families. The potentially large demands of behavioral treatment can be disrupted by a lack of motivation for complete implementation and noncooperation in the family. We use a behavioral contracting approach designed to increase cooperation and understanding of each family member's responsibilities with treatment. If the family is unable to agree to the goals of treatment, it does not begin.

Assessment of family stress and disturbance, as well as the physical home environment is important because they have been associated with slow response to treatment, treatment failure, and relapse. Couchells, Johnson, Carter, and Walker (1981) reported that families seeking help for bed-wetting are more likely to be experiencing stress than those families who do not seek treatment. Family disturbances and high maternal anxiety have been associated with slow response to treatment (Morgan & Young, 1975). Dische et al. (1983) reported that marital discord, mental or physical handicap of family members, poor maternal coping skills, and unusual family living arrangements were predictors of behavioral treatment failure and relapse.

Having the parents complete the Locke-Wallace Marital Adjustment Test (MAT) (Locke & Wallace, 1959) may indicate significant marital distress (MAT scores below 85 for either spouse) that could interfere with urine alarm treatment. Among single parents, typically mothers, the Beck Depression Inventory (BDI) (Beck, Rush, Shaw, & Emery, 1980) may identify significant parental distress (scores above 15) that may require therapeutic attention prior to starting behavior therapy for enuresis. Finally, the Symptom Checklist (SCL-90-R) (Derogatis, 1977) is useful in screening for significant levels of global psychiatric distress. Clinically significant elevations in any of the preceding areas of psychological functioning would allow the health care provider to judge whether prior marital or family therapy is necessary to prevent a negative outcome when behavior therapy is used for enuresis.

A 2-week baseline of wetting frequency should be established. Parents can complete record forms that include wet or dry nights, the size of the wet spot, and whether the child spontaneously awakened to void in the toilet. As a general rule of thumb, the more frequently the child wets, the longer it will take for the child to stop bed-wetting (Hallgren, 1957). It is important to determine whether a child is a multiple wetter (i.e., wets more than once per night). This may not be apparent until urine alarm treatment begins, as there is often only one large wet spot in the morning. Multiple wetters typically require more time to reach the success criterion of 14 consecutive dry nights, and informing parents accordingly contributes to realistic expectations about progress and avoids discouragement and possible dropout.

Even with patient and family information that has been associated with a poorer outcome, it should be pointed out that, all things being equal, 60% of bed-wetters treated with FSHT will cease wetting. The point is, if you were to guess the outcome of a monosymptomatic bed-wetter treated with FSHT prior to knowing anything about the child, it would most likely be a successful one. However, being aware of correlates of treatment outcome may further improve the odds of success.

What Is FSHT and How Is It Properly Implemented?

This program was designed to provide parents and children with an inexpensive, easy-to-use, and effective combination package treatment for simple bed-wetting. Our goal was to develop the strongest possible combination of behavioral procedures, and we created a full set of support materials for the package that would facilitate its home use. The treatment program has been described in detail in a self-help book for parents and teachers (Houts & Liebert, 1984). Full Spectrum Home Training includes urine alarm training, cleanliness training, retention control training, and overlearning, as well as several additional features designed to enhance its effectiveness and simplify its use.

From its inception, FSHT has been done in a single session, in groups, to minimize the financial cost to families. Parents and children filled out an explicit behavioral contract together as a trainer modeled each of the procedures point by point. A manual containing explanations and support materials was provided to parents ("Parent Guide"), and a wall chart ("Daily Steps to a Dry Bed") was given to the child. Through systematic research previously reviewed, the program has evolved to include the addition of overlearning and then the "graduated" overlearning to address our dissatisfaction with a 24% relapse rate. This addition has reduced the relapse rate to approximately 10% today.

Our research with this treatment program has also sought to deliver the treatment in a single session via a didactic videotape to further minimize costs to families. Compared with delivery by a professional, the delivery by videotape was considerably less effective (Houts et al., 1987). Therefore, we do not suggest that parents administer this treatment without having some assistance from a professional who can monitor the child's progress and make minor modifications to the program where needed. Nevertheless, the program can be carried out with minimal professional assistance, and in our current clinical work we typically follow a four-visit protocol.

Implementing Full Spectrum Home Training

All children who receive this treatment should be medically screened to rule out organic causes for their bed-wetting; the program is appropriate for children whose problem is primary nocturnal enuresis. Provided children meet these screening criteria, then the treatment program can generally be administered in the home after an initial training session.

At the first visit, the Family Support Agreement is completed and all aspects of the training are demonstrated. It is also important to "demystify" the problem by pointing out to the child and family how common the disorder is and emphasize that the problem is not a willful and defiant act. The stage must be set for effective collaboration between the child, parent, and therapist. At the second visit, which occurs the following week, the procedures are reviewed to ensure that the family is doing everything correctly and keeping accurate records. After the second visit, the family is contacted by telephone to track the child's progress and to solve any minor problems of implementation. The third visit occurs when the child attains 14 dry nights in a row. At this visit, the procedures for overlearning are introduced, and the family returns for the fourth visit when the child attains 14 consecutive dry nights in overlearning. Once a child completes overlearning, the alarm is removed and the training stops. Children are followed for 1 year to monitor relapse, and if a child returns to regular wetting, the alarm is reinstated until the child is dry for 14 consecutive dry nights.

In the following discussion of Full Spectrum training, we have emphasized some of our more recent modifications to the procedures based on clinical experience. We are in the process of collecting systematic research data on the efficacy of these modifications, and they are presented here as suggestions for parents and professionals who may want to implement the training described in more detail in *Bed-Wetting: A Guide for Parents and Children* (Houts & Liebert, 1984).

Figure 12.3 shows the Family Support Agreement of Full Spectrum Home Training. This is a behavioral contract that the trainer assists the parents and child in completing at the initial training session where each step of the program is described. The Family Support Agreement specifies exactly what the child and parents must do to carry out all the procedures of Full Spectrum Home Training. We have found that having parents and children sign this written agreement and refer back to it during the training helps to remind them of their mutual commitment and obligations, especially at those points when they get discouraged or confused about what to do.

As shown in Item 9 of the Family Support Agreement (Figure 12.3), Full Spectrum Home Training includes a version of retention control training that we call self-control training. Parents and children do this procedure once a day during a specified 2-hour period. The child begins by drinking a large glass of water. If the child feels the need to urinate, the child tells the parent about this, and the parent instructs the child to postpone going to the bathroom for 3 minutes. If the child can wait 3 minutes and then use

1. _____ & _____ agree to carry out the training procedures exactly as described in order to accomplish the mutually desired goal of a dry bed.

2. Training will be carried out for at least 84 days (12 weeks).

3. Parents and family agree not to punish, scold, ridicule, or refer to "bed-wetting" in a negative way during the training.

4. Both parents and child understand that training is most effective when the child is not overtired or stressed.
Therefore _____ & _____ agree that _____ P.M. is a reasonable bedtime, and _____ agrees to go to bed at that time every night.

5. NO RESTRICTIONS ON LIQUIDS. _____ will be allowed to drink as much liquid as desired at all times.

6. Parents and family agree to provide support, help, and understanding to _____ . They will praise him/her when dry and provide encouragement that progress will be made. However, they understand that the training itself includes sufficient pressure and agree they will not urge him/her to try harder or do better.

7. Parents and family agree not to complain about the effects of the training on them or about the urine alarm, but to support and help instead.
_____ also agrees not to complain about the training and to cooperate fully.

8. The family will provide a relatively stress-free environment at home during training.

9. _____ & _____ agree to participate in Self-Control Training once a day during the hours of _____ & _____ as explained in the Parent Guide.
Parents will give _____ money for each success according to the Reward Schedule for Self-Control Training.

10. _____ agrees to follow the procedure of Cleanliness Training as outlined on the wall chart and to put wet sheets and underwear in _____ .
Parents agree to keep clean sheets and clean underwear in the _____ in the child's room for him/her to use when remaking the bed.

11. Parents agree to wake _____ immediately if the buzzer rings and he/she does not wake up.
IT IS ESSENTIAL THAT THE PERSON RESPONSIBLE FOR WAKING THE CHILD WILL BE ABLE TO HEAR AND BE AWAKENED BY THE ALARM. NOTHING ELSE SHOULD BE DONE TO WAKE THE CHILD DURING THE NIGHT. THE ALARM MUST DO THIS.

12. Parents agree to check the batteries regularly and to have replacement batteries ready when needed. Parents will also check the absorbent pockets for wear and replace these when needed.

13. _____ & _____ agree that *only* _____ will touch the alarm, except for alarm testing as described above.

Figure 12.3 Family Support Agreement Used in Full Spectrum Home Training.

(Continued)

14. Parents agree to assume all responsibilities associated with training for a dry bed as spelled out in the Parent Guide.
   _____ agrees to follow the Daily Steps to a Dry Bed outlined on the wall chart.

15. Overlearning. When _____ has been dry for 14 consecutive nights, the Overlearning procedures will be followed until the child is dry for 14 more nights in a row. Overlearning will be explained when the child returns for the second follow-up appointment.

16. It is understood that every child has an occasional wet bed, especially when sick or under stress. Do Not Worry About This. Tell Your Child Not To Worry.

_____
(Child's Signature)

_____
(Parent's Signature)

_____
(Parent's Signature)

_____
(Witness or Other Family Member)

Figure 12.3   *(Continued)*

the toilet, the child is given a nickel. When the child completes a holding goal, the next day a new goal of 3 minutes longer is set and the reward increases by a nickel for each new goal. This part of the training is completed when the child successfully completes a 45-minute goal in step-by-step fashion. It is helpful to point out to the family that partial or inconsistent implementation of self-control training will only lengthen treatment and may reduce its overall effectiveness.

Parents make some common mistakes in implementing self-control training. For example, the father of a 6-year-old boy mistakenly allowed his son to hold for as long as possible rather than follow the step-by-step procedure of increasing the holding time in 3-minute increments. This defeated the purpose of training the child to discriminate between the different sensations associated with different levels of bladder filling. This child had little difficulty holding for 3 minutes, but he did not know his own bodily feelings well enough to be able to urinate at the end of 3 minutes after first feeling the need. In the early stages of self-control training, the challenge is for the child to be able to urinate at a specified time. Only later, as the holding time approaches 45 minutes, does the challenge become one of holding back and thereby increasing functional bladder capacity. Another common mistake is for parents to forget to time the child. This can be easily overcome by setting a kitchen or oven timer with an alarm that can signal when the holding time is past.

Full Spectrum Home Training also includes cleanliness training (see Item 10 in Figure 12.3) which requires the child to remake the bed after the alarm has sounded. The steps involved in cleanliness training are displayed on a wall chart ("Daily Steps to a Dry Bed") that is placed in the child's room. This wall chart also displays a record of the child's progress and is colored in either "wet" or "dry" for each day of the training. We have found that parents and children may not comply with cleanliness training, especially if the child has wet just enough to make the alarm sound but not so much as to get the bed wet. This can occur with the newer alarm devices (e.g., Palco's Wet-Stop) which will sound immediately when the child wets the underpants and stops any further urination. To make sure that the child is fully awake after a wetting episode, we instruct parents to have the child go through with the full procedure of remaking the bed even if the sheets are not wet.

Item 11 of the Family Support Agreement in Figure 12.3 emphasizes the importance of waking the child immediately after the alarm sounds. This is the most important part of urine alarm training. It is especially important to do this consistently for the first 3 weeks of the training so that the child can learn to respond to the alarm and wake without assistance from parents. In our instructions to families, we make it very clear that there is nothing magical about using an alarm. Parents and children are told that the alarm is used solely for the purpose of signaling to wake the child immediately after wetting starts. We have recommended that the parent must be able to hear the alarm sound. Using a baby monitor device to be aware of the alarm sounding can be helpful in this regard. Waking up, not the alarm itself, is the important thing. Also, children are instructed to follow the rule of getting out of bed and standing up before turning off the alarm. Parents are told never to turn off the alarm for the child. Parents are also asked to record each wet, its time of occurrence, the size of the wet spot, and whether children awoke on their own to urinate in the toilet. This information is useful to the therapist in monitoring progress and the need to use other treatment components such as a waking schedule for children not waking to the alarm. This information is important for the child and parent to document improvements in wetting to reinforce perseverance during the many weeks of treatment.

Full Spectrum Home Training incorporates overlearning (Item 15 of Figure 12.3) to prevent relapse once a child attains 14 consecutive dry nights. In our previous work, we implemented overlearning by having the child drink 16 ounces of water during the hour before bedtime once the child had attained 14 consecutive dry nights. This nightly drinking continued until the child attained 14 more consecutive dry nights while drinking the water. Whereas this way of implementing overlearning has consistently resulted in reducing relapse by 50% compared with simple urine alarm training without overlearning, we have noted that some children who failed to achieve 14 more dry nights in overlearning also failed to recover from the relapse induced by overlearning. Therefore, we have modified the implementation of overlearning by gradually increasing the amount of water that a child drinks before going to bed. Our preliminary results from this gradual approach to overlearning suggest that the rate of relapse can be reduced yet another 50%.

The gradual approach to overlearning begins by determining a maximum amount of water for a child to drink. This is done by the formula, 1 ounce for each year of age plus 2 ounces (Berger, Maizels, Moran, Conway, & Firlit, 1983). Thus, for an 8-year-old child, the maximum amount would be 10 ounces. Children then begin the overlearning process by drinking 4 ounces of water 15 minutes before bedtime. If they remain dry for two nights while drinking 4 ounces, then the amount of water increases to 6 ounces. If they remain dry for two nights at the 6-ounce amount, then the water is increased by 2 more ounces to 8 ounces. The water increases continue in this fashion, 2 ounces more for every 2 consecutive dry nights, until the child's maximum amount is reached. The child continues to drink this maximum amount until 14 consecutive dry nights are attained as measured from the beginning of overlearning. About one third of the children who achieve an initial arrest (14 consecutive dry nights) go on to complete this form of overlearning without having a wet night in overlearning. Most, however, do experience some wetting during overlearning, typically as they approach the goal of drinking their maximum amount. When a child has a wet night during overlearning, the child is instructed to drink the amount of water previously drunk on the most recent preceding dry night. The child then drinks this amount until dry for 5 consecutive nights, after which time the amount increases by 2 ounces for every two consecutive dry nights until the maximum amount is reached. Obviously, parents must keep accurate records to implement this procedure correctly.

Most children can attain the goal of a lasting cure for bed-wetting by following the basic steps of Full Spectrum Home Training. Parents should seek professional assistance to monitor their child's progress and to determine what modifications of the basic procedures, if any, are needed for their child to be successful. Discussed in the following section, the most common implementation problems with FSHT include waking difficulties and delayed responding that can lead to increased frustration and hopelessness in the child if not attended to by the therapist in a prompt and effective way. Our clinical observations suggest that perhaps only 2 out of 10 children will become disenchanted with the treatment and want to quit following a wet just short of the 14 consecutive dry nights success criterion. Assisting the child in setting realistic expectations and high-lighting treatment progress documented in the treatment records are two of the most important things a professional can do. Our research (Houts et al., 1987) and clinical observations lead us to believe that a family report of prior urine alarm treatment failures are the result of the absence of needed therapist supervision and guidance. The importance of proper therapist guidance to prevent or manage premature quitting of the treatment is described in the following section.

WHAT COMMON IMPLEMENTATION PROBLEMS ARE ENCOUNTERED WITH FSHT?

The two most important difficulties with implementing FSHT are problems in waking the child and problems in the delayed response of some children, each of which can lead to frustration and termination of treatment before the child becomes dry.

Waking Problems

Urine alarm treatments such as FSHT will only work if a child is systematically awakened immediately after a wetting episode begins. Although numerous studies have failed to find a reliable relationship between depth of sleep (as measured by electroencephalography) and wetting episodes, we have found that some children are more difficult to arouse than others. Some of the most difficult cases are those where a child fails to wake up to the sound of the urine alarm. In these cases, it is crucial to establish a waking routine early in the treatment. This requires having the child get out of bed and get to his or her feet before disconnecting and turning off the urine alarm. With younger children who are especially difficult to arouse, it may be necessary for one parent to sleep in this child's room to ensure that the child is awakened immediately when the alarm sounds.

It is also important to make sure that the child is fully awake. Children can do rather remarkable things in a sleepwalking state. We have found it useful to check the child's mental alertness by asking the child to perform short-term memory tasks such as repeating the home phone number backwards. Families also find it useful to establish a wake-up password that is decided on just before the child goes to bed. If the alarm sounds, the child is asked to repeat the password as a test to see if the child is fully awake.

If after 2 weeks of assistance, a child is still not waking to the urine alarm, it is useful to implement a waking schedule (Azrin et al., 1974) to disrupt the child's sleep pattern. Parents are instructed to wake the child hourly using minimal prompts throughout the first night. At each awakening, the child is praised for a dry bed and encouraged to void in the toilet. The second night forward, the waking schedule continues with the child being awakened once each night. Following a dry night, the parents wake the child 30 minutes earlier than the previous night. If the child wets during the night, then the time of waking remains the same as the previous night. The nightly waking ends when the scheduled time for waking the child has moved forward to within 30 minutes immediately following bedtime. The procedure is very demanding for the whole family and should be used only if absolutely necessary to train a child to awaken to the alarm. It should also be remembered that urine alarm treatments for bed-wetting are not perfect, and 1 or 2 of every 10 children will fail to cease bed-wetting with this treatment.

Delayed Response Problems

In FSHT, the first goal is for the child to attain 14 consecutive dry nights. Overlearning is then started, and the child completes the treatment when 14 additional consecutive dry nights are attained while drinking water before bedtime. Most children reach the first goal within 8 weeks of treatment, and they take an average additional 4 weeks to complete overlearning. Some children will not attain the first 14 consecutive dry nights even after 12 weeks of treatment, and their delayed response is often frustrating to them and to their parents.

One way to deal with the problem of delayed response is to keep parents and children focused on the progress that is being made. This requires regular follow-up and supportive therapy sessions with a family. Even though children may not attain 14 consecutive dry nights in the first 8 weeks of treatment, they almost always show evidence of progress. Signs of progress include (a) a reduction in the number of nights that the child needed adult assistance to awaken, (b) a reduction in wetting to once per night among children who started out wetting two or three times each night, (c) a reduction in wetting frequency, (d) a reduction in the size of the wet spot, and (e) an increase in the interval between bedtime and the first wetting episode.

Children who are multiple wetters are especially likely to be delayed responders. These children may also be good candidates for combined behavioral and pharmacotherapy, which requires close collaboration with a physician. To date, the research on combined treatments is very sparse. More research is needed to test the efficacy of such combinations, especially with difficult cases such as multiple wetters. At present, only two investigations have considered such combinations, and both report positive findings. Philpott and Flasher (1970) initially intended to compare imipramine with basic urine alarm treatment but decided that, if the urine alarm was not producing a satisfactory result, imipramine would be added. Thus, 27 boys and 6 girls received this combination treatment. Of those children, 21 boys and 4 girls experienced some positive change, and the authors concluded that the addition of imipramine to the urine alarm enhanced the therapeutic effect. In the second investigation, Sukhai, Mol, and Harris (1989) compared the combination of the urine alarm and desmopressin (DDAVP) with the alarm and a placebo pill. The combined treatment was more effective than the alarm with placebo in terms of increasing the number of dry nights during treatment. Neither of these studies provided long-term follow-up and, as is typical of outcome studies of pharmacological treatments for enuresis, outcome was reported in average reductions of wet nights rather than the percentage of children who ceased bed-wetting. Nevertheless, they both point to the potential usefulness of combining the immediate effects of pharmacological agents with the more lasting effects of multicomponent behavioral treatments. Combining FSHT with DDAVP for multiple wetters may reduce the frustration of parents and children who would otherwise be at risk for treatment dropout due to delays in reaching the success criteria. How and at what point to withdraw the medication are questions that need to be answered by future research.

CASE MATERIAL

HISTORY

Travis was a 9-year-old male who had been wetting since infancy. He was the third child of four in a two-parent home. Travis attained daytime bladder and bowel control by the age of 2½ and had no indication of urinary tract infection or other physical anomaly based on a medical examination. There was a positive family history of bed-wetting in the biological father and paternal grandfather. Travis suffered from no apparent psychological problems.

CLINICAL ASSESSMENT

During the clinical interview with Travis and his mother, it was reported that Travis was a very well-behaved child who was also an exceptional student and athlete (i.e., honor roll, black belt in Taekwondo). The parent's responses to the Child Behavior Checklist in fact revealed no significant clinical elevations for Travis in any area. However, both Travis and his mother admitted that he was embarrassed by his bed-wetting in that his 6-year-old brother no longer wet. Travis was also unwilling to participate in sleepovers with his friends for fear of wetting. Travis's mother reported that he wet the bed on the average of 5 out of 7 nights of the week and had done so since he was toilet trained. Two weeks of baseline recording of wet nights prior to the clinical interview confirmed this reported frequency. Travis was described as a deep sleeper, but was usually dry when sleeping away from home.

Travis's parents completed the Enuresis Tolerance Scale (ETS; Morgan & Young, 1975) and the Locke-Wallace Marital Adjustment Test (MAT; Locke & Wallace, 1959), which revealed no extreme beliefs about Travis's bed-wetting nor significant dissatisfaction with their marriage. Both parents were very concerned about Travis's self-esteem being affected because of the continued wetting and did not punish him for the problem.

TREATMENT

A week later, Travis and his parents attended a one-hour training session for FSHT during which the problem of enuresis was demystified, each component of treatment was reviewed, and all treatment materials were given to the family. This session involved the completion of the Family Support Agreement as described previously. Travis and his parents agreed to carry out all components of treatment for a minimum of 16 weeks and they all signed the contract. In addition, the parents were provided with a treatment manual and wall chart, instructed in how to keep treatment records, and given a urine alarm (Palco Wet-Stop).

The following week, Travis and his parents met the therapist to review treatment progress. Travis was well into his Self-Control Training and had achieved 5 out of 7 dry nights. The therapist praised Travis for his progress and emphasized the need to adhere to all treatment components. Travis was then scheduled to return to clinic every two to three weeks to monitor progress.

During the next 8 weeks, Travis obtained 12 consecutive dry nights on two separate occasions. However, he also failed to complete Self-Control Training. Problem solving with the parents revealed that the onset of the school year and the mother returning to the workforce contributed to a disruption in treatment and the need to reestablish treatment schedules and closer supervision. Another 10 consecutive days of dryness followed by a wet seemed to overwhelm Travis, and he began to deny he had wet and hid his underwear. Travis's parents scheduled an extra meeting with the therapist in hopes of preventing Travis from quitting prematurely. Praising Travis for his perseverance, reviewing his progress to date, and highlighting his overall accomplishments (e.g., honor student, black belt in Taekwondo) that resulted from not giving up, seemed to rejuvenate his enthusiasm and commitment to be successful. At this point, Travis immediately obtained his 14-day success criterion and began overlearning. Travis completed overlearning in three more weeks of treatment with only two additional wets. Though the treatment lasted a total of 19 weeks, both Travis and his parents were extremely pleased with his success and he was eager to fully participate in future sleepovers. Travis remained dry at one year follow-up.

CONCLUSION

When a parent is concerned about a child who has enuresis, the close collaboration between a behavioral psychologist and a physician is critical for the proper treatment of the child. It is important to get a careful assessment to determine contributing factors in the enuresis. Children who have daytime wetting or those whose nighttime wetting has resumed after a period of one year or more of consecutive dry nights may require rather extensive medical examination and treatment. All children, even those who are simple bed-wetters without apparent complications, should first be examined by their pediatrician. If the problem is simple bed-wetting, or primary nocturnal enuresis without medical complications, then the parent can assist the child to overcome the problem through home-implemented behavioral treatment. However, we do not recommend implementing home training without the assistance of a qualified and knowledgeable professional.

Full Spectrum Home Training is the treatment of choice in most cases. If the family is an intact family and the parents are generally supportive and understanding of the child, this program can be carried out by having the parents follow the detailed instructions provided in the parent guide. For such families, weekly consultation may not be necessary, though the professional should provide some support and follow-up even if only via telephone contact. For other families, weekly consultation with a professional may be necessary to keep the family motivated and to ensure that the procedures are followed carefully. Most cases of simple bed-wetting can be successfully treated with these methods.

Whereas medication treatment is not generally a permanent solution to enuresis, it may be the best alternative for some children, especially those for whom the enuresis has become a major barrier to social development and self-esteem and whose families are unable to implement a program of behavior therapy. In such cases, desmopressin (DDAVP) may provide some temporary and safe control over the problem and enable the child to participate in activities that require sleeping over such as camping trips or summer camp.

Because prolonged, uncontrolled wetting can result in damage to self-esteem, it is important to seek a permanent solution to the problem. When families are experiencing difficulties such as marital problems or excessive stress due to parents' work schedules, they should get help to solve these problems before attempting to implement behavioral treatment for a child's bed-wetting. Like most parent training approaches to child problems, Full Spectrum Home Training for primary enuresis requires that parents work together to support the child and provide a consistent environment where the child can learn new skills.

In dealing with a child who wets, there is no substitute for a caring and concerned family, particularly one that understands children rarely choose to be enuretic. In the United States, 5 to 7 million school-age children exhibit enuresis, and given the availability of effective treatments for simple bed-wetting, it is possible that parents and professionals can become partners in providing the help needed to deal with this age-old problem of childhood.

REFERENCES

Achenbach, T. M., & Edelbrock, C. (1983). *Manual for the child behavior checklist.* Burlington: Department of Psychiatry, University of Vermont.

American Academy of Pediatrics Committee on Radiology. (1980). Excretory urography for evaluation of enuresis. *Pediatrics, 65,* 644–655.

American Psychiatric Association. (1994). *Diagnostic and statistical manual of mental disorders* (3rd ed. Rev.). Washington, DC: Author.

Arnold, S. J., & Ginsberg, A. (1973). Enuresis, incidence and pertinence of genitourinary disease in healthy enuretic children. *Urology, 2,* 437–443.

Azrin, N. H., & Besalel, V. A. (1979). *A parent's guide to bedwetting control.* New York: Simon & Schuster.

Azrin, N. H., Sneed, T. J., & Foxx, R. M. (1974). Dry-bed training: Rapid elimination of childhood enuresis. *Behaviour Research and Therapy, 12,* 147–156.

Azrin, N. H., & Thienes, P. M. (1978). Rapid elimination of enuresis by intensive learning without a conditioning apparatus. *Behavior Therapy, 9,* 342–354.

Azrin, N. H., Thienes-Hontos, P., & Besalel-Azrin, V. (1979). Elimination of enuresis without a conditioning apparatus: An extension by office instruction of the child and parents. *Behavior Therapy, 10,* 14–19.

Baker, B. L. (1969). Symptom treatment and symptom substitution in enuresis. *Journal of Abnormal Psychology, 74,* 42–49.

Bakwin, H. (1973). The genetics of enuresis. In I. Kolvin, R. C. MacKeith, & S. R. Meadow (Eds.), *Bladder control and enuresis* (pp. 73–77). London: Heinemann.

Barclay, D. R. (1990). *Effects of a waking schedule as a function of children's arousability in the treatment of primary enuresis.* Unpublished master's thesis, Memphis State University, Memphis, TN.

Beck, A. T., Rush, A. J., Shaw, B. F., & Emery, G. (1980). *Cognitive therapy of depression.* New York: Guilford Press.

Berger, R. M., Maizels, M., Moran, G. C., Conway, J. J., & Firlit, C. F. (1983). Bladder capacity (ounces) equals age (years) plus 2 predicts normal bladder capacity and aids in diagnosis of abnormal voiding patterns. *The Journal of Urology, 129,* 347–349.

Bollard, J. (1982). A 2-year follow-up of bedwetters treated with dry-bed training and standard conditioning. *Behaviour Research and Therapy, 20,* 571–580.

Bollard, J., & Nettelbeck, T. (1988). *Bedwetting: A treatment manual for professional staff.* Unpublished manuscript, Adelaide Children's Hospital, Adelaide, South Australia.

Bostock, J. (1958). Exterior gestation, primitive sleep, enuresis and asthma: A study in aetiology. *Medical Journal of Australia, 149,* 185.

Boyd, M. M. (1960). The depth of sleep in enuretic school children and in non-enuretic controls. *Journal of Psychosomatic Research, 4,* 274–281.

Butler, R. J., Brewin, C. R., & Forsythe, W. I. (1986). Maternal attributions and tolerance for nocturnal enuresis. *Behaviour Research and Therapy, 24,* 307–312.

Buttarazzi, P. J. (1977). Oxybutynin Chloride (Ditropan) in enuresis. *The Journal of Urology, 118,* 46.

Couchells, S. M., Johnson, S. B., Carter, R., & Walker, D. (1981). Behavioral and environmental characteristics of treated and untreated enuretic children and matched nonenuretic controls. *Journal of Pediatrics, 99,* 812–816.

De Jonge, G. A. (1973). Epidemiology of enuresis: A survey of the literature. In I. Kolvin, R. C. MacKeith, & S. R. Meadow (Eds.), *Bladder control and enuresis* (pp. 39–46). London: Heinemann.

Derogatis, L. R. (1977). *SCL-90: Administration, scoring & procedures manual for the revised version.* Baltimore: Clinical Psychometric Research.

Dische, S., Yule, W., Corbett, J., & Hand, D. (1983). Childhood nocturnal enuresis: Factors associated with outcome of treatment with an enuresis alarm. *Developmental Medicine and Neurology, 25,* 67–80.

Djurhuus, J. C., Norgaard, J. P., & Rittig, S. (1992). Monosymptomatic bedwetting. *Scandinavian Journal of Urology and Nephrology Supplementum, 141,* 7–19.

Doleys, D. M. (1977). Behavioral treatments for nocturnal enuresis in children: A review of the recent literature. *Psychological Bulletin, 84,* 30–54.

Doleys, D. M., Schwartz, M. S., & Ciminero, A. R. (1981). Elimination problems: Enuresis and encopresis. In E. J. Mash & L. G. Terdal (Eds.), *Behavioral assessment of childhood disorders* (pp. 679–710). New York: Guilford Press.

Duche, D. J. (1973). Patterns of micturition in infancy. An introduction to the study of enuresis. In I. Kolvin, R. C. MacKeith, & S. R. Meadow (Eds.), *Bladder control and enuresis* (pp. 23–27). London: Heinemann.

Eiberg, H., Berendt, I., & Mohr, J. (1995). Assignment of dominant inherited nocturnal enuresis (ENUR1) to chromosome 13q. *Nature Genetics, 10,* 354–356.

Esperanca, M., & Gerrard, J. W. (1969). Nocturnal enuresis: Comparison of the effect of imipramine and dietary restriction on bladder capacity. *Canadian Medical Association Journal, 101,* 65–68.

Essen, J., & Peckham, C. (1976). Nocturnal enuresis in childhood. *Developmental Medicine and Child Neurology, 18,* 577–589.

Fergusson, D. M., Horwood, L. J., & Shannon, F. T. (1986). Factors related to the age of attainment of nocturnal bladder control: An 8 year longitudinal study. *Pediatrics, 78,* 884–890.

Fielding, D. (1980). The response of day and night wetting children and children who wet only at night to retention control training and the enuresis alarm. *Behaviour Research and Therapy, 18,* 305–317.

Fielding, D., & Doleys, D. M. (1989). Elimination problems: Enuresis and encopresis. In E. J. Mash & L. G. Terdal (Eds.), *Behavioral assessment of childhood disorders* (pp. 586–623). New York: Guilford Press.

Finley, W. W. (1971). An EEG study of the sleep of enuretics at three age levels. *Clinical Electroencephalography, 2,* 35–39.

Forsythe, W. I., & Redmond, A. (1974). Enuresis and spontaneous cure rate: Study of 1129 enuretics. *Archives of Disease in Childhood, 49,* 259–263.

Freud, S. (1959). Fragment of an analysis of a case of hysteria. In A. Strachey & J. Strachey (Eds.), *Sigmund Freud: Collected papers* (pp. 13–146). New York: Basic Books.

Friman, P. C. (1986). A preventive context for enuresis. *Pediatric Clinics of North America, 33*(4), 871–886.

Geffken, G., Johnson, S. B., & Walker, D. (1986). Behavioral interventions for childhood nocturnal enuresis: The differential effect of bladder capacity on treatment progress and outcome. *Health Psychology, 5*, 261–272.

George, C. P. L., Messerli, F. H., Genest, J., Nowaczynski, W., Boucher, R., Kuchel, O., & Rojo-Ortega, M. (1975). Diurnal variation of plasma vasopressin in man. *Journal of Clinical Endocrinology and Metabolism, 41*, 332–338.

Graham, P. (1973). Depth of sleep and enuresis: A critical review. In I. Kolvin, R. C. MacKeith, & S. R. Meadow (Eds.), *Bladder control and enuresis* (pp. 78–83). London: Heinemann.

Hallgren, B. (1957). Enuresis: A clinical and genetic study. *Acta Psychiatrica et Neurologica Scandinavica, 32*(Suppl. 114), 1–159.

Haque, M., Ellerstein, N. S., Gundy, J. H., Shelov, S. P., Weiss, J. C., McIntire, M. S., Olness, K. N., Jones, D. J., Heagarty, M. C., & Starfield, B. H. (1981). Parental perceptions of enuresis: A collaborative study. *American Journal of Diseases of Childhood, 135*, 809–811.

Houts, A. C. (1991). Nocturnal enuresis as a biobehavioral problem. *Behavior Therapy, 22*, 133–151.

Houts, A. C., Berman, J. S., & Abramson, H. A. (1994). The effectiveness of psychological and pharmacological treatments for nocturnal enuresis. *Journal of Consulting and Clinical Psychology, 62*, 737–745.

Houts, A. C., & Liebert, R. M. (1984). *Bedwetting: A guide for parents and children.* Springfield, IL: Thomas.

Houts, A. C., Liebert, R. M., & Padawer, W. (1983). A delivery system for the treatment of primary enuresis. *Journal of Abnormal Child Psychology, 11*, 513–519.

Houts, A. C., Peterson, J. K., & Liebert, R. M. (1984). Effect of prior imipramine treatment on the results of conditioning therapy in children with enuresis. *Journal of Pediatric Psychology, 9*, 505–509.

Houts, A. C., Peterson, J. K., & Whelan, J. P. (1986). Prevention of relapse in full-spectrum home training for primary enuresis: A components analysis. *Behavior Therapy, 17*, 462–469.

Houts, A. C., Whelan, J. P., & Peterson, J. K. (1987). Filmed vs. live delivery of full-spectrum home training for primary enuresis: Presenting the information is not enough. *Journal of Consulting and Clinical Psychology, 55*, 902–906.

James, L. E., & Foreman, M. E. (1973). A-B status of behavior therapy technicians as related to success of Mowrer's conditioning treatment for enuresis. *Journal of Consulting and Clinical Psychology, 41*, 224–229.

Jarvelin, M. R. (1989). Developmental history and neurological findings in enuretic children. *Developmental Medicine and Child Neurology, 31*, 728–736.

Jarvelin, M. R., Huttunen, N., Seppanen, J., Seppanen, U., & Moilanen, I. (1990). Screening of urinary tract abnormalities among day and nightwetting children. *Scandinavian Journal of Urology and Nephrology, 24*, 181–189.

Jarvelin, M. R., Moilanen, I., Kangas, P., Moring, K., Vikevainen-Tervonen, L., Huttunen, N. P., & Seppanen, J. (1991). Aetiological and precipitating factors for childhood enuresis. *Acta Pediatrica Scandinavia, 80,* 361–369.

Jarvelin, M. R., Vikevainen-Tervonen, L., Moilanen, I., & Huttunen, N. P. (1988). Enuresis in seven-year-old children. *Acta Pediatrica Scandinavia, 77,* 148–153.

Kaffman, M., & Elizur, E. (1977). Infants who become enuretics: A longitudinal study of 161 kibbutz children. *Monographs of the Society for Research in Child Development, 42*(2, Serial No. 170), 1–54.

Kass, E. J. (1991). Approaching enuresis in an uncomplicated way. *Contemporary Urology, 3,* 15–24.

Kawauchi, A., Watanabe, H., Kitamori, T., Imada, N., & Ohne, T. (1993). The possibility of centripetal stimulation from the urinary bladder for vasopressin excretion. *Journal of Kyoto Prefectural University of Medicine, 102,* 747–752.

Kimmel, H. D., & Kimmel, E. (1970). An instrumental conditioning method for the treatment of enuresis. *Journal of Behavior Therapy and Experimental Psychiatry, 1,* 121–123.

Klauber, G. T. (1989). Clinical efficacy and safety of desmopressin in the treatment of nocturnal enuresis. *Pediatrics, 114,* 719–722.

Levine, A. (1943). Enuresis in the navy. *American Journal of Psychiatry, 100,* 320–325.

Locke, H. J., & Wallace, K. M. (1959). Short marital adjustment and prediction tests: Their reliability and validity. *Marriage and Family Living, 21,* 251–255.

Lovibond, S. H. (1964). *Conditioning and enuresis.* Oxford, England: Pergamon Press.

MacLean, R. E. G. (1960). Imipramine hydrochloride (Tofranil) and enuresis. *American Journal of Psychiatry, 117,* 551.

Mellon, M. W., & Houts, A. C. (1995). Elimination disorders. In R. T. Ammerman & M. Hersen (Eds.), *Handbook of child behavior therapy in the psychiatric setting* (pp. 341–366). New York: Wiley.

Mikkelsen, E. J., Rapoport, J. L., Nee, L., Gruenau, C., Mendelson, W., & Gillin, J. C. (1980). Childhood enuresis: I. Sleep patterns and psychopathology. *Archives of General Psychiatry, 37,* 1139–1144.

Moffatt, M. E. K. (1989). Nocturnal enuresis: Psychologic implications of treatment and nontreatment. *Journal of Pediatrics, 114*(4, Pt. 2), 697–704.

Moffatt, M. E. K., Harlos, S., Kirshen, A. J., & Burd, L. (1993). Desmopressin acetate and nocturnal enuresis: How much do we know? *Pediatrics, 92,* 420–425.

Moffatt, M. E. K., Kato, C., & Pless, I. B. (1987). Improvements in self-concept after treatment of nocturnal enuresis: A randomized clinical trial. *Journal of Pediatrics, 110,* 647–652.

Morgan, R. T. T., & Young, G. C. (1975). Parental attitudes and the conditioning treatment of childhood enuresis. *Behaviour Research and Therapy, 13,* 197–199.

Mowrer, O. H., & Mowrer, W. M. (1938). Enuresis: A method for its study and treatment. *American Journal of Orthopsychiatry, 8,* 436–459.

Norgaard, J. P. (1989). Urodynamics in enuretics: II. A pressure/flow study. *Neurourology and Urodynamics, 8,* 213–217.

Norgaard, J. P., Hansen, J. H., Neilsen, J. B., Rittig, S., & Djurhuus, J. C. (1989a). Nocturnal studies in enuretics: A polygraphic study of sleep-stages and bladder activity. *Scandinavian Journal of Urology and Nephrology Supplementum, 125,* 73–78.

Norgaard, J. P., Hansen, J. H., Wildschiotz, G., Sorensen, S., Rittig, S., & Djurhuus, J. C. (1989). Sleep cystometries in children with nocturnal enuresis. *The Journal of Urology, 141,* 1156–1159.

Norgaard, J. P., Pedersen, E. B., & Djurhuus, J. C. (1985). Diurnal anti-diuretic-hormone levels in enuretics. *The Journal of Urology, 134,* 1029–1031.

Norgaard, J. P., Rittig, S., & Djurhuus, J. C. (1989). Nocturnal enuresis: An approach to treatment based on pathogenesis. *Pediatrics, 14,* 705–710.

Ornitz, E. M., Hanna, G. L., & de Traversay, J. (1992). Prestimulation-induced startle modulation in attention-deficit hyperactivity disorder and nocturnal enuresis. *Psychophysiology, 29,* 437–450.

Perlmutter, A. D. (1976). Enuresis. In P. Kelalis & L. King (Eds.), *Clinical pediatric urology* (pp. 2116–2124). Philadelphia: Saunders.

Philpott, M. G., & Flasher, M. C. (1970). The treatment of enuresis: Further clinical experience with imipramine. *British Journal of Clinical Practice, 24,* 327–329.

Pierce, C. M., Whitman, R. M., Mass, T. W., & Gay, M. L. (1961). Enuresis and dreaming: Experimental studies. *Archives of General Psychiatry, 4,* 166–170.

Redman, J. F., & Seibert, J. J. (1979). The uroradiographic evaluation of the enuretic child. *The Journal of Urology, 122,* 799–801.

Ritvo, E. R., Ornitz, E. M., Gottlieb, F., Poussaint, A. F., Maron, B. J., Ditman, K. S., & Blinn, K. A. (1969). Arousal and nonarousal enuretic events. *American Journal of Psychiatry, 126*(1), 115–122.

Rushton, H. G. (1989). Nocturnal enuresis: Epidemiology, evaluation, and currently available treatment options. *Journal of Pediatrics, 114,* 691–696.

Rutter, M. (1973). Indications for research: III. In I. Kolvin, R. C. MacKeith, & S. R. Meadow (Eds.), *Bladder control and enuresis* (pp. 292–300). London: Heinemann.

Rutter, M., Yule, W., & Graham, P. (1973). Enuresis and behavioral deviance. In I. Kolvin, R. C. MacKeith, & S. R. Meadow (Eds.), *Bladder control and enuresis* (pp. 137–147). London: Heinemann.

Sacks, S., & DeLeon, G. (1973). Case histories and shorter communications: Conditioning of two types of enuretics. *Behaviour Research and Therapy, 11,* 653–654.

Scott, M. A., Barclay, D. R., & Houts, A. C. (1990). Childhood enuresis: Etiology, assessment, and current behavioral treatment. In M. Hersen, R. M. Eisler, & P. M. Miller (Eds.), *Progress in behavior modification* (pp. 83–117). Beverly Hills, CA: Sage.

Shelov, S. P., Gundy, J., Weiss, J. C., McIntire, M. S., Olness, K., Staub, H. P., Jones, D. J., Haque, M., Ellerstein, N. S., Heagarty, M. C., & Starfield, B. (1981). Enuresis: A contrast of attitudes of parents and physicians. *Pediatrics, 67,* 707–710.

Stansfeld, J. M. (1973). Enuresis and urinary tract infection. In I. Kolvin, R. C. MacKeith, & S. R. Meadow (Eds.), *Bladder control and enuresis* (pp. 102–103). London: Heinemann.

Starfield, B. (1967). Functional bladder capacity in enuretic and nonenuretic children. *Pediatrics, 70,* 777–781.

Starfield, B., & Mellits, E. D. (1968). Increase in functional bladder capacity and improvements in enuresis. *Pediatrics, 72,* 483–487.

Stromgren, A., & Thomsen, P. H. (1990). Personality traits in young adults with a history of conditioning-treated childhood enuresis. *Acta Psychiatrics Scandinavia, 81,* 538–541.

Sukhai, R. N., Mol, J., & Harris, A. S. (1989). Combined therapy of enuresis alarm and desmopressin in the treatment of nocturnal enuresis. *European Journal of Pediatrics, 148,* 465–467.

Thompson, I. M., & Lauvetz, R. (1976). Oxybutinin in bladder spasm, neurogenic bladder, and enuresis. *Urology, 8,* 452–454.

Thorne, F. C. (1944). The incidence of nocturnal enuresis after age of 5 years. *American Journal of Psychiatry, 100,* 686–689.

Verhulst, F. C., van der Lee, J. H., Akkerhuis, G. W., Sanders-Woudstra, J. A. R., Timmer, F. C., & Donkhorst, I. D. (1985). The prevalence of nocturnal enuresis: Do *DSM III* criteria need to be changed? A brief research report. *Journal of Child Psychology and Psychiatry, 26,* 989–993.

Wanigaratne, S., Wallace, W., Pullin, J., Keaney, F., & Farmer, R. (1990). *Relapse prevention for addictive behaviors.* Oxford, England: Blackwell Scientific.

Watanabe, H., & Azuma, Y. (1989). A proposal for a classification system of enuresis based on overnight simultaneous monitoring of electroencephalography and cystometry. *Sleep, 12,* 257–264.

Watanabe, H., & Kawauchi, A. (1994). Nocturnal enuresis: Social aspects and treatment perspectives in Japan. *Scandinavian Journal of Nephrology, 163*(Suppl.), 29–38.

Watanabe, H., Kawauchi, A., Kitamori, T., & Azuma, Y. (1994). Treatment system for nocturnal enuresis according to an original classification system. *Pediatric Urology, 25,* 43–50.

Werry, J. S., Dowrick, P. W., Lampen, E. L., & Vamos, M. J. (1975). Imipramine in enuresis: Psychological and physiological effects. *Journal of Child Psychology and Psychiatry, 16,* 289–299.

Whelan, J. P., & Houts, A. C. (1990). Effects of a waking schedule on the outcome of primary enuretic children treated with Full-Spectrum Home Training. *Health Psychology, 9,* 164–176.

Young, G. C., & Morgan, R. T. T. (1972). Overlearning in the conditioning treatment of enuresis: A long-term follow-up study. *Behaviour Research and Therapy, 10,* 419–420.

Young, G. C., & Morgan, R. T. T. (1973). Conditioning treatment of enuresis: Auditory intensity. *Behaviour Research and Therapy, 11,* 411–416.

Zaleski, A., Gerrard, J. W., & Shokeir, M. K. K. (1973). Nocturnal enuresis: The importance of a small bladder capacity. In I. Kolvin, R. C. MacKeith, & S. R. Meadow (Eds.), *Bladder control and enuresis* (pp. 95–101). London: Heinemann.

CHAPTER 13

Parents as Therapists for Children's Food Refusal Problems

KAREN S. BUDD, CARY S. CHUGH, and SHARON L. BERRY

OVER THE past 25 years, parent training has become a treatment strategy of choice for many mild to moderate psychological problems in children, due to the cost-effectiveness and demonstrated therapeutic merit of this approach (e.g., Dangel & Polster, 1984; Mash, Hamerlynck, & Handy, 1976; Wright, Stroud, & Keenan, 1993). Wright, Schaefer, and Solomons (1979) assert that every hour of parent consultation with a professional is likely to yield hundreds of hours of changed interactions and different experiences for the child. A parent-mediated approach is presumably most well suited to overt child behavior problems, which are subject to change by teaching parents specific behavioral techniques to apply in the child's natural environment (Graziano & Diament, 1992).

This chapter describes the use of parents as therapists for their child's food refusal problems. Considering that feeding is a core, life-sustaining activity, and the earliest area in which the parent and infant work together toward a common goal—satiation of hunger—disturbances in the feeding process are likely to engender considerable parental concern. Food refusal problems differ from socially defined child behavior problems (e.g., noncompliance or aggression) in that medical, developmental, and dietary variables often play a role in precipitating or maintaining

This chapter was supported in part by Grant No. 1-R03-MH47539 from the National Institute of Mental Health and by a grant from the DePaul University Research Council, both to the first author. Sharon Berry is now at Children's Health Care, Minneapolis.

418

food refusal. However, as with many other behaviors, feeding difficulties typically are responsive to social contingencies. This chapter provides a clinical description of chronic food refusal, delineates a taxonomy of etiological and maintaining variables to consider in planning intervention, reviews common elements of behavioral parent training to deal with mealtime problems, and provides several case examples of feeding problems and parent-mediated interventions from our own clinical work.

SCOPE OF THE PROBLEM

Pediatric feeding problems include a wide array of concerns, such as food refusal, swallowing disorders, developmental delays in eating skills, obesity, vomiting, rumination, and pica (Ginsberg, 1988; Linscheid, Budd, & Rasnake, 1995; Luiselli, 1989). Estimates of the prevalence of feeding problems in children aged 12 years and under vary from around 20% (Beautrais, Fergusson, & Shannon, 1982; Lindberg, Bohlin, & Hagekull, 1991) to 30%–45% (Bentovim, 1970), and as high as 62% (Reau, Senturia, Lebailly, & Christoffel, 1996). Reisinger and Bires (1980) found that, during well-child pediatric visits in the first 2 years of their child's life, parents sought advice on feeding issues more often than on other child care concerns. However, the bulk of parental questions relate to common problems (e.g., finicky eating habits, spitting up, mild overeating or undereating, and colic). These mild feeding difficulties have been addressed elsewhere (Budd & Chugh, in press) and will not be covered here.

Chronic food refusal is characterized by the persistent, voluntary intake of a limited variety of food groups or textures, or a restriction in the total amount of food a child ingests, to the extent that the pattern has negative medical, developmental, or behavioral consequences (Werle, Murphy, & Budd, 1993; Williamson, Prather, Heffer, & Kelly, 1988). Some children with chronic food refusal receive a diagnosis of failure-to-thrive (FTT), given when the child's weight falls below the fifth percentile for age on standardized growth charts, when actual weight is less than 80% to 85% of the child's ideal body weight, or when the child's weight gain decelerates precipitously (Drotar, 1995). FTT is not synonymous with chronic food refusal, however, as some children remain within normal growth limits despite highly selective eating habits.

RATIONALE FOR INVOLVING PARENTS

The logic of a parent training approach for treating children's feeding problems derives from three related points. First, parents are the primary feeders during infancy and early childhood, and they serve as their child's main socialization agents about food (Birch, 1990; Satter, 1986).

Particularly in infancy, feeding accounts for more interaction time between the parent and child than any other activity. Because parents are responsible for the child's nurturance, it makes sense to include them as active participants in feeding treatment.

Second, numerous findings point to the role of maladaptive parent-child interactions in the development of some feeding problems. Parent-child conflicts in the feeding process (Chatoor & Egan, 1983), parental knowledge deficits regarding dietary needs for a developing child (Pugliese, Weyman-Daum, Moses, & Lifshitz, 1987), and inconsistent or inappropriate responses to the child's behaviors during the meal (Bradley, Casey, & Wortham, 1984; Pollitt, Eichler, & Chan, 1975) exemplify possible contributors to problematic mealtime behaviors. Sanders, Patel, Le Grice, and Shepherd (1993) found that parents and their children with persistent feeding difficulties showed higher levels of aversive interactions than did their non-problem counterparts. Additionally, parents of children with feeding problems tend to view their children more negatively than parents of children without feeding problems (Hagekull & Dahl, 1987). These findings suggest the relevance of addressing the parent-child relationship in treating children with chronic food refusal.

Third, applied research has demonstrated that parents can effectively modify children's food refusal problems by changing the social contingencies of mealtime interactions (e.g., Bernal, 1972; Hatcher, 1979; Linscheid, Tarnowski, Rasnake, & Brams, 1987; Werle et al., 1993, in press). Parents have been trained to address feeding problems in both inpatient and outpatient settings. The available research suggests that, when parents are available and motivated to participate in feeding intervention, they are effective treatment agents.

Some feeding professionals have cautioned that treating children via outpatient parent training is less efficient than inpatient treatment by a professional, and that reliance on parents is inappropriate for severely resistant or complex cases, due to possible health risks for the child and the negative impact on parent-child interactions (Blackman & Nelson, 1985; Linscheid, Oliver, Blyler, & Palmer, 1978). However, these issues must be weighed against the ultimate need to modify the child's everyday feeding environment, the negative effects of hospitalization on children, and pragmatic restrictions on hospitalizing children except for clear medical necessity (cf. Kedesdy & Budd, in press).

TAXONOMY OF VARIABLES
CONTRIBUTING TO FOOD REFUSAL

Food refusal problems occur for reasons ranging from biological to environmental, with these variables often interacting to create complex patterns of behavior. The following paragraphs provide a brief overview of normal feeding development as a frame of reference for considering feeding problems, followed by delineation of potential factors associated with children's food refusal.

Feeding is similar to other basic childhood skills, in that it develops in stages over time. Eating responses in the neonate are thought to be motivated reflexively due to physiological sensations of hunger (Linscheid, 1992). As the infant grows and develops, however, primitive reflexes begin to disappear, usually between 3 and 5 months of age (O'Brien, Repp, Williams, & Christophersen, 1991). Reflexive sucking gradually is supplemented or replaced with other oral-motor skills, including munching (5 months); tongue lateralization (7 months); biting (7 months); and the development of a mature chewing pattern (between 8 and 36 months) (Howard, 1984). Increasing oral-motor capacity and motor coordination allow the child to take in a wider variety of foods and become more active in the feeding process. Textured foods (e.g., pureed foods, infant cereal) are introduced at 4 to 6 months, finger feeding is initiated around 7 months, and use of a utensil by 12 months of age. By 15 months, the infant begins to engage in self-feeding (Christophersen & Hall, 1978).

Maturational influences (Erikson, 1950) are presumed to account in part for appetite changes during the toddler years, from a relatively stable to a more erratic and unpredictable pattern. As the child strives to master his or her world, feeding struggles and strong food preferences are likely to emerge (Bentovim, 1970). Although these difficulties usually are transient and relatively minor, feeding problems can reach clinically significant levels when precipitated by one or more of the factors to be described.

Medical and Developmental Variables

Kedesdy and Budd (in press) describe eight potential etiologic areas affecting children's feeding problems, including three categories that pertain mainly to medical and developmental precipitants. These areas are chronic and acute illnesses, physical competence factors (neuromotor, structural, or anatomic dysfunction), and child constitution (temperament, developmental functioning).

Food refusal may be a direct result of an organic or disease process in children, and underlying medical issues must always be considered and treated when food refusal becomes apparent. Symptoms of poor appetite, poor growth, and/or distress associated with feeding are often found with children born with gastroesophageal reflux (Linscheid et al., 1995). Other illnesses that may lead to food refusal are endocrine dysfunction, constitutional bone disease, or food allergies.

Food refusal also may be associated with secondary treatment for a medical problem. Children treated with chemotherapy regimens for cancer often experience related loss of appetite. Treatment of short-gut syndrome, in which part of the intestine is surgically resected, often entails a period of nonoral nutrition (e.g., through a feeding tube) during recovery from surgery (Linscheid et al., 1987). Even a brief period (e.g., 2 to 3 weeks) on supplemental forms of nutrition can lead to difficulties resuming or initiating oral feeding patterns (Handen, Mandell, & Russo, 1986). Similarly, chronic inflammation and pain associated with swallowing can lead to long-term resistance to oral intake, which may take many weeks to resolve despite successful intervention with medications or surgery. These examples of iatrogenic effects of medical treatment can set the stage for food refusal problems.

Children born prematurely or with congenital anomalies experience handicapping developmental conditions that complicate feeding practices, ranging from swallowing disorders, poor muscle tone, difficulties with establishing a strong suck, and poor coordination (Eicher, 1992). Early oral-motor sensitivity, tactile defensiveness, or an easy gag reflex may contribute to the development of feeding problems in young children, often requiring extensive therapy (e.g., physical; occupational; speech) to resolve the subsequent difficulties with growth and weight gain (Morris & Klein, 1987).

Dietary Factors

Many factors including lack of understanding about children's feeding needs (e.g., Pugliese et al., 1987), economic issues, or chaotic family schedules can complicate parents' selection of appropriate foods for their child's nutritional needs. (Pipes & Trahms, 1993). Some parents have developed their own beliefs about how to feed their child to avoid difficulties they have faced in their own lives (e.g., obesity; sugar cravings). Some of our pediatrician colleagues describe "yuppie parents," who select menu choices based on long-term personal issues at the expense of their child's early needs for nutrition and weight gain. Other parents rely on convenience foods that are high in fat and sodium.

Two potential areas of feeding difficulty related to dietary factors include initially making the transition from liquids to solids and learning to eat textured foods (e.g., crackers, meats, apples) in general. These developmental progressions, which normally occur in the first and second years of life, respectively, can become a source of food refusal problems if not mastered. Feeding specialists generally assume that the time around 7 to 10 months of age is a "sensitive period" for accepting coarser textures, based on findings of long-term feeding resistance in children who were unable to eat textured foods during this period (Illingworth & Lister, 1964). Although the notion of a sensitive period is difficult to confirm experimentally, the hypothesis provides a conceptual framework for considering whether the child's developmental experiences with varied textures may have contributed to current feeding difficulties.

Some children develop their own "picky eating" patterns by selecting a restricted menu of food items they are willing to eat. For example, one 4-year-old child would eat only "white foods" such as milk, white grape juice, and dry cereal. Another child, aged 3 years, would eat only a few kinds of crackers or dry cereal, and he became highly distressed if pushed to eat anything outside this repertoire. Persistent and highly restricted food preferences are more commonly reported in children with developmental and emotional disabilities (Ginsberg, 1988). One 6-year-old boy with autism self-restricted his intake to rice cakes, pretzels, cereal, and sweets.

Menu issues also can be complicated by a chronic medical condition requiring a nutritional balancing act (Pipes & Trahms, 1993). Children with renal disease, metabolic disorders, or diabetes must be careful about avoiding certain foods and increasing others. Dietary restrictions can become more problematic for children during school years, when peer influences increase in importance.

SOCIAL INTERACTIONS

Most parents view eating as a social event, and disruption of the pleasure anticipated with feeding a child is distressing and painful. Parents then begin to dread mealtimes, and their worry and anxiety are easily transmitted to the child, creating difficult feeding patterns. Although often viewed as a simple interchange lasting several minutes, feeding involves a complex set of reciprocal interactions. These include the timing of meals and snacks, accurate interpretation of cues related to hunger and satiety, pacing of feeding, and accommodation to temperament factors such as fussiness or general responsiveness of the child (Kedesdy & Budd, in press; Satter, 1986).

Parents play a key role in determining their children's behavior, in that parents' reactions can be experienced by the child as rewarding or punitive. According to operant conditioning principles (Bijou & Baer, 1965), children engage more often in behaviors that are rewarded and refrain from behaviors that are ignored or punished. Over the course of thousands of parent-child interactions during meals, children experience differential contingencies that influence their eating patterns.

For example, once a child begins to gag or spit out food that has been offered, it is natural for parents to stop offering it immediately. Some parents simply replace the rejected food with another choice in an effort to get the child to eat. This approach can backfire, however, in that the parents' response may reinforce the child's food refusal. At other times, there is insufficient reinforcement to continue eating, such as the use of physical touch, contingent attention, or social/verbal praise. One mother whose child was hospitalized with food refusal and FTT described that she had a hard time responding to the child in a positive manner while feeding, claiming, "I never talk to any of my babies 'til after they are a year old." This mother's parenting style appeared to contribute to the child's lack of interest in food.

ENVIRONMENTAL CONTEXT

The physical and temporal context in which feeding occurs may play a role in feeding difficulties with children (Kedesdy & Budd, in press; Mathisen, Skuse, Wolke, & Reilly, 1989; Werle et al., in press). Potentially important environmental variables include the physical setting of the eating area (e.g., distractions; toys), the seating arrangement (e.g., proximity to parents; quality of support in chair), and the scheduling of meals (e.g., how often meals and snacks occur; whether there is sufficient time between feeding opportunities for the child to experience hunger).

Many parents, out of desperation, begin to "entertain" their children in an effort to facilitate eating, resulting in a powerful child who will only eat in circumscribed situations (e.g., out of the high chair; in front of the television; along with a presentation of toys). One 2-year-old boy with multiple medical and developmental complications ate only in front of the television, where his mother spoon-fed him as he watched "Barney" videotapes. Children may do better or worse with intake while in a social situation; some children eat better in the presence of models who share the meal, whereas others (e.g., easily distracted children or those with oral-motor weakness) may do better when fed alone in a quiet setting.

FAMILY SYSTEM VARIABLES

Other factors that can play a role in the feeding process may be unique to a specific family, such as the amount of time parents can devote to feeding a child with difficulties. Both too much and too little time focused on the feeding situation can become problematic. Parents with other children and those who work outside the home may have limited time or patience to address feeding problems. Other stressors that may disrupt a parent's sense of competence with feeding include financial issues, marital conflict, or illness in a family member (Wahler & Hann, 1986). Multiple caregivers who feed the child may create difficulties, especially if there is limited consistency from one person to the next.

THE PARENT TRAINING PROGRAM

Because a number of factors may contribute to pediatric feeding difficulties, individualized assessment is needed to develop a treatment plan. Although there is no single way to approach parent training regarding feeding refusal, it is useful to keep two goals in mind: (a) promote immediate success; and (b) build a foundation for additional interventions over time.

Particularly when parents are being trained to implement treatment, it is advisable to start with small, manageable steps rather than to intervene with the most disruptive problem area at the beginning. For example, a 3-year-old female was referred for poor weight gain, limited intake, and behavioral feeding problems. Before directly intervening with the feeding problems, it was recommended that the parents first eliminate the pacifier (which at that time was in constant use) to promote both oral-motor skills and language acquisition. Initially, the girl's parents were opposed to this step, because they were afraid of the intensity of her response when the pacifier was removed. However, when coached in ignoring these tantrums and providing alternative distractions, they were successful within 2 days, and subsequently they were more optimistic that they could alter the established feeding problems.

The following sections provide a brief overview of behavioral feeding assessment, followed by common intervention strategies associated with the taxonomy of variables previously outlined. Italicized terms refer to specific behavioral strategies and learning principles involved in feeding treatment.

ASSESSMENT

Behavioral feeding assessment begins with a review of the child's medical and developmental history, together with information from a current medical examination to identify or rule out contributing physical conditions. Children with severe or life-threatening food refusal problems may be assessed in an inpatient setting, where health care professionals carry out feedings (Babbitt et al., 1994). Outpatient assessment consists of a clinical interview with the parent (and child, depending on age), 3- to 7-day diet histories or food diaries kept by the parent, and direct observation of one or more sample mealtimes (cf. Linscheid et al., 1995; Linscheid & Rasnake, 1985; Luiselli, 1989). These methods are used to clarify the feeding problems, the child's preferences for various foods and textures, the amount and variety of food the child is currently eating, social practices around eating, and eating-related behaviors (e.g., tantrums, choking, playing with food). The evaluator also explores other behavioral and contextual factors that may not relate directly to mealtime behavior (e.g., child's activity level, availability of age-appropriate food, maternal insularity, family impoverishment) (Heffer & Kelley, 1994). Standardized measures may be helpful when concerns arise about issues such as the child's developmental performance, parental stress levels, or overall parenting knowledge (cf. Kedesdy & Budd, in press). Other health professionals (e.g., nutritionists; speech-language pathologists) can provide helpful information on particular areas of concern.

Direct observation of the parent and child during a meal is a core component of the assessment. Such observations can reveal clues (e.g., aversive or noncontingent parent-child interaction patterns, abnormal eating patterns, or distractors affecting the child's intake) that may not be apparent from the clinical interview or medical records. For practical reasons, mealtime observations usually involve having the parent bring typical foods for the child to eat during the clinic session. Repeated observation of feeding at subsequent sessions reveals any changes from intervention or additional problems that need attention.

On occasion, clinic sessions provide an unrepresentative picture of mealtime issues, and selective home observations may be productive (Drotar & Crawford, 1987). One 2-year-old girl with FTT and limited intake was seen in a clinic feeding session, where she was sociable and cooperative with feeding requests. It was not until two home visits were conducted that the clinician had the opportunity to see what her parents described as typical problems. During a family meal, she became distracted by toys at the table and ate little. At the next home visit, her newborn sister's crying disrupted the meal; when her mother left the table to attend to the baby, the toddler inserted a very large bite of food in her mouth and then followed her mother. When she returned to the table four minutes later, she was still chewing on the same bite. Treatment recommendations focused on having the parents remove mealtime distractions and cut food into small bite-size pieces, which improved the child's feeding patterns. The utility of home observations is illustrated again in a case example later in this chapter.

TREATMENT OF MEDICAL AND DEVELOPMENTAL VARIABLES

It is important to work collaboratively with medical staff to identify and treat any organic component to food refusal. For example, a child may require medications or supplemental nonoral nutrition through a gastrostomy tube, which should be incorporated into the intervention program. With infants and toddlers, a major objective is to keep the child actively sucking, even if the organic problem precludes oral intake for a period of time (Wolf & Glass, 1992). Trying to reestablish the sucking response at a later time can be very difficult, whereas maintaining the suck, even when the child does not eat actively by mouth, often is easier. It is recommended that parents offer a pacifier or finger (child's or parent's) throughout the day on a scheduled basis, similar to the typical meal/snack schedule. If possible, placing small drops of fluid in the child's mouth with a finger or dropper also maintains the sucking activity.

Some medical conditions may lead to avoidance of certain foods due to negative conditioning (e.g., vomiting, gagging, or pain) associated with eating. To reverse the effects of aversive conditioning, *desensitization* procedures may be used. Desensitization involves pairing a conditioned aversive stimulus with the positive events or with the absence of negative events. Siegel (1982) described use of desensitization in treating a 6-year-old boy who refused most solid foods. In this case, the child watched television to serve as a distracting activity while eating, which was combined with the delivery of positive reinforcement (i.e., praise, preferred foods) for gradual steps toward eating. Notice that some events (e.g., television) can facilitate eating in some children and disrupt it in others; similarly, a stimulus may serve a short-term objective but require gradual removal or replacement to promote more adaptive eating habits.

Developmental complications (e.g., cerebral palsy, mental retardation) often result in long-term delays in children's acquisition of feeding skills. Parent training in these cases involves a task analysis of the child's current feeding skills and a program to teach parents the techniques of shaping, fading, and positive reinforcement of steps toward self-feeding (Luiselli, 1989). Shaping involves reinforcing successive approximations toward the desired behavior, whereas fading involves gradually removing the instructions, motor assistance, and reinforcement as the child acquires more control over the desired behavior (e.g., Leibowitz & Holcer, 1974). The treatment regimen often includes adjunctive rehabilitative therapy to maximize coordination, strength, and adaptive skills (Morris & Klein, 1987). Adaptive equipment, such as supported chairs or specialized feeding utensils, may be prescribed to enhance self-feeding skills.

Generally, medical and/or developmental factors contributing to feeding refusal can be addressed simultaneously with dietary, social, environmental, and family factors, rather than waiting until medical or developmental issues are resolved before proceeding with further interventions.

TREATMENT OF DIETARY FACTORS

Possible areas of intervention regarding nutritional variables include improving levels of vitamins and minerals, providing more varied food groups and textures, and making serving sizes and total quantity of intake appropriate to the child's health needs (Christophersen & Hall, 1978). When assessment (often by a nutritional specialist) indicates that the child has nutritional inadequacies, parents should receive educational guidelines regarding recommended nutritional supplements or vitamins to be used on a short-term basis, while expanding the variety of foods eaten during treatment. A diet history completed with a 9-year-old boy referred for picky eating patterns showed that his restricted intake severely interfered with calcium needs. Parents decided that it was better to begin with calcium supplements while the feeding problems were addressed than to push high-calcium foods the child had previously rejected.

Repeated exposure to new types and textures of foods is a common intervention strategy when a child's intake is limited in specific areas (Linscheid et al., 1987). This technique is supported by the work of Birch (1990) and her colleagues, showing positive relationships between children's exposure, sampling, and preference for novel foods. In clinical cases of food refusal, repeated exposure is accomplished by offering small amounts of the new foods frequently across meals, together with *prompts* (verbal instructions or gestures) and reinforcement as needed to encourage the child to accept one to two bites of the new foods. If these techniques are insufficient to create change, it often is necessary to shape the desired intake by making access to favorite foods contingent on trying a less preferred food. For example, a 5-year-old boy with chronic medical problems preferred the ease of drinking fluids over eating solid foods, even though he had the necessary skills for chewing and swallowing. One treatment intervention used by his parents was to allow drinking only after he had eaten one bite of solid foods, gradually increasing the expected number of bites before he would be given a drink.

Repeated exposure, prompts, and reinforcement also are techniques used to transition a child to textured foods (Werle et al., 1993). Parents should be cautioned that occasional gagging and choking may occur, and they often need support to follow the plan systematically (not sporadically) for at least five to six trials at each meal. It is helpful to identify "easier" textured foods, with which the child is more comfortable, and to make access to a favorite food or drink contingent on trying the textured food. Most parents can identify their child's favorite foods, which can be offered as incentives, even if it means serving cookies or ice cream at each meal.

TREATMENT OF SOCIAL INTERACTIONS

Parents are taught to use their attention contingently during meals to increase the frequency of desired behaviors (eating nutritious foods) and reduce the frequency of undesired behaviors (throwing or spitting out food, gagging). A basic component of virtually all parent-mediated feeding intervention is *differential social attention,* which involves providing immediate praise or other positive attention (clapping, hugs, or smiles) as a child eats in a desired manner and providing minimal attention to undesired behaviors (e.g., Bernal, 1972). For some parents, this means shifting the focus of their attention from being noncontingent to being contingent on child behaviors they wish to increase. Parents are taught to view their attention, not as "entertainment," but rather as a strategic tool to support positive eating patterns. Other parents, who initially provide minimal attention or mainly offer disciplinary input during meals, are taught to track desired child eating responses and provide positive attention on an intermittent basis (e.g., once per minute).

Some children are more receptive to tangible reinforcement strategies than to social attention. One mother learned that she could get her daughter to eat more consistently if the mother colored during the meal. She taught her child, "As long as you eat, then I will color," which was successful in increasing her child's intake. Other parents use variations on this approach, such as reading from a book or showing the child a windup toy after the child takes a bite. These steps work best when the child has preferred activities that can be interspersed during the meal, and when the activities do not seriously distract the child from eating.

Although contingent positive attention is the basic strategy used to modify parent-child social interactions, other techniques, including *modeling* (e.g., Greer, Dorow, Williams, McCorkle, & Asnes, 1991) or *time-out* (e.g., MacArthur, Ballard, & Artinian, 1986) have been included as components in some feeding interventions. Informal modeling is a means of promoting behavior change indirectly by having a sibling or other person demonstrate the desired eating behavior and receive reinforcement. Time-out can involve briefly removing the food from the child, turning the child's chair, or removing the child from the table.

Occasionally, feeding treatment incorporates negative reinforcement, in which an aversive stimulus is removed contingent on a desired behavior to strengthen the desired feeding response. One technique for reducing food refusal and promoting acceptance has been called "contingency contacting" (Hoch, Babbitt, Coe, Krell, & Hackbert, 1994). This technique entails holding a bite of food at the child's mouth until it is accepted, while ignoring or blocking inappropriate behaviors, and immediately providing reinforcement for food acceptance. Hoch and colleagues (1994) demonstrated that positive reinforcement of acceptances resulted in little change in feeding patterns for two boys hospitalized with severe food refusal problems, whereas the addition of contingency contacting led to dramatic improvements. The use of aversive techniques is complicated when parents are being trained to implement them at home because parents need to be well versed in their use and have a sound repertoire of positive techniques prior to instituting the negative techniques. Many parents resist using aversive procedures during meals and end up using them inconsistently, if at all. However, when opportunities exist for training parents over several sessions, when parents find the techniques acceptable, and when positive techniques alone are not sufficient, these techniques can substantially increase the effectiveness of intervention (cf. Ahearn, Kerwin, Eicher, Shantz, & Swearingin, 1996).

TREATMENT FOR ENVIRONMENTAL VARIABLES

The structure and physical conditions present during meals can influence child behavior by setting the occasion for reinforcement of either appropriate or inappropriate feeding patterns. Providing the child with his or her own plate and fork sets the occasion for self-feeding, but it also provides an opportunity for a child who is feeding-resistant or not hungry to throw food and utensils. Sitting a toddler in a well-supported chair at a table for meals provides greater physical support for eating than allowing the child to sit on the parent's lap, cruise past a table of food, or juggle food while seated on the floor. *Stimulus control* involves arranging antecedent variables and reinforcing desired behavior that occurs in the presence of the variables. Stimulus control procedures often are included in parent training programs to enhance the consistency and positive atmosphere for eating, although the impact of stimulus control and contextual variables on eating is rarely examined systematically (Werle et al., in press).

It is generally recommended that parents establish routine times for meals and snacks so they are predictable and maximize the likelihood of the child's hunger (Christophersen & Hall, 1978; Linscheid & Rasnake, 1985). Beyond infancy, three meals and two to three snacks daily are commonly recommended. It is important to teach parents to avoid additional eating opportunities between meals, even when the child asks to eat. This rule can be difficult for parents of children with feeding problems, given their strong desire to get the child to eat.

Length of meals and snacks can be an issue for children who dawdle or play with food. Meals usually should be limited to 20 to 30 minutes (Linscheid & Rasnake, 1985), unless the child has oral-motor problems that require extra feeding time. Positive incentives to encourage eating within a reasonable time frame include offering preferred activities contingent on finishing the meal (e.g., "once you eat all your lunch, we can go to the park"). Alternatively, setting a timer can provide a clear cue of meal length. Parents should be vigilant over the rules they state; if they say, "one more bite" is needed to end the meal, they should keep to this plan and fight the urge to push more food if the child seems to be accepting.

TREATMENT OF FAMILY SYSTEM VARIABLES

When two parents are available in the family, it is helpful to involve both of them in feeding treatment. They can work as a team so that one feeds and the other handles other family concerns, and they can alternate the feeding responsibility. It is imperative that all the child's caretakers (e.g., grandparents, babysitter) learn and follow the same feeding plan.

Some family issues may be beyond the scope of the parent training program, but it is important to be aware of them in planning treatment. For example, marital conflict may dictate who is available and willing to participate in intervention. If a family's personal or cultural beliefs support a different view of the feeding problem (e.g., that the child is physically ill and incapable of responding to parent intervention), it is important to identify this roadblock and try to resolve it through discussion rather than proceeding with parent training (Drotar, Wilson, & Sturm, 1989).

CASE EXAMPLES

In each of the three cases presented here, medical and/or developmental issues complicated the feeding process. In addition, dietary, social, environmental, and/or family system variables played a role in each case. After initially addressing the organic factors, intervention consisted of teaching the parents to use specific behavioral techniques to modify parent-child mealtime interactions. Specific written recommendations were provided after each session, in addition to follow-up telephone calls to monitor progress and fine-tune the feeding plan. Training methods included instruction and coaching, as well as behavioral rehearsal during feeding, verbal feedback, and shaping improved feeding habits.

CASE EXAMPLE 1: BRIAN

Background

Brian, a 26-month-old African American boy, was born prematurely with toxic levels of cocaine and alcohol. Medical records indicate that Brian had many complications, including bronchopulmonary disease, surgical repair of a hernia, developmental delay, mild oral-motor difficulties, and chronic malnutrition. Brian was placed with his current foster parents at around 6 months of age and was being considered for adoption at the time of assessment. Although his foster mother reported that Brian had always been a picky eater, his feeding difficulties worsened after having surgery for a hernia at 7 months of age. Upon referral, Brian was below the fifth percentile for height and 96% of his ideal body weight. Eating a restricted diet and fussiness during meals were the main parental concerns at the time of initial assessment.

Assessment and Formulation

During an initial outpatient feeding evaluation, Brian cooperated well with feeding, accepting his foster mother's offerings of food for the most part, and he also showed that he was capable of self-feeding (eating three bites per minute). In fact, the foster mother said she had never seen Brian eat as well as during this meal. Because no problems were observed during the clinic session, two home visits were scheduled. The first of these meals, which included four other foster children, also went very well, with Brian eating a wide variety of foods and cooperating well. During the second home visit, however, Brian refused much more food than he accepted and only ate a few bites in total. The foster mother reported that this was typical of Brian when he was not feeling well.

Assessment suggested that Brian had a variable feeding repertoire, which fluctuated somewhat based on immediate health factors. His foster mother had an adaptive social repertoire for supporting Brian's desired behavior, allowed Brian to pace his intake of food, and skillfully spread her attention across Brian and the other siblings. She used direct instructions when appropriate to alter Brian's behavior (e.g., regulate bite size). When Brian was eating poorly, however, the foster mother's tone became more irritable, and she persisted in offering food despite Brian's repeated refusals. She also tried offering foods that had not been originally presented and allowed Brian to sit on her lap and play with his food during the meal. None of these methods resulted in Brian's food acceptance.

Intervention

Two clinic sessions and four home visits were conducted from 26 to 33 months of age, with periodic phone consultation to assist the foster mother in carrying out the treatment plan. Parent training focused on strengthening her use of contingent social attention when Brian was not cooperating with meals and rearranging aspects of the environmental structure for mealtimes. Recommendations included the following:

1. Foster parents were told to ignore Brian's inappropriate feeding behavior (refusals, whining), and instead praise Brian for engaging in even small steps toward desired eating (e.g., looking at the food, sitting at the table). They were encouraged to allow Brian to continue self-feeding at his own pace when cooperating with eating.
2. Brian was to be removed from the table and the meal ended when he became fussy and showed he was uninterested in eating for a full 5 minutes. Additional food choices were not to be offered during the meal.

3. Brian was to remain seated in his high chair throughout the meal, rather than being placed in his foster mother's lap when he became fidgety or disruptive.

Outcome

At a 4-month follow-up, the foster mother exhibited changes in her interactions with Brian by praising him more often and by not attending to his inappropriate behaviors. She also indicated that she allowed him to leave the dining area when he became irritable or fussy. At a later follow-up, she said that Brian's interest in food had increased, and at his most recent medical evaluation, his pediatrician characterized him as a "healthy boy."

CASE EXAMPLE 2: EMILY

Background

Emily, age 20 months, was an only child born to older parents. She was referred for outpatient services at a medical center by the gastroenterology service for difficulties with eating and weight gain. She was born at 31 weeks gestation, with a birth weight of 2 pounds, 11 ounces. Emily was diagnosed with dysphagia (i.e., difficulty with swallowing) and laryngomalacia (i.e., softening of the tissues of the larynx) with subsequent surgical reconstruction. In addition, she had required tube placement surgery for frequent ear infections. At the time of the referral, medical staff and parents were concerned that Emily did not eat enough by mouth to sustain her nutritional needs, with both nasogastric feedings in the past and gastrostomy tube feedings currently. Speech therapy was in place for oral-motor delay.

In addition to the medical problems, behavioral factors played a role with feeding, including abrupt temperament shifts, generalized fussiness, and spitting out food at the beginning of every meal. Emily had a history of gastroesophageal reflux but was also known to self-induce vomiting when angry or when offered textured foods.

Assessment and Formulation

Clinic assessment suggested that Emily's resistance to oral feeding stemmed from a combination of early medical and developmental difficulties present at birth. Subsequently, she missed the developmental periods for transitioning to solids and textured foods due to medical problems. Temperamentally, she was irritable and fussy in general, and she had developed behavioral patterns that were intimidating to her parents. An observation of feeding in the office revealed immediately how strong her resistance to feeding had become, as she immediately made a "raspberry" when spoon-fed by her mother, spitting food everywhere in the room and on her mother. Generally, feeding stopped at this point.

Intervention

Four outpatient sessions were conducted from 20 to 26 months of age, each including observations of feeding. Contingency management strategies were used more often as Emily grew older, such as the use of a modified time-out procedure to discourage spitting patterns and throwing food. Recommendations included the following:

1. Parents were coached to alter their response to the spitting patterns by persisting with feeding and teaching Emily that this behavior would no longer work to stop the meal. As this behavior changed almost immediately when their response was altered, parents gained self-confidence in their ability to feed Emily.
2. Meals were limited to 20 minutes with no additional food or drinks provided between five to six scheduled meals and snacks.
3. Parents used differential social attention (i.e., social conversation, windup toys, verbal praise) contingently to encourage improved eating and discourage spitting or throwing of food. In addition, they were coached in the use of a modified time-out procedure, where they turned her high chair around briefly with no reinforcement or attention.
4. Preferred foods were offered initially to maximize food intake, but over time, parents used these preferred foods to reward bites of nonpreferred textured foods, so that Emily gradually moved from eating only strained baby foods to also eating table foods with texture by the end of treatment.
5. Parents began to reinforce self-feeding skills while continuing to feed Emily at each meal, in order to increase intake at the same time that they fostered development of independent feeding skills.

Outcome

Parent training was effective in reducing the behavioral factors that interfered with intake and the pleasure of mealtime. Parents no longer dreaded feeding Emily and gained confidence in their ability to manage her resistance. She moved from strained baby foods to regular table foods with texture. Parents were able to successfully eliminate the spitting and vomiting patterns. Parents were encouraged to continue ignoring the temperamental shifts and generalized fussiness that characterized many of her interactions with others.

CASE EXAMPLE 3: SAMUEL

Background

Samuel was an 8-year-old male referred to an outpatient medical center because he stopped eating solid foods due to perceived problems with swallowing. During the preceding 4 months, Samuel had experienced two episodes of strep throat, during which time he became more finicky with eating despite having always been a "good eater." Over time, he gradually eliminated more and more foods, to the point that intake was severely restricted to only liquids and clear broth. Gagging was prominent when any solid foods were offered. His early feeding history included being breast-fed until age 3½ years but generally eating virtually everything until recently. Samuel was perceived by his parents as exhibiting a strong personality; although he was not a "worrier" by nature, he appeared shy and was described as someone "who keeps stuff inside." He was an above-average student with no identified management problems at home or school.

ASSESSMENT AND FORMULATION

Assessment suggested that Samuel's refusal to eat solid foods stemmed from his perception that swallowing was dangerous and frightening. This fear presumably developed from the classical conditioning experience of painful swallowing, secondary to a documented virus (strep) but generalizing to eating in general once the virus was over. The goal of intervention was to break the association between fear of swallowing and eating, using a desensitization model.

Intervention

A one-session consultation was conducted, during which Samuel was expected to eat solid foods (thereby breaking through the established fear), knowing that a rehabilitation swallow study had already been completed and indicated normal functioning. The parents brought dinner from a fast-food restaurant as instructed, and Samuel was informed that he must eat one chicken nugget and several french fries before he could return home. He began by eating the french fries, dipping them first in a sauce which somehow reduced the fear of eating for him. However, Samuel chewed the piece of chicken until it was literally liquefied in his mouth, continuing to hold the liquid and swallowing only with self-induced coughing. Parents left the room while Samuel was instructed that he needed to swallow all of the liquid in his mouth before he could leave, resulting in a full 30 minutes before this was accomplished. Guidelines given to the parents included the following:

1. It is now clear that Samuel can be expected to eat solid foods without a significant problem, given that he ate a small amount of food in the office. In addition, the results of the swallow study show that he has no medical obstruction to swallowing and digesting solid food.
2. Previously preferred foods were recommended.
3. A contingency management plan was implemented to reward Samuel with desired privileges (e.g., TV; playing outdoors; use of the computer) for eating expected foods at both breakfast and dinner. This plan could only succeed if the parents were convinced that there was nothing mechanical or organic interfering with eating, and if they were willing to remain firm with applying consequences with the behavioral plan.

Outcome

Telephone follow-up with the parents revealed that Samuel was eating better with solid foods in general, was swallowing with less effort, and was less resistant to eating in general. He did lose privileges on occasion, but once he began eating normally he was able to earn privileges on a daily basis.

CONCLUSION

Given the central nature of feeding interactions to parenting, persistent food refusal problems in children often are accompanied by parental feelings of anxiety and failure, and the parent-child relationship becomes strained. Working with parents in the treatment of their children's food refusal problems not only teaches the parents new ways of interacting with their children, but also gives them a sense of success and competence in rearing their children.

This chapter has outlined a taxonomy of variables to consider in the assessment and treatment of chronic food refusal. In addition to social contingencies of the parent-child relationship, medical and developmental variables, dietary factors, the environmental context, and family system variables all need to be taken into account when designing an appropriate intervention. Through direct and indirect assessment of these problems, the contributions of each of these variables can be discerned and used to guide treatment. Behavioral techniques commonly used in the treatment of feeding problems have been discussed here; case examples have been offered to demonstrate applications of parent training to clinical cases.

REFERENCES

Ahearn, W. H., Kerwin, M. E., Eicher, P. S., Shantz, J., & Swearingin, W. (1996). An alternating treatments comparison of two intensive treatments for food refusal. *Journal of Applied Behavior Analysis, 29,* 321–332.

Babbitt, R. L., Hoch, T. A., Coe, D. A., Cataldo, M. F., Kelly, K. J., Stackhouse, C., & Permam, J. A. (1994). Behavioral assessment and treatment of pediatric feeding disorders. *Journal of Behavioral and Developmental Pediatrics, 15,* 278–291.

Beautrais, A. L., Fergusson, D. M., & Shannon, F. T. (1982). Family life events and behavioral problems in preschool-aged children. *Pediatrics, 70,* 774–779.

Bentovim, A. (1970). The clinical approach to feeding disorders of childhood. *Journal of Psychosomatic Research, 14,* 267–276.

Bernal, M. E. (1972). Behavioral treatment of a child's eating problem. *Journal of Behaviour Therapy and Experimental Psychiatry, 3,* 43–50.

Bijou, S. W., & Baer, D. M. (1965). *Child development: I. A systematic and empirical theory.* Englewood Cliffs, NJ: Prentice-Hall.

Birch, L. L. (1990). The control of food intake by young children: The role of learning. In E. D. Capaldi & T. L. Powley (Eds.), *Taste, experience, and feeding* (pp. 116–135). Washington, DC: American Psychological Association.

Blackman, J. A., & Nelson, C. L. A. (1985). Reinstituting oral feedings in children fed by gastrostomy tube. *Clinical Pediatrics, 24,* 434–438.

Bradley, R. H., Casey, P. M., & Wortham, B. (1984). Home environments of low SES non-organic failure-to-thrive infants. *Merrill-Palmer Quarterly, 30,* 393–402.

Budd, K. S., & Chugh, C. S. (in press). Common feeding problems in young children. In T. H. Ollendick & R. J. Prinz (Eds.), *Advances in clinical child psychology* (Vol. 20). New York: Plenum Press.

Chatoor, I., & Egan, J. (1983). Nonorganic failure to thrive and dwarfism due to food refusal: A separation disorder. *Journal of the American Academy of Child Psychiatry, 22,* 294–301.

Christophersen, E. R., & Hall, C. L. (1978). Eating patterns and associated problems encountered in normal children. *Issues in Comprehensive Pediatric Nursing, 3,* 1–16.

Dangel, R. F., & Polster, R. A. (Eds.). (1984). *Parent training.* New York: Guilford Press.

Drotar, D. (1995). Failure to thrive (growth deficiency). In M. Roberts (Ed.), *Handbook of pediatric psychology* (2nd ed., pp. 516–536). New York: Guilford Press.

Drotar, D., & Crawford, P. (1987). Using home observation in the clinical assessment of children. *Journal of Clinical Child Psychology, 16,* 342–349.

Drotar, D., Wilson, F., & Sturm, L. (1989). Parent intervention in failure-to-thrive. In C. E. Schaefer & J. M. Briesmeister (Eds.), *Handbook of parent training: Parents as co-therapists for children's behavior problems* (pp. 364–391). New York: Wiley.

Eicher, P. M. (1992). Feeding the child with disabilities. In M. L. Batshaw & Y. M. Perret (Eds.), *Children with disabilities: A medical primer* (3rd ed., pp. 197–211). Baltimore: Brookes.

Erikson, E. (1950). *Childhood and society.* New York: Norton.

Ginsberg, A. J. (1988). Feeding disorders in the developmentally disabled popu-lation. In D. E. Russo & J. H. Kedesdy (Eds.), *Behavioral medicine with the devel-opmentally disabled* (pp. 21–41). New York: Plenum Press.

Graziano, A. M., & Diament, D. M. (1992). Parent behavioral training: An exami-nation of the paradigm. *Behavior Modification, 16,* 3–38.

Greer, R. D., Dorow, L., Williams, G., McCorkle, N., & Asnes, R. (1991). Peer-mediated procedures to induce swallowing and food acceptance in young children. *Journal of Applied Behavior Analysis, 24,* 783–790.

Hagekull, B., & Dahl, M. (1987). Infants with and without feeding difficulties: Maternal experiences. *International Journal of Eating Disorders, 6,* 83–98.

Handen, B. L., Mandell, F., & Russo, D. C. (1986). Feeding induction in children who refuse to eat. *American Journal of Development in Children, 140,* 52–54.

Hatcher, R. P. (1979). Treatment of food refusal in a two-year-old child. *Journal of Behaviour Therapy and Experimental Psychiatry, 10,* 363–367.

Heffer, R. W., & Kelley, M. L. (1994). Nonorganic failure to thrive: Developmental outcomes and psychosocial assessment and intervention issues. *Research in Developmental Disabilities, 15,* 247–268.

Hoch, T. A., Babbitt, R. L., Coe, D. A., Krell, D. M., & Hackbert, L. (1994). Con-tingency contacting: Combining positive reinforcement and escape extinc-tion procedures to treat persistent food refusal. *Behavior Modification, 18,* 106–128.

Howard, R. B. (1984). The infant feeding experience. In R. B. Howard & H. S. Winter (Eds.), *Nutrition and feeding of infants and toddlers* (pp. 21–39). Boston: Little, Brown.

Illingworth, R. S., & Lister, J. (1964). The critical or sensitive period, with special reference to certain feeding problems in infants and children. *Journal of Pedi-atrics, 65,* 839–848.

Kedesdy, J. H., & Budd, K. S. (in press). *Childhood feeding disorders: Biobehavioral assessment and intervention.* Baltimore: Brookes.

Leibowitz, J. M., & Holcer, P. (1974). Building and maintaining self-feeding skills in a retarded child. *American Journal of Occupational Therapy, 28,* 545–548.

Lindberg, L., Bohlin, G., & Hagekull, B. (1991). Early feeding problems in a nor-mal population. *International Journal of Eating Disorders, 10,* 395–405.

Linscheid, T. R. (1992). Eating problems in children. In C. E. Walker & M. C. Roberts (Eds.), *Handbook of clinical child psychology* (2nd ed., pp. 451–473). New York: Wiley.

Linscheid, T. R., Budd, K. S., & Rasnake, K. L. (1995). Pediatric feeding disorders. In M. C. Roberts (Ed.), *Handbook of pediatric psychology* (2nd ed., pp. 501–515). New York: Guilford Press.

Linscheid, T. R., Oliver, J., Blyler, E., & Palmer, S. (1978). Brief hospitalization for the behavioral treatment of feeding problems in the developmentally dis-abled. *Journal of Pediatric Psychology, 3,* 72–76.

Linscheid, T. R., & Rasnake, L. K. (1985). Behavioral approaches to the treatment of failure to thrive. In D. Drotar (Ed.), *New directions in failure to thrive: Implica-tions for research and practice* (pp. 279–294). New York: Plenum Press.

Linscheid, T. R., Tarnowski, K. J., Rasnake, L. K., & Brams, J. S. (1987). Behavioral treatment of food refusal in a child with short-gut syndrome. *Journal of Pediatric Psychology, 12,* 451–459.

Luiselli, J. K. (1989). Behavioral assessment and treatment of pediatric feeding disorders in developmental disabilities. In M. Hersen, R. M. Eisler, & P. M. Miller (Eds.), *Progress in behavior modification* (Vol. 24, pp. 91–131). Newbury Park, CA: Sage.

MacArthur, J., Ballard, K. D., & Artinian, M. (1986). Teaching independent eating to a developmentally handicapped child showing chronic food refusal and disruption at mealtimes. *Australia and New Zealand Journal of Developmental Disabilities, 12,* 203–210.

Mash, E. J., Hamerlynck, L. A., & Handy, L. C. (Eds.). (1976). *Behavior modification approaches to parenting.* New York: Brunner/Mazel.

Mathisen, B., Skuse, D., Wolke, D., & Reilly, S. (1989). Oral-motor dysfunction and failure to thrive among inner-city infants. *Developmental Medicine and Child Neurology, 31,* 293–302.

Morris, S. E., & Klein, M. D. (1987). *Pre-feeding skills: A comprehensive resource for feeding development.* Tucson, AZ: Therapy Skill Builders.

O'Brien, S., Repp, A. C., Williams, G. E., & Christophersen, E. R. (1991). Pediatric feeding disorders. *Behavior Modification, 15,* 394–418.

Pipes, P. L., & Trahms, C. M. (Eds.). (1993). *Nutrition in infancy and childhood* (5th ed.). St. Louis: Mosby.

Pollitt, E., Eichler, A. W., & Chan, C. K. (1975). Psychosocial development and behavior of mothers of failure-to-thrive children. *American Journal of Orthopsychiatry, 45,* 525–537.

Pugliese, M. T., Weyman-Daum, M., Moses, N., & Lifshitz, F. (1987). Parental health beliefs as a cause of nonorganic failure to thrive. *Pediatrics, 80,* 175–181.

Reau, N. R., Senturia, Y. D., Lebailly, S. A., & Christoffel, K. K. (1996). Infant and toddler feeding patterns and problems: Normative data and a new direction. *Journal of Developmental and Behavioral Pediatrics, 17,* 149–153.

Reisinger, K. S., & Bires, J. A. (1980). Anticipatory guidance in pediatric practice. *Pediatrics, 66,* 889–892.

Sanders, M. R., Patel, R. K., Le Grice, B., & Shepherd, R. W. (1993). Children with persistent feeding difficulties: An observational analysis of the feeding interactions of problem and non-problem eaters. *Health Psychology, 12,* 64–73.

Satter, E. (1986). *Child of mine: Feeding with love and good sense.* Palo Alto, CA: Bull.

Siegel, L. J. (1982). Classical and operant procedures in the treatment of a case of food aversion in a young child. *Journal of Clinical Child Psychology, 11,* 167–172.

Wahler, R. G., & Hann, D. M. (1986). A behavioral systems perspective in childhood psychopathology: Expanding the three-term operant contingency. In N. A. Krasnegor, J. D. Arasteh, & M. F. Cataldo (Eds.), *Child health behavior: A behavioral pediatrics perspective* (pp. 146–167). New York: Wiley.

Werle, M. A., Murphy, T. B., & Budd, K. S. (1993). Treating chronic food refusal in young children: Home-based parent training. *Journal of Applied Behavior Analysis, 26,* 421–433.

Werle, M. A., Murphy, T. B., & Budd, K. S. (in press). Broadening the parameters of investigation in treating young children's chronic food refusal. *Behavior Therapy.*

Williamson, D. A., Prather, R. C., Heffer, R. W., & Kelly, M. L. (1988). Eating disorders: Psychological therapies. In J. L. Matson (Ed.), *Handbook of treatment approaches in childhood psychopathology* (pp. 367–396). New York: Plenum Press.

Wolf, L. S., & Glass, R. P. (1992). *Feeding and swallowing disorders in infancy.* Tucson, AZ: Therapy Skill Builders.

Wright, L., Schaefer, A. B., & Solomons, G. (1979). *Encyclopedia of pediatric psychology.* Baltimore: University Park Press.

Wright, L., Stroud, R., & Keenan, M. (1993). Indirect treatment of children via parent training: A burgeoning form of secondary prevention. *Applied and Preventive Psychology, 2,* 191–200.

PART FIVE

SPECIAL NEEDS PARENTS AND CHILDREN

In Chapter 14, Weiss and Wolchik describe a cognitive-behavioral parent training program designed to counter the negative impact of one of the most prevalent stressors experienced by children in our culture: divorce. The authors present a program entitled "New Beginnings," a theory-driven, research-based approach for children of divorce. The intervention plan not only seeks to reduce the stressors associated with divorce, it also emphasizes skill acquisition. In the final analysis, these skills improve and enhance the coping strategies of the children as well as the mothers. The program focuses on the custodial mothers because they are typically the primary agents of change. When the coping and adjustment process of either the child and/or the mother improves, it mutually benefits both parties and strengthens and stabilizes the mother-child relationship.

The authors also present a multifaceted definition of divorce that emphasizes the staggering impact of changes within the family on the children, specifically, and the family members, in general. Weiss and Wolchik conceptualize divorce as an ongoing process of multiple environmental changes that accompany the restructuring of the family unit. The adjustment problems of children are viewed as a consequence of the stressful environmental events that occur during the transition in the family structure as well as the protective resources available to the child.

The New Beginnings intervention program delineates the crucial tasks of specific training sessions and exercises. The sessions are uniquely designed to offer the mothers an overview of the program, help the participants grasp the impact of divorce on children, and teach the parenting skills of "Family Fun Time." The program offers occasions for positive, supportive, and caring contact between the children and the mothers. By providing sessions geared for "One-on-One Time," the program is aimed at changing negative behavioral and interactive cycles into positive ones that offer the youngsters a chance to feel valued. Sessions are also designed to improve listening and responding skills. In addition, the parents are trained in anger management skills that keep mothers from arguing with their ex-spouses in front of their children. The program with its individual sessions and exercises is designed to benefit the kids.

In Chapter 15, Sheeber and McDevitt offer an approach to parent guidance based on an understanding of children's temperament to modify and improve parent-child interactions. The goal is to reduce the stress in the parent-child unit that may occur from a mismatch between the child's temperament and the parents' behaviors. The authors provide an extensive discussion and critique of the pioneering study of children's temperament, the New York Longitudinal Study. With this research as a foundation, Sheeber and McDevitt concentrate on key variables, such as parent-child interactions, parental adjustment, and child behavior problems. The authors indicate that the key to understanding and formulating temperament-focused interventions is the realization that children manifest individual differences in behavior associated with temperament. These differences in behavioral styles affect parental responses to their children as well as an understanding of the children's behaviors. The temperament-focused intervention approach also helps parents to understand, expect, and appreciate individual behavioral diversity in children.

Sheeber and McDevitt identify four essential interventions for temperament-based problems: education of the parents about temperamental differences, individual behavioral assessment, environmental intervention, and the use of parent support groups. They offer a sound empirical base and clinically verified rationale for each of the four interventions. They also clarify which strategy is most suitable and appropriate for specific problems. Detailed case material illustrates the theoretical and practical value of temperament-focused parent guidance.

Following a historical review of behavioral parent training, from its inception to more recent innovations and modifications, Blechman tackles some of the major limitations of a traditional parent training intervention approach in Chapter 16. Blechman points out that classic parent training relies on the child's compliance with the requests of parents, teachers, therapists, and other adult authority figures and thus has had limited prevention potential for high-risk youngsters. In essence, high-risk adolescents are not only likely to be noncompliant, they do not know how to cope prosocially. For example, they do not know how to fulfill their needs for self-esteem and social approval in a socially acceptable manner that benefits themselves and others. The author notes that for parent training to realize its potential it must meet the needs of parents of antisocial youth and must take place within a moral context that promotes prosocial coping among high-risk adolescents and their families.

Blechman describes the coping-competence theory, a construct that provides a theoretical basis for intervention with antisocial youth and their families. The coping-competence theory holds that the youngster's current coping mechanisms directly influence future life outcomes while mediating the indirect impact of other risk and protection variables available to the child. The theory also highlights and advocates the youngster's acceptance of responsibility for actions and behaviors. The coping-competence theory addresses the initial acquisition of maladaptive antisocial coping strategies. It also posits that any lasting reduction in antisocial behavior results from prosocial coping techniques. The theory focuses on the importance of parenting and family processes which influence the child's coping styles as well as the intervention-related role of school, neighborhood, and societal risk factors.

The coping-competence theory provides a theoretical and philosophical foundation for Prosocial Family Therapy (PFT), a three-phase intervention program that outlines a series of tasks to reduce antisocial behaviors and enhance such factors as communications and problem-solving skills. The author recounts family case histories which demonstrate the approach, identify measures to assess clinically significant improvement in postintervention phases, and illustrate the effectiveness of each phase of Prosocial Family Therapy in reducing and changing the maladaptive coping strategies of a high-risk population within a moral context.

In Chapter 17, Bratton submits a creative parent training intervention format that seeks to improve the quality of the parent-child relationship following a divorce. Filial/Family Play Therapy is a structured methodological approach that trains parents to become therapeutic agents of change. The parents are trained in the implementation of child-centered play therapy skills designed to alleviate their child's problems. At its core, Filial/Family Therapy is a prolific and effective method of strengthening the parent-child relationship. It seeks to increase parental acceptance and decrease parental stress while also reducing the child's problematic behaviors. Because play is an integral and essential part of a child's life, the goals of this therapy are accomplished within the framework of play.

Bratton offers an extensive description of the 10-week Filial/Family Play Therapy Model. Parents are instructed in the basic methodology of child-centered play therapy, particularly as it applies to the treatment of children who are experiencing difficulties in adjusting to their parents' divorce. Within the child-centered play setting, parents learn to convey acceptance, empathy, and encouragement. The parents also learn effective limit setting. The approach presented in Chapter 17 not only facilitates the child's adjustment to the divorce and the problems associated with the divorce process, it also offers the parents a sense of mastery and competence over numerous parenting skills that can be generalized to many situations. As an added bonus, the Filial Therapy approach helps the parents reduce any feelings of guilt or helplessness that may result when parents depend on a professional for problem resolution. The competencies of the parents are enhanced and emphasized; they are the agents of therapeutic change. The sense of competency that follows the mastery of parenting and relational skills is particularly crucial for single parents who are going through the difficulties and adjustments inherent in a divorce and the subsequent restructuring of the family unit.

CHAPTER 14

New Beginnings: An Empirically-Based Intervention Program for Divorced Mothers to Help Their Children Adjust to Divorce

LILLIE WEISS and SHARLENE WOLCHIK

PARENTAL DIVORCE is one of the most prevalent stressors experienced by children in our society and can have serious negative effects on children, including elevated aggression (e.g., Felner, Stolberg, & Cowen, 1975; Hetherington, Cox, & Cox, 1978; Zill 1983), elevated anxiety (Wyman, Cowen, Hightower, & Pedro-Carroll, 1985), poor academic performance (e.g., Guidubaldi, Cleminshaw, Perry, & McLoughlin, 1983; Zill, 1983), poor self-concept (e.g., Parish & Wigle, 1985), and poor peer relationships (e.g., Guidubaldi et al., 1983; Hetherington, Cox, & Cox, 1981). A recent meta-analysis (Amato & Keith, 1991) showed that children of divorce scored lower than children from intact families on a variety of measures of adjustment. Further, children of divorce are over represented in treatment settings (Zill, 1983). Given the high prevalence of divorce and its potential negative effects, facilitating children's postdivorce adjustment is an important focus for preventive mental health programs.

In this chapter, we describe New Beginnings, a theory-driven, research-based program for children of divorce, which uses custodial mothers as change agents. The program is part of a research grant funded by the National Institute of Mental Health to compare the effects of three programs to help children adjust after divorce. It is not our purpose to provide a comprehensive review of the overall research design and/or findings of the intervention, but rather to describe the "nuts-and-bolts" of the parent training program. We will first briefly describe the research findings and theoretical framework on which the program is based and later outline the specifics of the parent training program.We will then provide a general overview and follow it with a description of each session. We will also review some general guidelines and process issues for group leaders.

THEORY AND RESEARCH

Making the link between research findings and an intervention program is a complex task. The development of New Beginnings involved four steps:

1. Examining the existing literature for theoretical frameworks and empirical studies on the development of adjustment problems in children of divorce.
2. Conducting generative studies to provide further insight into the processes that may lead to adjustment problems.
3. Developing an intervention designed to affect the critical processes identified in the research.
4. Evaluating the intervention using a randomized field trial.

There is growing consensus that divorce is best conceptualized as an ongoing process of multiple environmental changes that accompany the restructuring of the family unit rather than as a single, dichotomous event (Felner, Farber, & Primavera, 1983; Felner, Terre, & Rowlinson, 1988; Hetherington, 1979; Kurdek, 1981) and that children's adjustment to divorce is affected by the number and type of environmental events they experience. The underlying theoretical model of the intervention program is consistent with this consensus. In broad strokes, the adjustment problems of children are viewed as a consequence of both the *stressful environmental events* that may occur during this transition in family structure and of the *protective resources* available to the child (e.g., Felner et al., 1983; Kurdek, 1981; Sandler, Wolchik, & Braver, 1988).

This general framework organizes the results of previous research that show consistent empirical support for significant associations between children's adjustment after divorce and the following environmental and interpersonal factors: (a) *the quality of the child's relationship with the custodial parent* (e.g., Fogas, Wolchik, & Braver, 1987; Guidubaldi, Cleminshaw, Perry, Nastasi, & Lightel, 1986; Stolberg & Bush, 1985); (b) *discipline strategies* (e.g., Baldwin & Skinner, 1989; Fogas et al., 1987; Santrock & Warshak, 1979); (c) *amount of contact between the child and the noncustodial parent* (e.g., Guidubaldi et al., 1986; Hetherington et al., 1981; Warren et al., 1984); and (d) *negative divorce-related events, including interparental conflict* (e.g., Guiduabaldi et al., 1986; Hetherington et al., 1978; Long, Forehand, Fauber, & Brody, 1987; Sandler et al., 1988; Stolberg & Anker, 1984). A parent-based intervention was designed to affect these putative mediators, with changes in these mediating variables, in turn, being expected to lead to positive changes in children's psychological adjustment. Figure 14.1 depicts the hypothesized relations between putative variables targeted for change and children's adjustment problems

The specific intervention procedures used to modify each of these constructs are shown in Table 14.1. Wherever possible, techniques were used that previously have been shown to be effective in changing the mediating processes. For example, in selecting techniques to enhance the quality of the custodial parent-child relationship, we relied heavily on Forehand's and Patterson's work with families (Forehand & McMahon, 1981; Patterson, 1975). The specific change techniques included: positive family activities (Family Fun Time), One-on-One Time, monitoring and reinforcing children's positive behaviors, and listening skills (mirroring, continuing, summary, and feeling responses). Discipline was enhanced by self-monitoring discipline strategies and by practicing using consistent consequences to increase or decrease the frequency of two specific behaviors. Anger management training (Novaco, 1975) was used to decrease interparental conflict. Contact with the noncustodial parent was addressed by discussion of the impact of this relationship on the child's well-being and by identification and removal of obstacles such as restrictions on telephone calls, inflexible visitation arrangements, and fighting during visitation pick ups and drop offs.

Custodial parents were used as change agents rather than the children themselves because many of the divorce-related events that are harmful to children are within the parent's control and beyond the child's (e.g., the level of overt conflict between the parents). Also, research has demonstrated that a warm and accepting relationship with the custodial parent is associated with more positive divorce adjustment (Fogas et al., 1987; Hetherington et al., 1978; Santrock & Warshak, 1979; Wallerstein & Kelly, 1980). By working with parents, we can enhance and/or mobilize this protective resource. Finally, parents have been shown to be effective change agents for a wide variety of behavior problems (Graziano & Diament, 1992; Patterson, 1992; Wright, Stroud, & Keenan, 1993).

The efficacy of this program has been evaluated in two randomized, experimental field trials (Wolchik et al., 1993). In the first small-scale trial, we used an experimental versus delayed intervention control group design. The second trial addressed whether the positive effects of our program for mothers could be replicated and whether a combined

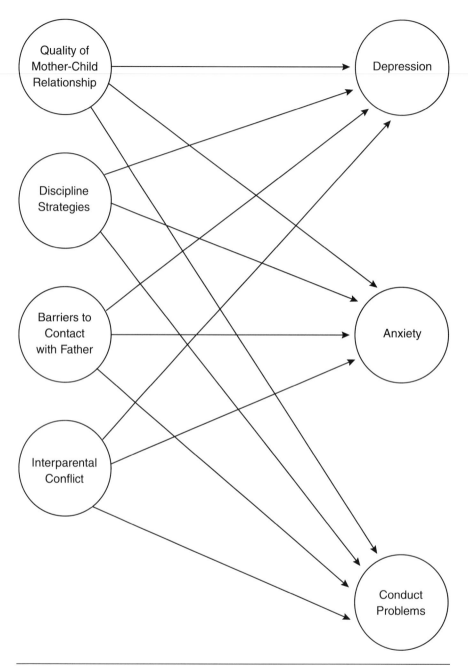

Figure 14.1   Hypothesized Relations between Putative Mediating Variables Targeted for Change and Children's Adjustments.

Table 14.1

Theory of the Intervention: Putative Mediators and Intervention Techniques

Putative Mediators	Intervention Techniques
Quality of mother relationship	Family Fun Time One-on-One Time Catch 'em Being Good Listening skills
Effective discipline	Clear expectations and rules Monitoring misbehaviors and consequences Increased consistency
Contact with father	Education about importance of child's relationship with father Reduction of obstacles to visitation
Negative divorce-related events including interparental conflict	Anger management skills Listening skills

program involving concurrent, separate groups for mothers and their children produced additive effects. In this trial, a low-dose self-study, guided reading intervention was used as the control condition. Because this chapter focuses on the program for mothers, we describe the findings from the first trial as well as the results of the analyses that compared the mother-only program versus self-study condition in the second trial.

The program for mothers was highly similar in the two trials. However, in addition to the four putative mediators described earlier, an increase in the amount and quality of support children received from nonparental adults was targeted in the Wolchik et al. (1993) study. The focus on non-parental support was deleted in the second trial to accommodate an expanded discipline section.

In both trials, several steps were taken to ensure high levels of intervention fidelity. First, sessions were delivered using detailed descriptions of content and format. Second, extensive training (30 hours prior to the start of the program and 1.5 hours/week during program delivery) and supervision (1.5 hours/week) were provided. Training included readings and didactic presentations about the theoretical and empirical bases for the program, videotapes of prior program sessions, and role plays of session material. Weekly supervision addressed problems encountered in conducting the previous session, including skill acquisition and homework compliance difficulties. Third, extensive process evaluation data were collected. These steps led to exceptionally high levels of program fidelity.

Data analyses indicated that the mother program led to positive effects on the mediators of mother-child relationship quality and discipline, and children's mental health outcomes. For some of the putative mediators and outcomes, the magnitude of intervention effects differed depending on preintervention functioning, with effects being most marked among those with the poorest initial levels. Evidence also indicated that changes in mother-child relationship quality partially mediated the program effects on children's mental health outcomes.

THE PARENT TRAINING PROGRAM

The orientation of the program is cognitive-behavioral, with a strong emphasis on skills acquisition or enhancement. It consists of eleven $1\frac{3}{4}$-hour weekly structured group sessions and two 1-hour individual sessions after weeks 3 and 6 to problem solve and facilitate the use of program skills. Each group is led by two masters' level counselors and is composed of eight to ten custodial or primary residential mothers. The format is of a psychoeducational group, with each session consisting of a short lecture with active group participation, skills demonstration and practice, homework assignments using skills with the children at home, and homework review and problem solving.

The program makes use of general group principles together with cooperative or active learning principles so that participants learn to do the skills correctly and to apply them outside the group sessions. The group sessions are both didactic and experiential. The didactic material is presented in a conversational, interactive learning style, allowing time for active participation. Much of the learning of the particular skills and concepts is experiential, with group exercises and role play aimed at learning the skills accurately and applying them outside the group session.

An old proverb states: "*Tell* me and I may forget. *Show* me and I may remember. *Involve* me and I will learn." As much as possible, we make use of active learning principles to maximize *involvement* for most effective learning. We also *show* (via films, demonstrations, modeling, etc.) rather than tell. We try to *tell* or lecture as little as necessary, and even in the didactic components, whenever possible, we ask participants questions and use their responses to make key teaching points.

The format for each session is essentially the same. Except for Session 1 which starts out in a large group, the sessions begin with the group splitting into two for homework review with individual leaders. The two groups then join and meet as a large group for the bulk of the session, where new material is introduced and skills are practiced in dyads or small groups. Each group leader is assigned the mothers with whom she meets with at the beginning of every session for homework review. However, for skills practice, different groups are chosen at each session by group leaders. The composition of these groups is usually planned before each session and strategized by group leaders to maximize effective learning of skills.

PROGRAM OVERVIEW

The program is basically a skills acquisition program, with cumulative skills building on each other (Table 14.2). The beginning sessions of the program teach skills to enhance the quality of the mother-child relationship and to reverse the negative cycle of communication between mother and child that frequently accompanies divorce. Improving mother-child communication early in the program helps reduce children's misbehaviors so that there is less need to address those in later sessions. It prevents little problems from turning into big ones and eliminates many problem behaviors altogether. As mothers spend more time being with and listening to their children, they can avoid many current and potential discipline issues later on. In sessions 1 and 2, we teach three skills (Family Fun Time, One-on-One Time, and Catch 'em Being Good) that mothers are to do each week of the program and indefinitely. This is followed by the Listening module in sessions 3, 4, and 5. Session 6 focuses on shielding children from negative divorce experiences, primarily interparental conflict. Session 7 is further practice of listening skills, followed by the Discipline module in sessions 8, 9, and 10. The last session is a review and closure.

Table 14.2
Central Topics Covered in Each Section

Program Overview	
Session 1	Introduction, 2 + 2 = 5, and Family Fun Time
Session 2	Cycling, One-on-One Time, and Catch 'em Being Good
Session 3	Listening 1: listen
Individual Session	Trouble shooting use of program activities
Session 4	Listening 2: think
Session 5	Listening 3: respond
Session 6	Shielding kids from negative divorce experiences
Individual Session	Time with dad
Session 7	Practicing listening skills
Session 8	Managing kids' behavior 1
Session 9	Managing kids' behavior 2
Session 10	Managing kids' behavior 3
Session 11	Review, closure, and graduation

THERAPIST QUALIFICATIONS AND CHARACTERISTICS

Therapists are masters' level counselors in psychology or related behavioral health fields. We use a structured interview when hiring group leaders to assess their theoretical orientation, knowledge of divorce-related issues, experience in leading groups and teaching parenting skills, ability to stay on task and adhere to a structured program, and comfort with being videotaped and supervised. In addition, we try to choose leaders with good interpersonal skills and the ability to be warm and empathetic and inspire confidence. We want leaders who can be nurturing and firm at the same time—in short, "good parents." Most of our leaders so far have been female, although we have had male leaders as well. Competence, not gender, is the more important factor in our selection. We also try to select leaders who are conscientious and demonstrate a great deal of involvement and follow-through. We demand a great deal of our group leaders, just as they demand of the mothers in the program. They are—like good parents—"chiefs, cooks, and bottle washers," as well as coaches and cheerleaders. Not all of our leaders have been parents themselves, although there are obvious advantages to having firsthand experience.

Leaders receive initial and ongoing training. The initial training sessions consist of seven 2- or 2½-hour meetings that cover general issues and specific content of the sessions. In addition, leaders are required to complete additional outside readings in preparation for the training sessions. Once the group starts, they receive 2 hours of weekly training before each session and an hour and a half of supervision after each session. They also spend time by themselves and with coleaders preparing and rehearsing each session and troubleshooting any anticipated problems. Once the groups start, the total time for preparation, training, conducting the sessions, paperwork, and supervision is about 10 to 12 hours per week.

Supervision and training are important components of the program. Just as actors need direction, even with a detailed script, leaders spend a great deal of time in supervision to maximize the success of the program. The supervision and training has been done by the two authors, both clinical psychologists with a great deal of experience in leading and supervising psychoeducational groups. The supervisors help leaders with any problems they may be having and ensure that they are conducting the session the way it is outlined in the manual. During supervision, leaders and supervisors review each mother's progress, view segments of the videotape of the session and problem solve any issues and difficulties. In our supervision and training sessions, we use the same principles and methods as those used in the group sessions, (e.g., active learning, role play, open discussions, demonstrations).

CLIENT CHARACTERISTICS

To be eligible for the group, a mother must have been divorced within the past two years without remarrying and have at least one child between 9 and 12 living with her. Although the age group for children for this intervention was between 9 and 12, we have used this program with younger and older children as well. An additional requirement for participating in the program was that neither the mother nor the child be in treatment for psychological problems at the time. Mothers were recruited through random sampling of court records of filing for divorce, media articles, and presentations to school personnel. Because the intervention was designed to be preventive, families were also excluded where the child had test scores indicating clinical levels of depression or extreme levels of externalizing problems or the child endorsed an item about suicidal ideation. These families were immediately referred for treatment.

MATERIALS

Leaders are provided with the *New Beginnings Parenting Program Leader Manual* (Wolchik, Westover, Sandler, & Martin, 1992), which includes the content and format of each session detailed in lengthy session outlines as well as all of the handouts provided to participants. Other materials include a film developed specifically for this program to demonstrate some of the program skills as well as posters and cue cards to use in teaching. A flipchart is also necessary to integrate lectures with members' responses.

DESCRIPTION OF SESSIONS

ORIENTATION INTERVIEW

Once a family is deemed to be eligible for the intervention following the successful completion of a home interview, the mother is scheduled for an hour-long orientation with the group leader. The purpose of the orientation interview is to establish rapport, to gather information about the family, to provide some information about the groups, and to establish proper norms for attendance and participation.

The group leader asks for the names, ages, and a brief description of each child, as well as any special concerns about any of the children, attempting to normalize these concerns and relate them to the goals of the program. In addition, the mother is asked about her current relationship with her exspouse as well as the child's relationship with him, including any special problems. These responses are used to introduce the goals of the program that are to improve the emotional adjustment of children, maintain a close relationship with them and help them talk about their concerns, learn more effective ways of managing their behavior, and shield them from divorce-related stressors, particularly from being caught in the middle between parents.

The group format is then described to the mother. She is told that she will be meeting in a group with 8 or 9 other women for 11 weeks in addition to 2 individual sessions. The group leader stresses that the group is an educational experience to teach skills that will help children adjust to the divorce. Although the parent will learn skills which she can use with all of her children, we focus intensively on one child in each family during the group meetings. She is also reminded that the group is primarily for the children's adjustment.

The importance of completing homework assignments and attending all sessions is stressed, and mothers are asked to make a commitment to be at all of the group meetings and individual sessions. If there is some hesitation about making a commitment, the group leader deals with this at the beginning. Since steady attendance and practicing the skills at home are very important components of the program, it is essential to set these norms in the initial interview. Mothers are also asked about additional concerns, and these are dealt with in the session.

The research design included two conditions: one for parents only, and one where the target child attended an 11-week group program as well on the same night. Mothers in the parent-child condition are also given information on what their child will be learning in his or her group. In addition, mothers are asked if they need babysitting for the other siblings while they attend the group, and arrangements for child care on the premises are made.

Session 1: Introduction, 2 + 2 = 5, and Family Fun Time

Purpose

The purpose of Session 1 is to provide an overview of the program, discuss the impact of divorce on children, and teach the parenting skill of Family Fun Time. Other goals include building rapport, trust, and group cohesion; establishing leader credibility; and motivating mothers to do homework.

Group Norms

This is probably the most important session because it sets the tone for future sessions. This is where we try to establish group norms, (e.g., punctuality, attendance, commitment to following through with the program and completing homework assignments). Leaders do whatever is possible to motivate mothers to attend the program and to follow through. By being role models themselves (e.g., being prepared, following through on assignments, and "going the extra mile"), leaders can set good group norms. We establish norms for being on time by starting *exactly* on time and also warning the group that we'll be "moving along" often and apologizing ahead of time for cutting members off. We try to limit off-task talk and stories and adhere to the time schedule as much as possible.

In this and other sessions, leaders try to achieve *group cohesion* and give *hope* along with providing information. We want mothers to recognize that there are benefits for them and their children so that they will do whatever is needed to make those changes, and we use every opportunity to link changes in children's behavior to mothers' hard work and effort. Providing hope and encouragement is essential because we require a great deal of work from the mothers, and it may take some time before they see the tangible results of their efforts.

Introductions

Leaders introduce themselves and talk about their training, background, and experience to establish credibility. When talking about themselves, they keep in mind that mothers are asking themselves, "Why should I listen to and believe what she or he has to say?" Then mothers introduce themselves, giving their names, length of time since the divorce, names and ages of children, and what they do for a living. We try to keep the introductions at a comfortable level. This is not group therapy nor the beginning of a women's divorce adjustment group. Even though mothers have been told at the orientation that this is not group therapy, when they get there, it may look very much like group therapy to them. Some mothers may be hurting and very much need to talk about their divorces or exhusbands and may see this as an opportunity to "vent" or to "bash" or perhaps just to elicit some support. We try to limit this since it can be very confusing to other group members if a mother takes the floor and begins to do the work that properly belongs in group therapy. When this happens, we acknowledge the mother's feelings and try to return her to answering the questions that leaders have posed for the introductions. One strategy to keep group members from getting sidetracked is to ask them to distinguish between their roles as parents versus exwives.

Following the introductions, mothers sign a participation contract not to discuss other mothers' personal issues outside of the meetings, to attend every meeting, be on time, and do all of the homework assignments. In addition, they agree to let group leaders know when they are having trouble with the assignments, and the leaders in turn agree to work with mothers to tailor the material to their child's needs. The participation contract is filled out in duplicate, one for leaders and one for mothers.

After the contract is signed, leaders provide information about the program, stating that its purpose is to help children adjust to divorce and stressing that children are the targets of this program. The program is *not* a divorce adjustment group for mothers, although if children are coping well, the parents' adjustment will be made easier. In addition, mothers are told that the program is RESEARCH-driven, MOM-driven, and HOMEWORK-driven. It is based on research-proven strategies, and mothers are the most powerful agents of change in their families. The homework IS the program: mothers who do the homework *will* see changes in their families and those who don't, *won't*.

Mothers are then asked what changes they would like to see in their families as a result of participating in this program. The purpose of this exercise is to normalize problems that they are experiencing as well as to shape their expectations so they fit well with the program goals and instill hope by showing a good fit between their expectations and the program. Leaders reinforce realistic expectations (e.g., reducing the stress level at home, feeling closer to kids, helping kids open up more, decreasing fighting and reducing feelings of being "out of control") and screen out unrealistic expectations (e.g., getting the exhusband to be more responsible). These expectations are tied into program activities that will address those expectations. Initially, for example, if a mother mentions that she hopes to get her children to talk more to her, we point out that we will be spending a great deal of time on effective listening to get children talking more openly. Each mother's expectations are written on a flipchart, and this information is referred to frequently in later sessions. For example, leaders can state, "As I recall, Judy, you mentioned in our first week that one of your goals was to get Johnny to stop fighting with his brothers. Tonight's instruction on discipline will teach you skills to help make that happen." Leaders keep this list in front of their manual to use in supervision and to personalize planning strategies for each mother.

Impact of Divorce: 2 + 2 = 5

The next exercise, 2 + 2 = 5, provides the foundation and rationale for the whole program and lays the groundwork for the next 10 weeks. The first purpose of the exercise is to do some normalizing that divorce is problematic and that there are good, valid reasons for this being a difficult time for families. The second reason is to instill hope that we know about and can provide solutions to their problems.

In the 2 + 2 = 5 exercise or the divorce equation, we develop the idea that the problems children have in adjusting to divorce plus the problems mothers have in adjusting to divorce add up with synergistic effects to create a sum greater than the total of its parts; in this case, a family situation characterized by stress, fighting, and other problems. It conveys to mothers that these are understandable, predictable, and *correctable* occurrences that are common after divorce. After stating that divorce is a period of transition and changes, group members are asked what problems and changes have occurred in their worlds and in their children's. Their responses are arranged on flipcharts as in Figure 14.2 and augmented with other problems and changes from that equation to deliver the punchline at the end that with so much change, they get more than they bargained for: 2 + 2 doesn't equal 4 but 5!

Hope is instilled by providing solutions to these divorce problems which lays the groundwork and rationale for the rest of the program. The solutions are the targeted mediators: increasing warm and positive contact with mothers, shielding children from the negative effects of divorce experiences and keeping them out of the war zone, supporting contact between children and their fathers and improving discipline skills. The presentation of the solutions is used to introduce the rest of the program and lead into the rationale for Family Fun Time.

Family Fun Time

Family Fun Time increases positive and warm contact with children and is a skill that mothers are asked to do every week so that it becomes a positive family routine that children can count on. Many divorced families think of themselves as "broken" or "incomplete" families. Doing a pleasurable

Changes in Kids' World:
- Loss of familiar routine
- Loss of family structure
- Loss of family organization
- Loss of a certain future: "Who will take care of me?"
- Loss of contact with extended family
- Fewer "nice" things
- Loss of house; loss of own room

Changes in Mom's World:
- More expenses and less money
- More work and less time
- More work and less help
- Setting up a new home
- Competing with dad for kids' favor
- No one to consult with, no one to say "Nice job!"

Relationship between Mom and Kids after Divorce:
- Increased distance between mom and kids
- Instability
- Kids unhappy
- Mom unhappy
- Not as much fun to be mom
- Tension, fights, chaos
- Less tolerant of kids' misbehaviors
- Unrealistic expectations for kids and moms

Problems with Kids:
- Aggressiveness
- Anger
- Not minding
- School problems
- Attention demands
- Afraid to be alone
- Withdrawal
- Depression

Mom's Emotions:
- Depressed
- Angry
- Guilty
- Impatient
- Overwhelmed
- Afraid

$$2 \qquad + \qquad 2 \qquad = \qquad 5$$

Figure 14.2 The Divorce Equation.

activity as a family every week provides children with a sense of family and helps create a new family tradition. Just as the name connotes, Family Fun Time has two essential components: it includes only the *Family* and it has to be *Fun*. It happens once a week, every week, and children decide what to do. In addition, it has to be an *Activity* where interaction between family members occurs (e.g., playing games together) and not a *Passivity* such as watching a movie together. The only rules for this activity are that it has to be inexpensive, not include any problem solving, complaining, teasing, or fighting, and it has to be fun! Examples of fun activities include going out for ice cream together, playing basketball or board games, having a slumber party in the living room, or going to the park. We have been impressed with the many creative and inexpensive ways to have fun that children have come up with. Leaders role play how to introduce Family Fun Time to children and answer questions about how to adapt it to the different families. Then the group is split into two small groups where mothers have an opportunity to role play the skill and receive feedback.

The homework for the first week is to introduce Family Fun Time to the family, plan what to do, and do it. Mothers are also asked to fill out a sheet listing their children's positive qualities which they will use in Session 2. They are given homework sheets to write out how their assignments went. They bring this homework to the next session. Leaders read the homework each week, make comments, and then give it back to the mothers. This has been a very effective way for mothers to communicate with leaders the problems or questions they have and for leaders to provide feedback, problem solve, and give encouragement to mothers.

SESSION 2: CYCLING, ONE-ON-ONE TIME, AND CATCH 'EM BEING GOOD

Purpose

The goals of this session are to teach mothers how to change negative cycles into positive ones and to introduce two more skills that parents do weekly: One-on-One Time and Catch 'em Being Good. We continue to build group cohesion to help mothers see the group as a place to problem solve and to get mothers comfortable practicing skills in a group setting.

Cycling: Negative and Positive

After reviewing the homework and collecting homework sheets in the small groups, leaders discuss how the changes resulting from divorce can lead to a negative cycle of stress, with children's behavior affecting mothers and vice-versa. These changes lead to a picture of children who are aggressive, mind less, act angry, talk back, and mothers who ignore good behaviors, yell, use less consistent discipline, control with power and authority, and make fewer demands for responsible behavior from their children. These negative ways of interacting escalate, and the negative cycle feeds itself. Mothers are told that *they* are the ones who can change the negative cycle into a positive one. When they change their behaviors, their children will begin to respond differently to them, although this *won't happen overnight*. As mothers recognize good behaviors and ignore bad, show lots of attention and have fewer power struggles, they reverse the negative cycle of divorce. By doing the activities they will learn in group, they can make the bond between them and their children stronger. The next two skills taught in the session—One-on-One Time and Catch 'em Being Good—help do that.

One-on-One Time

One-on-One Time is regular, *short* (15 minutes) periods of scheduled time that mothers spend with their children where children experience acceptance in as pure a form as it comes. In One-on-One Time, the child selects a 15-minute activity to do as the mother gives undivided positive attention. Here children feel that everything they do is right and nothing they do is wrong. Group leaders show film segments of One-on-One Time and also demonstrate the skill using role play. Activities could include playing at the child's hobby together, going out for a coke, playing a card game, or having the child teach the parent to play a video game. The mother does not compete or try to win, criticize, ask questions, or teach. She is to follow the child's lead instead of directing. We emphasize that One-on-One Time is the *attitude* of warmth, caring, and unconditional acceptance rather than just the *rote* application of the skill, and that it takes *work*. We also stress that this is one of the most powerful activities—children love it! Mothers get a chance to experience the power of this tool when they practice the skill, playing the part of mother and also the child. When they are asked how it feels to play the part of the child, they use terms like "special," "the focus of attention," and "important." This helps them understand the goal of this skill which is to make children feel loved and valued. We encourage them to try it even if it feels awkward at first.

Catch 'em Being Good

The second skill, Catch 'em Being Good also helps children feel valued and is an important step in creating the positive cycle. It involves catching children in the act of being good. It is a method of positive discipline to get children to do what parents want. Mothers are shown a film segment to demonstrate the skill and told to "catch" their children being "good" instead of focusing on "bad" behaviors. They can notice their children's behaviors, ideas, or personal characteristics and "catch 'em being good" in both physical (e.g., a hug) and verbal (e.g., "nice going!") ways. They are to praise the behavior and not the child and to be careful about giving backhanded compliments such as "it's about time you did such a nice job of cleaning your room." Mothers practice using this skill by reviewing the information sheet they had filled out the week before on their children's positive qualities. For homework, they are to do One-on-One Time once or twice with each child (depending on the number of children in the family) and to catch their children being good as often as they can.

SESSION 3: LISTENING I: LISTEN

Purpose

Session 3 is the first of three sessions devoted to improving listening skills. Its goals are to provide a rationale for good listening, to introduce the three parts of effective listening (Listen, Think, Respond) and to teach the first part—the 5 Talk-to-Me's.

Rationale for Good Listening

Good listening tells children "I love you," "I'm here for you," and "what you say is valuable." These messages are major factors in promoting children's adjustment after a divorce. Good listening raises children's self-esteem, and when parents listen, children feel comfortable sharing their concerns with them and get closer to them. Mothers are told that good listening is not easy and requires lots of practice.

Good Listening: The Big Picture

Mothers view two film segments to demonstrate the difference between bad and good listening and to introduce "The Big Picture" or three parts of effective listening. As can be seen from Figure 14.3, the process is circular, continuous, and ongoing. This session focuses on the first part of effective listening.

The 5 Talk-to-Me's

We discuss ways for mothers to let their children know that they are interested in what they are saying and to keep them talking. These are: (a) *Big Ears*: being "all ears" and tuning in to what their children are saying; (b) *Good Body Language*: (e.g., facing the speaker and making eye contact); (c) *Good Openers*: open vs. closed questions; (d) *Mmm-Hmms* (nodding, "yeah," "right"); and (e) *Say Mores* (phrases such as "tell me more about that" or "what else happened?" that encourage the speaker to say more). The first three "talk-to-me's" get the conversation off to a good

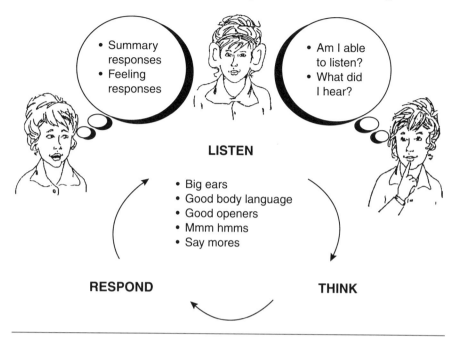

Figure 14.3 Good Listening.

start; the last two are ways to keep the conversation going. Leaders use role play to demonstrate these skills and later have mothers practice them in small groups.

The first individual session is scheduled after Session 3 to review and troubleshoot the skills taught so far in the program.

SESSION 4: LISTENING II: THINK

Purpose

The goals of this session are to teach mothers to think before they respond and to use summary responses when they respond.

Think Before You Respond

Stopping to think before responding allows time to "tailor" responses to the child's needs and helps mothers make responses that help their child feel heard and understood. Parents frequently rush into a response without thinking in an attempt to "fix" the situation. When mothers respond automatically without thinking first, they miss important information, frustrate their children by giving advice when it's not needed, and undermine their child's self-esteem and competence by solving a problem that the child could have solved himself with encouragement. Mothers are taught to ask themselves two questions before responding: (a) Am I able to use the 5 Talk-to-Me's? and (b) What did I hear? If they are unable to give their child their full attention by using the 5 Talk-to-Me's, they are taught how to postpone listening until a later time. In response to the second question, they are taught how to mirror by repeating exactly what they heard. Mirroring is done silently and prepares mothers for summary responses.

Summary Responses

After teaching parents to stop and think, we move on to the third part of effective listening—responding. We start with summary responses that condense the message heard, unlike mirroring responses that repeat the message word for word. Summary responses are like classnotes or highlights. They ask the question, "This is what I heard . . . did I get it right?" To summarize accurately, mothers learn to mirror first. After they have mirrored, they condense the mirrored message and give the summary response in a way that asks, "Did I get it right?" This invites their children to correct their understanding if they are off. Accurate summary responses don't add anything, they don't guess at feelings or interpret what's going on—they simply summarize. After leaders demonstrate summary responses, mothers practice these skills, receiving corrective feedback.

Learning to mirror and summarize is not easy, and there is a very strong tendency on the part of mothers to give advice and attempt a quick fix. Of all the listening traps, this is probably the one that is easiest for mothers to get into, and group leaders need to point this out when it happens. Soon mothers learn to catch themselves when they go for the quick fix. In this and other sessions, leaders model the listening skills in their interactions so that mothers can themselves feel what it's like to be listened to and have an opportunity to observe good listening.

SESSION 5: LISTENING III: RESPOND

Purpose

The goals of this session are to teach mothers feeling responses, to give them practice in putting all the listening skills together, and to teach them guided problem solving for those times when listening isn't enough.

Feeling Responses

Feeling responses ask the question "Is this how you feel?" They are used sparingly when the child is talking about an emotional issue. When making feeling responses, mothers try to identify what their child is feeling, using their gut reaction, intuition, or previous experience. Or they can put themselves in their child's place and imagine how they would feel in that situation. Feeling responses, like summary responses, are tentative, to allow the child time to correct them. Leaders role play and use film segments to demonstrate summary and feeling responses and then have mothers practice using them. These are *not* easy skills to learn, and when mothers have difficulty reaching for the feelings underneath the message, they are encouraged to use global responses such as "feel bad" or "feel upset."

Putting It All Together: Listen, Think, Respond

Mothers break up into small groups and practice putting all the skills together by role playing scenarios of situations that elicit feeling responses. Some of the scenes deal with tough issues like feelings about the father. Mothers are encouraged to use their listening skills to help their children with their feelings about the divorce and the changes that have occurred.

When Listening Isn't Enough

Sometimes children bring up problems that listening won't fix. Group leaders do a role play to demonstrate the steps in guiding children through problem solving: (a) use good listening skills, (b) ask the child to come up with possible solutions, (c) give a list of options if the child can't identify solutions by himself, and (d) allow the child to select an option to try if all options are possible and equally good or help him evaluate positive and negative outcomes for each if they are not.

SESSION 6: SHIELDING KIDS FROM NEGATIVE DIVORCE EXPERIENCES

Purpose

The purpose of this session is to educate mothers about the importance of keeping children out of the war zone and to teach them anger management skills to prevent their children from witnessing interparental conflict.

The War Zone

We try to help mothers see the war zone through their children's eyes and teach them what they can do to protect their children. We first give mothers a list of war zone experiences, such as arguing with the ex-spouse while the child is in the room or bad-mouthing by either parent or asking about the new partners. We ask them to circle those that their child has experienced within the past couple of months. After mothers briefly share their experiences, we stress that of all the negative things that children experience during divorce, *being caught in the war zone is the most stressful.*

We show a video illustrating how children feel when they are caught in the middle: responsible, angry, anxious, and unsure about whether they should love their mother or their father. We provide them with a handout based on the research done by the developers of this program that shows the many ways that children get caught in the middle and how stressful these situations are for them. Mothers are sometimes surprised to learn that sometimes even a simple question such as "What did you do at Dad's house?" can be very stressful.

Parents' bad-mouthing each other is particularly stressful, and although mothers cannot control what their ex-spouse says about them, they can control their behavior by ignoring the bad-mouthing that their children may relate to them. Many mothers feel this is unfair and that they need to defend themselves by bad-mouthing back and telling their children the truth. We acknowledge that it is tough to ignore the bad-mouthing, but it is in the best interest of their children to do so. We help them generate some self-statements such as "I'm not going to put my child in the middle" or "Just because he's a jerk, I don't have to be one" to ignore their spouse's bad-mouthing and limit the damage. Sometimes it is helpful for mothers to hear that their children will learn the "truth" about their father on their own, when they are developmentally ready. We tell them that one of the biggest gifts that mothers can give their children during divorce is the message that it's okay to love both parents. Although they cannot prevent their ex-spouse from saying bad things about them, they can choose not to retaliate. When they retaliate, their child pays too big a price. We have each mother choose a self-statement that she can use to stop bad-mouthing her exhusband in front of the children. We encourage her to find "adult ears" to listen to her anger and frustration. We do not ask her to stop bad-mouthing her exhusband altogether—*only to stop bad-mouthing in front of the children.*

Parents aren't the only ones who say bad things. Grandparents and other relatives are often just as angry or even angrier at the mother's exhusband than she is. Leaders role play how to make assertive requests to relatives to keep them from bad-mouthing the children's father in front of them.

Anger Management

Research clearly shows that watching parents argue is extremely stressful and leads to aggression, depression, and anxiety. When parents argue in private, the effects aren't as harmful. We teach anger management skills to keep mothers from arguing with their exspouse in front of their children. The goal of anger management is not to swallow anger but to *control* it. Mothers are taught to use "I messages" to make assertive requests when they speak to their exspouse in private instead of striking out, which only escalates the situation. They learn to use self-talk to help them keep their anger under control. Group leaders role play using anger management self-statements to keep from arguing in front of the children. Mothers are asked to identify self-statements that will work for them to help them before, during, and after a confrontation with their exhusband. Then they get an opportunity to practice these, using their anger management skills as leaders role play the exspouse.

The second individual session is scheduled after this session to discuss the child's relationship with the father. Obstacles that mothers put up are discussed, and mothers are encouraged to remove those obstacles.

Session 7: Practicing Listening Skills

Purpose

The goal of this session is to help mothers use the skills they have learned to listen to their children's concerns. In the parent and child group, mothers practice the listening skills they have learned in previous sessions and then meet with their children to practice those skills. In the parent-only group, the whole session is devoted to practicing listening skills.

The "Big Kahuna"

Following a review of the program skills, parents identify their "Big Kahunas": those issues that their child may raise which feel as overwhelming as a huge tidal wave. We had been told that Big Kahuna is a name for huge tidal waves in Hawaii, but one of our group leaders who lived there said the phrase had a different meaning. However, the name has stuck, and mothers and leaders frequently use it to refer to the worst possible thing your child could tell you. Group leaders pick two of the Big Kahunas and role play how to listen effectively to issues that children may bring up that may be difficult for them to hear, such as, "I want to move in with Dad" or "I don't want you to go out with Jim."

Comprehensive Skills Practice

In the parent-child group, parents and children meet together and the child reads prepared positive and negative "I message" statements to the mother, such as, "I feel happy when you give me a hug and I'd like you to do it more often" or "I feel mad when you work so much. I'd feel better if you spend time with me." Mothers get a chance to practice their listening skills in responding to these messages, as leaders coach and give feedback.

Parents and children return to their respective groups following the joint session where they are frequently relieved to hear that their children's Big Kahunas are not as bad as they had imagined and where they are congratulated for doing a good job! In the parent-only group, mothers practice using listening skills to respond to difficult situations.

SESSION 8: MANAGING KIDS' BEHAVIOR I

Purpose

Session 8 is the first of three sessions devoted to managing children's behavior more effectively. It provides an introduction to discipline and teaches the first step of effective discipline: setting clear and realistic expectations for behavior. Sessions 9 and 10 teach the next two steps: developing a change plan and using the plan, evaluating it, and re-evaluating it as needed.

Discipline When Half the Team Is Gone

Discipline presents a big challenge for divorced mothers for several reasons. Unlike intact families, parents can't work together to discipline. In addition, the stress mothers and children experience may lead to negative cycles of interaction and cooperation falls apart. Mothers need children to take on more responsibilities around the house so there are more opportunities for discipline if things don't get done but mothers have less time and energy to supervise. In some families, because children often have more say in family decisions, it is more difficult for them to accept the mother as the disciplinarian. Thus, after divorce, mothers have less help in discipline and more complex discipline problems.

The first step in helping mothers make some positive changes in their discipline styles is a self-assessment. Mothers record their responses to five discipline scenarios to assess which one of three discipline styles most fits them. Leaders then use role plays to demonstrate the three styles of Attila the Mom, Pam Permissive, and Freida Fair and Firm who has realistic expectations and reasonable consequences, who clearly communicates those, and who is consistent in enforcing them.

Leaders also explore some of the myths about the children's misbehavior (that they are punishing her for the divorce, that they are rotten or bad kids or that they are sadistic and want to drive her crazy) and point out the realities: that children may not be getting enough of her attention in positive ways, they may be angry and expressing their feelings, they may be "testing the limits" or they may not be clear about what the rules are. That is why it is so important to set clear and realistic expectations.

Adopting Clear and Realistic Expectations

Clear expectations provide children with structure and help them know what parents want from them. They involve specific behaviors ("my child should not talk back when asked to do something") rather than broad qualities ("she should not be sassy"). In addition, expectations should be realistic and age-appropriate. Mothers get some practice in identifying clear and realistic expectations by taking turns reading different expectations and evaluating whether these are clear and realistic and why. Leaders help them change the unrealistic expectations into more realistic ones and the unclear expectations into clear ones.

Mothers then come up with a clear and realistic expectation for a behavior they want to change in their child, and leaders help each mother develop a plan for monitoring the behavior. Mothers are told that good managers don't just walk in and start making changes; rather they monitor and evaluate the problem first. If the behavior is one that occurs many times every hour, mothers pick one hour per day to pay attention to how many times the behavior occurs. If the behavior is only associated with a certain event, for example, arguing at the dinner table, mothers keep track of how many times it happens at each dinner for that week. If it occurs only a few times per day, they pick several days and record how many times the behavior happens on each of those days. Mothers frequently choose common behaviors such as fighting with siblings, not completing homework, or not going to bed when told to.

Session 9: Managing Kids' Behavior II

Purpose

Session 9 teaches the second step of effective discipline: developing a change plan for decreasing a misbehavior. It teaches mothers how to choose consequences for behaviors and how to communicate their expectations to children.

Developing a Change Plan

After reviewing and problem solving each mother's change plan, we show mothers two brief film segments to demonstrate the difference between effective and ineffective discipline and to introduce the second step of effective discipline: Developing a change plan that includes reasonable and enforceable consequences, communicating expectations and consequences clearly to children, and planning to use the consequences consistently.

Kinds of Consequences

We review the types of consequences to use when children meet mothers' expectations and when they do not, relating those to the problem behaviors mothers have counted. Mothers are told that positive attention is one of the easiest and most powerful tools for getting children to meet their parents' expectations. Positive attention can be in the form of compliments, thank you's, or providing special privileges like staying out late for a special event.

We provide a menu of six choices of consequences to use when children do not meet expectations. The consequences are presented in the order of least to most harsh. We encourage mothers to choose the consequence that is the least harsh but is still likely to decrease her child's misbehavior. The goal is to make discipline as easy as it can be for both mothers and children. We want mothers to use the least harsh, fairest, most enforceable, and *easiest* consequences possible. The consequences are presented in an interactive lecture format, using role play and examples from the group to demonstrate each type of consequences:

1. *Ignoring* behavior where the child is seeking attention or trying to manipulate by constant questions or complaints and *rewarding* appropriate behavior instead;
2. *Increased supervision* (e.g., calling home from work to check on child's whereabouts);
3. *"Don't bail them out"* (e.g., if Johnny is late for dinner, the family begins without him);
4. *"Abuse it, lose it"* (Lauren leaves her mitt on the field and it gets stolen; she has to replace it with money she saved from her allowance);
5. *Taking away meaningful privileges* (e.g., Nintendo time, staying up late); and
6. *Giving something unpleasant* (e.g., extra work, earlier bedtime).

In choosing a consequence for misbehaviors, mothers ask themselves if it is a fair consequence, if they can consistently follow through with it, if it will help their child learn about the consequences of his own behavior for himself, and if it is the least harsh consequence that will decrease the misbehavior.

Leaders role play communicating expectations and consequences to children and stress the importance of being consistent in implementing the consequences. Because many stressed parents discipline according to their emotional state, they punish more often and more severely when they are angry or anxious and let things slide by when they are happy. This inconsistency can spell disaster for children. Mothers are told to use their anger management skills and to use self-statements such as "I don't need to lose it" or "I can choose not to let her push my buttons" to help them not punish when they are angry. Leaders then help each mother select a consequence for the misbehavior she counted last week and to commit to a time when she will talk to her child about the change plan. They also schedule a telephone appointment with each mother in the middle of the week to see how the plan is going.

SESSION 10: MANAGING KIDS' BEHAVIOR III

Purpose

Session 10 introduces the third step of effective discipline: Evaluating the change plan and revising it if necessary. In this session, leaders help parents develop a change plan to increase a positive behavior and give them practice with developing plans for other behaviors they would like to change in the future.

Using the Change Plan, Evaluating It, and Revising It

Managing children's behavior is an ongoing process—it's not something mothers do once and forget about. If the misbehaviors that mothers are managing are not decreasing, they can ask themselves if their expectations are clear and their consequences enforceable and meaningful, if they have communicated those clearly to their child and if the child understood, and if they have been consistent in giving positive attention or negative consequences when he or she met or didn't meet the expectation. We tell mothers that some misbehaviors take more time than others to change and sometimes things get worse before they get better. We also tell them that as children get older, their expectations should be re-evaluated for appropriateness at regular intervals.

Increasing Positive Behaviors

We help parents develop a change plan for increasing positive behaviors. Positive behaviors are *not* the opposite of misbehaviors. Positive behaviors are the "extra credit" behaviors, the ones you could walk away from or ignore when they don't occur. These are the "it would be nice if they did" behaviors; but not doing these behaviors is not the same as misbehaving. Some examples of positive behaviors that mothers have reported include taking the initiative to do more than the minimal requirements (e.g., putting flowers in a vase when setting the table, spontaneously giving part of their allowance to charity or displaying some unusually cooperative and kind behaviors without being asked). Mothers are taught shaping as a way to increase positive behaviors. They then practice working on a change plan to increase positive behaviors and also get some practice in developing change plans for future misbehaviors.

SESSION 11: REVIEW, CLOSURE, AND GRADUATION

The last session is basically a review of everything that has been learned in the group. We discuss the changes that each mother has made as well as ways to maintain the changes. We tell mothers that setbacks and

problems are an inherent part of making change and to use future problems as a cue to review and renew the skills so that they can turn the setback around. They are given homework diaries for the next six months so
that they can continue to monitor their use of the program skills. We also
help them plan ahead and problem solve for future problems. Following a
brief closure exercise where mothers share the changes they and their
children have made, we have a brief graduation ceremony where leaders
hand out diplomas as they make personalized, positive comments about
each mother. The last group session culminates with eating cake to cele-
brate a job well done!

CASE STUDY

Olivia is a 35-year-old married woman whose husband left her for another woman. She has two children, Gary, 9 and Anna, 8, who have become increasingly quiet and distant since the divorce. She is concerned
that Gary in particular doesn't talk about his feelings and that he has become increasingly rude and defiant to her. Olivia tries to get Gary to talk
and also to mind her, but the more she tries, the more withdrawn and defiant he becomes. She reports that he treats her "pretty much the way my
ex-spouse does"—with little respect and much belittlement. Olivia is self-
effacing and believes that she doesn't deserve much respect. She feels that
she doesn't have any control over Gary. At times she becomes so frustrated with him that she resorts to spanking which only escalates the
negative cycle. Olivia's ex-husband calls her frequently and berates her in
front of the children. Since he is a mental health professional, she is convinced that he knows best and allows him to berate her.

   Although Olivia felt like a child herself, she recognized that she had to
act the parent. She tried the program activities with her children—Family
Fun Time, One-on-One Time, and Catch 'em Being Good. She was surprised that Gary looked forward to these activities and that she was starting to change the negative cycle of her relationship with him. She also
started using her listening skills when Gary expressed his anger, and
Gary was able to express his feelings about the divorce in more appropriate ways. Finally, Olivia learned some anger management skills and refused to participate in verbal fights with her ex-spouse in front of the
children. Although Olivia alternated between being Pam Permissive and
Attila the Mom in her discipline styles, she recognized that she had to
make some changes for the children's sakes. Even though there was some
testing of limits and "things got worse before they got better," she was
able to become more consistent in managing her children's behavior, and
her relationships with them improved. Olivia didn't make these changes
overnight, and she needed a great deal of support and instruction from

group leaders and other mothers to effect these changes in herself and her children. Olivia's story comes in different variations, with many mothers reporting significant changes in their children and in themselves at the end of the program.

GENERAL GUIDELINES FOR GROUP LEADERS

The general guidelines provided for conducting these sessions are based on our experience in leading and supervising groups. Many of these guidelines are commonsense and involve basic therapy and learning principles. However, all of the problems or mistakes have been encountered in some form or other by our group leaders.

1. *Be prepared!* No matter how experienced or skilled you are, you cannot "wing" these sessions. It is important to have the material down pat. Each group session requires several hours of preparation before conducting it. These include learning the material thoroughly on your own, rehearsing with your coleader, two hours of training before each session, and an hour and a half of supervision after each session.
2. *Practice the skills you are using.* We have found that one of the best ways to familiarize yourself with the program is to practice the skills with your own child if you are a parent or with a "borrowed" child. Many of the listening and anger management skills can also be practiced with adults, and the One-on-One can be practiced with a pet!
3. *Always have a dress rehearsal before you do the group.* Much of this is done in the pregroup training session. Be aware of everything that can possibly go wrong. Make certain that the supplies are all there and ready so that you are not spending the session rewinding tapes and looking for papers. The session should flow *smoothly.*

STAYING FOCUSED

1. *Remember that the program is primarily for the mental health of the children.* It is *not* a therapy group for divorced mothers, and tempted as you might get to be the mother's therapist, you are there *to help her* be a better mother so her children can benefit. Remember that the program is primarily:

   TO BENEFIT THE KIDS.
   TO BENEFIT THE KIDS.
   TO BENEFIT THE KIDS.

2. *Remind yourself that this is not group therapy.* This is a *psychoeducational* group with both *psychological* and *educational* components. The emphasis is *not* on catharsis for mothers, but on learning within a group environment, using group principles to facilitate this process. Although group principles are very important here (e.g., cohesiveness, providing hope, support, sharing), please keep in mind that this is primarily a *class* for mothers, and your job is to make sure they *learn* the skills and *practice* them at home.

3. *Make certain that the program is followed as written.* This is a research-based program, and it is *critical* that it conforms as much as possible to the format and content outlined in the manual. Whereas we do not expect group leaders to just memorize the lines, we expect you to present the material in such a way that all the *points* in the session outline are made. We want to make certain that you follow this script and not your own, even if you have had a great deal of experience in working with divorced mothers.

4. *Do not allow yourself to get sidetracked.* Unlike an unstructured therapy group, where you have the flexibility to "switch gears" and go with the flow of the group members if they want to discuss one topic instead of another, you do not have the same flexibility here. If group members would prefer to talk about other relevant divorce topics, either let them know that this will come up in another session or discuss it with them individually afterwards.

5. *Stick to the time schedule as much as possible.* Always come *at least* five minutes early to group. Start *exactly* on time and end on time. Don't let one member dominate the group with her issues. Also, be considerate of your coleader and allow her to stick to the schedule. Don't waste precious group time moving chairs, rewinding videos or giving handouts. Always think of the strategy for the best possible flow of sessions.

6. *Use teaching methods to get the most effective use of exercises.*
   (a) *Use group members' comments to illustrate key points.*
   (b) *Show first, then tell.* It is more effective to first demonstrate an activity, then discuss what you did. Let the group come up with the answers.
   (c) *Set up skills practice with plenty of structure.* Always model first the skills you are teaching. Whenever possible, have the "best" group member follow you for more modeling and learning.
   (d) *Reinforce for baby steps.* Some mothers may have a lot of difficulty with the skills and get threatened if they don't do well.

7. *Emphasize the importance of homework.* Homework provides mothers with valuable opportunities to practice the skills they have learned

with their children. Parents who practice at home see improvements in their relationships with their children and their children's adjustment. Those who *don't,* do not see changes in their children's adjustment. It is essential *not* to create a group culture which allows members to forego homework. Preventing such group norms can be accomplished by:

(a) Emphasizing the importance of doing the homework assignments.

(b) Assessing whether each mother did the assignment during homework review and problem solving if a mother didn't get it done.

(c) Reinforcing mothers over and over for all their efforts.

(d) Making the link between changes in their children's behaviors and completing the homework.

(e) Using other mothers' success experiences to emphasize the importance of practicing the skills at home.

(f) Using the group to directly or indirectly exert pressure (group principles of vicarious learning and group pressure can be powerful motivators)!

(g) Setting up group norms that convey the importance of homework, (e.g., including homework completion in the participation contract).

(h) Making written comments on homework sheets to reinforce and problem solve. (If leaders put much effort into giving written input to mothers, mothers are more likely to model the behavior. In addition, they will look forward to getting individualized written feedback each week, which is a powerful reinforcer.) We also put stickers and smiley faces on homework sheets. We started this practice after some mothers expressed a wish to get those just as their children did. Leaders can provide feedback and nurturance with those stickers.

(i) Using modeling, leader's attention and reinforcement, as well as changes in children's behavior as incentives for completing the homework.

8. *Emphasize attendance and commitment.* Set up group norms for attendance. Follow up when a group member doesn't show and make every possible effort to have her attend regularly. Make-up sessions before each meeting are available for missed sessions. However, if a mother misses more than three sessions, she will be unable to keep up with the program and will need to drop out.

9. *Stress program prestige and leader credibility.*

10. *Remind yourself over and over that all your hard work is:*

> TO BENEFIT THE KIDS.
> TO BENEFIT THE KIDS.
> TO BENEFIT THE KIDS.

PROCESS ISSUES

Whereas some of the following suggestions may seem elementary and basic for many group leaders, we want to spell them out anyway based on previous experience.

1. *Create an atmosphere that encourages participation.* Leaders can do much of this in their interviews with mothers before the initial group session to establish rapport and trust and to prepare them for the group. Environmental factors can do a great deal to create a comfortable atmosphere (e.g., comfortable seating, refreshments). Similarly, some environments can inhibit participation (e.g., outside observers or stark, businesslike rooms). Try to make the physical setting as pleasant as possible within the existing limitations.

2. *Use basic clinical skills to establish group cohesion.* The following suggestions can be used to increase member interaction:

   (a) Promote interaction among group members rather than make the group a one-way communication between leaders and individual members. Tempting as it may be to give a long monologue when asked a question, involving the group can increase cohesion. Comments such as "Can anyone else relate to that?," "Let's have a show of hands," or "How many of you have experienced that?," can quickly change an authoritarian group structure to a more democratic one and prevent one member from monopolizing the session.

   (b) Pointing out similarities between group members ("This sounds like what happened to Debbie") and stating the obvious ("We're all moms") can promote cohesion and bridge educational and class differences.

   (c) Normalize divorce-related experiences as common occurrences so that mothers do not feel that they are abnormal.

   (d) Comment on the group process to increase interaction ("It looks like we're having a difficult time coming up with solutions").

   (e) Use small group activities and cooperative learning structures to increase cohesion.

(f) Recognize and validate in a warm and supportive way the difficult feelings mothers are having and the difficulty they may have in sharing these feelings.

It is important to note that whereas these suggestions can increase group participation, they may not always be appropriate, especially when time is a factor. You have to balance how much attention you pay to group process and how much to content, and there is a lot of content to cover in these meetings!

It is normal for groups to bond at different rates, and certain factors such as group composition may make it easier for some groups to develop group cohesiveness earlier than others. Some groups just bond more slowly than others, and it is not unusual, particularly in beginning sessions, for participants to be quiet until they feel comfortable to share. If there are still lots of uncomfortable silences after several group sessions, try to figure out what the "pink elephant" is in the room that is inhibiting interaction.

3. *Empowering mothers.* After divorce, many mothers are depressed, and like Olivia, feel badly about themselves as mothers. Your comments in group can make a real difference in how they feel about their parenting abilities and themselves. Leaders can do this by repeatedly making the link between changes in mothers' behaviors and the changes they are seeing in their children and by reinforcing them for practicing the program skills. It is also important to be vigilant for small changes in their children. Point these out to mothers as signs that they are making the program work!

4. *Use modeling to establish group norms and to maximize learning.* Leaders can model appropriate group norms (e.g., being on time, following through, being prepared). In addition, they can model the appropriate skills (e.g., listening). They can reflect back, summarize, make good eye contact, and so on to model good listening skills.

5. *Be aware of any unresolved issues with your exspouse or children that may make it difficult for you to model some of the skills.* Discuss those with your supervisor to make certain they do not interfere with your demonstrating the skills. Group members can pick up through subtle innuendos and verbal and nonverbal cues some of those attitudes that may negate many of our key points (e.g., the destructiveness of bad-mouthing).

6. *Self-disclosure.* Disclose only if it benefits the mothers and not for your benefit. A rule of thumb is to disclose only resolved issues and not unresolved ones. For example, it may be helpful to state that you had a similar problem with your child or ex-spouse *many* years ago and this is how you resolved it, but not that you still have

the problem and are at a loss as to what to do. (Mothers may either lose hope or feel that you are incompetent if you are unable to do what you are teaching them!)

7. *Make certain to inform your supervisor of any potential clinical problems or crises as they arise.* Although we screen mothers before the group, some problems or issues may come up from time to time.

If all of this seems like a great deal of work on your part, you are right: it is! But it is well worth it. We want this program to WORK! In the long run, this is being done:

TO BENEFIT THE KIDS.
TO BENEFIT THE KIDS.
TO BENEFIT THE KIDS.

CONCLUSION

Statistical analyses of the data demonstrate that an empirically-based intervention program for divorced mothers can make a significant difference in helping children adjust to divorce. Several features of this program deserve attention. Working with parents alone can help mitigate and cushion many of the potentially harmful effects of divorce. Teaching parents skills as a preventive tool can help make them more effective parents. We do not provide them with the fish but teach them how to fish. Although they cannot prevent, control, or "fix" the events that happen in their children's lives, they can learn lifelong skills to build a protective armor and secure base for children to withstand those stressors. Whereas much of the success of the program is because its content is based on sound theoretical and empirical principles, process issues are also very important in helping mothers make changes. Like Olivia, many mothers feel out of control and need nurturance themselves. Providing mothers with warmth and acceptance at the same time that we are empowering them and teaching them skills helps them be more effective mothers to their children and helps prevent future problems.

REFERENCES

Amato, P. R., & Keith, B. (1991). Parental divorce and the well-being of children: A meta-analysis. *Psychological Bulletin, 110,* 26–46.

Baldwin, D. V., & Skinner, M. L. (1989). Structural model for anti-social behavior: Generalization to single-mother families. *Developmental Psychology, 25,* 45–50.

Felner, R. D., Farber, S. S., & Primavera, J. (1983). Transitions and stressful life events: A model for primary prevention. In R. D. Felner, L. A. Jason,

J. N. Moritsugu, & S. S. Farber (Eds.), *Preventive psychology: Theory, research, and practice.* New York: Pergamon Press.

Felner, R. D., Stolberg, A., & Cowen, E. L. (1975). Crisis events and school mental health referral patterns of young children. *Journal of Consulting and Clinical Psychology, 43,* 305–310.

Felner, R. D., Terre, L., & Rowlinson, R. T. (1988). A life transition framework for understanding marital dissolution and family reorganization. In S. A. Wolchik & P. Karoly (Eds.), *Children of divorce: Empirical perspectives on adjustment* (pp. 35–65). New York: Gardner Press.

Fogas, B. S., Wolchik, S. A., & Braver, S. L. (1987, August). *Parenting behavior and psychopathology in children of divorce: Buffering effects.* Paper presented at the American Psychological Association Convention, New York.

Forehand, R., & McMahon, R. J. (1981). *Helping the noncompliant child: A clinician's guide to parent teaching.* New York: Guilford Press.

Graziano, A. M., & Diament, D. M. (1992). Parent behavioral training. An examination of the paradigm. *Behavior Modification, 16,* 3–38.

Guidubaldi, J., Cleminshaw, H. K., Perry, J. D., & McLoughlin, C. S. (1983). The impact of parental divorce on children: Report of the nationwide NASP study. *School Psychology Review, 12,* 300–323.

Guidubaldi, J., Cleminshaw, H. K., Perry, J. D., Nastasi, B. K., & Lightel, J. (1986). The role of selected family environment factors in children's post-divorce adjustment. *Family Relations, 35,* 141–151.

Hetherington, E. M. (1979). Divorce: A child's perspective. *American Psychologist, 34,* 851–858.

Hetherington, E. M., Cox, M., & Cox, R. (1978). The aftermath of divorce. In J. H. Stevens, Jr. & M. Matthews (Eds.), *Mother-child, father-child relations* (pp. 149–176). Washington, DC: National Association for the Education of Young Children.

Hetherington, E. M., Cox, M., & Cox, R. (1981). Effects of divorce on parents and children. In M. Lamb (Ed.), *Nontraditional families* (pp. 233–288). Hillsdale, NJ: Erlbaum.

Kurdek, L. A. (1981). An integrative perspective on children's divorce adjustment. *American Psychologist, 36,* 856–866.

Long, N., Forehand, R., Fauber, R., & Brody, G. (1987). Self-perceived and independently observed competence of young adolescents as a function of parental marital conflict and recent divorce. *Journal of Abnormal Child Psychology, 15,* 15–27.

Novaco, R. A. (1975). *Anger control: The development and evaluation of an experimental treatment.* Lexington, MA: Heath.

Parish, T., & Wigle, S. (1985). A longitudinal study of the impact of divorce on adolescents' evaluation of self and parents. *Adolescence, 20,* 239–244.

Patterson, G. R. (1975). *Families: Application of social learning to family life.* Champaign, IL: Research Press.

Patterson, G. R. (1992). Developmental changes in antisocial behavior. In R. D. Peters, R. J. McMahon, & V. L. Quinsey (Eds.), *Aggression and violence throughout the life span* (pp. 52–82). Newbury Park, CA: Sage.

Sandler, I. N., Wolchik, S. A., & Braver, S. L. (1988). The stressors of children's post-divorce environments. In S. A. Wolchik & P. Karoly (Eds.), *Children of divorce: Empirical perspectives on adjustment* (pp. 111–143). New York: Gardner Press.

Santrock, J. W., & Warshak, R. (1979). Father custody and social development in boys and girls. *Journal of Social Issues, 35,* 112–125.

Stolberg, A. L., & Anker, J. M. (1984). Cognitive and behavioral changes in children resulting from parental divorce and consequent environmental changes. *Journal of Divorce, 7,* 23–41.

Stolberg, A. L., & Bush, J. P. (1985). A path analysis of factors predicting children's divorce adjustment. *Journal of Clinical Child Psychology, 14,* 49–54.

Wallerstein, J. S., & Kelly, J. B. (1980). *Surviving the breakup: How children and parents cope with divorce.* New York: Basic Books.

Warren, N. J., Grew, R. S., Ilgen, E. L., Konans, J. T., Bourgoondien, M. E., & Amara, I. A. (1984). *Parenting after divorce: Preventive programs for divorcing families.* Paper presented at the meeting of the National Institute of Mental Health, Washington, DC.

Wolchik, S. A., West, S. G., Westover, S., Sandler, I. N., Martin, A., Lustig, J., Tien, J., & Fisher, J. (1993). The children of divorce parenting intervention: Outcome evaluation of an empirically based program. *American Journal of Community Psychology, 21*(3), 293–331.

Wolchik, S. A., Westover, S., Sandler, I. N., & Martin, A. (1992). *New Beginnings parenting programs reader manual.* Unpublished manual.

Wright, L., Stroud, R., & Keenan, M. (1993). Indirect treatment of children via parent training: A burgeoning form of secondary prevention. *Applied and Preventive Psychology, 2,* 191–200.

Wyman, P. A., Cowen, E. L., Hightower, A. D., & Pedro-Carroll, J. L. (1985). Perceived competence, self-esteem, and anxiety in latency-aged children of divorce. *Journal of Clinical Child Psychology, 14,* 20–26.

Zill, N. (1983). *Happy, healthy, and insecure: A portrait of middle childhood in America.* Garden City, NY: Doubleday.

CHAPTER 15

Temperament-Focused Parent Training

LISA B. SHEEBER and SEAN C. MCDEVITT

TEMPERAMENT-FOCUSED parent guidance is an approach that relies on using an understanding of children's temperament to improve parent-child interactions, reduce parental distress, and promote healthy child development. Unlike many of the approaches covered in this Handbook, temperament-focused guidance is not necessarily, or even typically, conceptualized as an intervention for the treatment of child psychopathology. Instead, the goal is to reduce the stress in the parent-child system that may develop as a function of a mismatch between child characteristics and parent behavior. This approach has applications in families of behaviorally or emotionally disordered children as well as in families with children who are psychologically healthy. This approach also differs from some of the others in this book in having parental comfort and adjustment to parenting as an explicit objective of the intervention. Temperament-focused guidance helps parents to develop an understanding of children's temperament characteristics to facilitate smoother parent-child interactions in the service of healthier child development and more relaxed and enjoyable parenting.

As temperament-focused parent guidance takes a variety of forms that share the use of temperament information to facilitate parenting, our goal in this chapter is to outline the basic concepts and methods that characterize this broad-based approach. We begin with a definition of child temperament and a brief discussion of the literature regarding the relationship between child temperament and parental adjustment, parent-child interactions, and child psychopathology. We then provide an overview of temperament-focused parent guidance that includes its historical and conceptual underpinnings as well as a discussion of the types of educational and clinical interventions that comprise this approach. Several temperament-focused interventions illustrating the range of ways in which temperament information can be used in parent guidance are highlighted. Where available, a summary of research findings relevant to evaluating the effectiveness of the interventions is provided. We then address the cautions and concerns that have been raised about the use of temperament data in parent guidance. One program, conducted by the first author (Sheeber & Johnson, 1994), is then presented in more detail. We conclude with a discussion of accomplishments to date, current limitations, and future directions.

TEMPERAMENT

DEFINITIONS AND HISTORICAL BACKGROUND

Stella Chess is often quoted as saying, "All parents are environmentalists until they have their second child." With the second child comes the knowledge that the contribution of particular parenting practices, though of unquestionable importance, is nonetheless finite, and the recognition that from very early on, children demonstrate temperamental differences that influence both the way that they respond to their environment and the way parents and other caretakers respond to them. This same awareness, on the part of Stella Chess and Alexander Thomas, was the impetus for the New York Longitudinal Study (NYLS; Thomas, Chess, Birch, Hertzig, & Korn, 1963) which in turn, sparked much of the current interest in child temperament.

When the NYLS began in the 1950s, child psychiatry was dominated by a strong environmentalist perspective. For all their obvious differences, the psychoanalytic and behavioral traditions had in common the belief that infants were born tabula rasa. Consequently, differences in personality and adjustment were thought to arise solely as a function of environmental influences—with mothers' parenting behaviors being the key determinant of their children's development. In reaction to this zeitgeist, and in response to their own clinical and personal observations, Thomas and Chess initiated the NYLS to investigate the role of children's inborn, early appearing individual differences on their later development.

Thomas and Chess defined temperament as behavioral style, and indicated that it referred to the *how* rather than the *what* (content) or *why* (motivation) of behavior. Using parent descriptions of childrens' behavior, they identified nine dimensions of behavioral style that differentiated between children, and were thought to be relevant to their developmental outcomes. These dimensions were activity, rhythmicity in biological functioning, approach versus withdrawal to novel stimuli, adaptability to change, persistence, distractibility, quality of mood, intensity of mood, and threshold of responsiveness to sensory stimulation. Central to their conceptualization, moreover, was the idea that positive development occurred when there was a good fit between the child's characteristics and those of the environment; such a goodness of fit was said to result "when the properties of the environment and its expectations and demands are in accord with the organisms' own capacities, motivations, and style of behavior" (Chess & Thomas, 1992). Several key developmental and clinical implications followed from this goodness-of-fit model. First, effective parenting required sensitivity to child characteristics. Second, both parental adjustment to parenting and the quality of parent-child interactions were influenced by child characteristics. Finally, behavior problems developed as a function of a poor fit between child characteristics and the demands and resources of the environment.

Though most clinical work to date has derived from the Thomas and Chess model, it should be noted that there are currently a number of distinct approaches to defining and understanding temperamental differences in infancy and childhood (Goldsmith et al., 1987). These other approaches to conceptualizing temperament have primarily been used by researchers interested in basic developmental processes rather than in applications. Nonetheless, as summarized by Goldsmith et al. (1987), there is fairly widespread agreement across models that temperament characteristics reflect relatively stable individual differences in behavioral tendencies that emerge early in life and are at least partially biological in origin. Moreover, there is broad, if not universal recognition, that temperament characteristics or at least their behavioral expression, may be modified by environmental factors (Bates, 1994; McDevitt, 1994; Rothbart & Ahadi, 1994).

Among clinicians, the primary interest in these child temperament characteristics derives from their association with important outcome variables including parent-child interactions, parental adjustment, and child psychopathology. Temperamental characteristics are neither positive or negative in themselves but derive their functional significance from the contexts in which they are expressed. At times, they may function as risk factors predisposing to problems or dysfunction; in other contexts, they may function as protective factors or be unrelated to the appearance of problems or disorders (Carey & McDevitt, 1995). In the following section, we briefly explore the relationship between temperament characteristics and clinical outcomes in childhood.

RELATION TO PARENTING AND CHILD BEHAVIOR PROBLEMS

As initially posited by Thomas and Chess (1977), there is evidence that parents who perceive their children to have more difficult temperament characteristics, particularly negative mood and high intensity of emotional expression, have less satisfying parenting experiences. They report more negative affect, less self-confidence in parenting, and greater disruption in family functioning than do parents of temperamentally easier children (e.g., Hagekull & Bohlin, 1989; Sheeber & Johnson, 1992). Child temperament characteristics may also relate to the quality of parent-child interactions (e.g., Allen & Prior, 1995; Gauvain & Fagot, 1995). For example, a number of studies have indicated that infant irritability is associated with less positive mother-child interactions (e.g., Schuler, Black, & Starr, 1995; van den Boom, 1989). However, it is important to note that reviews of the available research have concluded that the nature and strength of the associations between child temperament characteristics and parenting have not been clearly established (Bates, 1989; Crockenberg, 1986; Sanson & Rothbart, 1995). It has been hypothesized that the failure to adequately consider interactions with nontemperamental characteristics of the child, as well as with characteristics of the caregiver and the broader environment may account for the inconsistent findings (Crockenberg, 1986; Sanson & Rothbart, 1995). This hypothesis is consistent with the goodness-of-fit model in suggesting that the developmental significance of child temperament characteristics depends on the context within which the child interacts.

Finally, there is clear evidence of an association between children's temperament characteristics and their risk for psychopathology. Notably these associations exist both concurrently (e.g., Maziade, Caron, Cote, Boutin, & Thivierge, 1989; Goodyer, Ashby, Altham, Vize, & Cooper, 1993) and predictively over time (e.g., Caspi, Henry, McGee, Moffitt, & Silva, 1995; Rende, 1993). Moreover, there appears to be a specificity of effects over time, such that particular temperament traits are predictive of behavioral and emotional difficulties in theoretically coherent ways (e.g., Bates, 1990; Caspi et al., 1995). For example, in the Caspi study (Caspi et al., 1995), early lack of control was associated with the development of externalizing behaviors in later childhood, whereas approach responses were inversely associated with later anxiety. As noted by Rutter (1987), one interpretation of this type of empirical relationship is that extreme temperament characteristics are, in fact, early symptoms of childhood disorder. Alternatively, as initially suggested by Thomas and Chess (1977), behavioral and emotional problems, may develop in part as a result of a poor fit between the child's temperament characteristics and the demands of the environment. That is, the stress caused by disconsonant interactions may result in the development of behavioral disorder. Though the concept of goodness of fit has proven easier to describe than to operationalize (see Bates, 1989), it appears that examining child temperament in the context of environmental characteristics may be important in understanding the development of behavioral disorders (Maziade et al., 1989; Tschann, Kaiser, Chesney, Alkon, & Boyce, 1996). For example, in the Tschann et al. study, the association between difficult temperament characteristics (defined as a factor including distractibility, persistence, activity, mood, and intensity) and both internalizing and externalizing behaviors was strongest for children living in high-conflict families.

In summary, the past several decades have resulted in a body of evidence supporting many of Thomas and Chess's initial hypotheses regarding the relations between child temperament, parental adjustment, parent-child interactions, and the development of child behavior problems. Because of the brevity of this review, we have necessarily taken a broad brush approach that glosses over both conceptual debates and methodological limitations; the reader is therefore referred to Bates (1989) and Sanson and Rothbart (1995) for more comprehensive reviews of the research literature. Nonetheless, as summarized by Rutter (1987, 1989) it is clear that child temperament characteristics have important implications for child development. The associations between child temperament and developmental outcomes have led to an increased interest in the use of temperament information in providing parent guidance. In particular, evidence that child temperament interacts with parenting behavior to predict child behavior problems (Sanson & Rothbart, 1995) is particularly salient because if problems develop as a function of a poor fit between child characteristics and parental behaviors, then assisting parents in adapting their approaches to their children's styles may result in healthier outcomes for the children as well as more satisfying parenting experiences.

TEMPERAMENT-FOCUSED PARENT TRAINING

THOMAS AND CHESS INITIATIVE

As originally formulated, temperament-focused parent training had two components (Thomas & Chess, 1977). During the initial education component, the focus was on acquainting parents with the notion of temperament and providing insight into the child's temperament characteristics. The expectation was that a better understanding of the child's characteristics, and an appreciation of temperament as reflecting inborn characteristics would reduce parents' negative feelings and allow them to respond to their child with less anger and apprehension. During the intervention component, the implications of temperament for managing child behavior were explored. Consistent with the goodness-of-fit frame-work, training focused on developing behavior management strategies that were congruent with the child's temperament characteristics. In their writings, Thomas and Chess have provided numerous examples of parent guidance for temperament-environment fit conflicts.

In an early report, Thomas, Chess, and Birch (1968) described their use of temperament-based guidance in 42 cases in which a mismatch between child temperament and parenting styles was thought to be responsible for the development or maintenance of behavior problems of sufficient severity to warrant psychiatric attention. As the use of temperament-based parent guidance originated in the NYLS as a clinical process of dealing with parents' concerns about their children's behavior, all but one case was initiated based on parents' questions or concerns. The approach involved meeting individually with parents to clarify the mismatch between child characteristics and parenting style, to provide behavior management strategies tailored to the child's style, and to give parents the opportunity to discuss their feelings about parenting. Chess and Thomas (1986) reported an overall success rate of 50% for this sample and indicated that the degree of improvement was related both to the amount of behavioral change exhibited by the parents and to the children's specific temperament profile.

As a function of the clinical and anecdotal nature of this report, it is difficult to evaluate the effectiveness of the Thomas and Chess intervention. In particular, the absence of a control group, the reliance on clinical judgment as an outcome measure, and the lack of statistical analyses for both between group and pre- to postintervention comparisons are problematic. Therefore, the overarching contribution of Thomas and Chess's work has been less in demonstrating the effectiveness of their model, than in developing and describing a framework for integrating an understanding of and respect for children's individual differences into clinical work with parents. Their narrative reports and numerous examples of parent guidance for specific temperament-management mismatches have been instrumental in the ongoing application of temperament information in parent education and counseling. In fact, though research in developmental and personality psychology has led to the development of a number of approaches to defining and measuring temperament, nearly all current approaches to temperament-based parent guidance have relied on the Thomas and Chess model of temperament and their goodness-of-fit concept.

SHARED CHARACTERISTICS OF TEMPERAMENT-FOCUSED INTERVENTIONS

Most temperament-focused interventions are based on a set of fundamental assumptions initially articulated by Thomas and Chess and as described earlier, largely supported by research over the past three decades. Central among these is the idea that from an early age, children demonstrate individual differences in behavior along dimensions that can be construed as temperament. Moreover, it is held that these variations in behavioral style have implications for understanding, and perhaps predicting, children's behavioral difficulties and reactions to environmental demands, as well as parents' responses to their children and adjustment to the demands of parenting. Finally, the use of temperament information in parent guidance is predicated on the idea that children's temperamental individuality makes universal prescriptions for good parenting impossible and necessitates the tailoring of parenting behaviors to children's behavioral styles.

Temperament-based interventions also share the common objective of helping parents to understand and respect individual behavioral differences in children. This is intended to reduce parents' negative feelings about themselves and their children. Many intervention approaches are geared as well toward helping parents develop new parenting strategies. Though as discussed later, guidance regarding parenting strategies is not common to all temperament-focused approaches, programs that incorporate this component are typically structured around the goodness-of-fit framework. As described by Lerner, Baker, and Lerner (1985) poorness of fit can be addressed by interventions directed either at the individual or contextual level. In working with young children, the context, in the form of parental expectations, behavior, and attributions is the most viable target of intervention. Hence, temperament-focused interventions are aimed at modifying parenting behavior, *not* child temperament. A notable example of an intervention geared toward improving the goodness of fit between child characteristics and the parenting context is that designed by van den Boom (1994) for mothers of temperamentally irritable infants. Earlier research indicated that infant irritability was associated with patterns of mother-child interactions that resulted in the development of attachment difficulties (van den Boom, 1989). In particular, the high levels of infant irritability appeared to reduce maternal sensitive responsiveness and mothers' use of less effective soothing strategies contributed to the infants' continued irritability. Hence, the infants' temperamental irritability contributed to a poor fit between their needs for effective maternal soothing and mothers' decreasing responsiveness. The intervention consisted of individual coaching sessions in which mothers were helped to understand their childrens' signals and implement effective responses. This resulted in better quality interactions, greater infant exploration, and better attachment status in dyads participating in the intervention relative to comparison dyads. Thus without attempting to alter the infants' temperamental style, the environment, in the form of maternal parenting behavior was modified to improve the fit between the infants' needs and maternal behavior.

Although the primary focus is on altering parent behavior, it is also possible to use other intervention strategies, including developmentally appropriate teaching strategies to help children to recognize their own behavioral patterns and develop techniques for adapting to situational demands (Chess & Thomas, 1986; Turecki & Tonner, 1985). Thus, if parents empathize with the difficulty that a shy child has in venturing into kindergarten or a distractible child has in staying focused to complete chores, and they can frame suggestions or demands to take these difficulties into account (e.g., I know you're feeling shy, why don't you sit beside your sister until you feel more at home). The child then develops both an understanding of the situations he or she finds challenging and an awareness of ways to master the challenge. Additionally, increasing self-awareness and helping children develop strategies for managing difficult situations will likely be particularly important as children enter adolescence and take on increasing responsibility for their own behavior (Carey & McDevitt, 1995; Chess & Thomas, 1986). Therefore, though the interventions are primarily targeted at parents, the potential benefit of temperament-focused interventions in increasing children's self-awareness and competence in meeting developmental challenges should not be overlooked.

INTERVENTION STRATEGIES IN TEMPERAMENT-BASED GUIDANCE

Carey and McDevitt (1995) have identified four types of intervention for temperament-based problems:

1. Parent education about the existence of temperamental differences.
2. Individual behavioral assessment with feedback to the parent about the child's temperament profile.
3. Environmental intervention aimed at changing the interaction between the child's temperament and its context (e.g., the demands of the situation).
4. Parent support groups aimed at sharing experiences of and techniques for dealing with temperament-related concerns.

However, the existing approaches to providing temperament-based guidance nearly always combine two or more of these interventions. In the sections that follow, we describe each type of intervention in more detail and highlight several temperament-focused intervention programs to illustrate the range of ways in which temperament information is being used in work with parents. The extent to which empirical evaluation data is available for each of the interventions will also be described. Evaluation is in its beginning stages, however, and thus the effectiveness of the intervention strategies is not well established for any of the four types.

Parent Education

Parent education about temperament can take many forms. In the simplest clinical intervention, it involves a brief discussion with the parent about the existence of temperamental differences and the importance of individuality in behavior and development. Many parents believe (or worry) that differences between their two children's behavior or the differences between their child and a neighbor or friend's child must be due to differences in child rearing. When their child's behavior is less acceptable to them, as irritability in a newborn or impersistence in a school child may be, they may blame themselves for being poor parents or attribute difficulties to child psychopathology or character flaws (e.g., willfullness, laziness, and the like). The simple act of education may be helpful in relieving stress and guilt. It may also assist parents in relaxing and being more at ease with the child by sensitizing them to the uniqueness of their offspring's personality. Proponents of this approach have suggested that pediatric professionals' relationship with new (and not so new) parents may place them in unique position to provide this type of guidance (e.g., Carey & McDevitt, 1995; Medoff-Cooper, 1994). General information of this sort has also been provided to parents in written form (Cameron, Rice, Hansen, & Rosen, 1994; Koroloff, 1990).

General education about temperament and its impact on development and parenting is also available to parents in books and on-line sources (e.g., HTTP://B-DI.COM). There are several well-known books including *Raising Your Spirited Child* (Kurcinka, 1991), *Know Your Child* (Chess & Thomas, 1987), *The Difficult Child* (Turecki & Tonner, 1985, 1989), and *Your Child's Temperament. What It Is. What It Does. How to Work with It* (Carey & Jablow, 1997). Though most parents of psychologically healthy children will come across these books by browsing or word of mouth, bibliotherapy may also be a beneficial component of family therapy. For a bright, literate parent, clinical experience shows that reading such books can rapidly accelerate therapy or enrich understanding of basic concepts and issues related to temperament-environment mismatch.

There are more complex approaches to parent education as well. One of the more established is the Kaiser Temperament Program (Cameron et al., 1994) run by Preventive Ounce, a nonprofit preventive mental health organization in Northern California. Cameron and Rice use a prevention-focused educational model in which infant temperament is assessed by questionnaire, and anticipatory guidance is provided based on predictions of the parenting challenges likely to be posed by infants with given temperament styles. This HMO program involves parent education of an entire population of parents who are HMO subscribers. The intent is to identify and deal with behavioral issues starting in infancy with an educative "wellness" approach to temperament.

The intervention begins with a mass mailing of temperament questionnaires to HMO subscribers when their infants are 4 months old. Parents who return the questionnaires are provided with a definition of child temperament, a description of their child's temperament profile, information regarding the behavioral challenges that may occur in the next year, and suggestions for how to deal with potential problems should they arise. This information is provided in writing or in brief meetings with a temperament counselor depending on the parents' preference as well as the child's temperament profile.

A notable aspect of the Kaiser program is the ongoing evaluation research that has been a component of the program since its inception (Cameron & Rice, 1986). Data collected by the project indicates moderate to high levels of satisfaction with the information among the 50% to 70% of participants who return the outcome questionnaires (Cameron, Hansen, & Rosen, 1991; Cameron & Rice, 1986). Similar results were obtained by Ostergren (1997) in an independent replication; in this study, the information was considered most useful by less educated parents and parents who perceived their infants to be difficult. It is unclear, however, whether the guidance is effective in reducing the occurrence of behavioral challenges or helping parents to understand or manage their infants' behavior (Cameron et al., 1991; Cameron, Rice, Rosen, & Chesterman, 1996); in fact, it appears that written guidance alone may sensitize parents to problems without equipping them to improve management.

A recent evaluation provided preliminary evidence that the written guidance may decrease the number of pediatric visits for highly active and irritable infants (Cameron et al., 1996). Based on anecdotal data, the investigators have attributed this decrease to parents' greater understanding that their children's behavioral style was normal and not attributable to poor parenting practices. However, there was no evidence that infants of parents receiving the guidance demonstrated fewer problems or that these parents felt more capable of handling the difficulties that arose. Thus the conclusion remains speculative.

Individual Behavioral Assessment

The clinical approach to temperament assessment for use in pediatric and other settings has been explicated by Carey (1992; Carey & McDevitt, 1995). The professional conducts an assessment, consonant with the skills and training of his or her profession, to determine whether the concerns raised about the child's behavior are related to temperament, and if so, to determine the contributing behavioral styles. Unlike the educational approach discussed previously, this intervention is initiated when a concern has been raised about the child's adjustment.

The temperament component of this approach involves use of interview or questionnaire data to generate a temperament profile that can be used to educate the parents about the child's characteristics. Through discussion, the parents may be helped to draw connections between those characteristics and their experiences interacting with their child. This process allows the parents to develop a deeper understanding of the child's temperamental individuality and its impact on the parent-child relationship. Clinical experience suggests that when used appropriately, this technique can inform the parents, improve the accuracy of their view of the child, and relieve guilt while avoiding labeling or blaming of the child. Even without specific advice on management, this process of identifying the child's characteristics may provide parents with enough insight for them to make shifts in their parenting behavior to promote smoother interactions and reduce child difficulties (Carey, 1989). Additionally, identification of the child's temperament profile may lead to recommendations for parenting strategies as described in the next section.

This approach to intervention is appropriate when a temperament-environment mismatch is hypothesized to be contributing to child behavior problems or parent-child conflict whether or not the child evidences a diagnoseable behavioral disorder. Many children (most of them quite normal) have significant temperament-environment conflicts that cause stress in relationships. These may be addressed by professionals because of their functional significance even though behavioral disorder many not be present. Additionally, many children who do have behavioral or psychiatric disorders also have temperament-environment mismatches that can be addressed to achieve a better overall goodness of fit.

The second author (McDevitt, Hegvik, & Esterman, 1996) has developed software for use in conjunction with the Carey Scale Questionnaires. This software standardizes the written feedback to parents regarding their children's temperament. Two computer programs are available, the Carey Temperament Scales Report Writer and the Carey Temperament Scales Profile Writer. The Profile Writer generates a bar graph with standardized scores showing the temperament profile and gives a description of the nine scales and their definitions. The Report Writer is more extensive and generates two written reports (one for the professional and, if appropriate, one for the parent) that interpret scores on each of the nine dimensions (as high, midrange, or low) printing them in order of deviation from the mean. The interpretations assist the parent and professional in understanding the infant or child's behavioral style and give suggestions for the management of behavioral difficulties. The Report Writer also performs three validity checks on parent reports: social desirability, missing data, and ratings-perceptions discrepancy. The latter refers to a discrepancy between the ratings on the temperament scales and parents' global impressions of the child's temperament. Appropriate advisories are printed (for the professional only) to consider the type of invalidity and their impact on the overall assessment. Thus, if the rating-perception discrepancy indicates that a parent is experiencing the child as being more difficult than the ratings demonstrate, it may suggest that the parent's perceptions are being influenced by other sources of stress and thus point to an avenue that the clinician needs to explore more fully. The availability of this software should make temperament-focused interventions more accessible and assist professionals in providing structured and focused evaluations.

Environmental Intervention

The third approach to temperament-focused parent guidance involves helping parents to modify the demands of the settings in which the child interacts as a means of reducing the poorness of fit. When this work is done in individual counseling, the professional works with the parents to identify situations in which the demands being placed on the child are discordant with the child's temperament style and helps them to make changes to better accommodate the child's temperamental qualities. For example, a highly active child may have difficulty in the evenings because she hasn't had adequate opportunity during the day to spend her abundant energies. She becomes restless and complains, perhaps having an occassional tantrum or being reprimanded for running in the house or jumping on her bed. As part of the temperament assessment, the relationship between this girl's temperamental quality of high activity and the behavioral problems she is demonstrating in the evening can be clarified for her parents. Then through discussion, a series of changes can be planned that will reduce the significant mismatch in the environment and result in less disruptive child behavior. By scheduling active play, the situation may be modified to reduce her restlessness and improve the tenor of evenings in the household. Similarly, Weissbluth (1989a, 1989b) describes a series of interventions designed to remedy infant sleep disturbances resulting from an interaction between temperamental qualities such as low rhythmicity and low sensory threshold and parental responses that by ignoring the temperamental cause of the problem serve to exacerbate it. Such environmental interventions can be used on an "as needed" basis in the course of clinical work by medical or mental health practitioners who are sensitive to the impact of temperamental differences and goodness-of-fit issues on the development of behavioral and emotional difficulties in children (e.g., Bates, 1989; Carey & McDevitt, 1995). Additionally, several programs using (e.g., Smith, 1994; Turecki, 1989) or evaluating the use of (Sheeber & Johnson, 1994) temperament information in environmental interventions have been developed.

One such program was started as a community prevention project in rural eastern Oregon (Smith, 1994). Initially, the intervention was divided into four phases: (a) assessment; (b) parent-child relationship strengthening; (c) specific parenting advice and support; and (d) continued availability. Parents met for individual sessions with a paraprofessional trained in temperament concepts; the number of sessions was variable with intervention time ranging from 4 weeks to over a year. Though there were no selection criteria, the majority of participating families had children who met criteria for psychiatric disorders. The intervention was often conducted in conjunction with other psychological or psychiatric treatments.

Evaluation data have consisted of consumer satisfaction measures and a behavior rating scale. Participants who returned the assessment materials (N=80 [68%]) reported that they found the program to be "helpful" or "very helpful." Additionally, among a smaller subset of participants (N=52), significant pre-post changes were observed on the Eyberg Child Behavior Inventory (Koroloff, 1992). Although these results are encouraging, the absence of a control group is problematic.

More recently, the Oregon group has developed Temperament Talk (1995), a group-oriented, 8-week program designed to assist parents through education about temperamental characteristics, relationship building, and the teaching of specific parenting and behavioral management strategies. Two to ten parents meet for eight weekly 90-minute sessions. Leaders guides and suggestions for implementation are provided as well as an extensive collection of parenting suggestions for behavioral issues. The program is aimed primarily at children with subclinical behavioral problems though it can be used in conjunction with mental health services. Although the program has reportedly received extensive field-testing, evaluation data are primarily user satisfaction ratings rather than measures of either parenting or behavioral change in children.

A second program (Sheeber & Johnson, 1994) is a group-based psycho-educational intervention aimed at helping parents of temperamentally difficult preschool children to understand their children's temperament style and develop congruent parenting approaches. The intervention was largely based on the comprehensive approach developed by Turecki (Turecki & Tonner, 1985). It was modified to include recommendations offered by Chess and Thomas (1986, 1987), to reflect our understanding of child temperament and behavior management, and to facilitate conducting the program within a group format.

As described in detail in the Case Material section, the training program has two components: (a) education regarding child temperament and its role as a contributor to child behavior; and (b) training in techniques to manage temperament-related behavior problems.

Two evaluations of this intervention have been conducted. Only mothers participated in the first evaluation and too few fathers participated in the second analyses for statistical comparisons to be conducted. In each, parents initially self-referred to the program based on community advertisements and were then screened. Criteria for participation were difficult child temperament and the presence of reported parenting difficulties. Child temperament was assessed by parent questionnaire, and "difficulty" was defined as elevations on a minimum of three temperament characteristics previously shown to be predictive of poor child, parental, or familial adjustment. The flexibility of this inclusion criteria is in line with the goodness-of-fit model in recognizing that various child temperament characteristics may be predictive of difficulties within different families. Parenting difficulties were likewise assessed based on standardized self-report instruments. Results of the first investigation (Sheeber & Johnson, 1994) indicated that relative to mothers in a wait-list control condition, mothers who participated in the parent-training program reported increased satisfaction with parent-child relationships, greater perceived parenting competence, and decreases in depression, anxiety, child behavior problems, and family disruption. These gains were maintained at a 2-month follow-up assessment. In the second evaluation (Sheeber, Goldberg, Galvinhill, Hershberger, & Sorensen, 1996), the parent-training program was compared with a wait-list control condition as well as to a social support condition. In the latter, group leaders served as facilitators whose role was to raise questions and help structure the group's problem-solving. Each session had a specified topic, and group members were encouraged to discuss their parenting experiences and exchange ideas on managing difficult behavior. At posttreatment, mothers in the temperament-guidance condition reported fewer conduct problems and greater attachment to their children than did mothers in the support and wait-list conditions. Moreover, relative to mothers in the support condition, they reported less depression, less family disruption, and greater self-perceived competence in parenting. No differences emerged between mothers in the support and wait-list conditions. Participants in the two active conditions were reassessed at 6 and 12 months postintervention; however, between-group differences were not maintained. This pattern of results suggests that the benefits obtained by those participating in the parent training program were not primarily attributable to nonspecific factors such as social support or expectations for change engendered by involvement in a parenting program.

Parent Support Groups

A final approach to temperament-based interventions is the use of support groups for parents of temperamentally difficult children. The goal of these programs is to provide parents with a venue for sharing concerns and learning from others in similar situations. Initially, this approach was used in conjunction with a program of more structured parent guidance (Turecki, 1989). However, support groups also exist as independent interventions. One such program is the Difficult Child Support Association of British Columbia (DCSA; Anderson, 1994). This program was organized by two parents using the model provided in Turecki's Difficult Child book (Turecki & Tonner, 1985). The DCSA operates on a twice monthly meeting schedule and is mainly focused on active mutual support and dissemination of information about parenting. The DCSA program emphasizes understanding of normal individual differences, the importance of task mastery in child development, distinguishing normal from deviant behavior, reducing stress from temperament-environment interaction, and understanding the effects of marital and family stress on children's behavior as well as the interaction of temperament and medical problems. In addition to meetings, the DCSA has a quarterly newsletter and a volunteer professional advisory group. Members also educate community professionals about the goals and methods of the group.

CAUTIONS REGARDING TEMPERAMENT-FOCUSED GUIDANCE

Before concluding the discussion of approaches to temperament-focused guidance, it is important to address concerns that have been raised regarding clinical and educational applications of temperament information. A primary concern relates to the use of temperament measures for large-scale screening and prevention programs. One problem is that it has not been determined that the current generation of temperament measures has adequate sensitivity and specificity to identify cases at risk for behavioral difficulties from among a large sample of individuals. This is a function both of the psychometric properties of the measures and of the level of association between temperament characteristics and behavioral disturbance (Bates, 1989; Rothbart, 1982). Additionally, without professional guidance, there is a risk that the information may be misunderstood or misused (Carey & McDevitt, 1989). Relevant to this point is the preliminary data from the Kaiser project (Cameron et al., 1991, 1996) indicating that in the absence of individual counseling, receipt of a temperament profile and written anticipatory guidance may sensitize parents to behavioral concerns without increasing their self-perceived understanding or felt competence to manage the difficulties. Thus the consensus reached among participants at the 1988 symposium on clinical and educational applications of temperament research (Carey & McDevitt, 1989) that routine screening for temperament risk factors in all infants or children in any population is unjustified by current experiences, seems to us to remain valid. The clinicians and researchers participating in this conference recommended that health services personnel interested in screening for problems in developmental-behavioral area would do better to attend to: (a) parental concern about the child or the parent-child relationship; and/or (b) evidence of problems in the area of behavioral adjustment. If clinical problems are noted, then as described earlier, the use of temperament data can have value as part of a comprehensive assessment. Nonetheless, because we sympathize with the need for medical professionals to address parents questions regarding normal developmental challenges and because we expect that temperament information may well be helpful in this regard (see Cameron & Rice, 1986), we concur with Bates' (1989) assessment that there is a place for experimental use of such approaches so long as the programs are "well connected to the evolving literature and . . . have strong evaluation research components" (p. 348).

It is important to recognize, however, that concerns about imperfections in measurement do not need to rule out the clinical use of temperament information by skilled professionals. It should be noted in this regard that the reliability of temperament assessment is multifaceted. Temperament is not immutable and it is to be expected that changes brought about by interactions with the environment will be reflected in reduced stability of measurement (Thomas & Chess, 1977). Moreover, the longitudinal stability of parent report of temperament has been found to vary according to the child's age. After infancy, moderate stability coefficients have been obtained over the course of a couple of years (Guerin & Gottfried, 1994; Mufson, Fendrich, & Warner, 1990). In fact, after about the age of 3 years, the 1-year stability of temperament approaches the level of 1-month test-retest reliability (median $r = .70$; McDevitt, 1986). It is unclear whether the instability observed in infancy is based on birth and perinatal factors, the greater importance of environment in early life, or measurement difficulties (see Carey & McDevitt, 1995, for an in-depth discussion). Nonetheless, parents may benefit from understanding and adapting to their infants' early behavioral style even if that style does not predict the infants' later behavior (see Medoff-Cooper, 1994). Similarly, we do not foresee any danger in broad education about infants' and children's individual differences that serves to normalize parents' experiences.

A second concern relates to temperament-focused guidance more broadly because of its purported reliance on the concept of difficult temperament (Sanson & Rothbart, 1995). In particular, it has been suggested that the "difficult" label may be stigmatizing and self-fullfilling; that in placing blame within the child it ignores the role of the child-environment fit; and that it suggests that parents' efforts should be directed at modifying the child's temperament expressions. These concerns reflect an understanding of temperament-based guidance that is in marked contrast to our conceptualization. Though interest in temperament-based guidance developed, in part, out of a recognition that certain temperament characteristics can be a source of difficulty for parents, and though the "difficult" nomenclature may be used as a shorthand in professional communication, it is not a clinically useful concept (for many of the reasons Sanson and Rothbart articulate as well as because of its sheer vagueness) and we would argue, it is hence, *not* the basis of temperament-based guidance. As described earlier, the guidance is focused instead on helping parents to understand and respect their children's individuality and develop parenting approaches that are consonant with a child's style. Finally, we are unaware of any outcome data indicating that "labeling as 'difficult' or 'easy' may be one basis for the finding that extreme temperament characteristics are generally more stable than moderate characteristics" as hypothesized by Sanson and Rothbart (1995, p. 314). Nonetheless, as we've discussed, there is too little research data available regarding the outcomes of temperament-based interventions—and not surprisingly, this includes negative outcomes. So though the cautions raised do not strike us as so substantial as to counter the potential benefits to be achieved by temperament-focused guidance, we would certainly be in favor of efforts to assess, and if necessary address, potentially detrimental effects.

CASE MATERIAL: A GROUP PARENT-TRAINING INTERVENTION

To illustrate the use of temperament information in parent guidance, the group program conducted by the first author will be presented in more detail. As discussed, the goal of the intervention is to help parents to respect their children's individuality and tailor demands so as to be congruent with their temperament style. The program is intended for parents who are finding their children's behavioral style challenging; it is not intended as a treatment for psychopathology and has not been evaluated as an adjunct to other behavioral or psychiatric interventions. Typically, groups consist of parents from between four and eight families. The groups meet weekly for 1½- to 2-hour sessions over the course of 9 weeks. Homework is assigned at the end of each session and discussed at the beginning of the next.

TEMPERAMENT EDUCATION AND SELF-ASSESSMENT (SESSIONS 1–3)

The initial portion of the program is designed to familiarize parents with the nature of child temperament and help them understand its role as a contributor to child behavior problems. Parents are provided definitions for the nine dimensions of child temperament identified by Thomas and

Chess and several activities are used to help familiarize them with these dimensions. These include identifying relevant temperament traits from vignettes that portray children in various activities; having parents complete temperament questionnaires about themselves; and having them peruse the temperament questionnaires that they completed about their children. These activities have the additional benefit of helping parents to start drawing connections between children's temperament styles and behaviors that they perceive as difficult or challenging.

In addition to the temperament dimensions, group leaders try to convey several key ideas during these early sessions; these are summarized in Table 15.1. Two points are of particular importance. First, it is essential that temperament characteristics be understood to be descriptors and not evaluations. To this end, parents are led through a process of identifying the benefits and drawbacks of each temperament dimension. Thus, for example, parents can appreciate that though low distractibility can be very challenging in a crying infant or tantrumming toddler because the child is harder to soothe, it is an advantageous characteristic in a school-age child, who can be counted on to complete homework or chores without too much interruption or fuss. Of course, this is more difficult for some temperament characteristics than others. Most notably, group leaders admit to having trouble identifying a compelling benefit of negative mood (though one father was able to console himself by considering it to be an "artistic" temperament). Nonetheless, acknowledgment of the characteristic as being part of the child's temperamental makeup and not a function of either willfulness or poor parenting is a useful step in reducing parents' guilt and irritation, and setting the stage for planning effective interventions for behaviors such as whining, complaining, or crying that may be expressions of frequent negative mood.

Second, group leaders highlight the goodness-of-fit framework and establish that it is the guiding principle of the program. They stress that the specific temperament characteristics that parents find challenging depend on numerous factors including the child's age, the family's living environment, and the parents' own characteristics and values. Thus parents can see that a child's low adaptability may present particular challenges for a parent whose job demands entail frequent moves, irregular hours, or frequent after-hours calls that interrupt the family's evening routines. Group leaders explain, moreover, that difficulties arise when there is a poor fit between the child's temperament characteristics and the demands placed on him or her, and indicate that the goal of the program is to help parents tailor their approaches to maximize their children's success. Thus, difficulty is defined as being a function not of child characteristics or poor parenting practices, but of a mismatch between the two.

Table 15.1
Key Concepts Presented in Initial Sessions

Temperament Concepts

1. **Temperament refers to the style of behavior.** It is the manner in which a child approaches and engages in different tasks. For example, in playing a game, aspects of behavioral style may be evident in how much a child runs around (activity), how upset he or she is if the rules are changed (adaptability), and how easily he or she can leave the game if called in for dinner (persistence).

2. **Temperament refers to characteristics that are, at least in part, biological in origin.** However, they will be affected by parenting and other environmental influences.

3. **Temperament characteristics are relatively stable.** However, because children's behavior is a function of both innate characteristics and environmental influences, the expression of temperament traits will vary across situations. Similarly, because of maturation, learning, and different environmental conditions, some changes in temperament and its expression are expected over time.

4. **Temperament characteristics are neither good nor bad.** You may find some temperament characteristics more challenging than others at different ages and in different situations. Also, which characteristics you find difficult will likely depend, at least in part, on your own expectations, lifestyle, and temperamental dispositions.

5. **Perfectly healthy, normal children display temperament characteristics that you may find challenging.** Your child may demonstrate temperamental traits that can make parenting difficult, but this does not mean that your child is emotionally disturbed, hyperactive, or in any way "abnormal." Relatedly, it also doesn't mean that you've been a bad parent.

6. **Goodness of fit refers to the match between child characteristics and the demands placed on him and her by the environment.** A good fit is one in which demands and expectations are in line with the child's temperament style and capabilities. A poor fit may contribute to parent-child conflict and increasing behavior problems. Learning about your child's temperament style will help you to tailor your parenting approaches to achieve a good fit.

7. **A poor fit between a child's temperament style and the demands of the situation means that the tasks at hand will be harder or less enjoyable for the child.** As a parent, you experience your children's difficulties with them. It will be important to come to see that they are sharing their difficulties with you, not creating them for you, as it may feel at times.

An additional component of these early sessions is a self-assessment. Parents are guided through a process of determining where their children fall on each of the temperament dimensions, identifying specific behaviors that they find problematic, and drawing preliminary connections between problem behaviors and the temperament characteristics. This process includes reviewing the temperament questionnaire they completed about their child, an informal weeklong period of observing the children's behavior, and guided group discussion and review. Group leaders do not provide parents with a temperament profile of their children but rather guide them through a process of making their own determinations. Finally, during these beginning sessions, parents discuss their experiences related to parenting a child whose behavior is challenging or difficult. The role of these early sessions is to normalize both child behavior and parent affect, to define the group as a supportive and productive place to work, and to familiarize parents with temperament ideas as a building block to later sessions.

TEMPERAMENT-GUIDED INTERVENTIONS (SESSIONS 4–7)

The middle sessions focus on techniques to help parents manage temperament-related behavior problems. Each session addresses behavioral difficulties that are associated with particular temperament characteristics. Because a large number of common early childhood behavior problems reflecting an even broader range of temperament attributes are addressed, there is no expectation that each family will adopt, or even try the full range of techniques presented. In fact, parents are encouraged to think of the strategies presented in this phase of the program as a "cafeteria" menu. The cafeteria approach makes the most sense given the heterogeneity of children's temperament characteristics as well as individual differences in the behavior that parents find difficult. Additionally, group leaders indicate that their suggestions in no way exhaust the available options. Group members are advised to make changes in accordance with their own needs and styles so long as they stay within the conceptual framework of the goodness-of-fit model. Members are encouraged to discuss proposed modifications both to facilitate sharing of ideas among group participants and to check that approaches used by group members are congruent with this model.

For each set of behavioral difficulties, the first step is to recognize the temperament characteristic(s) contributing to the behavior. Vignettes describing a child engaging in the target behavior are read and through discussion parents identify the relevant temperament traits, much as they did in the earlier sessions. This format is used throughout the program both because the repetition is an aid in understanding and remembering the particular temperament dimensions and also because the goal is for parents to get in the habit of thinking about their children's temperament styles as a way of making sense of behavior problems.

Once the temperament characteristics are identified, parents are provided with management approaches that use this information to make parenting demands more congruent with their children's style. The overriding framework here (borrowed gratefully from the thinking of

Chess & Thomas), is that though a child's temperament makeup often cannot or should not be a barrier to meeting developmentally appropriate challenges (i.e., shyness doesn't preclude the need to start kindergarten) it can (and our bias is should) be taken into consideration in deciding which demands are really important as well as how to tailor demands to make them as manageable as possible. Thus, parents of a child who is nonrhythmic in appetite might decide to allow the child to eat prepared meals when hungry rather than insist that he or she eat at family mealtimes. Where the demands are necessary, a defining feature of nearly all the management approaches is the focus on the antecedents of child behavior. Our primary objective is to frame demands in a manner that maximizes the child's ability to meet them. For example, parents would be encouraged and taught ways to give a persistent child advance notice before requiring him or her to move from one activity to another. Similarly, parents of a child with initial withdrawal responses to new situations would be taught to prepare the child for upcoming events and be encouraged to allow the child to join activities at his or her own pace. With guidance from group leaders, parents make decisions about when it will be helpful to label the temperament style for the child to help him or her to gain self-awareness (e.g., I know its hard to calm down when you're so excited so we're going to . . .) and when it is best to use the knowledge to guide parenting approaches without labeling it for the child.

Secondary to this focus on making demands consonant with the children's temperament style, parents are also instructed in the use of social consequences, such as praise and ignoring, to facilitate performance of desired behaviors. For example, the persistent child who could be encouraged to leave a play activity to come to dinner or the timid child who could be encouraged to gradually join a group of other children would be praised for these accomplishments. In this way, parents learn to implement behavior management strategies to shape desired behaviors while being respectful of the challenges their children face as a function of their temperament characteristics.

WRAPPING UP (SESSIONS 8 AND 9)

In the next-to-final session, attention is directed toward problem behaviors that do not easily conform to a temperament conceptualization. In this session, parents are provided with help in choosing consequences for undesirable behaviors and further encouraged in the use of positive reinforcement for appropriate child behavior. At the end of the session, parents identify strategies to try during the coming week. These efforts are discussed at the final session. The remainder of the final session is devoted to a post-intervention assessment.

CONCLUSIONS AND FUTURE DIRECTIONS

Subsequent to the pioneering efforts of Thomas and Chess, a new generation of clinicians, educators, and to a lesser extent, researchers have been developing models for the application of temperament concepts to parent guidance and training. They have brought to this task a respect for children's individual differences, an understanding that these differences have implications for parent-child interactions and child development, and the belief that Thomas and Chess's model of improving the fit between child and environmental characteristics will result in better outcomes for children and parents. As we hope this chapter has demonstrated, the result has been the development of a broad range of creative approaches to applying information about children's individual differences and the importance of goodness of fit between child and environmental characteristics, to the job of helping parents to raise happy, healthy, and competent children. Thus, temperament concepts have become increasingly available to parents in clinical services and in the form of self-help books, on-line resources, and parent-support programs.

Unfortunately, the clinical science has not kept apace of this progress. As discussed earlier, very few studies assessing the effectiveness of temperament-based guidance have been conducted in the 20 years since Thomas and Chess published the results of their initial clinical evaluation (Thomas et al., 1968). Of course, and many would say of necessity, it is not unusual for clinical applications to progress well ahead of their empirical validation. Thus, it is perhaps not surprising that though there are a number of reasonably well-defined interventions that could be replicated and empirically validated, this work is in its very early stages. Therefore, as we turn to future directions, we think that the empirical evaluation of the effectiveness of temperament-focused parent guidance stands as the preeminent challenge. So with the perhaps immodest goal of fostering interest in improving the balance between clinical application and scientific validation, we begin with suggestions for research in this area. We conclude with some thoughts on future clinical directions.

RESEARCH DIRECTIONS

First, starting at the broadest, most basic level, controlled outcome studies are needed to determine whether (and which) temperament-focused interventions are successful in achieving stated goals for improvements in child behavior and emotional adjustment, parent-child interactions, and parental adjustment and satisfaction with parenting. To this end, researchers need to be attentive to the state of the art in such areas as the use of reliable, well-validated outcome measures, inclusion of multisource and multimethod assessment batteries, use of appropriate and well-matched comparison groups, and reliance on manualized treatments to facilitate replication (Peterson & Bell-Dolan, 1995). Though assessment of consumer satisfaction, particularly as part of a broader approach to measuring clinical significance, will be beneficial, the more detailed information to be gained from measures assessing the specific areas that the interventions are purported to affect are also needed. As temperament-based interventions often target nonclinical populations, researchers will need to consider how to conceptualize and assess positive changes in families who were not initially demonstrating clinical levels of behavior problems or emotional distress. Longitudinal designs that enable researchers to assess maintenance and consolidation of treatment gains will also be of interest.

Second, in the context of treatment outcome evaluations, it will be important to address the possibility that interventions can have unintended negative effects. To some extent, this goal will be accomplished in the natural course of controlled treatment studies in that differentially worse outcomes for participants in the temperament-focused interventions would be apparent. However, to the extent that particular negative outcomes are of concern, it may be necessary to proactively design studies for assessing these outcomes. So, for example, Sanson and Rothbart's (1995) concern that labeling temperament characteristics may result in a self-fullfilling prophecy could be framed as a testable hypothesis in which the relative stability of temperament attributes for individuals participating and not participating in temperament-based interventions could be assessed. It will also be beneficial to focus on identifying (as the Kaiser group has been doing) treatment and participant variables that are predictive of positive change. This will enable researchers and clinicians to engage in a self-correcting process that improves both the treatments and the ability to target those clients most likely to benefit from them.

At the next level, it will be beneficial to demonstrate that the outcomes of parenting programs in which guidance is tailored to children's temperament styles compare favorably with those obtained from standard behavior management approaches. From a theoretical perspective, temperament-based approaches should be superior in those cases in which a temperament-environment mismatch is accounting for difficulties and should be less effective when other factors are operative. In evaluating this hypothesis, outcomes can be broadly conceptualized to include reduction in behavior problems, improvements in child and parent mood or perceived self-competence, improvement in parent-child interactions, or consumer satisfaction with the guidance offered and results obtained. This recommendation is less relevant to early wellness-based approaches like the Kaiser program in that, by design, their program is compared with the "usual standard" of pediatric care, which necessarily includes addressing parents' questions about normal infancy and childhood concerns such as crying, eating, and sleeping problems.

Finally, for both theoretical and practical reasons, it will also be important to identify the mechanisms by which change occurs. Two mechanisms have been posited by proponents of temperament-based parent guidance: (a) Education increases parents' appreciation of normal individual differences as well as their understanding of their own children's behavioral styles and thus reduces unnecessary distress; and (b) the improvement in fit between child and environmental characteristics that develops either naturally as a function of this increased understanding or through specific clinician recommendations results in decreased stress and consequently, better child (and parent) adjustment. To date, it is unclear whether when treatments are effective, it is for the reasons posited. For example, as regards the benefits hypothesized to ensue from increased understanding of temperament concepts, Sheeber and Johnson (1994) reported that in addition to improvements in maternal and child functioning, mothers also demonstrated a significant increase in knowledge about child temperament; though this was interpreted to provide partial support for the role of temperament knowledge in treatment gains, assessment of the correlation between knowledge and outcome would provide a more direct test. Moreover, no one has examined whether parenting strategies change as a function of temperament-based guidance in such a way as to improve the goodness of fit. This is likely to present a particular challenge to researchers given the difficulty of operationalizing goodness of fit. Nonetheless, it will be an important step in validating the use of temperament-based interventions.

CLINICAL DIRECTIONS

Because the research has lagged behind clinical gains, most of our recommendations for immediate future directions concern the evaluation of approaches already in use. However, there are certainly interesting clinical endeavors to look forward to as well. First, findings in the developmental literature are beginning to suggest that the fit between children's behavioral style and parenting approaches may be relevant to children's cognitive development (Wachs & Gandour, 1983) as well as to the attainment of specific developmental competencies such as internalization of rules (Kochanska, 1995) and maturation of problem-solving skills (Fagot, 1996). Thus, there may eventually be a role for temperament-based guidance in helping parents to promote the development of beneficial competencies. Additionally, as our knowledge base regarding the mechanisms by which the relations between temperament and behavior problems develop, this knowledge will certainly inform our clinical thinking and may lead to more focused intervention approaches. Similarly, the burgeoning research regarding biological factors in temperament are likely to have significant treatment implications (Bates, 1994).

For the present, professionals who deal with infants and children where concerns about behavior are being addressed have a number of promising techniques to choose from in developing a partnership with parents. As additional data accumulate on the efficacy of various programs and intervention strategies, these techniques will no doubt be refined and strengthened in the pursuit of enhancing the parent-child relationship and promoting healthy child-environment interaction.

REFERENCES

Allen, K., & Prior, M. (1995). Assessment of the validity of easy and difficult temperament through observed mother-child behaviors. *International Journal of Behavioral Development, 18*(4), 609–630.

Anderson, C. J. (1994). Parent support groups. In W. B. Carey & S. C. McDevitt (Eds.), *Prevention and early intervention: Individual differences as risk factors for the mental health of children. A Festschrift for Stella Chess and Alexander Thomas* (pp. 267–275). New York: Brunner/Mazel.

Bates, J. E. (1989). Application of temperament concepts. In G. A. Kohnstamm, J. E. Bates, & M. K. Rothbart (Eds.), *Temperament in childhood* (pp. 321–356). Chichester, England: Wiley.

Bates, J. E. (1990). Conceptual and empirical linkages between temperament and behavior problems: A commentary on the Sanson, Prior, and Kyrios study. *Merrill-Palmer Quarterly, 36*, 193–199.

Bates, J. E. (1994). Introduction. In J. E. Bates & T. D. Wachs (Eds.), *Temperament: Individual differences at the interface of biology and behavior.* Washington, DC: American Psychological Association.

Cameron, J. R., Hansen, R., & Rosen, D. (1991). Preventing behavioral problems in infancy through temperament assessment and parental support programs within health maintenance organizations. In J. H. Johnson & S. B. Johnson (Eds.), *Advances in child health psychology* (pp. 127–139). Gainesville: University of Florida Press.

Cameron, J. R., & Rice, D. (1986). Developing anticipatory guidance programs based on early assessment of infant temperament: Two tests of a prevention model. *Journal of Pediatric Psychology, 11*(2), 221–234.

Cameron, J. R., Rice, D., Hansen, R., & Rosen, D. (1994). Developing temperament guidance programs within pediatric practice. In W. B. Carey & S. C. McDevitt (Eds.), *Prevention and early intervention: Individual differences as risk factors for the mental health of children. A Festschrift for Stella Chess and Alexander Thomas* (pp. 226–236). New York: Brunner/Mazel.

Cameron, J. R., Rice, D., Rosen, D., & Chesterman, E. (1996). *Evaluating the clinical and cost effectiveness of a temperament-based anticipatory guidance program for parents of infants in an HMO setting.* Manuscript submitted for publication.

Carey, W. B. (1989). Clinical use of temperament data in pediatrics. In W. B. Carey & S. C. McDevitt (Eds.), *Clinical and educational applications of temperament research* (pp. 127–140). Berwyn, PA: Swets North America.

Carey, W. B. (1992). Pediatric assessment of behavioral adjustment and behavioral style. In M. D. Levine, W. B. Carey, & A. C. Crocker (Eds.), *Developmental-behavioral pediatrics* (2nd ed., pp. 609–616). Philadelphia: Saunders.

Carey, W. B., & Jablow, M. M. (1997). *Your child's temperament. What it is. What it does. How to work with it.* New York: Simon & Schuster.

Carey, W. B., & McDevitt, S. C. (1989). *Clinical and educational applications of temperament research.* Berwyn, PA: Swets North America.

Carey, W. B., & McDevitt, S. C. (1995). *Coping with children's temperament: A guide for professionals.* New York: Basic Books.

Caspi, A., Henry, B., McGee, R. O., Moffitt, T. E., & Silva, P. A. (1995). Temperamental origins of child and adolescent behavior problems: From age three to age fifteen. *Child Development, 66*(1), 37–54.

Chess, S., & Thomas, A. (1986). *Temperament in clinical practice.* New York: Guilford Press.

Chess, S., & Thomas, A. (1987). *Know your child.* New York: Basic Books.

Chess, S., & Thomas, A. (1992). Dynamics of individual behavioral development. In M. D. Levine, W. B. Carey, & A. C. Crocker (Eds.), *Developmental-behavioral pediatrics* (2nd ed., pp. 84–94). Philadelphia: Saunders.

Crockenberg, S. B. (1986). Are temperamental differences in babies associated with predictable differences in care giving? In J. V. Lerner & R. M. Lerner (Eds.), *Temperament and social interaction in infants and children* (pp. 53–74). San Francisco: Jossey-Bass.

Fagot, B. (1996, October). *Temperament and parent guidance.* Paper presented at the Occasional Temperament Conference, Eugene, OR.

Gauvain, M., & Fagot, B. (1995). Child temperament as a mediator of mother-toddler problem-solving. *Social Development, 4*(3), 257–276.

Goldsmith, H. H., Buss, A. H., Plomin, R., Rothbart, M. K., Thomas, A., Chess, S., Hinde, R. A., & McCall, R. B. (1987). Roundtable: What is temperament? Four approaches. *Child Development, 58*, 505–529.

Goodyer, I. M., Ashby, L., Altham, P. M. E., Vize, C., & Cooper, P. J. (1993). Temperament and major depression in 11 to 16 year olds. *Journal of Child Psychology and Psychiatry, 34*(8), 1409–1423.

Guerin, D. W., & Gottfried, A. W. (1994). Developmental stability and change in parent reports of temperament: A ten-year longitudinal investigation from infancy through preadolescence. *Merrill-Palmer Quarterly, 40*(3), 334–355.

Hagekull, G., & Bohlin, G. (1989). Greater impact of infant temperament in multiparous mothers' adaptation. In W. B. Carey & S. C. McDevitt (Eds.), *Clinical and educational applications of temperament research* (pp. 97–102). Berwyn, PA: Swets North America.

Kochanska, G. (1995). Children's temperament, mother's discipline, and security of attachment: Multiple pathways to emerging internalization. *Child Development, 66*(3), 597–615.

Koroloff, N. (1990, March). *Getting a great start: Part II. Early intervention demonstration projects-January 1988 to June 1989.* Portland State University, Regional Research Institute for Human Services.

Koroloff, N. (1992, February). *Starting right: Part II. Early identification demonstration projects-January 1991 to July 1991.* Portland State University, Regional Research Institute for Human Services.

Kurcinka, M. S. (1991). *Raising your spirited child.* New York: HarperCollins.

Lerner, J. V., Baker, N., & Lerner, R. M. (1985). A person-context goodness of fit model of adjustment. In P. Kendall (Ed.), *Advances in cognitive-behavioral research and therapy* (Vol. 4, pp. 111–136). New York: Academic Press.

Maziade, M., Caron, C., Cote, R., Boutin, P., & Thivierge, J. (1989). Extreme temperament and diagnosis: A study in a psychiatric sample of consecutive children. *Archives of General Psychiatry, 47,* 477–484.

McDevitt, S. C. (1986). Continuity and discontinuity of temperament in infancy and early childhood. In R. Plomin & J. Dunn (Eds.), *The study of temperament: Changes, continuities and challenges* (pp. 27–38). Hillsdale, NJ: Erlbaum.

McDevitt, S. C. (1994). Assessment of individual differences in the temperament of children: Evaluation of interactions. In W. B. Carey & S. C. McDevitt (Eds.), *Prevention and early intervention: Individual differences as risk factors for the mental health of children. A Festschrift for Stella Chess and Alexander Thomas* (pp. 193–204). New York: Brunner/Mazel.

McDevitt, S. C., Hegvik, R. L., & Esterman, M. (1996, October). *Carey temperament scales report writer and profile writer software: Methods for providing written feedback about temperament to caregivers.* Paper presented at the Occasional Temperament Conference, Eugene, OR.

Medoff-Cooper, B. (1994). Specific prevention and intervention strategies used to accommodate individual needs of newborn infants. In W. B. Carey & S. C. McDevitt (Eds.), *Prevention and early intervention: Individual differences as risk factors for the mental health of children. A Festschrift for Stella Chess and Alexander Thomas* (pp. 205–214). New York: Brunner/Mazel.

Mufson, L., Fendrich, M., & Warner, V. (1990). The stability of temperament by child and mother reports over two years. *Journal of the American Academy of Child and Adolescent Psychiatry, 29*(3), 386–391.

Ostergren, C. S. (1997). Differential utility of temperament-based guidance materials for parents of infants. *Family Relations, 46*(1), 63–71.

Peterson, L., & Bell-Dolan, D. (1995). Treatment outcome research in child psychology: Realistic coping with the "Ten Commandments of Methodology." *Journal of Clinical Child Psychology, 24*(2), 149–162.

Rende, R. D. (1993). Longitudinal relations between temperament traits and behavioral syndromes in middle childhood. *Journal of the American Academy of Child and Adolescent Psychiatry, 32*(2), 287–290.

Rothbart, M. K. (1982). The concept of difficult temperament: A critical analysis of Thomas, Chess, and Korn. *Merrill-Palmer Quarterly, 28,* 35–40.

Rothbart, M. K., & Ahadi, S. A. (1994). Temperament and the development of personality. *Journal of Abnormal Psychology, 103,* 55–66.

Rutter, M. (1987). Temperament, personality, and personality disorder. *British Journal of Psychiatry, 150,* 443–458.

Rutter, M. (1989). Temperament: Conceptual issues and clinical implications. In G. A. Kohnstamm, J. E. Bates, & M. K. Rothbart (Eds.), *Temperament in childhood* (pp. 463–482). Chichester, England: Wiley.

Sanson, A., & Rothbart, M. K. (1995). Child temperament and parenting. In M. H. Bornstein (Ed.), *Handbook of parenting: Vol. 4. Applied and practical parenting.* Mahwah, NJ: Erlbaum.

Schuler, M. E., Black, M. M., & Starr, R. H. (1995). Determinants of mother-infant interaction: Effects of prenatal exposure, social support, and infant temperament. *Journal of Clinical Child Psychology, 24*(4), 397–405.

Sheeber, L. B., Goldberg, H., Galvinhill, P., Hershberger, K., & Sorensen, E. D. (1996, October). *Evaluation of a temperament-focused parent-training program: A replication and extension.* Paper presented at the Occasional Temperament Conference, Eugene, OR.

Sheeber, L. B., & Johnson, J. H. (1992). Applicability of the impact on family scale for assessing families with behaviorally difficult children. *Psychological Reports, 71,* 155–159.

Sheeber, L. B., & Johnson, J. H. (1994). Evaluation of a temperament-focused parent-training program. *Journal of Clinical Child Psychology, 23,* 249–259.

Smith, B. (1994). The temperament program: Community-based prevention of behavior disorders in children. In W. B. Carey & S. C. McDevitt (Eds.), *Prevention and early intervention: Individual differences as risk factors for the mental health of children. A Festschrift for Stella Chess and Alexander Thomas* (pp. 257–266). New York: Brunner/Mazel.

Thomas, A., & Chess, S. (1977). *Temperament and development.* New York: Bruner/Mazel.

Thomas, A., Chess, S., & Birch, H. (1968). *Temperament and behavior disorders in children.* New York: New York University Press.

Thomas, A., Chess, S., Birch, H. G., Hertzig, M. E., & Korn, S. (1963). *Behavioral individuality in early childhood.* New York: New York University Press.

Tschann, J. M., Kaiser, P., Chesney, M. A., Alkon, A., & Boyce, W. T. (1996). Resilience and vulnerability among preschool children: Family functioning, temperament, and behavior problems. *Journal of the American Academy of Child and Adolescent Psychiatry, 35*(2), 184–192.

Turecki, S. (1989). The difficult child center. In W. B. Carey & S. C. McDevitt (Eds.), *Clinical and educational applications of temperament research* (pp. 141–154). Berwyn, PA: Swets North America.

Turecki, S., & Tonner, L. (1985). *The difficult child.* New York: Bantam Books.

Turecki, S., & Tonner, L. (1989). *The difficult child* (Rev. ed.). New York: Bantam Books.

van den Boom, D. (1989). Neonatal irritability and the development of attachment. In G. A. Kohnstamm, J. E. Bates, & M. K. Rothbart (Eds.), *Temperament in childhood* (pp. 299–318). Chichester, England: Wiley.

van den Boom, D. (1994). The influence of temperament and mothering on attachment and exploration: An experimental manipulation of sensitive responsiveness among lower-class mothers with irritable infants. *Child Development, 65*(5), 1457–1477.

Wachs, T. D., & Gandour, M. J. (1983). Temperament, environment, and six-month cognitive-intellectual development: A test of the organismic specificity hypothesis. *International Journal of Behavioral Development, 6,* 135–152.

Weissbluth, M. (1989a). Sleep-loss stress and temperamental difficultness: Psychobiological processes and practical considerations. In G. A. Kohnstamm, J. E. Bates, & M. K. Rothbart (Eds.), *Temperament in childhood* (pp. 357–376). Chichester, England: Wiley.

Weissbluth, M. (1989b). *Sleep-temperament interactions: Clinical and educational applications of temperament research* (pp. 113–116). Berwyn, PA: Swets North America.

CHAPTER 16

Parent Training in Moral Context: Prosocial Family Therapy

ELAINE A. BLECHMAN

AT ITS INCEPTION in the early to mid-1960s (R. Hawkins, Peterson, Schweid, & Bijou, 1966; Wahler, Winkel, Peterson, & Morrison, 1965; Williams, 1959), behavioral parent training was a little-known but revolutionary method of enabling parents to treat their children's behavior problems. Almost four decades later, parent training is in widespread and varied use and considered a promising approach for the prevention of adolescent crime and substance abuse (Kazdin, 1990).

The classic behavioral parent-training programs (PT) are manualized interventions designed to teach parents how their children's behavior can be modified through the systematic application of social-learning principles and enhanced parental supervision and monitoring (e.g., Blechman, 1985; Forehand & McMahon, 1981; Patterson, 1975). PT presumably brings about reductions in deviant child behavior when parents, acting as natural change agents, employ operant conditioning principles (e.g., positive reinforcement of desirable behavior) and strategies (e.g., time-out for disruptive behavior) to re-engineer their children's social environment. Thus, PT differs from child-focused interventions that variously attribute change to (a) a child's relationship with a therapist who acts as a substitute parent; (b) resolution of a child's unconscious conflicts; or (c) a child's self-actualization. PT also

For support of the work described here, I thank the Boulder County District Attorney, Alex Hunter, the Assistant District Attorney, Phil Miller, and the Juvenile Diversion Coordinators Jim Kennedy and Patty Baker. Kevin Hall and Amy Helstrom made substantial contributions to the work described in this chapter.

508

differs from family-focused interventions that attribute change to a more adaptive family power structure or to a therapist's strategic use of tactics with otherwise treatment-resistant families. PT procedures are always specified in procedural manuals developed for particular problems and audiences. As a result, PT is a much better target for outcome research than alternative interventions that rely heavily on ad hoc clinician ingenuity. Manuals have been responsible for PT's widespread application to self-help and group education of parents and to diverse behavioral and medical problems of childhood and adolescence.

PT has always targeted some form of deviant child behavior including noncompliance in preschool children, externalizing behavior problems in school-aged children, disruptive behavior disorders, and delinquency in children and adolescents. PT's psychoeducational approach implicitly presumes that all parents of deviant children are psychologically healthy, law-abiding adults who conform to conventional social norms and commonsense at home, at work, and in the community and are able and willing to adopt new methods of child-rearing.

Perhaps due to the mismatch between assumptions about the parents of deviant children and reality, classic PT has never been shown to work well with parents who do not conform to middle-class norms and who do rely on maladaptive, substance-dependent coping strategies inside and outside the family. Thus, in a cross-site collaborative study, Blechman and colleagues (1981) demonstrated that the parents who stay in PT are a distinctly biased sample of highly motivated and well-functioning adults. Parents who fare least well in PT are poorly educated, low-income, socially insular single mothers whose problems extend far beyond child noncompliance (Wahler & Dumas, 1984). Marital distress, parent depression, and poverty all interfere with engagement and success in parent training (Sanders, 1992). Even among those parents who complete the recommended course of training, improved child behavior at home often does not generalize to school or community (Forehand et al., 1979). Long-term follow-up studies suggest that after training, 30 to 50% of parents and 25 to 50% of teachers report that children continue to have behavior problems in the deviant or clinical range (Schmaling & Jacobson, 1987) indicating that classic PT does not have clinically significant results even for the biased, highly motivated parents who stay the course.

Because classic PT values child compliance with parental and other adult requests above all else, it has limited prevention potential for high-risk youth. Most adolescent gang members are quite capable of following orders and rules. Their problem is that they usually choose to follow orders and rules that hurt other people and, in the long run, themselves. High-risk adolescents are expert at antisocial coping, solving problems by breaking laws that were designed to protect innocent people and preserve the social fabric. High-risk adolescents do not know how to cope prosocially, satisfying their needs for self-esteem, social approval, and material wealth in ways that help others as well as themselves. The parents of high-risk youth often share their children's maladaptive coping strategies. For parent training to realize its prevention potential, it must attract parents of antisocial youth; and take place in a moral context (Baer, 1984; Blechman, 1984), promoting prosocial coping among high-risk youth and their multiproblem families (Blechman, 1981, 1991), and engaging the mechanisms involved in the etiology of antisocial behavior.

ETIOLOGICAL THEORIES RELEVANT TO PARENT TRAINING

In this chapter, the term antisocial behavior is used to connote antisocial, substance abusing behavior. Proposed explanations of the etiology of such behavior (cf. for reviews, J. Hawkins, Catalano, & Miller, 1992; Newcomb & Harlow, 1986; Petraitis, Flay, & Miller, 1995) can be reduced to the following 10 theories. Each theory, explicitly or implicitly, implicates parenting behavior in the etiology of antisocial behavior. However, the theories differ in their emphasis on the crucial importance of parenting behavior. In some theories, parenting is the keystone proximal risk-protection variable believed to mediate the influence of distal risk and protection variables and, in some, parenting behavior represents a distal risk-protection variable.

HOST-VARIABLES THEORY

Variations on the host-variable theory implicate the centrality of diverse intrapersonal factors in the etiology of antisocial behavior including genetic endowment, physiology, personality styles, and behavioral dispositions. This theory posits that from birth onward, host variables mediate the effects of risk factors such as a socially disorganized neighborhood, family history of substance abuse, and inept parenting skills, thereby disposing youth to antisocial behavior (Ball, Carroll, & Rounsaville, 1994; Cloninger, 1987; Newcomb & Earlywine, 1996; Newcomb & McGee, 1991; Wills, Duhamel, & Vaccaro, 1995; Zuckerman, 1987).

CONFORMITY THEORY

Variations on conformity theory emphasize the etiological role of conventional values, problem behavior, and general deviance in the development of antisocial behavior. Conformity theory posits that conventional beliefs (e.g., in the benefits of education) and conventional behavior (e.g., church attendance) protect against drug use, criminal behavior, and risky sexual behavior (Felix-Ortiz & Newcomb, 1992; Jessor, Donovan, & Costa, 1991; McGee & Newcomb, 1992).

SOCIAL-COGNITIONS THEORY

Variations on social-cognitions theory emphasize the central etiological role of perceived norms, reasoned action, and labeling in the development of antisocial behavior. Social-cognitions theory posits that a hostile social-cognitive style involving an external locus of control, limited self-efficacy, low self-worth, and distrust of others' motives and intentions is a key risk factor for antisocial behavior (Dodge, 1993; Robinson, Garber, & Hilsman, 1995). Furthermore, perceptions that substance abuse is normative among peers (Burton, Sussman, Hansen, Johnson, & Flay, 1989); favorable attitudes about the usefulness of substance abuse (Graham, Marks, & Hansen, 1991) for enhancing self-image and making friends (Aloise-Young, Graham, & Hansen, 1994); and intentions to use drugs and alcohol (Laflin, Moore-Hirschi, Weis, & Hayes, 1994) are key risk factors for substance abuse.

COPING THEORY

Variations on coping theory emphasize the central etiological significance of self-esteem, self-derogation, defense mechanisms, and learned habits. In essence, coping theory posits that maladaptive coping with stress (including self-medication against uncontrollable stress with drugs), although it may be a youth's only means of survival and the basis for self-esteem, leads to childhood behavior problems, adolescent substance abuse, and bad life outcomes while adaptive, prosocial, self-controlled coping leads to good life outcomes (Blechman, 1996; Blechman, Prinz, & Dumas, 1995; Brunswick, Lewis, & Messeri, 1992; Gottfredson & Hirschi, 1990; Grunberg & Baum, 1985; Kaplan, 1980, 1996; Kaplan & Peck, 1992; Labouvie, 1986; Newcomb & Harlow, 1986; Perlmutter, 1987; Wills, 1986).

BEHAVIOR-CONTINUITY THEORY

Variations on behavior-continuity theory emphasize the central contributions of early-onset, cross-context aggression, persistent heterogeneity, flocking, and fledgling psychopathy to later antisocial behavior. This theory posits that early and serious childhood behavior problems (e.g., conduct disorder, hyperactivity) manifest in home, school, and neighborhood predispose youth to adolescent association with deviant peers, substance abuse, and delinquency (Dobkin, Tremblay, Masse, & Vitaro, 1995;

Loeber, Green, Keenan, & Lahey, 1995; Lynam, 1996; Nagan & Farrington, 1992; Pulkkinen & Tremblay, 1992; Thornberry, Lizotte, Krohn, Farnworth, & Jang, 1994).

LANGUAGE THEORY

Variations on language theory emphasize that limited receptive and expressive language skills promote attention problems and disruptive behavior, illiteracy, school failure, delinquency, and unemployment; while rich language skills allow a child to cope with adversity via humor or distracting hobbies such as reading and to bond with parents, teachers, and mentors (Achenbach, Howell, McConaughy, & Stanger, 1995; Farrington, Gallagher, Morley, St. Ledger, & West, 1986; Fergusson, Horwood, & Lynskey, 1995; Werner & Smith, 1992; White, Moffitt, Earls, Robins, & Silva, 1990).

PARENTING THEORY

Variations on parenting theory emphasize the centrality of bonding, cultural identity, social control, differential association, and social learning processes in the etiology of antisocial behavior. This theory posits that parents who lack warmth and socialization skills (particularly monitoring/supervising skills) set children up for school failure, association with deviant peers, and delinquency (Akers, 1977; Aseltine, 1995; Catalano, Kosterman, Hawkins, Newcomb, & Abbott, 1996; Harnish, Dodge, & Valente, 1995; Kandel, 1996; Patterson & Dishion, 1985; Stoolmiller & Dishion, 1993). In contrast, warm, skilled parents form secure attachments to children, enabling children to identify with family and ethnic culture, bond with teachers and school, and adopt conventional values (Brook, Whiteman, Gordon, & Cohen, 1989; Hirschi, 1969; O'Donnell, Hawkins, & Abbott, 1995; Oetting, 1993; Rutter, 1978).

FAMILY PROCESS THEORY

This theory posits that youth are unusually vulnerable to deviant peers and bad life outcomes when they lack conventional mentors or role models and come from a multiproblem family characterized by ineffective communication and headed by substance abusing, criminal, or psychologically impaired parents who cope maladaptively with stress and conflicts within the family, on the job, and in the community (Achenbach et al., 1995; Blackson, Tarter, Loeber, Ammerman, & Windle, 1996; Blechman, 1990; Blechman & McEnroe, 1985; Castro, Maddahian, Newcomb, & Bentler, 1987; Loeber et al., 1995; Pulkkinen & Pitkanen, 1994; Shedler & Block, 1990; Weintraub, 1991; Werner & Smith, 1992).

SOCIETAL CONTEXT THEORY

Variations on societal-context theory emphasize the central role of the large-scale neighborhood, community, and societal context in the etiology of antisocial behavior. This theory posits that media influences (e.g., violent television) and neighborhood influences (e.g., few conventional adult role models, few informal social controls, many deviant role models, freely available drugs) breed antisocial behavior (Brewster, 1994; Connell, Halpern-Felsher, Clifford, Crichlow, & Usinger, 1995; Eliot, Huizinga, & Ageton, 1985; Garbarino & Sherman, 1980; Hirschi, 1969; Kupersmidt, Griesler, DeRosier, Patterson, & Davis, 1995; Quinton, 1988; Wills, Blechman, & McNamara, 1996).

ECONOMIC THEORY

Variations on economic theory emphasize the central etiological role in antisocial behavior of material deprivation, pessimism about opportunities for future advancement, and social strain. This theory posits that poverty is "the ultimate cause" of all bad life outcomes, mediating the effects of numerous other risk factors (Felner et al., 1995; Schorr, 1988).

CLASSIC PARENT TRAINING AND ETIOLOGICAL THEORIES

Of all etiological theories, classic PT is most closely related to parenting theory. PT's keystone assumption is that any parent can learn to use reinforcement principles to modify any child's antisocial behavior and that the cessation of antisocial behavior is a sufficient outcome of intervention. Over the years, the limitations of parenting theory as a platform for intervention with antisocial youth became apparent. Tied to parenting theory, classic PT ignores issues raised by theories concerned with host variables, conformity, social cognitions, language, coping, behavior continuity, family process, societal context, and economics. An accumulation of evidence lending some support to each of the 10 major etiological theories suggests that the singular focus of parent training may be a fatal flaw and argues strongly for a reconsideration of parent-training's theoretical underpinnings and clinical objectives.

COPING-COMPETENCE THEORY

With colleagues and students, I have developed coping-competence theory to provide a theoretical platform for interventions with antisocial youth and their families (Blechman, 1996; Blechman & Culhane, 1993; Blechman et al., 1995). Coping-competence theory, shown as a latent model in Figure 16.1, proposes that youths' current coping strategies directly influence

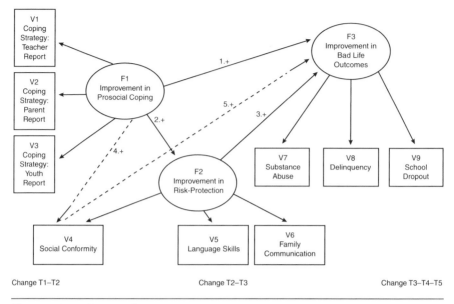

Figure 16.1 Coping-Competence Theory as a Latent Mode.

their future life outcomes while mediating the indirect influences of other risk and protection variables located in self, family, peer group, school, and neighborhood contexts and emphasized in the 10 theories identified above.

RESPONSIBILITY

A major philosophical question rarely addressed in psychological theories of human development concerns youths' responsibilities for their own actions and life outcomes. Do youth have any responsibility for their own antisocial behavior, or are they merely passive victims of inept parents, rejecting peers, poverty, and disorganized neighborhoods? In coping-competence theory, use of the term "bad life outcomes" rather than "problem behaviors" or "general deviance" emphasizes that youths' own actions have substantial influence on their future "life events" (McGee & Newcomb, 1992; Pillow, Zautra, & Sandler, 1996). Despite the contributions of uncontrollable and unfortunate risk and protective factors, each time a youth knowingly and intentionally commits an antisocial act, the youth is regarded by the law as responsible for the social consequences of the act. Similarly, it is reasonable to regard the youth as responsible for the personal consequences of antisocial behavior in the form of such bad life outcomes as police arrest and school failure.

The Parent-Training Paradox

How is it possible within a deterministic, behavioral perspective to expect responsible, prosocial behavior from youth who have been maltreated or neglected since conception? Why should we expect great success in parent training from a mother who was abused as a child and gave birth as a teenager to several difficult-to-manage children? What prepares youth to assume responsible control over their own behavior in the absence of parental monitoring, supervision, and contingency management? Unintentionally, parent-training interventions represent a paradox. On the one hand, all behavior is viewed as determined by forces in the social-environment. On the other hand, the implicit aim of parent training is self-controlled behavior on the part of parents and children who formerly demonstrated a remarkable absence of self-control.

A Compensatory Model of Antisocial Behavior

A potential resolution of the parent-training paradox is supplied by Marlatt et al.'s two-stage compensatory model of addiction (Marlatt, Baer, Donovan, & Kivlahan, 1988). The compensatory model posits that an addict is not responsible for the initial acquisition of addictive behavior but can take responsibility for reversing addictive behavior patterns. In fact, only addicts themselves can assume self-control over their addictive behavior. Compensating for the risk factors that originally caused addictive behavior, addicts can permanently replace their addictive behavior patterns with drug-free methods of self-gratification. Similarly, coping-competence theory posits that the initial acquisition of antisocial behavior is shaped by diverse uncontrollable risk factors while change comes about when antisocial youth learn to rely on prosocial and drug-free coping strategies. Key implications of coping-competence theory for intervention with antisocial youth are outlined next.

Acquisition of Antisocial Behavior

Coping-competence theory posits that the initial acquisition of maladaptive antisocial coping strategies is a product of multiple interacting risk factors including host factors such as temperament and genetic endowment, family factors such as parental warmth and supervision, school factors such as availability of afterschool programs for poorly supervised youth, neighborhood factors such as absence of conventional role models, societal factors such as endorsement of antisocial behavior by highly visible sports personalities, and economic factors that limit parents' access to assistance in childrearing and limit youths' access to better schools and neighborhoods.

Acquisition of Prosocial Coping

Coping-competence theory posits that lasting reduction in antisocial behavior can only result from increased reliance on prosocial coping strategies for purposes of survival, stress reduction, and problem solving. Mere suppression of antisocial behavior will result in an empty shell of a person like the delinquent subjected to aversive conditioning in the film *A Clockwork Orange*. Amelioration of one or more prominent risk factors (e.g., economics, societal context) may reduce reliance on antisocial coping or heighten reliance on prosocial coping. At best, some naturally occurring turnabout event in the youth's life or an artificially contrived intervention directed at youth, family, school, or neighborhood will turn former risk factors into stress-buffering, competence-enhancing protective factors. The more risk liabilities that are converted into protective assets, the greater the likelihood that youth will replace antisocial with prosocial coping strategies. Thus, coping-competence theory, as Figure 16.1 shows, posits that of all risk factors, coping exercises the most proximal and direct influence on future antisocial behavior and related bad life outcomes. By their influence on coping, other risk factors have a distal, indirect, mediated influence on future antisocial behavior and life outcomes.

Prosocial Parents and Prosocial Families

Coping-competence theory assigns central roles to two distal risk factors—parenting and family process—that directly influence children's coping styles and, thereby, indirectly influence children's propensity for antisocial behavior and vulnerability to bad life outcomes. In the natural course of development, children are much more likely to rely heavily on prosocial coping if their parents are effective socialization agents and if family communication emphasizes prosocial considerations: making decisions and taking actions that benefit self, family, and society. A family-based intervention is much more likely to encourage the adoption of prosocial coping strategies if it enables parents to become effective socialization agents for all children in the family and if it turns the family communication process in a prosocial direction. From this perspective, classic parent training's disregard for the values that parents teach their children and for the quality of familywide communication (parent-parent, parent-child, child-sibling) is insufficient. Adherents of classic PT may argue that by encouraging the use of positive reinforcement and discouraging the use of punishment, PT routinely does attend to values (i.e., reward is better than punishment) and communication (e.g., "Catch children being good.") Critics might respond that in classic PT parents do not learn the value of postconventional moral reasoning or to communicate in ways that promote each family member's autonomy. Arguably, a family-based intervention that is successful in a moral context promotes prosocial coping by all family members, buffering children against the adverse effects of host, neighborhood, peer group, school, societal, and economic risk factors and buffering parents against the typical risks of parenthood such as marital dissatisfaction and maternal depression.

Prosocial Schools and Communities

The natural and the contrived acquisition of prosocial coping is most easily arranged with the involvement of a child's family. At the same time, coping-competence theory recognizes the intervention-related role of indirect school, neighborhood, and societal risk factors. Appropriately designed interventions can be put in place in settings that consistently promote prosocial coping. These programs can be used to supplement family-based interventions or to substitute for family-based interventions when parents are unable or unwilling to be involved (Blechman, 1996).

PROSOCIAL FAMILY THERAPY

Prosocial Family Therapy (PFT), the product of earlier interventions developed for high-risk youth in the home, at school, and in the peer group (e.g., Blechman, 1985; Blechman, Dumas, & Prinz, 1994; Prinz, Blechman, & Dumas, 1994), purposefully builds on the strengths of classic parent training. PFT is a manualized skill-building intervention that specifies general principles of skill acquisition (e.g., positive reinforcement of prosocial coping by other family members and by natural consequences, observational learning of prosocial communication from other family members), related procedures (e.g., parent reinforcement of a good day without community problems, a reunion task during which the family exchanges information about recent experiences), and a process of prosocial counselor-family communication designed to motivate the whole family to work hard at skill acquisition despite crises that ordinarily derail family therapy. The description that follows provides specifics of PFT as it is currently applied in my clinic for delinquent youth.

PFT CLIENTS AND COUNSELORS

PFT represents a secondary prevention approach to high-risk youth (who are already engaged in some form of problem behavior) and their multi-problem, crisis-ridden families (who have many difficulties other than the behavior problems of the index high-risk youth) (Blechman, 1991). PFT involves in intervention, the high-risk youth, all siblings who live at home, and all adults who are involved in caretaker roles. PFT counselors have at least a master's degree in a social or behavioral science discipline (e.g., psychology, sociology), prior experience working with troubled children and families, and continuous training and supervision in PFT.

PFT Communication

PFT counselors are trained to use prosocial communication strategies (defined as solving problems in ways that help self and others) to achieve several purposes: heighten clients' motivation for change; promote a goal-oriented, problem-solving attitude; and demonstrate a coping style that involves sensitivity to others' opinions and needs. The PFT manual specifies and defines an array of communication tactics and their applicability to problems frequently encountered in therapy with families of adolescents such as Miller and Rollnick's (1991) "motivational interviewing" strategies. Counselors are free to communicate in ways that are consistent with their own personal styles as long as they stay within the broad limits specified in the manual. In this way, PFT specifies supposedly non-specific aspects of intervention that are believed by many clinicians to account for much of the success of any therapy (Barlow, 1994).

Communication about Motivation

PFT counselors rely heavily on brief open-ended questions (as opposed to close-ended questions, instructions, or statements) to encourage family members to make self-motivational, self-instructional, and self-explanatory statements. PFT counselors carefully formulate their open-ended questions with a desired effect (and answer) in mind. Like good lawyers, PFT counselors never ask a question without knowing in advance what answers they will get. They use brief linking statements to tie a concern just expressed by a family member to a task in the current session. During standard PFT meetings, PFT counselors use prosocial communication strategies to keep family members on track as they move from one task to another. During supplementary PFT meetings convened to confront new crises, PFT counselors use prosocial communication strategies to enable family members to cope in ways that will not interfere with, and may even augment, their progress in PFT.

PFT Structure

Pinpointing Community, Home, and Personal Problems.   In PFT, all families address all children's community problems (trouble outside the home), home problems (trouble inside the home), and personal problems (trouble with one's self). However, the intake counselor helps each family pinpoint an operational definition of these problems that suits the family's own experiences and that lends itself to quantification during weekly telephone interviews (see Appendix C). Thus, community problems are defined in general as complaints or reports of trouble regarding a child's behavior received by a parent or guardian from police, school personnel, neighbors, or other credible sources in the community. A family might define community problems as, "Teacher calls and says that Susan was suspended," or "Neighbors call and complain that kids trespassed on their property." Home problems are defined in general as problem behaviors at home, such as "Violates curfew," or "Arrives home intoxicated." Personal problems are defined in general as emotional problems that a child recognizes and finds troubling (as opposed to emotional or behavioral problems that largely concern others and would be classified as community or home problems). When a child is troubled by suicidal thoughts, these thoughts would be labeled as personal problems. When a child makes suicidal threats and denies their significance, these threats would be labeled as home problems.

PFT Phases

PFT has three phases. In Phase 1 (3-month intervention), there are 14 regularly scheduled weekly meetings. In Phase 2 (3-month short-term follow-up), there are 3 optional monthly check-up meetings. In Phase 3 (3-year-term follow-up), there are 6 optional twice yearly check-up meetings. In our current work, attendance at regularly scheduled weekly Phase 1 meetings (standard meetings) is required by the district attorney's office to satisfy conditions of juvenile offenders' diversion contracts. Attendance at Phase 2 and 3 standard meetings is optional. In any PFT phase, the PFT counselor may schedule additional supplementary meetings for various purposes, such as crisis management, coordination of intervention plans across social systems and health-care providers, and specialized skill training. Records of requests for and attendance at standard and supplementary meetings provide a behavioral index of a family's engagement in and satisfaction with PFT.

    Standard PFT Meetings and Tasks.   Standard, 50-minute, PFT meetings in Phases 1–3 include discovery, reunion, rules, and plan tasks during which the family assesses, formulates, troubleshoots, and revises plans to resolve youths' community, home, and personal problems. The family's plan represents a contingency contract (see Appendix B for plan form). The standard meeting always concludes with a wrap-up in which the PFT counselor summarizes progress to date and brings up for discussion any "unfinished business" (matters that family members raised earlier in the meeting that were not directly relevant to the task at hand). The approximate length of the discovery task is 10 minutes; the reunion task, 8 minutes; the rules task, 3 minutes; the plan task, 20 minutes; and the wrap-up, 9 minutes. In Phase 1, the initial standard meeting is scheduled for 90, rather than 50 minutes, providing extra time for counselor and family to get to know each other and for introduction and explanation of each task.

The Discovery Task.   The discovery task opens each PFT meeting and ritualizes a process of information exchange in which family members gain understanding of one another's efforts to change their behavior and accommodate to group goals. The discovery task is meant to encourage an interest in observable behavior as a basis for problem solving and an optimistic attitude about the possibilities for behavior change. During the discovery task, the family inspects data collected via telephone interview during the previous week (see Appendix C) and, as appropriate, compares these data with previous week's data. As relevant, the family and counselor formulate hypotheses based on these data regarding the need for a new plan or the need to revise an existing plan.

The Reunion Task.   The reunion task ritualizes a process of information exchange in which family members gain increasing understanding of one another's points of view. The weekly reunion is meant to encourage communication bouts in which each family member has uncensored opportunity to disclose events and feelings of personal importance and in which each other member has an opportunity to appreciate the speaker's unique qualities. In their initial Phase 1 reunion, family members each take turns as speaker mentioning "two things that make me special" and as listener. In subsequent reunions, listeners each mention "one good thing and one bad thing that happened to me since our last reunion." The PFT counselor assigns each family member a turn to talk so that across reunion tasks (over meetings) each family member will have an equal opportunity to talk first and last. During the talk turn, the speaker holds a timer, stops talking when the buzzer goes off, and hands the timer to the next speaker. The time allocated for the reunion task is divided equally among family members. At the end of the reunion task, family members attempt to recall the central meaning or message of other's statements, verify whether others' accurately understood their messages, and try to accurately restate others' messages that they did not earlier comprehend. In bigger families, each speaker will have less talk time than in smaller families, reflecting the reality of family life.

The Rules Task.   The rules task is meant to promote a familywide interest in equitable self-governance and an appreciation of the benefits of self-imposed behavioral constraints. During the rules task, the counselor introduces a prototype rule (e.g., "Parents reward kids for a good day without community problems") relevant to the family's current focus and uses open-ended questions to encourage discussion of the benefits of such a rule (e.g., "How would you benefit if your family had a rule like this?" "Maybe my mom would give me some of the stuff I want." "Maybe

I could get a good night's sleep and not worry about hearing from the police again.") At the end of the rules task, the counselor typically makes a linking statement that connects the benefits of the general rule for good days (e.g., in the community) to the upcoming plan task during which the family will construct their version of this general rule.

The Plan Task. The plan task is meant to increase family members' beliefs in their abilities to cope prosocially with family problems, albeit with the help of the PFT counselor. The plan task engages the family in formulating, troubleshooting, and revising realistic plans, or contingency contracts, to solve current family problems. The PFT counselor typically structures the plan task via open-ended questions designed to enable family members to formulate elements of a plan relevant to their current focus (e.g., community problems) (see Appendices A and B). The counselor often uses a series of leading questions to elicit self-motivational and self-advising responses. For example, a counselor might use an open-ended question ("What can you do when it has not been a good day?") to elicit from a parent the statement that, "Well, I can just say 'tomorrow is another day' and leave it at that." The counselor's highly structured although open-ended questions are purposefully designed to avoid off-track past-oriented attributions of blame and guilt or quasi-insightful explorations of the underlying reasons why other family members are so inadequate (e.g., "If only I had been able to stay home with John when he was an infant, maybe John would be a more responsible son.") Instead, the counselor's open-ended questions are designed to keep family members engaged in the problem-solving process, figuring out mutually acceptable means of overcoming obstacles to mutual success.

Supplementary PFT Meetings

Supplementary PFT meetings are scheduled in addition to (but not as replacements for) standard PFT meetings. PFT counselors schedule these meetings at the request of family members or on their own initiative for several purposes: (a) Enable the family to cope with a new crisis (e.g., arrest of a younger sibling) without interrupting progress in PFT; (b) Enable the family to cope with a chronic problem (e.g., family violence) without interrupting progress in PFT; (c) Coordinate an intervention plan (e.g., regarding community problems) across school, juvenile-justice, and mental-health systems; (d) Provide specialized skill training to a family member who is involved in PFT (e.g., relaxation training to mother) that will heighten the family's chances for success in PFT; and, (e) Coordinate PFT with treatment of a family member not engaged in PFT (e.g., father serving a prison sentence for prior sexual abuse of his now delinquent daughter).

SOCIALLY SIGNIFICANT RESULTS

Two strategies are used to insure that as a direct result of PFT each family achieves socially significant short- and long-term results that would be deemed satisfactory by family members, by teachers and police, and by experienced clinicians. First, each family begins PFT by confronting what they have identified as their most challenging problem type (community, home, or personal). Second, each family persists in focusing on their highest priority problems until the trend of telephone data show an evident improvement. The usual criterion for initial success and phase change is three more good days (with no evidence of problems that day) per week over baseline. When criterion is reached, the family expands their plan to include a focus on their second (and later their third) highest priority problems. Although every family addresses community, home, and personal problems during PFT, the order of focus on problems varies between families. When referral has been prompted by a daughter's delinquency, the family would focus on community problems first and would move on to deal with home and personal problems only after achieving evident success in increasing the number of "good days" per week without community problems on the part of the index high-risk youth or siblings. When referral has been prompted by a son's delinquency, and evidence emerged during intake of suicidal thoughts, threats, and attempts, the family would begin by focusing on personal problems (i.e., suicidal affect, cognitions, and behavior) and expand their plan to deal with community problems only after achieving success in increasing the number of good days per week without personal problems. When the index high-risk youth is an only child and her community problems are relatively mild and infrequent, the family might make speedy progress in resolving community, home, and personal problems within Phase 1 of intervention. When the index high-risk youth and his five siblings all have severe and frequent community problems, it may take the family all of Phase 1 to reach criterion for community problems.

RELAPSE PREVENTION

Classic PT assumes that a brief course of intervention will suffice for all families. However, there is good reason to believe that only a small segment of highly motivated and not very troubled families will derive lasting benefits from brief intervention. Most families will derive some benefits during a brief course of intervention (Phase 1) but will quickly relapse once support is withdrawn for maintenance of newly acquired skills and development of still needed skills. Therefore, at intake to PFT, families are given a rationale and signed up for a rich meeting schedule in Phase 1 and an increasingly thinner meeting schedule in Phase 2 and 3. The rationale prepares families for a honeymoon effect in Phase 1 and for predictable problems in maintaining gains and avoiding relapse in Phases 2 and 3. While families are expected to commit themselves to weekly attendance in Phase 1, attendance in Phases 2 and 3 is purely voluntary and is used as an index of treatment engagement and satisfaction. The three mock families described here are composites of families of juvenile offenders in Boulder County, Colorado, who have contracted with the Juvenile Diversion Program to participate in treatment for up to six months in order to avoid sentencing by a judge. Their contracts would be revoked and they would be subject to sentencing if they received no treatment of any kind for six months from the date of the arrest (during Phases 1 and 2 of PFT). They are, therefore, not obliged to participate in Phase 3 check-ups. We use data about a family's attendance at meetings in Phases 1 to 3 to gauge the intensity and duration of intervention they received and to test for a dose-response relationship. As described in the examples that follow, PFT's multiple phases are adequate for the needs of families of varying size, problem severity, and chronicity.

ADHERENCE TO PROTOCOL

The PFT manual specifies the procedures that define the intervention. Evidence that counselors are adhering to the manual is crucial. If there is evidence of change but not of adherence, change cannot be attributed to intervention but might be due to the quality of counselor-client relationship or to other unknown variables. If there is no evidence of change or of adherence, lack of change cannot be attributed to intervention since the counselor did not adhere to protocol. After each meeting, the counselor completes a fidelity checklist (see Appendix A) describing adherence to prescribed procedures and communication style. A trained observer completes the same checklist after watching a videotape of the meeting. Discrepancies between checklist data and the PFT manual are discussed in weekly supervision.

INTERNAL VALIDITY OF RESULTS

Regardless of variations between families in the way problems are defined, the order in which problems are confronted, or the time taken to reach criterion with the highest-priority problem, all families move through PFT in a multiple-baseline, single-case experimental design (within family, across problems). The multiple-baseline design shown in Figures 16.2, 16.4, and 16.5 can offer credible evidence of internal validity, such that improvement is clearly attributable to PFT plans (see Appendix B) rather than to the relationship between PFT counselor and family or to any extraneous threats to internal validity such as maturation or regression to the mean (see also Blechman & Hall 1997). The multiple-baseline design can either insure that intervention is effective, or, when intervention is ineffective, this design allows fine-tuning and changes of course until intervention is effective. Consistent with human-research requirements, families have the right to withdraw from intervention at any time.

EXAMPLE 1: SUCCESS IN PHASE 1

The Smith family illustrates core elements in PFT and the most rapid pattern of progress through PFT. Jane Smith is a 35-year-old single mother; 12-year-old John Smith is her only child. The Smiths entered PFT as an alternative to sentencing by a judge after John was arrested for his first offense, stealing a car with three older boys. Like all families wishing to qualify for an alternative to sentencing, the Smiths took part in a standardized assessment that was scheduled for repetition at the 6-month, 1-year, and 2-year anniversaries of John's arrest. Conducted by means of structured interview, the assessment battery included measures of parent depression (BDI, Beck, Ward, Mendelson, Mock, & Erbaugh, 1961), child externalizing and internalizing behavior problems (CBCL, Achenbach, 1991), and child substance use (Oetting, 1993).

Problem Definition and Weekly Data Collection

At intake, the Smiths defined community problems as any misconduct reports about John by police, neighbors, or teachers to Jane, they defined home problems as any noncompliance with Jane's requests; and, they considered John's self-reported anxiety attacks, triggered by fears that his mother would die, to be personal problems. Immediately after intake, in each of the next 14 weeks, and just before the 6-month, 1-year, and 2-year check-up meetings, the Smiths received regularly scheduled weekly phone calls during which they reported (Figure 16.2) the daily frequency of community, home, and personal problems (as defined by them). During the telephone interview (Figure 16.3), the Smiths also rated average mood for that week [1 (terrible) to 10 (delighted)] (Andrews & Withey, 1976), optimism about the future [1 (not at all optimistic) to 10 (very optimistic)], and satisfaction with intervention [1 (not at all satisfied) to 10 (very satisfied)].

Baseline Problem Data

As the top graph in Figure 16.2 shows, in three weeks of baseline (Weeks 1–3), there was no spontaneous improvement in community, home, or personal problems, ruling out the possibility that the Smiths' behavior

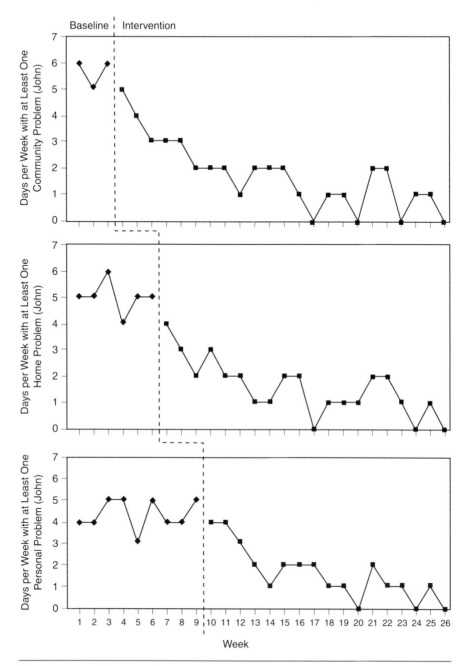

Figure 16.2 Number of Days per Week That John Smith Had at Least One Community, Home, or Personal Problem as Reported by His Mother, Jane, in Telephone Interviews during Phase 1 (Weeks 1–14) and Phase 2 (Weeks 15–26).

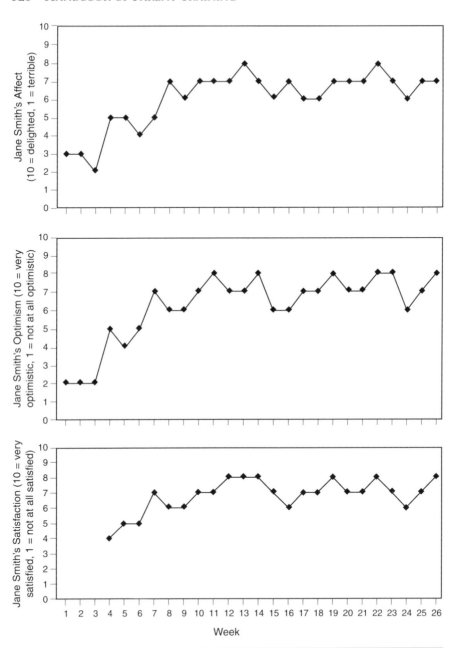

Figure 16.3 Jane Smith's Reports of Affect, Optimism, and Satisfaction with Intervention in Telephone Interviews during Phase 1 (Weeks 1–14) and Phase 2 (Weeks 15–26). Satisfaction Is Not Assessed Prior to the First PFT Standard Meeting.

might change as a result of starting treatment and establishing a trusting relationship with clinical staff. Examination of satisfaction ratings in Figure 16.3 shows that the process of baseline data collection (Weeks 1–3) was, as expected, not accompanied by any improvement in mood, optimism, or satisfaction.

Beginning PFT

In Week 4, after three weeks' of baseline data collection via telephone interview, the Smiths met with the PFT counselor for the first time. After introducing herself, the counselor spent about 10 minutes establishing a connection with the family, by (a) clarifying information that the Smiths had already provided to the intake interviewer and the telephone interviewer and using open-ended questions to encourage the Smiths to state their priorities for intervention; (b) explaining the overall purpose of PFT and the counselor's responsibility (i.e., help the Smiths resolve community, home, and personal problems); (c) clarifying the family's role in PFT (i.e., on-time attendance at all meetings, honesty, openness to change, consideration for others' feelings, and most important, willingness to solve problems in ways that lead to long-term benefits for self and others); (d) describing the PFT tasks (discovery, reunion, rules, plan, and wrap-up) that would enable the Smiths to solve current and future community, home, and personal problems; and (e) explaining the three phases of PFT including the check-up meetings in Phases 2 and 3. The counselor explained that the Smiths would encounter the same five tasks in each PFT meeting. By Week 14, the Smiths would become so used to these tasks that they would become familiar family rituals and part of their daily routines at home. In the next 40 minutes of the first (Week 4) PFT meeting, the counselor guided the Smiths through the five PFT tasks.

The Discovery Task: What's Happening with Problem Behavior in Our Family?   In their first discovery task, the Smiths looked at graphs of baseline data for community, home, and personal problems (Figure 16.2), agreed that one more good day each week (free from community problems) was a reasonable goal and that it would be time to address home problems once the number of good days per week was three more than in the last baseline week. Thus, the Smiths would move on to address home problems following a week with three good days free from any community problems. Using open-ended questions, the counselor enabled John Smith to articulate why the family was working to reduce reports to mother (even if inaccurate) of community problems and to reduce mother's reports to the telephone interviewer (even if inaccurate) of problem behavior (i.e., "Because the reason I'm here is that the police think I'm always getting in trouble. Because if my mom thinks I have fewer problems with the police, she'll hassle me less and get off my case.") At the end of the discovery task, the counselor made a linking statement that connected the benefits of accurate knowledge about problem behavior and awareness of the variability of problem behavior to the upcoming plan task.

The Reunion Task: What Are the Different Points of View of Members of Our Family?   In their first reunion task, mother mentioned that what made her special "is my hard work. I work a full-time job and I spend all my free time taking care of my house and trying to be a good mother to my son." John said, "I'm special because I'm the only one in my class that doesn't do drugs. I could get any stuff I wanted, but I don't." While one person spoke the other took a turn as a listener trying to understand and remember what the speaker had said. At the end of the reunion task, the counselor used open-ended questions and descriptive praise to encourage an interest in and an appreciation of one another's unique point of view and thoughtful behavior during the reunion (e.g., listening without interruption; remembering accurately the other's statements).

The Plan Task.   When introducing the family to their first plan task, the counselor asked, "John, remind me, what have you and your mom agreed is a good day for community problems?" ("A day without any calls from the police.") "Mom, when will you decide that this has been a good day?" ("Six P.M. would be a good time. I'm home from work at five, and by six I know what's been happening.") "Now is the time for us to put together a reward menu with rewards that you, John, would like to earn at the end of a good day and at the end of a good week. What are your ideas?" "Mom, what are your ideas?" "You've got a menu that you both find acceptable and you understand that John gets choices from the menu only at the end of a good day. Now, Mom, what would be a good thing for you to do when it hasn't been such a good day?" By the end of the plan task, the counselor was able to clarify and put in writing terms of an agreement acceptable to John and mom. The Smiths took home their copy of the plan together with a chart that enabled them to keep track of good days and earned rewards.

The Wrap-Up Task.   The approximately 10-minute wrap-up provides a time for family members to discuss matters other than the current focus of intervention. Throughout the Week 4 meeting, when the Smiths brought up other matters (e.g., mother's curiosity about the benefits of military school as an alternative to PFT), the counselor suggested that these would be wonderful topics for discussion during the wrap-up. The counselor opened the wrap-up by a linking statement that restated the progress the family had made during the preceding plan task. She then summarized mother's question about military school and used open-ended questions to help mother clarify the costs and benefits of military school versus PFT. She was able to motivate mother for PFT (and to remotivate her in subsequent wrap-ups) by asking, "How does your son feel about you right now?" ("He's very angry at me. I think he hates me.") "How would you like your son to feel about you?" ("I want him to feel as much love for me as I do for him, even when I'm angry at him.") "How much contact would you like to have with your son when he's married and has his own children, your grandchildren?" ("I'd like to see him and his wife and my grandchildren a whole lot.") "Now that your son is having a lot of problems, if you send him off to military school rather than working things through with him at home, how do you think he'll feel about you? How much contact will he want to have with you when he's older?" ("I get it. So military school might help with behavior problems and might make me feel better right now, but in the long run it might hurt my relationship with my son.")

Troubleshooting and Modifying Plans.   In Weeks 5 and 6, during the discovery task, the counselor reviewed with the Smiths the results of their community-problem plan. During the plan task, they made modifications in the community plan to improve the plan's success. The counselor began the plan task each time with a linking statement that recalled what the Smiths had said earlier during the discovery task about reasons why some days were good days, and some days were not. The counselor then used open-ended questions to solicit relevant modifications from John and his mother that would make the plan easier to implement and more effective. Since mom had been giving some rewards noncontingently, she agreed to give them out only when John earned them. Since community complaints often did not surface until days after the reported incident, mom and John agreed that the day when mom received a problem report would be considered "not a good day." In weeks following formulation of home- and personal-problem plans (e.g., Weeks 8–9, 11–12), plans were revised in a similar fashion.

Monitoring and Expanding Plans.   The plan formulated in the Week 4 meeting targeted only community problems. Weekly telephone reports tracked changes in community problem behavior that were observed and discussed in the Week 5 and 6 discovery tasks. For home and personal problems, no intervention plans were instituted and baseline data collection via telephone continued until improvement in community problems was evident. As Figure 16.2 shows, following Week 4 institution of the Smiths' community plan, there was a gradual improvement in community problems (one more good day per week during the next three weeks). By Week 7, the Smiths were ready to expand their plan to include home problems. At this point, John earned rewards for a day without community or home problems. Continued improvement in community problems and the onset of improvement in home problems is evident in Figure 16.2. By Week 10, the Smiths expanded their plan to include community, home, and personal problems. At this point, John earned rewards for good days free from any of these three types of problems. As Figure 16.2 shows, the Smiths' institution of their third and most comprehensive plan was followed by continued improvement in community and home problems and the onset of success with personal problems and by maintenance of improvement in post-intervention phases. Moreover, as Figure 16.3 shows, improvements in mother's mood, optimism about the future, and satisfaction with life paralleled improvements in her son's behavior. Had mother's mood, for example, not improved by Week 14, the counselor would have used open-ended questions to clarify what steps mother could take to feel better in order to insure that maternal depression does not interfere with long-term maintenance and generalization of the gains achieved during intervention. A similar strategy would have been pursued given low levels of optimism or satisfaction despite improvement in child behavior problems.

Measuring Clinically Significant Improvement in Post-Intervention Phases

Progress of the sort the Smiths achieved with self-reported frequencies of community, home, and personal problems is crucial but insufficient. At intake, mother rated John in the deviant range for externalizing behavior problems on the Child Behavior Checklist (CBCL) (Achenbach, 1991). If intervention achieved clinically significant improvement, John's CBCL externalizing score would have to drop into the normal range and stay there and his internalizing score would have to remain in the normal range as it was at intake. By the 6-month anniversary of John's arrest, 2 months after Week 14 of intervention, clinically significant improvements on CBCL externalizing behavior problems (without increases in internalizing problems) were evident. At 1- and 2-year check-ups, clinically significant improvement was maintained.

Clinical Decision Making

Only because of continuous data collection in a multiple-baseline design is it possible to be certain that improvement in behavior problems is definitely attributable to PFT and not to extratherapy events such as remoralization (Frank & Frank, 1991). Without such certainty, a clinician might have downplayed the importance of adherence to community, home, and personal plans that, as the data show, accounted for significant reductions in behavior problems. Or, a clinician might have agreed with mother's initial impulse to send her son away to military school rather than attempt to help him change with support from the family. While successful resolution of problems was achieved in PFT Phase 1, longitudinal assessment in Phases 2 and 3 insured that success was maintained and that no new problems emerged.

EXAMPLE 2: GRADUAL SUCCESS ACROSS PHASES 1 TO 3

The Johnson family illustrates how a large family and a history of criminal behavior among parents and siblings can delay the course of improvement in community problems and necessitate much more than brief Phase 1 intervention.

The Johnson family is a blended family with two parents and four of their six children living at home, ranging in age from 14-year-old Sheila (mother's child from a previous marriage) to 20-year-old Bill (father's child from a previous relationship). Father's 30-year-old son is in jail on a charge of armed robbery. The Johnsons entered PFT after Sheila's third arrest for shoplifting. During intake, Sheila reported sexual abuse by an uncle who was subsequently required by the court to receive treatment and to no longer visit the Johnson's home or to see Sheila elsewhere except when supervised by both parents. Police records indicated that Bill had been arrested six times since age 9 and that both parents and two other siblings had criminal records. As Figure 16.4 shows, the Johnsons instituted a community plan in Week 4 for all four children and worked on fine-tuning this plan until Week 14. By Week 14, there was some improvement in all siblings' community, home, and personal problems but during this time the family never met criterion for reduction of all children's community problems. For this reason, the Johnsons did not formulate home and personal problem plans during Phase 1. The family attended Phase 2 and Phase 3 check-ups to fine tune the community problems plan for all siblings and achieved and maintained criterion for this plan by the 12-month anniversary of Sheila's arrest, with continued maintenance at subsequent Phase 3 check-ups.

Clinical Decision Making

Without continuous data collection in a multiple-baseline design, slow but steady improvement in community problems might never have been noticed or might have been attributed mistakenly to extratherapy events (such as a change in police standards for arrests of juveniles). Lacking this information, a clinician might have despaired of involving the family in Sheila's treatment and might, instead, have considered a foster-family or institutional placement for her. For this family, a brief intervention in Phase 1 was insufficient; meetings in Phases 2 and 3 and longitudinal follow-ups were essential for clinically significant progress.

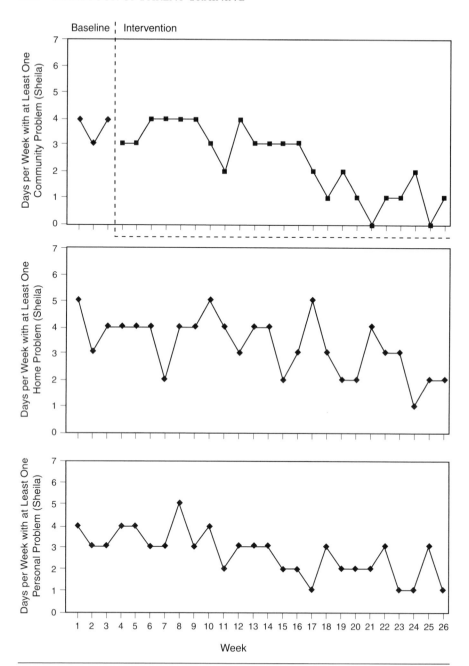

Figure 16.4 Number of Days per Week That Sheila Johnson Had at Least One Community, Home, or Personal Problem as Reported by Her Father, Harry, in Weekly Telephone Interviews during Phase 1 (Weeks 1–14) and Phase 2 (Weeks 15–26).

The Robinson family illustrates how severe maternal depression can aggravate children's home problems despite a plan that successfully reduces community problems.

The Robinson family includes a single mother, who has recently been hospitalized for her third episode of major depressive disorder, her 10-year-old daughter Pamela, and her 16-year-old son Frankie. The Robinsons entered PFT after Frankie's arrest for assaulting a classmate with a knife. Last year, Frankie was expelled from school after threatening his teacher with a knife. At home, Frankie has frequent, violent temper tantrums and on several occasions has assaulted and beat up his sister and threatened his mother with a knife. Pamela has recently been expelled from school for using threats of violence to extort money from younger children. As Figure 16.5 shows, the Robinsons instituted a community plan for Frankie and Pamela in Week 4; by Week 8 there was evident reduction in community problems for both siblings. In Week 9, a plan for community and home problems was introduced. By Week 14, both siblings' community problems were evidently improved, but home problems were only slightly better. At the first Phase 2 check-up (Week 18), examination of telephone interview data indicated that a decrement in mother's self-reported mood reliably preceded increases in siblings' home problems. In Week 19, the counselor taught mother some simple relaxation and meditation techniques for use two times a day for 20 minutes and at the first sign of worsening mood. With no alteration of the community and home plan, a pattern of gradual improvement in mother's mood and in siblings' community and home problems emerged across Phases 2 and 3. Improvement in community and home problems appeared to generalize to siblings' personal problems (e.g., Frankie's bedwetting, Pamela's nailbiting). Mother's self-reported optimism about the future and satisfaction with intervention was evidently better at the 6-month anniversary of Frankie's arrest.

Clinical Decision Making

Without continuous data collection in a multiple-baseline design regarding children's behavior problems and mother's mood, improvement in community problems might have been overshadowed by worsening home problems. Similarly, the covariation between mother's mood and increased home problems might never have been noticed and used to modify intervention. Lacking information about the interdependence of children's home problems and mother's mood, both Frankie and his mother might have been referred for pharmacotherapy. Brief intervention in Phase 1 was insufficient for this family; inclusion of Phases 2 and 3 and

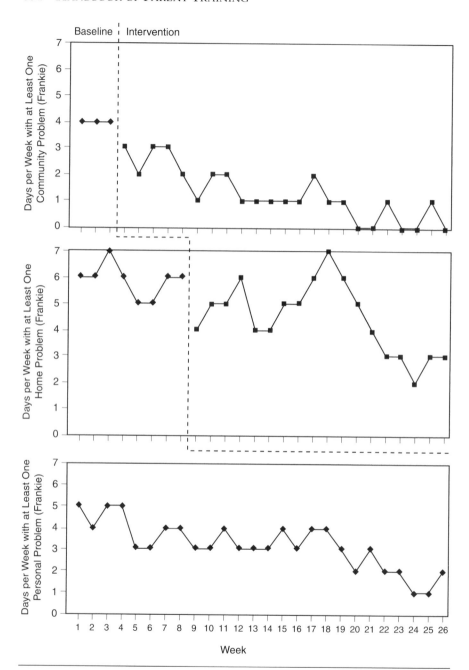

Figure 16.5 Number of Days per Week That Frankie Robinson Had at Least One Community, Home, or Personal Problem as Reported by His Mother, Susan, in Weekly Telephone Interviews during Phase 1 (Weeks 1–14) and Phase 2 (Weeks 15–26).

of longitudinal data collection was essential for clinically significant progress.

PFT's CHECK-UP MODEL

Consistent with the time limitations and economic constraints of managed care, PFT includes three phases. In Phase 1, 14 weekly meetings focus on achieving improvement, at the very least, in community problems. Some families, like the Smiths, are able to address community, home, and personal problems in Phase 1. In Phase 2, 3 monthly check-up meetings focus on continuing previously achieved improvement and expanding improvement to new problems using the same tasks included in Phase 2 meetings. Without Phase 2, families like the Johnsons and the Robinsons who have serious and long-standing problems among many family members would not be able to achieve and maintain reasonable outcomes. In Phase 3, 4 biannual check-ups focus on continued maintenance and expansion of improvement using the same tasks included in Phase 1 meetings. Weekly telephone data collection in a multiple-baseline design during Phase 1 allows each family to progress through intervention at their own pace as illustrated by the Smith, Johnson, and Robinson families in Figures 16.2, 16.4, and 16.5. Weekly telephone data collection in Phase 2 provides information needed to troubleshoot plans at Phase 2 monthly check-ups. Bimonthly telephone data collection in Phase 3 protects against relapse and prepares for productive biannual Phase 3 check-ups.

CONCLUSIONS

Forehand and Kotchik (1996) have described how innovative approaches to behavioral family therapy have evolved from classic PT to benefit otherwise ill-served groups (e.g., children of maritally distressed parents). There is an obvious need to adapt classic PT to suit high-risk adolescents. Serketich and Dumas (1996) in a meta-analysis of 117 studies on the outcome of classic PT concluded that results support the short-term effectiveness of PT to modify young (preschool and elementary school) children's antisocial behavior at home and school, and to improve parental adjustment. Ruma, Burke, and Thompson (1996) examined archival data from 304 mothers who attended group PT and tested for age effects on statistical and clinical significance of improvements in child behavior problems following program participation. Adolescents began intervention with significantly more severe behavior problems than younger children and adolescents had a significantly lower recovery rate following intervention than younger children.

Prosocial Family Therapy (PFT) is designed specifically for high-risk adolescents who, together with other family members, currently rely on maladaptive antisocial coping strategies that hurt themselves and others (Pulkkinen, 1996; Magura & Laudet, 1996). PFT retains the core strengths of classic PT including manualization; use of a single-case experimental design to document internal validity; pinpointing of problems by family members; use of daily reports of problem frequency to gauge the success of intervention plans; and, pursuit of socially significant short- and long-term results. PFT goes beyond classic PT by manualizing the mode of communication between counselors and families; including all children (not just the index youth) in intervention plans; including three phases in intervention to assure maintenance over at least two follow-up years; including crisis management procedures to accommodate the needs of severely distressed families with long-standing, familywide problems; and, using data about family members' moods, optimism, and satisfaction with intervention to detect potential obstacles to progress.

In a 1984 review of the parent-training discipline, Don Baer asked "whether there is a larger context within which parent training is the only logical thing to do on as wide a scale as we can do it" and pointed out that a context I called "competence" (Blechman, 1984) might have just that function. In the intervening years, I have defined family competence as a context that promotes prosocial coping with emotional, social, and cognitive challenges. In this chapter, I have described how Prosocial Family Therapy may enable antisocial youth and their families to cope with life's adversities in a moral context, doing well by doing good.

Appendix A
PFT Counselor Post-Session Checklist

PFT Counselor Name: _____ Date: _____

Client Family Name: _____ Time: _____

PFT Session Number: _____

#		Yes	No	PC	DKNA
1	Were required attendees (referred juvenile & CBCL parent) on time?				
2	**Discovery Task:** Was the Discovery Task conducted?				
3	Did you clarify linkage & purposes of the Discovery Task?				
4	Did you review each graph with the entire family?				
5	Did you confirm that family members understood the data review?				
6	Did you confirm that family members understood the need to introduce a new plan?				
7	Did you confirm that family members understood the need to revise an existing plan?				
8	Did the family spend at least 10 minutes on the Discovery Task?				
9	**Reunion Task:** Was the Reunion Task conducted?				
10	Did you clarify linkage of the Reunion Task?				
11	Did you clarify the purposes and rules of the Reunion Task?				
12	Did you troubleshoot typical problems before the Reunion Task?				
13	Did family members make self-motivational statements before the Reunion Task?				
14	Did the family follow the rules for the Reunion Task?				
15	Did all family members get a chance to say one good and one bad thing that happened in the past week within their allotted time?				
16	Did you encourage accurate recall of at least one statement made by each family member, and did you encourage checking with others to determine if recall was accurate?				
17	Did family members make self-rewarding statements following Reunion?				
18	**Family Rules Task:** Was the Family Rules Task conducted?				
19	Did you clarify linkage and purposes of the Family Rules Task?				
20	Did you review all previously discussed family rules?				
21	Did you introduce a new family rule?				
22	**Plan Task:** Was the Plan Task conducted?				
23	Did you confirm linkage and purposes of the Plan Task?				

(continued)

#		Yes	No	PC	DKNA
24	Consistent with the data, did the family create a new community plan?				
25	Consistent with the data, did the family revise an existing community plan?				
26	Consistent with the data, did the family create a new home plan?				
27	Consistent with the data, did the family revise an existing home plan?				
28	Consistent with the data, did the family create a new personal plan?				
29	Consistent with the data, did the family revise an existing personal plan?				
30	Clarified with all family members 1 definition of a good day for all siblings?				
31	Did you clarify which type/s of problem/s this good day deals with?				
32	Did you clarify with all family members by whom and when a good day is determined?				
33	Did you clarify with all family members one individual reward menu for daily success applicable to all siblings?				
34	Did you clarify with all family members one group reward menu for weekly success applicable to all siblings?				
35	Did you clarify that reward menu choices are available only if a good day?				
36	Did you clarify how parents will respond to the absence of a good day?				
37	Did you clarify that added punishment for the absence of a good day is not to be instituted?				
38	Did you review natural punishments of no good day?				
39	Did you troubleshoot the plan with all family members?				
40	Did the family make self-motivational statements about the plan?				
41	Did you fill out a Family Plan form, attach Family Plan Progress Report forms, and give a copy to the family (and place a copy in the client file)?				
42	**Wrap-up:** Was Wrap-up conducted?				
43	Is follow-up needed by you or others re: Wrap-up content? (describe on reverse)				
44	Did you schedule a crisis management session? (why/when on reverse)				
45	Did you end the session on an optimistic note?				

Write additional comments on attached sheets. Include: When did you have difficulty using prosocial communication (PC)? and What will you do next time you encounter this problem?

Appendix B
PFT Family Plan

Family's name: _____   Date plan created/modified: _____

Relating to (check one): ____ community problems   ____ community & home problems
                         ____ community, home, & personal problems

Definition of a good day:

_____

What time every day is a good day declared:

_____

Who must be present for this to happen:

_____

What happens if it is a good day for one kid?

_____

What happens if five out of seven days are good days for all kids?

_____

Reward Menu (for Daily Rewards)

Kid's Name	Reward	Who Gives It?	When Given?

Group Reward Menu (for Weekly Group Rewards for All Kids)

Reward	Who Gives It?	When Given?

Appendix C
PFT Weekly Telephone Interview Data Sheet Form

Parent targeted for interview (include last name): _____

Juvenile referred for counseling (include last name): _____

Siblings' names: _____

Staff member name: _____ Date: _____ Time: _____

#	Before Asking Questions	Yes	No	DKNA
1	Did you greet the family member in a cordial way?			
2	Did you indicate who you were and why you were calling (i.e., "I am _____. I am calling on behalf of the PAL Center at the University of Colorado to ask you a few questions as part of the PFT family counseling you are receiving.")?			
3	Did you ask to speak to the parent of the client who was targeted for the interview?			
4	Did you explain the directions to the family member before asking any questions (i.e., "Please refer to the forms provided by the PAL Center when I ask for the answers to questions for each of your kids.")?			
	Questions for Parent			
5	"Could you please tell me how many days in the last week _____ [referred youth] was reported to have community problems? If so, what kind of problems, which days, with who?"			
6	"Could you please tell me how many days in the last week _____ [referred youth] was in trouble at home? If so, what kind of problems, which days, with who?"			
7	"Could you please tell me how many days in the last week _____ [referred youth] had personal problems? If so, what kind of problems, which days?"			
8	"Could you please tell me how many days in the last week _____ [name of sibling] was reported to have community problems? If so, what kind of problems, which days, with who?"			

	Questions for Parent	
9	"Could you please tell me how many days in the last week [name of sibling] was in trouble at home? If so, what kind of problems, which days, with who?"	
10	"Could you please tell me how many days in the last week [name of sibling] has had personal problems? If so, what kind of problems, which days?"	
11	"Could you please tell me how many days in the last week [name of sibling] was reported to have community problems? If so, what kind of problems, which days, with who?"	
12	"Could you please tell me how many days in the last week [name of sibling] was in trouble at home? If so, what kind of problems, which days, with who?"	
13	"Could you please tell me how many days in the last week [name of sibling] has had personal problems? If so, what kind of problems, which days?"	
	NOTE: If more space is required due to additional siblings, use additional forms as needed & staple them to this form.	

Calculate number of days with no community problems with referred child: _____

Calculate number of days with no home problems with referred child: _____

Calculate number of days with no personal problems with referred child: _____

14	"Regarding community problems, [referred youth] had _____ good days this week. Is this correct?"	
15	"Regarding home problems, [referred youth] had _____ good days this week. Is this correct?"	
16	"Regarding personal problems, [referred youth] had _____ good days this week. Is this correct?"	
17	"On a scale from 1 to 10, 1 being 'terrible' and 10 being 'delighted,' how do you feel about your emotional well-being?"	

(continued)

	Questions for Parent	
18	"On a scale from 1 to 10, 10 being very optimistic, how optimistic are you that PFT counseling is, or will be, helping your family?"	
19	"Has your family begun making family plans in PFT sessions?"	
20	IF YES TO 19: "On a scale from 1 to 10, 10 being very well, how well do you think that your family plans are helping your family?"	
21	IF YES TO 19: "What problems with the plan should I tell your counselor about?"	
22	Family member thanked? [yes/no:]	
23	Next PFT session date & time:	
24	Next telephone interview date & time:	
	Questions for Referred Youth (if present)	
25	"Regarding community problems, [Mom/Dad] reported that you had good days this week. Is that correct?"	
26	IF NO TO 25: "Would you please explain?"	
27	"Regarding home problems, [Mom/Dad] reported that you had good days this week. Is that correct?"	
28	IF NO TO 27: "Would you please explain?"	
29	"Regarding personal problems, [Mom/Dad] reported that you had good days this week. Is that correct?"	
30	IF NO TO 29: "Would you please explain?"	
31	IF YES TO 19: "Is there anything you want me to tell your counselor?"	

Write additional comments on the bottom or back of this form, or attach additional sheets.

REFERENCES

Achenbach, T. M. (1991). *Manual for the Child Behavior Checklist/4-18 and 1991 profile.* Burlington: University of Vermont Press.

Achenbach, T. M., Howell, C. T., McConaughy, S. H., & Stanger, C. (1995). Six-year predictors of problems in a national sample of children and youth: II. Signs of disturbance. *Journal of the American Academy of Child and Adolescent Psychiatry, 34,* 488–498.

Akers, R. L. (1977). *Deviant behavior: A social learning perspective.* Belmont, CA: Wadsworth.

Aloise-Young, P. A., Graham, J. W., & Hansen, W. B. (1994). Peer influence on smoking initiation during early adolescence: A comparison of group members and group outsiders. *Journal of Applied Psychology, 79,* 281–287.

Andrews, F. M., & Withey, S. B. (1976). *Social indicators of America's perceptions of life quality.* New York: Plenum Press.

Aseltine, R. H. (1995). A reconsideration of parental and peer influences on adolescent deviance. *Journal of Health and Social Behavior, 36,* 103–121.

Baer, D. M. (1984). Future directions?: Or, is it useful to ask, "Where did we go wrong?" before we go? In R. F. Dangel & R. A. Polster (Eds.), *Parent training: Foundations of research and practice* (pp. 547–556). New York: Guilford Press.

Ball, S. A., Carroll, K. M., & Rounsaville, B. J. (1994). Sensation seeking, substance abuse, and psychopathology in treatment-seeking and community cocaine abusers. *Journal of Consulting and Clinical Psychology, 62,* 1053–1057.

Barlow, D. H. (1994). Psychological interventions in the era of managed competition. *Clinical Psychology: Science and Practice, 1,* 109–122.

Beck, A. T., Ward, C. H., Mendelson, M., Mock, J., & Erbaugh, J. (1961). An inventory for measuring depression. *Archives of General Psychiatry, 4,* 561–571.

Blackson, T. C., Tarter, R. E., Loeber, R., Ammerman, R. T., & Windle, M. (1996). The influence of paternal substance abuse and difficult temperament in fathers and sons on son's disengagement from family to deviant peers. *Journal of Youth and Adolescence, 25,* 389–411.

Blechman, E. A. (1974). A new way to teach contracting: The family contract game. *Psychotherapy, 11,* 294.

Blechman, E. A. (1981). Toward comprehensive behavioral family intervention: An algorithm for matching families and interventions. *Behavior Modification, 5,* 221–236.

Blechman, E. A. (1984). Competent parents, competent children: Behavioral objectives of parent training. In R. F. Dangel & R. A. Polster (Eds.), *Parent training: Foundations of research and practice* (pp. 34–66). New York: Guilford Press.

Blechman, E. A. (1985). *Solving child behavior problems: At home and at school.* Champaign, IL: Research Press.

Blechman, E. A. (1990). A new look at emotions and the family: A model of effective family communication. In E. A. Blechman (Ed.), *Emotions and the family: For better or for worse* (pp. 201–224). New York: Erlbaum.

Blechman, E. A. (1991). Effective communication: Enabling the multi-problem family to change. In P. Cowan & M. Hetherington (Eds.), *Advances in family research: II. Family transitions* (pp. 219–246). New York: Erlbaum.

Blechman, E. A. (1996). Coping, competency, and aggression prevention: Part 2. Universal, school-based prevention. *Applied and Preventive Psychology, 5,* 19–35.

Blechman, E. A., Budd, K. S., Christopherson, E. R., Syzkula, S., Wahler, R., Embry, H., Kogan, K., O'Leary, K. D., & Riner, L. S. (1981). Engagement in behavioral family therapy. *Behavior Therapy, 12,* 461–472.

Blechman, E. A., & Culhane, S. E. (1993). Early adolescence and the development of aggression, depression, coping, and competence. *Journal of Early Adolescence, 13,* 361–382.

Blechman, E. A., Dumas, J. E., & Prinz, R. J. (1994). Prosocial coping by youth exposed to violence. *Journal of Child and Adolescent Group Therapy, 4,* 205–227.

Blechman, E. A., & Hall, K. (1997). *Prosocial family therapy: A manualized prevention intervention for juvenile offenders.* Unpublished manuscript, University of Colorado at Boulder.

Blechman, E. A., & McEnroe, M. J. (1985). Effective family problem solving. *Child Development, 56,* 429–437.

Blechman, E. A., Prinz, R. J., & Dumas, J. E. (1995). Coping, competence, and aggression prevention: Part 1. Developmental model. *Applied and Preventive Psychology, 4,* 211–232.

Brewster, K. L. (1994). Race differences in sexual activity among adolescent women: The role of neighborhood characteristics. *American Sociological Review, 59,* 408–424.

Brook, J. S., Whiteman, M., Gordon, A. S., & Cohen, P. (1989). Changes in drug involvement: A longitudinal study of childhood and adolescent determinants. *Psychological Reports, 65,* 707–726.

Brunswick, A. F., Lewis, C. S., & Messeri, P. A. (1992). Drug use and stress: Testing a coping model in an urban African-American sample. *Journal of Community Psychology, 20,* 148–162.

Burton, D., Sussman, S., Hansen, W. B., Johnson, C. A., & Flay, B. R. (1989). Image attributions and smoking intentions among seventh grade students. *Journal of Applied Social Psychology, 19,* 656–664.

Castro, F. G., Maddahian, E., Newcomb, M. D., & Bentler, P. M. (1987). A multivariate model of the determinants of cigarette smoking among adolescents. *Journal of Health and Social Behavior, 28,* 273–289.

Catalano, R. F., Kosterman, R., Hawkins, J. D., Newcomb, M. D., & Abbott, R. D. (1996). Modeling the etiology of adolescent substance use: A test of the social development model. *Journal of Drug Issues, 26,* 429–455.

Cloninger, C. R. (1987). Neurogenetic adaptive mechanisms in alcoholism. *Science, 236,* 410–416.

Connell, J. P., Halpern-Felsher, B. L., Clifford, E., Crichlow, W., & Usinger, P. (1995). Hanging in there: Behavioral, psychological, and contextual factors affecting whether African-American adolescents stay in high school. *Journal of Adolescent Research, 10,* 41–63.

Dobkin, P. L., Tremblay, R. E., Masse, L. C., & Vitaro, F. (1995). Individual and peer characteristics in predicting boys' early onset of substance abuse: A seven-year longitudinal study. *Child Development, 66,* 1198–1214.

Dodge, K. A. (1993). Social-cognitive mechanisms in the development of conduct disorder and depression. *Annual Review of Psychology, 44,* 559–584.

Eliot, D., Huizinga, D., & Ageton, S. (1985). *Explaining delinquency and drug use.* Beverly Hills, CA: Sage.

Farrington, D. P., Gallagher, B., Morley, L., St. Ledger, R. J., & West, D. J. (1986). Unemployment, school leaving, and crime. *British Journal of Criminology, 26,* 335–356.

Felix-Ortiz, M., & Newcomb, M. D. (1992). Risk and protective factors for drug use among Latino and White adolescents. *Hispanic Journal of Behavioral Sciences, 14,* 291–309.

Felner, R. D., Brand, S., DuBois, D. L., Adan, A. M., Mulhall, P., & Evans, E. G. (1995). Socioeconomic disadvantage, proximal environmental experiences, and socioemotional and academic adjustment in early adolescence: Investigation of a mediated effects model. *Child Development, 66,* 774–792.

Fergusson, D. M., Horwood, L. J., & Lynskey, M. T. (1995). The stability of disruptive childhood behaviors. *Journal of Abnormal Child Psychology, 23,* 379–396.

Forehand, R., & Kotchik, B. A. (1996). Cultural diversity: A wake-up call for parent training. *Behavior Therapy, 27,* 187–206.

Forehand, R., & McMahon, R. (1981). *Helping the noncompliant child.* New York: Guilford Press.

Forehand, R., Sturgis, E. T., McMahon, R. J., Aguar, D., Green, K., Wells, K., & Breiner, J. (1979). Parent behavioral training to modify child noncompliance: Treatment generalization across time and from home to school. *Behavior Modification, 3,* 3–25.

Frank, J. D., & Frank, J. B. (1991). *Persuasion and healing: A comparative study of psychotherapy.* Baltimore: Johns Hopkins University Press.

Garbarino, J., & Sherman, D. (1980). High-risk neighborhoods and high-risk families: The human ecology of child maltreatment. *Child Development, 51,* 188–198.

Gottfredson, M. R., & Hirschi, T. (1990). *A general theory of crime.* Stanford, CA: Stanford University Press.

Graham, J. W., Marks, G., & Hansen, W. B. (1991). Social influence processes affecting adolescent substance use. *Journal of Applied Psychology, 76,* 291–298.

Grunberg, N. E., & Baum, A. (1985). Biological commonalities in stress and substance abuse. In S. Shiffman & T. A. Wills (Eds.), *Coping and substance use* (pp. 25–62). Orlando, FL: Academic Press.

Harnish, J. D., Dodge, K. A., & Valente, E. (1995). Mother-child interaction quality as a partial mediator of the roles of maternal depressive symptomatology and socioeconomic status in the development of child behavior problems. *Child Development, 66,* 739–753.

Hawkins, J. D., Catalano, R. F., & Miller, J. Y. (1992). Risk and protective factors for alcohol and other drug problems in adolescence and early adulthood: Implications for substance abuse prevention. *Psychological Bulletin, 112,* 64–105.

Hawkins, R. P., Peterson, R. F., Schweid, E., & Bijou, S. W. (1966). Behavior therapy in the home: Amelioration of problem parent-child relations with the parent in a therapeutic role. *Journal of Experimental Child Psychology, 4,* 99–107.

Hirschi, T. (1969). *Causes of delinquency.* Berkeley: University of California Press.

Jessor, R., Donovan, J. E., & Costa, F. M. (1991). *Beyond adolescence: Problem behavior and young adult development.* New York: Cambridge University Press.

Kandel, D. B. (1996). The parental and peer contexts of adolescent deviance: An algebra of interpersonal influences. *Journal of Drug Issues, 26,* 289–315.

Kaplan, H. B. (1980). *Deviant behavior in defense of self.* San Diego, CA: Academic Press.

Kaplan, H. B. (1996). Empirical validation of the applicability of an integrative theory of deviant behavior to the study of drug use. *Journal of Drug Issues, 26,* 345–377.

Kaplan, H. B., & Peck, B. M. (1992). Self-rejection, coping style, and mode of deviant response. *Social Science Quarterly, 73,* 903–919.

Kazdin, A. E. (1990). Psychotherapy for children and adolescents. *Annual Review of Psychology, 41,* 21–54.

Kupersmidt, J. B., Griesler, P. C., DeRosier, M. E., Patterson, C. J., & Davis, P. W. (1995). Childhood aggression and peer relations in the context of family and neighborhood factors. *Child Development, 66,* 360–375.

Labouvie, E. W. (1986). The coping function of adolescent alcohol and drug use. In R. K. Silbereisen, K. Eyferth, & G. Rudinger (Eds.), *Development as action in context* (pp. 229–240). New York: Springer.

Laflin, M. T., Moore-Hirschi, S., Weis, D. L., & Hayes, B. E. (1994). Use of the theory of reasoned action to predict drug and alcohol use. *International Journal of the Addictions, 29,* 927–940.

Loeber, R., Green, S. M., Keenan, K., & Lahey, B. B. (1995). Which boys will fare worse? Early predictors of the onset of conduct disorder in a six-year longitudinal study. *Journal of the American Academy of Child and Adolescent Psychiatry, 34,* 499–509.

Lynam, D. R. (1996). Early identification of chronic offenders: Who is the fledgling psychopath? *Psychological Bulletin, 120,* 209–234.

Magura, S., & Laudet, A. B. (1996). Parental substance abuse and child maltreatment: Review and implications for intervention. *Children and Youth Services Review, 18,* 193–220.

Marlatt, G. A., Baer, J. S., Donovan, D. M., & Kivlahan, D. R. (1988). Addictive behaviors: Etiology and treatment. In M. R. Rosenzweig & L. W. Porter (Eds.), *Annual Review of Psychology, 39,* 223–252.

McGee, L., & Newcomb, M. D. (1992). General deviance syndrome: Expanded hierarchical evaluations at four ages from early adolescence to adulthood. *Journal of Consulting and Clinical Psychology, 60,* 766–776.

Miller, W., & Rollnick, S. (1991). *Motivational interviewing.* New York: Guilford Press.

Nagan, D., & Farrington, D. P. (1992). The stability of criminal potential from childhood to adulthood. *Criminology, 30,* 235–260.

Newcomb, M. D., & Earlywine, M. (1996). Intrapersonal contributors to drug use: The willing host. *American Behavioral Scientist, 39,* 823–837.

Newcomb, M. D., & Harlow, L. L. (1986). Life events and substance use among adolescents: Mediating effects of perceived loss of control and meaninglessness in life. *Journal of Personality and Social Problems, 51,* 564–577.

Newcomb, M. D., & McGee, L. (1991). The influence of sensation seeking on general and specific problem behaviors from adolescence to young adulthood. *Journal of Personality and Social Psychology, 61,* 614–628.

O'Donnell, J., Hawkins, J. D., & Abbott, R. D. (1995). Predicting serious delinquency and substance use among aggressive boys. *Journal of Consulting and Clinical Psychology, 63,* 529–537.

Oetting, E. R. (1993). Orthogonal cultural identification: Theoretical links between cultural identification and substance use. In M. De La Rosa & J. Adrados (Eds.), *Drug abuse among minority youth: Advances in research and methodology* (Research Monograph No. 130). Rockville, MD: National Institute on Drug Abuse.

Patterson, G. R. (1975). *Families: Applications of social learning to family life.* Champaign, IL: Research Press.

Patterson, G. R., & Dishion, T. (1985). Contribution of families and peers to delinquency. *Criminology, 23,* 63–79.

Perlmutter, B. (1987). Delinquency and learning disabilities: Evidence for compensatory behaviors and adaptation. *Journal of Youth and Adolescence, 16,* 89–95.

Petraitis, J., Flay, B. R., & Miller, T. Q. (1995). Reviewing theories of adolescent substance use: Organizing pieces in the puzzle. *Psychological Bulletin, 117,* 67–86.

Pillow, D. R., Zautra, A. J., & Sandler, I. (1996). Major life events and minor stressors: Identifying mediational links in the stress process. *Journal of Personality and Social Psychology, 70,* 381–394.

Prinz, R. J., Blechman, E. A., & Dumas, J. E. (1994). An evaluation of peer coping skills training for childhood aggression. *Journal of Clinical Child Psychology, 23,* 193–203.

Pulkkinen, L. (1996). Proactive and reactive aggression in early adolescence as precursors to anti- and prosocial behavior in young adults. *Aggressive Behavior, 22,* 241–257.

Pulkkinen, L., & Pitkanen, T. (1994). A prospective study of the precursors to problem drinking in young adulthood. *Journal of Studies on Alcohol, 55,* 578–587.

Pulkkinen, L., & Tremblay, R. E. (1992). Patterns of boys' social adjustment in two cultures and at different ages: A longitudinal perspective. *International Journal of Behavioral Development, 15,* 527–553.

Quinton, D. (1988). Annotation: Urbanism and child mental health. *Journal of Child Psychology and Psychiatry, 29,* 11–20.

Robinson, N. S., Garber, J., & Hilsman, R. (1995). Cognitions and stress: Direct and moderating effects on depressive vs. externalizing symptoms during the junior high school transition. *Journal of Abnormal Psychology, 104,* 453–463.

Ruma, P. R., Burke, R. V., & Thompson, R. W. (1996). Group parent training: Is it effective for children of all ages? *Behavior Therapy, 27,* 159–169.

Rutter, M. (1978). Family, area, and school influences in the genesis of conduct disorders. In L. A. Hersov, M. Berger, & D. Shaffer (Eds.), *Aggression and antisocial behavior in childhood and adolescence* (pp. 95–113). Oxford, England: Pergamon Press.

Sanders, M. R. (1992). New directions in behavioral family intervention with children: From clinical management to prevention. *New Zealand Journal of Psychology, 21,* 25–36.

Schmaling, K. B., & Jacobson, N. S. (1987, November). *The clinical significance of treatment gains resulting from parent training interventions for children with conduct problems: An analysis of outcome data.* Paper presented at the meeting of the Association for Advancement of Behavior Therapy, Boston, MA.

Schorr, L. B. (1988). *Within our reach: Breaking the cycle of disadvantage.* New York: Anchor Press.

Serketich, W. J., & Dumas, J. E. (1996). The effectiveness of behavioral parent training to modify antisocial behavior in children: A meta-analysis. *Behavior Therapy, 27,* 171–186.

Shedler, J., & Block, J. (1990). Adolescent drug use and psychological health: A longitudinal inquiry. *American Psychologist, 45,* 612–630.

Stoolmiller, M., & Dishion, T. (1993). Predictors and consequences of unsupervised wandering for boys during transition to early adolescence. In J. B. Kupersmidt (Chair), *Peer influences on aggression and juvenile delinquency.* Paper presented at the annual meeting of the American Society for Criminology, Phoenix, AZ.

Thornberry, T. P., Lizotte, A. J., Krohn, M. D., Farnworth, M., & Jang, S. J. (1994). Delinquent peers, beliefs, and delinquent behavior: A longitudinal test of interactional theory. *Criminology, 32, 47–83.*

Wahler, R., & Dumas, J. (1984). Changing the observational coding styles of insular and noninsular mothers: A step toward maintenance of parent training effects. In R. F. Dangel & R. A. Polster (Eds.), *Parent training: Foundations of research and practice* (pp. 379–416). New York: Guilford Press.

Wahler, R. C., Winkel, G. H., Peterson, R. F., & Morrison, D. C. (1965). Mothers as behavior therapists for their own children. *Behaviour Research and Therapy, 3,* 113–134.

Weintraub, S. A. (1991). Children and adolescents at risk for substance abuse and psychopathology. *International Journal of the Addictions, 25,* 481–494.

Werner, E. E., & Smith, R. (1992). *Overcoming the odds: High risk children from birth to adulthood.* Ithaca, NY: Cornell University Press.

White, J. L., Moffitt, T. E., Earls, F., Robins, L., & Silva, P. A. (1990). How early can we tell? Predictors of childhood conduct disorder and adolescent delinquency. *Criminology, 28,* 507–533.

Williams, C. D. (1959). The elimination of tantrum behavior by extinction procedures. *Journal of Abnormal and Social Psychology, 59,* 269.

Wills, T. A. (1986). Stress and coping in early adolescence: Relationships to smoking and alcohol use in urban school samples. *Health Psychology, 5,* 503–529.

Wills, T. A., Blechman, E. A., & McNamara, G. (1996). Family support, coping, and competence. In E. M. Hetherington & E. A. Blechman (Eds.), *Stress, coping, and resiliency in children and the family* (pp. 107–134). Hillsdale, NJ: Erlbaum.

Wills, T. A., Duhamel, K., & Vaccaro, D. (1995). Activity and mood temperament as predictors of adolescent substance use: Test of a self-regulation mediational model. *Journal of Personality and Social Psychology, 68,* 901–916.

Zuckerman, M. (1987). Biological connection between sensation-seeking and drug abuse. In J. Engel & L. Oreland (Eds.), *Brain reward systems and abuse* (pp. 165–173). New York: Raven Press.

CHAPTER 17

Training Parents to Facilitate Their Child's Adjustment to Divorce Using the Filial/Family Play Therapy Approach

SUE CARLTON BRATTON

THIS CHAPTER describes a 10-week Filial/Family Play Therapy (FFPT) parent training model and its application to the treatment of children having difficulties adjusting to their parents' divorce. For the purpose of this chapter, the term filial/family play therapy and filial therapy refer to the same basic approach and are used interchangeably. The FFPT parent training model, based on the 10-week filial therapy model proposed by Landreth (1991), is a unique parenting approach aimed at fostering healthy parent-child relationships through training and supervising parents in the basic methodology of child-centered play therapy. Parents conduct weekly play therapy-type sessions with their child; learning to convey acceptance, empathy, and encouragement, as well as master the skills of effective limit setting.

FAMILIES TORN APART BY DIVORCE

In the last three decades, family life in the United States has changed dramatically. The single-parent family is the fastest growing family form in the United States today, primarily as a result of the escalating divorce rate, with one of every two marriages ending in divorce. In 1970, there were 3.8 million single-parent families with children under the age of 18;

in 1992 the number had increased to 10.5 million (U.S. Bureau of Census, 1992). Eighty percent of these parents were single as a result of separation or divorce. These changes in family structure and the resulting effects may, in part, explain the rapidly growing demand over the last three decades for mental health services for children and families.

Raising children is challenging and, at times, stressful even for the well-equipped two-parent family. These challenges and the accompanying stress are often compounded for divorcing parents as they adapt to changing roles. The consensus of research on the effects of divorce on children is that divorce often results in negative stresses and long-term adjustment of children to continued changes in their environment (Hamner & Turner, 1990). Parents' emotional turmoil, increased responsibilities, and social isolation, along with the children's emotional reaction to the loss of one parent, contribute to the stress experienced by these families (Tarshis, 1990). Single parents describe feeling overwhelmed by the practical and emotional demands of parenting and report a lack of support systems to aid in meeting these demands (Amato, 1993).

An increasing need to provide mental health services for single parents and their children has been well documented in the literature. Studies have reported that single parents and their children are at greater risk for emotional problems (Kitson & Morgan, 1990) than those who are married. Multiple studies have implicated divorce as a source of academic, behavioral, psychological, and social problems in children (Amato & Keith, 1991b; Hetherington, 1988; Wallerstein & Kelly, 1980). Furthermore, without intervention these problems often continue into adulthood (Amato & Keith, 1991a; Garber, 1991; Robins & Rutter, 1990).

The quality of the parent-child relationship following divorce has been found to strongly correlate with the child's well-being (Wallerstein & Kelly, 1980) and with the parent's adjustment as well (Johnson, 1986). However, a multitude of factors associated with divorce and single parenting has been identified that makes it especially difficult for parents to maintain healthy parent-child relationships and make positive contributions to their children's development. Parents' inability to effectively discipline, communicate, empathize, problem solve, and cope with their own stress are factors that can significantly influence children's adjustment to the disruption of their lives caused by separation and divorce (Ellwood & Stolberg, 1991; Holloway & Machida, 1991; Sandler, Tein, & West, 1994). Limited parental effectiveness often results in an increase in children's behavior problems, which in turn increases the anxiety and depression of divorced parents who are already feeling overwhelmed. Thus, effective parenting skills are needed at a time when parents are most likely to feel vulnerable, overwhelmed, and emotionally unavailable.

Therapy for the child is often sought as behavior problems increase and the parent feels overwhelmed and helpless to cope with the demands of single parenting. Although play therapy is a viable intervention for helping children who are having difficulties adjusting to divorce, the parent's sense of helplessness and inability to cope is generally not addressed; thus the parent-child relationship may continue to deteriorate. There is a critical need for innovative programs that strengthen the single parent's interest in and skills for promoting healthy parent-child interactions and at the same time provide them with the emotional support they need. Traditionally, society has focused little attention on the training of parents, believing that parenting is an "innate" ability. Furthermore, parent training as an intervention to ameliorate the emotional needs of children experiencing difficulty adjusting to divorce requires a conceptual shift for most clinicians who have been trained to intervene directly with the child who is experiencing problems (Ginsberg, 1989).

HISTORY AND DEVELOPMENT
OF FILIAL THERAPY

The concept of training parents to become therapeutic agents in their child's life can be traced to the early 1900s when Freud effectively utilized a father in treating his 5-year-old son's phobia. Freud (1959) was convinced that no one, but the father, could have made the same progress with the child. Freud attributed the successful treatment to the father's understanding of his child and to the special relationship between father and son. Bonnard (1950) and Jacobs (1949) also discussed the effectiveness of training parents to intervene in their child's problems. Fuchs (1957), on the advice of her father, Carl Rogers, utilized play therapy methods to help her daughter overcome anxiety related to toilet training. Not only was the problem resolved, but Fuchs also reported positive changes within herself. Moustakas (1959) also encouraged parents to conduct play therapy sessions at home with their child and wrote about the potential benefits to the child: ". . . In the play therapy relationship . . . the child finds that his parent really cares, wants to understand, and accepts him as he is" (pp. 275–277).

Bernard Guerney (1964) was the first to propose a structured program for training parents to become therapeutic agents in their child's life. Filial therapy was originally conceptualized by Guerney as a treatment program for children with emotional and behavioral problems. Louise Guerney worked with her husband in the early research and development of filial therapy, and she continues to be one of the leading proponents of this approach to helping children and families. Recognizing a shortage of professionals to meet the growing demands for mental health services for children, the Guerneys began developing a treatment methodology that would allow parents to create a therapeutic family system. They envisioned that such a system would (a) enhance and strengthen parents' relationships with their children, and (b) help to prevent children's future problems through healthy parent-child interactions (L. Guerney & Guerney, 1989). Assuming that the parent potentially has more emotional significance to the child than does the therapist, the objective of the Guerneys' approach was to train the parent to become the therapeutic agent in the child's life by utilizing the naturally existing bond between parent and child. Thus the term, "filial" therapy, was coined. The Guerneys relabeled filial therapy, calling it Child Relationship Enhancement Therapy (CREFT) in 1985 to more clearly describe the concept, but the term filial therapy continues to be widely used (L. Guerney & Guerney, 1989).

Since play is an integral part of children's lives and the main vehicle they use to express themselves and work through issues, filial therapy utilizes play as the developmentally appropriate means to fostering interaction between parent and child. The Guerneys advocate a structured small group training format in which parents are taught to utilize the principles and skills of child-centered play therapy in special weekly play sessions with their child and receive weekly supervision from the trained play therapist/facilitator (B. Guerney, 1977; L. Guerney & Guerney, 1989). This combination of didactic instruction, coupled with supervision in a supportive atmosphere provides a dynamic process that sets filial therapy training apart from other parent training programs, the majority of which are exclusively educational in nature.

Studies have shown that filial therapy is an innovative and proven method of strengthening parent-child relationships, increasing parental acceptance, decreasing parental stress, and decreasing children's problematic behavior (Bratton, 1993; Bratton & Landreth, 1995; Glass, 1986; B. Guerney & Stover, 1971; Lobaugh, 1991; Sywulak, 1977; Van Fleet, 1992). This approach has been found to be effective in increasing the level of self-esteem both in parents (Glass, 1986) and in children (Lobaugh, 1991). Filial therapy has been effectively used with emotionally disturbed children (Sensue, 1981), children with learning disabilities (L. Guerney, 1983), chronically ill children (Glazer-Waldman, 1991), children of single parents (Bratton, 1993), and children with an incarcerated parent (Harris, 1995; Lobaugh, 1991).

In addition to being a proven method of treatment for children and their families, filial therapy serves a preventative function as parents learn attitudes and skills that they will continue to utilize throughout their child's life. Thus, this approach offers the potential for long-term benefits for families torn apart by divorce by providing single parents with both the skill training and emotional support they need in order to learn to move toward healthier parent-child interactions. In addition to being an effective method of strengthening parent-child relationships, filial therapy is an economical and efficient means of providing treatment for single-parent families, who often have limited financial resources.

The utilization of a structured 10-week group format provides an economical treatment plan that benefits both parents *and* children, while allowing the therapist to help a great deal more children and families than time would allow in more traditional, individualized approaches. In addition, with the current emphasis in the managed health care field on time-limited treatment, the 10-week filial/family play therapy approach is attractive to insurance companies. The relational and therapeutic value of filial therapy combined with the economy and efficiency it offers makes this approach a viable intervention for children and parents who are experiencing difficulties related to divorce.

THE FILIAL/FAMILY PLAY THERAPY PARENT TRAINING PROGRAM

Although filial therapy was originally structured by the Guerneys as a 6- to 12-month training program for children with emotional and behavioral problems (B. Guerney, Guerney, & Andronico, 1966), Landreth (1991) proposed a 10-week training model to address the needs of parents with financial and time constraints. Landreth further emphasized that filial training is a preventative approach that can be helpful for all families, not just those experiencing severe problems. He found that parents could successfully learn the necessary skills to become therapeutic agents in their child's life in a carefully structured 10-week program. Several research studies utilizing Landreth's 10-week program have shown this time-limited approach to be highly effective with a variety of populations (Bratton & Landreth, 1995; Glass 1986; Glover, 1996; Harris, 1995; Lobaugh, 1991). My experience has been that getting all parents in a group to consistently attend longer than 10 weeks is difficult, regardless of their financial resources. However, the majority of parents are willing to make a commitment to attend 10 weeks, and group or individual follow-up sessions can be scheduled to address the needs of parents who require more training and/or support.

As in the Guerneys' model of filial therapy training, the 10-week FFPT training model utilizes both didactic and dynamic components and is designed to enhance the parent-child relationship by helping parents learn how to create an accepting and nonjudgmental environment in which their children will feel safe enough to express and explore thoughts and feelings. Utilizing a small support-group format, six to eight parents meet 2 hours weekly for 10 weeks. Parents are taught the basic methodology of child-centered play therapy through demonstration and role play, and then are required to practice these new skills with their child in weekly 30-minute special play sessions and report their experiences to the group. In addition, during the training period parents are scheduled on an individual basis to bring their child to the clinic for a parent-child play session that is videotaped and then critiqued during the following week's group training session. Through the viewing of these videotapes, supportive feedback from the facilitator and other parents, role playing, and a variety of didactic experiences, parents learn to convey acceptance, empathy, and encouragement to their children, as well as to master the skills of effective limit setting. Because the focus is on the parent-child relationship, special play times are always conducted with *one* child and *one* parent. Filial therapy is typically utilized with children ages 2 to 10, but the basic child-centered principles and skills can be adapted for older children and teens. Instead of a "play" time, more developmentally appropriate activities are substituted with the focus remaining on allowing the child to lead or choose the activity.

BASIC PREMISES UNDERLYING THE FILIAL/FAMILY PLAY THERAPY APPROACH

Filial therapy is notably different from most other forms of parent training, the majority of which are exclusively didactic in nature and focus primarily on helping parents learn to control their child's behavior through behavioral methods. Several major assumptions underline this unique approach to training parents. First, as in child-centered play therapy, filial therapy focuses on the importance of the relationship, in this case between the parent and child, with the parent serving as the therapeutic agent. This approach acknowledges the vital importance of the parent-child relationship in the healthy growth and development of children. The relationship is seen as the vehicle for the process of change; and as such the focus is on the process of relationship enhancement, not on finding a "quick fix" to a specific behavior problem. Parents are taught basic counseling/play therapy skills, focusing on learning to express empathy and acceptance in order to enhance their relationship with their child. According to Landreth (1991), "This new creative dynamic of empathic responding by parents becomes the creative process through which change occurs *within* parent and child and *between* parent and child" (p. 339).

Next, as in child-centered play therapy, the filial therapy approach acknowledges that learning, growth, and lasting change stem from within the child. Therefore, parents are taught to nurture an internal locus of control in their child, helping the child to become more self-directed within clearly established, consistent limits. This acceptance of and respect for the child's need for independence fosters the child's acceptance and trust of self. Self-directed play also provides the child with the freedom and opportunity to develop creativity, resourcefulness, and self-responsibility. Children experience for themselves what works and what doesn't, thus enhancing problem-solving skills and coping strategies. Landreth (1991) stated, "The power of this kind of freedom, within appropriate boundaries set by the parent, to direct oneself . . . is without a doubt, the most facilitative, growth enhancing experience that can be created" (p. 340).

Third, this approach assumes that parents can learn the skills necessary to be therapeutic with their children and that the parent can conceivably be more effective than a play therapist. This rationale rests on the assumptions that (a) parents have greater emotional significance to the child than any other adult, including a therapist; (b) children's problematic behaviors that have been influenced by parental attitudes can be more effectively ameliorated under similar conditions; and (c) parent-child misperceptions based on inconsistencies in the parent's expectations of the child can be more easily rectified by the parent learning to establish clear and consistent limits as to what is, and what is not, appropriate behavior according to the situation (Stover & Guerney, 1967). Additionally, as parents learn to accept their child unconditionally and learn more effective ways of interacting, there is greater potential for long-lasting change as parents continue to utilize these acquired skills and attitudes throughout their child's life. Stover and Guerney proposed further advantages of utilizing parents as therapeutic agents: (a) reducing feelings of guilt and helplessness parents may develop when dependent upon a professional for problem resolution, and (b) avoiding the problems that otherwise could be aroused when parents fail to develop appropriate new responses to the child's new behavioral patterns.

Next, filial therapy acknowledges that play is the developmentally appropriate means for fostering healthier parent-child interactions. Play therapists consider play the primary means of relating to and understanding the child's world. Through play, children express their feelings and needs, act out their experiences in an attempt to make sense of their world, develop a sense of control and mastery over their world, and develop effective problem-solving and coping strategies. Therefore, filial training focuses on helping parents understand and respond appropriately to their child's play. In addition, this approach utilizes an educational model in combination with a support group format, based on the assumption that most difficulties that parents experience with their children arise from a lack of knowledge and skill that is often compounded by the stressors in their life. Central to this approach is the belief that parents require support and encouragement to begin to make changes as they acquire new knowledge and skills, just as their children do.

Finally, this approach acknowledges the vital importance of parents experiencing success in order to gain confidence in their new role. Filial training is structured to ensure parent success in several ways. First, parents are asked to practice the skills they are learning *only* during a weekly 30-minute special play time. They are not asked or expected to completely change the way in which they interact with their child; in fact, they are initially told specifically *not* to practice these skills outside of the play time. This avoids the sense of failure that would inevitably ensue if parents were expected to utilize these new skills in *all* their interactions with their children. Typically, as parents gain confidence in their skills they will gradually begin to spontaneously and successfully utilize their new skills outside of the play sessions. Much attention is also paid to helping parents select the time and place they will conduct the play sessions each week, focusing on helping them commit to a set time when they are not likely to be stressed or hurried and can be emotionally available to the child. This is a particularly important strategy when working with divorced parents, who generally are overwhelmed by the practical and emotional demands of adjusting to their new role as single parent.

Again, the goal is to structure all aspects of training to promote success. Another means for ensuring success, particularly for single parents, is the facilitation of a warm, supportive atmosphere where parents experience the safety and freedom to share their concerns, as well as give and receive feedback from other parents. Finally, success is encouraged through the supervision of parents' videotaped and/or live play sessions. Parents don't just report on how their play sessions are progressing, they also demonstrate their skills, either live or videotaped, and receive supportive feedback and encouragement from the facilitator and the other group members.

GOALS OF FILIAL/FAMILY PLAY THERAPY

The overall goal of filial/family play therapy is to enhance and strengthen the parent-child relationship through improved family interactions and problem-solving strategies and through increased feelings of familial affection, warmth, and trust. Filial therapy offers significant benefits for both children and parents. Therapeutic goals for children include a reduction of symptoms and development of coping strategies, an increase in positive feelings of self-worth and confidence, and a more positive perception of parents. Broad therapeutic goals for parents include a greater understanding and acceptance of the child's emotional world, the development of more realistic and tolerant perceptions and attitudes toward both self and child, the development of more effective parenting skills based on developmentally appropriate strategies, and last, but not least, to help parents recapture the joy in parenting.

Group Format

The small support group format utilized in this approach is an important element in its effectiveness, particularly when training single parents who often have greater needs for emotional support as they adapt to their new role. The structure is much like group therapy where members sit in a circle to facilitate interaction. My experience is that six to nine parents is an optimal number to ensure that the facilitator can effectively provide supervision and that all parents have the opportunity to share. This kind of format requires a skilled therapist/facilitator who can balance the didactic and dynamic components of this approach, particularly in a 10-week model. There are specific skills that must be taught, modeled, and practiced in each session so that parents will experience success in their home play sessions. Often, parents need so much support that it is easy for the facilitator to get caught up in exploring feelings to the exclusion of providing the necessary training. In addition, many novice filial therapists lack experience and training in group facilitation and make the deadly mistake of allowing one or two parents to dominate group discussions, resulting in the other group members feeling left out and unimportant. Facilitators must also feel confident in their own skills as a play therapist in order to demonstrate and model specific play therapy skills for parents. Thus, minimal requirements for the facilitator include training and experience in basic counseling/communication skills, play therapy skills, and group facilitation skills. Another important skill for the facilitator, that is harder to measure, is spontaneity and creativity. Parents are more motivated to learn these new skills when the information and skills are presented in the context of their own lives. When the facilitator can seize the opportunity to teach or reinforce a skill as an issue is spontaneously presented by a parent, the potential for learning is enhanced. The potential for learning can be further heightened if the facilitator uses the opportunity to explore feelings and emotional reactions in the group. Encouragement of even the smallest success must be offered throughout the process. Generalizing a specific comment made by a parent to include the other parents' experience is another important strategy the facilitator should utilize to maximize learning.

Structure and Content of the Training Sessions

The basic outline for the 10 weekly 2-hour training sessions follows the methodology proposed by Landreth (1991) for a 10-week filial therapy training group. The optimal setting for conducting the training is a group room in a clinic that also houses a play therapy room with a two-way mirror and a space for providing child care for the children of the parents in the group. Providing child care is particularly necessary for single parents who often lack financial resources and/or the necessary support systems to assist in caring for their child while they attend training. Children seem to enjoy coming to the clinic and seeing where their parents are coming to learn "special ways of playing with them." Providing child care on-site also allows the therapist to conduct live demonstrations with each of the children, play sessions that can be observed by the rest of the parents.

Training Session 1

Parents introduce themselves and describe their families. They are asked to select one child that they will focus on during the 10-week training and asked to describe that child in more detail. The therapist addresses parents' concerns about other children in the family not having a special play time and suggests "special" activities for the other children to be involved in while the parent conducts a play session with the "child of focus," (e.g., a relative taking other children to the park or for an ice cream cone). Parents are asked what they hope to gain from this experience for themselves as well as for their child. Next, the therapist gives an overview of the filial/family play therapy training, focusing on the value of play in children's lives. The goals of the filial therapy training are explained, emphasizing the goal of parents developing sensitivity to their children and responding with empathy. A videotape is shown to demonstrate the skills of reflective listening and tracking behavior. The therapist further illustrates these skills through role play, with one of the parents playing as a child. Then parents are encouraged to practice empathic responses in a similar role-play situation. Through the use of a videotape, the parents are introduced to the facial expressions of children's various emotions. For their homework assignment, parents are asked to identify four emotions (happiness, sadness, anger, and surprise) in their children during the coming week and make a reflective response for each, writing down what happened, what the child did or said, and their response to the child.

Training Session 2

Session 2 begins, as do all subsequent sessions, with a review of the parents' homework assignment from the previous week. The therapist utilizes parents' responses from their homework to further elaborate on the skills of empathic responding, encouraging parents' efforts, even if they weren't entirely successful. Another demonstration of empathic responding by the therapist is generally helpful, with a parent volunteer role playing as their own child. The basic principles and guidelines of the

30-minute play sessions, as described by Landreth (1991), are explained to the parents:

1. The child should be completely free to determine how he will use the time. The child leads and the parent follows without making suggestions or asking questions.
2. The parent's major task is to empathize with the child, to understand the intent of his actions, and his thoughts and feelings.
3. The parent's next task is to communicate this understanding to the child by appropriate comments, particularly, whenever possible, by verbalizing the *feelings* that the child is actively experiencing.
4. The parent is to be clear and firm about the few "limits" that are placed on the child. Limits to be set are time limits, not breaking specified toys, and not physically hurting the parent.

Next, the parents are given a list of toys to be used during the special play times: inflatable bop bag, baby bottle, small container for water, small doll family, small domestic animal family, 1 to 2 stuffed wild animals, doctor kit with real Band-Aids, play money, dart gun with darts, rubber knife, handcuffs, rope, Lone Ranger-type mask, toy soldiers (2 colors), small car, deck of cards, ring-toss game, construction toy (e.g., Tinkertoys®), 8 crayons, assorted paper, blunt-edged scissors, tape, glue, Play-Doh®, small blanket or sheet, and a small sturdy cardboard box with lid (the kind copy paper comes in) that doubles as a storage box and dollhouse (cut out windows/door and mark off rooms with tape). The therapist demonstrates each of the toys and shares the rationale for each. The parents are reminded that to add to the specialness of their play time with their child, the toys are to be used only for the play sessions. Next, the therapist demonstrates a typical play session using one of the children, if child care is provided on-site. If this option is not available, a videotaped demonstration can be shown. Parents are then shown the playroom and asked to pair-up and take turns role playing a parent-child play session. The focus of the role play is for parents to practice skills of observing, listening, and reflective communication. For homework, parents are given several scenarios to respond to in writing, practicing their reflection skills. Parents are also asked to put their toy kit together and select a specific time and location for the home play sessions. Parents are directed to choose a location that offers the fewest distractions to the child and the greatest freedom from worry about breaking things or making a mess. The therapist emphasizes the importance of selecting a specific time of the day and week when parents are less likely to be hurried or stressed and when there will be no interruptions from others.

Training Session 3

The session begins with a discussion of the homework assignment on reflective communication followed from a report by each parent as to when and where they will have their special play time with their child. The major focus for this session is preparing parents for their first home play session.

Parents are given a handout that outlines basic principles for conducting play sessions that are based on guidelines proposed by Landreth (1991) and L. Guerney (1972):

Do's

1. Do set the stage—convey the freedom of the special play time.

    "During our special play time, you can play with the toys in lots of the ways you'd like to."

    "In here, that's up to you . . . you can decide . . . that can be whatever you want it to be."

2. Do let the child lead.

    "You want me to put that on" . . . (whisper technique) "what should I say" . . . "show me what you want me to do."

3. Do track child's play.

    "You're filling that all the way to the top" . . . "You've decided you want to paint next" . . . . "You've got 'em all lined up just how you want them."

4. Do reflect the child's feelings.

    "You like how you look in that" . . . "that kinda surprised you" . . . "You really like how that feels on your hands" . . . "You really wish that we could play longer" . . . "you don't like the way that turned out."

5. Do set firm and consistent limits.

    "I know you'd like to play with the play dough on the floor, but it's not for putting on the floor . . . you can play with it on the tray."

6. Do salute the child's power and encourage effort.

    "You worked hard on that and you did it" . . . "you figured it out" . . . "You've got a plan for how you want to _____" . . . "You know just how you want that _____" . . . . "Sounds like you know lots about _____ ."

7. Do join in the child's play as a follower.

    "You want me to be the robber and I'm supposed to wear the black mask" . . . "Now I'm supposed to go to jail until you say I can get out."

8. Do be verbally active.

Don'ts

1. Don't criticize any behavior.
2. Don't praise the child.
3. Don't ask leading questions.
4. Don't allow interruptions of the session.
5. Don't give information or teach.
6. Don't preach.
7. Don't initiate new behavior.
8. Don't be passive, quiet.

Next, parents view a live or videotaped play session conducted by the therapist and are asked to note when they hear the therapist using the "Do's" listed on the handout. Parents are encouraged to share their observations and ask questions, and then to immediately put their knowledge into action by role-playing in the playroom. At the end of the session, homework is assigned and the first parent is scheduled to come to the clinic to be videotaped with their child (sometime before next week's filial session, but after the parent has had their first home play session). *Note:* The therapist should select a parent in the group who seems to pick up readily on the skills being taught. Most parents are apprehensive about being videotaped knowing that their tape will be viewed by the entire group of parents at next week's session; therefore, much encouragement and support is needed throughout the process. In some groups, there will not be a parent ready to demonstrate his/her new skills on videotape this early in the training process; therefore, videotaping can be delayed one week. Some flexibility in the structure of training is necessary to ensure that parents experience success.

Homework for this week is for parents to prepare for and conduct their first home play session. Parents are instructed to tell their child one day ahead about the play session and explain to their child that they are having these "special" play sessions because, "mom (or dad) is going to class to learn how to play with you in a special way." Parents then reinforce the "specialness" of this time together by assisting their child in making a "Special Play Session—Do Not Disturb" sign to be put on the front door during the play times. In addition to the handout outlining the basic principles, parents are given additional guidelines for ensuring a successful play session: Encourage the child to use the bathroom prior to the play session, take the phone off the hook, and don't answer the door. Parents are instructed to begin the session by telling the child, "We will have 30 minutes of special play time—you may choose to play with the toys in lots of the ways you like to" and letting the child lead from this point. Other reminders are given: Play actively with the child if the child requests your participation; set limits on behaviors that make you feel uncomfortable; avoid identifying toys by name because this can stifle creativity—instead, call them "it," "that," "her," "him," and so on; give the child a 5-minute advance notice before terminating the session; and do not exceed the time limit by more than 2 to 3 minutes. Parents are instructed to make notes about their reactions to specific happenings in the play session, focusing on what the child did or said and their response to their child.

Training Session 4

This session begins with each parent reporting on their first home play session with their child. The therapist uses examples from the parents' comments to reinforce the basic principles of filial therapy, to point out difficult situations, and to focus on how the parents felt during the sessions. Much of the time is spent with parents asking for help on how to respond to certain situations. Role play is an effective strategy to address specific questions, with the therapist playing the parent asking the question and the parent playing the child. The therapist's primary task is to find something in each parent's sharing that can be encouraged and supported. Next, the parent who came in to be videotaped receives supportive feedback from the therapist and other group members as the video is viewed by the group. Although anxiety producing, parents having the opportunity to view and critique themselves as they practice these new skills is an invaluable part of the learning process. The use of videotapes also offers more opportunities for vicarious learning for other group members. In this first video critique, the therapist's main task is to encourage and build on every small success in skill development; correction is kept to a minimum. Limit-setting during the play sessions is discussed in more detail and parents are taught a three-step method of setting limits developed by Landreth (1991):

1. Recognize the feeling.
2. State the limit.
3. Provide an acceptable alternative or something to look forward to.

An issue that is always brought up by at least one parent is that the child is enjoying the play session and doesn't want to stop when the time is up. Parents are reminded that it is their responsibility to end the sessions even though children may want to continue playing, and that this situation is a perfect opportunity to practice limit setting, "Joey, I know you'd like to play with the soldiers longer, *but* our special play time is over for today. You can choose to play with the soldiers next week," or for the younger child who may need a more immediate alternative, "Joey, I know you want to play longer, *but* our special play time is over for today. . . . We can go outside and play on the swing." This topic usually generates much discussion among parents about how this technique can be applied in every day interactions with their children as well as during the special play sessions, but parents are asked to refrain from using the technique outside of the play session (for now). If time permits, a short video of the use of limit setting in a play session is shown and the parents spend the rest of the time role-playing situations where a limit needs to be set. Parents are instructed to continue the home play sessions and to notice one intense feeling in themselves during their session this week. They are briefly introduced to a structured method for choice-giving, "Joey, would you like to have one cookie or two?" and instructed to practice giving one choice this week (outside of the play session). Two parents are scheduled to come to the clinic before next week's training session to be videotaped with their children. (Again, it is helpful if the parents will conduct their next home play session before coming in to be taped—more experience assures greater success on their video.)

Training Sessions 5 through 9

The next five sessions all follow the same general format: first each parent reports about his or her home play session of the previous week and then, the videotaped play sessions of two parents are shown. As reporting occurs each week, the therapist has two primary tasks: to find something to encourage in each parent and to use parents' comments to reinforce the basic filial therapy principles. The therapist continues to encourage parents to be aware of their own feelings during the play sessions and asks each parent to specify what they would like to do differently in their next play session. The weekly supervision of the videotaped sessions, along with the dynamics of group interaction, are crucial elements in the success of the filial therapy training. Parents are also helped to see that they are not alone in their child-rearing difficulties by the therapist commenting frequently on experiences shared by several parents. As parents begin to share experiences that indicate that they are developing new coping strategies outside the play sessions, the therapist quickly acknowledges them in order to help parents gain confidence and feel empowered. The parents' confidence in their newly learned skills becomes more evident toward the end of training as they begin to participate more freely in critiquing each other's skills. Parents being able to recognize what the videotaped parent is doing correctly and then giving constructive feedback concerning what that parent might try differently is an invaluable part of the learning process. By the eighth session, parents generally begin to volunteer comments on changes they see in themselves and in their child. Parents are reminded each week of the importance of consistency in conducting their home play sessions (same time, same place—even if the child asks for changes and/or it would be more convenient for the parent to change). Each week two more parents are scheduled to come to the clinic for videotaping. (My goal is that over the course of training, each parent will have two opportunities to be videotaped and receive focused feedback.)

Training Session 10

The final session is used primarily as a review and to bring closure to the group. The videotapes of the last two parents are viewed by the group, and their comments are utilized by the therapist to summarize and generalize learnings. The therapist asks the parents to think back to the beginning of the sessions and consider the progress they and their children have made. Parents are then asked to reflect on the process and what has been the most important learning for them. They are asked to speculate about how they believe this experience will continue to impact their life and that of their child. As they respond, the therapist encourages and reinforces their comments through the examples of progress they have already shared. The importance of continuing the home play sessions is emphasized and the parents each sign a contract, making a commitment to continue the play sessions for "x" number of weeks. Parents are told, "If you stop the play sessions now, the message is that you were playing with your child because you had to, not because you wanted to." My experience is that parents will typically commit to continuing the play sessions until the follow-up training session, which is generally scheduled to be held in 4 to 6 weeks. The parents are also encouraged to set up their own support group, meeting weekly at the park or some other location where the children can play and the parents can talk. It's important to get one parent to volunteer to coordinate the weekly meeting time and place. My experience is that single parents are particularly open to this idea and will follow through.

Follow-Up Training Session

Parents are sent a postcard reminding them about the follow-up session. Providing child care is very important, because the children want to come back "to the place that has that room with all those neat toys." The session begins by giving parents the opportunity to briefly share their experiences in their play sessions since the last meeting, focusing on changes they have observed in themselves and in their child. The therapist utilizes this sharing time to reinforce the basic filial principles and encourage each parent's growth since the beginning of training. The majority of the session is focused on helping parents generalize their skills outside the play sessions, asking for examples of when they have used their new skills successfully. This is a very empowering experience for the parents, as they begin to realize that what they have to share is helpful to another parent who is experiencing a similar difficulty with his or her child. Parents are encouraged to continue meeting weekly with each other to offer support. If there is enough interest, another follow-up training session can be scheduled to be held in approximately three months.

CASE STUDY

This case study was selected because it illustrates the flexibility of this approach and how it can be adapted to meet the specific needs of one parent within the context of the group training. This case illustrates how the basic principles of this approach were utilized with an extremely challenging parent to benefit both parent and child.

BACKGROUND INFORMATION

Kathy White (pseudonym), a single, 30-year-old graduate student and mother of two, brought her 7-year-old son, Robert, to play therapy because he was acting out at home and at school. Kathy described Robert as out of control, angry, and oppositional. Kathy was struggling both financially and emotionally, and reported that she didn't know what she would do if she didn't get some help. Although she described many frustrations in her life, she perceived that Robert was the primary source of her misery. The school also reported that Robert was a behavior problem, describing him as manipulative, disobedient, and aggressive, often to the point of hurting other children. However, the school also described Robert as a very bright and creative child and had recently placed him in a class for gifted children. Kathy, a Caucasian, had been divorced from Robert's father, James, an African American, since Robert was 3. James lived out of state and saw his children infrequently. Robert expressed a desire to see his father more, but had many conflicting feelings about his dad. Kathy and James' relationship was very hostile. According to Kathy, James rarely paid child support, and didn't follow through on his promises to her or the children. She also reported that the few times he had picked-up the children for a visit that he had not brought them back when he was supposed to and that she had involved the police. In addition, Kathy blamed James for getting her pregnant and expressed concern that her children had to cope with being biracial. She suggested this as a possible cause of Robert's behavior problems.

ASSESSMENT

The needs of the family were assessed through a detailed parent intake, information obtained from the school, and a structured family art activity, where the family is given two drawing tasks to complete as a family (one verbal and one nonverbal), with the therapist's primary role to observe and note family interactions. Typically, a parent-child play observation may be utilized to further assess parent-child dynamics, but in this case, it was obvious from observing the family activity that there were serious problems in the parent-child relationship and that much of Robert's behavior appeared to be in response to Kathy's extremely critical and controlling parenting style. Filial therapy was suggested as a way in which Kathy could regain control as a parent and help Robert learn self-control. Control was an important issue for Kathy; therefore, discussing the potential benefits of filial therapy in terms of "gaining control" was particularly beneficial in helping Kathy "buy in" to participating in the training. (Kathy had initially expressed no interest in participating in her son's therapy.) In addition, it was obvious from talking with Kathy and observing her interactions with her children that she would need a great deal of support and encouragement in order to be successful in learning more effective ways of interacting with Robert.

TRAINING

Kathy immediately stood out in the filial group made up of seven other single parents. She arrived 20 minutes late to the first training session, screaming at Robert and Mary from the time they entered the front door of the clinic and all the way down a long hallway until she left the children in the child care area. The other parents in the group could hear what was going on and seemed embarrassed and unsure of how to respond as Kathy entered the room looking defeated and helpless. After several awkward minutes, Kathy seemed to relax and genuinely enjoy the experience of being with the other parents. She later told me that being in the group was like an oasis in her week, a time when she didn't have to "deal with the kids." This pattern of being late and struggling with the children, continued for the next three weeks. Each time the family's arrival caused a disruption in the filial training group, as well as in the entire clinic. At this point in the filial training (Session 4), Kathy appeared to be feeling somewhat supported emotionally, but she did not seem to be benefiting from the skill training. She seldom had anything positive to share with the group; rather her tendency was to focus on the negative. Her first home play session was disastrous, and lasted only a few minutes before Robert got mad and walked out of the room. Clearly Kathy needed even more support than the 2-hour training group provided in order to be successful in learning these new skills. Therefore it was decided that in order to intensify the training and provide more individual support, Kathy would conduct her weekly play sessions at the clinic under supervision, rather than at home, and also continue to attend the group training.

This proved to be a very effective strategy. Kathy and Robert came to the clinic a few days later. I met with Kathy briefly to review the basic procedure and methods for the play session while Robert played in the waiting room. Kathy expressed much reluctance and doubt in her ability, so we determined that while Kathy observed behind the two-way mirror, I would do a brief demonstration with Robert, modeling the play therapy skills I wanted Kathy to practice in her play session. The process was explained to Robert and he was shown where mom would be while he was playing with me. After a brief demonstration (10 minutes), Kathy and I discussed what she had seen me do, and then she went into the playroom and played with Robert for 10 minutes. I chose to limit the time, in the belief that Kathy could be successful in responding empathically to Robert for a 10-minute period. I observed behind the mirror, noting any new behavior I could encourage and reinforce. Kathy received immediate feedback after her session and we role-played a few instances when she had struggled with how to respond. We then repeated the entire process of my modeling specific skills with Robert, followed by Kathy immediately going into the playroom with Robert to practice, followed by supportive feedback. Although I felt that this one-on-one supervision with Kathy was successful and definitely necessary, she still had a long way to go, in terms of skill level and attitude, in order to catch up with the rest of the group.

After this individual training/supervision session with Kathy, there was a subtle change in her behavior in the next group training (Session 5). She appeared slightly more confident and was able to share two positive comments about her experience in the play session, although she continued to focus primarily on the negative. Kathy and Robert continued to come to the clinic for their weekly special play time for the remainder of the 10 weeks. Progress was slow, but Kathy made small gains weekly. Her greatest growth in her second and third play sessions was in allowing Robert to direct the play, but she continued to appear uncomfortable in her role. Kathy's greatest area for growth was in conveying acceptance, which is the foundation for this approach. In addition, Kathy initially had great difficulty effectively setting limits on Robert's behavior in the play room, generally reverting to "don't do that" or "I told you to stop that," after which Robert would respond by getting angry. Most of these incidents centered around Robert's use of a Nerfball shooter that shot the ball out with a great deal of force and made a very loud noise. Kathy did not like Robert to play with this gun, therefore it was Robert's favorite toy! Robert was a master at "pushing his mom's buttons."

Kathy was extremely critical of herself, as well as Robert; therefore helping Kathy become more self-accepting became a focus of our interactions. As Kathy seemed to feel more accepted by me and the other group members, she appeared to relax more in her interactions with Robert. As

Kathy was able to relax, she began to show more acceptance of Robert's behavior in *some* situations. This acceptance did not extend to those situations when Kathy perceived Robert's behavior as aggressive. For example, when Robert would shoot the Nerfball shooter, as he did in every session, Kathy perceived that as aggressive behavior directed at her; and she had a very difficult time responding appropriately. By the fourth play session, Kathy had learned to refrain from responding negatively to this activity, but she still could not convey verbal acceptance and her nonverbals clearly conveyed nonacceptance. The most dramatic turn in the course of training happened in Kathy's fifth play session with Robert. (This play session took place after the eighth week of parent training in which there had been much discussion about unconditional acceptance and the importance of accepting both positive and *negative* feelings and behaviors. Kathy appeared very emotional as the parents discussed their own needs for the same kind of acceptance.) For the first time, Kathy was able to convey acceptance of Robert's aggressive behavior by reflecting how she thought he was feeling. The change in Robert's behavior was dramatic; he immediately became calmer, and after a few minutes stopped playing with the Nerfball shooter. He went over to the easel and began to paint for the rest of the play session, eventually inviting his mom to participate. Kathy was noticeably more relaxed, and throughout the remainder of the session responded much more effectively to Robert's feelings and his behavior. During feedback after the play session, Kathy expressed amazement at the change in Robert's behavior and commented on how much more she enjoyed this session. I helped Kathy take credit for facilitating this change through her improved responses, particularly her reflection of Robert's feelings of aggression toward her. She told me that the discussion in last week's training about the importance of accepting children's negative feelings had been on her mind all week, and that she had genuinely felt more accepting in the session today, even when Robert was aggressive. We viewed the segment of her video where she had reflected that Robert was angry with her. Kathy was overwhelmed with emotion as she observed the dramatic effect her responses had on Robert's behavior. Kathy shared that growing up she had never had anyone accept her negative feelings, and that she had felt that people were always criticizing her. (This kind of comment is common as parents begin to make a connection between their own feelings and experiences and the parenting difficulties they are having.)

Kathy continued to need much support, but she was now making greater strides in each session. Perhaps the greatest change was in her interactions with Robert and Mary when they arrived at the clinic each week. They often arrived early, sitting in the waiting room and reading or talking together. Kathy's demeanor was more confident and relaxed. She decided she was ready for her first home play session in the tenth week of training and reported that both she and Robert enjoyed it. Kathy came in for supervision one more time after the group ended and attended a follow-up group training session held 4 weeks later and another one held 3 months after that. Kathy reported that Robert's behavior at home had improved and that Robert's behavior at school had dramatically changed. I again encouraged Kathy to take credit for facilitating the changes she was seeing. Kathy continued to call occasionally over the next two years with concerns about Robert and/or Mary, but mostly she seemed to need support and encouragement. She tended to isolate herself and had few friends, although she did keep in contact with one mother from the filial training group. Kathy showed more improvement than any parent I have ever trained, but her skill level at the end of 10 weeks was among the weakest in her group. The greatest shift I observed was in her attitude of acceptance toward Robert and toward herself. Kathy still had many intrapersonal obstacles to overcome and continued to struggle emotionally and financially, but through the confidence and skills she gained in filial training, Kathy was now better equipped to handle the challenges she faced as a single parent. The last time I saw Robert, he was a charming, confident 9-year-old, doing very well at school. He, too, appeared to continue to benefit from the filial training and a much-improved relationship with his mom.

CONCLUSIONS

This chapter has presented a detailed description of a 10-week Filial/Family Play Therapy parent training model and its application to the treatment of children having difficulty adjusting to divorce. This approach focuses on fostering a healthy parent-child relationship through training and supervising parents in the basic methodology of child-centered play therapy. Research substantiates filial therapy training as an effective intervention for single parents that has preventive, educational, and clinical implications (Bratton, 1993). Single parent families form an increasing portion of the population with particular needs. Children of divorce often need help in adjusting to changes in their environment, especially the separation from one parent. A healthy parent-child relationship, particularly with the custodial parent, is essential to the present and future mental health of these children. However, a multitude of factors associated with divorce and single parenting have been identified that make it especially difficult for parents to maintain a healthy relationship with their child and make positive contributions to their child's development. Filial therapy offers significant possibilities for promoting the well-being of single parent families by equipping parents with healthy parenting and relational skills, while providing them and their children with the emotional support they need.

REFERENCES

Amato, P. R. (1993). Children's adjustment to divorce: Theories, hypotheses, and empirical support. *Journal of Marriage and the Family, 55,* 23–38.

Amato, P. R., & Keith, B. (1991a). Parental divorce and the well-being of children: A meta-analysis. *Psychological Bulletin, 110* 26–46.

Amato, P. R., & Keith, B. (1991b). Parental divorce and adult well-being of children: A meta-analysis. *Psychological Bulletin, 110,* 26–46.

Bonnard, A. (1950). The mother as therapist in a case of obsessional neurosis. *Psychoanalytic Study of the Child, 5,* 391–408.

Bratton, S. (1993). *Filial therapy with single parents.* Unpublished doctoral dissertation, University of North Texas, Denton.

Bratton, S., & Landreth, G., (1995). Filial therapy with single parents: Effects on parental acceptance, empathy and stress. *International Journal of Play Therapy, 4,* 61–80.

Ellwood, M. S., & Stolberg, A. L. (1991). A preliminary investigation of family systems influences on individual divorce adjustment. *Journal of Divorce and Remarriage, 15,* 157–174.

Freud, S. (1959). *Analysis of a phobia in a five-year-old boy. Collected papers: Case histories.* New York: Basic Books.

Fuchs, N. (1957). Play therapy at home. *Merrill-Palmer Quarterly, 3,* 89–95.

Garber, R. J. (1991). Long-term effects of divorce on the self-esteem of young adults. *Journal of Divorce and Remarriage, 17,* 131–137.

Ginsberg, B. G. (1989). Training parents as therapeutic agents with foster/adoptive children using the filial approach. In C. E. Schaefer & J. M. Briesmeister (Eds.), *Handbook of parent training* (pp. 442–478). New York: Wiley.

Glass, N. (1986). *Parents as therapeutic agents: A study of the effects of filial therapy.* Unpublished doctoral dissertation, North Texas State University, Denton.

Glazer-Waldman, H. (1991). *Filial therapy: CPR training for families with chronically ill children.* Unpublished masters thesis, University of North Texas, Denton.

Glover, G. J. (1996). *Filial therapy with native americans on the Flathead reservation.* Unpublished doctoral dissertation, University of North Texas, Denton.

Guerney, B. (1964). Filial therapy: Description and rationale. *Journal of Consulting Psychology, 28*(4), 303–310.

Guerney, B. (1977). *Relationship enhancement: Skill training programs for therapy, problem prevention, and enrichment.* San Francisco: Jossey-Bass.

Guerney, B., Burton, J., Silverberg, D., & Shapiro, E. (1965). Use of adult responses to codify children's behavior in a play situation. *Perceptual and Motor Skills, 20,* 614–616.

Guerney, B., Guerney, L., & Andronico, M. (1966). Filial therapy. *Yale Scientific Magazine, 40,* 6–14.

Guerney, B., & Stover, L. (1971). *Filial therapy: Final report on MH 18254-01.* Unpublished manuscript, Pennsylvania State University.

Guerney, B., Stover, L., & DeMerritt, S. (1968). A measurement of empathy for parent-child interaction. *Journal of Genetic Psychology, 112,* 49–55.

Guerney, L. (1972). *Play therapy: A training manual for parents.* Unpublished manuscript, Pennsylvania State University at State College.

Guerney, L. (1983). Play therapy with learning disabled children. In C. Schaefer & K. O'Connor (Eds.), *Handbook of play therapy* (pp. 419–435). New York: Wiley.

Guerney, L., & Guerney, B. (1985). The relationship enhancement family of family therapies. In L. L'Abate & M. A. Milan (Eds.), *Handbook of social skills training and research* (pp. 506–525). Somerset, NY: Wiley.

Guerney, L., & Guerney, B. (1989). Child relationship enhancement: Family therapy and parent education. Person-centered approaches with families [Special issue]. *Person Centered Review, 4,* 344–357.

Hamner, T., & Turner, P. (1990). *Parenting in contemporary society* (2nd ed.). Englewood Cliffs, NJ: Prentice-Hall.

Harris, Z. L. (1995). *Filial therapy with incarcerated mothers.* Unpublished doctoral dissertation, University of North Texas, Denton.

Hetherington, E. M. (1988). Family relations six years after divorce. In E. M. Hetherington & R. D. Parke (Eds.), *Contemporary readings in child psychology* (pp. 423–438). New York: McGraw-Hill.

Holloway, S., & Machida, S. (1991). Child-rearing effectiveness of divorced mothers: Relationship to coping strategies and social support. *Journal of Divorce and Remarriage, 14* (3/4), 179–200.

Jacobs, L. (1949). Methods used in the education of mothers: A contribution to the handling and treatment of developmental difficulties in children under five years of age. *Psychoanalytic Study of the Child, 3–4,* 408–422.

Johnson, B. (1986). Single mothers following separation and divorce: Making it on your own. *Family Relations, 35,* 189–197.

Kitson, G. C., & Morgan, L. A. (1990). The multiple consequences of divorce. *Journal of Marriage and the Family, 52,* 913–924.

Landreth, G. (1991). *Play therapy: The art of the relationship.* Muncie, IN: Accelerated Development.

Lobaugh, A. (1991). *Filial therapy with incarcerated parents.* Unpublished doctoral dissertation, University of North Texas, Denton.

Moustakas, C. (1959). *Psychotherapy with children: The living relationships.* New York: Harper & Row.

Robins, L., & Rutter, M. (Eds.). (1990). *Straight and devious pathways from childhood to adulthood.* Cambridge, England: Cambridge University Press.

Sandler, I., Tein, J., & West, S. G. (1994). Coping, stress, and the psychological symptoms of children of divorce: A cross-sectional and longitudinal study. *Child Development, 65,* 1744–1763.

Sensue, M. (1981). Filial therapy follow-up study: Effects on parental acceptance and child adjustment (Doctoral dissertation, Pennsylvania State University, 1981). *Dissertation Abstracts International, 42,* 0148A.

Stover, L., & Guerney, B. (1967). The efficacy of training procedures for mothers in filial therapy. *Psychotherapy: Theory, Research, and Practice, 4*(3), 110-115.

Stover, L., Guerney, B., & O'Connell, M. (1971). Measurements of acceptance, allowing self-direction, involvement, and empathy in adult-child interaction. *Journal of Psychology, 77,* 261-269.

Sywulak, A. (1977). The effect of filial therapy on parental acceptance and child adjustment (Doctoral dissertation, Pennsylvania State University, 1977). *Dissertation Abstract International, 38,* 6180B.

Tarshis, E. (1990). *An evaluation of a systematic skills training program for single parents.* Unpublished doctoral dissertation, Boston University, Boston.

U.S. Bureau of the Census. (1992). *Households, families, and children: A 30-year perspective. Current Populations Reports* (Series P23, No. 181). Washington, DC: U.S. Government Printing Office.

Van Fleet, R. (1992). Using filial therapy to strengthen families with chronically ill children. In L. VandeCreek, S. Knapp, & T. L. Jackson (Eds.), *Innovations in clinical practice: A source book* (Vol. 11, pp. 87–97). Sarasota, FL: Professional Resource Press.

Wallerstein, J., & Kelly, J. (1980). *Surviving the breakup: How children and parents cope with divorce.* New York: Basic Books.

Author Index

Subject Index